The Songs of Aristophanes

The Songs of Aristophanes

L. P. E. PARKER

CLARENDON PRESS · OXFORD

1997

Oxford University Press, Great Clarendon Street, Oxford OX2 6DP

Oxford   New York

Athens   Auckland   Bangkok   Bogota   Bombay
Buenos Aires   Calcutta   Cape Town   Dar es Salaam
Delhi   Florence   Hong Kong   Istanbul   Karachi
Kuala Lumpur   Madras   Madrid   Melbourne
Mexico City   Nairobi   Paris   Singapore
Taipei   Tokyo   Toronto

and associated companies in
Berlin   Ibadan

Oxford is a trade mark of Oxford University Press

Published in the United States
by Oxford University Press Inc., New York

British Library Cataloguing in Publication Data
Data available

Library of Congress Cataloging in Publication Data
The songs of Aristophanes / L.P.E. Parker.
Includes bibliographical references
1. Aristophanes—Versification. 2. Greek language—Metrics and
rhythmics. 3. Greek drama (Comedy)—History and criticism.
4. Satire, Greek—History and criticism. 5. Greek poetry—History
and criticism. I. Title.
PA3888.Z7P37   1995   882'.01—dc20   95–22080
ISBN --19-814944-1

1 3 5 7 9 10 8 6 4 2

Typeset by Regent Typesetting, London
Printed in Great Britain on acid-free paper by
Bookcraft (Bath) Ltd., Midsomer Norton

τῷ φαλακρῷ

Preface

THE prime reason for studying metre is to enrich our literary appreciation and understanding of ancient poetry, and I should like this book
above all to make more accessible to readers of Aristophanes an aspect
of his art that is generally regarded as technical and difficult, and is, in
consequence, often neglected. The text and commentary are arranged
play by play, and I have sought to show the role played by lyric metres
in dramatic structure, to distinguish levels of metrical style, and to draw
attention to the affinities and significance of different types of rhythm.
In commenting on each passage, I have started with observations of
literary significance, and anyone who does not wish to pursue the techni-
calities of metre and text need read no further. Only in a few passages has
it proved impossible to separate literary and textual discussion. There is,
I have no doubt, much more to be observed about the aesthetic role of
metre in the plays, and I hope that the book will serve as an enabling tool
to more talented critics than myself.

The metrical introduction is designed specifically as a guide to the
structures and history of the various metres used by Aristophanes. But
much of Aristophanes' lyric is metrically quite simple, and I hope that
the book will be of more general use not only to mature scholars but to
younger students of Greek poetry, for whom the introduction and scansions may provide a practical introduction to Greek lyric metre.

The importance of metre to textual criticism is, of course, well recognized. With that in mind, I have provided fuller textual notes than are
usually found in editions of *cantica*. My text is also, generally, conservative—more so than might be thought desirable in a 'reading' edition.
I have often refrained from introducing attractive conjectures the better
to show what is actually in the MSS. I have, however, adopted simple
conjectures, and also some more elaborate ones, where that seemed the
best way to show the metrical improvements they produce. The book is
not, however, meant to take the place of a critical edition, but to offer

guidance on the metrical aspects of textual problems. Thus, I have kept textual discussions short, confining myself as far as possible to metrical considerations. I have used the facsimiles of R and V, and have consulted the Triclinian MS, L. Otherwise, my reports of MS readings come from published sources. I have reported the readings of Triclinius and the Aldine extensively, not because they cast light on what Aristophanes may have written, but because of their importance in the history of the application of metrical scholarship to the plays. In particular, it is easy to get a false impression of Triclinius' methods and competence from ordinary critical editions, since they record only his more successful efforts.

The work could have been made much longer in two ways, but I have chosen comparative brevity. Firstly, I have avoided prolonged discussion of alternative colometries and metrical interpretations, unless they are of major theoretical significance or seem to offer really strong competitive attractions to the ones I have adopted. I have examined every song afresh, and chosen for each what seems to me the simplest and most coherent interpretation. Secondly, I have been economical in citing parallels. Most metrical phrases in Greek are multi-purpose, and their presence in a variety of contexts is of no special significance. I have quoted parallels to demonstrate the acceptability of metrical rarities and to illustrate what seem to me to be genuine and significant affinities in metrical style. General information on the distribution and use of metrical forms is, of course, to be found in the introduction.

The idea of this book came to me when I learned that A. M. Dale had, apparently, left no scansions of Aristophanes. I am very grateful for encouragement, initially from the late Professor T. B. L. Webster and Professor E. W. Handley, and later from Professor J. P. Barron and from Ms Hilary O'Shea of the Oxford University Press. Sir Kenneth Dover has encouraged me in my work over many years, and has, in particular, read the portion of the introduction which deals with the history of the text. He also, most kindly, provided me with full information on the MS colometries of *Frogs*. I have had most enlightening discussions with two Oxford colleagues: Miss N. V. Dunbar has worked through more than one draft of my scansions of *Birds* and Mr N. G. Wilson has read my text and commentaries on *Ach.* and *Lys.* He has also kindly lent me photographs of the MS E. I owe an incalculable debt to Dr Colin Austin, who has read the whole MS, provided countless corrections and valuable observations, has drawn my attention to important work which I should otherwise have missed, and has then read the proofs as well. For the remaining errors and perversities I am entirely to blame.

Going further back in time, I must record my indebtedness to the late Sir Denys Page, who introduced me to the study both of Greek lyric metre and the text of Aristophanes, and to A. M. Dale, who generously used her immense knowledge and exceptional sensitivity to rhythm to guide my early research, without ever seeking to impose her own views. It will be seen that I do not invariably agree with her ideas about Aristophanes, but harm has come not so much from the ideas themselves as from the uncritical acceptance accorded to them. Although an exacting scholar, Dale brought to the study of Greek metre a fine literary sense and an enlivening imagination which makes her work unique.

Finally, I must thank the reader of the Press, Mr Cordy, and Mr Smith of Regent Typesetting for their skilful and patient work on a very difficult manuscript.

L. P. E. P.

Oxford
July 1995

Contents

Symbols   xiii

Abbreviations and Metrical Terminology   xv

List of Manuscripts Cited   xviii

I. INTRODUCTION

1. The Art of Aristophanes' Lyric   3

2. The Metres of Aristophanes   18
   - Metrical Structures   18
     - I. Colon and verse   18
     - II. Strophic structure   21
   - Iambic   27
   - Trochaic   35
   - Cretic   40
   - Dactylic   48
   - Anapaestic   55
   - Ionic   61
   - Dochmiac   65
   - Choriambic   70
     - I. Aeolic-choriambic   70
     - II. Iambo-choriambic   78
   - Dactylo-epitrite   85
   - APPENDIX: Notes on Prosody   91
     - I. Epic correption   91
     - II. Lengthening before plosive + liquid or nasal   92

3. Metre and the Transmission of the Text   94
   - The Poet to Triclinius   94
   - Triclinius to Brunck   106
   - Brunck to the Present   113

II. THE PLAYS

Acharnians 122

Knights 160

Clouds 184

Wasps 214

Peace 262

Birds 296

Lysistrata 358

Thesmophoriazusae 396

Frogs 454

Ecclesiazusae 524

Wealth 554

Select Bibliography 562

Index 573

Symbols

–	long syllable (in a scansion), long position (in a metrical scheme)
◡	short syllable (in a scansion), short position (in a metrical scheme)
‿	short syllable at verse-end (*brevis in fine versus*, *b.f.v.*). The symbol usually represents a short syllable in a long position (*syllaba brevis in elemento longo*, *brevis in longo*). I have, however, also used it in the few places where verse-end undoubtedly falls after short anceps (as may, for example, happen in acatalectic trochees)
⊔, ⊔	triseme, i.e. in Greek musical notation, a long with the time-value of three shorts (◡ – or – ◡)
×	anceps position, i.e. a position in a metrical scheme or in a lacuna in the text which may be occupied by either a long or a short syllable
. . . .	aeolic base in its Attic form (– ◡, ◡ –, or ◡ ◡ ◡) in a metrical scheme
◡̄, ◡◡̲, etc.	where two quantities are marked one above the other in a scansion, the upper is that of the strophe, the lower that of the antistrophe
◡͡◡	double short produced by resolution
∧	at the beginning of a colon marks it as acephalous (headless), meaning that the first position is missing. Thus, ∧◡ ◡ – ◡ – is the acephalous version of – ◡ ◡ – ◡ –
|	word-end corresponding in strophe and antistrophe, or, in astropha, at a significant point
||	verse-end (metrical pause). Verse-end may be indicated by hiatus in strophe, or antistrophe, or both (||ᴴ or ||_H or ||ʜ), by *brevis in longo* (‿̲|| or ‿̄|| or ‿||), or by *anceps iuxta anceps* (– ||a.a., or ‿ ||a.a.). Examples of *anceps iuxta breve* are problematic and are discussed where they occur in the text. Probable verse-ends not confirmed by any of these

	phenomena are not marked in the scansions, although attention is drawn to them in the commentary
|||	stanza-end
=	corresponds with, in strophic responsion
ǀ	marks syllable-boundary between plosive and liquid or nasal, or, in older terminology, between mute and liquid when they 'make position', e.g.: ἐριβǀρεμέτας. The strong combinations, βλ, γλ, γν, γμ, δν, δμ, which regularly make position, are not marked

Cola in synartesis (i.e. not divided by word-end from the preceding colon) are recessed, and described thus: glyc + pher. + is also sometimes used to mark off sections of verses which may be felt as distinct cola. Sequences too long for one line, but not clearly divisible into cola, are described thus: 5 ia.

References to whole stanzas are given by the number of the first line only, with ff., thus: 'see *Ach.* 263 ff.' or 'see *Ach.* 204 ff. = 218 ff.'

In metrical schemes and scansions repeating metra are spaced to show the structure of the verse, e.g.: ᴗ – ᴗ –   ᴗ – ᴗ –. Some cola which are open to different interpretations are spaced differently according to context. Thus, lec may be – ᴗ –   ×– ᴗ – (in an iambic context), – ᴗ –×   – ᴗ – (in a trochaic context), or – ᴗ –×– ᴗ – (uncertain).

Abbreviations and Metrical Terminology

Colon Lengths

colarion	short colon
monom	monometer
dim	dimeter
trim	trimeter
tetram	tetrameter
pent	pentameter
hex	hexameter
trip	tripody

Types of Variation

cat	catalectic (see Parker, *CQ* 26 (1976), 14–28)
dragged	· · · – – – for – ⏑ – in the cadence of aeolo-choriambic cola
sync	syncopated: with one or more positions not occupied by a syllable, e.g. × – ⏑ – – ⏑ – × – ⏑ – = ia trim sync. See Introduction, *Iambic* and *Trochaic*

Types of Metron

an	anapaest: ⏑⏑ ⏖ ⏑⏑ ⏖
ba	bacchiac: ⏑ – –
cr	cretic: – ⏑ –
cho	choriambic: – ⏑ ⏑ –
da	dactylic: – ⏑ ⏑ or – –
δ	dochmiac: × – – × –
hypod	hypodochmiac: – ⏑ – ⏑ –
ia	iambic: × – ⏑ –
ion	ionic: ⏑ ⏑ – –
mol	molossus: – – –
sp	spondee: – –
tro	trochaic: – ⏑ – ×

Dactylo-epitrite Code

D	$- \cup \cup - \cup \cup -$
d	$- \cup \cup -$
e	$- \cup -$
D prol	D prolonged: $- \cup \cup - \cup \cup - \cup \cup -$
×	link-anceps in metrical schemes
– or $\cup$	link-anceps in scansions
E	$- \cup - \cup -$

Aeolo-choriambic Cola

adon	adonean: $- \cup \cup - -$
aeol da	aeolic dactyls: see below, p. 70
asclepiad	see below, p. 70
decasyll	decasyllable: $\times - \cup \cup - \cup - \cup - -$
dodrans A	$- \cup \cup - \cup -$
dodrans B	$- \times - \cup \cup -$
enneasyll	enneasyllable: $\times - \cup - \cup \cup - \cup -$
enopl	enoplian: see below, pp. 77–8.
glyc	glyconic: $\cdots \;\; \cdots - \cup \cup - \cup -$
hag	hagesichorean: $\times - \cup \cup - \cup - -$
heptasyll	heptasyllable: $\times - \cup - \cup \cup -$
hexasyll	hexasyllable: $\cdots \;\; \cdots - \cup \cup -$
hipp	hipponactean: $\cdots \;\; \cdots - \cup \cup - \cup - -$
ibyc	ibycean: $- \cup \cup - \cup \cup - \cup -$
phal	phalaecian hendecasyllable: $\cdots \;\; \cdots - \cup \cup - \cup - \cup - -$
pher	pherecratean: $\cdots \;\; \cdots - \cup \cup - -$
pol	polyschematist: $\cdots \;\; \cdots - \times - \cup \cup -$
reiz	reizianum: $\times - \cup \cup - -$
tel	telesillean: $\times - \cup \cup - \cup -$

Other Cola

anac	anacreontic (anaclomenon): $\cup \cup - \cup - \cup - -$ or, occasion-ally, $\cup \cup - - - \cup - -$
arist	aristophanean: $- \cup \cup - \cup - -$ (see below, pp. 82–4)
da tetram A	dactylic tetrameter ending in $- -$
da tetram B	dactylic tetrameter ending in $- \cup \cup$
hem	hemiepes: $- \cup \cup - \cup \cup -$ (D)
iambel	iambelegus: $\times - \cup - \times - \cup \cup - \cup \cup -$ (– e – D)
ith	ithyphallic: $- \cup - \;\; \cup - -$

lec   lecythion: $-\cup-\times-\cup-$ (see above, p. xiv)

paroem   paroemiac: $\overset{\smile}{\frown}-\overset{\smile}{\frown}-\overset{\smile}{\frown}--$ (most often, a catalectic ana-
       paestic dimeter)

Dicola

archil   archilochean: $\times-\cup\cup-\cup\cup-\times-\cup-\cup--$

eupol   eupolidean: $\cdot\cdot\;\;\cdot\cdot-\times-\cup\cup-|\cdot\cdot\;\;\cdot\cdot-\times-\cup-$ (polyschema-
       tist + lecythion, with the first two positions of the lecythion
       treated as aeolic base (see Parker, *PCPS* 214 (1988), 115–22))

euripid   euripidean: $\times-\cup-\;\;\times-\cup-|\;\;-\cup-\;\;\cup--$ (iambic
       dimeter + ithyphallic). Also, $\times-\cup-\;\;\times-\cup-|\;\;-\cup-$
       $\times-\cup-$ (iambic dimeter + lec)

List of Manuscripts Cited

The symbols are those devised by J. W. White (*CPh* 1 (1906), 1–20). The MSS which contain *Frogs* are described in detail by C. N. Eberline, *Studies in the Manuscript Tradition of the Ranae of Aristophanes*, 1–48. On the Triclinian MSS, see W. J. W. Koster, *Autour d'un manuscrit d'Aristophane écrit par Démétrius Triclinius*, and M. A. Turyn, *The Byzantine Manuscript Tradition of the Tragedies of Euripides* (on P20), and N. G. Wilson, *CQ* 12 (1962), 32–47 (on L). On Triclinian influence on other MSS, see Dover, *Frogs* 81–3.

A Paris, Bibliothèque Nationale, Ancien fonds grec 2712, *c*.1300.
   Wealth, Clouds, Frogs, Knights, Birds, Ach., Ecc. (1–282)

B ibid., Ancien fonds grec 2715, 16th c.
   Knights, Ach., Wasps, Lys. (1–61, 132–199, 268–819, 890–1097, 1237–end), *Ecc.* (1–1135), *Peace* (1–947, 1012–1300)

C ibid., Ancien fonds grec 2717, 16th c.
   Knights, Ach., Wasps, Wealth, Frogs, Birds, Peace (1–947, 1012–1354, 1357), *Lys.* (as B)

Ct6 Cambridge, Trinity College Library, R.1.42, 15th c.
   Wealth, Clouds, Frogs
   Brunck's MS.

E Modena, Biblioteca Estense, α.U.5.10, late 14th–early 15th c.
   Wealth, Clouds, Frogs, Knights, Birds (1–220, 662–end), *Ach.*

H Copenhagen, Det Kongelige Bibliotek, Gamle Kongelig Samling 1980, 15th c.
   Wealth, Clouds, Frogs, Knights, Ach., Wasps, Birds, Peace (as C), *Lys.* (as B)

L Oxford, Bodleian Library, Holkham gr. 88, early 15th c.
   Wealth, Clouds, Frogs, Knights, Ach., Wasps, Birds, Peace 1–1268)
   Triclinius' second edition

M Milan, Biblioteca Ambrosiana, L 39 sup., early 14th c.
   Wealth, Clouds, Frogs, Knights, Birds (1–1641)

M4 ibid., C 222 inf., *c*.1300
   Wealth, Clouds, Frogs (1–1196, 1251–end)
   (=K in Dover, *Frogs*)

Mu1   Munich, Bayerische Staatsbibliothek, gr. 137, 15th c.
Wealth, Clouds, Frogs, Ecc. (= N in von Velsen, *Ecc.*)

Mu2   ibid., gr. 492, 15th c.
Thesm., Lys.
(= G in von Velsen, *Thesm.*)

Mu4   ibid., gr. 533, 15th–16th c.
Wealth (1–203)

Np1   Naples, Biblioteca Nazionale, II.F.22, end of 14th c.
Wealth, Clouds, Frogs

Np2   ibid., II.F.27, 14th c.
Wealth, Clouds

P20   Paris, Bibliothèque Nationale, Suppl. gr. 463, early 14th c.
Wealth, Clouds, Frogs
Corrections and annotations in Triclinius' hand

Pe1   Perugia, Biblioteca Augusta del Comune di Perugia, H 56, 15th c.
Frogs, Ecc.
(= Λ in Ussher, *Ecc.*)

R   Ravenna, Biblioteca Classense, 429, mid-10th c.
All the surviving plays
Facsimile: Leiden 1904

U   Rome, Biblioteca Apostolica Vaticana, Urbinas gr. 141, 14th c.
Wealth, Clouds, Frogs, Birds

V   Venice, Biblioteca Marciana, gr. 474, 11th or 12th c.
Wealth, Clouds, Frogs, Knights, Birds, Peace, Wasps
Facsimile: London and Boston 1902

Vb1   Rome, Biblioteca Apostolica Vaticana, Barberinianus I 45, 15th c.
Ach., Ecc. (1–1135), *Knights*

Vb3   ibid., Barberinianus I 126, 14th c.
Wealth, Clouds, Frogs

Vp2   ibid., Palatinus gr. 67, 15th c.
Wealth, Clouds, Frogs, Knights, Ach., Wasps, Birds, Peace (as C), *Lys.* (as B)
(= P in Zacher and van Herwerden, *Peace*, and MacDowell, *Wasps*)

Vp3   ibid., Palatinus gr. 128, 15th c.
Knights, Ach., Wasps
(= P in von Velsen, *Knights*, and J in MacDowell, *Wasps*)

Vs1   Rome, Biblioteca Apostolica Vaticana, Reginensis gr. 147, early 14th c.
Wealth, Clouds, Frogs
(= Rs in Koster *et al.*, *Scholia*)

Vv5   ibid., gr. 1294, 14th c.
       Wealth, Clouds, Frogs, Knights (1–270)
       (= Vat in von Velsen, *Knights*)

Γ   Florence, Biblioteca Mediceo-Laurenziana 31.15, 14th c.
       Ach., Ecc., Knights, Birds (1–1419), *Wasps* (421–1396, 1494–end),
       Peace (378–490, 548–837, 893–947, 1012–1126, 1190–1300)
       Leiden, Bibliotheek der Rijksuniversiteit, Vossianus gr. 52.
       Lys. (1–61, 132–99, 268–819, 890–1034), *Birds* (1492–1765).

Θ   Florence, Biblioteca Mediceo-Laurenziana, Conventi Soppressi 140,
       14th c.
       Wealth, Clouds, Knights, Frogs

Σ vet. *Scholia vetera*

I INTRODUCTION

1 The Art of Aristophanes' Lyric

εἶτα Κρατίνου μεμνημένος, ὃς πολλῷ ῥεύσας ποτ' ἐπαίνῳ
διὰ τῶν ἀφελῶν πεδίων ἔρρει . . .
ᾆσαι δ' οὐκ ἦν ἐν συμποσίῳ πλὴν "Δωροῖ συκοπέδιλε"
καὶ "τέκτονες εὐπαλάμων ὕμνων". οὕτως ἤνθησεν ἐκεῖνος.

(*Knights* 526–30)

ᾆσον δή μοι σκόλιόν τι λαβὼν Ἀλκαίου κἀνακρέοντος

(*Banqueters*, PCG 235)

πρῶτον μὲν αὐτὸν τὴν λύραν λαβόντ' ἐγὼ 'κέλευσα
ᾆσαι Σιμωνίδου μέλος, τὸν Κριὸν ὡς ἐπέχθη . . .
ἔπειτα δ' ἐκέλευσ' αὐτὸν ἀλλὰ μυρρίνην λαβόντα
τῶν Αἰσχύλου λέξαι τί μοι . . .
ὅμως δὲ τὸν θυμὸν δακὼν ἔφην, "σὺ δ' ἀλλὰ τούτων
λέξον τι τῶν νεωτέρων, ἅττ' ἐστὶ τὰ σοφὰ ταῦτα."
ὁ δ' εὐθὺς ἦσ' Εὐριπίδου ῥῆσίν τιν' . . .

(*Clouds* 1355 ff.)

τὰ Στησιχόρου τε καὶ Ἀλκμᾶνος Σιμωνίδου τε
ἀρχαῖον ἀείδειν . . .

(Eupolis, *Helots*, PCG 148. 1–2)

The first passage quoted gives an idea of what success (beyond the instant lionization described in *Peace* 769–74) meant to Aristophanes and his fellow comic poets. It also gives a glimpse of the social milieu that produced both Attic tragedy and comedy. Secondly, this and the other passages form part of the evidence that the performances at symposia covered a much wider range than the little verses preserved by Athenaeus (694c–95f) which make up much of the section of *carmina convivialia* in Page, *PMG* (884–917). Stanzas from the great lyric poets of the last century or two, extracts (including speeches) from tragedy, both contemporary and of the last generation, lyrics from comedy, all were included in the repertoire.

We have accounts of the order of events at symposia, all of which may go back ultimately to the same authority, the Aristotelian, Dicaearchus (see R. Reitzenstein, *Epigramm und Skolion*, 3–44). First came the paean, with libations, then short stanzas sung by each guest in turn as he held the myrtle branch, then the virtuoso performances by οἱ συνετοὶ δοκοῦντες, those of the guests with musical skills above the average. It was surely such performers—professionals or gifted amateurs—and their listeners who will have been among the most discerning members of the audiences of Aristophanes and his fellow comedians. The repertoire may not, of course, have been enormously wide. A song by Ben Jonson was well known in Victorian drawing-rooms, but only *one* ('Drink to me only with thine eyes . . .'). But, at any rate, the range of styles represented was wide, and what Aristophanes chose to parody, to quote from, to allude to must reflect it, just as the range of parody one finds in numbers of *Punch* of the 1930s, 1940s and 1950s reflects a range of poetry read in schools which has now vanished from the syllabus. Indeed, the lyric of Aristophanes is a product of the very last creative phase of what John Herington has called the 'song-culture' of early and classical Greece (*Poetry into Drama*, 3 ff.). Song, of course, played an important part elsewhere in the life of Aristophanes' contemporaries—in private life (serenades and other types of folk-song) and on all sorts of public occasions—and versions of those different types of song are to be found everywhere in Aristophanes' plays. But the symposium both provided an environment congenial to the standard stuff of Aristophanic humour and sharpened the musical perceptions of the individual, and at the same time developed the eclecti-cism characteristic of Attic drama in general, and, distinctively, of old comedy.

It is worth the risk of stating the obvious to point out that Aristophanes' contemporaries were able to recognize not only verbal allusion but rhythmic allusion, not only verbal stylistic level but musical stylistic level. This is perhaps the widest gulf between their powers of appreciation and ours. Our only resort is to try to educate the eye and the mind, and through them, as far as we can, the ear, by the study of the nearest thing we have to musical scores: scansions. We need, in particular, to collect precise data on the metrical practices of 'serious' poets, if we are to reach any sort of perception of how, where, and why Aristophanes' rhythms differ from theirs. Most types of Greek metre are neutral or highly adaptable, and precise usage and context have to be examined if we are to distinguish allusion and parody from the common stock of Attic dramatic lyric. Crude, mechanical classifications will not do. Moreover, stylistic level of diction, content, and metre do not have to proceed in step in comedy, and critical appreciation of comic lyric depends to a great extent on the recognition of divergences and clashes. Thus, a pair of 'noble' syncopated iambic trimeters marks the climax of the turd-throwing incident at *Ach.* 1169–73. Again, dactylic, with its epic associations is a 'noble' metre (see below, 48), and the vastly extended run in which the chorus of *OC* (228–34) express their horror and outrage at the presence of Oedipus is adapted at *Ecc.* 1169–76 to listing the ingredients of a dinner.

Parody of high lyric appears on a small scale in early plays (*Clouds* 1154–66, *Wasps* 316–33) and comes into its own in *Thesm.* and *Frogs*. It is, however, an extremely delicate matter to identify specifically *metrical* parody (see especially on *Thesm.* 1015 ff., *Frogs* 1264 ff. and 1284 ff., 1309 ff. and 1331 ff.). The run of dactyls at *Ecc.* 1169–76, referred to above, may be an example. *Frogs* 1354–5:

δάκρυα δάκρυά τ' ἀπ' ὀμμάτων
ἔβαλον ἔβαλον ἁ τλάμων

∪ ⌢ ∪ ⌢   ∪ – ∪ –
∪ ⌢ ∪ ⌢   – – –

with its tribrach division of resolution, does indeed mimic Euripidean practice, but it does not exaggerate it, as we expect of parody. Rather the reverse (see below, 29–30 and 34). In any case, the metrical pattern is no more than a by-product of the verbal pattern.

It is often assumed that parody is designed to ridicule its original, but that is not necessarily so. Parody (or pastiche) can be used to point up a whole range of incongruities and parallelisms (*Private Eye*'s recurrent treatments of Israelo-Arab relations in the style of the *Authorized Version*; Michael Frayn's Shakespearean sherry-party and countless other Shakespearean 'parodies'). In fact, writers on Aristophanes commonly use 'parody' in a loose sense to cover all sorts of pastiche and allusion. *Peace* 775 ff. = 796 ff. provides an interesting example of allusion, both verbal and metrical, with something beyond purely humorous intent:

> Μοῦσα, σὺ μὲν πολέμους ἀπωσαμένη μετ' ἐμοῦ
> τοῦ φίλου χόρευσον,
> κλείουσα θεῶν τε γάμους
> ἀνδρῶν τε δαῖτας καὶ θαλίας μακάρων·
> σοὶ γὰρ τάδ' ἐξ ἀρχῆς μέλει.
> ἢν δέ σε Καρκίνος ἐλθὼν
> ἀντιβολῇ μετὰ τῶν παίδων χορεῦσαι,
> μήθ' ὑπάκουε μήτ' ἔλ-
> θῃς συνέριθος αὐτοῖς,
> ἀλλὰ νόμιζε πάντας
> ὄρτυγας οἰκογενεῖς, γυλιαύχενας ὀρχηστὰς
> νανοφυεῖς, σφυράδων ἀποκνίσματα μηχανοδίφας·
> καὶ γὰρ ἔφασχ' ὁ πατὴρ ὃ παρ' ἐλπίδας
> εἶχε τὸ δρᾶμα γαλῆν τῆς ἑσπέρας ἀπάγξαι.
> τοιάδε χρὴ Χαρίτων δαμώματα καλλικόμων
> τὸν σοφὸν ποιητὴν
> ὑμνεῖν, ὅταν ἠρινὰ μὲν
> φωνῇ χελιδὼν ἡδομένη κελαδῇ,
> χορὸν δὲ μὴ 'χῃ Μόρσιμος
> μηδὲ Μελάνθιος, οὗ δὴ
> πικροτάτην ὄπα γηρύσαντος ἤκουσ'
> ἡνίκα τῶν τραγῳδῶν
> τὸν χορὸν εἶχον ἀδελ-
> φός τε καὶ αὐτός, ἄμφω
> Γοργόνες ὀψοφάγοι, βατιδοσκόποι Ἅρπυιαι,
> γραοσόβαι μιαροί, τραγομάσχαλοι ἰχθυολῦμαι·
> ὧν καταχρεμψαμένη μέγα καὶ πλατὺ
> Μοῦσα θεὰ μετ' ἐμοῦ ξύμπαιζε τὴν ἑορτήν.

> i ‒◡◡‒◡◡‒| ◡̲ ‒◡◡‒◡◡‒
>   ‒◡‒| ◡‒‒
>   ‒ ‒◡◡‒◡◡‒

```
      –   –⏑– –|   –⏑⏑–|⏑⏑ –
      –   –⏑– –   –⏑–||ᴴ
 ii –⏑⏑–⏑⏑|–  –
     –⏑⏑–|⏑⏑– –  –⏑– –
           –⏑⏑–⏑––
           –⏑⏑–⏑––
           –⏑⏑–⏑––
iii –⏑⏑|  –⏑⏑  –|⏑⏑  –⏑⏑|  ––  –
        –⏑⏑  –|⏑⏑  –|⏑⏑  –⏑⏑|  –⏑⏑  ––||ᴴ
 iv –⏑⏑  –⏑⏑  –|⏑⏑  –⏑⏑
        –⏑⏑–⏑⏑–|  –  –⏑–  ⏑––|||
```

The stanza is constructed in four sections, the first being pure dactylo-epitrite, the metre *par excellence* of Dorian choral lyric. The only pure dactylo-epitrite stanza in Aristophanes is *Knights* 1264 ff. = 1290 ff., the song of the second parabasis, which begins with a quotation from Pindar, and where the well-established association between the metre and aristocratic athleticism suits the chorus. Dactylo-epitrite in Aristophanes does not seem to be significant *per se*, but in the *Peace* and *Knights* stanzas it is combined with verbal allusion. The second section makes a transition, without word-end, from dactylo-epitrite to a sequence of three catalectic cola, still in synartesis. The third section is dactylic, and the fourth begins dactylic, returning to dactylo-epitrite at the close. According to *Σ vet.*, the first sections of both strophe and antistrophe incorporate quotations from Stesichorus. Stesichorus' *Oresteia* in its entirety can hardly have been a party-piece, but one can imagine that an extract from it could have served as an independent song. The fragments embedded here look suitably convivial. Aristophanes' contribution cannot be disentangled completely and with certainty, but the matey μετ' ἐμοῦ τοῦ φίλου is surely his and the prosaic τὸν σοφὸν ποιητήν is known to be. But there is no evident clash of style within the lines such as would make them laughable. Rather, Aristophanes has produced a sort of domesticated version of high lyric, and 'parody of Stesichorus' is no way to describe it. The first part of the stanza must be interpreted in the light of the second part, which is devoted to invective against contemporary tragic poets, Carcinus and his sons in the strophe, Morsimus and Melanthius, brothers presumably, in the antistrophe.

Another master of poetic invective, Byron, embeds a quotation from Milton in his dedication of *Don Juan* 'to Robert Southey Esq., poet laureate':

> If, fallen in evil days on evil tongues,
>   Milton appealed to the Avenger, Time,
> If Time, the Avenger, execrates his wrongs,
>   And makes the word 'Miltonic' mean '*Sublime*',
> *He* deigned not to belie his soul in songs,
>   Nor turn his very talent to a crime;
> *He* did not loath the Sire to laud the Son,
> But closed the tyrant-hater he begun.
>
> Think'st thou, could he—the blind Old Man—arise
>   Like Samuel from the grave . . .
> Would *he* adore a sultan? *He* obey
> The intellectual eunuch Castlereagh?

The adapted quotation from *Paradise Lost* does not stand out in its Byronic context, but it belongs in its true context to quite a different poetic register:

> Standing on Earth, not rapt above the Pole,
> More safe I sing, with mortal voice, unchang'd
> To Hoarce or mute, though fall'n on evil dayes,
> On evil dayes though fall'n, and evil tongues . . .

Milton's words, harmoniously absorbed, give a touch of elevation to Byron's verse, help to produce a poetic and emotional high point, sustained by 'Think'st thou . . .' at the beginning of the next stanza (elsewhere in the poem, except in the address to Italy in stanza 16, Byron uses the conversational 'you'). Thereafter, a stylistic descent has to be made to versified invective rhetoric. Byron makes his intentions perfectly clear: the truly great poet of an earlier age is being enlisted as an ally against Byron's contemporary, and the alliance is expressed through a sort of momentary identification.

Aristophanes is not explicit. None the less, the absorption of Stesichorus' words suggests an alliance between the grand old poet, the skilled poet-comedian ($\sigma o \phi \acute{\iota} a$ is Pindar's word for poetic skill), and the

Muse who inspires both against the bogus, would-be-grand poets of the present day. After the opening in 'domesticated' Stesichorean style, Aristophanes, too, has to make the descent to invective. In both strophe and antistrophe the change is quite abrupt. Only, in the strophe there is a clean syntactical break coinciding with verse-end at 780, whereas in the antistrophe the descent begins earlier, when Morsimus is paired παρὰ προσδοκίαν with the swallow in parallel μέν . . . δέ clauses. The colon three times repeated at 785–88 = 806–9 acquired the name 'aristophanean', but it is by no means particularly associated with comedy: Aeschylus and Euripides both use it in sequence (see below, 83). Indeed, catalectic cola appear in synartesis more often in Aeschylus than elsewhere (Parker, *CQ* 26 (1976), 25). Stylistically, then, the sequence of catalectic cola in synartesis can be taken as neutral, or possibly even dignified, but I think it is not fanciful to suggest that it creates, by rhythmic means, a sort of tension, which is released with the flow of colourful abuse in dactyls. This dactylic passage deserves scrutiny. First, there is a striking sequence of three longs at the end of the first colon, produced by a spondaic metron followed by catalexis, an extreme rarity in extant drama (see below, ad loc.). Then, there is the extraordinarily close correspondence of word-end in strophe and antistrophe. Correspondence of this type is found occasionally in tragic lyric and, much more rarely, in Aristophanes. Given the association of both dactyls and compound epithets with high poetry, it is natural to look for parody here. We know nothing of the lyric of Carcinus or Morsimus or Melanthius, but it is worth turning to Morsimus' great-uncle: the sequence of epithets and substantives in dactylic runs is not un-Aeschylean: See *Ag.* 154–5:

> . . . μίμνει γὰρ φοβερὰ παλίνορτος,
> οἰκονόμος δολία, μνάμων Μῆνις τεκνόποινος

> . . . ‒‒ ‒◡◡ ‒◡◡ ‒‒
> ‒◡◡ ‒◡◡ ‒‒ ‒‒ ‒◡◡ ‒‒

For coincidence of word-end in strophe and antistrophe, compare *Ag.* 104–5 = 122–4:

> ‒◡◡ ‒◡◡ ‒◡◡ ‒|◡◡| ‒◡◡| ‒‒
> ‒◡◡ ‒|◡◡ ‒|◡◡ ‒|◡◡ ‒‒

Finally, there is a return to dactylo-epitrite, and, in the antistrophe, the song does indeed come full circle with the second address to the Muse, who is invited this time to behave in a way which marks her decisively as the muse of Aristophanes.

This song, like *Ach.* 1150 ff. = 1162 ff. and *Frogs* 674 ff. = 706 ff., belongs to a genre which might be called 'ornate invective'. Aristophanes, of course, produced much simpler invective songs, such as *Ach.* 836 ff. and *Frogs* 420 ff., much closer to what one assumes to have been the more or less extempore popular prototype. But if one wanted to pillory someone in late fifth-century Athens a highly effective way would surely have been through a song good in its own right, something that would catch on and go the rounds as a party-piece.

Students of Aristophanes owe much to Michael Silk for a study of the comedian's lyric that dispels the haze of piety and wishful thinking and applies sure literary judgement to genuine analysis (*YCS* 26 (1980), 99–151). It will be observed that I too use the stylistic classification 'low', 'middle', and 'high', but this is no more than a starting point, needing considerable refinement and adaptation to produce illuminating results. The functions of Aristophanic lyric are too various and its registers too diverse to be ranged, as it were, at different points along a single axis. One aspect of Aristophanes' lyric to which Silk does not give full value is its function as a constituent of a type of musical drama. Aristophanes was *not* a lyric poet. Some of the lyrics of tragedy may seem to us entirely satisfactory as independent poems. That is partly a matter of their quality, but partly also of our own deficiency of sensibility, which blunts awareness of the organic relationship between song and dramatic situation, song and surrounding dialogue in Attic tragedy. A proportion of Aristophanes' song is of virtually no poetic significance. It is in lyric metre because the genre requires it, because that is how choruses express themselves, because lyric metre and song confer of themselves a certain impetus and heightening of excitement.

> Hail the valiant fellow who
> Did this deed of derring-do!
> Honours wait on such a one;
> By my head, 'twas bravely done!
> (W. S. Gilbert, *Yeomen of the Guard*, Act II)

Here, the relative 'who' at the end of a line marks this as verse of comic type. Otherwise it is quite characterless. It is hard to find anything as flat in Aristophanes, but, as a piece of direct comment on the action, one might choose *Ach.* 1037 ff. (= 1008 ff.):

X. ἀνὴρ ἐνηύρηκέν τι ταῖς
   σπονδαῖσιν ἡδύ, κοὐκ ἔοικεν οὐδενὶ μεταδώσειν.
Δ. κατάχει σὺ τῆς χορδῆς τὸ μέλι. τὰς σηπίας στάθευε.
X. ἤκουσας ὀρθιασμάτων; Δ. ὀπτᾶτε τἀγχέλεια.
X. ἀποκτενεῖς λιμῷ 'με καὶ
   τοὺς γείτονας κνίσῃ τε καὶ
   φωνῇ τοιαῦτα λάσκων.

```
‒ ‒ ∪ ‒    ‒ ‒ ∪ ‒
    ‒ ‒ ∪ ‒    ∪ ‒ ∪ ‒
    ∪ ‒ ∪ ⌢⌣    ∪ ‒ ‒
⌢⌣ ‒ ∪ ‒    ‒ ‒ ∪ ⌢⌣    ‒ ‒ ∪ ‒    ∪ ‒ ‿ ‖ ᴴ
‒ ‒ ∪ ‒    ∪ ‒ ∪ ‒    ‒ ‒ ∪ ‒    ∪ ‒ ‿ ‖ ᴴ
∪ ‒ ∪ ‒    ‒ ‒ ∪ ‒
    ‒ ‒ ∪ ‒    ‒ ‒ ∪ ‒
    ‒ ‒ ∪ ‒    ∪ ‒ ‒ ‖‖‖
```

Metrically, this could hardly be less adventurous. The verse gains some character from the rhyming effect at 1044–5 (=1015–16), noted by Silk, but the real quality of the stanza comes from the way in which Dicaeopolis' culinary instructions, perhaps delivered in recitative, fit neatly into the song, producing a sort of accidental duet. This is not paratragedy, but the technique has affinities with dialogues in tragedy between a highly emotional and a calmer character, where the first uses lyric metre and the second spoken metre. In tragedy, as here at 1042–3, a verse may actually be shared between two characters, one of whom is speaking and the other singing, e.g. *Her.* 1184–1190:

Θ. εὔφημα φώνει. Α. βουλομένοισιν ἐπαγγέλλῃ.
Θ. ὦ δεινὰ λέξας. Α. οἰχόμεθ' οἰχόμεθα πτανοί.
Θ. τί φῄς; τί δράσας; Α. μαινομένῳ πιτύλῳ πλαγχθείς.

Th. ‒ ‒ ∪ ‒ ‒ A. ‒ ∪ ∪ ‒ ∪ ∪ ‒ ‒ ‒

Th. –   –◡–   –   A. –◡◡–◡◡–   ¬ –
Th. –   –◡–   –   A. –◡◡–◡◡–   – –

Here, Theseus repeatedly begins iambic trimeters which are completed by the distraught Amphitryon as dactylo-epitrite. The parallel is not close: Amphitryon uses much more obtrusively lyric rhythms than the Acharnians. None the less, they are more impassioned than Dicaeopolis, for he has the food and they haven't. The art that makes Aristophanes' stanza entertaining and distinctive is in large measure that of the dramatist, hardly at all that of the lyric poet.

Again, lyric often has important structural functions in Aristophanes' plays. The device of separating strophe and antistrophe will have given strong definition to the intervening episode: the audience would recognize the returning 'tune'. The use of lyric stanzas to frame or punctuate in this way is very common. See, for example, *Peace* 346 ff. = 385 ff. = 582 ff., 939 ff. = 1023 ff., *Birds* 451 ff. = 539 ff., 1188 ff. = 1262 ff., *Lys.* 476 ff. = 541 ff., *Frogs* 895 ff. = 992 ff. with 1099 ff. = 1109 ff. Passages in recitative interspersed with songs produce changes of tempo. Diversity is provided by lyrical interludes, little cantatas, as it were: *Wasps* 273–345, *Lys.* 1247–1321, *Thesm.* 947–1000, *Frogs* 209–67, 316–459. Some plays have their individual rhythmic characters, defined both by the predominance of one or more metres and the exclusion of others (see *Ach.*, *Knights*, *Clouds*). A play can also be marked off into sections by changes in the predominant rhythm (see *Wasps*, *Peace*, *Clouds*, *Lys.*). Most of these effects are likely to pass unperceived by modern readers, who are grappling with language and content. Modern audiences are not much better off: they cannot pick up the rhythms of the lyric, and recitative is commonly spoken rather than chanted in modern productions.

The most difficult problem for the modern critic of Aristophanes is posed by those apparently 'serious' lyrics which have earned him the hyperbolical tributes quoted by Silk at the beginning of his paper. P. W. Harsh's 'some of the finest lyrics produced by the human genius' (*A Handbook of Classical Drama*, 264 ff.) will do as a sample. Silk's criticisms of Aristophanes' 'high' lyrics are, in detail, justified, but questions still remain. What was Aristophanes trying to do in these songs? What did his original audience, or its more discerning members, make of them? Was Aristophanes trying to write like Sophocles and Euripides and failing? Or was he, in spite of superficial similarities, aiming at something altogether different?

Birds is a play much admired for its lyrical qualities, and the parabasis-song (737 ff. = 769 ff.) is certainly not meant to be comic. As Sir Kenneth Dover says, it uses 'the vocabulary and imagery of tragic and lyric poetry to bring the birds, as part of the order of nature, into a relation with the gods which is independent of man' (*Aristophanic Comedy*, 147 ff.). None the less, the combinations of substantive and epithet are conventional, and the passage of parody from *Thesm.* (43–51), appositely quoted by Dover, makes it very hard to believe that Aristophanes did not know it:

> ἐχέτω δὲ πνοὰς νήνεμος αἰθήρ
> κῦμα δὲ πόντου μὴ κελαδείτω
> γλαυκόν . . .
> πτηνῶν τε γένη κατακοιμάσθω,
> θηρῶν τ' ἀγρίων πόδες ὑλοδρόμων
> μὴ λυέσθων.

The humour in *Thesm.* is complex, lying in the dramatic situation, in the use of the duet technique (much more farcically than in *Ach.* 1037 ff.) and in the contrast between the *nugae canorae* of the Servant's prelude and the grotesque description of Agathon's processes of composition at 52–7. Returning to *Birds* 737 ff., one observes that the strophe looks in some degree like a re-hash of the Hoopoe's anapaests at 209 ff.: 742 μελίας ἐπὶ φυλλοκόμου (215 διὰ φυλλοκόμου μίλακος), 744 γέννος ξουθῆς (214 γέννος ξουθῆς), 744–5 μελέων . . . νόμους ἱεροὺς (210 νόμους ἱερῶν ὕμνων). An attentive listener could hardly fail to notice this in performance.

In the antistrophe, the cry of the swans is well imagined, but the expression is flat by comparison with, say, Pindar's description of the effect of the sound of the lyre at the beginning of *Pyth.* I. But this comparison is *mal à propos*. It is the interspersed bird-noises that give the clue to the type of composition we are dealing with. Like the Hoopoe's invocation at 227 ff., this is a *jeu d'esprit*, a musical set-piece, in the same genre as the Frogs' Boating Song — and Rossini's Cats' Duet. The fun lies in the composer's skill in mimicking the authentic sound of a bird or animal while keeping within current musical conventions. Words, as has

often been pointed out, were much more important in ancient Greek
song than, generally, in that of modern Europe — and even in modern
Europe comic opera is an exception. But here, in the Birds' song, the
words are genuinely secondary. The loss of the music and of the whole
musical convention is highly damaging to such a song, far more so than
to high lyric.

The first song of the Cloud-chorus (275 ff. = 298 ff.) presents a
different, but not completely unrelated, problem. Again, the idea of
clouds floating over the Attic countryside is finely imagined, but the
poetic realization of the idea seems comparatively weak. Even if Silk's
accusations of 'triteness, inflation and pervasive lack of point' are somewhat harsh, I do not think it can be denied that the song is over-loaded
with conventional and predictable poetic language. Silk entertains the
idea, at first sight plausible, of parody. One thinks of those κυκλίων
χορῶν ᾀσματοκάμπται whom the Clouds are said to inspire (333). He
rejects it, however, on two grounds: parodic grotesqueness is not
obvious, and the antistrophe, the praise of Athens, must be serious.
Implicit here is a principle which deserves to be stated explicitly: that in
Aristophanes strophe and antistrophe match not only in metre but in
stylistic type, level, and mood. This is only incidentally connected with
the idea (which is, in any case, of limited validity) that certain types
of metre suit certain ideas and emotions. Rather, it is a matter of the
rhythmic architecture of the individual stanza, of the symbiosis of words
and tune, which even requires that where there is a shift of mood and
style within a stanza the corresponding stanza shall generally move in
step, a phenomenon well illustrated by *Peace* 775 ff. = 796 ff., analysed
above. It is also, distinctively, a feature of *comic* technique; a product of
the clashes, contrasts, and allusions that characterize comic lyric, and
which have no parallel in tragedy. Silk assumes the principle without
investigation, but I think that it is valid. There is, of course, an element
of the subjective in assessing stylistic type, level, and, above all, mood,
but I cannot find in Aristophanes any example of a whole stanza which
is clearly meant to raise a laugh corresponding with one that is not.
There are a few minor divergences within stanzas, of which the clearest
is *Birds* 1315–16 = 1327–8.

The metre of *Clouds* 275 ff. = 298 ff. does little to solve the problem of
that particular stanza: it is very nearly pure dactylic, and dactylic so

nearly undiluted in stanzas of such length is found only in Euripides among the surviving tragedians (see, for example, *Hcld.* 608 ff. = 618 ff. and *Supp.* 271–85; there are other pure dactylic stanzas in plays later than *Clouds*). So one can hazard that rhythmically this is a composition in the modern tragic style, not, say, a pastiche of Aeschylus. What relation, if any, it may have had with contemporary dithyramb we have no means of knowing. Dactylic dignity, however, can be either real or bogus, and it is just possible that here the metre is adaptable to both effects, so that, despite Aristophanes' normal practice, the strophe can be parodic and the antistrophe 'straight'. But it is also possible that both strophe and antistrophe belong to a type of verse which adopts the stylistic colour of high poetry without burlesque intent, and which, where the plot requires it, provides a substitute for τὸ σεμνόν which is assimilable into the poetic context of comedy. Aristophanic comedy does not demand stylistic coherence as tragedy does (gradual shifts, sudden contrasts, incongruities are part of the art), but it cannot accommodate true high lyric. That is beyond the limits of the genre. Yet there are moments and characters in comedy that are not laughable, and they demand their own kind of lyric, a kind of lyric for which the stylistic levels of pseudo-Longinus do not allow, and which, habitually, we do not recognize in classical Greek poetry. *Faute de mieux*, it can be called 'light verse'. To please, it must be interesting in conception and elegant in execution. It uses similar techniques to high poetry, without being either high poetry or parody of high poetry. It may be, then, that *Clouds* 275 ff. is to be appreciated as well-turned verse, designed to join with spectacle and music to produce a complete theatrical experience, not to be subjected to close analysis as lyric poetry.

It remains to look in Aristophanes for verse that is good independently of being witty or humorous, independently of its lost music and even of its dramatic function, verse that qualifies for that elusive genre, comic poetry. I should choose as an example *Ach.* 971 ff. = 988 ff. The metre, as with so much of the lyric in this play, is, except for the clausular trochees, cretic: $- \cup -$ and $- \cup \, \widetilde{\frown}$. Resolved and unresolved metra are not distributed at random, but in a clearly perceptible pattern identical in strophe and antistrophe. This is not the rule in cretic songs: some are strict in the matter, some not. The extreme rhythmic regularity of this song, verging almost on recitative style, distances it as far as may be from tragic lyric. There is also quite a lot of correspondence of word-end. All this points to consciously artistic composition. While Aristophanes shows a general fondness for cretic in his earliest plays, the predominance of the rhythm in *Ach.* is exceptional. Recurrent metrical motifs in individual plays, rhythmical 'signatures', as it were, will, no doubt, have contributed in both tragedy and comedy to making the play a unified aesthetic whole, but other considerations that may have caused an Attic dramatist to choose a particular rhythm for a particular play are much more obscure. Cretic, however, was connected as a matter of history with the ἀνδρεία traditionally attributed to the Cretans and with their energetic dances in armour (see below, 40), and its use in this play may well express the energy and virility of the venerable charcoal-burners: Ἀχάρναι δὲ παλαίφατον εὐάνορες (Pindar, *Nem.* 2. 16). I find surprising Silk's classification of this song among those that begin high and end low. The stylistic level, like the metre, seems to me to be uniform throughout. Strophe and antistrophe begin with tributes to the wisdom and consequent bliss of Dicaeopolis. The strophe continues with the depiction in metaphor of war as a drunken gatecrasher wrecking a pleasant party. The parallel metaphorical section of the antistrophe is the old men's love-song to Reconciliation:

ὦ Κύπριδι τῇ καλῇ καὶ Χάρισι ταῖς φίλαις ξύντροφε Διαλλαγή,
ὡς καλὸν ἔχουσα τὸ πρόσωπον ἄρ' ἐλάνθανες.
πῶς ἂν ἐμὲ καὶ σέ τις Ἔρως ξυναγάγοι λαβών,
ὥσπερ ὁ γεγραμμένος, ἔχων στέφανον ἀνθέμων;
ἢ πάνυ γερόντιον ἴσως νενόμικάς με σύ;
ἀλλά σε λαβὼν τρία δοκῶ γ' ἂν ἔτι προσβαλεῖν·
πρῶτα μὲν ἂν ἀμπελίδος ὄρχον ἐλάσαι μακρόν,
εἶτα παρὰ τόνδε νέα μοσχίδια συκίδων,
καὶ τὸ τρίτον ἡμερίδος ὄσχον, ὁ γέρων ὁδί,
καὶ περὶ τὸ χωρίον ἐλάδας ἅπαν ἐν κύκλῳ,
ὥστ' ἀλείφεσθαί σ' ἀπ' αὐτῶν κἀμὲ ταῖς νουμηνίαις.

Note first of all the unobtrusive but rare skill with which Aristophanes has reproduced the authentic quality of natural speech within a rigid and elaborate metrical framework. One might think of Catullus as another ancient poet who possessed this particular gift. The personification of Ἔρως is removed both from the realm of high poetry and from the banal and given a touching naïvety and literalness by ὥσπερ ὁ γεγραμμένος, 'just like the one in the picture'. 'The remainder of the song', to quote Dover, 'appears to describe the planting and cultivation of vines, figs and olives, but nearly all the words chosen are also slang words for the male and female genitals and so constitute a description of some details of sexual intercourse' (*Aristophanic Comedy*, 47). True, no doubt, but it is a pity to stop there. The extended passage of *double entendre* recalls Anacreon, *PMG* 417, πῶλε Θρηκίη . . . But in that poem, characteristically of Anacreon's heterosexual love-poetry, the tone is hostile and the metaphor is of dominance and aggression, while Aristophanes' symbolism is of fertility and peace. προσβαλεῖν at 994 belongs to the ordinary (and graphic) Greek colloquial language of sex, but Jeffrey Henderson's assumption (*The Maculate Muse*, 170) that the old men are contemplating gang-rape is an over-literal inference from the necessary plurality of the chorus. They express themselves like wooers, not like rapists, and they are envisaging a continuing way of life. As they look forward individually to cultivating their own land in peace, they also look forward to individual enjoyment of Diallage. The idea belongs to the same area of symbolism as the 'marriage' of Trygaeus to Opora at the end of *Peace*. The similarity of technique with Anacreon highlights the difference in emotional tone. Moreover, there is a double layer of symbolism in Aristophanes: the vines, figs, and olives are also the slow-yielding crops which are only worth planting in times of peace and stability. The sexual metaphor conveys the sensual intensity of the old countryman's love for his land. One could hardly look for a better illustration of the passage than Norman Douglas's reminiscence of the Mediterranean countryside: 'I remember watching an old man stubbornly digging a field by himself. He toiled through the flaming hours, and what he lacked in strength was made up in the craftiness, *maliʒia*, born of long love of the soil' (*Old Calabria*, ch. 8).

2 The Metres of Aristophanes

I. *Colon and verse*

Since Boeckh observed the significance of verse-end in lyric (*Pindari carmina quae supersunt* (Leipzig, 1811–21)), texts of Pindar have been laid out in verses. In texts of dramatic lyric, however, editors, while often (and necessarily) correcting and rearranging the colometries inherited from medieval MSS, still, for the most part, divide into cola of dimeter- or trimeter-length. A major reason for this is the comparative difficulty of finding verse-end in dramatic lyric, where the metrical pattern is generally repeated only once, instead of eight or ten times, as often in Pindar. It is also arguable that presentation in short cola makes it easier for the metrically-conscious reader to distinguish the rhythm. Not infrequently, however, division into short cola makes metrical nonsense. No editor now follows the MSS RV in disguising the dactylic hexameters that feature in lyric by dividing them into

$$- \cup \cup - \cup \cup -$$
$$\cup \cup - \cup \cup - \cup \cup - -$$

Again, a verse like $- \cup \cup - \quad - \cup \cup - \quad - \cup \cup - \quad \cup - -$ is comprehensible as a sequence of identical rhythmic phrases with a contrasting clausula. It makes far less sense as a pair of 'dimeters':

$$- \cup \cup - \quad - \cup \cup -$$
$$- \cup \cup - \quad \cup - -$$

But the combinations of iambic dimeter + catalectic iambic dimeter and trochaic dimeter + catalectic trochaic dimeter present a problem. Both combinations are familiar in comedy as recitative verses, with regular word-end between the constituent cola. Should those sequences, then, be printed as tetrameters when they occur in lyric? It is difficult, indeed

impossible, to be consistent in this matter. The metrical shape and context of the individual passage may seem to suggest either a dimeter or a
tetrameter division. We cannot, in any case, be sure that the distinctions
that our typographical conventions force upon us would have had any
meaning for the poet and his contemporaries.

The relationship between word-end and colon-end is not simple. In
aeolo-choriambic, cola are clearly recognizable, whether or not they are
marked off by word-end. Thus, ·· ··−◡◡−◡− ·· ··−◡◡−− is
clearly two cola, whether or not word-end falls between the eighth and
ninth positions. In metres composed in repeating metra, however, we
have little except coincidence of word-end with metron-end to guide
us. If an undivided sequence of, say, four iambic metra occurs among
unambiguous dimeters, we may surmise that the prevailing movement
will have caused the original hearers to phrase the sequence as

$$\times - \cup - \quad \times - \cup -$$
$$\times - \cup - \quad \times - \cup -$$

Something of the kind may apply at *Frogs* 384–8 = 389–93, where the
strophe is divided into dimeters by word-end, while the antistrophe is
only divided into 6 metra + 4 metra. But this is only conjecture. In the
mammoth run of dactyls at *Ecc.* 1169–76 (to take an extreme example),
we have no way of identifying cola.

It is, however, important to take note of coincidence of word-end in
strophe and antistrophe if it falls at a point which could be the junction
between cola. Coincidence of word-end is a signal from the poet. To
take an example from outside Aristophanes, at *Her.* 763–6 = 772–6,
Diggle divides:

$$\cup - | \cup - |$$
$$- \cup \cup - | \quad \cup - \cup | -$$
$$- \cup \cup - | \quad \cup - - |$$
$$\cup - \cup - \quad - \cup \cup - |$$
$$\cup - \cup - \quad - \cup \cup - |$$
$$\cup \overarc{\cup} \cup \overarc{\cup} \quad \cup - - |$$

The second and third cola (−◡◡− ×−◡− −◡◡− ◡−−)
make up a combination common in iambo-choriambic (see below,

p. 79), but to produce it Diggle has ignored a signal from the poet. Dale divides:

$$\cup - | \cup - | \quad - \cup \cup - |$$
$$\cup - \cup | - \quad - \cup \cup - | \quad \cup - - |$$
$$\cup - \cup - \quad - \cup \cup - |$$
$$\cup - \cup - | \quad - \cup \cup - |$$
$$\cup \,\widehat{}\, \cup \,\widehat{}\, | \quad \cup - - |$$

By following coincidence of word-end more closely, Dale has produced a simpler and more coherent pattern, and has shown how insistently Euripides has marked off the phrase ◡ − ◡ −   − ◡ ◡ −. Again, at *Ach.* 1160–1 = 1171–2, the traditional colometry, common to RV and the Aldine, produces 'dimeters' in flagrant disregard of coinciding word-end:

$$\cup - - \quad - \cup -$$
$$- - \cup - | \quad - - \cup -$$
$$- \cup - \quad \cup - - |||$$

Elmsley, following word-end, produced a pair of syncopated iambic trimeters — and (unawares, no doubt) a metrical joke: the account of an eminently untragic occurrence reaches its climax in tragic rhythm (see below, ad loc.). Preserving the dimeter division is misplaced piety, since it entails disregarding the guidance in articulating the passage that the poet himself has provided.

There are, however, many passages where more than one division would make sense. Thus, at *Lys.* 327–9 = 341–3

$$- - \cup - \quad - \cup \cup - | \quad - \cup \cup - \quad \cup - \smile ||$$
$$\underset{\smile}{} \,\widehat{}\, \cup - \quad - \cup \cup - | \quad - \cup \cup - | \quad - \cup \cup - \quad \cup - - |$$

could, given the pattern of corresponding word-end, be laid out as

$$- - \cup - \quad - \cup \cup - |$$
$$- \cup \cup - \quad \cup - \smile ||$$
$$\underset{\smile}{} \,\widehat{}\, \cup - \quad - \cup \cup - |$$
$$- \cup \cup - |$$
$$- \cup \cup - \quad \cup - - |$$

Both divisions express something about the rhythm of the passage.

While certainty is often impossible, every stanza must be examined without preconceptions and with careful attention to any signals, such as corresponding word-end, which the text may offer.

II. *Strophic structure*

The key to strophic structure has, not unnaturally, been sought in numerical patterning, and in some metrically-uniform stanzas marked off in sections by recurring catalexis, counting metra does indeed show a kind of symmetry. Thus, the pure iambic stanza, *Ach.* 929 ff. = 940 ff., divides into 7 7 2 2 7. In the same play, 1008 ff. = 1037 ff., again pure iambic, falls into 6 4 4 6. *Ach.* 284 ff. = 335 ff. is not metrically uniform, but there the stanza divides into near-symmetrical halves, in which changes of metre reinforce a numerical pattern: (i) 4 tro, 5 ∪ ∪ −, 4 tro, 12 cr; (ii) 4 tro, 5 cr, 4 tro, 12 cr. In many stanzas, however, metron-counting yields no readily intelligible result. That applies even to metrically-uniform stanzas. Thus, counting metra in the sections marked off by catalexis in the pure trochaic stanza, *Wasps* 1265 ff., gives 6 4 8 5 6. Another pure trochaic stanza, *Thesm.* 459 ff., divides into 7 11. In polymetric lyric, metron-counting becomes altogether questionable. In what sense can metra so different in length as the anapaest and the dactyl be treated as equivalent? The glyconic is commonly seen as equivalent to a dimeter. But what measure, in that case, is to be attributed to the telesillean and the lesser asclepiad? Even so relatively sensitive and flexible a metron-counter as Walther Kraus (*Strophengestaltung in der griechischen Tragödie*, i. *Aischylos und Sophokles* (Vienna, 1959); see Parker, *CR* 1959) shows dangerously procrustean tendencies.

Alternation is an obvious pattern which has a long history in Greek poetry going back to the elegiac couplet and the epodic metres of Archilochus. One whole stanza in Aristophanes, *Clouds* 1345 ff., is based on it; the couplet ia trim, reiz is repeated three times. Elsewhere, alternating cola make up part of a stanza. See, for example, *Ach.* 1218–25 (ia trim, δ; ia trim, ia dim cat), *Birds* 233–6 (tro trim, δ), 1748–51 (da tetram, da trim), *Lys.* 1287–90 (da tetram, ibyc). The dactylo-epitrite passage at *Clouds* 465–75 makes a tantalizing approximation to alternation:

−∪∪−∪∪−   ∪   −∪∪−∪∪−

−   −∪∪−∪∪−   ∪   −∪−   −

$$- \cup \cup - \cup \cup - \quad - \quad - \cup \cup - \cup \cup - \quad -$$
$$- \cup \cup - \cup \cup - \quad - \quad - \cup - \quad -$$
$$- \cup \cup - \cup \cup - \quad - \quad - \cup \cup - \cup \cup -$$

The third verse differs from the first and fifth only by the added final anceps; the second differs from the fourth by the initial anceps. One may guess that for the poet and his contemporaries the avoidance of exact symmetry here gave interest and piquancy to the rhythms.

A far more common method of pattern-making in Greek lyric, however, is to use the contrast between catalectic and acatalectic cola, that is between blunt ending (. . . $\cup - |$) and pendent (. . . $\cup - - |$). In its most elementary form, the contrast is exemplified in various dicola made up of dimeter + catalectic dimeter:

iambic (blunt, pendent):

$$\times - \cup - \quad \times - \cup - | \quad \times - \cup - \quad \cup - -$$

trochaic (pendent, blunt):

$$- \cup - \times \quad - \cup - \times | \quad - \cup - \times \quad - \cup -$$

priapean (blunt, pendent):

$$.. \quad ..- \cup \cup - \cup - | \quad .. \quad ..- \cup \cup - -$$

Two, three, or four acatalectic cola with catalectic clausula make up simple lyric stanzas. A stanza of this type made up of two or three glyconics with pherecratean clausula first appears in Anacreon (*PMG* 357–61). Aristophanes more than once uses a version made up of telesilleans with reizianum as clausula:

$$\times - \cup \cup - \cup -$$
$$\times - \cup \cup - \cup -$$
$$\times - \cup \cup - \cup -$$
$$\times - \cup \cup - -$$

See *Peace* 856 ff. = 909 ff., 1329 ff., *Birds* 1731 ff. = 1737 ff., *Frogs* 448 ff. = 454 ff., and, with a syncopated iambic tetrameter prefixed, *Ecc.* 289 ff. = 300 ff. The fact that *Peace* 1329 ff. and *Birds* 1731 ff. = 1737 ff. are wedding songs suggests traditional usage (see on *Peace* 1329 ff.). Stanzas of such demotic simplicity are rare in literary lyric, even in Aristophanes, but both he and the tragedians frequently use sequences of this kind as components in longer and more complicated stanzas. The following four stanzas can serve as a conspectus of the range of sophistication of Attic lyric. All are predominantly in the same or kindred types of metre, and all rely to a great extent on versions of the glyconic-pherecratean stanza of Anacreon.

A. *Knights* 973 ff. = 985 ff.:

> i   – ⏑̅ – ⏑ ⏑ – ⏑ –
>
>   – – – ⏑ ⏑ – ⏑ –
>
>   – – – ⏑ ⏑ – ⏑ –
>
>   – ⏑ – ⏑ ⏑ – –
>
> ii   – – – ⏑ ⏑ – ⏑ –
>
>   – – – ⏑ ⏑ – ⏑ –
>
>   – – – ⏑ ⏑ – ⏑ –
>
>   – ⏑̅ – ⏑ ⏑ – –
>
> iii   – – – ⏑ ⏑ – ⏑ –
>
>   – ⏑̆ – ⏑ ⏑ – ⏑ –
>
>   – ⏑̅ – ⏑ ⏑ – ⏑ –
>
>   – – – ⏑ ⏑ – ⏑̆ |||

In this song, which was clearly intended to catch on with sections of the public hostile to Cleon, Aristophanes simply repeats Anacreon's quatrain three times over.

B. *Knights* 551 ff. = 581 ff.:

> i   – ⏑ ⏑ –   ⏑ – ⏑ –
>
>   – ⏑ ⏑ –   ⏑̅ – ⏑ –
>
>   – ⏑ ⏑ –   ⏑ – ⏑ –
>
>   – ⏑ ⏑ –   ⏑ – ⏑ –
>
>   – ⏑ ⏑ –   ⏑ – –
>
> ii   – ⏑ ⏑ –   ⏑ – ⏑ –
>
>   – ⏑ ⏑ –   ⏑ – ⏑ –
>
>   – ⏑ ⏑ –   ⏑ – –
>
> iii   – – – ⏑ ⏑ – – ⏑ ⏑ – –
>
>   – – – ⏑ ⏑ – – ⏑ ⏑ – ⏑̆ ||
>
> iv   – ⏑̆ – ⏑ ⏑ – ⏑ –
>
>   – ⏑̆ – ⏑ ⏑ – ⏑ –
>
>   – – – ⏑ ⏑ – ⏑ –
>
>   – – – ⏑ ⏑ – ⏑̆ |||

This hymn shows a distinct advance in metrical sophistication. There are now four sections, of which the last is the basic quatrain. The first also follows the pattern of repeated blunt colon rounded off by its own catalectic form, but the cola used are the choriambo-iambic dimeter, with the cognate aristophanean as clausula. The second section begins as if to repeat the first, but comes to its catalectic close after two cola instead of four. The third section marks the high point (an invocation in the strophe), and Aristophanes introduces a pair of catalectic lesser asclepiads, more exotic members of the same family of rhythms from the eastern Aegean.

C. *Clouds* 563 ff. = 595 ff.:

<pre>
  i   – ∪ ∪ –   ∪ – ∪ –
      – ∪ ∪ –   ∪ – ∪ –
      – ∪ ∪ –   ∪ – –
 ii   – ∪ ∪ –   ∪ – ∪ –
        – ∪ ∪ –| – ∪ ∪ –   ∪ – ∪ –
        – ∪ ∪ –   ∪ – ⌣ ||
iii   – ∪ ∪   – ∪ ∪   – ∪ ∪   – ∪ ∪
        – ∪ ∪   – ∪ ∪   – ∪ ∪   – ∪ ∪   – –
 iv   – – ∪ –   – ∪ ∪ –
        ⌣ – – – – ∪ ∪ –
      – ⌣ – ∪ ∪ – ∪ –
      – – – ∪ ∪ – ⌣ |||
</pre>

This is, again, a hymn. It is sung by an exceptionally dignified chorus (see below, p. 192–7), and shows still further elaboration. Like B, the stanza begins with two sections in choriambo-iambic: blunt cola rounded off by aristophaneans. But the second section differs from the first in that the second colon is lengthened by an extra choriamb. Section iii introduces dactylic, a metre of different origin, although found in company with choriambic cola as early as Alcman (*PMG* 1). Finally, the quatrain returns, but not in its ordinary, simple form, for the first two blunt cola are not glyconics, but an iambo-choriambic dimeter and a polyschematist.

D. *OC* 668 ff. = 681 ff.:

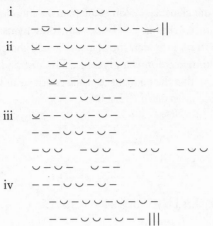

This, of course, is the first strophic pair of one of the most famous lyrics in tragedy, Sophocles' Colonus song. While using, for the most part, the most common cola, Sophocles has introduced a greater element of the unexpected than Aristophanes, even in C. Every section begins with a glyconic, and in ii the glyconic does actually lead into the familiar quatrain. Section i features the common contrast of blunt and pendent, but the glyconic is followed not by a pherecratean, but by a longer pendent colon, a hendecasyllable. Section iii starts with two glyconics, as if to repeat the simple rhythms of ii, but a short dactylic interlude breaks in abruptly (not tidily, after catalexis, as in C). Nor do the dactyls end in an orthodox spondee (see p. 48). Instead, in defiance of normal practice in Greek metre, double short is followed by anceps, and the section ends with a catalectic iambic dimeter. Section iv seems about to repeat section i, but the second colon extends the glyconic only by ∪ −, instead of ∪ − −, and the clausula is the catalectic version of this new colon.

The sequence of acatalectic cola with catalectic clausula (a a b, a a a b, etc.) is not the only pattern to exploit the contrast of blunt and pendent. For the simple iambic lampoon-song at *Frogs* 416 ff., Aristophanes uses a short repeating stanza of two catalectic dimeters, with acatalectic trimeter as clausula:

$$\times - \cup - \qquad \cup - -$$
$$- - \cup - \qquad \cup - -$$
$$\times - \cup - \qquad \times - \cup - \qquad \times - \cup -$$

The normal relation between catalectic and acatalectic has been reversed, and the clausular colon stands out all the more by its greater length. For the ephymnia at *Ag.* 366 ff., Aeschylus uses an aeolo-choriambic quatrain in which the clausula is still the pherecratean, but only the penultimate colon is a glyconic. The first and second cola are pherecrateans, so that the pendent clausula contrasts only with the colon that immediately precedes it (b b a b):

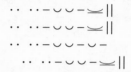

Aristophanes makes play with aeolo-choriambic variations of this kind on a larger scale at *Wasps* 317–23 and *Frogs* 1251 ff. In *Frogs* 1370 ff. and 1482 ff. = 1491 ff., he makes similar patterns with the trochaic dimeter (a) and its catalectic form, the lecythion (b), adding to each stanza a clausula unusual in trochees, − ‿ − ‿   − − (c): b b b a a a a c and b b b a b a a a c. There is, however, a further patterning device which gives these stanzas a touch of distinction and sophistication: resolution, producing strategically-placed runs of three, or sometimes six, short syllables. 1370 ff.:

The fourth colon begins with a fully resolved metron, like the second and third, but defeats expectation by turning out to be acatalectic. In the sixth colon, the resolved first long of the second metron comes as a surprise, for the hearer has become accustomed to alternation between resolved and unresolved metra. The sequence of three metra with resolution in the sixth and seventh cola builds up a tension which is released by the unresolved second metron of colon 7. The last colon again brings a surprise: there is no initial resolution, and $--$ takes the place of $-\smile-$, the normal catalectic rhythm in trochees.

Stanzas quite often gain their effect by surprise, by cheating expectations based on familiar metrical patterns (e.g. *OC* 668 ff. = 681 ff.), or created by the poet himself (e.g. *Frogs* 1370 ff.). One more example will suffice: the three corresponding stanzas of the hymn to Iacchus at *Frogs* 398 ff.:

$$\smile-\smile\;\underset{\smile\smile}{=}\qquad \smile-\smile|\underset{\smile\smile}{}\qquad \smile-\underset{=}{}\|$$

$$--\smile-\quad -|\underset{\smile\smile}{}\;\underset{\smile\smile}{=}\quad \smile--$$

$$--\smile-$$

$$\underset{\smile}{=}-\smile-\quad \underset{\smile}{=}-\smile-\quad --\smile-\quad \smile-\underset{=}{}\;\|$$

$$\smile-\smile\smile\smile\quad \smile-\smile|-\quad \smile-\smile\smile\;\||\|$$

The first two verses are mildly surprising in themselves, since the catalectic trimeter is far less familiar than the acatalectic, and both prepare the hearer for the familiar verse by the caesura. The single metron of the third colon puzzles the ear; the familiar iambic tetrameter provides a resolution. The refrain, in the form of an acatalectic trimeter, comes unexpectedly after the definitive-sounding tetrameter, and, at the same time, half-echoes the opening verse, with its caesura.

Numerical patterns, patterns of repetition and near-repetition, of defeated expectation, of contrasting close can be recognized by anyone sensitive to rhythm. It must, however, be admitted that the structure of much dramatic lyric remains obscure to us. Astrophic monodic lyric in particular often seems merely to ramble on. In fact, its freedom and flexibility may well have provided an important means of expression. The most fruitful approach is to be alert to every type of signal, not to look for some universal structural principle.

IAMBIC

Metron: $\times-\smile-$

Iambic is one of several types of Greek metre based on the sequence $\ldots\times-\smile-\times\ldots$ (see Dale, *LM²*, 71–2, *Collected Papers*, 174 ff.). In the fully-developed lyric iambic of Attic drama, two types of variation are possible: resolution of one or both longs ($\times\widehat{}\smile-$, $\times-\smile\widehat{}$,

$\times \widehat{\smile}\smile\widehat{\smile}$) and syncopation, meaning the suppression of anceps (to produce $-\smile-$ 'cretic'), or of short (to produce $\smile--$ 'bacchiac', or $---$ 'molossus'), or, occasionally, of both ($--$ 'spondee'). Word-end between shorts produced by resolution ('split resolution') is generally avoided, especially before and after long anceps (Parker, *CQ* 18 (1968), 241–69). In serious poetry, word-end is avoided after long anceps ('extended Porson's Law', Parker, *CQ* 16 (1966), 1–26). The bacchiac provides the catalectic rhythm for iambic, and is normally preceded or followed by word-end (Dale, *LM²*, 72, Parker, *CQ* 26 (1976), 20). Bacchiacs are also sometimes found in sequence.

The word ἴαμβος occurs for the first time in Archilochus (*IEG²* 215), in a context which suggests that it is not a metrical term. Sir Kenneth Dover (*Entretiens Hardt*, 10 (1963), 183–212) suggests that Archilochus used the term ἴαμβοι for all his poems, regardless of metre, and that its reference was to 'the type of occasion for which they were composed'. The use of the term to designate a poetic genre not confined to iambic metre continued beyond the fifth century (Aristotle, *Rhet.* 1418^b) and through the Hellenistic period.

As well as the term, the earliest literary use of the iambic metre is found in Archilochus. The only lengths that definitely occur in his fragments are the trimeter and dimeter. There are fewer than half a dozen examples of resolution, and never more than one in a verse. Syncopation is confined to the final bacchiac of the catalectic trimeter ($\times-\smile-$ $\times-\smile-$ $\smile--$) and the short colon known as 'ithyphallic' ($-\smile-$ $\smile--$), which he uses in compound verses. Iambic, with and without catalexis, is also well represented in the fragments of Alcman (catalectic trimeter: *PMG* 14, 19, 30, 59(a); acatalectic tetrameter: 15; indeterminate longer sequences: 16, 20). The catalectic tetrameter is found in Hipponax (*IEG²* 119), the acatalectic in Alcaeus (*PLF* 374). Anacreon seems to have used iambic dimeters in sequence: *PMG* 427–8 (acatalectic) and 429 (catalectic).

Archilochus and Hipponax were celebrated as writers of invective, and Archilochus at least was treated in old comedy as a congenial literary figure (witness Cratinus' play Ἀρχίλοχοι and the widespread comic use of dicola on the Archilochean model). But the association of iambic metre with invective and burlesque goes back to folk usage (see the Homeric *Hymn to Demeter*, 202ff., with Richardson on 213–17, and

Aristotle, *Poetics* 1448[b]). A literary version of an invective cult-song is to be found at *Frogs* 420–34, and an iambic lampoon-song outside a cult context at *Ach.* 836–59. Compare Eupolis, *PCG* 99 and 386.

The traditional use of iambic does not seem to have been confined to ritual invective. The lampoon-song at *Frogs* 420 ff. is preceded by hymns to Demeter (384 ff.) and Iacchus (398 ff.), both, equally, in very simple iambic. There is an iambic hymn at *Thesm.* 969 ff. = 977 ff., and other hymns in that play include substantial iambic passages (312–31 and 351–71). Dicaeopolis' solo hymn to Phales at *Ach.* 263–79 is also in simple iambic, and is, we may guess, a literary version of some kind of traditional song. It seems safe to assume that iambic was commonly used for ritual invective and popular hymnody because it was the easiest and most natural rhythm in which an ordinary Greek could compose. Aristotle, in explaining its predominance as the spoken metre of drama, calls it μάλιστα . . . λεκτικὸν τῶν μέτρων (*Poetics* 1449[a]). Again, the fact that no other metre, except for a few dochmiacs, features in the lyric of *Wealth* is a clear indication of loss of interest in, and appreciation of, the sophisticated and subtly allusive use of metre which characterizes the earlier plays, and of decline into the simple and popular.

In addition to dialogue and song, iambic is extensively used in comic recitative: in catalectic tetrameters in sequence and in systems of dimeters rounded off by catalexis (e.g. *Knights* 367–81). In Attic drama, song, recitative, and speech do not seem to have been distinguished with the sharpness and clarity that the terms imply to a modern sensibility. Thus, a dialogue in which one character 'sings' and another 'speaks' is not uncommon in tragedy. In Aristophanes, the characteristic recitative verse, the catalectic tetrameter, is often found, singly or in sequence, in lyric contexts, and it is often far from clear what method of delivery was intended: recitative and song merge. Simple iambic, closely akin to recitative, is common in a range of songs in which the chorus involves itself closely and directly in the action: when it carries on a dialogue with a character (*Ach.* 929 ff., 1008 ff., *Peace* 512 ff., 856 ff., 939 ff., *Birds* 406 ff., *Thesm.* 707 ff., *Frogs* 209 ff.); or exhorts and advises him (*Knights* 756 ff., *Wasps* 729 ff., *Clouds* 1345 ff., *Ecc.* 478 ff.); or comments on his actions (*Clouds* 1303 ff.). Dialogue, exhortation, advice, and comment are not, of course, mutually exclusive.

The Attic tragedians developed highly sophisticated forms of iambic, far removed from the simple and popular. Resolution was exploited for expressive purposes, especially for lamentation. It is found in threnetic passages in Aeschylus (*Sept.* 848 ff., *Cho.* 22 ff.), Sophocles (*Trach.* 947 ff.), and, above all, Euripides (*Med.* 206, *Andr.* 492–3, *Her.* 113 ff. = 125 ff., *Tro.* 1313 = 1329, *Hel.* 195 = 214, 1117–18 = 1133–4, *IT* 863, *Phoen.* 1030–1 = 1054–5, *Or.* 1414, 1416, *IA* 1334). There is a strong tendency in resolved iambic not merely to avoid split resolution, but to compose resolved metra in trisyllabic words, e.g. *Trach.* 947–8 (= 950–1):

$$\pi\acute{o}\tau\epsilon\rho\alpha\ \pi\rho\acute{o}\tau\epsilon\rho o\nu\ \acute{\epsilon}\pi\iota\sigma\tau\acute{\epsilon}\nu\omega,$$
$$\pi\acute{o}\tau\epsilon\rho\alpha\ \mu\acute{\epsilon}\lambda\epsilon\alpha\ \pi\epsilon\rho\alpha\iota\tau\acute{\epsilon}\rho\omega$$

$$\cup \widehat{} \mid \cup \widehat{} \mid \quad \cup - \cup -$$
$$\cup \widehat{} \mid \cup \widehat{} \mid \quad \cup - \cup -$$

(Cf. *Ant.* 108 = 126, *El.* 209–10 = 229–30, *Phil.* 1210, *OC* 186, 538 = 545). In Euripides, there are iambic dimeters which are completely resolved and divided trisyllabically throughout, e.g. *Or.* 1416:

$$\dot{\alpha}\nu\dot{\alpha}\ \delta\dot{\epsilon}\ \delta\rho o\mu\acute{\alpha}\delta\epsilon\varsigma\ \acute{\epsilon}\theta o\rho o\nu\ \acute{\epsilon}\theta o\rho o\nu$$
$$\cup \widehat{} \mid \cup \widehat{} \mid \quad \cup \widehat{} \mid \cup \widehat{} \mid$$

(Cf. *Andr.* 491, *Tro.* 1288, *Phoen.* 1030 = 1054, *Ba.* 600, *IA* 1334). As in the example quoted, Euripides' fondness for repeating words is often exemplified in his resolved iambic. Aristophanes parodies threnetic resolution at *Ach.* 1191 and *Frogs* 1338, 1354–5. By contrast, he makes a distinctively comic use of resolution in *Birds* 853 ff. = 897 ff., to mimic twittering.

Syncopation, used with freedom, not merely to produce catalexis, or in certain fixed cola, is characteristic of tragedy, and of Aeschylus in particular. The rhythm is especially well represented in *Ag.* There, the trimeter length is common, resolution and long anceps are avoided, the same verse-form is often repeated within the stanza, and there is a tendency for word-end and metron-end to coincide, e.g. *Ag.* 192–7:

$$\pi\nu o\alpha\grave{\iota}\ \delta'\ \dot{\alpha}\pi\grave{o}\ \Sigma\tau\rho\acute{\upsilon}\mu o\nu o\varsigma\ \mu o\lambda o\hat{\upsilon}\sigma\alpha\iota$$
$$\kappa\alpha\kappa\acute{o}\sigma\chi o\lambda o\iota\ \nu\acute{\eta}\sigma\tau\iota\delta\epsilon\varsigma\ \delta\acute{\upsilon}\sigma o\rho\mu o\iota$$
$$\beta\rho o\tau\hat{\omega}\nu\ \acute{\alpha}\lambda\alpha\iota,$$
$$\nu\alpha\hat{\omega}\nu\ \langle\tau\epsilon\rangle\ \kappa\alpha\grave{\iota}\ \pi\epsilon\iota\sigma\mu\acute{\alpha}\tau\omega\nu\ \dot{\alpha}\phi\epsilon\iota\delta\epsilon\hat{\iota}\varsigma$$
$$\pi\alpha\lambda\iota\mu\mu\acute{\eta}\kappa\eta\ \chi\rho\acute{o}\nu o\nu\ \tau\iota\theta\epsilon\hat{\iota}\sigma\alpha\iota\ \ldots$$

∪ – ∪ –   – ∪ –| ∪ – –
∪ – ∪ –| – ∪ –| ∪ – –
∪ – ∪ –
– – ∪ –   – ∪ –| ∪ – –
∪ – –   – ∪ –| ∪ – –

A fragment of Cratinus, *PCG* 258, suggests burlesque of Aeschylus:

> Στάσις δὲ καὶ πρεσβυγενὴς
> Χρόνος ἀλλήλοισι μιγέντε
> μέγιστον τίκτετον τύραννον
> ὃν δὴ κεφαληγερέταν
> θεοὶ καλέουσι

∪ – ∪ –   – ∪ ∪ –
∪ ∪ – – – ∪ ∪ – ◡||
∪ – –| – ∪ –| ∪ – –
– – ∪ ∪ – ∪ ∪ –
∪ – ∪ ∪ – ∪

The metrical context is enigmatic, but the third colon stands out as authentically Aeschylean in rhythm. Typically (although not, of course, exclusively) Aeschylean is also the symbolical genealogy (cf. *Ag.* 385–6, 750–6, 764–6, and see Fraenkel on 386). The diction, however, is banal, and the collocation of syllables τον τικ τε τον τυ possibly a trifle absurd.

Excluding examples of the simple catalectic trimeter (× – ∪ – × – ∪ –   ∪ – –), there are 18 syncopated trimeters in Aristophanes:

(a) × – ∪ –   – ∪ –   × – ∪ –   6 (*Ach.* 1196, 1205, 1207, *Clouds* 1154, 1155, *Wasps* 732=746)

(b) × – ∪ –   – ∪ –   ∪ – –   6 (*Ach.* 1161=1173, 1197, 1203, 1210, *Birds* 636, *Thesm.* 1033)

(c) ∪ – –   – ∪ –   × – ∪ –   3 (*Ach.* 1159–60=1171–2, *Birds* 629, 630)

(d) ∪ – –   – ∪ –   ∪ – –   1 (*Birds* 858=902)

(e) – –   – ∪ –   ∪ – –   1 (*Lys.* 1261).

Of these verses, no fewer than six come from the paratragic duet between Dicaeopolis and Lamachus at the end of *Ach. Clouds* 1154–5 and

Thesm. 1033 are also paratragic. In almost all the other passages, the chorus is in serious mood. *Wasps* 732=746 reflects a moment of urgency and passion, and *Birds* 629, 630 and 636 one of emotional exaltation. *Lys.* 1261 comes in the Spartan song, a composition *sui generis*, which seems, in spite of the dialect, to be non-burlesque. Given the evidence that syncopated iambic trimeters belong to the grand style, the combination of the verse with low content at *Birds* 858=902 and, more decisively, *Ach.* 1161=1173 suggests a musical joke.

In Sophocles, pure, or nearly pure, iambic stanzas are rare (see *Trach.* 132–40, 205–24 and *OT* 190 ff.=203 ff.). Iambic trimeters appear as clausulae to stanzas in other metres, sometimes with a more or less substantial preceding section in iambic (*Ant.* 856=875, 954=965, 976=987, *El.* 127=144, 172=192, 1089=1096, *OC* 1084=1095, 1567=1578, *OT* 668=696). The pure, or nearly pure, iambic stanza returns in Euripides, but with less syncopation, fewer trimeter-lengths, and more resolution. See, for example, *Supp.* 798 ff.=811 ff., 918 ff., 1123 ff.=1132 ff., 1139 ff.= 1146 ff., 1153 ff.=1159 ff., *Tro.* 1302 ff.=1317 ff. The result is quite different from the lapidary stanzas of Aeschylus.

Bacchiacs in sequence are found in Aeschylus and Euripides, and occasionally (strategically placed) in Aristophanes. See further below, on *Thesm.* 1018–19 and 1136 ff. Molossi in sequence are much rarer. See below, on *Birds* 1720 ff.

While generally in Greek lyric different types of metre are divided from each other at least by word-end, iambic forms compounds comparatively readily. The combination of iambic and choriambic metra is common enough to constitute a distinct type of metre (see below, on *Iambo-Choriambic*). In quotation from Aeschylus, an iambic metron introduces dactyls at *Frogs* 1264, 1269, 1285, 1291. An iambic metron leads into cretics at *Birds* 410–15, *Lys.* 476=541, 614–5=636–7, 1047=1061=1193=1207. Iambic dimeter in synartesis with reizianum is a recurrent combination: *Ach.* 840–1=846–7, 852–3=858–9, *Clouds* 1304=1312, *Lys.* 1302–3. Iambic leads into dochmiac at *Wasps* 729–30. More rarely, iambic follows another rhythm without intervening word-end: dochmiac runs into iambic at *Thesm.* 1028–9 and *Frogs* 883–4, and telesillean into iambic at *Thesm.* 1020–1.

In Sophocles and Euripides, trisyllabic dactyl is occasionally found immediately preceding iamb (. . . $-\cup\cup$ $\times-\cup-$), a collocation which breaks the embargo on short beside anceps (see Stinton, *CR* 15 (1965), 142 ff. = *Collected Papers* (1990), 11, and D. S. Raven, *AJP* 86 (1965), 225 ff. and below, under *Dactylic*). There are a few possible examples of this phenomenon in Aristophanes: *Lys.* 277–8 (susceptible to other analyses and almost certainly corrupt), *Thesm.* 127–8, *Frogs* 674–5 = 706–7. The *Thesm.* and *Frogs* passages are both in the metrical grand style.

In the spoken iambic of comedy, double short is quite freely substituted for anceps or short (⌣ ⌣ – ⌣ –, ×– ⌣ ⌣ –). The same substitution is found, though less often, in recitative, e.g. *Knights* 414:

ἀπομαγδαλιὰς σιτούμενος τοσοῦτος ἐκτραφείην

⌢ – ⌢ –   – – ⌣ –   ⌣ – ⌣ –   ⌣ – –

and 921:

τῶν δᾳδίων ἀπαρυστέον

– – ⌣ –   ⌢ – ⌣ –

In lyric it is exceedingly rare. At *Ach.* 849, the MSS offer ⌢ for ⌣, but there sense is dubious as well as metre. There are, at most, five examples of ⌢ for ×: *Ach.* 1040 (κατάχει), *Clouds* 812 (ταχέως. ταχέως is judged un-Aristophanic by Dover, ad loc., but see *Wasps* 1068 νεανικὴν, 1070 νεανιῶν and, perhaps, *Thesm.* 465 ὕβρεως), *Peace* 947 (τὸ κανοῦν, which may be recitative), *Lys.* 345 (πολιοῦχε, unless the ι is consonantalized), *Thesm.* 680 (μανίαις).

Aristophanes breaks the extended Porson's Law in his lyric iambics, just as he breaks the original Law in his spoken trimeters and recitative. There are some forty examples of word-end after long anceps in his lyric, not softened by elision and not including caesurae in trimeters in lyric contexts. In his spoken iambic, it is possible to identify paratragic trimeters in which the Law is observed. The position is much less clear in lyric. Word-end after long anceps is not found in some unmistakably paratragic iambic, such as the antiphonal lament between Dicaeopolis and Lamachus at *Ach.* 1190 ff., and the monodies at *Clouds* 1154 ff. and *Thesm.* 1015 ff. It is, however, also absent from some characteristically comic stanzas: *Knights* 756 ff. = 836 ff., *Peace* 512 ff., *Wealth* 290 ff. = 296 ff., 302 ff. = 309 ff. One is tempted to suspect that its presence or absence is fortuitous.

Where long anceps occurs in combination with resolution, particular restrictions seem to apply. Long anceps is in itself out of keeping with the 'pattering' rhythm of heavily resolved passages. But metra immediately preceded by word-end where the long anceps is followed by resolved long without word-end (| – ‿͡‿ ‿ –) are not rare: there are eighteen examples. In comparison, resolution preceding long anceps is rare, with or without intervening word-end. There are three examples of ×– ‿ ͡‿ | – – ‿ – (*Ach.* 1011–12, *Thesm.* 318–19 and 970–1), and four of ×– ‿ ͡‿ ͡ – – ‿ – (*Frogs* 398, *Ecc* 485, *Wealth* 314). *Wealth* 314 is a particularly ungainly verse, with two occurrences:

τὴν ῥῖνα· σὺ δ᾽ Ἀρίστυλλος ὑποχάσκων ἐρεῖς

– – ‿ ͡‿   – – ‿ ͡‿   – – ‿ –

Rarest of all is word-end after long anceps with following resolution: – | ͡‿ ‿ –. *Frogs* 405 is a catalectic trimeter, and word-end falls at the caesura point:

κἀπ᾽ εὐτελείᾳ τόδε τὸ σανδαλίσκον

– – ‿ –   – | ͡‿ ‿ –   ‿ – –

Wasps 1337 is much harsher, but there seems no other reason to doubt the text:

ἀρχαῖά γ᾽ ὑμῶν· ἀρά γ᾽ ἴσθ᾽ ὡς οὐδ᾽ ἀκούων ἀνέχομαι

– – ‿ –   – – ‿ –   – – ‿ –   – | ͡‿ ‿ –

Thesm. 720 (λόγους τε λέξεις ἀνοσίους, ‿ – ‿ –   – | ͡‿ ‿ –) is in close proximity to a textually problematic passage.

In contrast with his treatment of Porson's Law, Aristophanes is at one with the tragedians in generally avoiding split resolution. *Frogs* 1353–5 juxtaposes a particularly harsh example of split resolution with the neat division into trisyllables which is common in tragedy and elsewhere in Aristophanes:

ἐμοὶ δ᾽ ἄχε᾽ ἄχεα κατέλιπε,
δάκρυα δάκρυά τ᾽ ἀπ᾽ ὀμμάτων
ἔβαλον ἔβαλον ἁ τλάμων.

‿ – ‿ ͡⏑   ‿ ͡⏑ ‿ ͡‿
‿ ͡‿ | ‿ ͡‿   ‿ – ‿ –
‿ ͡‿ | ‿ ͡‿ | – – –

The passage is, it may be observed, paratragic (see Parker, *CQ* 18 (1968), 241–69).

On correspondence between ×– ‿ – and – ‿ ‿ –, see below, on *Iambo-Choriambic*.

TROCHAIC

Metron: – ‿ –×

Trochaic rhythm can be seen as derived, like iambic, from the sequence . . . ×– ‿ –× . . ., but the sequence is articulated into metra moving in the opposite direction. It can be modified on the same principles as iambic: by resolution (⌒ ‿ ⌒×) and syncopation (– ‿ – 'cretic', – – ‿ 'palimbacchiac', – – – 'molossus', – – 'spondee'). Where the catalectic rhythm of iambic is pendent (‿ – –), that of trochaic is blunt (– ‿ –). Period-end after full trochee (thus after anceps) is uncommon. Poets rarely shift from iambic to trochaic rhythm without a clear break: demonstrable metrical pause, or at least word-end, where metrical pause can be posited (on period-end after full trochee and on transitions between iambic and trochaic, see further Parker, in Craik, '*Owls to Athens*', 331–48).

The name 'trochee' is connected with τρέχειν, and ancient authorities characterize the rhythm as fast-moving and undignified: ὁ δὲ τροχαῖος κορδακικώτερος· δηλοῖ δὲ τὰ τετράμετρα· ἔστι γὰρ τροχερὸς ῥυθμὸς τὰ τετράμετρα (Aristotle, *Rhet.* 3. 8. 1408ᵇ. Cf. *Poetics* 1449ᵃ and Hephaestion, Cons. 78. 4–6). Usage confirms to some extent that the metre was felt to have a different character from iambic.

Like iambic, literary trochaic appears in Archilochus: his fragments include examples of the standard verse of recitative trochaic, the catalectic tetrameter (*IEG*² 88–167) and also of a catalectic trimeter (*IEG*² 197, cf. Hephaestion, Cons. 18. 11–13). Alcman uses trochees in polymetric choral lyric: *PMG* 1 includes dimeters and trimeters, and also the catalectic dimeter, or 'lecythion' (– ‿ –×   – ‿ –). This colon plays an important and interesting role in Greek lyric. In iambic contexts, it can be interpreted as syncopated iambic: ((×)– ‿ –   ×– ‿ –), and, for us at least, it is ambiguous. Whether it was also so for the Greeks we do not know. As always in such matters, the supposed sprightliness of the trochee should not be over-stressed: an epitaph in catalectic tetrameters is attributed to Anacreon (*PMG* 419).

Associations with pre-literary forms of verse seem less easy to trace for trochaic than for iambic, although some literary trochaic verse of a popular kind was certainly included in the 'iambic' genre. Archaic poets classified in Hellenistic times as iambists (Archilochus and Hipponax) used trochees, and trochaic tetrameters are quoted from the ἴαμβοι of Aristophanes' near-contemporary, Hermippus (*IEG²* 267–8). Among the fragments of Anacreon there are two in very simple combinations of acatalectic and catalectic dimeters which suggest popular poetry (*PMG* 347 and 417). The first of these is in the same metre as the drinking-song by Timocreon of Rhodes (*PMG* 731) to which Aristophanes alludes at *Ach.* 532. *Birds* 1470 ff. is an invective song in the same sort of simple trochaic, although the content is much enriched by literary fantasy. *Wasps* 1265–74, a simple combination of full and catalectic trochees, although not in stanzas, also has invective content. Trochees also feature in the love-songs of *Ecc.* (893–99, 900–910), which are presumably based on popular models, but their relationship with those models is wholly obscure (see below, ad loc.).

The catalectic trochaic tetrameter is used in recitative in Aeschylus, and reappears in Euripides. It is much used by Aristophanes, and features among the fragments of his Athenian contemporaries and (extensively) among those of the Sicilian comedian, Epicharmus. The character of trochaic as the 'running' metre is manifest in its use by choruses who enter at speed (and, more often than not, in aggressive mood): the old Acharnians, the knights, the farmers of *Peace*. Contrast these with the choruses who enter with iambic tetrameters: the old men of *Wasps*, stumbling along in semi-darkness, led by their sons; the old men of *Lys.*, labouring under their faggots; the women of *Ecc.*, proceeding resolutely, but with caution, and probably impeded by wearing men's boots; the weak old men of *Wealth*, making what speed they can, but not running (259 σὺ δ' ἀξιοῖς ἴσως με θεῖν . . .).

Like the iambic tetrameter, the trochaic tetrameter frequently appears interspersed in lyric stanzas as a sung verse, as well as in sequence in recitative. Another type of trochaic recitative is found in the earlier plays of Aristophanes, always as a pendant to tetrameters. See *Knights* 284–302, *Peace* 338–45, 571–81, 651–6, 1156–8 = 1188–90, *Birds* 387–99.

These passages are traditionally set out in dimeters, but in fact the phrasing is highly flexible and expressive. Thus, at *Knights* 284 ff., after a rapid-fire exchange of dimeters, the Sausage-Seller and Cleon each produce a longer run as a *coup de grâce*: the Sausage-Seller gets in two dimeters, but Cleon wins with two dimeters *and* an unbroken catalectic tetrameter. The reader needs to be alert to effects of this kind, which traditional colometries tend to conceal.

It is consistent with the allegedly lively and potentially undignified character of trochaic that it is generally rare in tragic lyric. Aeschylus uses lecythia freely (e.g. *Eum.* 508 ff. = 517 ff., 996 ff. = 1002 ff.), but the contexts in which he uses them can be iambic (e.g. *Cho.* 800ff. = 812 ff., *Eum.* 916 ff. = 938 ff.). Syncopated passages are often interpretable either as trochaic or iambic. At *Eum.* 490 ff. = 499 ff., the unsyncopated trochaic dimeter at 496 = 505 suggests that the lecythia and cretics which make up the rest of the stanza may be interpreted as trochaic. At *Pers.* 638 = 645 and, apparently, *PV* 694, a single trochaic metron follows iambic. The same rhythmic conceit appears in Sophocles (*Trach.* 499–509, *Ant.* 364 = 375) and Euripides (*Supp.* 368 = 372, 374 = 378, 376 = 380, *Or.* 967 = 978). In the earlier and the undated plays of Sophocles there are very few trochaic passages. Apart from the single metra already mentioned, there are half a dozen cola with some syncopation at *El.* 1281–7, a doubtful verse in an iambic context at *Trach.* 133, another at *OT* 894–5 = 908–9. There is more unambiguous trochaic in *OC* than in any other play of Sophocles (more, indeed, than in all the other plays put together). This may be the result of Euripidean influence: in Euripides too there is very little trochaic in the early and middle plays. In the plays from 412 onwards, however, *Hel.*, *Phoen.*, *Or.*, *Ba.*, *IA*, a new and distinctively tragic trochaic appears in highly emotional passages. It is characterized, in particular, by frequent resolution, much in the manner of threnetic resolution in iambic. The most extreme examples are to be found in *Hel.* (where one may suspect self-parody), e.g. 174–8 (= 185–90):

πάθεσι πάθεα, μέλεσι μέλεα,   ⌢ ⌣ ⌢ ⌣   ⌢ ⌣ ⌢ ⌣

μουσεῖα θρηνήμασι ξυνῳδὰ   – – ⌣   – – ⌣   – ⌣ – ⌣

πέμψειε Φερσέφασσα   – – ⌣   – ⌣ – ⌣

φόνια, χάριτας ἵν' ἐπὶ δάκρυσι   ⌢ ⌣ ⌢ ⌣   ⌢ ⌣ ⌢ ⌣

παρ' ἐμέθεν ὑπὸ μέλαθρα νύχια   ⌢ ⌣ ⌢ ⌣   ⌢ ⌣ ⌢ ⌣

παιᾶνα νέκυσιν ὀλομένοις λάβῃ.   – – ⌣   ⌢ ⌣ ⌢ ⌣   – ⌣ –

Here, in addition to the resolution, the use of the rare, syncopated metron, the palimbacchiac, heightens the exoticism. Compare *Hel.* 244–51, 348–52, 363–6, 372–4, *Or.* 1468–70, *Phoen.* 247–9 = 258–60 (rounding off a sequence of lecythia, in the Aeschylean manner), 638–47 = 657–66 (full dimeters interspersed with lecythia), 1567–9, 1756–7, *Ba.* 600–3, *IA* 1306–9, 1495. It is this fashion that Sophocles may well have been following in introducing highly-resolved trochees in *OC* (1220–3 = 1235–8, 1681 = 1708, 1689 = 1715, 1731–6 = 1744–50. Trisyllabic word-division is common in resolved trochees, as in resolved iambs (see above, 30).

Aristophanes was prompt to parody *Helen* in his play of the following year, *Thesm.*, and he includes emotional trochees (1042–5). Compare *Frogs* 1105–6. Earlier, however, in *Birds* (1720–1) he had used highly-resolved trochaic (like highly-resolved iambic) to mimic twittering, and in plays from 411 onwards there are passages in highly-resolved trochees which are not manifestly parodic (*Lys.* 1279 ff., *Frogs* 1370 ff., 1482 ff. = 1491 ff.). The more or less simultaneous appearance of resolved trochaic in Euripides and Aristophanes is interesting.

By far the most common use of trochees in Aristophanes is in the type of simple lyric which springs directly from the action. For such songs, trochaic is even more common than iambic. Examples of the genre in pure (or nearly pure) trochaic are *Wasps* 334–78, *Frogs* 534–48 = 589–604 (dialogues between the chorus and a character or characters); *Thesm.* 459–65, 434–42 = 520–30 (comment on the action); *Thesm.* 663–6, 966–8 (self-exhortation); *Frogs* 895–904 = 992–1003, 1099–1108 = 1109–18, 1370–7, 1482–90 = 1491–9 (comment and exhortation addressed to characters). It will be noticed that most of these songs belong to the later plays. Even more common in songs of this type, especially in the earlier plays, is the combination of trochaic with cretic ($- \cup -$, $- \cup \wideparen{\cup\cup}$). This combination is used for dialogue at *Ach.* 284–301 = 335–46, *Knights* 303–32 = 382–406, *Wasps* 403–87; for self-exhortation and comment at *Ach.* 280–3, *Lys.* 658–71 = 682–95, *Thesm.* 966–8; for exhortation and comment addressed to a character at *Knights* 616–24 = 683–90.

Cretic is the type of metre most commonly found in combination with trochaic. Indeed, in two songs (*Wasps* 1062 = 1093, 1064 = 1095 and *Lys.* 785 = 807, 787 = 811) there is correspondence between $- \cup -\times$ and

$- \cup \mathrel{\widehat{\cup\cup}}$. The equal number of syllables in these two metra may have helped to produce an approximation to correspondence in the music of strophe and antistrophe, but these cases are not enough to form the basis for a general theory of correspondence by syllable-counting. Correspondence of $- \cup - \times$ to $- \cup -$, which would be required at *Thesm.* 967 if 966–8 is not a mesode, would be unique. Trochaic and anapaestic occur in close proximity in several passages: *Wasps* 1009–14, *Birds* 240–1, 255–9, *Thesm.* 667 ff., 707 ff. So do trochaic and dactylic: *Birds* 737 ff. *Lys.* 1250, *Frogs* 1340 ff. Trochaic features in polymetric songs: *Birds* 229 ff., *Lys.* 1247 ff., *Thesm* 101 ff., 707 ff., 1015 ff., *Frogs* 1331 ff., etc. The interesting interchange of iambic and trochaic in the episode of the frogs' boating song (*Frogs* 209 ff.) is discussed below, ad loc.

Substitution of double short for anceps or short is even rarer in Aristophanes' lyric trochees than in his iambs. At *Wasps* 406, ἐντέτατ᾽ ὀξύ ($- \cup \cup - \cup$) is surely corrupt. At *Thesm.* 436, the MS reading δεινότερον produces $- \cup - \cup \cup$. οἷα κατεστωμύλατο ($- \cup \cup - - - \cup \mathrel{\widehat{\cup}}$) at 461 in the same play looks in isolation like a choriambo-iambic dimeter, but the rest of the stanza is pure trochaic, suggesting that the colon is a lecythion, with $\cup \cup$ for $\cup$ in the first metron.

Word-end after long anceps is permitted quite freely in Aristophanes' trochaic, as in his iambic. However, word-end after anceps in trochees means coincidence between word-end and metron-end: the cut goes with metrical phrasing instead of against it.

Verse-end in Greek generally follows true long. In trochaic, where the metron ends with anceps, this can only be achieved by catalexis ($- \cup - (\times)$), and indeed verse-end in trochees without catalexis is rare. In the few examples of full trochaic metra at verse-end in Attic drama, anceps is more often long than short. There is, however, an exceptional concentration of examples with short anceps in *Birds* 229–41. Other examples in Aristophanes are *Wasps* 1014 (long), *Ecc.* 899 (short), and *Thesm.* 105 and 112 (long) and 114 (short).

Fully-resolved trochaic metra are not found in plays earlier than *Birds*. In *Birds* and later plays, there are 27 examples (counting corresponding pairs as one), but only two of these (*Thesm.* 1044 and *Frogs* 993) have long anceps ($\mathrel{\widehat{\cup\cup}} \cup \mathrel{\widehat{\cup\cup}} -$). When one long is resolved, it is the first that is so treated nearly three times as often as the second: there are 67 examples of ⏖ ⏑ –×, compared with 27 of – ⏑ ⏖×. And again, the following anceps is far more often short than long (– ⏑ ⏖ ⏑ 21, – ⏑ ⏖ – 6). This is consistent with the general incompatibility of long anceps with resolution in iambic (see above, p. 34). On the other hand, where resolution *follows* anceps in consecutive metra, without metrical pause, the difference in treatment of long and short anceps is much less striking. There are 38 examples of – ⏑ – ⏑   ⏖ ⏑ –×, compared with 23 of – ⏑ – –   ⏖ ⏑ –×.

Split resolution is avoided in trochees, as in iambs. The strongest examples are: *Wasps* 412 (-*ούμενον, ὅτι*   – ⏑ ⏖ ⏑) and *Lys.* 1262 (-*οκτόνε, μόλε* – ⏑ ⏖ ⏑). Both are textually problematic. *Wasps* 342 (. . . *τι περὶ τῶν νε-* ⏖ ⏑ – ⏑) also involves emendation. *Wasps* 1067 (-*τις ἐρέτης ἐ-* ⏖ ⏑ – ⏑) and *Lys.* 1056 (-*ετ' ἀποδῷ* ⏖ ⏑ –, in a catalectic metron) are both weak breaks.

Metron: – ⏑ –

The term 'cretic' goes back at least to the later fifth century. Hephaestion (Cons. 40. 7) says that the rhythm is so called 'by the poets themselves', and quotes Cratinus (*PCG* 237): ἔγειρε δὴ νῦν, Μοῦσα, Κρητικὸν μέλος. Then follows a sequence of – ⏑ –, with its resolved form, – ⏑ ⏖. Ephorus, quoted by Strabo (see *FGrHist* 70 F 149), characterizes the rhythm as συντονώτατος, 'most energetic', and associates it with the armed dances of the Curetes and with Thaletas of Gortyn. According to Pseudo-Plutarch (*De musica*, 1134d), Thaletas introduced the cretic rhythm into song from pipe-music, and also, with others, carried out the second organization of music at Sparta (1134b). The earliest specimen of cretic that we have is, indeed, from Sparta: Alcman, *PMG* 58 (quoted by Hephaestion, Cons. 19–22):

Ἀφροδίτα μὲν οὐκ ἔστι, μάργος δ' Ἔρως οἷα ⟨παῖς⟩ παίσδει . . .
– ⏑ –   – ⏑ –   – ⏑ –   – ⏑ –   – ⏑ –   – –

Here, – – seems to be used as the catalectic version of – ⏑ – (cf. *PMG* 967), but it does not seem to have become established, in drama at least,

as the clausular rhythm of cretic in the same way as, say, ∪ – – became
for iambic. Usually, pure cretic sequences just stop (like dochmiacs, see
below, p. 65) with a full metron. Hephaestion goes on to say that whole
poems have been written in cretic, and quotes in illustration a sequence
from Bacchylides (Snell–Maehler, fr. 16). A longer sequence from
Bacchylides, including one resolved metron (– ∪ ⌣⌣), is quoted by
Dionysius of Halicarnassus (*De comp. verb.* 25. 206 = Snell–Maehler, fr.
15), and the first words of the same passage are quoted by an anonymous
metrician (Studemund, *Anecdota varia Graeca*, 225. 26–30), who asserts
that the cretic rhythm is congenial to the hyporcheme. The association
with dancing (and vigorous dancing) is consistent with the relatively
frequent use of the rhythm in comedy (see below, pp. 45–6). The term
'paeon', used by ancient metrical writers for the resolved forms of
cretic, is an unnecessary complication.

Pindar, in *Ol.* 2, uses an individual version of cretic which admits, in
addition to – ∪ –, – ∪ ⌣⌣, and ⌣⌣ ∪ –, a sort of prolonged cretic,
– ∪ – ∪ –, acephalous metra (∧ ∪ –, ∧ ∪ ⌣⌣) at the beginning of the
verse, and occasional ancipitia, most often at the beginning or end of the
verse. The strophe scans as follows:

∪   – ∪ –   – ∪ –   ⌣‖H
∧ ∪ ⌣⌣ (once ∧ ∪ –)   – ∪ –   – ∪ ⌣⌣   – ∪ ⌣⌣   – ∪ ⌣‖
–   – ∪ –   – ∪ ⌣⌣   – ∪ ⌣⌣ (once – ∪ –)   –   – ∪ –   ⌣⌣ ∪ ⌣‖H
– ∪ –   ⌣⌣ ∪ ⌣‖H
–   – ∪ ⌣⌣   – ∪ –   ⌣⌣ ∪ –   – ∪ – (once ⌣⌣ ∪ –)‖H
∧ ∪ –   – ∪ ⌣⌣   – ∪ ⌣⌣   – ∪ – ∪ –   – ∪ –   ⌣‖H
–   – ∪ –   ⌣⌣ ∪ –   ∪   – ∪ – ∪ ∪ ⌣‖‖

Pindar seems here to use the anceps position, like the link anceps in
dactylo-epitrite (see below, p. 85), as a sort of loose position which
may be placed before, after, or between cretic metra, without coalescing
with the cretic to form an iambic or trochaic metron, and so without
establishing a direction of movement (see also Parker 'Trochee to Iamb,
Iamb to Trochee', in Craik, '*Owls to Athens*', 337–8).

Cretic-shaped metra are, of course, produced by syncopation in
iambic and trochaic (see above, pp. 27–8 and 35), but the ancient
testimony seems to put beyond doubt that there really was a true and
distinct cretic metre. Apart from the sources quoted above (in particular,

Dionysius of Halicarnassus, *De comp. verb.* 25), *P. Oxy.* 2687 preserves
fragments of a treatise on rhythm, probably Aristoxenus' Ῥυθμικὰ
Στοιχεῖα, and there a cretic metron equivalent to five shorts seems to
be envisaged. Unfortunately, however, the fragments, though extensive,
are highly obscure, and the problem of how to distinguish true cretics
from iambic and trochaic 'cretics' (produced by syncopation) remains
unsolved (on *P. Oxy.* 2687, see Rossi, in *Aristoxenica, Menandrea
Fragmenta Philosophica*, 11–30).

Metrically uniform cretic stanzas can, one supposes, be safely identified as true cretic, but there is only one such stanza in Attic tragedy: A.
Supp. 418 ff. = 423 ff. There is also a self-contained run of twelve cretics
at *Or.* 1419–24. Otherwise, the tragedians combine cretics, or apparent
cretics, more or less enigmatically, with iambic, trochaic, or dochmiac
(see further below).

In a verse like ∪ – ∪ –   – ∪ –   ∪ – – (e.g. *Ag.* 192 = 205), there is
no temptation to regard – ∪ – as anything other than a syncopated
iambic metron, perhaps equivalent rhythmically to six shorts (⌐ ∪ –).
There are, however, longer cretic sequences sandwiched between
unambiguous iambic metra, e.g. *Pers.* 1014 = 1026 × – ∪ –   – ∪ –
– ∪ –   ∪ – – (cf. S. *El.* 1085–6 = 1093–4, 1407 = 1428, *OT* 1337–8 =
1357–8, *Alc.* 465 = 475); *Ag.* 378–9 = 396–7 × – ∪ –   – ∪ –   – ∪ –
– ∪ –   ∪ – – (cf. *OT* 652–3 = 681–2). Akin to these are verses in
which a sequence of cretics closes with a full iambic metron or a
bacchiac, e.g. *Cho.* 783 (=794):

   νῦν παραιτουμένα μοι, πάτερ Ζεῦ θεῶν Ὀλυμπίων
   – ∪ –   – ∪ –   – ∪ –   – ∪ –   ∪ – ∪ –

Cf. *Pers.* 126–9 = 133–4, 982–3 = 995–6, *Cho.* 585–6 = 594–5, *Eum.*
956–7 = 976–7.

In Sophocles' *Ichneutae* (Radt, fr. 314), there are two choruses which
combine iambic and cretic. 329 ff. = 371 ff. scans thus:

   ∪ – ∪ –   – ∪ –   – ∪ –   – ∪ –
   – ∪ –   – ∪ –   – ∪ –   – ∪ –   ∪ – –
   ∪ – ∪ –   – ∪ –   – ∪ –
   – ∪ –   – ∪ –   – ∪ –   – ∪ –   – ∪ –   – ∪ –   – ∪ –
   – ∪ –   – ∪ –   ∪ – ‿ ||
   ∪ – ∪ –   ∪ – ∪ –   – ∪ –   – ∪ –   ∪ – – |||

In 235 ff. = 281 ff., the cretic element is less pronounced. These stanzas are distinct from anything in surviving tragedy by the uniformity of the rhythm, not by its nature. There are short passages in tragedy which seem metrically indistinguishable, e.g. *OT* 649–53 (= 678–82):

Χο. πιθοῦ θελήσας φρονήσας τ', ἄναξ, λίσσομαι—
Οι. τί σοι θέλεις δῆτ' εἰκάθω;
Χο. τὸν οὔτε πρὶν νήπιον νῦν τ' ἐν ὅρκῳ μέγαν καταίδεσαι.

⏑ – ⏑ –   – ⏑ –   – ⏑ –   – ⏑ –
⏑ – ⏑ –   – – ⏑ –
⏑ – ⏑ –   – ⏑ –   – ⏑ –   – ⏑ –   ⏑ – ⏑ –

Apparent cretics are, of course, also produced by syncopation in trochaic. Thus, at *Eum.* 323–4 = 336–7, a run of cretics ends with a trochaic metron, and both there and in a few other passages cretics seem to be used to make a transition between trochaic and iambic, e.g. *OC* 1681–3 (= 1708–10):

ἄσκοποι δὲ πλάκες ἔμαρψεν
ἐν ἀφανεῖ τινι μόρῳ φερόμενον
τάλαινα, νῷν δ' ὀλεθ|ρία

– ⏑ – ⏑   ⌢ ⏑ – ⏑
⌢ ⏑ –   ⌢ ⏑ –   ⌢ ⏑ –
⏑ – ⏑ –   ⏑ – ⏑ –

In tragedy, cretics are also quite often found in company with dochmiacs. S. *El.* 1384–5 (= 1391–2) illustrates well the affinity between the two metres:

ἴδεθ' ὅπου προνέμεται
τὸ δυσέριστον αἷμα φυσῶν Ἄρης

⌢ ⏑ –   ⌢ ⏑ –
⏑ ⌢ – ⏑ –   ⏑ – – ⏑ –

Cf. *Or.* 317–18 = 333–4. One cannot, of course, say with certainty whether the cretics found in dochmiac contexts are true cretics or syncopated iambic metra. Unsyncopated iambic is also found in dochmiac contexts.

An examination of all resolved cretics in tragedy shows that ⌢ ⏑ – is far more common than – ⏑ ⌢. In Aeschylus it is more than six times as common, in Sophocles and Euripides about three times. This observation includes cretics which either are or may be produced by syncopation, since the level of uncertainty makes it impracticable to try to examine only true cretics. ⌢ ⌣ − is found in every type of context: iambic, trochaic, dochmiac, and polymetric. It is the only form used in one of the largest concentrations of cretics in tragedy, the ephymnia at *Eum.* 328 ff., 354 ff., and 372 ff. On the other hand, in the pure cretic stanza at A. *Supp.* 418 ff. = 423 ff., − ⌣ ⌢ is more common than ⌢ ⌣ −. There is an interesting analogy here with Pindar's practice. In the cretic poem, *Ol.* 2 (see above, p. 41), − ⌣ ⌢ is more common than ⌢ ⌣ −. In dactylo-epitrite, however, ⌢ ⌣ − is much more common than − ⌣ ⌢. Compare Bacchylides, Snell–Maehler, fr. 15 (see above, p. 41). It is tempting to conjecture that − ⌣ ⌢ is favoured in true cretic. In that case, the examples of − ⌣ ⌢ − ⌣ − listed by J. Diggle (*Studies on the Text of Euripides*, 119) may not involve resolution before syncopation. ×− ⌣ ⌢ − ⌣ − would be a different phenomenon, because the initial iambic metron would indicate that the following − ⌣ − was a syncopated iambic metron. Unfortunately, however, the evidence is not clear-cut: − ⌣ ⌢ is occasionally found in unambiguous iambic, e.g. *Ag.* 407–8 = 424–5, *Hel.* 232, 243–4. A. M. Dale (*LM*[2] 99), observing the tragic preference for ⌢ ⌣ − over − ⌣ ⌢, saw an analogy with the preference for iambs over trochees, for 'rising' over 'falling' rhythm. It should, however, be noted that the actual incidence of ⌢ ⌣ − and − ⌣ ⌢ in tragedy does not suggest that one has an affinity with iambic and the other with trochaic. For example, in *OC* 1681–3 = 1708–10, quoted above, ⌢ ⌣ − looks like a syncopated version of the preceding trochaic metron, ⌢ ⌣ − ⌣. Compare *Ba.* 589–90:

ὁ Διόνυσος ἀνὰ μέλαθ∤ρα·
σέβετέ νιν,
σέβομεν ὤ.

⌢ ⌣ − ⌣   ⌢ ⌣ − ⌣
⌢ ⌣ −
⌢ ⌣ − ||

⌢ ⌣ − is not found in correspondence with − ⌣ ⌢, nor are the two types of resolved metron ever found side by side in the same verse.

I have in the past (*CQ* 18 (1968), 241–69) examined the incidence of split resolution in cretics. To the examples of $- \cup \widehat{\smile\smile}$ collected there, I should now be inclined to add another two from Euripides, *Or.* 186 (ἥσυχον ὕπ-) and, with elision, *Or.* 1423 (*Τυνδαρίδ᾽ ὁ*). The figures are not impressive: $\widehat{\smile\smile} \cup -$ is found three times, and $- \cup \widehat{\smile\smile}$ seven times, but, given the comparative rarity of $- \cup \widehat{\smile\smile}$, the higher incidence of split resolution may be significant. Comic practice (see below) suggests that it is.

There are several more or less plausible examples of completely resolved cretics ($\widehat{\smile\smile} \cup \widehat{\smile\smile}$): *Ag.* 1142 = 1153, *Cho.* 152–3 (scanning cr ia ia cr, which avoids split resolution), *Alc.* 266, *Andr.* 1204 (where, if the text is sound, $\widehat{\smile\smile} \cup \widehat{\smile\smile}$ corresponds with $- \cup -$), *Her.* 131, *IT* 881, *Ion* 1095 (corresponding with $\widehat{\smile\smile} \cup -$), 1449, and *Phoen.* 1288–9 = 1299–1300 (where a dochmiac follows $\cup \cup \cup \cup \cup \cup \cup \cup \cup \cup \cup \cup$, which is analysable as either cr ia or ia cr).

In comedy, the tetrameter $- \cup \widehat{\smile\smile} \quad - \cup \widehat{\smile\smile} \quad - \cup \widehat{\smile\smile} \quad - \cup -$ is used in sequence extensively enough to be regarded as a standard verse-form. It appears as a recitative verse, rounded off by a trochaic tetra-meter, in the epirrhematic sections of the second parabasis of *Wasps* (1275–83, 1284–91). Closely akin to these recitative passages is the almost-pure cretic stanza, *Ach.* 971 ff. = 988 ff. (see further below, ad loc.). Verses of this type are found among the fragments of Aristophanes (*PCG* 112 from Γεωργοί, and 347 from Θεσμοφοριάζουσαι β′). There is a pair among the fragments of Eupolis (*PCG* 173 from Κόλακες), and a longer version, with $- \cup \widehat{\smile\smile}$ four times instead of three, is quoted by Hephaestion from Theopompus (*PCG* 39). A pair of tetrameters of a slightly different pattern is quoted from an unspecified play of Aristophanes by the *Suda* (*PCG* 719):

It is not clear whether these verses are lyric or recitative.

Cretic is well represented in the lyric of Aristophanes' early plays, above all in *Ach.*, where it is tempting to see the rhythm as reflecting the virile and vehement character of the chorus. There is a pure cretic song in *Knights* (303 ff. = 382 ff.) and substantial cretic runs in 324 ff. = 397 ff. and 616 ff. = 683 ff. In *Wasps*, there are two pairs of cretic tetrameters at 418–19 and 428–9, and the enraged chorus uses cretics extensively at 468–87. *Peace* 346 ff. = 385 ff. = 582 ff. combines cretic with trochaic tetrameters in much the same way as *Ach.* 204 ff. = 218 ff. and 284 ff. = 335 ff. *Peace* 1127 ff. = 1159 ff. opens with a pair of cretics, and passes from iambic to trochaic via a sequence of twelve cretics. The choruses of all these plays are male and more or less aggressive. The chorus of *Clouds*, in contrast, does not use cretics at all.

An interesting feature of *Birds* is a new and recurrent association of cretics with anapaests. The sequence of twelve cretics in the polymetric song at 229 ff. follows immediately on an anapaestic verse. In the antistrophe of 327 ff. = 343 ff. a run of cretics follows a run of anapaests (on this stanza, see further below, p. 59). Finally, 1058 ff. = 1088 ff. is composed of purely spondaic anapaests and cretics of the forms $-\smile-$ and $-\smile\widetilde{}$. It is worth noting here that a fragment from Ταγηνισταί (*PCG* 520) has a substantial run of cretics following three anapaestic metra of the form $\smile\smile\smile\smile--$.

Cretics return in quantity in the lyric of *Lys.*: 476 ff. = 541 ff., 614 ff. = 636 ff., 658 ff. = 682 ff., 781 ff. = 805 ff., 1043 ff. = 1058 ff. = 1189 ff. = 1203 ff. The metre is, however, treated with much greater freedom and subtlety than in the earlier plays. While cretics continue to be associated with trochees, the trochees come in various lengths, while, in the same contexts, there are cretic verses which open with an iambic metron, as in *Ichneutae* 329 ff. = 371 ff. (see above, p. 42). This pattern first appeared in *Birds* 406 ff. Another combination reminiscent of *Birds* is that of cretic and and anapaest at *Lys.* 476 ff. = 541 ff. The use of $-\smile\widetilde{}\quad-\smile-$, instead of $-\smile-\times\quad-\smile-$, as clausula to both sung and recitative trochees in the part of the play preceding the reconciliation of the two semichoruses must be significant. The principle that resolution cannot immediately precede syncopation would indicate that these are true cretics, not syncopated trochees, but that principle is of dubious validity (see J. Diggle, *Studies on the Text of Euripides*, 18–21 and 119). The largest concentration of cretics in any play later than *Lys.* is in Euripidean parody at *Frogs* 1356–60, where the metre is appropriately used to summon Cretan assistance and to invoke Dictynna.

In contrast with tragedy, the predominant form of resolved cretic in comedy is overwhelmingly $-\smile\widetilde{}$. A verse from Γεωργοί (*PCG* 113) is quoted by Hephaestion specifically as an example of $\widetilde{}\smile-$. Otherwise, there is no example of $\widetilde{}\smile-$ in any play earlier than *Birds*, except, possibly, for the highly problematic *Ach.* 300–1 (where

∾ ⏑ –, if admitted, would be in otherwise unparalleled correspondence with – ⏑ ∾ (see further below, ad loc.). Even in the later plays, ∾ ⏑ – remains rare. If one excludes lecythia of the form ∾ ⏑ –×– ⏑ – in trochaic contexts (where the resolution presumably belongs to the initial trochaic metron), it is found at *Birds* 246, *Lys.* 1263 (the Spartan's song), *Frogs* 245 (trochaic), 1359–60 (twice, in tragic parody), *Ecc.* 907 (trochaic), 953=961, 958=967. – ⏑ ∾ is the only resolved form found in other comic fragments. In – ⏑ ∾ split resolution is not uncommon: there are more than fifty occurrences. In contrast, resolution is never split in the few examples of ∾ ⏑ –. There are fully resolved cretics (∾ ⏑ ∾) at *Lys.* 1257 (the Spartan's song) and *Frogs* 1337 (parody of Euripides).

Cretics are implicated in some of the most notable failures of normal correspondence in Aristophanes. The repeated correspondence of – ⏑ – with ⏑ ⏑ – in *Wasps* 273 ff.=281 ff. does not conform to any recognizable pattern. Otherwise, cretics are found in unorthodox correspondences of two distinct types: correspondence with dochmiacs, and with full trochaic metra. At *Birds* 333–5=349–51, pairs of cretics in the antistrophe correspond with dochmiacs in the strophe, the number of syllables in corresponding cretic pairs and dochmiacs being always the same: ×∾ ∾ ⏑ ∾ corresponds with – ⏑ ∾   – ⏑ ∾, and ×∾ ∾ ⏑ – with – ⏑ ∾   – ⏑ –. There is a single example of the same phenomenon at *Wasps* 339=370 (⏑ ∾ ∾ ⏑ –=– ⏑ ∾   – ⏑ –). Cretics apparently correspond with full trochaic metra at *Wasps* 1062=1093, 1064=1095, *Lys.* 785=809, 787=811, 788=812, and, possibly, *Ecc.* 900=906 and 901=907. In most of these passages, – ⏑ ∾ corresponds with – ⏑ – ⏑. The exceptions are *Lys.* 785=809 (– ⏑ ∾ =– ⏑ – –), *Ecc.* 900=906 (– ⏑ – =– ⏑ – ⏑) and 901=907 (∾ ⏑ – =– ⏑ – ⏑), where the preceding trochaic metron is resolved, ∾ ⏑ – ⏑). The two passages from *Ecc.* can be emended fairly easily (see further below, ad loc.). In these stanzas, there is a strong presumption that the cretics, which are so closely interwoven with trochees, are in fact syncopated trochaic metra.

As in tragedy, – ⏑ ∾ is not found in correspondence with ∾ ⏑ – (see above, on *Ach.* 300–1). There is, if the text is sound, an example of ∾ ⏑ –   – ⏑ ∾ at *Birds* 246. There is no example of – ⏑ ∾ ∾ ⏑ – (unless one were to accept the MS reading at *Birds* 334).

DACTYLIC

Metron: $- \cup \cup$ or $- -$ The spondaic form is normally required at verse-end.

δάκτυλος as a metrical term makes its only appearance in classical Greek at *Clouds* 651 ff. The rhythm first appears in Greek in the dactylic hexameter of epic, and it is thus hardly surprising that Aristotle (*Poetics* 1459[b]) characterizes it as στασιμώτατον καὶ ὀγκωδέστατον τῶν μέτρων. Whether or not this is largely a matter of literary association, dactylic in comedy is confined to the more ornate songs, and brings with it connotations of dignity, real or bogus.

Archilochus used tetrameters ending $- -$ (Dale's 'A-type') and $- \cup \cup$ (Dale's 'B-type') as ingredients in his epodes (Hephaestion, Cons. 21. 15 and 19. 9–10, with 22. 10–11; cf. *IEG²* 195 and 188). Hephaestion asserts (Cons. 50. 6; cf. *IEG²* 190) that the final metron of Archilochus' B-type tetrameters might take the form $- \cup -$, as well as $- \cup \cup$. However, since Hephaestion believed that the final positions of *all* cola might be either long or short (ἀδιάφορον), he may merely be citing a corrupt verse which appeared to confirm his theory—a practice that metricians at all periods find hard to resist on occasion. See below, on *Peace* 114 ff. The practice of combining dactylic with iambic, and, in particular, the use of short iambic or iambo-trochaic cola (ithyphallics or lecythia) as clausulae to dactyls continues into Attic dramatic lyric.

Alcman used hexameters in sequence, and, according, again, to Hephaestion (Cons. 22. 12), composed whole strophae in tetrameters ending $- \cup \cup$, of which he quotes three cola (*PMG* 27). This raises the problem of how these stanzas ended: was $- \cup \cup$ really followed by metrical pause, or is Hephaestion's statement a matter of misunderstanding or carelessness in exposition? The answer, if we knew it, would be relevant to *Peace* 116 (see below, ad loc.). Evidence of Hephaestion's indifference to the significance of clausular rhythms is not hard to find: see, for example, his account (such as it is) of the telesillean (Cons. 35. 10–11). Alcman (*PMG* 17) also combines 'B-type' with 'A-type' tetrameters, and *PMG* 56 combines both with a hexameter, in a manner very similar to *Peace* 114–18, although the direct object of parody there is probably Euripidean (see below, ad loc.). *PMG* 1 is composed in stanzas combining trochaic with aeolo-choriambic (in the form of the colon $\times - \cup \cup - \cup - -$) which end with:

$$- \cup \cup \quad - \cup \cup \quad - \cup \cup \quad - \cup \cup$$
$$- \cup \cup - \cup \cup - \left\{ \begin{matrix} \cup \ - \ - \\ \cup \cup - \end{matrix} \right.$$

Apart from the unique freedom of responsion, the stanza is interesting both as the earliest known example of a polymetric strophe and as providing our earliest example of a dactylic interlude or finale in a stanza composed in other metres, a pattern which recurs in drama.

The name of Ibycus is attached to the colon $- \cup \cup - \cup \cup - \cup -$ (see below, p. 77), which he combines with its own pendent version and with dactylic in *PMG* 286:

$$- \cup \cup - \cup \cup - \cup -$$
$$- \cup \cup - \cup \cup - \cup -$$
$$- \cup \cup - \cup \cup - \cup -$$
$$- \cup \cup \quad - \cup \cup \quad - - \quad - \cup \cup$$
$$- \cup \cup \quad - \cup \cup \quad - \cup \cup \quad - \cup \cup$$
$$- \cup \cup \quad - \cup \cup \quad - \cup \cup \quad - \cup \cup$$
$$- \cup \cup - \cup \cup - \cup - -$$

There are textual uncertainties in the latter part of the stanza, but it undoubtedly includes a long dactylic sequence. Aristophanes uses dactylic tetrameters alternating with ibyceans at *Lys.* 1286–90. Both *PMG* 286 and the fragment preserved by Plato (*Parmenides* 137a = *PMG* 287) are self-contained reflections on love which seem well adapted to performance at symposia. So Ibycus' influence could have reached Aristophanes through the Athenian popular repertoire. On the other hand, at *Thesm.* 161, Agathon is made to refer with approval to 'the famous Ibycus', and later in that play (1136–59) Aristophanes blends ibycean and dactylic in a highly unusual composition (see further ad loc.). This suggests the possibility that Aristophanes' flirtation with ibycean-type metre in the plays of 411 may reflect a fashion set by Agathon.

In tragic lyric, the most common dactylic lengths are still the hexameter and the tetrameter, and in 'B-type' tetrameters all poets have a strong tendency to introduce caesura either after the third long or the fifth short, to compose them, in fact, like hexameters which stop dead at the bucolic diaeresis: $-\cup\cup$ $-\cup\cup$ $-|\cup|\cup$ $-\cup\cup$. This tendency starts as early as Alcman, all of whose tetrameters of this type have one caesura or the other. In fact, patterns of caesura and bucolic diaeresis are quite often used to harmonize different dactylic lengths, e.g.: *Hcld.* 619–21:

ἀλλὰ σὺ μὴ προπίτνων| τὰ θεῶν φέρε,| μηδ' ὑπεράλγει| φροντίδα λύπᾳ· |
εὐδόκιμον γὰρ ἔχει| θανάτου μέρος|

$-\cup\cup$ $-\cup\cup$ $-|\cup\cup$ $-\cup\cup|$ $-\cup\cup$ $--|$
$-\cup\cup$ $--|$
$-\cup\cup$ $-\cup\cup$ $-|\cup\cup$ $-\cup\cup|$

(The pattern is the same in the strophe, 608–10, except that the caesura in 608 is very weak: θεῶν| ἄτερ). For patterning of this kind on a larger scale exactly reproduced in correspondence, see *OT* 151–8 = 159–66. Aristophanes uses the technique at *Peace* 114 ff., and a variation of it at *Frogs* 814 ff. (see below, ad loc.). For corresponding word-end in dactyls with a less obvious harmonizing function, see *Clouds* 275 ff. = 298 ff.

A comparatively rare, but interesting, dactylic length is the trimeter. In the form $--$ $-\cup\cup$ $--$ it is identical with one form of pherecratean, and with the even rarer anapaestic tripody (see p. 58). There are signs that the poets themselves sometimes exploited this ambiguity. In tragedy, $--$ $-\cup\cup$ $--$ occurs in dactylic contexts at *Pers.* 588–9 = 595–6 (following $-\cup\cup$ $-\cup\cup$ $--$ and preceding $-\cup\cup-\cup--$), 906, *Ag.* 117 = 135, *Eum.* 351 = 362, *Phoen.* 794–5 = 811–12, *Ba.* 169 (in synartesis with the preceding run of dactyls). Aristophanes makes similar use of $--$ $-\cup\cup$ $--$ in Euripidean parody at *Frogs* 1341. In *Birds* 1748 ff., he makes repeated use of the trimeter in the form $-\cup\cup$ $-\cup\cup$ $--$, and at *Thesm.* 1136 ff. he uses the same form in a context which suggests a catalectic form of the ibycean: $-\cup\cup-\cup\cup-(\cup)-$, as well as ambiguity with the pherecratean.

In Aeschylus, there are several predominantly dactylic stanzas. The triad which opens the first choral song of *Ag.* is notable. There is a slight admixture of iambic: in particular, a single iambic metron introduces a dactylic colon, e.g. 107–8 (=126–7):

ὅπως Ἀχαι-
ῶν δίθρονον κράτος Ἑλλάδος ἥβας

‿ – ‿ –

– ‿ ‿   – ‿ ‿   – ‿ ‿   – –

Cf. 115–16=133–4. The parody of Aeschylean lyric at *Frogs* 1264–95 has close affinities with this stanza, and the fact that it is largely pieced together from quotations from Aeschylus proves that there were other similar stanzas in lost plays. Other dactylic stanzas in the surviving plays are, however, shorter and simpler: *Eum.* 347 ff.=360 ff. (2 da pent, da trim, da hex, lec as clausula), 368 ff.=377 ff. (3 da pent, lec as clausula), 1032 ff.=1036 ff. (da tetram, da pent, da trim), 1040 ff.=1044 ff. (2 da tetram, da tetram cat, acephalous da tetr), *Pers.* 852 ff.=857 ff. (2 da tetram, – ‿ –   – –, da hex, ith as clausula), 864 ff.=871 ff. (7 da, lec, 7 da, ith as clausula), 880 ff.=889 ff. (da pent, lec, 11 da, ith as clausula), 896–907 (7 da, 2 da tetram, da pent, 7 da, – –   – ‿ ‿   – –, ith as clausula). It will be observed that the pentameter is a favourite dactylic length in Aeschylus. The four dactylic stanzas with lecythion as clausula at *Frogs* 814–29 have a clear affinity with these short Aeschylean stanzas, and *Frogs* 875–84 is particularly close in metrical style to *Pers.* 897–905.

In Sophocles, *OT* 151 ff.=159 ff. closely resembles the longer Aeschylean dactylic stanzas of *Ag.*, but it is unique in the surviving plays. Sophocles' most distinctive use of dactyls is in passages of lamentation, particularly in lyric dialogues (κομμοί), strophic (e.g. *El.* 121–250) or astrophic (e.g. *Phil.* 1170–1217, *OC* 207–53). These songs include substantial dactylic sections, mostly in tetrameters. *El.* 233–242 features an interesting drift from anapaests into dactyls and back. Compare *Birds* 229 ff. There is a sequence of 26 dactyls at *OC* 229–35, in which the first four and last four metra are marked off by word-end, but cola are not otherwise distinguishable. It is possible that this passage represents a fashion in late fifth-century tragedy which is parodied in the run of 28 dactyls at *Ecc.* 1168–83. It may even be that Aristophanes is specifically parodying *OC* (see further below, ad loc.).

Allowing for the larger number of surviving plays, predominantly dactylic stanzas are about as common in Euripides as in Aeschylus.

Indeed, the dactylo-iambic stanza at *Hipp.* 1102 ff. = 1111 ff. seems clearly reminiscent of Aeschylus, with its opening hexameter, followed by

$$\cup - \cup -$$
$$- \cup \cup \quad - \cup \cup \quad - \cup \cup \quad - -$$

The acephalous tetrameter at 1109 = 1117 ($\cup \cup \quad - \cup \cup \quad - \cup \cup \quad - -$) may also be Aeschylean (see below, on *Frogs* 1264 ff.). But the stanza also includes an un-Aeschylean exoticism: an iambic metron following two dactyls at 1108 = 1116, on which see below, p. 53. Like Sophocles, Euripides uses dactyls in laments: *Andr.* 1173–96, *Hel.* 375–85, *Phoen.* 1495–1580 and, notably, *Supp.* 271–85 and *Tro.* 595–607 (both in almost pure hexameters). Note also Helen's brief introductory solo of two hexameters and one pentameter at *Hel.* 164–66. Unlike Sophocles, however, he uses dactyls not only for interludes in stanzas composed largely in other metres, but to make up whole stanzas almost or completely undiluted: *Hcld.* 608 ff. = 618 ff., *Phoen.* 784 ff. = 801 ff. (as well as *Supp.* 271 ff., *Andr.* 1173 ff. = 1186 ff. and *Tro.* 595 ff., noted above).

Sequences of dactylic hexameters which may have been delivered in recitative rather than song are found in Sophocles and Euripides: *Trach.* 1010 ff., *Phil.* 839 ff., *Supp.* 271 ff., *Tro.* 595 ff.

Dactyls are not widely used in Aristophanes' lyric. They first appear as an interlude in a stanza combining cretic, iambic, and trochaic at *Knights* 324 ff. = 397 ff. *Clouds* 275 ff. = 298 ff. is an almost purely dactylic stanza of Euripidean type, and there is a dactylic interlude in *Clouds* 563 ff. = 595 ff. The Clouds are a dignified chorus, and their relatively extensive use of dactyls no doubt reflects that. *Peace* 114 ff. is a miniature paratragic dactylic lament, and in 789 ff. = 810 ff. in the same play, there is a substantial dactylic passage which is probably tragic burlesque. The metre appears three times in *Birds*. There is a substantial dactylic interlude at 250–3 in the Hoopoe's invocation, which may allude to Alcman and which modulates into anapaests through an ambiguous colon in a manner reminiscent of S. *El.* 233–42. The parabasis-song, 737 ff. = 769 ff., is predominantly dactylic, with an admixture of trochaic and iambic. Even more dactylic is the chorus's last major contribution to the grand finale, 1748–54, the celebration of Zeus' thunderbolt.

In *Lys.* and *Thesm.*, dactylic is confined to interludes (*Lys.* 1247 ff. and 1279 ff., *Thesm.* 101 ff., 1015 ff., and 1136 ff.). The possibility of metrical allusion to Ibycus in these two plays of the same year has already been mentioned (p. 49). In the section of *Frogs* devoted to the poets' contest, dactylic features extensively, not only in the mutual parody by the two poets (1264 ff., 1285 ff., 1331 ff.), but also in songs by the chorus which are not specifically parodic (814 ff. and 875 ff.). Dactylic appears for the last time in Aristophanes in the monster sequence, *Ecc.* 1170–6, already mentioned (p. 51).

Strictly outside the scope of lyric, dactylic hexameters are used in comedy for mock oracles and epic burlesque. Aristophanes uses mock oracles at *Knights* 197–201, *Birds* 967–88 and *Lys.* 770–6, and, on a large scale, at *Knights* 1015–95. At *Peace* 1063–1114, there is an extended passage in hexameters, combining oracular and epic parody. *Frogs* ends with hexameters (1528–33), like Cratinus' Χείρωνες (*PCG* 255). However, the fragments of some other comedians suggest a much greater fondness for parody of epic. From Hermippus are preserved two quite long passages of burlesque hexameters (*PCG* 23 and 77); from Plato, thirteen lines of mock epic (*PCG* 173), as well as a mock oracle (*PCG* 3). Pherecrates, *PCG* 162 is a sequence of thirteen hexameters. Hexameter fragments from Cratinus are not long, but they are quite numerous (*PCG* 94, 149, 150, 183, 222–4, 253, 255, 349). In contrast, there are only two hexameters among the fragments of Eupolis (*PCG* 249 and 315) and four at most among those of Aristophanes: 29 (an oracle), 267 and 383 (both of which could, however, be part of ana-paestic tetrameters), and 284 (problematic). This may be accidental, or it may be that Aristophanes and Eupolis were at one in regarding epic parody as in danger of being overworked.

Finally, it is worth noting a few oddities which Aristophanes' dactyls share with those of the tragedians. A possible exception to the general rule that the final metron of a dactylic sequence must be a spondee has been noted above (p. 48) in Alcman. In Attic drama, there are a few passages in which $- \cup \cup$ is followed by hiatus, and so, presumably, by verse-end. The only (possible) example in Aristophanes is *Peace* 116 (see further below, ad loc.).

Another oddity sometimes found in the dactyls of later tragedy is the sequence . . . $- \cup \cup \times$ . . ., which contravenes the general principle in Greek metre that short and anceps do not stand side by side within the same verse, e.g. *OT* 176–7 (=188–9):

κρεῖσσον ἀμαιμακέτου πυρὸς ὄρμενον
ἀκτὰν πρὸς ἑσπέρου θεοῦ

‒ ᴗ ᴗ   ‒ ᴗ ᴗ   ‒ ᴗ ᴗ   ‒ ᴗ ᴗ
‒ ‒ ᴗ ‒   ᴗ ‒ ‒

The Sophoclean examples are listed by D. S. Raven, *AJP* 86 (1965), 229, and also by T. C. W. Stinton, *CR* 15 (1965), 142 = *Collected Papers* (1990), 11. The phenomenon is found in Euripides at *Alc.* 464–5 = 474–5, *Hipp.* 1108 = 1116, *Andr.* 278–9 = 288–9, *El.* 456–7 = 468–9, 459–60 = 471–2, *Phoen.* 1580–1 (?), *Or.* 1011–12, *IA* 1332 (reading ἀνδράσιν ἀνευρεῖν) and, without intervening word-end, at *Hec.* 167–8 = 209–10 and *Hel.* 384–5. At *IA* 229–30, dactyl is followed by dochmiac without intervening word-end. Where there is word-end (as in the majority of cases) between dactyl and anceps, we have the option of assuming verse-end after ‒ ᴗ ᴗ. There is no certain example of the phenomenon in Aristophanes, but more or less probable examples are *Clouds* 290 = 313, *Lys.* 277–8, *Thesm.* 127–8, *Frogs* 674–5 = 706–7.

A few apparently dactylic cola end . . . ᴗ ᴗ ‒, instead of the normal ‒ ‒. These can legitimately be called 'catalectic'. I have discussed the theory of catalexis in dactyls in *CQ* 26 (1976), 18–19. Examples of catalectic dactyls in tragedy are *Eum.* 1035 = 1039, 1042 = 1046, *Andr.* 274 = 284, E. *Supp.* 179, E. *El.* 141 = 157, 452 = 464, *IT* 1134–5 = 1149–50, *Phoen.* 1489–91 and *Rhes.* 26–7 = 44–5. In Aristophanes, *Peace* 789 = 810 is identical metrically with *Andr.* 274 = 284; there are three catalectic cola in *Birds* 737 ff. = 769 ff., and two more at *Frogs* 879 and 881.

There are occasional cola in dactylic contexts which begin with double-short and which are most obviously identified as acephalous dactylic. Tragic examples are *Eum.* 1043 (see below, on *Frogs* 1284 ff.), *OT* 170 = 181, *Hipp.* 1109 = 1117, 1122 = 1133, *Andr.* 124 = 133, 278 = 288, 296 = 303, 298 = 306, *Phoen.* 1547–8 and, from a satyr-play, *Cyc.* 360. The most plausible examples in Aristophanes are *Birds* 742 = 776 (with catalexis as well) and *Frogs* 1265 etc. (a repeated refrain in parody of Aeschylus). *Birds* 1313 ff. = 1325 ff. is an enigmatic stanza which may feature acephalous and catalectic dactyls (see further below ad loc.). *Clouds* 290 = 313 begins not with ᴗ ᴗ, but with ‒ .

Resolution in dactyls is altogether exceptional. The most comprehensive list for tragedy is provided by J. Diggle (*PCPS* 200 (1974), 26): *Alc.*

120–1 = 130–1, *Andr.* 490 (=482), *Phoen.* 796 (=813). In Aristophanes, there is a possible example at *Birds* 1752, and *Ecc.* 1171 has two in succession.

ANAPAESTIC

Metron: ⌣⌣ ⎯⎯ ⌣⌣ ⎯⎯

Anapaestic is predominantly a recitative metre, and its use in lyric tends to reflect that. In the earliest surviving anapaestic poetry, the metron seems to be ⌣⌣ – ⌣⌣ –, and ⌣ ⌣ – . . . remains the dominant movement thereafter. But in Attic poetry, double short and long are admitted in all four positions, so that an anapaestic dimeter can even take the form – ⌣ ⌣ – ⌣ ⌣   – ⌣ ⌣ – ⌣ ⌣ (e.g. *Ag.* 1553). ⌣ ⌣ ⌣ ⌣ ('pro-celeumatic') is, however, only admitted in sung anapaests. Syncopation is used only to produce catalexis, and a clausular catalectic metron may only take the forms ⌣ ⌣ – – or – – –. Word-end between metra (diaeresis) is usual.

In Hephaestion's arithmetical scheme (Cons. 11. 9), the anapaestic 'foot' (⌣ ⌣ –) is the opposite of the dactyl. However, he shows aware-ness by his use of the terms 'syzygy', 'tetrameter', etc. that the unit of movement is in reality twice that length (Cons. 24, 15 ff.). From tradi-tional anapaestic poetry two specimens of Spartan marching songs survive. *PMG* 857 is a catalectic tetrameter:

ἄγετ᾽, ὦ Σπάρτας ἔνοπλοι κοῦροι ποτὶ τὰν Ἄρεως κίνασιν
⌣ ⌣ – – –   ⌣ ⌣ – – –   ⌣ ⌣ – ⌣ ⌣ –   – – –

Hephaestion, who quotes the verse, says that some metricians attempted to distinguish between tetrameters ending ⌣ ⌣ – – and – – –, and called the latter type Λακωνικόν. The other song (*PMG* 856) is a sequence of six catalectic dimeters of the form ⌣⌣ – ⌣⌣ –| ⌣⌣ – –. The catalectic dimeter is also called 'paroemiac' from its use in proverbs (Hephaestion, Cons. 26. 17 ff.). But, unfortunately, that term has wider and vaguer uses. For example, the anapaestic dimeter must not be con-fused (as Hephaestion confuses it) with ×– ⌣ ⌣ – ⌣ ⌣ –×, the first part of the archilochean dicolon, which is entirely different in composition, usage, and affinities (see on *Wasps* 1518 ff.).

In Attic tragedy, recitative anapaests appear in 'systems', punctuated by catalexis. These systems are traditionally set out in dimeters, with occasional monometers. The metrical reality of the anapaestic dimeter has been questioned (see West, *BICS* 24 (1977), 89–103), but whether the traditional colometry of anapaestic systems is correct in principle and in detail (in particular in excluding the trimeter) is a different question from whether or not the anapaestic dimeter is a real metrical entity. There is no more reason to doubt the reality of the anapaestic dimeter than that of any other acatalectic colon in repeating metra. In particular, the catalectic anapaestic tetrameter is built on the contrast between full dimeter and catalectic dimeter, in the same way as other dicola (Parker, *CQ* 26 (1976), 14): both cola must be felt as rhythmic entities.

Tragic anapaestic systems can be of any length from two or three cola to over fifty. In three plays of Aeschylus (*Pers.*, *Supp.*, *Ag.*) and also in *PV*, the chorus enters with an anapaestic system, and in two of those plays (*Pers.* and *Supp.*) the entrance of the chorus actually begins the play. There is no anapaestic opening to a play in Sophocles, although in *Aj.* the chorus enters with anapaests at the end of the prologue (as in *Ag.*). Two plays in the Euripidean corpus, *IA* and *Rhes.*, begin, in the form in which we have them, with anapaests, but that may not be authentic (see Ritchie, *The Authenticity of the Rhesus*, 101 ff.). However, according to Σ *vet.* on *Thesm.* 1065, the words ὦ νὺξ ἱερά ... δι' Ὀλύμπου actually *began* the prologue of Euripides' *Andromeda* (see Nauck², Euripides 114). Recitative anapaests are often used in duets, sometimes between a character and the chorus, sometimes between two characters. Sometimes both parties use anapaests, sometimes one uses lyric. Short anapaestic systems sometimes embody the reflections of the chorus on events. They also occasionally serve to announce the entrances of characters. There is an exceptional concentration of these anapaestic introductions in *Ant.* (155 ff., 376 ff., 526 ff., 626 ff., 801 ff., 1257 ff.), which is the more striking because there is none in any other surviving play of Sophocles. While such introductions are much more commonly made in iambic trimeters, there is an imposing specimen of the anapaestic introduction combined with reflection at *Ag.* 783–809, which functions as a processional chant. The anapaestic close, short or long, is very common in tragedy. Plays which end with anapaests are: *Sept.*, *Cho.*, *PV*, all of Sophocles (except *OT*), all of Euripides (except

Cyc., *Tro.*, *Ion.*, *IA*). While recitative anapaests undoubtedly have processional uses and an association with entrances and exits, the term 'marching anapaests' (*Märschanapäste*), if used as equivalent to 'recitative anapaests', is an exaggeration.

Lyric anapaests admit sequences of catalectic dimeters and also contiguous double short (. . .⏑ ⏑ ⏑ ⏑. . .). They are also sometimes heavily spondaic. Some passages in sung anapaests are, however, scarcely distinguishable rhythmically from recitative. In tragedy, the association of lyric anapaests with mourning (*Klaganapäste*) is stronger than that of recitative anapaests with marching. They are used extensively in a number of structurally elaborate scenes of lamentation, of which the earliest to survive is *Pers.* 907–1001 (Xerxes and the chorus). At *Ag.* 1448–1576, the chorus's interventions include anapaests, but in this aberrant specimen of the genre the dead man's wife, instead of joining in the lament, uses recitative anapaests. The one surviving example in Sophocles is *El.* 86–250. Euripidean examples are *Med.* 96–183, *Hec.* 59–196, *Tro.* 98–229, *IT* 123–235. In *Ion* there are two anapaestic monodies. That of Creusa (859–922) is classifiable as lamentation, but not so Ion's opening solo (82–183), which starts with recitative anapaests and includes a section in lyric anapaests (144–83). The dying Hippolytus (*Hipp.* 1370–8) begins his lamentations with anapaests. There are short anapaestic passages at *Cyc.* 73–4 and 79–81, *Phoen.* 825–7, and in the Phrygian's monody in *Or.* 1395, 1397–8, 1403–6, 1426–9, 1434–5, 1484–8. In the anapaestic dialogue between Agamemnon and the Old Man at *IA* 1–48, 115–63, Agamemnon uses lyric anapaests at 115–42, and Iphigenia's monody (1279–1335) includes an anapaestic section, 1319–29. On Euripidean monodies, see further below on *Frogs* 1331 ff.

Sophocles and Euripides seem occasionally to exploit rhythmic ambiguity between anapaests and dactyls: see S. *El.* 233–42 (see Dale, *LM*², 53), *Phoen.* 826–31, *IA* 1319–32. There is also a recurrent association of anapaests with dochmiacs, which seems less comprehensible to us. Repeatedly in *Pers.* 932 ff. = 940 ff. Aeschylus uses a form of anapaestic metron, ⏑ ⏑ ⏑ ⏑ ⏑ ⏑ –, which is identical with a form of dochmiac (⏑ ‿ ‿ ⏑ –; cf. *Hipp.* 1371). Dochmiacs of other types are found sporadically in anapaestic contexts: ⏑ ‿ – ⏑ – (*Hec.* 185, *Ion* 894), – ‿ – ⏓ – (S. *El.* 243–5, 854=862, *Hec.* 190, *Ion* 147–8, 895), – – – – – (*Hec.* 158=201, *IT* 126–7, *Ion* 178, 907–9), – ‿ ‿ ⏑ – (S.

El. 205=225). Conversely, short anapaestic sections are occasionally found in predominantly dochmiac contexts: *Hec.* 1070–3, 1076–7, *Her.* 882–3, *Ion* 505–8, *Phoen.* 110. A particularly intriguing manifestation of the affinity between anapaests and dochmiacs is a sort of hybrid colon which is typically found in conjunction with dochmiacs in anapaestic contexts. Thus, at *Ion* 894–6, two ordinary dochmiacs (∪ ‿ – ∪ – and – ∪ ∪ – – –) are followed by ∪ ∪ ∪ ∪ – – –. This last colon has one short too many for a dochmiac and one long too many for an anapaest. Compare *Ion* 149–50, 905 (again ∪ ∪ ∪ ∪ – – –), 508 (∪ ∪ – ∪ ∪ – –), *Cyc.* 81 and *Phaethon* 84=92 (– – – ∪ ∪ –).

Another colon which defies the normal rules of anapaestic structure is the tripody. Almost all the examples cited could be analysed in some other way, but anapaestic contexts invite anapaestic analysis. In Sophocles, – ∪ ∪ – – – – is found twice immediately before anapaests: *El.* 129=145 and *Phil.* 828=844. – – – – – – occurs in a purely anapaestic context at *Tro.* 144, and, in synartesis with a dochmiac, among anapaests at *Hec.* 157=200. Both cola are made up of two trisyllabic words: – – – | – – –. At *Tro.* 148 and *Ion* 904, the same colon occurs with anapaestic word-division (– – | – – – – and – – | – – | – –). So does *IT* 146: – – | ∪ ∪ – | ∪ ∪ –. *IT* 213 and 220 (both obelized by Diggle) are divided trisyllabically (∪ ∪ ∪ | ∪ ∪ ∪ | – – – and ∪ ∪ ∪ | ∪ ∪ ∪ | ∪ ∪ ∪ | ∪ ∪ ∪). Dale (*LM²*, 64–5) 'very tentatively' interpreted these sequences of three shorts as 'light anapaests', equivalent to ∪ ∪ –. *IT* 232, however, has clear anapaestic division:

σύγγονον, ὃν ἔλιπον ἐπιμαστίδιον
ἔτι βρέφος, ἔτι νέον, ἔτι θάλος

– ∪ ∪ | ∪ ∪ ∪ ∪ | ∪ ∪ – ∪ ∪ –
∪ ∪ ∪ ∪ | ∪ ∪ ∪ ∪ | ∪ ∪ ∪ ∪

Hephaestion (*Cons.* 25. 10–13) tells us that the catalectic anapaestic tetrameter was extensively used in Sicilian comedy by Epicharmus and, before him, by 'Aristoxenus of Selinus'. 'Aristoxenus' is enigmatic; from Epicharmus, only one tetrameter survives (Kaibel 114). In Attic comedy, it is an important recitative verse. In particular, long sequences are found in parabases: *Ach.* 626–64, *Knights* 507–50, *Wasps* 1015–59, *Peace* 729–74, *Birds* 685–736, *Thesm.* 785–813. Indeed, Aristophanes several times refers to the first recitative section of the parabasis, the parabasis proper, as 'the anapaests': (*Ach.* 627, *Knights* 504, *Peace* 735, *Birds* 684). Another characteristic use of the tetrameter is in scenes of debate and persuasion: *Knights* 761–835, *Clouds* 961–1023, *Wasps* 546–728, *Birds* 460–628, *Lys.* 484–607, *Frogs* 1004–98, *Ecc.* 581–709, *Plut.* 487–618. Such sequences normally end with a short anapaestic system.

Independent recitative systems are variously used. Two plays, *Clouds* and *Thesm.*, end, like many tragedies, with a short anapaestic coda. Processional anapaests are used at *Ach.* 1142–8, *Knights* 498–506 and *Frogs* 1500–27 to speed a character on his way. Trygaeus (*Peace* 81–101, 154–72) chants in anapaests as the beetle carries him heavenwards. Anapaests are used in parody in the lament of the frustrated Cinesias at *Lys.* 954–79 (compare Hippolytus' recitative at *Hipp.* 1347–69) and in the vacuously pompous chant of Agathon's servant, with irreverent interruptions from the Kinsman (*Thesm.* 39–62).

In contrast to tragedy, Aristophanes uses lyric anapaests only in short passages. *Frogs* 372 ff. = 377 ff. is a pure anapaestic stanza, but a short one. *Peace* 463 ff. = 490 ff. is almost entirely anapaestic, and *Birds* 1058 ff. = 1088 ff. is predominantly so. This last song contains the largest concentration of anapaests in the surviving plays: nine dimeters. The stylistic significance of the anapaests in the latter two passages is not obvious. Both are heavily spondaic, in the manner of tragic lyric, but the *Peace* song seems to accompany energetic miming, while the *Birds* song calls for hieratic solemnity. *Frogs* 372 ff. = 377 ff. is a lyric version of an anapaestic processional song. In obvious allusion to this use of the metre, Aristophanes sometimes begins a stanza with a few anapaests to give a send-off to a character or to the chorus itself: *Wasps* 1009–10, *Clouds* 510–11 (for the phrase ἀλλ' ἴθι χαίρων opening recitative anapaests, cf. *Knights* 498 and *Peace* 729), *Thesm.* 953, *Ecc.* 478. *Frogs* 895 = 992 is exceptional in that the opening anapaestic dimeter is not a send-off or an exhortation of any kind. The anapaestic passage at *Frogs* 1332–6 parodies tragic 'mourning anapaests', but there is no parody *in extenso* of Sophoclean or Euripidean anapaestic laments.

Sequences of four or more shorts are used in the anapaests of *Birds* to suggest twittering, one supposes (241, 327–30 = 343–6), and also by the agitated and ineffectual old men of *Lys.* (481–3) and, in correspondence, by the sprightly old women (545–8). Hephaestion (Cons. 27. 25 cf. *PCG* 718, but see below, p. 69) quotes from Aristophanes an anapaestic dimeter of the form ∪∪∪∪ ∪∪∪∪ ∪∪∪∪ ∪∪–. But the colon probably owes its individual mention in Hephaestion to Hellenistic and later metrical experiments (see, for example, *PMG* 1033), rather than to any specific connection with Aristophanes.

Aristophanes juxtaposes anapaests and dactyls at *Birds* 250–7, but, rather than exploiting possible ambiguity, he differentiates the two rhythms sharply by making the anapaests almost wholly spondaic. The association between anapaest and dochmiac is exemplified in *Birds* 327–35 and *Clouds* 1164–70. The MS text of *Birds* 633 offers a single anapaestic metron among dochmiacs. The combination of anapaests with cretics, found at *Birds* 343 ff. and *Lys.* 476 ff. = 541 ff. is peculiar to Aristophanes in surviving Attic drama.

There are several (possible) anapaestic tripodies in Aristophanes:

Birds 328 = 344 ∪∪∪∪ ∪∪∪∪ ∪∪∪∪ (cf. *IT* 232, above)
Birds 330 = 346 ∪∪∪∪ ∪∪∪∪ – –
Lys. 479 = 543 ∪∪–| ∪∪–| ∪∪– (the anapaestic word-division is once softened by elision in the antistrophe)
Lys. 482 = 547 ∪∪∪∪| ∪∪–| ∪∪–
Frogs 374 = 380 – – –|– – – (cf. *Tro.* 144 and *Hec.* 157 = 200, above)

There are also three cola in the monody, *Frogs* 1331 ff., which could be interpreted as choriambic, but which could also in the context be anapaestic tripodies:

1338   φόνια φόνια δερκόμενον   ∪∪∪∪∪∪–∪∪–
                                     (cf. *Lys.* 482 = 547)
1339   μεγάλους ὄνυχας ἔχοντα   ∪∪–∪∪∪∪–⌣
1346b προσέχουσ᾽ ἔτυχον ἐμαυτῆς   ∪∪–∪∪∪∪– –

Dindorf's emendation of *Frogs* 1335 produces – – –∪∪– –, a colon in appearance identical with one form of the aeolo-choriambic pherecratean, but which Pherecrates himself used in sequence and claimed to have 'invented' in his σύμπτυκτοι ἀνάπαιστοι (*PCG* 84). σύμπτυκτος ('folded up') must be a humorous coinage by Pherecrates, and it does not seem ever to have become a standard term of ancient metrics. It is explained as 'contracted' (i.e. spondaic) in a scholium on Pindar, *Ol.* 4, str. 7, which is not included among the *scholia vetera* by

Irigoin or Tessier. But even if the note is Alexandrian in origin, rather
than Byzantine, there is no reason to think that its author was doing anything other than guessing. Hephaestion, in his confused description of
the colon, refers to double catalexis (δικατάληκτον). This may or may
not be a useful lead, but some kind of syncopation seems a possible
explanation. In that case, Pherecrates' colon may have been equivalent
to a full dimeter, rather than to a tripody. For pherecratean in close
proximity to anapaests, see *Wasps* 317 ff., *Frogs* 1331 ff.

IONIC

Metron: ◡ ◡ − −

  Ionic is not a standard comic metre. Aristophanes uses it either allusively or in his more ornate and literary compositions.

  Hephaestion (Cons. 37. 22) says that 'whole songs have been composed in ionic'. He quotes an ionic tetrameter from Alcman (*PMG* 46):

  Ϝέκατον μὲν Διὸς υἱὸν τάδε Μῶσαι κροκόπεπλοι
  ◡ ◡ − −   ◡ ◡ − −   ◡ ◡ − −   ◡ ◡ − −

Such tetrameters are also found among the fragments of Alcaeus (*PLF*
10. Cf. Horace, *Odes* 3. 12) and Anacreon (*PMG* 352, 409). Hephaestion
also quotes a curious catalectic trimeter from Anacreon (*PMG* 411(b)):

  Διονύσου σαῦλαι Βασσαρίδες
  ◡ ◡ − −   − − −   ◡ ◡ −

Here, not only is the last metron syncopated to produce a blunt close,
but the two shorts of the second metron are 'contracted' to a long. A
much more important variation was also introduced by Anacreon: the
colon ◡ ◡ − ◡ − ◡ − −, known as the 'anacreontic' or 'anaclomenon'.
The latter name stems from the theory that the colon was evolved from
the normal dimeter by 'anaclasis', or the switching of the fourth and fifth
positions:

  ◡ ◡ − | − ◡ | ◡ − −
  ◡ ◡ − | ◡ − | ◡ − −

Be that as it may, Anacreon produced poems in anacreontics diversified
by ordinary dimeters (e.g. *PMG* 395: stanzas composed of 4 anac, dim,
anac). A variation not easily accounted for by the hypothesis of anaclasis

seems also to be found in Anacreon, *P. Oxy.* 2321. 4. 3 (*PMG* 346, fr. 4. 3):]. ωι πολλὴν ὀφείλω. Here, the fourth position is long instead of short: ∪ ∪]‒ ‒ ‒ ∪ ‒ ‒.

In Attic drama, the use of anacreontics in the comastic song at *Cyc.* 495 ff. seems unsurprising, in view of the character of much of Anacreon's poetry. However, a (somewhat corrupt) scholium on *PV* 128 (quoted at *PMG* 412), after mentioning that Anacreon visited Athens, seems to assert that the tragedians used his rhythms in threnetic passages. This is to some extent borne out by *Cho.* 325–30=357–61 and S. *El.* 1067–8=1077–80. There is a warning here against assuming the anacreontic to have been a 'catchy' or 'tripping' rhythm.

It is also important not to use the anacreontic to deduce the existence of ionic metra of the form ∪ ∪ ‒ ∪ and ‒ ∪ ‒ ‒ which can be identified in other contexts. The sequence ∪ ∪ ‒ ∪ is never found preceding an ordinary ionic metron (i.e. ∪ ∪ ‒ ∪ ∪ ∪ ‒ ‒), and ‒ ∪ ‒ ‒ is only found following ∪ ∪ ‒ ∪ or (occasionally) ∪ ∪ ‒ ‒ or ∪ ∪.

From the early tragedian, Phrynichus, Hephaestion quotes a catalectic tetrameter: ∪ ∪ ‒ ‒   ∪ ∪ ‒ ‒   ∪ ∪ ‒ ‒   ∪ ∪ ‒. This is interesting, in view of the use of ionic at *Wasps* 273=281 and 291 ff.=303 ff. by a chorus of old men who have been described (219–20) as singers of the old songs of Phrynichus. In Attic poetry, the syncopated metron ∪ ∪ ‒ appears at the opening of a sequence as well as at the close. In Aristophanes, see, for example, *Wasps* 273=81, 276, 301=314. There are also a few examples of ∪ ∪ ‒ in sequence. At *Pers.* 952=965, ∪ ∪ ‒ ∪ ∪ ‒ ∪ ∪ ‒ (νυχίαν πλάκα κερσάμενος = Σαλαμινιάσι στυφελοῦ) occurs in what appears to be an ionic stanza. *Thesm.* 101 (∪ ∪ ‒ ∪ ∪ ‒) may be compared with *Ba.* 64, although Euripides' is the later play. Generally, ∪ ∪ ‒, unless in sequence, is either preceded or followed by word-end—is, in fact, treated like the bacchiac in iambic. Exceptions are *Phil.* 1178, E. *Supp.* 51 and *Pers.* 102–7=108–13 (where the phenomenon occurs three times in the same stanza).

Rare tragic variations are: (*a*) contraction, producing ‒ ‒ ‒ (*Ba.* 81, cf. Anacreon, *PMG* 411(b) cited above), and (*b*) resolution, producing ∪ ∪ ∪ ∪ ‒ (*Ba.* 79=95) or ∪ ∪ ‒ ∪ ∪ (*Ba.* 372, 398). The only (possible) examples of ‒ ‒ ‒ in Aristophanes are at *Knights* 559–60= 589–90, but there a choriambic analysis seems preferable. The most plausible example of resolution is at *Thesm.* 122. The variation on the anacreontic, ∪∪ − − − ∪ − −, is found occasionally in Aeschylus (see on *Frogs* 323 ff. = 340 ff.). Aristophanes uses it with surprising frequency, given the relatively small amount of ionic in his surviving plays: *Wasps* 296 (antistrophe corrupt), *Thesm.* 101 ff., *Frogs* 323 ff. = 340 ff. This last passage features some unusual correspondence, which is discussed below, ad loc.

The incidence of the metre in tragedy gives some support to the idea that ionic was thought of as a suitable rhythm for orientals. In Aeschylus, there is an exceptional concentration of pure, or almost pure, ionic stanzas in *Pers.*, and the largest concentration of ionics in Euripides is in *Ba.*, where the Asian bacchants use undiluted ionic stanzas repeatedly in the first half of the play. Eupolis (*PCG* 207), deriding Hyperbolus as barbarian and servile, adopts an ionic verse from *Pers.* (65):

$$πεπέρακεν μὲν ὁ περσέπτολις ἤδη Μαρικᾶς$$
$$∪∪−− \quad ∪∪−− \quad ∪∪−− \quad ∪∪−$$

Hephaestion (Cons. 38. 6) attributes a catalectic tetrameter to the comedian Phrynichus (*PCG* 76), and Marius Victorinus (*GrL* vi. 95. 2) claims that he used them extensively. But the metre is, in fact, exceedingly rare among the fragments of Old Comedy.

In Aristophanes, apart from the parodos of *Wasps*, the hymn to Iacchus at *Frogs* 323 ff. = 340 ff. is the only predominantly ionic song. E. R. Dodds (*Bacchae* (1960²), 72) conjectured that ionic was a metre associated with the worship of Dionysus. Apart from the hymn in *Frogs* and the ionic choruses in *Ba.*, Dodds adduces such phrases as ἴτε Βάκχαι, and the Paean to Dionysus of Philodamus of Scarphaea (J. U. Powell, *Collectanea Alexandrina*, 167). But the evidence is rather thin. The Paean of Philodamus dates from the second half of the fourth century, and contains only one unambiguous ionic colon (see below, on *Knights* 551 ff. = 581 ff.).

While ionic composed in repeating metra and the anacreontic with its variations are easily identifiable, the limits of the genus are controversial. Anacreon 346 (*P. Oxy.* 2321) features the stanza:

$$− ∪ ∪ − ∪ − ∪ − −$$
$$∪ ∪ − ∪ − ∪ − −$$
$$∪ ∪ − − \quad ∪ ∪ − ∪ − −$$

This can easily be rearranged into choriambo-iambic cola in synartesis:

$$- \cup \cup - \quad \cup - \cup -$$
$$- \cup \cup - \quad \cup - \cup -$$
$$- \cup \cup - \quad - \cup \cup - \quad \cup - -$$

However, the apparently choriambic opening to sequences of anacreontics recurs in tragedy (see, in particular, *Pers.* 647 ff. = 652 ff., S. *El.* 1066 = 1078, *Phil.* 687 ff. = 703 ff., and, with iambic prefix, *Ag.* 447 ff. = 466 ff., *Sept.* 720 ff. = 727 ff.). A comparable type of ambiguity is typically sophoclean: that between choriambic and ionic sequences. Thus, at *OT* 483 ff. = 498 ff., the stanza opens with:

$$- \cup \cup - \quad - \cup \cup - \quad - \cup \cup - \quad - \cup \cup -$$
$$- \cup \cup - \quad - \cup \cup - \quad - \cup \cup - \quad - \cup \cup -$$
$$\cup \cup - - \quad \cup \cup - - \quad \cup \cup - - \quad \cup \cup -$$

Attempting to extend the definition of ionic to cover sequences opening with a choriamb forces us to assume methods of structural variation otherwise unknown in Greek metre, and also risks extending the genus until it loses all clarity of definition. On the other hand, the mingling of different types of metre is characteristic of dramatic lyric, and I prefer to exclude cola beginning $- \cup \cup$ from ionic. There is, in fact, very little ambiguity in Aristophanes. A passage where probable choriambic has been identified as ionic by some scholars is *Knights* 559–60 = 589–90.

Hephaestion (*Cons.* 35–6) believed in a reverse type of metron, the ionic *a majore* ($- - \cup \cup$), but he quotes in support a mixture of cola beginning $- - \cup \cup$ (including the telesillean with long initial anceps: $- - \cup \cup - \cup -$), most of which are undoubtedly choriambic. Here, it should be borne in mind that Hephaestion's list of 'feet' (*Cons.* 10 ff.) is the product of an exercise in permutations and combinations. So the ionic, $\cup \cup - -$, entails $- - \cup \cup$, just as the choriamb, $- \cup \cup -$, entails the 'antispast', $\cup - - \cup$.

DOCHMIAC

Metron: ×--×-.

All the longs may be resolved, but syncopation does not occur. In consequence, there is no catalectic form.

The δοχμιακόν of Hephaestion is ∪--∪- (Cons. 32. 5). Choeroboscus, in a long note (Cons. 239. 7ff.), offers alternative analyses ('antispast' + syllable or iamb + paeon), and attributes the name to the ῥυθμικοί. The metre as now understood was identified and its rules of variation formulated by Hermann's pupil, Seidler (*De Versibus Dochmiacis* (Leipzig, 1811)).

Except for the curious *Fragmentum Grenfellianum* (J. U. Powell, *Collectanea Alexandrina*, 177–9), dochmiacs are confined to Attic drama. Dochmiac-shaped phrases are to be found sporadically in Pindar, but the characteristic variations of response are absent, and there are no sustained passages in the rhythm.

Mathematically, there are 32 possible forms of dochmiac, but at least half a dozen of these are never found. Five of the unused forms listed by N. C. Conomis (*Hermes* 92 (1964), 23) feature long second anceps followed by resolved final long (e.g. ----∪∪, -∪∪--∪∪). West (*GM*, 109) would exclude as many as eleven forms. Moreover, of the approximately 2000 dochmiacs in Attic drama, some two-thirds are accounted for by three types: ∪⌢-∪- (about 650), ∪--∪- (about 500), -∪∪-∪- (about 250). There are also about 90 examples of ∪⌢⌢∪- and 60 of ∪⌢⌢∪⌢. These two highly-resolved forms are particularly favoured by Euripides. -∪∪-∪- owes its position as one of the most common forms to Aeschylus. A. *Supp.* 656ff.=667ff. is an interesting example of harmonization of this type of dochmiac with iambo-choriambic cola (-∪∪-∪-- and -∪∪-∪-∪-).

Individual dochmiacs are often marked off by word-end. In Aeschylus, 72% of dochmiacs are self-contained in this way, in Sophocles 66%, and in Euripides 60% (Parker, *BICS* 5 (1958), 17).

In Aeschylus and Euripides, the metre is much used in astrophic passages: there are about 100 astrophic dochmiacs in Aeschylus and over 600 in Euripides. Sophocles, however, hardly uses dochmiacs in astropha. I find only three (of the form -∪∪-∪-), followed by two hypodochmiacs, at *El.* 244–6. Dochmiacs in correspondence often match exactly, but do not have to. In Aeschylus there are about 140 exactly matching pairs to 46 non-matching pairs, in Sophocles 105 to 34, in Euripides 172 to 69. Correspondence between different types of dochmiac is limited by what are, clearly, principles of compatibility. Thus, a dochmiac with two short ancipitia may not correspond with one with two long ancipitia. I have found two exceptions in Sophocles: *Ant.* 1320=1344, ἐγὼ φάμ᾽ ἔτυμον (‿ – – ‿ ῀)=πρὸς πότερον ἴδω, πᾷ (– ῀ ῀ – –), where the text is not above suspicion, and *OC* 1561=1573 μήτ᾽ ἐπὶ βαρυαχεῖ (– ῀ ῀ – –)=φύλακα παρ᾽ Ἀΐδᾳ (‿ ῀ ῀ ‿ –), where the scansion βαρυᾰχεῖ, offered by LSJ, is a desperate expedient. In correspondence, the ratio of resolved long may either be the same, e.g. 1:1: *Hipp.* 821=840 ‿ ῀ – ‿ – = ‿ – ῀ ‿ –, or may differ by one, e.g. 0:1 and 1:2: *Sept.* 115=132:

> καχλάζει πνοαῖς Ἄρεος ὀρόμενον
> ἐπίλυσιν φόβων, ἐπίλυσιν δίδου
> ‿ ῀ – ‿ –   ‿ ῀ ῁ ‿ ⏔

The only exception to this seems to be *Or.* 330=346 (‿ ῀ ῀ ‿ ῀ = ‿ ῀ – ‿ –).

Very occasionally, double short seems to be substituted for anceps in dochmiacs. Some of the most plausible examples are *Aj.* 402=420 ῀ ῀ – – – = – ῀ – – –, *Tro.* 311=328 ‿ ῀ ῀ ῀ – = ‿ – ῀ ῀ ῀ ῀, *Phoen.* 1295=1307 ῀ ῀ – – – = ῀ ῀ – ‿ –.

Metricians have been tempted to identify as 'dochmiac equivalents' various phrases found in dochmiac contexts which cannot be derived by any normal process of metrical variation from ×– –×–. By far the best authenticated of these is the hypodochmiac, – ‿ – ‿ –, which is even found corresponding with normal dochmiacs (e.g. *PV* 577=595, *Hipp.* 832=850, *Med.* 1252=1262). It should be noted, however, that – ‿ – ‿ – is also found in contexts where there are no dochmiacs (e.g. *OT* 1208–9=1217–19, *Med.* 155=180, *Phoen.* 1023–5=1047–8, *Or.* 992–3).

Dochmiac is often found in combination with iambic, and it is tempting to speculate that the rhythm is somehow derived from iambic. A fact which makes this doubtful is that split resolution seems to be quite freely admitted in dochmiacs, whereas it is rare in iambic (see Parker, *CQ* 18

(1968), 264 ff.). The affinity of dochmiacs with cretics is even closer, and the manifest resemblance of certain forms of the two types of metre can be exploited, e.g. *Ant.* 1264 (=1286):

> ὦ κτανόντας τε καὶ
> θανόντας βλέποντες ἐμφυλίους

> $- \cup -\quad - \cup -$

> $\cup - - \cup -\quad\ \cup - - \cup -$

and S. *El.* 1384–5 (=1391–7)

> ἴδεθ᾽ ὅπου προνέμεται
> ὁ δυσέριστον αἷμα φυσῶν Ἄρης

> $\overset{\frown}{} \cup -\quad\ \overset{\frown}{} \cup -$

> $\overset{\frown}{} \cup - \cup -\quad\ \cup - - \cup -$

Other passages which combine dochmiacs with cretics are *Sept.* 170–1 = 178–9, *Ag.* 1143 = 1154, *Eum.* 270–1 (see also above, p. 43).

Of all Greek metres, dochmiac is the one that has the clearest expressive function. It is the metre of violent emotion: anger, grief, fear, even, in later tragedy, tumultuous joy (see further below, on *Clouds* 1154 ff.). Where a play opens with the chorus in a dangerous situation, dochmiacs may appear early (e.g. *Sept.*, A. *Supp.*), or they may appear late, used by the protagonist at a point of emotional climax (e.g. *Ant.*, *OT*).

There are 113 certain or highly probable dochmiacs in Aristophanes, and their incidence by type and play is shown in the table, p. 68. The first group, A, covers the three most common forms of dochmiac, the second, B, the more heavily resolved forms, the third, C, the forms which are both relatively uncommon and have no more than one long resolved.

Dochmiacs in Aristophanes are not necessarily paratragic. In the play with more dochmiacs than any other, *Ach.*, the chorus uses them to express extreme agitation in the short songs interspersed with dialogue at 358–571, but, apart from the Homeric reference at 390 and the opening of the invocation to Lamachus at 566, the diction is not elevated and the most common forms of dochmiac are heavily predominant. Dochmiacs are, in fact, being used to express emotion in a way that is comic, but not parodic. Only the two examples of $- \cup \cup - \cup -$ at 1219 and 1221, which may well be dochmiacs, occur in a paratragic context. The chorus of

TABLE

			Ach.	Clouds	Wasps	Birds	Thesm.	Wealth
A	28	∪ – – ∪ –	18		2	3	1	4
	25	∪ ⁓ – ∪ –	6	2	3	6	6	2
	20	– ⁓ – ∪ –	5	5	3	4	3	
	73		29	7	8	13	10	6
B	12	∪ ⁓ ⁓ ∪ ⁓	2			5	5	
	6	∪ ⁓ ⁓ ∪ –			1	2	3	
	4	– ⁓ ⁓ ∪ ⁓				3	1	
	7	⁓ ∪ – ∪ ⁓	2			3	2	
	1	– ⁓ ⁓ ∪ –				1		
	30		4		1	14	11	
C	3	– – – ∪ –	2			1		
	3	– ∪ ∪ – – –				1	2	
	2	∪ ⁓ – – –					2	
	1	∪ – – – –					1	
	1	∪ – ⁓ ∪ –					1	
	10		2			2	6	
	113		35	7	9	29	27	6

Birds is generally excitable and, both literally and figuratively, twittery. They use frequent resolution in dochmiacs just as they use it in other metres, and dochmiacs are scattered through their songs without any particular emotional significance. There is just one moment of concentrated emotion where dochmiacs are used in the characteristic way: the declaration of war on the gods at 1188 ff. and the corresponding affirmation at 1262 ff. that the strategy has worked. In *Thesm.*, dochmiacs are pointedly used with parodic intent, and the frequency of highly-resolved forms reflects Euripidean preferences. The dochmiacs of Strepsiades' monody at *Clouds* 1153 ff. are, again, parodic, although we are not in a position to know what exactly is being parodied. So, too, is the little choric burst at *Wealth* 637 ff. In both *Clouds* and *Wealth*, only the most common forms of dochmiac are used, and both passages are songs of joy.

In general, Aristophanes' use of dochmiacs is unadventurous. There are hypodochmiacs at *Thesm.* 1039 and 1054, but, like the tragedians, he does not confine the phrase – ∪ – ∪ – to dochmiac contexts: see *Birds*

904 ff. There is one possible example of ⏑ ⏑ for ×: *Birds* 430. Diaeresis between dochmiacs is common, but not as common as in any of the tragedians. Of Aristophanes' dochmiacs 59, or 52 per cent, are self-contained. Like Aeschylus and Euripides, he tends to use dochmiacs in astropha (70 out of 113). Where there is correspondence, however, it is very close. The only exceptions to exact correspondence are: ⏑ ⏖ – ⏑ – = – ⏖ – ⏑ – *Wasps* 730 (twice), 736, *Birds* 1190 (twice), and ⏑ – – ⏑ – = – – – – ⏑ – *Birds* 1195. All the more remarkable is the passage at *Birds* 332–5 where five times in succession a dochmiac corresponds with two cretics. At *Wasps* 339=370, too, what appears to be a dochmiac corresponds with – ⏑ ⏖ – ⏑ –. These passsages are best seen in the light of the known affinity between dochmiacs and cretics (see above).

In the fragments of Old Comedy, dochmiacs are only identifiable with a fair degree of certainty in Aristophanes. This does not put us in a position to deduce that Aristophanes introduced the dochmiac to comedy, because the variability of dochmiacs makes them hard to identify in fragmentary form. Probable dochmiac fragments in Aristophanes are *PCG* 717:

> τί γὰρ ἐπὶ κακότροπον ἔμολε τότε βίον
> ἀδικομηχάνῳ τέχνῃ;
>
> ⏑ ⏖ ⏖ ⏑ ⏖ | ⏑ ⏖ ⏖ ⏑ ⏑ ‖
> ⏑ ⏖ – ⏑ – | ⏑ – . . .

and 718:

> τίς ὄρεα βαθύκομα τάδ᾽ ἐπέσυτο βροτῶν;
> ⏑ ⏖ ⏖ ⏑ ⏖ | ⏑ ⏖ ⏖ ⏑ –

The way in which word-end divides the passages into dochmiac lengths reinforces the identification. Hephaestion's description of the second fragment as anapaestic need not be taken seriously, since he clearly had very little understanding of dochmiacs.

CHORIAMBIC

I. *Aeolo-choriambic*

This very large and variable class of metres is based on the phrase
– ∪ ∪ – ∪ – (dodrans). The unit of analysis is the colon. Another dis-
tinguishing feature is the 'base': originally, two consecutive ancipitia
(× ×) at the beginning of the colon. The combination base + dodrans
produces the simplest and most common aeolo-choriambic colon, the
glyconic (× × – ∪ ∪ – ∪ –). In the Lesbian poets, where the metre first
appears, the base takes the forms – ∪, ∪ –, – –, and occasionally ∪ ∪
(Sappho, *PLF* 94. 22, 98. 8, and perhaps 47. 2). A couple of times in
Sappho, a reversed version of the glyconic, × × – ∪ – ∪ ∪ – (polyschematist), appears in correspondence with the standard form: *PLF* 95.
9, 96. 7; cf. Anacreon, *PMG* 349. 1). Aeolic verse is strict in syllable-
counting: resolution is absent.

Methods of variation are numerous and nomenclature opulent.
Glyconic + bacchiac produces the phalaecian, Catullus' hendecasyllable
(× × – ∪ ∪ – ∪ – ∪ – –). Base + pendent dodrans makes the hipponactean (× × – ∪ ∪ – ∪ – –). The basic colon can be expanded internally in two ways: (*a*) by the insertion of one or more – ∪ ∪ between
base and dodrans (e.g. × × – ∪ ∪ – ∪ ∪ – ∪ ∪ – ∪ –, Sappho, *PLF*
44), producing the so-called 'aeolic dactyls', or (*b*) by the insertion, in
the same way, of one or more – ∪ ∪ – (e.g. × × – ∪ ∪ – – ∪ ∪ – ∪ –),
making the 'asclepiadic' metres. The aeolic base can also be reduced to
a single anceps, as in the telesillean (× – ∪ ∪ – ∪ –, *PMG* 717) and its
catalectic form, the reizianum (× – ∪ ∪ – –). Alcman, who appears not
to use cola with full base, includes a pendent equivalent of the telesillean
(× – ∪ ∪ – ∪ – –, hagesichorean) in *PMG* 1. Base can also be omitted
completely.

Anacreon uses simple aeolo-choriambic stanzas made up of two,
three, or four glyconics, with the catalectic form of the glyconic, the
pherecratean (× × – ∪ ∪ – –), as clausula. Asclepiadic cola are also
found among his fragments (*PMG* 375, 376). *PMG* 378 (quoted at *Birds*
1372) is in asclepiadic cola, with ∪ ∪ ∪ ∪ – instead of base. This is
probably most easily explained as an iambic metron with resolution, for
the combination of iambic and choriambic is consistent with Anacreon's

metrical style (see below, p. 78). Sophocles also occasionally substitutes an iambic metron for base in asclepiad-type verses (e.g. *Aj.* 228=252, 1185=1192, *Ant.* 785=795). The alternative explanation, that the verse could be a version of *PMG* 381b ($- \cup \cup - - - \cup \cup - - \cup \cup - \cup - -$), is less plausible. Resolution in a choriamb is a rarity anywhere, and there is no other evidence that Anacreon permitted it (see further below, on *Birds* 1372).

Nor does Anacreon admit double-short base, though the form may still occur in some non-Lesbian popular poetry (*PMG* 903. 1 and, just possibly, 892. 1, but there $\cup \cup$ may well be equivalent to half-base; see below). In Attic literary poetry it seems clear that the base was no longer conceived as two ancipitia. Forms found are $- \cup$, $\cup -$, and $- -$, and in Sophocles and Euripides $\cup \cup \cup$ (there is a possible example of a phere-cratean with base $\cup \cup \cup$ in Aeschylus, at *Ag.* 698=716). Base in the form $\cup \cup \cup$ (by resolution of long in $- \times$ or $\times -$) opens up the possibility of half-base in the form $\cup \cup$. There are thus three theoreti-cally possible explanations of aeolo-choriambic cola beginning $\cup \cup$: (i) 'headlessness' ($(-) \cup \cup - \cup -$), (ii) resolution of half-base, (iii) sur-vival of double-short base from Lesbian aeolic. There is no convincing evidence of (iii) in literary poetry. Different metrical contexts make (i) or (ii) seem more or less plausible in individual passages. There may be a very few examples of base in the form $- \cup \cup$, but $\cup \cup -$ is never certainly found (see below, on *Wasps* 1461=1473, *Thesm.* 1136 ff., and *Frogs* 1322). The virtual exclusion of these two forms precludes the idea that Attic poets simply conceived base as long and anceps in indetermin-ate order. For that reason, I use the special symbol $\cdot \cdot \ \ \cdot \cdot$ for base in its Attic form (cf. *PCPS* 214 (1988), 115). Correspondence between different forms of base is restricted: $\cup \cup \cup$ does not normally corre-spond with other forms, and $- \cup$ and $\cup -$ hardly ever correspond with each other (see further I. K. Itsumi, *CQ* 34 (1984), 67–75).

In the polyschematist as used by Sophocles, Euripides, and Aristophanes, the second position of the reversed dodrans is treated as anceps (not $- \cup - \cup \cup -$, but $- \times - \cup \cup -$). Failure to recognize the reversed dodrans and its variations (e.g. $\times - \times - \cup \cup -$, aeolic hepta-syllable) has led to much confusion and misinterpretation of the aeolic cola of drama. Much more rarely, the penultimate position of the standard dodrans is lengthened ($- \cup \cup - - -$). This phenomenon was termed 'drag' by Dale. Resolution of long is admitted as an occasional licence in dramatic aeolo-choriambic. There are exceptional concentrations of such resolutions in *Phoen.* 202 ff. = 214 ff. and *IA* 164 ff. = 185 ff.

Simple groupings of glyconics with pherecratean clausula in the manner of Anacreon, and minor variations on that pattern, are found everywhere in Attic drama as constituents of stanzas (see above, pp. 22–5). However, the tragedians (Sophocles in particular) also use aeolo-choriambic cola with great freedom and sophistication in complex combinations with more or less closely related rhythms. Asclepiadic cola (usually with base in the form – –) are used above all by Sophocles, although it is interesting to note that the fragments of the early tragedian Phrynichus include greater asclepiads (*TrGF* 3 F 6).

Popular convivial songs feature various short, aeolo-choriambic stanza-forms. The most famous is the stanza used in the patriotic 'Harmodius' songs (*PMG* 893–6; cf. 884–90):

$$.. \ .. - \cup \cup - \cup - \cup - -$$
$$.. \ .. - \cup \cup - \cup - \cup - -$$
$$\cup \cup - \cup - \quad - \cup \cup -$$
$$- \cup \cup - \cup - \quad - \cup \cup - \cup -$$

For other aeolo-choriambic songs, see *PMG* 891, 892, 897, 902–5. Popular convivial songs are sometimes quoted by Aristophanes (see especially *Wasps* 1226–46). The Harmodius stanza-form is used allusively at *Ecc.* 938 ff. = 942 ff.

In Aristophanes, aeolo-choriambic is completely absent (but for one clausular reizianum) from *Ach.* However, in the play of the following year, *Knights*, it is quite strongly represented. The use of the metre there may possibly reflect some cult connection with Poseidon Ἵππιος (see below, p. 161). Thereafter, the metre is present in every play (though only sparsely in *Birds* and *Lys.*) until *Wealth*, when it is again absent. Only four types of colon are at all common in Aristophanes: telesillean, reizianum, glyconic and pherecratean. Other cola are mostly confined to the later plays and to the more literary and sophisticated types of composition. Some are found only in parody and quotation.

1. *Telesillean*: ×– ⏑ ⏑ – ⏑ –: 108
   There are 78 cola with long initial anceps, of which one is 'dragged'
   (– – ⏑ ⏑ – – –, *Thesm.* 129), 28 with short. *Thesm.* 1020 and the
   corresponding pair of cola of the form ⏑ ⏑ – ⏑ ⏑ – ⏑ – at *Ecc.*
   972=975b may well be telesillean with double-short half-base (see
   further below, on *Ecc.* 969 ff.=973 ff.). There are concentrations of
   telesilleans in *Knights* 1111 ff.=1131 ff., in the wedding-songs at
   Peace 1329–66 and *Birds* 1731 ff.=1737 ff., and in the processional
   song at *Ecc.* 289 ff.=300 ff. On the telesilllean in wedding-songs, see
   below on *Peace* 1329 ff. There is no obvious explanation for the use
   of the metre in *Ecc.* (see further ad loc.).

2. *Reizianum*: ×– ⏑ ⏑ – –: about 60 (the number depends on the very
   uncertain text of *Peace* 1329–66).
   There are 32 cola with long initial anceps, 25–30 with short.
   The high proportion of cola with short anceps is, at least in part,
   attributable to the recurring refrain Ὑμήν, Ὑμέναι' ὤ.
   Aristophanes uses the reizianum as clausula not only to aeolo-
   choriambic, but also to iambic: *Ach.* 841=846=853=859, *Wasps*
   874=890 (immediately preceded by – ⏑ ⏑ – ⏑ –), *Clouds*
   1304=1313, and *Lys.* 1303. In an iambic hymn at *Thesm.*
   969 ff.=977 ff., a pair of reiziana make a contrasting inset in mid-
   stanza (972–3=981–2). At *Lys.* 1269, a reizianum among trochees
   may highlight the invocation ὦ δεῦρ' ἴθι, δεῦρο. *Clouds*
   1345 ff.=1391 ff. is a short and simple stanza, made up of alternating
   iambic trimeters and reiziana.

3. *Glyconic*: ·· ··– ⏑ ⏑ – ⏑ –: 53
   Base in the form – – is three times as common as base in the
   form – ⏑ (36 : 12). Other forms of base are very rare and confined
   to just one play, *Frogs*. ⏑ ⏑ ⏑ occurs there three times, once in a
   choral song (1251), and twice in parody of Euripides (1317 and
   1327). ⏑ – – ⏑ ⏑ – ⏑ – occurs only once, in the same parody of
   Euripides (1323). *Frogs* 1322, where, if the MS reading is correct,
   base takes the form ⏑ ⏑ –, is a notorious problem, which is discussed ad loc.

4. *Pherecratean*: ·· ··– ⏑ ⏑ – –: 33
   As in glyconics, base in the form – – is approximately three times
   as common as – ⏑ (17 : 6). ⏑ ⏑ ⏑ occurs three times, again late in

the poet's career: *Thesm.* 991 (where it corresponds with $\smile -$),
Thesm. 1046, *Frogs* 1253. Base in the form $\smile -$ is relatively common
in the pherecratean; there are seven examples: *Birds* 1381,
1736–7 = 1742–3, 1754, *Thesm.* 996. This is less surprising than it
might seem, since five examples are accounted for by the refrain
Ὑμὴν ὢ Ὑμέναι' ὢ (compare the relatively high incidence of short
initial anceps in the reizianum).

5. *Polyschematist*: $\cdot\cdot\ \cdot\cdot -\times-\smile\smile-$: 13?
More than half the examples (8) are in *Wasps* 1450 ff. = 1462 ff., where
this colon, in combination with the iambo-choriambic dimeter
($\times-\smile-\ \ -\smile\smile-$) provides the basic rhythm. Otherwise, there
are single cola scattered here and there. At *Clouds* 572 = 604,
$\triangledown----\smile\smile-$ occurs in synartesis with an iambo-choriambic
dimeter. At *Lys.* 1247, $-----\smile\smile-$ opens the metrically
enigmatic Spartan song. The Euripidean parody at *Frogs* 1331 ff.
opens with $---\smile-\smile\smile-$, with an added $--$ at the end.
Earlier, at 1325, 'Aeschylus', singing in his own person, produces
$-----\smile\smile-$. The colon $\smile\smile\smile\smile\smile\smile-\smile\smile-$ occurs three
times in the two parodies of Euripides. At 1337a, it is most probably
to be interpreted as an anapaestic tripody (see further ad loc.). At
1312 and 1321, it is definitely in an aeolo-choriambic context, but
this does not preclude interpretation as iambo-choriambic dimeter
(cf. 1316). Resolved long in aeolic metre ($\smile\smile\smile\overwidehat{\smile\smile}\smile-\smile\smile-$)
is exotic, but, on the other hand, at 1312 iambic interpretation
of the first six syllables produces split resolution ($\smile\overwidehat{\smile\smile}\smile\overwidehat{\smile\smile}$).
$\smile----\smile\smile-$ occurs at *Ecc.* 917 and 923.

6. *Aeolic heptasyllable*; $\times-\smile-\smile\smile-$: 8
This colon, in which half-base precedes the reversed dodrans,
stands in the same relationship to the polyschematist as the
telesillean to the glyconic. However, while in Aristophanes' polyschematists the reversed dodrans more often than not takes the form
$---\smile\smile-$, in the heptasyllable it is always $-\smile-\smile\smile-$. The
colon is found only in the later plays: *Lys.* 1300, *Thesm.* 106, 110,
113, 119, 125, *Ecc.* 916, 922. All the specimens in *Thesm.* 101–29
have the first long of the dodrans resolved ($\times\overwidehat{\smile\smile}\smile-\smile\smile-$).
At *Thesm.* 120, a heptasyllable is followed by a colon which
adds the cadence . . . $\smile-$ and features another unusual resolution:

⏑ – – ⏑ – ⏑ ⏑ ⏑͡⏑ ⏑ –. It is tantalizing that we have no way of knowing whether the unusual resolutions parody Agathon's practice.

7. *Dodrans A* – ⏑ ⏑ – ⏑ –: 9

At *Wasps* 873=890, – ⏑ ⏑ – ⏑ – forms the first half of a double
clausula to an iambic stanza (the second half is a reizianum). The
dragged version (– ⏑ ⏑ – – –) makes a distinctive opening to *Birds*
676–84. Otherwise, the colon is confined to quotations or pastiche
of scolia (*Wasps* 1245–7, *Ecc.* 941=945).

8. *Reversed dodrans (dodrans B)* – × – ⏑ ⏑ –: 2

Birds 938, in Pindaric parody, is made up of – ⏑ – ⏑ ⏑ – and
what appears to be a heavily resolved version of the same colon:
⏑͡⏑ ⏑ – ⏑ ⏑ ⏑͡⏑.

9. *Acephalous dodrans*: ⏑ ⏑ – ⏑ –: 2

Ecc. 940=944. This curious colon, followed by a choriamb, makes
up the third verse of the Harmodius stanza (see above, p. 72).

10. *Adonean*: – ⏑ ⏑ – –: 3

Lys. 1293 (the Athenian song), *Ecc.* 918, 924.

11. *Hexasyllable*: ⏑ – – – ⏑ ⏑ – (presumably ·· ··– ⏑ ⏑ –): 2

This colon is found at *Thesm.* 992=997, following a pherecratean,
in a context which is otherwise iambic and aeolo-choriambic.

12. *Hagesichorean*: × – ⏑ ⏑ – ⏑ – –: 1? 2?

This pendent version of the telesillean occurs at *Wasps* 1241, in a
quotation from a scolion. The next verse, × – ⏑ ⏑ – ⏑ – – – ⏑ –, is
analysable either as another hagesichorean + cretic, or, perhaps
more probably, as telesillean + iamb (see further ad loc.).

13. *Phalaecian* (hendecasyllable): ·· ··– ⏑ ⏑ – ⏑ – ⏑ – –: 7

The first two verses of the Harmodius song (see above, p. 72) are
phalaecians, and Aristophanes uses the colon only in quotation from
or pastiche of scolia: *Wasps* 1226, 1227, 1248, *Ecc.* 938–9=942–3. In
parody of Euripides, at *Frogs* 1314, he uses a similar colon with
half-base (× – ⏑ ⏑ – ⏑ – ⏑ – –), which is actually used by
Euripides at *Alc.* 462=472. At *Birds* 1411 and 1415, the sycophant
sings two cola of the form ⏑ ⏑ – ⏑ ⏑ – ⏑ – ⏑ – –, following a
greater asclepiad. This colon could be explained as a version of
× – ⏑ ⏑ – ⏑ – ⏑ – –, with half-base treated as long and resolved,
but it also appears in Euripides, at *Alc.* 437=446 and 442=452, in
what seems to be a 'free dactylo-epitrite' context (see below, p. 88).

14. *Hipponactean*: ·· ··– ∪ ∪ – ∪ – –: 1.

This pendent version of the glyconic occurs at *Frogs* 1309 in parody of Euripides.

15. *Asclepiads*

– – – ∪ ∪ – – ∪ ∪ – –:

Knights 559–60=589–90. A pair of these cola, identifiable as the catalectic form of the lesser asclepiad, forms a climax in mid-stanza. See further ad loc.

– – – ∪ ∪ – – ∪ ∪ – – ∪ ∪ – ∪ –:

Wasps 1238 and *Birds* 1410. Greater asclepiad. The *Wasps* verse is a quotation; the *Birds* verse an adapted quotation.

– ∪ ∪ – – ∪ ∪ – – ∪ ∪ – – –:

Birds 1725. The sequence of choriambs suggests that this colon may be best classified with the asclepiads, although it lacks the other distinctive features of aeolo-choriambic, base and the cadence . . . – ∪ ∪ – ∪ –. The context is trochaic.

– ∪ ∪ – – ∪ ∪ – – ∪ ∪ – ∪ –:

Thesm. 102. This colon, a greater asclepiad without base, precedes an iambo-choriambic dimeter in parody of Agathon.

– – ∪ ∪ – – ∪ ∪ – –:

Frogs 1347. This colon occurs in parody of Euripides. It seems to be a version with half-base of the colon found at *Knights* 559–60=589–90.

– ∪ ∪ – – ∪ ∪ – –:

Thesm. 109. The same colon, without base.

16. *Aeolic Dactyls*

– – – ∪ ∪ – ∪ ∪ – ∪ ∪ – ∪ –:

Wasps 1232–5. This authentic Lesbian aeolic colon is found in an adapted quotation from Alcaeus.

– – – ∪ ∪ – ∪ ∪ – ∪ ∪ ⌢ ∪ – –:

Ecc. 571. A pendent version of the same colon, with resolution of one long, introduces a dactylo-epitrite stanza.

– – ∪ ∪ – ∪ ∪ – ∪ ∪ – ∪ –

– – ∪ ∪ – ∪ ∪ – ∪ ∪ – ∪ – –:

Thesm. 1157–9. Versions with half-base, blunt and pendent, conclude the metrically distinctive hymn at *Thesm.* 1136 ff.

⏑ – ⏑ ⏑ – ⏑ ⏑ – ⏑ –:

Frogs 1313. This colon, which looks like a shortened version of the original Lesbian aeolic dactyl (see *Wasps* 1232 above), precedes an aeolic decasyllable (see 13 above) in pseudo-Euripidean monody. It cannot, however, be straight quotation from Euripides (see further ad loc.).

.. ..– ⏑ ⏑ – ⏑ ⏑ –:

Clouds 703=807 (base – ⏑), *Thesm.* 1155 (base ⏑ ⏑ ⏑), *Frogs* 1323 (base ⏑ –). This seems to be a truncated version of .. ..– ⏑ ⏑ – ⏑ ⏑ – ⏑ – (see *Frogs* 1313 above). There is a version with half-base at *Lys.* 1301 (the Spartan song). At *Birds* 936, ⏑ ⏑ ⏑ – ⏑ ⏑ – ⏑ ⏑ – figures in a dactylo-epitrite context, in quotation from or pastiche of Pindar.

17. *Enoplians*

A. M. Dale used the term 'prosodiac-enoplian' for a number of cola which she grouped together as a type of aeolic. I. K. Itsumi (*BICS* 38 (1991–3), 243–61) and, very briefly, M. L. West (*GM* 195, 199, under 'En(h)oplian' and 'Prosodiac') have cast justified doubt on the constitution of this category and its relationship with aeolic. I retain the term 'enoplian' for cola beginning either with – ⏑ ⏑ – or with ⏑ ⏑ –, which feature repeated – ⏑ ⏑ and the aeolo-choriambic cadence . . . – ⏑ ⏑ – ⏑ –.

– ⏑ ⏑ – ⏑ ⏑ – ⏑ – (ibycean):

Ibycus does not seem to have used the standard aeolo-choriambic cola favoured by his colleague in Samos, Anacreon. The colon named after him, which he used in conjunction with ordinary dactylic (*PMG* 286), does, however, have the aeolo-choriambic cadence. Another fragment of Ibycus, *PMG* 282, features a colon which looks like a lesser asclepiad without base (cf. Anacreon, *PMG* 381b, cited above, p. 71): – ⏑ ⏑ – – ⏑ ⏑ – ⏑ –. In Aristophanes, ibyceans appear only in the plays of 411: in the Athenian song at *Lys.* 1279 ff. and in the hymn at *Thesm.* 1136 ff. In both songs, the colon is combined with dactylic, as in Ibycus. *Thesm.* 161 raises the interesting possibility that this may reflect a fashion in serious poetry of the time (see further below, on *Thesm.* 1136 ff.).

$- \cup \cup - \cup \cup - -$:

Thesm. 1139, 1154. The colon is identifiable by the context as the catalectic form of the ibycean (not as dactylo-epitrite, D ✕).

$- \cup \cup - \cup \cup - \cup \cup - \cup -$:

This lengthened form of the ibycean appears, with the normal form, in the Athenian song at *Lys.* 1284.

$\cup \cup - \cup \cup - \cup \cup - \cup \cup - \cup \cup - \cup \cup - \cup -$:

Frogs 1352. This long sequence occurs in parody of Euripides, and Euripides does indeed use such sequences (for references, see ad loc.). There is nothing else like it in Aristophanes.

II. *Iambo-choriambic*

Among the fragments of Anacreon there are verses made up of choriambs ($- \cup \cup -$) combined with iambs ($\times - \cup -$, or, in catalexis, $\cup - -$). The metre may be aeolic in origin: Anacreon, *PMG* 381(b), is identical metrically with Sappho, *PLF* 128:

$$- \cup \cup - \quad - \cup \cup - \quad - \cup \cup - \quad \cup - -$$

Anacreon also used metres of asclepiad type (*PMG* 375–77), and iambo-choriambic could be seen as related to these. It differs, however, in two important respects: aeolic base is not used, and, while in the aeolo-choriambic dodrans ($- \cup \cup - \cup -$) the coda . . . $\cup -$ is not detachable, the iambo-choriambic $\cup - -$ is a metron capable of independent analysis. In fact, iambo-choriambic is unique in being apparently constructed with two different types of metron. Moreover, the choriamb is not merely a version of the iamb with the first two positions reversed. The two metra differ fundamentally in that the iamb includes an anceps position and the choriamb does not. There are, however, a very few passages in Attic drama where, at least in the received text, choriamb corresponds to iamb. The most plausible examples in tragedy are in Sophocles: *Phil.* 1099=1121 and 1138=1161. For Aristophanes, see below on *Ach.* 1150=1161, *Wasps* 526 ff.=631 ff., *Lys.* 326=340, 331=345. The occasional substitution of choriamb for iamb to accommodate proper names in the first metron of the spoken trimeters of tragedy may be a convenient licence inspired by the combination of choriamb and iamb in lyric.

Anacreon, *PMG* 378. 1 is quoted at *Birds* 1372:

⏑⏓⏑– –⏑⏑– –⏑⏑– ⏑– –

The first metron here is most probably iambic (see below, ad loc.). In later poetry, verses with initial iamb, central choriambs and final bacchiac are well attested, e.g. *Aj.* 227–8=251–2 (see below, p. 80), Cratinus, *PCG* 184, *Lys.* 319–20, 328=342. In *Aj.* 1185–6=1192–3, initial iamb is resolved, as in Anacreon. In *Lys.* 329=343, long anceps in the antistrophe (– ⏓ ⏑ –) makes iambic analysis incontestable. Compare S. *El.* 823–4=837–8.

In Anacreon, *PMG* 380, the iambic and choriambic constituents are differently distributed:

–⏑⏑– –⏑⏑– ⏑–⏑– ⏑– –

This verse has affinities with the metre of *PMG* 388, which is composed in five-colon stanzas (traditionally set out as two, two, one). There, the dimeters –⏑⏑– –⏑⏑–, –⏑⏑– ×–⏑–, and ×–⏑– ×–⏑– are used interchangeably, except that the first and third cola of the stanza are most often purely choriambic, while the fifth is always purely iambic. *PMG* 385 and 386 are dicola constructed on a principle familiar from the various recitative tetrameters of Attic comedy: the second colon is the catalectic version of the first:

–⏑⏑– ×–⏑– –⏑⏑– ⏑– –

Indeed, the verse actually came to be used in comic recitative, e.g. Eupolis, *PCG* 172, Aristophanes, *PCG* 30, 31. Less predictably, perhaps, the same dicolon (or minor variations on it) is sometimes used by Aeschylus to round off a stanza: *Supp.* 352–3 (=363–4, corrupt), *Eum.* 556–7=564–5 and *Ag.* 225–7=235–7.

Lyric trimeters in which a choriamb appears as either the first or second metron seem to be distinctively tragic:

A. ×–⏑– –⏑⏑– ×–⏑–
    Pers. 1017–20=1030–2, *OC* 1050=1065, E. *El.* 181–2=204–5, *Hipp.* 877, *Or.* 811=823, *Rhes.* 242=254.
B. ×–⏑– –⏑⏑– ⏑– –
    Pers. 1016=1027, *Ag.* 141, *Aj.* 705=718, *Ant.* 806=823, *Med.* 431=439, *Her.* 352=368, 763–4=772–3, *Hel.* 1452=1466, *Ba.* 414–15=431–2, *Rhes.* 347=356 (cf. Anacreon, *PMG* 384).

C. $- \cup \cup -$ $- \cup -$ $\cup - -$

    Sept. 326=338, *Pers.* 1007=1013, A. *Supp.* 375=386, *OT* 1212=1222, *Andr.* 300=308, E. *Supp.* 619=627, 1130=1137.

Given the incidence of iambo-choriambic trimeters in tragedy, it is worth noting that there is only one such verse in Aristophanes: *Thesm.* 993=998 (type B), and this occurs in a hymn which is non-humorous and which shows a degree of metrical sophistication.

Aeschylus uses choriambs in quite long sequences, rounded off by bacchiac: *Sept.* 918–21=928–31 (8 cho), A. *Supp.* 544–6=553–5 (6 cho), *Ag.* 201–4=214–17 (7 cho). Sophocles and Euripides use shorter sequences: *Phil.* 1121–2 (3 cho; the corresponding verse, 1099–1100, is textually problematic, see above, p. 78), 1138–9 (4 cho; in the corresponding verse, 1161–2, $\cup - \cup -$ may correspond with $- \cup \cup -$, see above, p. 78), *OC* 1251 (2 cho), *Med.* 645–6=654–5, *Her.* 637–8=655–6, *Rhes.* 369=378 (all 3 cho). In Aristophanes, there are such sequences at *Ach.* 1150=1163, 1155=1166, and *Lys.* 326=340. In both passages there may be correspondence between $- \cup \cup -$ and $\times - \cup -$ (see above, p. 78). At *Birds* 1725, three choriambs end with a spondee.

Particularly characteristic of Sophocles are passages where asclepiadic and iambo-choriambic verses are juxtaposed in a way which throws their compatibility into relief: e.g. *Aj.* 228–30 (=252–4):

    ὤμοι, φοβοῦμαι τὸ προσέρπον. περίφαντος ἀνὴρ
    θανεῖται, παραπλήκτῳ χερὶ συγκατακτὰς

    $- - \cup -$ $- \cup \cup -$ $- \cup \cup -$ $\cup - -$
    $\cup -$ $- \cup \cup -$ $- \cup \cup -$ $\cup - -$

The dimeter $- \cup \cup -$ $\times - \cup -$ repeated, with its catalectic form, $- \cup \cup -$ $\cup - -$, as clausula, is occasionally used by Aeschylus and Sophocles in the same way as repeated glyconic with pherecratean (see above, p. 22): A. *Supp.* 101–3=108–11, 562–4=571–3, *Trach.* 119–21=129–31, *Phil.* 687–90=703–6. All these sequences end stanzas. In Aristophanes there are several sequences of the kind. The hymn at *Knights* 551 ff.=581 ff. begins with two in succession (and ends with a glyconic-pherecratean sequence). *Clouds* 563 ff.=595 ff. consists of two such sequences, the second of which is varied by an extra choriamb in the penultimate colon:

$$- \cup \cup - \quad \cup - \cup -$$
$$- \cup \cup - \quad - \cup \cup - \quad \cup - \cup -$$
$$- \cup \cup - \quad \cup - -$$

Wasps 526 ff. = 631 ff. is a single long sequence of the kind, varied only by the second colon, which is $- \cup \cup - \quad - \cup \cup -$, instead of $- \cup \cup - \quad \cup - \cup -$.

The reverse form of dimeter ($\times - \cup - \quad - \cup \cup -$) is sometimes used by the tragedians as the opening colon of stanzas in which it does not otherwise feature: A. *Supp.* 524=531, *Aj.* 1199=1211, *Ant.* 781=791, *OT* 463=473, *Hipp.* 1142, *Her.* 673=687, *Hel.* 1338–9=1353–4 (a double opening). In contrast, Aristophanes uses $\times - \cup - \quad - \cup \cup -$ as an opening colon only to stanzas in which iambo-choriambic is predominant: *Wasps* 526=631, 1450=1462, *Clouds* 949=1024 (cf. *Her.* 763 ff. = 772 ff., *Hel.* 1451 ff. = 1465 ff.).

The tragedians often interweave iambo-choriambic and aeolo-choriambic, exploiting, in particular, the resemblance between ia cho dim and pol. Thus, the first of the pair of dicola at *OT* 463–6=473–6 is made up of ia cho dim + ia dim cat, the second of pol + ia dim cat:

τίς ὄντιν᾽ ἁ θεσπιέπει-
α Δελφὶς ἦδε πέτρα
ἄρρητ᾽ ἀρρήτων τελέσαν-
τα φοινίαισι χερσίν;

$$\cup - \cup - \quad - \cup \cup -$$
$$\cup - \cup - \quad \cup - -$$
$$- - - - - \cup \cup -$$
$$\cup - \cup - \quad \cup - -$$

At *Or.* 810–11=822–3, Euripides, similarly, produces a pair of 'trimeters', of which the first is pol + ba, the second ia cho dim + ia (see above, p. 79):

πάλιν ἀνῆλθ᾽ ἐξ εὐτυχίας Ἀτρείδαις
πάλαι παλαιᾶς ἀπὸ συμφορᾶς δόμων

$$\cup \cup \cup - - - \cup \cup - \quad \cup - -$$
$$\cup - \cup - \quad - \cup \cup - \quad \cup - \cup -$$

At 814–15 = 826–7 in the same stanza, ia cho dim is in synartesis with pol:

οἰκτρότατα θοινάματα καὶ
σφάγια γενναίων τεκέων·

– ⌢ ⌣ –   – ⌣ ⌣ –

⌣ ⌣ ⌣ – – – ⌣ ⌣ –

Here, Euripides introduces into both cola the triple short which is a recurrent motif in the stanza. In view of passages like these, it is not surprising that metricians have been slow to recognize iambo-choriambic as a distinct metrical type. Wilamowitz (*GV* 212) saw pol and ia cho dim as versions of the same colon (' . . . ein Dimeter, dessen zweites Metron ein Choriamb ist; das erste erscheint als trochäisches Metron . . . aber auch als iambisch'), introducing a confusion that has persisted ever after. The crucial observation has been made by I. K. Itsumi (*CQ* 32 (1982), 67) that ✕ – ⌣ –   – ⌣ ⌣ – and ·· ··–✕– ⌣ ⌣ – never correspond. As Wilamowitz identified pol with ia cho dim, West (*GM* 31) classifies cho ia dim (– ⌣ ⌣ –   ✕ – ⌣ –) as 'anaclastic glyconic', citing Sappho, *PLF* 95.6, as an example of the 'anaclastic' in correspondence with the normal form. But Sappho 95 is too fragmentary for the metre of the poem to be securely identified, and all that survives of 6 is – ⌣ ⌣ – ⌣̣̆ [. Blass may well have been right to suspect corruption or misdivision (see Voigt, ad loc.). There is no reliable evidence for such a correspondence anywhere else in Greek poetry (see below, on *Wasps* 526 ff. = 631 ff.).

A colon which deserves separate treatment, especially in a study of Aristophanes, is the so-called aristophanean (– ⌣ ⌣ – ⌣ – –). The aristophanean can be interpreted as aeolo-choriambic: a pendent version of the dodrans, which, with base prefixed, makes up the hipponactean. But in iambo-choriambic it serves as the catalectic form of – ⌣ ⌣ – ✕ – ⌣ – (see above, p. 80). The colon is a favourite of Aeschylus, who uses it in a variety of contexts: aeolo-choriambic with iambo-choriambic (*Sept.* 303 = 320); iambic (*Pers.* 1045 = 1053, *Sept.* 771 = 777); dochmiac (*Sept.* 567 = 630, 688 = 694, 701 = 708, *Supp.* 396 = 406, etc.). At *Sept.* 688 = 694 and 701 = 708, he exploits the compatibility of – ⌣ ⌣ – ⌣ – – with his favoured form of dochmiac, – ⌣ ⌣ – ⌣ –. Aristophaneans are less common in Sophocles, and are most often found in aeolo-choriambic or iambo-choriambic contexts. Twice, however, the colon appears with dochmiacs: *Aj.* 353 = 361 and *OC* 1557 = 1569. In the latter passage, the affinity of – ⌣ ⌣ – ⌣ – – with – ⌣ ⌣ – ⌣ – is exploited in a way which might be consciously Aeschylean:

> εἰ θέμις ἐστί μοι τὰν ἀφανῆ θεὸν
> καὶ σὲ λιταῖς σεβίζειν,
> ἐννυχίων ἄναξ

$$- \cup \cup - \cup - \quad - \cup \cup - \cup -$$
$$- \cup \cup - \cup - -$$
$$- \cup \cup - \cup -$$

In Euripides, aristophaneans are almost exclusively confined to the earlier plays (*Alc.*, *Med.*, *Hec.*, *Hcld.*) and to iambo-choriambic and aeolo-choriambic contexts. At *Alc.* 414–15 (=402–3, corrupt), however, there is the Aeschylean combination of aristophanean with the dochmiac $- \cup \cup - \cup -$. There are two aristophaneans in *Rhes.*, one of which (350=359) serves as an unorthodox clausula to dactylo-epitrite. In later plays, there is one example at *El.* 710=724 and, strikingly, four in *Ba.* 105 ff. = 120 ff., where the stanza opens with a pair in synartesis:

> ὦ Σεμέλας τροφοὶ Θή-
> βαι, στεφανοῦσθε κισσῷ

The aristophanean is the only pendent choriambic colon found at all commonly in synartesis (see further Parker, *CQ* 26 (1976), 24–5). Use of the colon in sequence, sometimes in synartesis, sometimes not, is (apart from *Ba.* 105–6=120–1) confined to Aeschylus (*Supp.* 659–60=670–1, *Ag.* 199–200=212–13, 226–7=236–7, *Cho.* 387–91=411–14, 467–8=472–3) and Aristophanes (*Wasps* 534–7=638–41, *Peace* 785–7=807–9). The sequence of five aristophaneans from Αἰολοσίκων (*PCG* 9) looks like recitative. It may be this use of the colon which caused later metricians to attach Aristophanes' name to it, for in lyric he is not particularly lavish with it. He uses it occasionally in non-choriambic contexts: *Thesm.* 988 (as first colon of a double clausula to an otherwise iambic stanza) and twice in *Ecc.* 900 ff. = 906 ff. (as clausula to trochaic periods). But as an all-purpose clausula he makes far greater use of the reizianum (see above p. 73). He differs, also, from the tragedians in markedly associating the aristophanean with iambo-choriambic (typically as clausula to $- \cup \cup - \quad \times - \cup -$) rather than aeolo-choriambic. Only in two deliberately 'poetic' passages, *Birds* 905 and

Thesm. 990 ff. = 995 ff., is it closely associated with aeolo-choriambic (glyconic and pherecratean).

In general, Aristophanes uses iambo-choriambic in homogeneous blocks, rather than interwoven with aeolo-choriambic. *Clouds* 949 ff. = 1024 ff., *Wasps* 526 ff. = 631 ff.; and *Lys* 321 ff. = 335 ff. are pure, or very nearly pure, iambo-choriambic stanzas. Two hymns, *Knights* 551 ff. = 581 ff. and *Clouds* 563 ff. = 595 ff., are very similar in structure. In both, the first section is iambo-choriambic. A short central section follows (asclepiadic in *Knights*, dactylic in *Clouds*); then comes a final section of pure, or almost pure, aeolo-choriambic. Given that iambo-choriambic is not a very common type of metre, *Clouds* and *Wasps* contain quite large concentrations of it. Choriambic sequences ending in bacchiac occur at *Ach.* 1150 = 1163, 1154 = 1166. At *Clouds* 955–7 = 1030–2, three choriambs in sequence precede the dicolon – ᴗ ᴗ – ⨯ – ᴗ – – ᴗ ᴗ – ᴗ – –. A pair of varied dicola (ia cho dim + ia dim cat, ia cho dim + ar) opens a short stanza of the serenade at *Ecc.* 969 ff. = 973 ff. *PCG* 111 (from Γεωργοί) is a longer and more elaborate sequence alternating dicola with choriambic + bacchiac verses, and including a glyconic:

Εἰρήνη βαθύπλουτε καὶ ζευγάριον βοεικόν,
εἰ γὰρ ἐμοὶ παυσαμένῳ τοῦ πολέμου γένοιτο
σκάψαι τ᾽ἀποκλάσαι ⟨τε⟩ καὶ λουσαμένῳ διελκύσαι
τῆς τρυγός, ἄρτον λιπαρὸν καὶ ῥάφανον φέροντι

– – – ᴗ ᴗ – ᴗ –   – ᴗ ᴗ – ᴗ – ᴗ ‖
– ᴗ ᴗ –   – ᴗ ᴗ – | – ᴗ ᴗ –   ᴗ – –
– – ᴗ –   ᴗ – ᴗ –   – ᴗ ᴗ –   ᴗ – ᴗ –
– ᴗ ᴗ –   – ᴗ ᴗ –   – ᴗ ᴗ –   ᴗ – ᴗ̣ ‖

For the rare glyc + ar, cf. *Birds* 904–5. The pattern of varied dicola seems even to have invaded comic recitative: see Pherecrates, *PCG* 114 and 138, where, again, glyconic (and pherecratean) mingle with iambo-choriambic. The iambo-choriambic dimeter introducing aeolo-choriambic at *Frogs* 1316–21 is not surprising in parody of tragedy, just as the repeated triple short that harmonizes different cola at 1315–17 is very much in the tragic manner (cf. above, p. 81, on *Or.* 814–15 = 826–7).

DACTYLO-EPITRITE

In fully-developed dactylo-epitrite, anceps, usually long, seems to act as a link between different rhythmic phrases, of which the most common are –⏑⏑–⏑⏑– (hemiepes) and –⏑– (cretic), e.g. *Ol.* 3. 1–2:

Τυνδαρίδαις τε φιλοξείνοις ἁδεῖν καλλιπλοκάμῳ θ' Ἑλένᾳ
κλεινὰν Ἀκράγαντα γεραίρων εὔχομαι

–⏑⏑–⏑⏑– – –⏑– – –⏑⏑–⏑⏑–
– –⏑⏑–⏑⏑– – –⏑–

The original associations of the metre are with Dorian lyric and with composition in triads (strophe, antistrophe, and epode). The discovery of fragments of Stesichorus, extensive in metrical terms, has now made it possible to reconstruct the process by which dactylo-epitrite was formed.

Even in the purely 'dactylic' fragments of Stesichorus, contraction of double short to long is not distributed with the same freedom as in dactylic hexameters. Thus, the strophe of the *Geryoneis* (*P. Oxy.* 2617) shows both a pattern of contraction and a tendency to use it to mark off the phrase –⏑⏑–⏑⏑–:

⏕–⏕–⏑⏑––||
⏕–⏑⏑–⏕–⏑⏑–⏑⏑–⏕–⏑⏑––|
⏕–⏑⏑–⏕–⏑⏑–⏑⏑––||
⏕–⏕–⏑⏑–⏑⏑–⏕–⏑⏑–|
⏕–⏑⏑–⏕–⏕–⏕–⏑⏑–⏕–⏑⏑–|||

In the *Iliou Persis* (*P. Oxy.* 2619 and 2803) this tendency is more marked, and a few short phrases in iambo-trochaic rhythm (. . . ×–⏑–× . . .) are mingled with the dactyls. The strophe scans:

–⏕–⏑⏑–⏑⏑–⏑⏑–|⏕–⏑⏑–⏑⏑–|
–⏕–⏑⏑–⏕–⏑––|
–⏑⏑–⏑⏑–|⏕–⏑⏑–⏑⏑–|⏕–⏑⏑–⏑⏑–|⏕–⏑⏑–
⏑⏑–––⏑–|
–⏑⏑–⏑⏑–|⏓–⏑⏑–⏑⏑––––⏑––|||

Further, the 'contractible' double short ('biceps') that marks off the hemiepe is actually replaced in the final verse by anceps, even between two dactylic phrases. In the epode of this poem, anceps completely supplants biceps in this function. The *Thebaid* (*P. Lille* 76 a b c) shows correspondence between ⏑, –, and ⏑ ⏑ in the same link positions, but ⏑ never corresponds with ⏑ ⏑ in the same strophic pair. The *Nostoi* (*P. Oxy.* 2360) is made up exclusively of – ⏑ ⏑ – ⏑ ⏑ – and – ⏑ – linked by ancipitia. This is fully-developed dactylo-epitrite at its simplest.

The evidence of developed dactylo-epitrite would lead us not to expect to find in Stesichorus the cadence . . . – ⏑ ⏑ – ⏑ – (–), which is typical of aeolo-choriambic. *PMG* 211 (quoted by *Σ vet.* on *Peace* 800) scans ⏑ ⏑ – ⏑ – – ⏑ ⏑ – ⏑ – –, but this is merely a snatch without metrical context, and we cannot even be sure that it is correctly quoted. The reverse sequence, – ⏑ – ⏑ ⏑ – . . ., seems to appear in the first verse of the strophe at *P. Oxy.* 2618, which runs: – ⏑ – – – ⏑ – ⏑ ⏑ – ⏑ ⏑ – ⏑ ⏑ – ⏑ ⏑ – ⏑ ⏑ –. W. S. Barrett (see Page, *PCPS* 197 (1971), 96) has made the plausible suggestion that the first ⏑ ⏑ is biceps, linking – ⏑ – with a dactylic sequence (as it does in reverse in str. 2 of the *Iliou Persis*, *P. Oxy.* 2619 + 2803). The same explanation is applicable to a few verses, such as the 'archebulean' (⏑ ⏑ – ⏑ ⏑ – ⏑ ⏑ – ⏑ ⏑ – ⏑ – –), *PMG* 244 (cf. Caesius Bassus, vi. 256. 9 K), in which a dactylic sequence ends in . . . – ⏑ ⏑ – ⏑ – –. Here, the last ⏑ ⏑ would be the link biceps (see further, West, *GM* 48 n. 47). On Stesichorus' metres, see, in particular, West, *ZPE* 4 (1969), 135–49, and Haslam, *QUCC* 17 (1974), 7–57 and *GRBS* 19 (1978), 29–57.

It is impossible to distinguish cola within dactylo-epitrite verses because we do not know whether to take link anceps with what follows or with what precedes. For descriptive purposes, Paul Maas (*GM*, § 55) short-circuited the problem by the use of a code based on D (= – ⏑ ⏑ – ⏑ ⏑ –) and e (= – ⏑ –). I use a simplified form of this.

In the developed dactylo-epitrite of Pindar and Bacchylides, the choriamb (– ⏑ ⏑ – = d) appears as an occasional constituent, and link anceps is sometimes omitted. A spondee (– –) is also occasionally found at verse-beginning or verse-end. All three phenomena are exemplified in *Pyth.* 1. 2:

σύνδικον Μοῖσαν κτέανον· τᾶς ἀκούει μὲν βάσις ἀγλαΐας
ἀρχά

‒ ∪ ‒   ‒   ‒ ∪ ∪ ‒   ‒ ∪ ‒   ‒   ‒ ∪ ∪ ‒ ∪ ∪ ‒   ‒ ‒

(e‒de‒D‒‒)

There is no obvious explanation for ‒ ‒. In iambic and trochaic it is explicable as a doubly-syncopated metron ((✕)‒(∪)‒ or ‒(∪)‒(✕)), but syncopation is not otherwise found in dactylo-epitrite. However, explicable or not, ‒ ‒ already appears in the clausula ‒ ‒   ‒ ∪ ‒   ‒ in the embryonic dactylo-epitrite of Stesichorus (*P. Oxy.* 2618 and *P. Lille* 76 a b c). Occasionally, dactylic phrases are prolonged:

(*a*) ‒ ∪ ∪ ‒ ∪ ∪ ‒ ∪ ∪ ‒
Pyth. 4. 4: ἔνθα ποτὲ χ͏͏|ρυσέων Διὸς αἰετῶν πάρεδ|ρος
   ‒ ∪ ∪ ‒ ∪ ∪ ‒ ∪ ∪ ‒   ∪   ‒ ∪ ‒   ‒ (D prol ∪ e ‒)

(*b*) ‒ ∪ ∪ ‒ ∪ ∪ ‒ ∪ ∪ ‒ ∪ ∪ ‒
Pyth. 3. 4: Οὐρανίδα γόνον εὐρυμέδοντα Κρόνου
   ‒ ∪ ∪ ‒ ∪ ∪ ‒ ∪ ∪ ‒ ∪ ∪ ‒ (D prol)

Acephalous (headless) phrases sometimes occur at the beginning of a verse:

(*a*) ∧ ∪ ‒
Ol. 6. 6: συνοικιστήρ τε τᾶν κλεινᾶν Συρακοσσᾶν, τίνα κεν φύγοι
      ὕμνον
∧ ∪ ‒   ‒   ‒ ∪ ‒   ‒   ‒ ∪ ‒   ‒   ‒ ∪ ∪ ‒ ∪ ∪ ‒   ‒
(∧e‒e‒e‒D‒)

(*b*) ∧ ∪ ∪ ‒
Ol. 7. 1: φιάλαν ὡς εἴ τις ἀφ|νειᾶς ἀπὸ χειρὸς ἑλών
   ∧ ∪ ∪ ‒   ‒   ‒ ∪ ‒   ‒   ‒ ∪ ∪ ‒ ∪ ∪ ‒ (∧d‒e‒D)

(*c*) ∪ ∪ ‒ ∪ ∪ ‒
Pyth. 3. 23: μεταμώνια θηρεύων ἀκράντοις ἐλπίσιν
      ∧ ∪ ∪ ‒ ∪ ∪ ‒   ‒   ‒ ∪ ‒   ‒   ‒ ∪ ‒ (∧D‒e‒e)

Resolution of long and contraction of double short are generally excluded from dactylo-epitrite, except that resolution of one or other long is sometimes found in cretic phrases. ⌣̅ ∪ ‒ is found recurring at *Ol.* 7, ep. 5, *Pyth.* 1, ep. 3, 7, 10, *Pyth.* 4, str. 8, *Nem.* 1, ep. 1, *Isth.* 5, str. 2, 6 and ep. 6, *Isth.* 6, str. 7 (twice). ‒ ∪ ⌣̅ is found recurring at *Nem.*

10, str. 6, and *Isth*. 2, ep. 3. Otherwise, it occurs only as an occasional variation on $- \smile -$ (*Ol*. 3. 35, *Pyth*. 4. 184, 253, *Nem*. 5. 6, 10, 12, *Isth*. 3 + 4. 72b).

In the dactylo-epitrite poems of Pindar and Bacchylides, word-end tends to recur at the same points within the verse in stanza after stanza. There is a strong tendency in Bacchylides to avoid recurrent word-end after long anceps. The practice of reproducing the same pattern of word-end in every or nearly every repetition of a given verse means that he also tends to avoid word-end after short anceps, although less rigorously. Pindar does not avoid recurrent word-end after long anceps, but he shows a strong preference for word-end before anceps to word-end after it (see further, Parker, *CQ* 16 (1966), 4–9).

In tragedy, occasional phrases of dactylo-epitrite type (especially $- \smile \smile - \smile \smile -$) are found in a wide variety of contexts, and the first fascicule of A. M. Dale's *Metrical Analyses of Tragic Choruses*, which is devoted to dactylo-epitrite, in fact contains much material which owes its inclusion only to the presence of that phrase, and which is only tenuously related or not at all to true dactylo-epitrite. Fully developed dactylo-epitrite of the Pindaric type is recognizable (apart from the presence of $- \smile \smile - \smile \smile -$ and $- \smile -$) by the predominance of long anceps, lack of resolution, and, usually, by the way in which the rhythm seems to ramble on without repeating recognizable cola. Stanzas in Sophocles and Euripides in which dactylo-epitrite predominates are *Aj*. 172 ff. = 182 ff., *Ant*. 582 ff. = 593 ff. (where, at 583–4 = 594–5, there may be a survival of Stesichorean link biceps), *Trach*. 94 ff. = 103 ff., 821 ff. = 831 ff., *OT* 1086 ff. = 1098 ff., *OC* 1074 ff. = 1085 ff., *Med*. 410 ff. = 421 ff., 627 ff. = 635 ff., 824 ff. = 835 ff., 976 ff. = 982 ff., *Andr*. 766 ff. = 776 ff., 789 ff., E. *El*. 859 ff. = 873 ff., *Tro*. 799 ff. = 808 ff., *Hel*. 1137 ff., = 1157 ff., *Rhes*. 224 ff. = 233 ff. It will be observed that the play with the largest concentration of dactylo-epitrite is *Med*., followed by *Trach*. and *Andr*.

There are also certain tragic stanzas (e.g. *Trach*. 497 ff. = 507 ff., *Med*. 643 ff. = 652 ff., *Alc*. 435 ff. = 445 ff.) which seem to have affinities with the undeveloped dactylo-epitrite of Stesichorus, and which I tentatively class as 'free dactylo-epitrite' (see below on *Birds* 451 ff. = 539 ff.).

Dactylo-epitrite has no catalectic form, but interplay of blunt and pendent rhythm is achieved by recurrent word-end within the verse (see Parker, *BICS* 5 (1958), 20–3) and by the presence or absence of anceps at the end of the verse. The Attic tragedians, however, seem to have introduced a (strictly) alien phrase as clausula, the bacchiac, usually preceded by ×–∪– or –∪–. If we accept that in dactylo-epitrite contexts, as in iambic, bacchiac was a product of syncopation (∪–(∪)–), this clausular rhythm must have been very distinctive indeed. See, for example, *PV* 535=544, *OT*, 1095=1107, *OC* 1083=1094, *Med.* 420=430, 634=642, 981=988, *Andr.* 776=787.

Aristophanes uses dactylo-epitrite rarely, but to interesting effect. In two early plays its presence is clearly allusive. *Knights* 1264 ff. = 1290 ff., which is pure dactylo-epitrite with the characteristic Attic bacchiac clausula, begins with a quotation from Pindar, and the association of the metre, through the epinician genre, with equitation suits the chorus. At *Peace* 775 ff. = 796 ff., the first half of the stanza is in dactylo-epitrite and embodies quotations from Stesichorus (see further, p. 7). *Wasps* 273 ff. = 281 ff. is more enigmatic. The earlier lines, 219–20, lead us to expect that when the chorus sing they will adopt the musical style of Phrynichus, but the surviving fragments of Phrynichus' lyric are, not surprisingly, inadequate to show whether or how far this is so (see further below, ad loc.). The use of dactylo-epitrite at *Clouds* 457 ff. is consistent with this chorus's preference early in the play for rhythms associated with high poetry, but there is no more particular allusion perceptible to us.

Developed dactylo-epitrite in its ordinary form is only found in snatches in the later plays. The Poet at *Birds* 904 ff. introduces the metre among his Pindaric scraps. There is a short dactylo-epitrite passage at the end of the hymn at *Thesm.* 312 ff. (328–31) and another at *Frogs* 1362–4. The *Birds* and *Frogs* passages are both parodic, while the *Thesm.* hymn is a metrically sophisticated composition.

In the later plays there are three pure, or nearly pure, dactylo-epitrite stanzas, but these seem to hark back in their metrical style to Stesichorus. *Ecc.* 571 ff. opens with an apparently aeolo-choriambic verse: –––∪∪–∪∪–∪∪⌢∪––, which may be a reminiscence and adaptation of those Stesichorean verses, such as the archebulean, in which a dactylic run ends with … –⌣–∪–– (see above, p. 86). The rest of the stanza is made up of the ordinary phrases of Attic dactylo-epitrite (–∪∪–∪∪–, –∪–, and ∪––), but the preponderance of dactylic rhythm is striking. Even more striking are *Birds* 451 ff. = 539 ff. and *Frogs* 674 ff. = 706 ff., both of which feature long dactylic sequences which sometimes open with $\cup\cup$ in a manner reminiscent of Stesichorus (*P. Oxy.* 2617 and 2359).

Ecc. 571ff. ends (580) with an archilochean dicolon:

$$-\ -\ \cup\ \cup\ -\ \cup\ \cup\ -\ \cup\ -\ \cup\ -\ \cup\ -\ -$$

Although compatible with Attic dactylo-epitrite, this verse is quite distinct in origin. Archilochus' blends of dactylic with iambic rhythm are structurally completely different from Stesichorus'. Unlike Stesichorus, Archilochus uses catalexis to mark verse-end, and his dactylic, iambic (and trochaic) verses are almost invariably analysable into metra. The exception is a rhythmic phrase which he shares with Stesichorus, the hemiepes. In elegiac couplets, he uses a pair of hemiepe marked off by diaeresis ($-\cup\cup-\cup\cup-|\quad -\cup\cup-\cup\cup-$), alternating with dactylic hexameters. A hemiepes with anceps prefixed and followed by a catalectic iambic dimeter makes up the archilochean dicolon (*IEG*^{2} 168–71). See further on *Wasps* 1518.

APPENDIX: NOTES ON PROSODY

I. *Epic correption*

Dactyls

Clouds	290	τηλεσκόπῳ ὄμματι	
	298	παρθένοι ὀμβροφόροι	
	304–5	ἀναδείκνυται οὐρανίοις	
	306	καὶ ἀγάλματα	
	308–9	ἱερώταται εὐστέφανοι	
Peace	811	βατιδοσκόποι Ἅρπυιαι	
	813	τραγομάσχαλοι ἰχθυολῦμαι	
Birds	774	ὄχθῳ ἐφεζόμενοι	
Frogs	706	ἐγὼ ὄρθος	
	875	παρθένοι ἁγναί	
	1269	κόπῳ, Αἰσχύλε	
	1338	μοι ἀμφίπολοι	
	1340	ἀποκ|λύσω· ἰώ	
	1344	Νύμφαι ὀρεσσίγονοι (hem in dactylic context)	

Dactylo-epitrite

Clouds	466	ὄψομαι; ὥστε	(change of speaker)
	471	καὶ εἰς	
Frogs	714	ἐνδιατρίψει ἰδών	

Aeolo-choriambic, Iambo-choriambic

Knights	1133	τρόπῳ, ὡς	(tel)
	1137	τύχῃ ὄψον	(tel)
Clouds	513	τἀνθρώπῳ ὅτι	(ith or arist; see further ad loc.)
	567	καὶ ἁλμυρᾶς	(cho ia trim)
	595	μοι αὖτε	(cho ia dim)
Peace	809	καὶ αὐτός	(arist)
	1329	γύναι, εἰς	(tel)
Birds	676	φίλη, ὦ	(dodrans)
Thesm.	1149	πότ|νιαι ἄλσος	(ibyc)
	1157	ἐπηκόω ἤλθετε	(aeol da)
Ecc.	970	ὦ ἱκετεύω	(cho ia dim cat)

Ionic
　Wasps　291　μοι οὖν

Dochmiac
　Clouds　1170　ἰὼ ἰώ
　Thesm.　915　κύσω. ἄπαγε
　　　　　1028　πάλαι ἐφεστώς

Trochaic
　Wasps　1065　δὴ αἶδ᾽

Iambic
　Wasps　1338　ἰαιβοῖ αἰβοῖ

Epic correption is, as one would expect, most common in dactyls. It is comparatively less common in the Dorian metre, dactylo-epitrite, and more common in aeolo-choriambic and kindred metres, the metres of the eastern Aegean.

II. *Lengthening before plosive (mute) + liquid or nasal (other than the 'strong' combinations, βλ γλ γν γμ δν δμ)*

Dactylic
　Clouds　278　πατ|ρός
　　　　　284　βαρύβ|ρομον
　　　　　301　Κέκ|ροπος
　　　　　313　βαρύβ|ρομος
　Birds　769　κύκ|νοι
　　　　　1321　ἀγανόφ|ρονος
　Lys.　1289　ἀγανόφ|ρονος
　Frogs　814　ἐριβ|ρεμέτας
　　　　　1340　ἀποκ|λύσω
　Ecc　1172　-κιχ|λεπι-

Dactylo-epitrite
　Peace　805　πικ|ροτάτην
　Birds　950　χρυσόθ|ρονε　(quotation or parody of Pindar)
　Birds　1338　ἀτ|ρυγέτου　(quotation from Sophocles)
　Thesm.　116　ἀγ|ροτέραν　(parody of Agathon)
　Frogs　680　ἐριβ|ρέμεται

The following two examples come from the same scene as *Birds* 950. The metre is uncertain, but the context is pseudo-Pindaric:

Birds	930	πρόφ'ρων
	943	ἀκ'λεής

Aeolo-choriambic, iambo-choriambic, etc.

Wasps	1232–3	μέγα κ'ράτος	(quotation from Alcaeus)
Clouds	513	ὅτι π'ροήκων	(arist or ith; see further ad loc)
	597	πέτ'ραν	(arist)
Thesm.	1149	πότ'νιαι	(ibyc)
	1156	πολυποτ'νία	(ibyc)

Archilochean dicola

Wasps	1518	τέκ'να
	1521	ἀτ'ρυγέτοιο
	1523	κυκ'λοσοβεῖτε

Iambic

Lys.	1296	ἐκ'λιπῶᾱ
Thesm.	719	ἐνυβ'ριεῖς

Trochaic

Thesm.	463	πολύπ'λοκον

There is an obvious connexion between lengthening before plosive and liquid/nasal and metres typical of serious poetry: dactylic (the metre of epic) and dactylo-epitrite (the metre of Dorian lyric). Obviously, quotation from other poets reflects their prosodic practice, but so, perhaps, does allusion, witness the cluster of occurrences in the archilocheans of *Wasps* 1518 ff.

There is also a strong tendency for the phenomenon to be found in the kind of compound words that belong to the language of literary poetry. The only example split between words is in the quotation from Alcaeus at *Wasps* 1232–3.

3   Metre and the Transmission of the Text

The metrical history of the text of Aristophanes falls into three periods: from the poet himself to Triclinius, from Triclinius to Brunck, and from Brunck to the present. The first period is both the most mysterious and immeasurably the most important.

THE POET TO TRICLINIUS

In general, the plays of Aristophanes do not seem to have been revived on stage, which protected them, no doubt, from interpolation and other 'improvements' to which theatrical directors perennially subject dramatic classics. On the other hand, performance keeps alive a sense of dramatic form, and Aristophanic comedy is, formally, highly complex.[1]

Scholarly industry at Alexandria was prompt in applying itself to Aristophanes,[2] and it can safely be assumed that Aristophanes of Byzantium and those colleagues of his who first set out the lyric of tragedy in cola did the same for Old Comedy.[3] The degree of skill and understanding with which these original divisions were carried out is best revealed by the traditional colometry of Pindar, because for Pindar we have one point of certainty lacking for drama. Because of the comparatively large number of repetitions of the individual stanza-form it is possible to ascertain with almost complete certainty the incidence of verse-end, or metrical pause, which is marked, firstly, by obligatory word-end, secondly, by the admissibility of hiatus and *brevis in longo*. It is the finding of J. Irigoin[4] that in the traditional colometry of Pindar

---

[1] This is ingeniously illustrated by the diagrams at the end of T. Zieliński, *Die Gliederung der altattischen Komödie* (Leipzig, 1885).

[2] See P. Boudreaux, *Le Texte d'Aristophane et ses Commentateurs* (Paris, 1919); R. Pfeiffer, *History of Classical Scholarship: From the Beginnings to the end of the Hellenistic Age* (Oxford, 1968), 161 ff., 187 ff., 224; L. D. Reynolds and N. G. Wilson, *Scribes and Scholars*[3] (Oxford, 1991), 15–16.

[3] Dionysius of Halicarnassus, *De comp. Verb.* 22. 17 (cf. 26. 14).

[4] *Les Scholies métriques de Pindare* (Paris, 1958), 21.

7 per cent of verse-ends in the dactylo-epitrite poems do not coincide with the end of a colon, while in the twenty-one poems classified by Irigoin as 'iambic' the proportion rises to 21.6 per cent. This is not particularly creditable to the metricians of Alexandria, since in order to find verse-ends in Pindar it is not actually necessary to understand the significance of hiatus and *brevis in longo*. Careful observation of recurrent word-end will suffice. The task of setting out lyric poetry in cola was undoubtedly massive, and it would be unfair to suggest that Alexandrian scholars carried it out carelessly or incompetently. None the less, the study of traditional colometries has so far failed to support the idea that because the Alexandrians were so much closer in time to the date of composition they necessarily possessed crucial knowledge that we do not. The evidence points rather in the opposite direction.

The earliest name definitely connected with the study of Aristophanic metre is that of Heliodorus.[5] Two plays, *Clouds* and *Peace*, carry in some MSS (including V) the subscription κεκώλισται ἐκ τῶν (or πρὸς τὰ) Ἡλιοδώρου. In addition, Heliodorus is mentioned twice in the pre-Triclinian metrical scholia (Σ vet.). On *Peace* 1329–59, V has simply ὑμὴν ὑμέναι' ὦ· οὕτως Ἡλιόδωρος. On *Wasps* 1283, however, V preserves an important and problematic note relating to the size of the lacuna after 1285.[6] Heliodorus preceded Hephaestion, since the latter mentions him (Cons. 6. 16). Like Hephaestion, he produced an ἐγχειρίδιον (Cons. 81. 14). Marius Victorinus refers to him as '*inter*

---

[5] On Heliodorus, see: R. Westphal, *Metrik der Griechen*, i² (Leipzig, 1867), 214–26; C. Thiemann, *Heliodori Colometriae aristophaneae quantum superest*, (Halle, 1869); O. Hense, *Heliodoreische Untersuchungen*, Leipzig, 1870, and, after the publication of *P. Oxy.* 220, Pauly-Wissowa viii. 1 (1912), 28–40; W. J. W. Koster, *Autour d'un manuscrit d'Aristophane écrit par Démétrius Triclinius* (Groningen, 1957), esp. 87–93; D. Holwerda, 'De Heliodori Commentario metrico in Aristophanem', *Mnemosyne*, 17 (1964), 113–39 and 20 (1967), 247–72. J. W. White includes in his book, *The Verse of Greek Comedy* (London, 1912; repr. Hildesheim, 1969), a text of Σ vet., and, indeed, one of his major preoccupations is the reconstruction of the metrical theories of Heliodorus. Metrical scholia are, however, subject to extensive corruption. To most scribes they will have been by far the least comprehensible part of what they were copying, and they are full of numbers and easily confusible words: καταληκτικόν and ἀκατάληκτον, ἰαμβικόν and χοριαμβικόν. White's text is heavily emended, and too much of his interpretation rests on his emendations. Modern editions of the scholia of Aristophanes are in course of publication by Bouma's Boekhuis, Groningen, under the general editorship of W. J. W. Koster and D. Holwerda.

[6] *Scholia in Aristophanem*, II. i. *Scholia vetera et recentiora in Aristophanis Vespas*, W. J. W. Koster, (Groningen, 1978), 204. See also T. W. Allen, 'Miscellanea III', *CQ* 22 (1929), 28–9; D. Holwerda, *Mnemosyne*, 20 (1967), 261 ff.

Graecos huiusce artis [sc. *metricae*] *antistes aut primus aut solus.*[7] Close scrutiny of the evidence for dating serves neither to confirm nor refute Bergk's appealing conjecture that he was the *rhetor Heliodorus, Graecorum longe doctissimus* who went with Horace to Brundisium, but Horace could hardly have had a more useful friend than a Greek metrician.[8] A major preoccupation of the *Σ vet.* on Aristophanes is a method of indicating the relative length of cola by lay-out. Taking the iambic trimeter as the norm, longer cola (or verses) are to commence further to the left (ἐν ἐκθέσει) and shorter cola nearer to the middle of the column (ἐν εἰσθέσει). In *P. Oxy.* 2545 of *Knights* 1057–76 the hexameters begin 'about five letters further to the left' than the trimeters.[9] The papyrus is dated on palaeographical grounds by the editor, E. G. Turner, to the first century BC or the first century AD. This dating raises the possibility that Heliodorus may not have been the inventor of the system, nor even the first scholar to have applied it to the text of Aristophanes.

Apart from the dating, the major controversy relating to Heliodorus is whether and to what extent he represents a different strain of ancient metrical thought from Hephaestion. Choeroboscus, commenting on Hephaestion (Cons. 247. 11), reports a statement of Heliodorus that in paeonics (i.e. $- \cup -$, $- \cup \cup \cup$, $\cup \cup \cup -$) word-end coinciding with foot-end is κοσμία, because the pause thereby produced makes the foot hexaseme (that is to say equal to six shorts instead of five). This shows,

---

[7] Keil, *Grammatici Latini*, vi. 94. 7.

[8] *Sat.* 1. 5. 2–3. Hense (see above, n. 5) placed Heliodorus' prime in the mid-first century AD. According to Hense, the grammarian Seleucus, who lived at the time of Augustus and Tiberius, is quoted by Heliodorus. It is, of course, possible to quote one's contemporaries, and even one's juniors, but, in any case, the passage relied on by Hense (Priscian, *De metris Terent.*, Keil iii. 428) quotes Seleucus and Heliodorus as separate authorities for distinct phenomena. According to the *Suda*, Irenaeus, otherwise known as Minucius Pacatus, was a pupil of 'Heliodorus, the metrician' (Adler, ii. 533, 21 s. Εἰρηναῖος and iv. 4, 4 s. Πάκατος). Irenaeus is quoted by Erotian (ed. E. Nachmanson (Göteborg, 1918), 116. 6), who lived at the end of the first century AD, but if he can be identified with the *Pacatus rhetor* mentioned by the elder Seneca (*Controv.* 10, *praef.* 10), his date would be brought back to at least the beginning of the century. His master, Heliodorus, could then plausibly have been a member of Maecenas' circle. The question remains of whether the same man could be referred to as a *rhetor* and *grammaticus*. Quintilian (2. 1) suggests that in his own day the demarcation between the professions was tending to break down, and it is at least thought-provoking that we have evidence of a Heliodorus *rhetor* and a Heliodorus *grammaticus* and a Pacatus *rhetor* and a Pacatus *grammaticus*, at least within the same century.

[9] *P. Oxy.* xxxi. 55–7. *Σ vet.* on 1067a specifies ἐν ἐκθέσει ἐπικοὶ τρεῖς and on 1070a ἐν εἰσθέσει δὲ ἴαμβοι δέκα.

at least, an interest in rhythm and realization in performance which is alien to Hephaestion.

The metrical scholia on Pindar indubitably follow the method of Hephaestion. In his edition, Irigoin[10] compares the descriptions of metrically similar passages in Pindaric and Aristophanic scholia, and discerns no fundamentally different principles of analysis. There is, however, an important difference of character between the two sets of scholia. While the Pindaric scholia are little more than a mechanical description in Hephaestion's superabundant terminology, the Aristophanic scholia preserve evidence of serious scholarship and controversy. As in the non-metrical *scholia vetera*, there is mention of other texts with variant readings (e.g. on *Peace* 582, where the variant reported would actually damage correspondence). Moreover, some of the scholia reveal that their author is commenting on a colometry with which he does not agree, and that he knows texts with different colometries. Thus, on *Peace* 775–95=796–818, Σ *vet.* notes the existence of an alternative colometry 'which is actually better'.[11] The following portion of the note is corrupt, but seems again to express a preference for an alternative colometry to that on which the author is commenting. At 939ff. in the same play Σ *vet.* says that he suspects that there is an antistrophe separated from the strophe (ἐν διεχείᾳ), but that the stanza has come down in a different division (φέρεται δὲ ὡς διάφορον). He goes on to fault the received text, and to suggest emendation designed to restore correspondence. On *Clouds* 949 ff., he again remarks that there is an antistrophe, but that it is ἐν διεχείᾳ and διαφόρως κεκωλισμένην.[12] At *Peace* 1132 ff.=1164 ff., Σ *vet.* remarks on a divergence of colometry between strophe and antistrophe, but does not (at least in the mutilated state of the text) vouchsafe any views on the matter. The MSS R and V, however, preserve a corresponding division.

It would be wrong, moreover, to assume that all the Σ *vet.* were compiled from the work of a single metrician. Within the scholia there are inconsistencies and evidence of different views and different minds at work. The note on *Wasps* 1283, mentioned above (p. 95), is a case in

---

[10] *Les Scholies métriques*, 49–52.

[11] *Scholia in Aristophanem*, II.ii, *Scholia vetera et recentiora in Aristophanis Pacem*, D. Holwerda, 120–1 (on 775). See below, p. 101.

[12] *Scholia in Aristophanem*, I.iii.1. *Scholia vetera in Nubes*, D. Holwerda, 183.

point.[13] At *Clouds* 1345–50=1391–96, the metre of the antistrophe is clear and simple: three distichs of the form iambic trimeter, reizianum:

$$\times - \cup - \quad \times - \cup - \quad \times - \cup -$$
$$\times - \cup \cup - -$$

In the strophe, the text of the final distich (1349–50) is corrupt. The text of all the MSS, in the colometry of R, is:

ἀλλ' ἔσθ' ὅτῳ θρασύνεται·
δῆλον τὸ λῆμ' ἐστὶ τἀνθρώπου

$$- - \cup - \quad \cup - \cup -$$
$$- - \cup - - \cup - - -$$

Σ *vet.* E on 1345a describes this text and colometry. He sees the stanza as a miniature triad, the first distichs being a strophe and antistrophe, and the corrupt distich the epode. There is no suggestion that he was aware of a corresponding stanza. In the more meagre scholia on Vs1 however, 1391 is marked ἀντίστροφος and on 1350 the scholiast notes that ἐστὶ τἀνθρώπου is ὅμοιον to ἀλλ' οὐδ' ἐρεβίνθου (1396). In its surviving form, of course, it is not, but the two cola *ought* to correspond. Again, on the vexed pair of stanzas *Clouds* 1303–10=1311–20, Σ *vet.* E betrays no awareness of correspondence: the song is described as μέλος τοῦ χοροῦ κώλων ιη'. The less ample scholia on RV add nothing to E. The colon-division of RV, however, preserves a trace of what may once have been a corresponding division: 1303 and 1311, the first cola of strophe and antistrophe respectively, both appear as iambic trimeters. Σ *vet.* Vs1 shows awareness of correspondence: while including some of the same material as the rest, he remarks on 1319–20: τὰ β' κῶλα ταῦτα ἄνισά εἰσι ⟨τοῖς⟩ τῆς ᾠδῆς.[14]

Some fifteen passages of lyric from the surviving plays are preserved in published papyri, which range in date from the second to the seventh century AD (to take the earliest and latest dates proposed for individual papyri).[15] It has often been observed that the papyri of surviving plays of

[13] See above, n. 6.

[14] For a discussion of differences of authorship within the Σ *vet.* based on other passages, see D. Holwerda, *Mnemosyne*, 20 (1967), 258–66.

[15] For full references on the papyri, see C. Austin, *Comicorum Graecorum Fragmenta in papyris reperta* (Berlin and New York, 1973), and W. Luppe, 'Literarische Texte unter Ausschluss der Christlichen', *APF* 27 (1980), 232–50, and 'Literarische Texte: Drama', *APF* 38 (1992), 75–86.

Aristophanes diverge very little in text from the medieval MSS.[16] Equally, their colometry generally tallies with that of R. There are only four exceptions in published fragments.

1. *Ach.* 971–4. *P. Berol.* 13231. 5th–6th c. AD. The papyrus has the division described by Σ *vet.* 971a, which led to confusion and textual corruption in the medieval MSS. In particular, the papyrus treats οἵ’ ἔχει as a separate colon. R, or an ancestor of R, took the words to be an omission written in above the line and incorporated them into the following line in the wrong place. See further below, ad loc.

2. *Knights* 551–5 = 581–4. *P. Berol.* 13929+21105. 4th c. AD. The papyrus divides both strophe and antistrophe correctly, in the only possible way, to produce the scansion:

$$- \cup \cup - \quad \cup - \cup -$$
$$- \cup \cup - \quad \cup - \cup -$$
$$- \cup \cup - \quad \cup - \cup -$$
$$- \cup \cup - \quad \cup - \cup -$$

R diverges, firstly, by writing two cola to a line, the first pair in both strophe and antistrophe continuous, the second in two columns, with a clear gap between. Secondly, 581–4 is divided thus:

ὦ πολιοῦχε Παλλάς, ὦ τῆς ἱερωτάτης ἁπασῶν
πολέμῳ τε καὶ ποιη- ταῖς δυνάμει θ’ ὑπερφερού-
σης . . .

There is a simple mistake here which is common whenever a scribe is copying cola in synartesis, and which will be familiar to anyone who has ever copied much Greek lyric. At the end of the second colon, the scribe should have changed line at ἁπα-. Instead, he has run on to the end of the word before changing. The scribe of R can, in fact, be seen to have made this mistake from time to time and corrected it at once,[17] but here

---

[16] On the relationship between the metrical analyses of Σ *vet.* and the papyri in *Clouds* and *Frogs*, see Dover, *The Greeks and their Legacy*, ii. 249.

[17] e.g. at *Knights* 1113–16, R writes:

θρωποι δεδίασί σ’ ὥσπερ
περ ἄνδρα τύραννον,
ἀλλ’ εὐπαράγωγος εἶ,
θωπευόμενός τε χαιρεῖς
ρεῖς . . .

he is not to blame, since V and E make the same mistake. From 583 onwards, however, R rights himself, while VE continue in accidental anacreontics:

> πολέμῳ τε καὶ ποιηταῖς   ∪∪−∪−∪−−
> δυνάμει θ' ὑπερφερούσης   ∪∪−∪−∪−−
> μεδέουσα χώρας   ∪∪−∪−−

The mis-division is purely accidental, and has developed in two stages: first the simple run-on mistake at ἁπασῶν inherited by all the MSS, then the series of run-on mistakes in the following cola made by a common ancestor of VE. VE make a similar sequence of run-on mistakes in the last four cola of the stanza, where, again, R divides correctly.

   3. *Clouds* 955–8. *P. Berol.* 13219 (Dover *Π* 4), 5th–6th c. AD. Here RV lay the passage out in dicolon lengths:

> νῦν γὰρ ἅπας ἐνθάδε κίνδυνος ἀνεῖται σοφίας,
> ἧς πέρι τοῖς ἐμοῖς φίλοις ἐστὶν ἀγὼν μέγιστος

> −∪∪−   −∪∪−   −∪∪−   −∪∪−
> −∪∪−   ∪−∪−   −∪∪−   ∪−−

Division into single cola requires κίν-δυνος to be split between lines. According to Dover,[18] the majority of MSS other than RV fail to change line until the end of the word:

> νῦν γὰρ ἅπας ἐνθάδε κίνδυνος
> ἀνεῖται σοφίας

That is to say that they derive from a common ancestor who ran on by mistake. The papyrus, however, makes the opposite mistake, that of changing lines too early:

> [νυνγαραπασενθ]αδε
> [κινδυνοσανειταισο]φιας

Following word-end in stopping short is not such an easy mistake to make as running on, but the scribe of R does demonstrably make it occasionally,[19] and it could well have been made more frequently by a scribe

---

[18] *Clouds* (Oxford, 1968), p. cxiii.

[19] R follows word-end in stopping short twice in *Frogs* 392–5:

> πολλὰ δὲ [καὶ] σπουδαῖα
> καὶ τῆς σῆς ἑορτῆς ἀξίως

less concerned about copying colon-division correctly. It is the division
of the majority of MSS other than RV that is described by Triclinius in
his detailed analysis of the stanza and by the Σ *anon. rec.* The Σ *vet.* on
949 casts no light. He notes a failure of correspondence, but that is
accounted for by the state of the text at 1028–31.[20]

4. *Peace* 781–6. *PSI* 720. 3rd c. AD. R divides:

ἦν δέ σε Καρκίνος ἐλθὼν	$- \cup \cup - \cup \cup - -$
ἀντιβολῇ μετὰ τῶν παί-	$- \cup \cup - \cup \cup - -$
δων χορεῦσαι,	$- \cup - -$
μήθ᾽ ὑπακούσῃς μήτ᾽ ἐλ-	$- \cup \cup - - - -$
θῃς συνέριθος αὐτοῖς	$- \cup \cup - \cup - -$

The papyrus, however, offers:

ηνδεσεκα[	$- \cup \cup - [\cup \cup - -$
αντιβολημ[	$- \cup \cup - [\cup \cup -$
παιδωνχ[	$- - [\cup - -$
μηθυπακουση[	$- \cup \cup - - [- - -$
ξυνεριθ[	$\cup \cup - [\cup - -$

The division of the papyrus is generally less neat and plausible than
that of the MS, but this is one of the passages mentioned above
(p. 97) for which Σ *vet.* notes the existence of a variant colometry:
τινὲς δὲ συνάπτουσι τὸ η΄ καὶ τὸ θ΄ καὶ γίνεται ἐγκωμιολογικὸν
†εἰς† διπενθημιμερές, ὃ καὶ ἄμεινον.[21] The controversy is of a kind

> παίσαντα καὶ σκώψαντα
> νικήσαντα ταινιοῦσθαι.

V divides correctly. At *Ach.* 669, R stops one syllable short within a word, changing lines at
ἐρ|εθιζόμενος, instead of ἐρε|θιζόμενος. At *Clouds* 511–12 he writes:

> εὐτυχία γένοι τότ᾽ ἂν
> ἀνθρωπῳ . . .

Accentuation shows that the scribe was making a mistake of word-division here (τότ᾽ ἀνθρώπῳ
for -το τἀνθρώπῳ), and originally changed lines at what he thought was word-end (after τότ᾽).
Stopping short is not the only possible explanation here, but it is the simplest.

[20] *Scholia in Aristophanem*, 1.iii.2. *Scholia recentiora in Nubes*, W. J. W. Koster, 133–4 (Triclinius
on 949), 376 (Σ *anon. rec.*, 949a), and 1.iii.1 *Scholia vetera in Nubes*, D. Holwerda, 183.

[21] In *Mnemosyne*, 20 (1967), 261 ff., Holwerda favoured deleting ἐγκωμιολογικόν. In his
edition of 1982 (*Scholia in Aristophanem*, II.ii.121) his suspicions are turned upon εἰς only. In his discussion in *Mnemosyne*, he adduces the evidence of Choeroboscus (Consbruch 225. 16 ff.) that
Heliodorus favoured divisions which coincided with word-end (and for Heliodorus τῶν|παίδων
would probably have constituted word-end).

still common between a metrician who likes cola of equal length and one
who prefers to divide according to word-end (as he conceives it). The
scribe of the papyrus does not run 783–4 together, but he does divide
them as two 'penthemimers'. We may be tempted to wonder, particularly in view of the relatively early date of the papyrus, whether we have
here a genuine survival of the controversy recorded in Σ *vet.* The
papyrus's division of the next two cola is, however, rather implausible
metrically, and it is by no means impossible that the whole division is the
accidental product of a careless scribe who followed word-end in changing lines, too early at the end of the second colon, too late at the end of
the fourth.[22]

Just as the few divergences in colometry between the papyri and R
are most probably the result of scribal error, so, too, the many divergences in the same matter between medieval MSS are, in all probability,
accidental. *Frogs* 814–17 = 818–21 = 822–5 = 826–9 provides a good example. These four short, corresponding stanzas, made up of two dactylic
hexameters, a dactylic pentameter and a lecythion, are set out in RV in
seven cola:

$$- - - \cup \cup - \cup \cup -$$
$$\cup \cup - \cup \cup - -$$
$$- \cup \cup - \cup \cup - \cup \cup -$$
$$- - \cup \cup - -$$
$$- \cup \cup - \cup \cup -$$
$$\cup \cup - \cup \cup - -$$
$$- \cup - \cup - \cup -$$

This is done consistently, and must represent the deliberate division of
an ancient edition. The scribe of U consistently writes two cola to a line.
Since the stanza consists, in its traditional division, of an odd number of
cola, this causes him twice to run together the last colon of one stanza
with the first of the next, and, four times, to produce back-to-front hexa-

---

[22] It will be observed that I do not here take into account Snell's theory, based on the Bacchylides
papyrus, that the tendency of early scribes to change line at word-end accurately reproduces a
deliberate feature of Alexandrian colometry (*Bacchylidis carmina cum fragmentis, post* B. Snell,
ed. H. Maehler (Leipzig, 1970), *Praefatio*, p. xxxi). This is not the place for an extended discussion,
but, given the observable tendencies of medieval scribes, the fact that the inconsistencies in
the Bacchylides papyrus involve moves *towards* dividing at word-end is evidence that they are
accidental.

meters ($\cup\cup - \cup\cup - - - \cup\cup - \cup\cup - \cup\cup -$). A begins with three of
RV's cola crammed on to one line, and continues with one or, more
often, two cola to a line, apparently at random. His changes of line do,
however, always coincide with colon-end. The sole concern of the
scribe of M seems to have been to produce lines of equal length, regardless even of word-end. He even adds the first words of the following
iambic trimeter to the last colon of the song. Metrical structure is completely lost.[23]

Although, on the evidence of Σ *vet.*, there were editions with at least
some differences of colometry current in later antiquity, it is highly
unlikely that these have actually survived as differences between groups
of medieval MSS. At least, anyone trying to distinguish the vestiges of
deliberate differences from accidental ones would have to proceed with
extreme caution. There is, however, something to be learnt from the
observation of MSS colometries. Most obviously, they can help to
throw light on the relationships between the MSS. Thus, the finding of
D. Mervyn Jones[24] that for *Knights* E is closely related to V is borne out
by colon-division. The only divergences between the two MSS are at
331–2 (where E writes both cola on the same line) and, more interestingly, at 1145 and 1147, at both of which points E sides with R against V,
making a run-on mistake at 1145 and avoiding one at 1147. For
Acharnians, on the other hand, E shares the disordered division of the Φ
MSS, A and Γ.[25]

Of more particular interest to the student of metre is the light which
the colon-divisions of MSS can cast on the earliest colon-divisions and
the state of the text on which the earliest editors worked. As has already
been remarked, the colon-division of R tallies closely with the papyri; it
also tallies fairly closely with Σ *vet.* V is generally less reliable, but is,
none the less, occasionally right where R is wrong. These two MSS are
useful auxiliaries to the student of Σ *vet.*, and, where these scholia are

[23] On combination of cola and misdivision in MSS, see further Dover, *The Greeks and their
Legacy*, ii. 250–4.

[24] 'The MSS of Aristophanes' *Knights*', *CQ* 2 (1952), 168–85. See esp. 172: ' . . . the stichometry
of the lyrics exhibits quite clearly the separate existence of these groups; and it is apparent that each
group is descended from a separate hyparchetype.'

[25] E. Cary, *HSCP* 18 (1907), 168 ff. The colometry of the MSS of *Ach.* is reported by R. T. Elliott
in his edition of the play (Oxford, 1914). I am indebted to Mr N. G. Wilson for the loan of
photographs of part of E.

lacking, can be used to some extent as a substitute source of information on ancient colometry. Where R and/or V offer a corresponding division of strophe and antistrophe, that division must go back to antiquity, or at least to very early Byzantium. Where corresponding stanzas are given a non-corresponding, but metrically plausible, division, the likely explanation is that the earliest metricians to work on the text failed to recognize correspondence. These points deserve attention because many of the most important and difficult textual problems in Aristophanes' lyric involve correspondence. If a strophic pair of stanzas shows a failure of correspondence in the text and survives in a non-corresponding division in R(V), the most obvious (though not by any means the only possible) conclusion is that the textual corruption (if it is a corruption) was already present in the text at a very early date, and that its presence prevented the earliest editors from recognizing correspondence.[26]

An interesting and problematic case is *Acharnians* 929–39=940–51, which is preserved in a papyrus of the fifth or sixth century AD (*P. Berol.* 13231) in the same colometry as in RV. In the first section of the stanza, 929–33=940–6, there is a striking difference of division between strophe and antistrophe:

929–33 ἔνδησον, ὦ βέλτιστε, τῷ ξένῳ καλῶς
        τὴν ἐμπολὴν οὕτως ὅπως ἂν μὴ φέρων κατάξῃ.
        ἐμοὶ μελήσει ταῦτ' ἐπεί τοι καὶ ψοφεῖ
        λάλον τι καὶ πυρορραγὲς κἄλλως θεοῖσιν ἐχθρόν.

        — — ∪ —   — — ∪ —   ∪ — ∪ —
        — — ∪ —   — — ∪ —   — — ∪ —   ∪ — — ‖ ᴴ
        ∪ — ∪ —   — — ∪ —   — — ∪ —
        ∪ — ∪ —   ∪ — ∪ —   — — ∪ —   ∪ — —

This colometry is also described by Σ *vet.* on 929:[27]

---

[26] This is not to propound the view rejected by Dover (*The Greeks and their Legacy*, ii. 250) that 'R is peculiarly faithful to a standard ancient colometry'. In the first place, the hypothesis of a 'standard ancient colometry' needs itself to be treated with extreme caution. However, if one takes into account the type as well as the number of mistakes, R can, I believe, be seen to have taken a relatively high degree of care in copying a source which, in general, reproduced ancient colometry. Non-corresponding divisions of corresponding stanzas do not prove R's fallibility, unless one assumes that ancient colometricians could be relied on to spot correspondence.

[27] *Scholia in Aristophanem*, I.i ʙ, *Scholia in Aristophanis Acharnenses*, N. G. Wilson (Groningen, 1975), 119.

940–6: πῶς δ' ἂν πεποιθοίη τις ἀγ-   – – ◡ –   – – ◡ –
γείῳ τοιούτῳ χρώμενος   – – ◡ –   – – ◡ –
κατ' οἰκίαν   ◡ – ◡ –
τοσόνδ' ἀεὶ ψοφοῦντι;   ◡ – ◡ –   ◡ – ⌣ ‖ ᴴ
ἰσχυρόν ἐστιν, ὦγαθ', ὥστ'   – – ◡ –   ◡ – ◡ –
οὐκ ἂν καταγείη ποτ' εἴ-   – – ◡ –   – – ◡ –
περ ἐκ ποδῶν   ◡ – ◡ –
κατωκάρα κρέμαιτο   ◡ – ◡ –   ◡ – ⌣ ‖ ᴴ

I do not see how either division could be anything but deliberate, and the two are so different in principle that it is hard to believe that both could have been produced by the same metrician. It also seems unlikely that the author of the 'distich' division of 929–33 knew that the lines corresponded with 940–6, for if applied to those lines it loses one of its chief attractions, its coincidence with word-end. The next two cola, 935–6=946–7, have a corresponding division, and are observed to correspond by *Σ vet.* on 946. The last four cola of the stanza do not, in the MS text, correspond: there is an extra iambic metron in the antistrophe. *Σ vet.* on 948 shows no awareness of correspondence, but the colometry does, in fact, correspond as closely as it can:

    strophe   – – ◡ –   – – ◡ –
                          – – ◡ –   – – ◡ –
                          – – ◡ –
                          ◡ – ◡ –   ◡ – – |||

    antistrophe   – – ◡ –   – – ◡ –
                          ◡ – ◡ –   – – ◡ –
                          – – ◡ –   – – ◡ –
                          – – ◡ –   ◡ – – |||

It is not easy to see what has happened to these stanzas. A possible explanation is that they were originally given a corresponding division, but that, at some time in later antiquity, but before the compilation of *Σ vet.*, some scholar who did not recognize correspondence attempted a re-division of the beginning of the stanza. The extra metron in the latter part of the stanza could have been either cause, or, if it is interpolated, effect of the failure to recognize correspondence.[28]

---

[28] On this passage, see further ad. loc.

It would be pleasant to be able to believe that the Alexandrian editors worked on a sound text (perhaps even an official copy from the state archives of Athens[29]), that the original colometry was reverently preserved for the rest of antiquity, to be described by Heliodorus, and to survive, in however mutilated a form, in the papyri and medieval MSS; to believe, in short, that ancient editors conducted themselves in a manner wholly different from their Byzantine and modern successors. Apart, however, from sheer probability, the evidence makes such a belief untenable. According to the *Suda*,[30] a certain Eugenius, a γραμματικός of Constantinople, wrote on the colometry of fifteen tragedies in the fifth century AD. His work would seem to mark the end of a period of more than seven centuries in which, at least on and off, scholars were (or thought they were) competent to pronounce on metrical matters. The evidence of later periods suggests that the effect of metrical study on texts is not unlike that of αἰδώς on the life of men: μέγα σίνεται ἠδ' ὀνίνησιν.

TRICLINIUS TO BRUNCK

Demetrius Triclinius, in the early fourteenth century, produced the first recognizable major impact since antiquity of metrical scholarship on the text of Aristophanes. Some earlier Byzantine scholars had taken an interest in metre, but it does not appear that any before him possessed the knowledge and self-confidence to attempt major revisions of colometry and text.[31] Triclinius' activities were extensive and their effects long-lasting. He produced more than one recension of the text of Aristophanes, and his late work shows marked advances on the earlier.[32]

---

[29] It has been suggested that texts of the plays performed at the major festivals may have been kept in the state archives at Athens. But pseudo-Plutarch (*Lives of the Ten Orators*, 8. 841) says that Lycurgus (d. 324 BC) had official copies made of the plays of the three great tragedians to be deposited in the archives, and thus to protect the texts from actors' interpolation. Why do that if the texts were already there? The story may not be true, nor may that reported by Galen (*CMG* v. 10. 2 (1936), 79. 8) of how Ptolemy Philadelphus acquired the official texts for the library at Alexandria. In any case, both writers mention only tragedy, and our tragic texts do not seem to be free from actors' interpolations.

[30] Adler, ii. 442.

[31] See e.g. R. D. Dawe, *Studies in the Text of Sophocles*, i (Leiden, 1973), 59; O. L. Smith, 'Tricliniana', *C & M* 33 (1981–2), 246.

[32] On the Triclinian recensions, see K. Zacher, *Die Handschriften und Classen den*

To the student of Aristophanes, however, it is the latest recension that is of prime importance.

The identification of Triclinius' contribution to the metrical study of Aristophanes began with the work of Konrad Zacher on the Vatican MS 1294 (Vv5), which contains the 'Byzantine triad' (*Wealth, Clouds*, and *Frogs*) and 1–270 of *Knights*. In 1962, N. G. Wilson demonstrated that a manuscript in Oxford, Holkham gr. 88 (L), was a copy of the latest Triclinian recension of eight of the surviving plays, all, that is, except *Thesmophoriazusae, Ecclesiazusae*, and *Lysistrata*. The end of *Peace* (1286 ff.) is also missing. Wilson inferred from his specimen collations that, for the triad, L is a gemellus of Vv5.

Like his Byzantine predecessors in the study of metre, Triclinius relied heavily on Hephaestion; he used, if he did not fully understand, *Σ vet.*; and the exemplars he used were already divided into cola (an obvious point, though sometimes neglected). He is celebrated above all as the first scholar since the end of antiquity to have understood the principle of strophic responsion, and to have used it to emend lyric texts.

Aristophanesscholien, Bursian Suppl. 16 (Leipzig, 1888), 627 ff.; K. von Holzinger, *Vorstudien zur Beurteilung und Erklärertätigkeit des Demetrios Triklinios zu den Komödien des Aristophanes*, SB Wien 217.4 (Vienna and Leipzig, 1939), 6 ff.; W. J. W. Koster, *Autour d'un manuscrit d'Aristophane écrit par Démétrius Triclinius* (Groningen, 1957); M. A. Turyn, *The Byzantine Manuscript Tradition of the Tragedies of Euripides* (Urbana, Ill., 1957), 32 n. 49; N. G. Wilson, 'The Triclinian Edition of Aristophanes', *CQ* 12 (1962), 32–47; O. L. Smith, *Studies in the Scholia of Aeschylus, Mnemosyne* Suppl. 37 (Leiden, 1975), 95 ff. and 'Tricliniana', *C & M* 33 (1981–2), 32 ff., C. N. Eberline, *Studies in the Manuscript Tradition of the Ranae of Aristophanes* (Meisenheim am Glan, 1980).

Zacher identified two recensions of the plays of the Byzantine triad (*Wealth, Clouds, Frogs*), the earlier represented by Paris. gr. 2821 (P8) and the later by Vat. 1294 (Vv5), which contains, in addition to the triad, *Knights* 1–270. In 1955 Koster announced that Paris. Suppl. gr. 463 (P20, or, to Koster, Ps), which, again, contains the triad, was written by Triclinius himself, and represented an early state of his work on Aristophanes. On the other hand, he rejected Zacher's conclusion that P8 was an early Triclinian recension, and argued instead that it was post-Triclinian, by an anonymous scribe and based, with modifications of both commentary and text, on P20 and Vv5. Turyn, writing after the publication of Koster's initial announcement but before that of his book, identified the scribe of the body of the text in P20 not as Triclinius but as the writer of Angelicus 14 of Euripides. He accepted, however, that Triclinius had revised and corrected the text, and added scholia, both Thoman and his own (mostly metrical) and glosses. He posited three Triclinian recensions, represented, in sequence, by P8, P20, and Vv5. His view is accepted by O. L. Smith. Most recently, Eberline (op. cit. 113–23) ascribes P8 to 'a post-Triclinian editor who used Triclinian metrical scholia where he had them and wrote his own, using Triclinius' scholia as a model' where he did not. The capital point, however, which is generally accepted, is that P20 represents an early state of the Triclinian recension and that it shows Triclinius' metrical work actually in progress. See further, Smith, *C & M* 33 (1981–82), 239–43, and below, on *Wealth* 302 ff.

In a number of passages, his restorations have never been improved on.[33] Thus, in *Acharnians* he is responsible for ἔστιν (instead of ἔστ ') at 943, for ἐμὲ (instead of ἐμέ τε) at 991, for ἀπέλυσ' (instead of ἀπέλυσεν, ἀπέλυσαν, or ἀπέκλεισε) at 1155; in *Knights* for αἰμύλοις (for αἰμυλίοις) at 687, and for the supplement ἂν in 989. In other passages he can be seen to have identified a problem, even if he failed to solve it. See, for example, *Acharnians* 997 and *Knights* 1268 and 1273.[34]

Triclinius did not, however, confine himself to correcting failures of correspondence. Many of his emendations are evidently designed to improve metrical regularity and elegance, as he understood them. Thus, at *Wasps* 890 he saw that the reading νεωτέρων preserved in *Σ vet.* was preferable to γενναιοτέρων in the MS text. In addition, however, to adopting it, he supplemented both 890 and its corresponding colon, 873, to make a sort of unsyncopated iambic:

$$873 \quad \langle\dot{\omega}\varsigma\rangle \; \pi\alpha\upsilon\sigma\alpha\mu\acute{\epsilon}\nu\text{οι}\sigma\langle\iota \; \tau\hat{\omega}\nu\rangle \; \pi\lambda\acute{\alpha}\nu\omega\nu$$

$$\langle - \rangle - \cup \cup - \quad \langle \cup - \rangle \cup -$$

$$890 \quad \tau\hat{\omega}\nu \; \langle\nu\hat{\upsilon}\nu\rangle \; \gamma\epsilon \; \langle\sigma\text{ο}\hat{\upsilon}\rangle \; \nu\epsilon\omega\tau\acute{\epsilon}\rho\omega\nu$$

$$-\langle - \rangle\cup\langle - \rangle \quad \cup - \cup -$$

It was left to Reisig to restore 890 without disturbing 873. Again, at *Wasps* 747, the pre-Triclinian MSS have a mis-division, τοῖς ἴσοις. The simple correction, τοῖσι σοῖς, was eventually produced by Invernizi. Triclinius corrected the sense, but also embarked on a sustained but not

---

[33] On earlier Byzantine metricians, see J. Irigoin, *Les Scholies métriques de Pindare*, pp. 55 ff. On Triclinius' work in general, see N. G. Wilson, *Scholars of Byzantium* (London, 1983), 249–56; on the sources of his metrical knowledge and his use and understanding of *Σ vet.*, see Wilson, 252–3 and Smith, *Studies in the Scholia of Aeschylus*, 169 ff.; on his use of pre-existing colometries, see below, on *Wealth* 302 ff. Triclinius occasionally makes explicit claim to an emendation in his scholia (as with the deletion of τινάσσων at *Frogs* 340). Usually, however, his emendations have to be identified by deduction from their presence in MSS judged to be Triclinian, in conjunction with their absence, as far as we know, from pre-Triclinian MSS, and, to some extent, from their character. It must, however, be borne in mind that Triclinius' combination of knowledge and ignorance was vastly different from anything that one would expect from a modern scholar. The question of whether or to what extent he derived readings from sources now lost to us remains open. It is considered by Smith, loc. cit.

[34] For MS readings, see N. G. Wilson, *CQ* 12 (1962), 32–47. For *Ach.*, see also E. Cary, 'The Manuscript Tradition of the *Acharnenses*', *HSCP* 18 (1907), 157–211, and R. T. Elliott, *The Acharnians of Aristophanes* (Oxford, 1914); for *Knights*, D. Mervyn Jones, 'The Manuscripts of Aristophanes *Knights* II', *CQ* 5 (1955), 42; for *Wasps*, J. W. White and E. Cary, 'Collations of the Manuscripts of Aristophanes' *Vespae*', *HSCP* 30 (1919), 1–35.

wholly successful, effort to turn 746–7, with the corresponding cola, 732–3, into unsyncopated iambic trimeters:

732–3   εἰναί τις ὅστις ⟨δὴ⟩ τοιαῦτ' ἐνουθέτει.
  νῦν δὲ νῦν τις ⟨τῶν⟩ θεῶν παρὼν ἐμφανὴς . . .

  $-\,-\,\cup\,-\quad -\langle-\rangle\cup\,-\quad \cup\,-\,\cup\,-$
  $-\,\cup\,-\,-\langle-\rangle\cup\,-\,\cup\,-\quad -\,\cup\,-$

746–7   ἃ σοῦ ⟨παρα⟩κελεύοντος οὐκ ἐπείθετο.
  νῦν ⟨οὖν⟩ ἴσως τοῖς[ι] σοῖς λόγοισ⟨ι⟩ πείθεται

  $\cup\,-\langle\cup\,\cup\rangle\cup\quad -\,-\,\cup\,-\quad \cup\,-\,\cup\,\smile\,||$
  $-\langle-\rangle\cup\,-\quad -[\cup]-\cup\,-\quad \langle\cup\rangle-\cup\,-$

It is worth noting that, although 733 as a whole defeated his ingenuity, he did not leave it entirely alone. Brunck, misled by Triclinius into believing that an iambic trimeter was required there, produced one — a good example of the importance of being able to recognize Triclinius' work.

It seems that Triclinius' indefatigable meliorism led him to emend even perfectly sound texts. His penchant for producing unsyncopated iambic has already been illustrated. His treatment of *Ach.* 1190 ff. provides another striking example.[35] It is also possible to discern in his recension a partiality for something approximating to anapaests. *Frogs* 875–78 is a non-corresponding passage, consisting of a dactylic tetrameter and three hexameters. In the pre-Triclinian colometry, the hexameters are, as usual in lyric, split into two cola at the caesura, so as to produce:

  $-\,\cup\,\cup\,-\,\cup\,\cup\,-\,\cup\,\cup\,-\,-$
  $-\,-\,-\,\cup\,\cup\,-$
  $\cup\,\cup\,-\,\cup\,\cup\,-\,\cup\,\cup\,-\,\smile\,||\,$ H
  $-\,-\,-\,\cup\,\cup\,-$
  $\cup\,\cup\,-\,\cup\,\cup\,-\,\cup\,\cup\,-\,-$
  $-\,-\,-\,-\,\smile\,\cup$
  $\cup\,-\,\cup\,\cup\,-\,\cup\,\cup\,-\,\smile\,||$

By one deletion and one supplement, Triclinius produced a pattern of seductive neatness:

---

[35] See below, ad. loc.

[ὦ] Διὸς ἐννέα παρθένοι ἁγναὶ   ‿‿‑‿‿‑‿‿‑‑
Μοῦσαι, λεπτολόγους   ‑‑‑‿‿‑
συνετὰς φρένας αἳ καθορᾶτε   ‿‿‑‿‿‑‿‿‑‿‖ ᴴ
ἀνδρῶν γνωμοτύπων,   ‑‑‑‿‿‑
ὅταν εἰς ἔριν ὀξυμερίμνοις   ‿‿‑‿‿‑‿‿‑‑
ἔλθωσι στρεβλοῖσί⟨ν⟩   ‑‑‑‑‑‑
⟨τε⟩ παλαίσμασιν ἀντιλογοῦντες . . . ‿‿‑‿‿‑‿‿‑‿‖

Modern scholars have no cause for complacency when contemplating Triclinius. Producing patterns which appear to make sense by repetition is still a common resort when understanding fails us.

Triclinius exercised a powerful and lasting influence over the text of Aristophanes through the first printed edition of nine of the plays, the Aldine of 1498, edited by Marcus Musurus. The relationship between Triclinius' final recension and Musurus' text remains to be fully explored in the light of reliable collations of the Aldine for all the eight plays concerned. However, the material gathered by Wilson[36] shows that it was close. Moreover, Musurus used several MSS, not all of them Triclinian,[37] so that his adoption of Triclinian readings and colometry was a matter of deliberate choice. This contrasts with the practice of the first editor of *Lysistrata* and *Thesmophoriazusae* (Junta, 1516), who reproduced the colometry of R because it was his sole source for the text.[38]

It would seem that Musurus did well to respect Triclinius' metrical expertise, for his own was probably somewhat inferior. A specimen comparison of the text of *Frogs* in L and in the Aldine reveals, firstly, that the colometry is identical, except at 815–16, which are not divided in L. That this is merely a scribal error in L is, however, shown by the metrical scholium. In the lyric of *Frogs* there are 41 textual divergences between Triclinius and the Aldine;[39] 12 of these involve ephelcystic ν:

---

[36] *CQ* 12 (1962), 40 ff. See also, on *Knights*, D. Mervyn Jones, *CQ* 5 (1955), 40 ff.

[37] See L. D. Reynolds and N. G. Wilson, *Scribes and Scholars*, (Oxford, ³1991), 156–8, and K. Zacher, *Bursian* 71 (1892), 30–2.

[38] On the source of the Juntine edition, see W. G. Clark, *Journal of Philology*, 3 (1871), 153 ff., and F. von Velsen, *Über den Codex Urbinas der Lysistrata und der Thesmophoriazusen* (Halle, 1871). I have compared the colometry of the Junta with R.

[39] C. N. Eberline, *Studies in the Manuscript Tradition of the Ranae of Aristophanes* (Meisenheim am Glan, 1980), provides, for that play, a list of Triclinius' corrections to the text in P20 compared with the text of L Vv5 (51–73) and a selective list of readings of L Vv5 compared with other MSS influenced by the second Triclinian edition and the Aldine (124–33). Unfortunately, he has

Triclinius has it, Musurus omits it. This is not as trivial as it might seem. Triclinius sometimes adds *ν* unnecessarily, but never *contra metrum*. Musurus, however, seems not to have realized that ephelcystic *ν* is sometimes needed before a consonant to 'make position'. He omits it *contra metrum* at 421 (κἄστι(ν)), 544 (στρώμασι(ν)), 1484 (πολλοῖσι(ν)) and 1496 (σεμνοῖσι(ν)). Taking all the divergences into account, Musurus' text improves metrically on Triclinius in three passages (242 φθεγξώμεθ' T.: φθεγξόμεσθ' M.; 879 ὀψόμεναι T.: ἐποψόμεναι M.; 1270 Ἀτρέως τε T.: Ἀτρέως M.), but Triclinius has the advantage nine times in addition to the four passages involving ephelcystic *ν*, 711 κονίας T.: τε κονίας M.; 819 σκινδαλαμῶν T.: σκινδαλμῶν M.; 1106 ἀναδέρετον T.: ἀναδαίρετον M.; 1258 μέμψεταί T.: μέμψαιτό M.; 1376 ἐπιθόμην T.: ἐπειθόμην M.). All in all, the comparison tempts one to the conclusion that Musurus had little or no understanding of lyric metres. In the three passages where his reading is metrically preferable to that of Triclinius he has simply adopted a pre-Triclinian text, which he may have done for non-metrical reasons. Moreover, divergences between Musurus and Triclinius are generally minor: Musurus adopted most of Triclinius' more drastic textual interventions and handed them down to later editions.

J. W. White looked forward to the advent of an 'industrious man' to thoroughly investigate the Renaissance editions of Aristophanes. That man has yet to appear. Küster, the first editor to declare his sources with some degree of clarity, based his edition of 1710 on the Aldine above all.[40] Examination, once again, of *Frogs* reveals that in that play he reproduces the colometry of the Aldine exactly, except in two places. At 1100–1 he runs two cola together inadvertently (the Aldine, as often, prints the two cola on one line, marking the junction only with a capital letter). At 458–9 he divides, correctly, two cola which are run together

excluded from the latter list (among other minor divergences) differences in ephelcystic *ν*, dative plurals, and first person plural middle verb-endings, all of which are metrically significant. According to Eberline's reporting, Vv5 differs from L twice in the lyric of *Frogs* (351 and 599). In both passages the Aldine sides with Vv5. This, together with the fact that the Aldine does not reproduce L's error of colometry at 515–16, accords with Wilson's conclusion that L was not the representative of the Triclinian edition used by Musurus.

[40] L. Küster, *Aristophanis Comoediae* (Amsterdam, 1710), Praefatio ad Lectorem: 'Aldinae Editionis fidem in recensendo Textu prae aliis secutus sum, quippe quae haud paucis in locis probam et germanam Lectionem, a qua posteriores Editt. discesserunt retinuit.'

in the Aldine. In the text of the choruses he diverges a mere dozen times from the Aldine. The most significant divergences are: 433, where, by reading τουτονί for τοῦτον, he (wrongly) turns iambic into trochaic; 597, where, in the interests of sense, but *contra metrum*, he restores 'στι (as V) for the Triclinian τις; and 1313, where he restores κατὰ γωνίας, omitted by the Aldine. In fact, Küster preserves all the major Triclinian emendations and almost all the minor modifications, metrical and unmetrical, introduced by Musurus. Yet he did have access to pre-Triclinian texts. For *Frogs* he used collations of a MS 'Vaticano-Urbinas', which has been identified as Vat. Urb. 141 (U).[41] His text of the play was already set up when the collations reached him, but he records in his notes the passages in which he would have preferred the MS text to the one he had printed. In the lyric parts of the play there are only three: 230, where he prefers εἰκότως σύ γ᾽ (UA) to the Triclinian εἰκότως ⟨ἔγω⟩γ᾽; 346, where he rightly prefers ἀποσείονται to ἀποσείεται; 542, where he prefers, again rightly, οὐ γὰρ ἂν to the Triclinian οὐ γὰρ δή, 'quod metro magis convenit'. Outside the lyric passages, it is also interesting to observe that he noted in U a version of the anapaestic tetrameter 1019 with the correct median diaeresis. This, and a few other remarks, show that, to some extent, Küster could and did scan. Nevertheless, in metrical matters he depended almost entirely on the Aldine, and, through the Aldine, on Triclinius.

Good emendations of Aristophanes' lyric were certainly produced during the eighteenth century. Bentley above all (who contributed to Küster's edition) had, as his emendations show, a much clearer perception of metrical patterns and a better understanding of correspondence than Küster. None the less, the colometry of the first printed editions seems to have been passed on unchanged, and Triclinius' work continued to dominate the text of the plays he had edited. Brunck's edition of 1783 marks the beginning of a period in which editors show a striking loss of respect for the printed vulgate and an increasing belief in their own metrical competence.[42]

---

[41] On the identification of Küster's MSS, see J. W. White, 'The Manuscripts of Aristophanes II', *CPh* 1 (1906), 259.

[42] Early-19th-c. editors and commentators, notably Beck, Dindorf, and, somewhat later, Fritzsche, testify to the importance of Brunck's work. He is repeatedly cited on individual passages as the first editor to have modified the vulgate colometry.

BRUNCK TO THE PRESENT

Three factors come together in the late eighteenth century to break the dominance of the printed vulgate based on the Aldine: the discovery of pre-Triclinian MSS; a change of attitude towards MSS; the confidence engendered by better understanding of metrical patterns and of the structure of the plays.

Among the Paris MSS used by Brunck was A (Par. Reg. 2712).[43] Invernizi used R for his edition of 1794. Bekker made his first collation of V in 1812 and made the results available to Hermann and others. He collated both V and R again for his edition of 1829. It was, however, the use made of MSS rather than their mere discovery which caused the revolution. A notable contribution of Brunck to the colometry of printed texts of Aristophanes was the recognition and reconstitution of dactylic hexameters in lyric contexts, which had been laid out in two cola, as far as can be deduced, from Alexandrian times. Thus, he set out *Frogs* 814–29 as it appears in modern editions: in four stanzas, each consisting of two hexameters, pentameter and lecythion. At *Frogs* 875–8 he removed the Triclinian emendations,[44] and set the lines out as a dactylic tetrameter and three hexameters. Yet almost all the information used by Brunck had been available to Küster: the hexameter-division of 814–29 is suggested in an Aldine scholium,[45] and the pre-Triclinian text of 875–8, which Brunck got from A, should have been known to Küster from U. Apart from massive self-confidence, Brunck enjoyed only one advantage over Küster: he had actually seen the hexameter passages laid out, in part at least, in two cola to the line in A.[46]

Ignorance of lyric metre and delight in his newly discovered MS

[43] Brunck was the first editor to use single Roman capitals to designate MSS. Unfortunately, however, he was inconsistent in his usage. For *Lysistrata*, A denotes Par. Reg. 2715 (=White B), while for *Frogs*, A denotes Par. Reg. 2712 (=White A). For other plays he does not say what the letters represent. On Brunck's MSS, see J. W. White, 'The Manuscripts of Aristophanes II', *CPh* 1 (1906), 260, and Th. Gelzer, 'Eine Aristophaneshandschrift und ihre Besitzer', Κωμῳδοτραγήματα: *Studia . . . W. J. W. Koster in honorem* (Amsterdam, 1967), 44–5.

[44] See above, pp. 109–10.

[45] Recognizing hexameters at *Frogs* 814–29 was within the capacity even of the apprentice metrician who composed scholia to P8, see F. Jorsal, M. Kiil Jørgensen, and O. Smith, 'A Byzantine Metrical Commentary on Aristophanes' *Frogs*,' *C & M* 31 (1975), 332.

[46] See above, pp. 102 and 109. Küster does not seem to have examined U himself. Collations were supplied to him by the librarian of the Vatican library.

caused Invernizi simply to jettison the Aldine colometry and adopt that of R, right or wrong. Between 1809 and 1826, Invernizi's text was provided with a commentary in eleven volumes by C. D. Beck and Dindorf. Beck was Hermann's colleague at Leipzig, and Dindorf was the pupil of both. Moreover, Bothe's observations on the text of Aristophanes (*Ludovici Hotibii Rigensis Lectiones Aristophaneae*) had appeared in 1808. The Beck–Dindorf commentary makes curious reading: a considerable proportion of it is taken up with rescuing good readings rejected by their editor.[47] None the less, Invernizi's text marks an important reversal of attitude in editing: it exemplifies, even more clearly than Brunck's edition, the whole-hearted acceptance of a MS not merely as an auxiliary to correcting the vulgate, but as a superior source for the text.

However, the use of MSS needed to be complemented by an understanding of metrical patterns. Here, Hermann was the pioneer, and his work laid the foundations of modern metrical studies. His *Elementa Doctrinae Metricae* of 1816 remained a standard textbook for more than half a century, but the quality of his thought and method are, perhaps, better revealed by his earlier work, *De Metris Poetarum Graecorum et Romanorum Libri III* (Leipzig, 1796). In discussing passages from Aristophanes there, he was able to take advantage of the testimony of R. Anyone wishing to observe the difference between Hermann's use of that testimony and Invernizi's could well compare the latter's treatment of *Frogs* 324–53 in his edition with Hermann's in *De Metris*, 352–3 (cf. *Elementa*, 501–2).

Although Hermann was supreme in his logical analysis of metrical patterns, other scholars of the period produced important results by fine

---

[47] e.g. at *Frogs* 252 the Aldine (in common with VAML) has the metrically necessary πεισόμεσθα. Invernizi, however, printed πεισόμεθα from R. Beck remarks: 'πεισόμεσθα in Küst., Bergl. etc. recte est, neque quod metro adversatur, debebatur πεισόμεθα ab Inv. recipi.' At 391–5 in the same play, the Aldine has the impeccable sequence of four iambic dimeters with catalectic dimeter as clausula, which is found in all modern editions. Invernizi chose, however, to print R's highly disordered version:

> καὶ πολλὰ μὲν γέλοιά μ' εἰπεῖν
> πολλὰ δὲ καὶ σπουδαῖα,
> καὶ τῆς σῆς ἑορτῆς ἀξίως
> παίσαντα καὶ σκώψαντα
> νικήσαντα ταινιοῦσθαι

Beck notes: 'restituenda haec sunt, ut ante Inv.'

and precise observation of correspondence and of the particularities of the individual passage. For proof of this one need only look at Porson's treatment of *Frogs* 814–29 and *Wasps* 526–48 (see below, ad. loc.).

For more than a century after the publication of Brunck's edition, scholarly effort was steadily applied to producing greater metrical regularity and strictness of correspondence. The Teubner editions of individual plays produced between 1881 and 1909 by Adolf von Velsen and Konrad Zacher show the extreme development of this approach. They combine meticulous reporting of the earlier MSS, almost total neglect of the *recentiores* and the Aldine, and bold and extensive emendation. There is a certain contradiction between the scrupulosity with which von Velsen and Zacher report MS readings and the lack of respect for the testimony of MSS apparent in their treatment of the text.

The publication in 1912 of J. W. White's *The Verse of Greek Comedy* marks a reaction towards trust in the MS tradition and metrical permissiveness. White was prepared to accept that corresponding periods in the same metre might differ in length, as, for example, at *Ach.* 216=231, where, in the received text, eight cretics in the strophe correspond with seven in the antistrophe, or *Ach.* 937–9=948–51, where the antistrophe has been transmitted as longer by one iambic metron than the strophe.[48] However, a much more widely usable escape-route from the demand for strict correspondence was provided by the theory of Greek rhythm developed in the mid-nineteenth century by Rossbach and Westphal and J. H. H. Schmidt,[49] which was designed to assimilate classical Greek song to the rhythmical regularity of nineteenth-century European music. White was an early convert to this theory, and, indeed, sought to introduce it to English-speaking students by his translation (published in 1878) of Schmidt's *Leitfaden in der Rhythmik und Metrik der klassischen Sprachen* (Leipzig, 1869).[50]

---

[48] White, § 51. Other failures of correspondence of this kind that White accepts are: *Clouds* 1309–10=1315–20 (§ 581); *Wasps* 297=309 (§ 426), 544–5=646–7 (§ 566), 1275–83=1284–91 (§ 457); *Peace* 464–6=491–2 (§ 302); *Lys.* 330–4=344–9 (§ 563); *Frogs* 536–7=592–3 (§ 217), 896–7=993–4 (§ 214).

[49] For a very brief, but clear, summary of the theory (by a convert), see the introductory section of the 'Metrical Analysis' in Jebb's edition of *Oedipus Tyrannus* (³1893, pp. lxiii–lxvii). L.-E. Rossi traces the history of the theory and submits it to critical examination in *Metrica e critica stilistica* (Rome, 1963).

[50] *An Introduction to the Rhythmic and Metric of the Classical Languages* (Boston, 1878).

Interpreting a sequence like:

$$- \cup \cup \cup \quad - \cup - \cup \quad - \cup \cup \cup \quad - \cup - \cup \quad - \cup - - \quad - \cup -$$

in regular 'bars', involved, of course, assuming that the different types of metron must, in some way, have been equalized in delivery. For White, that assumption rendered easy the acceptance of syncopated metra in correspondence with full metra. Indeed he regarded the presence of such correspondences in the received text as confirmation of the theory (§§ 223 ff.). Furthermore, White accepted so-called 'logaoedic' metra in iambic and trochaic on the assumption that in a hypothetical pre-history of Greek metre $\cup - \cup -$, $- - - -$, $\cup \cup - \cup \cup -$, $- - \cup -$, $\cup - - -$, $\cup \cup - \cup -$, etc. were interchangeable (ch. VII, pp. 162 ff.). It might be thought that the degree of latitude allowed by such theories would have been enough to dispose of practically all the metrical problems posed by the text of Aristophanes. White was, however, conservative in the application of his principles. Thus, although according to the logaoedic theory $- \cup \cup - \cup \cup \cup - \cup -$ can be equivalent to $\cup \cup$ $\cup \cup \cup \cup - \cup -$, White does not accept the two in correspondence at *Lys.* 262–3 = 277–8, on the grounds that that is contrary to Aristophanes' practice. He obelizes 277–8 (§ 94). In some other passages he rejects explanations based on rhythmical equivalence in favour of the idea that the poet sometimes introduced deliberate variation of rhythm between strophe and antistrophe for expressive purposes. Thus, at *Birds* 333–5 = 349–51, he would accept neither the 'cyclic paeons' of Zieliński ($\cup \cup - = \cup \cup \cup -$, the long of the paeon having a time-value less than a 'full' long) nor the trochaic equivalences of Schroeder ($- \cup \cup \cup$ and $\cup \cup \cup \cup = - \cup - \cup$).[51] Instead, he saw an intentional change of rhythm: 'the chorus sings in dochmiac rhythm in the strophe, in paeonic in the antistrophe. Each rhythm is singularly appropriate to the sentiment expressed' (§ 463).

A. M. Dale accepts all the irregularities of correspondence that White accepts, and some that he does not.[52] But the rhythmical theories that for

---

[51] T. Zieliński, *Die Gliederung der altattischen Komoedie* (Leipzig, 1885), 331, Schroeder, *AC* 32 and 99.

[52] *The Lyric Metres of Greek Drama*, (Cambridge, ²1968). On periods of unequal length, see 207, with n. 1. Here, Dale includes in her list *Ecc.* 487, where White accepts emendation (§ 85), and *Peace* 585, which he regards as astrophic (§ 233). In addition, Dale treats irregularities of responsion in the following passages: 56–7: *Birds* 333–5 = 349–51, *Wasps* 339 = 370 (White emends,

White served to justify many of them could not be accepted by a scholar with Dale's justified hatred of self-supporting theoretical structures. Instead, she resorted to the idea that Aristophanes from time to time abandoned normal quantitative correspondence for syllable-counting. That popular influence should lead to the occasional abandonment of the quantitative principle is an uncomfortable conclusion for a metrician who, like Dale, firmly believed quantitative versification to be natural to Greek. She sometimes reinforces her defence of irregularities by references to dancing and to methods of delivery peculiar to comedy, which are, it must be said, highly speculative,[53] and insists that departures from the quantitative principle are merely occasional licences. It is a tribute to Dale's scholarly honesty and rigour that some very bold speculations of hers have come to be treated as if they represented well-tried metrical orthodoxy. None the less, the admission of syllable-counting is a drastic and dangerous solution. If it ever really was an audibly acceptable alternative to quantitative response, why is it so rare? For Dale, the determining factor was the recurrence in comedy of 'metrical irregularities traceably similar in type, where the text is otherwise irreproachable'.[54] But before apparent similarities can be aggregated, the textual credentials of the individual passages must survive the most careful scrutiny.[55]

A common defence of metrically suspect passages is that the text makes perfect sense and is unexceptionable linguistically. Take, for example, C. M. Bowra on the failures of correspondence in *Ecclesiazusae* 952–75:[56] '. . . the lines otherwise are not blatantly corrupt. They betray

§ 238); 65: *Thesm.* 439=525 (White regards as astrophic, § 414); 78: *Lys.* 262–3=277–8 (rejected as corrupt by White, § 94); 89: *Wasps* 1062 ff.=1093 ff.; 91: *Knights* 332=406, *Thesm.* 434 ff.=520 ff. (White: astrophic, § 414); 125: *Frogs* 323–36=340–53, with n. 1: *Wasps* 276=284; 189: *Wasps* 273–80=281–9; 190: *Birds* 333–4=349–50 (cf. 56).

[53] On syllable-counting, see LM^2 56–7, 65, 78–9, 89, 112, 190; on the idea that Euripides may occasionally have abandoned quantity and substituted 'diaeresis, syllable-grouping', see 64; on dancing and rhythm, 90–1; on the delivery of comic lyric, 207.

[54] LM^2 91.

[55] M. Platnauer offers a survey of correspondence, regular and irregular, in 'Antistrophic Variation in Aristophanes', *Greek Poetry and Life: Essays presented to Gilbert Murray* (Oxford, 1936), 241–56, but his discussions of individual passages are too perfunctory to be conclusive. More recently, two monographs have been devoted to the subject: E. Domingo, *La Responsión estrófica en Aristophanes*, (Salamanca, 1975), and C. Romano, *Responsioni libere nei canti di Aristofane*, (Rome, 1992).

[56] 'A Love-duet', *AJP* 79 (1958), 382 = *On Greek Margins* (1970), 155.

no defects of sense or syntax which would justify us in emending them, and this should make us wary of emendation for purely metrical reasons.' For Dale too, 'there is no reason other than metrical for emending the strophe' can be equivalent to 'there is no reason'.[57] Statements of this kind all too easily suggest that metre is somehow less important than language. What they actually mean (or should mean) is that we are aware that we know less about metre and about what is metrically acceptable than we do about language. Consequently, if a passage makes sense as it stands, it is just as well to leave it alone. That does not, however, mean that it can safely be treated as sound. Corrupters of verse texts do not necessarily make nonsense; sometimes they just make prose. This is particularly likely to happen with a poet like Aristophanes, who, for the most part, uses simple language. This is corruption by paraphrase. The process is well illustrated by a version of two famous lines from Wordsworth which appeared a few years ago in a letter to the *Times*:

> There are two voices; one is of the sea,
> The other of the mountains; each a mighty voice.[58]

The writer was, no doubt, quoting from memory, but the mistakes he makes can easily be paralleled from classical manuscripts: change from poetic inversion to prose order and substitution of prosaic 'the other' for the more literary 'one'. The meaning remains unchanged; the rhythm is not self-evidently unacceptable, and if the lines were to be transmitted to posterity in that form, I cannot see that they could ever be restored by conjecture. No critic following the principles we now observe in dealing with ancient texts would think of trying to emend. Another revealing example is the first line of Euripides' *Ion*, which in its received form breaks Porson's Law. Yet it has needed a piece of external testimony, Philodemus' quotation of the line in his *De Pietate* (*P. Herc.* 1088 II) to convince editors that the MS text is not what Euripides wrote.[59]

---

[57] *LM*[2] 189, à propos of *PV* 535=543.

[58]   Two voices are there; one is of the sea,
              One of the mountains; each a mighty voice . . .

'Thought of a Briton on the Subjugation of Switzerland'. The garbled version may be compared with R's version of *Frogs* 391–5, quoted in n. 47 above.

[59] D. L. Page drew attention to the fragment of Philodemus ('Various Conjectures', *PCPS* 187 (1961), 69), but his solution has been faulted by W. Luppe ('Atlas-Zitate im 1. Buch Philodems "De Pietate"', *CronErc* 13 (1983), 47–9).

The tendency to cherish metrical anomalies may be, in part, a mis-application of the principle that the *lectio difficilior* is to be preferred. This principle, an admission of defeat at the best of times, is not trans-ferable to metre, since it depends on the assumption that copyists tend, by accident or design, to make texts easier. To simplify requires some degree of understanding, and, while many copyists at most periods will have had some understanding of the Greek language, very few indeed at any time can have had any notion of lyric metres. The likelihood, then, is that the language will have been made simpler and more prosaic at the expense of the metre.[60]

These are not arguments for wholesale emendation, but for scepti-cism and restraint, and against the intellectual slither from 'the passage had better not be emended' to 'the passage is sound and fit to be used as evidence'. In dealing with problematic passages I have tried to present the evidence as fairly as possible. The reader may make his or her own judgement.[61]

---

[60] For a (very rare) example of metrical simplification going back, apparently, to antiquity, see *Peace* 939 = 1023.

[61] On metre and textual criticism, see P. Maas, 'Die neuen Responsionsfreiheiten bei Bakchylides und Pindar', *Jahresber. des Phil. Vereins zu Berlin*, 39 (1913), 289–320, § 2, and A. E. Housman, 'Prosody and Method', *CQ* (1927), 1–12 (= *The Classical Papers of A. E. Housman* III, ed. J. Diggle and F. R. D. Goodyear (Cambridge 1972), 1114–26). Housman's paper, in particular, should be studied by anyone disposed to defend metrical anomalies by aggregating examples.

II THE PLAYS

Acharnians

204–17 = 218–33	*Trochaic* tetrameters, then *cretics*.
263–79	Dicaeopolis' solo: *Iambic*, without syncopation.
280–3	*Trochees*, modulating into *cretics*.
284–301 = 335–46	Dicaeopolis and chorus: Dicaeopolis uses *trochaic* tetrameters; the chorus have one verse in *dactyls* (?), otherwise they use *cretics*.
358–65 = 385–92	*Dochmiacs*, then two *iambic* trimeters.
490–5	*Dochmiacs*, with two *iambic* trimeters.
566–71	*Dochmiacs*, with a little *iambic*.
665–75 = 692–702	*Cretics*.
836–41 = 842–7 (=848–53 = 854–9)	*Iambic*. Catalectic tetrameters and dimeters, with *reiȥianum* as clausula.
929–39 = 940–51	Dicaeopolis and chorus: *Iambic*.
971–87 = 988–99	*Cretics*, with *trochaic* tetrameter as clausula.
1008–17 = 1037–46	Dicaeopolis and chorus: *Iambic*.
1150–61 = 1162–73	*Iambo-choriambic*, *iambic*, with resolution and syncopation.
1190–1234	Dicaeopolis and Lamachus: *Iambic*, with resolution and syncopation, perhaps *dochmiac*. Then Dicaeopolis and chorus using *iambic* tetrameters.

Cretics are much used in the early plays of Aristophanes, but in none do they predominate as in *Acharnians*. It is at least highly plausible that the poet felt the rhythm to be not only suitable to comic dance but particularly suitable to the fierce and virile old men of this chorus. Most strikingly, pure, or almost pure, cretics are used in the parabasis-song (665 ff. = 692 ff.), in which the Acharnian Muse is characterized as φλεγυρὰ, πυρὸς ἔχουσα μένος, | ἔντονος, and in 971 ff. = 988 ff., where the chorus express in elaborate and sustained metaphor their hatred of war and passionate desire for peace. After this song, cretics disappear from the play, and, coincidentally, the chorus loses much of its significance as a character.

Very simple iambic, without syncopation (except in clausular bacchiac), is used in Dicaeopolis' hymn to Phales and in the lampoon-song, 836 ff. = 842 ff. = 848 ff. = 854 ff., both compositions which are presumably based on popular forms. In contrast, paratragic iambic appears in the elaborate lampoon-song, 1150 ff. = 1162 ff., and in the duet between Dicaeopolis and Lamachus at the end of the play (1190 ff.).

Dochmiacs are, naturally, used in moments of extreme passion and excitement 358 ff. = 385 ff., 490 ff., 566 ff.

The predominance of cretic and the absence of aeolo-choriambic (complete, except for the clausular reizianum at 841 = 847 = 853 = 859) combine to differentiate the rhythmic character of this play sharply from anything to be found in surviving tragedy of the period.

The play is constructed with a subtle symmetry, in paired scenes which contrast wealth with poverty, luxury with hardship (the Persian embassy and the Thracians; the Megarian and the Boeotian; Dercetes and the bridal party; finally, Dicaeopolis and Lamachus). Dicaeopolis exhibits the contrast by his own transmutation from refugee farmer and pseudo-Telephus to winner of the ἀσκός. The metrical structure of the play after the parabasis also exhibits a symmetry, subtly varied so as to be unobvious:

Parabasis.

Episode of the Megarian (poverty).

Simple iambic lampoon-song.

Episode of the Boeotian (wealth).

Simple iambic duet.

Short episode: departure of the Boeotian. Lamachus' servant.

Elaborate song in cretics, with some parabatic features.

Short episode: the herald.

Simple iambic duet, of which the strophe and antistrophe frame the episode of Dercetes (poverty).

Episodes of the bridal party (wealth) and of the burlesque of Lamachus' preparations (wealth and poverty, luxury and hardship).

Elaborate lampoon-song.

Episode of the paratragic messenger.

Paratragic duet of Dicaeopolis and Lamachus (luxury and hardship).

Exodos.

204–17 = 218–33

204–8   tro tetram cat IV

‒ ∪ ‒   ‒ ∪ ‒

ἐκπέφευγ᾽, οἴχεται

‒ ∪ ‒   ‒ ∪ ‒   ‒ ∪ ‒   ‒ ∪ ‿ ‖ₕ

210–11   φροῦδος. οἴμοι τάλας τῶν ἐτῶν τῶν ἐμῶν.

‒ ∪ ⏜   ‒ ∪ ⏜   ‒ ∪ ⏜   ‒ ∪ ‒

οὐκ ἂν ἐπ᾽ ἐμῆς γε νεότητος, ὅτ᾽ ἐγὼ φέρων

‒ ∪ ‒| ‒ ∪ ‿ ‖

ἀνθράκων φορτίον

‒ ∪ ‒   ‒|∪ ‒   ‒ ∪ ‒   ‒ ∪|‒   ‒ ∪ ‒

215   ἠκολούθουν Φαΰλλῳ τρέχων, ὧδε φαύλως ἂν ὁ

‒ ∪ ⌣| ‒ ∪ ⏜   ‒ ∪ ⏜   ‒ ∪ ⏜

σπονδοφόρος οὗτος ὑπ᾽ ἐμοῦ τότε διωκόμενος

‒ ∪ ⏜   ‒ ∪|⏜   ‒ ∪ ⌣   ‒ ∪ ‿ ‖‖‖

ἐξέφυγεν οὐδ᾽ ἂν ἐλαφρῶς ἂν ἀπεπλίξατο.

Like other aristophanic choruses who enter at speed (*Knights* 247 ff., *Peace* 301 ff.), the old Acharnians use trochees (Cf. Σ *vet.* 204 a (i)). Their change from recitative to song marks the moment of frustration and exasperation when they conclude that, because of their old age, their quarry has outrun them. The corresponding heightening of emotion in the antistrophe comes with the address to the gods. The stanza is in pure cretic, articulated by word-end and verse-end into 2 + 4, 4 + 2, 6 + 7. Sequences of resolved cretics come together and correspondence of resolution is close, but not perfect.

In the trochaic tetrameters at 222, ὄντας seems to have been lost by haplography and replaced by Triclinius.

At 231, the text of the MSS is shorter by one cretic than the antistrophe. Editors who accept this as an example of Aristophanic 'free

218–23 tro tetram cat IV

2 cr
ὅστις, ὦ Ζεῦ πάτερ

4 cr
225 καὶ θεοί, τοῖσιν ἐχθροῖσιν ἐσπείσατο,

4cr
οἷσι παρ' ἐμοῦ πόλεμος ἐχθοδοπὸς αὔξεται

2 cr
τῶν ἐμῶν χωρίων·

13 cr
230 κοὐκ ἀνήσω πρὶν ἂν σχοῖνος αὐτοῖσιν ἀντεμπαγῶ

⟨καὶ σκόλοψ⟩ ὀξύς, ὀδυνηρός, ἐπίκωπος, ἵνα

μήποτε πατῶσιν ἔτι τὰς ἐμὰς ἀμπέλους.

responsion' fail to notice that the hiatus at ἀντεμπαγῶ ‖ ὀξύς requires corresponding verse-end between article and substantive in the strophe: ὁ ‖ σπονδοφόρος, which is unparalleled and improbable in the last degree. Hermann's supplement, καὶ σκόλοψ, derived from the *Suda* (s. σκόλοψ. σκόλοψ αὐτοῖς καὶ σχοῖνος ἀντεμπάγω) must be right. It not only solves the problem of verse-end but provides a masculine substantive with which ὀξύς can agree (for σχοῖνος f. = reed, cf. Aristophanes, *PCG* 36). Blaydes's ἀνιαρός after ὀδυνηρός is unacceptable because it fails to solve the problem of verse-end in the strophe, but is interesting technically in that it shows how the loss of a word not of cretic form could produce the appearance of a missing cretic:

ὀξύς, ὀδυνηρός, ⟨ἀνιαρός⟩, ἐπίκωπος, ἵνα
$- \cup \widehat{\cup\cup} \quad - \cup \langle \widehat{\cup\cup} \quad - \cup \rangle \widehat{\cup\cup} \quad - \cup \widehat{\cup\cup}$

263–79

∪ – ∪ –　　∪ – ∪ –

Δ. Φαλῆς, ἑταῖρε Βακχ[ε]ίου,

– – ∪ –　∪ ⌢ ∪ –　∪ – ∪ –　∪ – ⌣ ‖ ʜ

264–5　ξύγκωμε, νυκτοπεριπλάνητε, μοιχέ, παιδεραστά,

– – ∪ –　∪ – ∪ –　– – ∪ –　– – ∪ –

ἕκτῳ σ' ἔτει προσεῖπον εἰς τὸν δῆμον ἐλθὼν ἄσμενος,

– – ∪ –　∪ ⌢ ∪ –　– – ∪ –　∪ – ∪ –

σπονδὰς ποιησάμενος ἐμαυτῷ, πραγμάτων τε καὶ μαχῶν

– – ∪ –　∪ – ∪ –

270　καὶ Λαμάχων ἀπαλλαγείς.

– – ∪ –　– – ∪ | –　∪ – ∪ –

πολλῷ γάρ ἐσθ' ἥδιον, ὦ Φαλῆς Φαλῆς,

– – ∪ –　– | – ∪ –　– – ∪ –

κλέπτουσαν εὑρόνθ' ὡρικὴν ὑληφόρον,

– – ∪ –　– | – ∪ –　– – ∪ –

τὴν Στρυμοδώρου Θρᾷτταν ἐκ τοῦ φελλέως,

∪ – ∪ –　– – ∪ ⌢　∪ – ∪ ⌢　∪ – ∪ –

275　μέσην λαβόντ' ἄραντα καταβαλόντα καταγιγαρτίσαι,

∪ – ∪ –

[ὦ] Φαλῆς, Φαλῆς.

∪ – ∪ –　– | – ∪ –　– – ∪ –

ἐὰν μεθ' ἡμῶν ξυμπίῃς, ἐκ κραιπάλης

∪ – ∪ –　– – | ∪ –　– – ∪ ⌣ ‖

ἔωθεν εἰρήνης ῥοφήσει[ς] τρύβλιον·

– – ∪ –　– – ∪ –　∪ – ∪ – ‖|

ἡ δ' ἀσπὶς ἐν τῷ φεψάλῳ κρεμήσεται.

Dicaeopolis' hymn to Phales is in simple iambic, unsyncopated except for the bacchiac at verse-end in 265, and, except for that and the *brevis in longo* at 278, articulated, as far as we can see, only by

ia dim

ia tetram cat

ia tetram

ia tetram

ia dim

ia trim

ia trim

ia trim

ia tetram

ia monom

ia trim

ia trim

ia trim

coincidence between word-end and metron-end. One guesses that the song is based on a traditional form, but there is no surviving parallel. Other simple iambic songs in Aristophanes which seem to be of traditional type are in short stanzas (see, in particular, *Frogs* 416–39). One might speculate that this is a solo, not a choral, hymn-form, but the fact that Dicaeopolis sings it as a solo does not prove that. In his miniature festival, he may be representing a choir, just as his daughter represents a whole troup of basket-carriers and his wife an ὄχλος.

The iambic trimeters in the song all have caesura, as in spoken iambic, except for the last (279), which is isolated both syntactically and metrically.

280–3

– ∪ – ∪ – ∪ – –

280 οὗτος αὐτός ἐστιν, οὗτος·

– ∪ – ∪ – ∪ – ∪

βάλλε, βάλλε, βάλλε, βάλλε,

– ∪ – ∪ – ∪ ◡͡◡

παῖε, παῖε τὸν μιαρόν·

– ∪ – – ∪ – |||

οὐ βαλεῖς; οὐ βαλεῖς;

The chorus break in with contrasting trochaic on Dicaeopolis' iambic hymn. The change of rhythm is calculated to startle. They then modulate into cretics through a lecythion.

Bergk sought to produce a neater division between trochees and cretics by reading παῖε πᾶς for παῖε παῖε in 282. Exhortations in that form are, indeed, found in Aristophanes, e.g. *Peace* 458 ὑπότεινε δὴ

284–301 = 335–46

– ∪ – ◡ –|∪ – ∪ – ∪ – ◡ – ∪ ‿ ‖ₕ

Δ. Ἡράκλεις, τουτὶ τί ἐστι; τὴν χύτραν συντρίψετε;

∪ ∪ – ∪ ∪ – ∪ ∪|– ∪ ∪ – ∪ ∪ – ‖ₕ

285 Χ. σὲ μὲν οὖν καταλεύσομεν, ὦ μιαρὰ κεφαλή.

– ∪ – ◡ – ∪ – – – ∪ –|◡ – ∪ ‿ ‖ₕ

Δ. ἀντὶ ποίας αἰτίας, ὦχαρνέων γεραίτατοι;

At 263, Βακχίου for Βακχείου is Scaliger's correction. At 276, Elmsley deleted ὦ. At 278, the change of the active form ῥοφήσεις to the middle form ῥοφήσει is also Elmsley's. The MSS offer active future forms of the second person at *Knights* 360 and *Peace* 716, but the middle form ῥοφήσομαι is guaranteed by metre at *Wasps* 814. Fraenkel's hesitation (*Beobachtungen*, 27 n. 1) 'to change three passages to bring them into line with one passage' neglects the fact that only the one passage is guaranteed to be right. On active and middle forms, see further Elliott, ad loc.

      tro dim

      tro dim

      tro cr

      cr dim

πᾶς, cf. *Peace* 512, *Frogs* 372. Bergk was, however, influenced by noting the quadruple βάλλε at *Rhesus* 675, with παῖε πᾶς at 685. If *Rhesus* is indeed an early work of Euripides (so Ritchie, *The Authenticity of the Rhesus of Euripides* (Cambridge, 1964)) there might be parody here. But the uncertainties are far too great to warrant interference with the text. For παῖε παῖε, cf. *Knights* 247, *Wasps* 456, *Peace* 1119.

      tro tetram cat
335 *Δ.* ὡς ἀποκτενῶ· κέκραχθ᾽· ἐγὼ γὰρ οὐκ ἀκούσομαι.

      ∧ 5 da cat?
  X. ἀπολεῖς ἄρ᾽ ὁμήλικα τόνδε φιλανθρακέα;

      tro tetram cat
  Δ. οὐδ᾽ ἐμοῦ λέγοντος ὑμεῖς ἀρτίως ἠκούσατε.

‒∪‒　‒∪‒　‒∪‒　‒∪⌣

Χ. τοῦτ' ἐρωτᾷς; ἀναίσχυντος εἶ καὶ βδελυρός,

‒∪⌣|　‒∪⌣　‒∪‒　‒∪⌣

290　　ὦ προδότα τῆς πατρίδος, ὅστις ἡμῶν μόνος

‒∪⌣　‒∪⌣　‒∪⌣　‒∪⌣‖

σπεισάμενος εἶτα δύνασαι πρὸς ἔμ' ἀποβλέπειν.

‒∪‒‒　‒∪‒⌥　‒∪‒∪　‒∪⌣‖ʜ

Δ. ἀντὶ δ' ὧν ἐσπεισάμην οὐκ ἰστέ'; ἀλλ' ἀκούσατε.

‒∪‒　‒∪⌣　‒∪⌣　‒∪‒|　‒∪⌣‖

295　Χ. σοῦ γ' ἀκούσωμεν; ἀπολεῖ· κατά σε χώσομεν τοῖς λίθοις.

‒∪‒⌣　‒∪‒⌥　‒∪‒‒　‒∪‒‖ʜ

Δ. μηδαμῶς πρὶν ἄν γ' ἀκούσητ'· ἀλλ' ἀνάσχεσθ', ὦγαθοί,

‒∪‒　‒∪‒　‒∪⌣　‒∪⌣

Χ. οὐκ ἀνασχήσομαι· μηδὲ λέγε μοι σὺ λόγον·

‒∪‒　‒∪⌣　‒∪⌣　‒∪⌣

300　　ὡς μεμίσηκά σε Κλέωνος ἔτι μᾶλλον ὃν †ἐγὼ

‒∪⌣　‒∪⌣　‒∪‒　‒∪‒|‖‖

κατατεμῶ τοῖσι(ν) ἱππεῦσί(ν) ποτ' ἐς καττύματα†

In this duet, Dicaeopolis, markedly the more reasonable and less excited party, uses recitative-type trochaic tetrameters, while the chorus use lyric, almost exclusively cretic. Their explosive first utterance is a double-short-single-long sequence which cannot be classified with certainty.

The song contains two major textual problems:

(1) The MS text at 300–1 looks like a deliberate attempt to produce iambic, but may be no more than accidental paraphrase (Introduction, p. 118). Σ *vet.* (300 a) already remarks that ποτὲ is redundant διὰ τὴν μετροποιΐαν (adding another, pleasantly zany, reason). ἐς (deleted by Elmsley) is possible linguistically, but not necessary (cf. *Knights* 768 κατατμηθείην λέπαδνα). Bothe's ejection of ἐγὼ would then give:

4 cr

X. ἀλλὰ νυν⟨ὶ⟩ λέγ', εἴ σοι δοκεῖ, †τόν τε Λακε-

+4 cr

δαιμόνιον αὐτὸν ὅ τι τῷ τρόπῳ σου 'στὶ φιλόν†

4 cr

340   ὡς τόδε τὸ λαρκίδιον οὐ προδώσω ποτέ.

tro tetram cat

Δ. τοὺς λίθους νῦν μοι χαμᾶζε πρῶτον ἐξεράσατε.

5 cr

X. οὑτοί σοι χαμαί, καὶ σὺ κατάθου πάλιν τὸ ξίφος.

tro tetram cat

Δ. ἀλλ' ὅπως μὴ 'ν τοῖς τρίβωσιν ἐγκάθηνταί που λίθοι.

4 cr

X. ἐκσέσεισται χαμᾶζ'. οὐχ ὁρᾷς σειόμενον;

4 cr

345   ἀλλὰ μή μοι πρόφασιν ἀλλὰ κατάθου τὸ βέλος.

4 cr

ὡς ὅδε γε σειστὸς ἅμα τῇ στροφῇ γίγνεται.

$$- \cup -$$
$$\widetilde{} \cup - \quad - \cup - \quad - \cup - \quad - \cup \widetilde{} \parallel$$

. . . μᾶλλον ὂν
κατατέμω τοῖσιν ἱππεῦσι καττύματα

Correspondence of resolution is less close in this song than in 204 ff. = 218 ff., 665 ff. = 692 ff., 971 ff. = 988 ff., but a cretic of the form $\widetilde{} \cup -$ is unparalleled in Aristophanes' early plays. The one exception is in a fragment from Γεωργοί, *PCG* 113. However, the fragment is quoted by Hephaestion (*Cons.* 41. 7) with a comment which, though mutilated, shows that he regarded it as exceptional. Moreover, we have no context or corresponding passage to prove the soundness of the text Hephaestion was quoting. The alternative is, with Meineke, to retain

ἐγώ (which has some force here: 'I will personally cut him up . . .') and
to read the uncompounded τεμῶ (Elmsley). For τέμνειν meaning 'to
cut up, chop up' see Sotades, *PCG* 1. 32. The fact that κατατέμνειν is
the ordinary word could well have led to its introduction.

(2) In the antistrophe, 338–9 presents a problem to which there is no
wholly satisfactory solution. Bentley's νυνὶ for νῦν restores the metre (as
does B's ἀλλὰ γὰρ νῦν, 'Yes, but . . .', see Denniston, *Particles* 104 (6)
(ii)). Otherwise, the text of the MSS other than R (which I print) scans
perfectly. The difficulty is the meaning. R differs from the rest at 338 by
adding τι after εἴ, omitting τε after τὸν and offering φίλος for φίλον.
Albert Mueller, adopting φίλος from R, proposed minimal emendation:
λέγ' . . . ὅτι τῳ τρόπῳ σούστι φίλος ('Say that he is dear to you in
some way'. Cf. Σ *vet.* 339). Rennie's emendation is less easy palaeographically, but more pointed in sense: λέγ' . . . αὐτόθεν ὅτῳ τρόπῳ
σούστι φίλος ('Tell us here and now how the Spartan is your friend').
Both solutions require a second λέγε to be understood with a different

$$358–65 = 385–92$$

$$\cup--\cup-| \quad \cup--\cup- \quad \cup--\cup-$$

τί οὖν οὐ λέγεις, ἐπίξηνον ἐξενεγκὼν θύραζ',

$$\cup\widetilde{}-\cup\widetilde{}| \quad \cup\widetilde{}-\cup-$$

360   ὅ τι ποτ', ὦ σχέτλιε, τὸ μέγα τοῦτ' ἔχεις;

$$\cup\widetilde{}\widetilde{}\cup\widetilde{} \quad \cup\widetilde{}-\cup-\parallel^{H}$$

πάνυ γὰρ ἐμέ γε πόθος ὅ τι φρονεῖς ἔχει.

364–5   trim II

$$490–5$$

$$\cup--\cup- \quad -\langle-\rangle-\cup-$$

490   τί δράσεις; τί φήσεις; ⟨εὖ⟩ ἴσθι νῦν

$$\cup--\cup- \quad \cup--\cup-$$

ἀναίσχυντος ὢν σιδηροῦς τ' ἀνήρ,

492–3   trim II

$$---\cup- \quad \cup--\cup-$$

ἀνὴρ οὐ τρέμει τὸ πρᾶγμ'. εἶα νῦν,

meaning from the first: 'Speak . . . and (say) . . .'. As parallels for
the double use of the verb with τε, Rennie adduces Pindar, *Pyth.* 1. 40
τιθέμεν . . . τε . . . 'to put . . . and (to make) . . .', and
IT 279–80: ἔδοξε . . . τε . . . 'he seemed . . . and (it seemed good) . . .'.
Accepting Reisig's γε for τε, with φίλον, D. L. Page (*WS* 69 (1956),
120–1) proposed: λέγ' . . . τόν γε Λ. αὐτὸν ὅ τι χὠ τρόπῳ σούστι
φίλον ('Say about the Lacedaemonian himself whatever you like and
in whatever way you like').

Emendation is required at two other points in the song. At 294, ἰστέ'
(ἰστέα) was proposed by W. G. Clark (*J.Phil.* 9 (1880), 12) for ἴστε,
the reading of the MSS other than R. Kock, supposing R's οὐκ ἰσατ' to
be an anagrammatization, suggested ἠκούσατ', which has been quite
widely accepted. The Triclinian MSS remove the hiatus by the typical
expedient of introducing γ' after ἴστε. At 336, ἄρ' ὁμήλικα is Reisig's
emendation of the unmetrical ἄρα τὸν ἥλικα (ἄρα θ' ἥλικα B).

     5 δ
385   τί ταῦτα στρέφει τεχνάζεις τε καὶ πορίζεις τριβάς;

    λαβὲ δ' ἐμοῦ γ' ἕνεκα παρ' Ἱερωνύμου
    2 δ
390   σκοτοδασυπυκνότριχά τιν' Ἅιδος κυνῆν,

391–2   trim II

    2 δ

    2 δ

    trim II
    2 δ

∪ − − ∪ −   ∪ − − ∪ ⌣ |||

ἐπειδήπερ αὐτὸς αἱρεῖ, λέγε.

566–71

∪ − − ∪ −   ∪ − − ∪ −

ἰὼ Λάμαχ', ὦ βλέπων ἀστραπάς,

∪ − − ∪ −   − ⌢ − ∪ −

βοήθησον, ὦ γοργολόφα, φανείς,

∪ − − ∪ −   ∪ − − ∪ ⌣ || ᴴ

ἰὼ Λάμαχ', ὦ φίλ', ὦ φυλέτα·

− ⌢ − ∪ −

εἴτε τις ἔστι τα-

∪ − ∪ −   ∪ − ∪ −

ξίαρχος ἢ στρατηγὸς ἢ

− ⌢ − ∪ −

570   τειχομάχας ἀνήρ,

∪ − − ∪ −   ∪ ⌢ − ∪ −   ∪ ⌢ − ∪ − |||

βοηθησάτω τις ἀνύσας· ἐγὼ γὰρ ἔχομαι μέσος.

Dochmiacs suggest a certain loss of control as the anger of the
Acharnians takes on a new tone of exasperation and bewilderment. Their
certainties are to be shaken in this scene and eventually demolished.

In 358–65=385–92 correspondence is exact between the various
forms of dochmiac. Coincidence of word-end in strophe and antistrophe
divides the stanza into 1, 3, 1, 2, but there is no real sense of a break until
after the fifth dochmiac.

In 358, οὐ, lost by haplography in RA, survives in E and the
Triclinian MSS. Γ has an erasure where it probably once was. In 361,
πάνυ γὰρ ἐμέ γε πόθος, making a fully-resolved dochmiac of
Euripidean type, is preserved by RAΓE. Triclinius, who supposed the
metre to be a mixture of cretic and bacchiac, substituted πόθος γὰρ
πάνυ με (∪ − − ∪ ∪ ∪). He did not, however, interfere with the antistrophe, although he recognized it as such (Σ Tric. 358c).

At 390, τιν' is Brunck's emendation for the MS τὴν.

2 δ

2 δ

2 δ

2 δ

1 δ

+2 ia

+1δ

3 δ

In the short utterance interjected by the chorus between Dicaeopolis' exhortation to his own soul and his formal ῥῆσις, iambic trimeters are combined with dochmiacs which are completely without resolution. The design may be to produce a rhythm more measured and compatible with iambic of spoken type.

At 490, εὖ is Meineke's supplement. For the hiatus, compare *Knights* 438 εὖ οἶδα, *Wasps* 425 εὖ εἰδῇ.

At 566, the MSS repeat ἰὼ before βλέπων, contrary to metre. ὢ is Hermann's correction. The combination of ἰὼ and ὢ gives rise to the same mistake in some MSS at E. *Med.* 1274:

$$\text{ἰὼ τλᾶμον, ὢ κακοτυχὲς γύναι}$$
$$\cup - - \cup - \quad \cup \overset{\frown}{} - \cup -$$

The combination of dochmiac and iambic at 569–70 is not self-evidently intolerable, but has been subject to editorial assaults from

Triclinius onwards. The Triclinian MSS, B and the Aldine have εἶτ᾽ ἔστι τις. On this basis, Fritzsche, by deleting τις, produced three iambs:

εἶτ᾽ ἔστι ταξίαρχος ἢ στρατηγὸς ἢ

⏤ ⏤ ⏑ ⏤   ⏑ ⏤ ⏑ ⏤   ⏑ ⏤ ⏑ ⏤

'whether he be a taxiarch, or etc., let someone come', rather than 'whether there is some taxiarch, etc.' It should, however, be noted that ἢ

665–75 = 692–702

⏤ ⏑ | ⏤   ⏤ ⏑ ⏗   ⏤ | ⏑ ⏗   ⏤ ⏑ ⏗

665   δεῦρο, Μοῦσ᾽, ἐλθέ, φλεγυρά, πυρὸς ἔχουσα μένος,

⏤ ⏑ ⏗   ⏤ ⏑ ⏤ ‖ᴴ

ἔντονος, Ἀχαρνική.

⏤ ⏑ ⏤   ⏤ ⏑ ⏤   ⏤ ⏑ ⏤   ⏤ ⏑ ⏗

οἷον ἐξ ἀνθράκων πρινίνων φέψαλος ἀν-

⏤ ⏑ ⏗   ⏤ ⏑ ⏗   ⏤ ⏑ ⏤ | ⏤ ⏑ ⏑ ‖ᴴ

ἤλατ᾽ ἐρεθιζόμενος οὐρίᾳ ῥιπίδι,

⏤ ⏑ ⏗   ⏤ ⏑ ⏗   ⏤ ⏑ | ⏗   ⏤ ⏑ ⏝ ‖ᴴ

670   ἡνίκ᾽ ἂν ἐπανθρακίδες ὦσι παρακείμεναι,

⏤ ⏑ | ⏗   ⏤ ⏑ ⏗   ⏤ ⏑ | ⏗   ⏤ ⏑ ⏝ ‖ᴴ

οἱ δὲ Θασίαν ἀνακυκῶσι λιπαράμπυκα,

⏤ ⏑ ⏤   ⏤ ⏑ ⏤   ⏤ | ⏑ ⏗   ⏤ ⏑ ⏗

οἱ δὲ μάττωσιν, οὕτω σοβαρὸν ἐλθὲ μέλος

⏤ ⏑ ⏢   ⏤ ⏑ ⏗

εὔτονον, ἀγροικότονον

⏤ ⏑ ⏢   ⏤ ⏑ ⏤   ⏤ ⏑ ⏤ ⫾⫾⫾

675   ὡς ἐμὲ λαβοῦσα τὸν δημότην.

The Acharnians return to cretics, their characteristic metre, for the parabasis-song. The stanza is articulated by verse-end and by corresponding coincidence of word-end and metron-end into 4 + 2, 8, 4, 4, 4 + 2 + 3. There is exact correspondence of resolution and frequent coincidence of word-end in strophe and antistrophe. The Muse is also

here is prepositive, so that these iambic metra do not make up an independent trimeter, like the trimeters found among dochmiacs at 492–3. Sommerstein observes that Fritzsche's version is actually found in one MS., *Laur. XXXI. 16*, a copy of B. But the omission of τις from the Triclinian text there is most unlikely to be anything other than a private error. The choice of text here must depend on meaning and metre.

4 cr
ταῦτα πῶς εἰκότα, γέροντ' ἀπολέσαι πολιὸν

2 cr
ἄνδρα περὶ κλεψύδραν,

4 cr
695   πολλὰ δὴ ξυμπονήσαντα καὶ θερμὸν ἀπο-

+4 cr
μορξάμενον ἀνδρικὸν ἱδρῶτα δὴ καὶ πολύν,

4 cr
ἄνδρ' ἀγαθὸν ὄντα Μαραθῶνι περὶ τὴν πόλιν;

4 cr
εἶτα Μαραθῶνι μὲν ὅτ' ἦμεν, ἐδιώκομεν,

4 cr
700   νῦν δ' ὑπ' ἀνδρῶν πονηρῶν σφόδρα διωκόμεθα,

2 cr
κᾆτα πρὸς ἁλισκόμεθα;

3 cr
πρὸς τάδε τίς ἀντερεῖ Μαρψίας;

invoked in cretics in a fragment of Cratinus' Τροφώνιος (*PCG* 237), a play of uncertain date. Fraenkel (*Beobachtungen*, 198–201) raises the possibility of the influence of traditional cult-poetry in the use of cretics in comedy. Here, however, the use of cretics is amply justified by the dramatic significance of the metre in this play, and the content and style of the song do not suggest traditional cult-poetry. Rather, the elaborate simile of the strophe which develops into an independent genre scene in Homeric style suggests literary antecedents. The antistrophe continues the subject of the preceding epirrheme.

$$836–41=842–7\ (=848–53=854–9)$$

‒ ‒ ◡ ‒　　‒ ‒ ◡ ‒　　‒ ‒ ◡ ‒　　◡ ‒ ⌣ ‖н

εὐδαιμονεῖ γ' ἄνθρωπος. οὐκ ἤκουσας οἷ προβαίνει

⌣ ‒ ◡ ‒　　⌐ ‒ ◡ ‒ |　　‒ ‒ ◡ ‒　　◡ ‒ ‒ ‖н

τὸ πρᾶγμα τοῦ βουλεύματος; καρπώσεται γὰρ ἀνὴρ

‒ ‒ ◡ ‒ |　　◡ ‒ ◡ ‒

ἐν τἀγορᾷ καθήμενος·

‒ ‒ ◡ ‒　　‒ ‒ ◡ ‒

κἂν εἰσίῃ τις Κτησίας

‒ ‒ ◡ ‒　　⌐ ‒ ◡ ‒

840　　ἢ συκοφάντης ἄλλος, οἱ-

⌐ ‒ ◡ ◡ ‒ ‒ |||

μώζων καθεδεῖται·

$$848–53=854–9\ (=836–41=842–7)$$

‒ ‒ ◡ ‒　　‒ ‒ ◡ ‒ |　　⌣ ‒ ◡ ‒　　◡ ‒ ‒

οὐδ' ἐντυχὼν ἐν τἀγορᾷ προσεισί σοι βαδίζων

⌣ ‒ ◡ ‒　　⌣ ‒ ◡ ‒ |　　⌐ ‒ ◡ ‒　　◡ ‒ ⌣ ‖н

Κρατῖνος †ἀεὶ† κεκαρμένος μοιχὸν μιᾷ μαχαίρᾳ,

◡ ⌢ ◡ ‒　　⌣ | ‒ ◡ ‒

850　　[οὐδ'] ὁ περιπόνηρος Ἀρτέμων,

⌣ ⌣ ◡ ‒　　‒ ‒ ◡ ‒

ὁ ταχὺς ἄγαν τὴν μουσικήν,

‒ ‒ ◡ ‒　　‒ ‒ ◡ ‒

ὄζων κακὸν τῶν μασχαλῶν

⌣ ‒ ◡ ◡ ‒ ‒ |||

πατρὸς Τραγασαίου·

Textual variants are few and insignificant. At 667, οἷον appears as a correction in Γ, but is otherwise confined to the Triclinian MSS. RAΓ¹E have οἴων. At 670, the Aldine omits ἂν, and is followed by printed texts until Brunck.

ia tetram cat
οὐδ' ἄλλος ἀνθρώπων ὑποψωνῶν σε πημανεῖ τι,

ia tetram cat
οὐδ' ἐξομόρξεται Πρέπις τὴν εὐρυπρωκτίαν σοι,

ia dim
οὐδ' ὠστιεῖ Κλεωνύμῳ·

ia dim
845   χλαῖναν δ' ἔχων φανὴν δίει

ia dim
κοὐ ξυντυχών σ' Ὑπέρβολος

+ reiz
δικῶν ἀναπλήσει·

ia tetram cat
οὐδ' αὖθις αὖ σε σκώψεται Παύσων ὁ παμπόνηρος

ia tetram cat
855   Λυσίστρατός τ' ἐν τἀγορᾷ, Χολαργέων ὄνειδος,

ia dim
ὁ περιαλουργὸς τοῖς κακοῖς,

ia dim
ῥιγῶν τε καὶ πεινῶν ἀεὶ

ia dim
πλεῖν ἢ τριάκονθ' ἡμέρας

+ reiz
τοῦ μηνὸς ἑκάστου.

The fantastic hypothesis of the private peace once established, the old men lose their active role. Thereafter, they admire the felicity of Dicaeopolis, affirm the value of peace, or sing lampoon-songs. This specimen of the latter genre is tenuously attached to the plot by the idea that Dicaeopolis in his private market will not be bothered by the tiresome people mentioned. For a similarly slender excuse for a lampoon song, see *Birds* 1470ff. = 1482ff., 1553ff. = 1694ff. For the use of iambic in a lampoon-song, compare *Frogs* 417ff. and Eupolis, *PCG* 99, 386. The Eupolis fragments are extremely simple metrically, consisting, apparently, of sequences of iambic metra, marked off by catalexis. Here, the tetrameter-lengths and the reizianum clausula give more definition to the stanza. Although all four stanzas correspond, the relation is perhaps slightly closer between the first and second on the one hand and

929–39 = 940–51

$- - \cup - \quad - - \cup | - \quad \cup - | \cup - \quad - - \cup -$

X. ἔνδησον, ὦ βέλτιστε, τῷ ξένῳ καλῶς τὴν ἐμπολὴν

931   οὕτως ὅπως ἂν μὴ φέρων κατάξῃ.

Δ. ἐμοὶ μελήσει ταῦτ' ἐπεί τοι καὶ ψοφεῖ λάλον τι καὶ

πυρορραγὲς κἄλλως θεοῖσιν ἐχθρόν.

935 X. τί χρήσεταί ποτ' αὐτῷ;

Δ. πάγχρηστον ἄγγος ἔσται,

κρατὴρ κακῶν, τριπτὴρ δικῶν, φαίνειν ὑπευθύνους λυχνοῦ-

χος καὶ κύλιξ τὰ πράγματ' ἐγκυκᾶσθαι.

the third and fourth on the other (corresponding word-end at 838=844, corresponding word-end, resolution, and verbal echo at 850=856).

In 844, the *Suda* and Zonaras offer ἐναπομόρξεται, which seems to be post-classical. For the literal and figurative uses of ἐξομόργνυμι, compare *Her.* 1399 αἷμα . . . ἐξομόρξωμαι πέπλοις and *Ba.* 344 ἐξομόρξῃ . . . μωρίαν ἐμοί. The latter passage is not, of course, as LSJ quaintly says, parodied here.

In 849, ἀεί produces ◡ ◡ for ◡, for which there is no reliable parallel in sung iambic (Introduction, p. 33), nor does the word seem to have much point in the context. Reisig's ἀποκεκαρμένος is attractive (Cf. *Thesm.* 838 σκαφίον ἀποκεκαρμένην 'with a bowl-cut').

In 850, οὐδ', interpolated by someone ignorant both of metre and of Anacreon, was excised by Bentley.

4 ia

940 X. πῶς δ' ἂν πεποιθοίη τις ἀγγείῳ τοιούτῳ χρώμενος

2 ia ba
κατ' οἰκίαν τοσόνδ' ἀεὶ ψοφοῦντι;

4 ia
Δ. ἰσχυρόν ἐστιν, ὦγάθ', ὥστ' οὐκ ἂν καταγείη ποτ' εἴ-

+2 ia ba
945   περ ἐκ ποδῶν κατωκάρα κρέμαιτο.

ia ba
X. ἤδη καλῶς ἔχει σοι.

ia ba
Θ. μέλλω γά τοι θερίδδειν.

4 ia
X. ἀλλ', ὦ ξένων βέλτιστε, συνθέριζε καὶ [τοῦτον λαβὼν]
προσβαλλ' ὅποι

+2 ia ba
950–1   βούλει φέρων πρὸς πάντα συκοφάντην.

This simple, iambic duet is articulated metrically by catalexis coinciding with change of speaker. The count of metra gives the structure: 7, 7, 2, 2, 7.

929–34 is preserved in *P. Berol.* 13231 (5th c. AD), with the same colon-division as in R, which is also that described by *Σ vet.* on 929, i.e. two pairs of distichs consisting of iambic trimeter and iambic tetrameter catalectic:

> Χο. ἔνδησον, ὦ βέλτιστε, τῷ ξένῳ καλῶς
> τὴν ἐμπολὴν οὕτως ὅπως ἂν μὴ φέρων κατάξῃ.
> Δι. ἐμοὶ μελήσει ταῦτ' ἐπεί τοι καὶ ψοφεῖ
> λάλον τι καὶ πυρορραγὲς κἄλλως θεοῖσιν ἐχθρόν.

The corresponding lines are also partially preserved in *Π*, which, wherever it survives, coincides with the division of R:

> Χο. πῶς δ'ἂν πεποιθοίη τις ἀγ-   — ‿ —   — ‿ —
> γείῳ τοιούτῳ χρώμενος   — ‿ —   — ‿ —
> κατ' οἰκίαν   ‿ — ‿ —
> τοσόνδ' ἀεὶ ψοφοῦντι;   ‿ — ‿ —   ‿ — ‿ ‖ н
> Δι. ἰσχυρόν ἐστιν, ὦγαθ', ὥστ'   — ‿ —   ‿ — ‿ —
> οὐκ ἂν καταγείη ποτ' εἴ-   — ‿ —   — ‿ —
> περ ἐκ ποδῶν   ‿ — ‿ —
> κατωκάρα κρέμαιτο.   ‿ — ‿ —   ‿ — ‿ ‖ н

The two divisions do not merely fail to correspond; they seem to have been made on different principles. The strophe, with its long lines and careful regard for word-end, looks like the work of, say, Adolph von

$$971{-}87 = 988{-}99$$

— ‿ —   — ‿ ⌢   — ‿ ⌢| — ‿ ⌢   — ‿ ⌣ ‖

εἶδες, ὦ πᾶσα πόλι, τὸν φρόνιμον ἄνδρα, τὸν ὑπέρσοφον

— ‿ —   — ‿ ⌢| — ‿ ⌢| — ‿ ⌘   — ‿ —

οἷ' ἔχει σπεισάμενος ἐμπορικὰ χρήματα διεμπολᾶν,

— ‿ ⌢   — ‿ —| — ‿ ⌢   — ‿ —| — ‿ ⌘   — ‿ —‖н

975–7   ὧν τὰ μὲν ἐν οἰκίᾳ χρήσιμα, τὰ δ' αὖ πρέπει χλιαρὰ
                                             [κατεσθίειν.

Velsen, while the antistrophe shows a devotion to dimeter-lengths and a brutal disregard of rhetorical division reminiscent of Radermacher. It is highly unlikely that either division could have been arrived at accidentally. If, however, the distich-division of the strophe is tried on the antistrophe, the attractive correspondence with word-end disappears (τοιού-τῳ and κατα-γείη are split between lines). The conclusion seems inescapable that the originator of the distich-division of 929–34 did not realize that he was dealing with corresponding stanzas.

Apart from the light it throws on the metrical history of the text, this observation is worth taking into account when considering the failure of correspondence in the second part of the stanza (937–9 = 948–51), where the antistrophe contains one more iambic metron than the strophe. The lines 948–51 survive in *Π*, with the same text and colometry as in R, which is also confirmed by *Σ vet.* on 948. But we have evidence that, at least in late antiquity, correspondence in these stanzas went unrecognized (except, possibly, at 935–6 = 946–7; see *Σ vet.* 946), so that the text was unprotected from interpolation. Bergk's deletion of τοῦτον λαβών has been widely and rightly accepted. Apart from the question of correspondence, the words disrupt the neat numerical pattern of metra, which is characteristically Aristophanic. The motive for the interpolation may have been a supposed need for a reference to this particular sycophant. πρόσβαλλε could mean 'inflict on' (like a misfortune, cf. *Pers.* 781 κακὸν . . . προσέβαλον πόλει), or 'apply to', 'throw against' (*Hipp.* 1233 ἀψῖδα πέτρῳ προσβαλών), or simply 'throw him on top of everything else [that your party is carrying] and take him wherever you like' (See K. Holzinger, *SAWW* 215.1 (1933), 35–69)

5 cr
ἐπτέρωταί τ' ἐπὶ τὸ δεῖπνον ἅμα καὶ μεγάλα δὴ φρονεῖ,

5 cr
τοῦ βίου δ' ἐξέβαλε δεῖγμα ⟨τάδε⟩ τὰ πτερὰ πρὸ τῶν
[θυρῶν.

6 cr
ὦ Κύπριδι τῇ καλῇ καὶ Χάρισι ταῖς φίλαις ξύντροφε
[Διαλλαγή,

$- \cup \widehat{\cup\cup} \quad - \cup \widehat{\cup\cup} \quad - \cup \widehat{\cup\cup} \quad - \cup - \parallel^H$

αὐτόματα πάντ᾽ ἀγαθὰ τῷδέ γε πορίζεται,

$- \cup \widehat{\cup\cup} \quad - \cup \widehat{\cup\cup} \quad - \cup \widehat{\cup\cup} \quad - \cup - \parallel^H$

οὐδέποτ᾽ ἐγὼ Πόλεμον οἴκαδ᾽ ὑποδέξομαι,

$- \cup \widehat{\cup\cup} \quad - \cup \widehat{\cup\cup} \quad - \cup \widehat{\cup\cup}| \quad - \cup -$

980   οὐδὲ παρ᾽ ἐμοί ποτε τὸν Ἁρμόδιον ᾁσεται

$- \cup \widehat{\cup\cup} \quad - \cup \widehat{\cup\cup} \quad - \cup \widehat{\cup\cup} \quad - \cup \cup \smile \parallel^H$

ξυγκατακλινείς, ὅτι παροινικὸς ἀνὴρ ἔφυ,

$- \cup \widehat{\cup\cup} \quad - \cup \widehat{\cup\cup} \quad - \cup| \widehat{\cup\cup} \quad - \cup -$

ὅστις ἐπὶ πάντ᾽ ἀγάθ᾽ ἔχοντας ἐπικωμάσας

$- \cup \widehat{\cup\cup}| \quad - \cup \widehat{\cup\cup}| \quad - \cup \widehat{\cup\cup} \quad - \cup \smile \parallel$

ἠργάσατο πάντα κακά, κἀνέτρεπε κἀξέχει

$- \cup \widehat{\cup\cup}| \quad - \cup \widehat{\cup\cup}| \quad - \cup \widehat{\cup\cup} \quad - \cup -$

κἀμάχετο, καὶ προσέτι πολλὰ προκαλουμένου·

$- \cup \widehat{\cup\cup} \quad - \cup \widehat{\cup\cup}| \quad - \cup \widehat{\cup\cup} \quad - \cup -$

985   "πῖνε, κατάκεισο, λαβὲ τήνδε φιλοτησίαν,"

$- \cup \widehat{\cup\cup} \quad - \cup \widehat{\cup\cup} \quad - \cup| \widehat{\cup\cup} \quad - \cup \smile \smile \parallel^H$

τὰς χάρακας ἧπτε πολὺ μᾶλλον ἔτι τῷ πυρί,

$- \cup - - \quad - \cup - \smile \quad - \cup| - - \quad - \cup - \parallel\parallel\parallel$

ἐξέχει θ᾽ ἡμῶν βίᾳ τὸν οἶνον ἐκ τῶν ἀμπέλων.

In this elaborate set-piece, the chorus, addressing 'the whole city', uses cretics for the last time. The resolved cretic, $- \cup \widehat{\cup\cup}$, is frequent, and correspondence of resolution is exact. There is also much correspondence of word-end and a tendency to divide into dimeter-lengths. The incidence of verse-end, however, points to a structure of 5, 5, 6, then nine tetrameters, with a catalectic trochaic tetrameter as clausula. Both strophe and antistrophe begin with invitations to admire Dicaeopolis, then the chorus turn to expressing their hatred of war and their longing for peace through the medium of imagery. The change of subject nearly, but not quite, coincides with the beginning of the tetrameter-section. In the strophe, the section on Dicaeopolis continues to the end

4 cr

990   ὡς καλὸν ἔχουσα τὸ πρόσωπον ἄρ' ἐλάνθανες.

4 cr

πῶς ἂν ἐμὲ καὶ σέ τις Ἔρως ξυναγάγοι λαβών,

4 cr

ὥσπερ ὁ γεγραμμένος, ἔχων στέφανον ἀνθέμων;

4 cr

ἢ πάνυ γερόντιον ἴσως νενόμικάς με σύ;

4 cr

ἀλλά σε λαβὼν τρία δοκῶ γ' ἂν ἔτι προσβαλεῖν·

4 cr

995   πρῶτα μὲν ἂν ἀμπελίδος ὄρχον ἐλάσαι μακρόν,

4 cr

εἶτα παρὰ τόνδε νέα μοσχίδια συκίδων,

4 cr

καὶ τὸ τρίτον ἡμερίδος ὦσχον, ὁ γέρων ὁδί,

4 cr

καὶ περὶ τὸ χωρίον ἐλᾴδας ἅπαν ἐν κύκλῳ,

tro tetram cat

ὥστ' ἀλείφεσθαί σ' ἀπ' αὐτῶν κἀμὲ ταῖς νουμηνίαις.

of the first tetrameter; in the antistrophe, the chorus begin their address to Διαλλαγή with the verse before the first tetrameter. While the song has evident parabatic features, I hesitate to call it a 'second parabasis', in which 971–7 = 988–9 would be ode and antode, and 978–87 = 990–9 epirrheme and antepirrheme. The poet has actually taken pains to avoid such clear-cut divisions. One may compare and contrast the second parabasis of *Wasps* (1265–91), which also features the cretic tetrameter $- \cup \widetilde{}$ $- \cup \widetilde{}$ $- \cup \widetilde{}$ $- \cup -$ (Introduction, p. 45) in its epirrhematic sections, but where the ode and antode are quite distinct metrically and rhetorically. (See also Introduction, pp. 15–17.)

At 971, almost all the MSS (including L, but not H Vp2) have εἶδες ὦ twice. Meineke chose to adopt that and assume a lacuna in the anti-strophe. This, however, destroys the symmetry of the stanza. Moreover, the repeated εἶδες ὦ is probably merely one of a number of errors in the transmission of both strophe and antistrophe caused, apparently, by the ancient colon-division. The division, described by Σ. *vet.* 971a and confirmed by *P. Berol.* 13231, was:

> εἶδες, ὦ
> πᾶσα πόλι, τὸν φρόνιμον ἄνδρα τὸν ὑπέρσοφον,
>   οἷ᾽ ἔχει
> σπεισάμενος ἐμπορικὰ χρήματα διεμπολᾶν,

$$- \cup -$$
$$- \cup - \quad \widehat{- \cup} \quad \widehat{- \cup} \quad \widehat{- \cup} \quad - \cup -$$
$$- \cup -$$
$$- \cup \widehat{} \quad - \cup \widehat{} \quad - \cup \widehat{} \quad - \cup -$$

The lay-out is based on good observation both of the pattern of resolu-tion and of the incidence of word-end, but it played havoc with copyists. Apart from the repeated εἶδες, ὦ, R at 972 has σπεισάμενος οἷ᾽ ἔχει, clearly as a result of seeing οἷ᾽ ἔχει above σπεισάμενος and assuming it to be an accidental omission. The words *are* actually omitted by other MSS and the Aldine. They are added after ὑπέρσοφον (at the end of the previous line) by the corrector of Γ and E and, in the right place, before σπεισάμενος, by the corrector of B. The ancient colometry continues to cause trouble in the antistrophe: ἐπτέρω- is omitted by all the MSS. It is preserved by lemmata in R and E, and was added to the text by the

$$1008\text{–}17 = 1037\text{–}46$$

$$- - \cup - \quad - - \cup -$$
Χ. ζηλῶ σε τῆς εὐβουλίας,

$$- - \cup | - \quad \widehat{} - \cup -$$
μᾶλλον δὲ τῆς εὐωχίας,

$$\widehat{} - \cup \widehat{} \quad \cup - -$$
1010   ἄνθρωπε, τῆς παρούσης.

$$\times - \cup - \quad - \cup \widehat{}$$
Δ. τί δῆτ᾽, ἐπειδὰν τὰς κίχλας

corrector of E. At 988, having written τοῦ βίου on a line by itself, as the colometry required, the scribe of R omitted the next line, which has been added by a different hand. Such was the crop of errors produced by a sophisticated colometry meeting scribal ignorance (see Introduction, p. 99).

At 981, παροινικὸς ('prone to drunkenness', cf. *Wasps* 1300) is a certain emendation by Elmsley for the MS παροίνιος ('suitable to accompany drinking'). For the idiom 'he is a such-and-such man', compare *Ach.* 491, *Wasps* 730, *Peace* 1120, *Lys.* 1030. Cobet's πάροινος ἀνήρ ('the man was by nature drunken') is metrically as well as linguistically inferior in that it destroys the correspondence of – ◡ ∽ to – ◡ ∽.

At 989, τάδε is Brunck's supplement.

At 997, where I adopt ὦσχον from Brunck's ὄσχον, the pre-Triclinian MSS have κλάδον, and the Triclinian ὄρχον. ὄρχον is evidently an uninspired metrical emendation derived from 995. Apart from the repetition, it leaves the presence of κλάδον in the MSS unexplained. What is needed is a word that could have been glossed by κλάδον. Another possibility is Bergk's ὄζον (which is actually glossed by κλάδον in L Ald at *Wasps* 1377). But ὦσχος is the rarer word, and has a special appropriateness to vines (Hesychius, s. ὦσχοι, cf. ὄσχαι, Athenaeus 11. 495f.). Aelian (*Letter* IV), imitating this passage, omits the ἡμερίς, possibly because the line was already corrupt in his text, or because it seemed to him redundant after the ἀμπελίς of 995.

5 ia ba

X. ἀνὴρ ἐνηύρηκέν τι ταῖς

σπονδαῖσιν ἡδύ, κοὐκ ἔοι-

κεν οὐδενὶ μεταδώσειν.

2 ia

1040 Δ. κατάχει σὺ τῆς χορδῆς τὸ μέλι·

‒ ‒ ᴗ ‒| ᴗ ‒ ᴗ ‖ ᴴ

ὀπτωμένας ἴδητε;

‒ ‒ ᴗ| ‒   ᴖ ‒ ᴗ ‒

Χ. οἶμαί σε καὶ τοῦτ᾽ εὖ λέγειν.

ᴗ ‒ ᴗ ‒   ᴗ ‒ ᴗ ‖ ᴴ

Δ. τὸ πῦρ ὑποσκάλευε.

ᴖ ‒ ᴗ ‒   ᴗ ‒ ᴗ ‒

1015 Χ. ἤκουσας ὡς μαγειρικῶς

‒ ‒ ᴗ ‒   ‒ ‒ ᴗ ‒

κομψῶς τε καὶ δειπνητικῶς

‒ ‒| ᴗ ‒   ᴗ ‒ ‒ |||

αὑτῷ διακονεῖται;

This duet, again in simple iambic, between the chorus and Dicaeopolis, balances the one at 929 ff. = 940 ff. Exact symmetry is, however, avoided, for here the strophe is divided from the antistrophe by the short Dercetes-episode. The song is constructed in four periods marked off by catalexis in the pattern 6, 4, 4, 6. But here too exact symmetry is avoided: the first period of four metra is sung by Dicaeopolis, while the second is divided between him and the chorus (2+2). The four-

1150–61 = 1162–73

‒ ᴗ ᴗ ‒   ‒ ᴗ ᴗ ‒| ‒ ᴗ ᴗ ‒   ‒ ᴗ ᴗ ‒   ᴗ ‒ ◡ ‖ ᴴ

1150 Ἀντίμαχον τὸν Ψακάδος, †τὸν ξυγγραφῆ, τὸν μελέων

                                       [ποιητήν,

‒ ᴗ ᴗ ‒   ᴗ ‒ ᴗ ‒   ‒ ᴗ ᴗ ‒   ᴗ ‒ ‒

ὡς μὲν ἁπλῷ λόγῳ κακῶς ἐξολέσειεν ὁ Ζεύς·

‒ ᴗ ᴗ ‒   ‒ ᴗ ᴗ| ‒   ‒ ᴗ ᴗ ‒   ‒ ᴗ ᴗ ‒   ᴗ ‒ ◡ ‖

1155 ὅς γ᾽ ἐμὲ τὸν τλήμονα Λήναια χορηγῶν ἀπέλυσ᾽ ἄδειπνον.

ᴗ ◠ ᴗ ◠   ᴗ ‒ ᴗ ‒

ὃν ἔτ᾽ ἐπίδοιμι τευθίδος

ia ba
τὰς σηπίας στάθευε.

2 ia
Χ. ἤκουσας ὀρθιασμάτων;

ia ba
Δ. ὀπτᾶτε τἀγχέλεια.

5 ia ba
Χ. ἀποκτενεῖς λιμῷ 'μὲ καὶ

1045   τοὺς γείτονας κνίσῃ τε καὶ

φωνῇ τοιαῦτα λάσκων.

metron periods are divided into dimeter lengths by word-end. The
six-metron periods are so divided in the strophe, but not in the antistrophe.

At 1017, the Triclinian MSS and the Aldine have αὐτῷ γε, presumably because Triclinius scanned διἄκονεῖται. ◡ ◡ for ╳ in 1040 suggests
that Dicaeopolis may be delivering his part in recitative (Introduction,
p. 33). At 1037, ἐνεύρηκεν is Dobree's correction of the MS ἀνεύρηκεν.

4 cho ba
τοῦτο μὲν αὐτῷ κακὸν ἕν· κᾆθ' ἕτερον νυκτερινὸν γένοιτο.

cho ia dim + cho ia dim cat
1165 ἠπιαλῶν γὰρ οἴκαδ' ἐξ ἱππασίας βαδίζων,

4 cho ba
εἶτα κατάξειέ τις αὐτοῦ μεθύων τῆς κεφαλῆς Ὀρέστης

2 ia
μαινόμενος· ὁ δὲ λίθον βαλεῖν

⏑⏜⏑|–‾ ‾–⏑–

δεόμενον, ἡ δ' ὠπτημένη

–‾–⏑|⏜ ⏑|⏝⏑–‾ ‾–⏑⏝‖ᴴ

σίζουσα πάραλος ἐπὶ τραπέζῃ κειμένη

⏑–‾–‾ –⏑–‾ –‾–⏑–

1160 ὀκέλλοι· κᾆτα μέλλοντος λαβεῖν

–‾–⏑–‾ –⏑–‾ ⏑–⏝‖‖‖

αὐτοῦ κύων ἁρπάσασα φεύγοι.

In this elaborate lampoon-song, the chorus abandon their dramatic character, sing as chorus-men and direct their attack on a single person, Antimachus. Metrically, it is the most sophisticated song in the play, and subtle metrical parody of tragedy appears here for the first time. The first section of the stanza (1150–5 = 1162–7), is iambo-choriambic, reminiscent of Anacreon in its constituents: Anacreon uses choriambic sequences ending in bacchiac (*PMG* 381(b), 382), and the second verse here is a dicolon found among his fragments (*PMG* 385, 386). The verses are not, however, anacreontic in their structure, for which the closest parallel is the alternation of dicola and choriambic verses in a fragment from Γεωργοί (*PCG* 111; Introduction, p. 84):

–‾–‾⏑⏑–⏑–‾ –⏑⏑–⏑–‾–

–⏑⏑–‾ –⏑⏑–| –⏑⏑–‾ ⏑––

–‾⏑–‾ ⏑–⏑–‾ –⏑⏑–‾ ⏑–⏑–

–⏑⏑–‾ –⏑⏑–‾ –⏑⏑–‾ ⏑–⏝̣‖

Aeschylus, too, uses choriambic sequences closing with bacchiac, but towards the end of stanzas and, apparently, with a climactic function (*Ag.* 201 ff. = 214 ff., *Sept.* 918 ff. = 929 ff., *Supp.* 544 ff. = 553 ff.). The second section is in iambic, unsyncopated, but quite heavily resolved. The stanza ends with two syncopated iambic trimeters. Strophe and antistrophe each recount an imaginary episode in which Antimachus meets with undignified catastrophe, and in each the increasing nobility of the metre towards the end of the stanza contrasts with the climax

2 ia

βουλόμενος ἐν σκότῳ λάβοι

ia trim

1170 τῇ χειρὶ πέλεθον ἀρτίως κεχεσμένον·

ia trim sync

ἐπᾴξειεν δ' ἔχων τὸν μάρμαρον,

ia trim sync cat

κἄπειθ' ἁμαρτὼν βάλοι Κρατῖνον.

in vulgarity of content. Sycopated iambic trimeters naturally suggest Aeschylus, but in fact Sophocles sometimes ends polymetric stanzas with an iambic section leading into one or two trimeters, e.g. *Ant.* 985–7 (=974–6):

ἀλαὸν ἀλαστόροισιν ὀμμάτων κύκλοις,
ἀραχθέντων ὑφ' αἱματηραῖς
χείρεσσι καὶ κερκίδων ἀκμαῖσιν.

∪◠∪ –   ∪ – ∪ ◠   ∪ – ∪ –
∪ – –   – ∪ –   ∪ – –
– – ∪ –   – ∪ –   ∪ – –

(see Introduction, p. 32).

1150 poses a textual problem which, because of our lack of information about Antimachus, is insoluble. Correspondence between iambic and choriambic metra is not unparalleled (Introduction, p. 78), but the verse could well be corrupt. Editors generally follow the lead of Σ *vet.* in endowing Antimachus with a humorously fictitious father called 'Psacas'. This is, of course, a typically Aristophanic type of joke (cf. 1131), and it is for that very reason possible that the explanation is the invention of a commentator. Hall–Geldart's τὸν ψακάδος ξυγγραφέα (ψακάδος being substituted παρὰ προσδοκίαν for ψηφίσματος) deserves attention.

In 1155, ἀπέλυσ' ἄδειπνον is a simple Triclinian emendation (LHVp2 Ald) for ἀπέλυσεν ἄδειπνον common to the other MSS except R, which has ἀπέκλεισε δείπνων from the scholium.

1190–1234

‾ ⏑ ‾   ‾ ⏑ ‾

1190 Λ. ἀτταταῖ ἀτταταῖ

⏑ ⏜| ⏑ ⏜| ⏑ ⏜| ⏑ ⏜| ⏑ ‾ ⏑ ‾

στυγερὰ τάδε γε κρυερὰ πάθεα· τάλας ἐγώ·

⏑ ‾ ⏑ ‾   ⏑ ⏜ ⏑ ⏜   ⏑ ‾ ⏑ ‾

διόλλυμαι δορὸς ὑπὸ πολεμίου τυπείς.

⏑ ‾ ⏑ ‾   ‾ ‾ ⏑ ‾   ⏑ ‾ ⏝ ‖

1195   ἐκεῖνο δ' οὖν αἰακτὸν [οἰμωκτὸν] ἂν γένοιτο [μοι]

⏑ ‾ ⏑ ⏜   ‾ ⏑ ‾   ⏑ ‾ ⏑ ‾

Δικαιόπολις εἴ μ' ἴδοι τετρωμένον

‾ ‾ ⏑ ‾   ‾ ⏑ ‾   ⏑ ‾ ⏝ ‖

κᾆτ' ἐγχάνοι ταῖς ἐμαῖς τύχαισιν.

‾ ⏑ ‾   ‾ ⏑ ‾

Δ. ἀτταταῖ ἀτταταῖ

‾ ‾ ⏑ ‾   ‾ ‾ ⏑ ‾   ⏑ ‾ ⏑ ⏝ ‖

τῶν τιτθίων, ὡς σκληρὰ καὶ κυδώνια.

⏑ ‾ ⏑ ‾   ⏑ ‾ ⏑ ‾   ‾ ‾ ⏑ ‾

1200   φιλήσατόν με μαλθακῶς, ὦ χρυσίω,

⏑ ⏜ ⏑ ‾   ‾ ‾ ⏑ ‾   ⏑ ‾ ‾

τὸ περιπεταστὸν κἀπιμανδαλωτόν.

‾ ‾ ⏑ ‾   ‾ ⏑ ‾   ⏑ ‾ ⏝ ‖ ʜ

τὸν γὰρ χοᾶ πρῶτος ἐκπέπωκα.

‾ ‾ ⏑ ‾   ⏑ ‾ ⏑ ‾   ⏑ ‾ ⏑ ‾

Λ. ὦ συμφορὰ τάλαινα τῶν ἐμῶν κακῶν.

⏑ ‾ ⏑ ‾   ‾ ⏑ ‾   ⏑ ‾ ⏑ ‾

1205   ἰὼ ἰὼ τραυμάτων ἐπωδύνων.

⏑ ‾ ⏑ ‾   ‾ ⏑ ‾   ⏑ ‾ ⏑ ‾

Δ. ἰὴ ἰή, χαῖρε, Λαμαχίππιον.

2 cr

ia trim

ia trim

ia trim cat

ia trim sync

ia trim sync cat

2 cr

ia trim

ia trim

ia trim cat

ia trim sync cat

ia trim

ia trim sync

ia trim sync

‿⌢‿–
Λ. στυγερὸς ἐγώ.

‿⌢‿–
μογερὸς ἐγώ.

‿⌢‿–
Δ. τί με σὺ κυνεῖς;

‿⌢‿–
τί με σὺ δάκνεις;

‿–‿– –‿– ‿– –
1210 Λ. τάλας ἐγὼ [τῆς ἐν μάχῃ] ξυμβολῆς βαρείας.

– –‿– ‿–‿– ‿–‿‿◡‖ʜ
Δ. τοῖς Χουσὶ γάρ τις ξυμβολὰς ἐπράττετο;
‿–‿– ‿–‿–
Λ. ἰὼ ⟨ἰώ⟩, Παιὰν Παιάν.

– –‿– – –‿– ‿–‿◡‖
Δ. ἀλλ' οὐχὶ νυνὶ τήμερον Παιώνια.

‿–‿– ‿–‿– ‿–‿–
Λ. λάβεσθέ μου, λάβεσθε τοῦ σκέλους· παπαῖ,

–‿– –‿–‖
1215   προσλάβεσθ', ὦ φίλοι.

‿–‿– – –‿– – –‿–
Δ. ἐμοῦ δέ γε σφὼ τοῦ πέους ἄμφω μέσου

–‿– –‿–‖ʜ
προσλάβεσθ', ὦ φίλαι.

– –‿– ‿–‿– ‿–‿–
Λ. εἰλιγγιῶ κάρα λίθῳ πεπληγμένος

–‿‿–‿–
καὶ σκοτοδινιῶ.

– –‿– ‿–‿– – –‿–
1220 Δ. κἀγὼ καθεύδειν βούλομαι καὶ στύομαι

1 ia

1 ia

1 ia

1 ia

ia trim sync cat

ia trim

2 ia

ia trim

ia trim

2 cr

ia trim

2 cr

ia trim

dodrans A? δ?

ia trim

‒ ᴗ ᴗ ‒ ᴗ ‒

καὶ σκοτοβινιῶ.

ᴗ ‒ ᴗ ‒   ᴗ ‒ ᴗ ‒   ‒ ‒ ᴗ ‒

Λ. θύραζέ μ' ἐξενέγκατ' εἰς τοῦ Πιττάλου

ᴗ ‒ ᴗ ‒   ᴗ ‒ ‿ ‖

παιωνίαισι χερσίν.

‒ ‒ ᴗ ‒   ᴗ ⁀ᴗ ᴗ ‒   ᴗ ⁀ᴗ ᴗ ‒

Δ. ὡς τοὺς κριτάς με φέρετε. ποῦ 'στιν ὁ βασιλεύς;

ᴗ ⁀ᴗ ᴗ ‒   ᴗ ‒ ‒ ‖‖‖

1225   ἀπόδοτέ μοι τὸν ἀσκόν.

1226–31

‒ ‒ ᴗ ‒   ᴗ ‒ ᴗ ‒

Χ. ἀλλ' ἑψόμεσθα σὴν χάριν

‒ ‒ ᴗ ‒   ᴗ ‒ ᴗ ‒   ‒ ‒ ᴗ ‒   ᴗ ‒ ‿ ‖‖‖

τήνελλα καλλίνικον ᾄδοντες σὲ καὶ τὸν ἀσκόν.

At 1097–1142, Dicaeopolis' preparations for his gourmet picnic burlesqued Lamachus' preparations for campaign. In this scene, his ecstasies of pleasure burlesque the agonies of the wounded Lamachus. Their duet evidently parodies the entry of an anguished hero in the final scene of a tragedy. An example close in date to this play is the entry of the fatally-injured Hippolytus at *Hipp.* 1347 ff. There, Hippolytus begins his monody in anapaests (following the chorus's introduction), then changes to iambic, with resolution (cf. 1190–1 in this passage) and syncopation and with two iambo-choriambic cola. The idea of two agonized heroes wailing in competition may have been less self-

Lamachus

1190–7   2 cr

                       2 ia trim

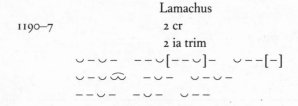

dodrans A? δ?

ia trim

ia dim cat

ia trim

ia dim cat

ia tetram cat VI
2 ia

ia tetram cat

evidently funny to a Greek audience, who were familiar with antiphonal
lamentation (e.g. *Tro.* 577–94, and see M. Alexiou, *The Ritual Lament
in Greek Tradition*, ch. 7). A notable feature of the passage is the
concentration of syncopated iambic trimeters. Out of a total of eighteen
such verses in Aristophanes' surviving plays, no less than six are here.

   A general textual and metrical problem of the passage is whether
Lamachus' and Dicaeopolis' uttterances ought to correspond exactly, or
only approximately. For a lyric dialogue with a degree of symmetry, but
without full correspondence, one may compare *Birds* 406–34, but here
correspondence is close enough to be tantalizing:

Dicaeopolis

1198–1205   2 cr

              2 ia trim

       ⏑‿⏑ –　– – ⏑ –　⏑ – –

      – – ⏑ –　– ⏑ –　⏑ – –

1204–5	ia trim
	∪ – ∪ – – ∪ – ∪ – ∪ –
1207–8	∪ ⌣͡⌣ ∪ – ∪ ⌣͡⌣ ∪ –
1210	∪ – ∪ – – ∪ – ∪ – –
1212	∪ – ⟨∪ –⟩ ∪ – ∪ –
1214–15	ia trim
	2 cr
1218–19	ia trim
	– ∪ ∪ – ∪ –
1222–3	ia trim
	ia dim cat

It is by no means impossible that Dicaeopolis has lost a line following 1201, although the sense does not betray it. Another line could well have been lost after 1205. Lamachus' exclamation may be mutilated. There are signs of mutilation to the text elsewhere in the latter part of this play: a line has been lost at 1094–5, and two half-lines at 1142. To produce correspondence between 1210 and 1211 requires fairly drastic re-writing. Bergk proposed τοῖς Χουσὶ τίς ξυμβολάς σ' ἔπραττεν; It may be that here the spoken-type trimeter is intended to surprise, mirroring rhythmically the comic contrast between Lamachus' tragic exclamation and the grotesquely prosaic interpretation that Dicaeopolis gives to it. But both emendation and explanation are unverifiable.

An interesting feature of the passage is the light it throws on Triclinius' metrical competence and editorial procedures. In LAld (and, in consequence, in printed editions for the following three centuries) the text is bespattered with minor supplements, mostly designed to eliminate syncopation, e.g.:

1197	κᾷτ' ἐγχάνοι ⟨γε⟩ ταῖς ἐμαῖσ⟨ιν ἂν⟩ τύχαις.
1201	τὸ περιπεταστὸν κἀ⟨να⟩πιμανδαλωτὸν ⟨ἄν⟩.
1202	τὸν γὰρ χοᾶ ⟨νῦν⟩ πρῶτος ἐκπέπωκα ⟨γε⟩.
1215, 1217	προσλάβεσθ⟨ε μ'⟩, ὦ φίλοι/αι

One Triclinian reading which is linguistically apt is the addition of οὖν after ἐκεῖνο δ' in 1195 (see Denniston, *Particles*, 462). Adopting that, together with Porson's deletion of οἰμωκτὸν and Dindorf's of μοι, produces a verse corresponding to 1201. The fact that R has an erasure after ἐκεῖνο δ' might tempt one to wonder whether Triclinius, in this

1206	∪‒∪‒ ‒∪‒ ∪‒∪‒
1209	∪⏓∪‒ ∪⏓∪‒
1211	‒‒∪‒ ‒‒∪‒ ∪‒∪⌣‖
1213	‒‒∪‒ ‒‒∪‒ ∪‒∪⌣‖
1216–7	ia trim
	2 cr
1220–1	ia trim
	‒∪∪‒∪‒
	ia trim
	ia dim cat

instance, derived οὖν from a source now lost to us, rather than from his own ingenuity.

At 1207–8, the MSS offer the cola in the order given, with considerable variation in attribution to speakers. Elmsley, following those (other than RAΓB) which attribute μογερὸς ἐγώ to Dicaeopolis, supposed that Dicaeopolis here bestows a maudlin kiss on Lamachus, who bites him in retaliation. More recently, editors (with the exception of Sommerstein) have preferred the closely antiphonal arrangement of Lenting:

> Λ. στυγερὸς ἐγώ.
> Δ. τί με σὺ κυνεῖς;
> Λ. μογερὸς ἐγώ.
> Δ. τί με σὺ δάκνεις;

(See further, Page, *WS* 69 (1956), 124–5, Dover, *Maia* 15 (1963), 25 = *Greek and the Greeks* (1987), 305). At 1210, τῆς ἐν μάχῃ was deleted by Dindorf.

At 1226, Lamachus utters his last lamentation in a catalectic iambic tetrameter, and Dicaeopolis and the chorus finish the play with an exchange in the same metre, except that 1232 is only a dimeter. Σ *vet.*, although mutilated, confirms that the text on which the metrical note was based was the same as ours. None the less, Elmsley may well have been right in suspecting that something which could have completed the tetrameter, perhaps τήνελλα καλλίνικον, has been lost after σὴν χάριν. The repetition of the phrase could easily have led to its loss (cf. *Birds* 1755 ff. below).

Knights

SYNOPSIS

303–13 = 382–90	*Cretics.*
322–34 = 397–408	*Cretics, trochaic* tetrameters, *dactylic, iambic.* Exceptional correspondence of lecythion with glyconic.
551–64 = 581–94	*Iambo-choriambic* and *aeolo-choriambic* (asclepiadic and glyconic).
616–23 = 683–90	*Trochees* and *cretics.*
756–60 = 836–40	*Iambic* (catalectic tetrameters and euripideans).
973–84 = 985–96	*Aeolo-choriambic* (glyconic).
1111–20 = 1121–30 = 1131–40 = 1141–50	The chorus and Demus: *Aeolo-choriambic* (telesillean).
1264–73 = 1290–9	*Dactylo-epitrite.*

With few characters and little diversity of incident, *Knights* depends heavily on the interchange of speech, song, and recitative for variety and pace. The first, second, fourth and fifth songs are in metres predominant in *Ach.*: cretic, trochaic, and iambic, with a few dactyls. Dochmiacs are absent from the play: neither the chorus nor any of the characters gives way to the kind of uncontrolled emotion typically expressed in that metre.

In the play as it stands, the last song is in pure dactylo-epitrite, the

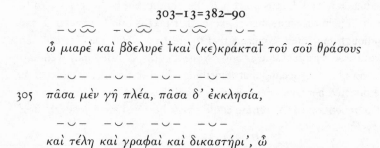

303–13=382–90

ὦ μιαρὲ καὶ βδελυρὲ †καὶ (κε)κράκτα† τοῦ σοῦ θράσους

305 πᾶσα μὲν γῆ πλέα, πᾶσα δ' ἐκκλησία,

καὶ τέλη καὶ γραφαὶ καὶ δικαστήρι', ὦ

only one of its kind in Aristophanes. As a metre common in Pindar's epinicians, dactylo-epitrite is surely chosen for its appropriateness to the social distinction and equestrian interests of the chorus.

The question remains of why aeolo-choriambic and iambo-choriambic feature so extensively in the play. At *Ol.* 1. 101–2, Pindar speaks of celebrating Hieron ἱππίῳ νόμῳ | Αἰοληΐδι μολπᾷ, and at *Pyth.* 2. 69 he mentions τὸ Καστόρειον . . . ἐν Αἰολίδεσσι χορδαῖς which he proposes to send to Hieron. Wilamowitz (*Pindaros*, 234) took ἵππιος νόμος in *Ol.* 1 to be a technical, musical term. That idea is rejected by Adolf Köhnken (*CQ* 24 (1974), 204), who prefers to see a reference to the theme and subject-matter of the poem. Αἰοληΐδι μολπᾷ and Αἰολίδεσσι χορδαῖς are, however, certainly technical, and *Ol.* 1 is, indeed, in a version of aeolo-choriambic. That *Pyth.* 2 is also in that metre is less significant, as the Καστόρειον mentioned at 69 is a different poem. Aeolic metre was, of course, widely used in all sorts of poetry in the fifth century, and Pindar himself did not confine his use of it to equestrian subjects. *Nem.* 3, composed for a pancratiast, is in aeolic metre, and said by Pindar to be so. But the fact that the poet chooses to draw attention to his use of it both for his poem in praise of Hieron and Poseidon Ἵππιος and for his 'Castor-song' suggests some special appropriateness. The metrical similarities between the parabasis-song in this play and Sophocles' 'Colonus-song' (*OC* 668–719) are discussed below (on 551 ff. = 581 ff.). None of this, of course, is more than suggestive.

The play as we have it ends abruptly and in iambic trimeters. There is not even an indication, as at the end of *Ach.*, that the chorus goes off singing. The conclusion that the end of the play is lost is hard to escape.

      4 cr
ἦν ἄρα πυρός †ἔτερα θερμότερα καὶ λόγων

      4 cr
ἐν πόλει τῶν ἀναιδῶν ἀναιδέστεροι·

      10 cr
385   καὶ τὸ πρᾶγμ' ἦν ἄρ' οὐ φαῦλον ὧδ' – ∪ –

‒∪‿ ‒∪‒   ‒∪‿ ‒∪‒

βορβοροτάραξι καὶ τὴν πόλιν ἅπασαν ἡ-

‒∪‿ ‒∪⌣ ‖

310   μῶν ἀνατετυρβακώς,

311–13   tro tetram cat II

At 284, the slanging-match between the Paphlagonian and the Sausage-seller runs into a rapid-fire exchange of dimeters. At 297–8, the Sausage-seller interjects two dimeters, but the Paphlagonian gets the upper hand with eight trochaic metra to the Sausage-seller's four. Moreover, the formal need to end his speech with catalexis before the choral song gives a tone of decisiveness: rhythmically, he has had the last word. It is at this point that the chorus intervenes in song, with a burst of abuse in cretics rounded off by a pair of catalectic trochaic tetrameters, which serves at 313 and 390 to lead into a short exchange in the same metre between the Paphlagonian and the Sausage-seller and (at 319–21) Demosthenes. At 375 ff., before the antistrophe, it is Demosthenes who asserts predominance, in the same way as the Paphlagonian before the strophe, but even more forcefully, with a run of thirteen trochees ending in catalexis. The chorus's νῦν γὰρ ἔχεται μέσος at 388 confirms that their side is now winning.

This strophic pair is interwoven with another, 322 ff. = 397 ff. The strophe 303 ff. is divided from the strophe 322 ff. by eight trochaic tetrameters (314–21), while the two antistrophes, 382 ff. and 397 ff., are divided by six trochaic tetrameters. It is not clear where the change from song to recitative would have taken place in performance. At 310–11 there is no strong rhetorical division according to the conventions of modern punctuation, but in fact 304–10 is syntactically self-contained, and the relative clauses of 311–13 come as an addendum.

The first verse of the stanza is corrupt in both strophe and antistrophe. The scansion given is based on the first two metra of the strophe and the last two of the antistrophe. If that is correct, the chorus begins with a rush of resolved cretics, then produces a sequence of unresolved ones, and winds up, at least in the strophe, with alternate resolved and unresolved. For the pattern of three resolved cretics and one unresolved, compare *Ach.* 978 ff. = 990 ff., and see Introduction, p. 45. For the alter-

ἀλλ᾽ ἔπιθι καὶ στρόβει, μηδὲν ὀλίγον ποίει·

νῦν γὰρ ἔχεται μέσος.

389–90   tro tetram cat II

nation, see Aristophanes, *PCG* 348, 719. In the final (alternate) sequence, at least, correspondence between resolved and unresolved metra may be exact, but there is a textual problem. It would be rash to assume that the versions of these stanzas that appear in modern texts are what Aristophanes wrote, or, unfortunately, that we can be sure of what the pattern of resolution originally was.

In 303, καὶ κεκράκτα is the reading of all the MSS, except for A and the first hands of Γ and Θ. It was also the reading on which the metrical analysis of Σ *vet.* (303–11) was based:

ὦ μιαρὲ καὶ βδελυρέ
καὶ κεκράκτα τοῦ σοῦ θράσους

$- \cup \widetilde{\cup\cup} \quad - \cup \widetilde{\cup\cup}$
$- \cup - \cup - - \cup -$

Nor does Σ *vet.* show any awareness of correspondence either here or on 382–8. The corruption, then, is ancient. ΑΓ'Θ' offer καὶ κράκτα. With deletion of καὶ this produces an unresolved cretic, and, with change of accent to κράκτα (Meineke) has found favour with many editors. However, κράκτης is not attested in classical Greek (see Neil, ad loc.), and the reading κράκτα is, in all probability, a mistake by haplography (aided by Byzantine usage) in the common ancestor of ΑΓΘ. No wholly satisfactory solution has been proposed. The corresponding verse, 302, does not provide reliable help, since in its pre-Triclinian form it does not scan at all. The Tricliinian MSS insert γ᾽ after πυρός to produce $- \cup \widetilde{\cup\cup}$ $- \cup \widetilde{\cup\cup} \quad - \cup \widetilde{\cup\cup} \quad - \cup -$. As simple metrical first-aid, von Velsen's θ᾽ is preferable linguistically. The fact that Σ *vet.* scans the whole stanza as cretics suggests that the corruption here is relatively recent. A more serious problem, however, is that the antistrophe is at least one metron shorter than the strophe, and was so in the text on which Σ *vet.*'s analysis is based. The solution most favoured by editors is to assume a lacuna after ὧδ᾽ in 385. That is not, however, inevitably right. The colometry described by Σ *vet.*, three cretic trimeters followed by four dimeters, when applied to the surviving text, follows rhetorical division quite closely, except at 382–4, where the division seems perverse:

> καὶ λόγων ἐν πόλει τῶν ἀναι-
> δῶν ἀναιδέστεροι· καὶ τὸ πρᾶγμ᾽ . . .

322–34 = 397–408

‒ ∪ ‒   ‒ ∪ ‒   ‒ ∪ ‒   ‒ ∪ ‒   ‒ ∪|‒   ‒ ∪ ‒
ἆρα δῆτ᾽ οὐκ ἀπ᾽ ἀρχῆς ἐδήλους ἀναίδειαν, ἥπερ μόνη

‒ ∪ ‒   ‒ ∪ ⏒ ||
325 προστατεῖ [τῶν] ῥητόρων;

326–7   tro tetram cat II

‒ ∪ ∪   ‒ ∪ ∪   ‒ ∪ ∪   ‒ ∪ ∪
ἀλλ᾽ ἐφάνη γὰρ ἀνὴρ ἕτερος πολὺ

‒ ∪ ∪   ‒ ∪ ∪   ‒ ∪ ∪| ‒ ‒
σοῦ μιαρώτερος ὥστε με χαίρειν,

‒ ∪ ‒ ‒   ‒ ∪ ‒ ∪   ‒ ∪ ‒ ⏓   ‒ ∪ ⏒ ||
330 ὅς σε παύσει καὶ πάρεισι, δῆλός ἐστιν, αὐτόθεν

⏓ ‒ ∪ ‒   ∪ ‒ ∪ ‒
πανουργίᾳ τε καὶ θράσει

‒ ∪ ‒ ∪ ‒ ∪ ⏔ ||
‒ ∪ ‒ ∪ ∪ ‒ ∪ ‒ ||
καὶ κοβαλικεύμασιν.

333–4   ia tetram cat II

The chorus's second stanza shows more metrical variety, but the different types of metre are divided neatly into homogeneous sections in the manner typical of Aristophanes. Once again, the question of how the trochaic tetrameters in the stanza were delivered must remain open. The pair at 326–7 = 400–1, however, seem parenthetic, while 330 = 404 are integral to the sense.

This suggests the possibility that the maker of the division was not working from the text as we have it. Hermann's supplement καὶ ⟨λόγοι τῶν⟩ λόγων would make three intelligible 'trimeters'. So would a lacuna after πυρός: ἦν ἄρα πυρὸς ⟨∪ ⌣ –⟩ ἕτερα. At 385, ἦν ἄρ' is the reading of R Γ²M against the other MSS' οὐκ ἄρ' ἦν.

6 cr

ὡς δὲ πρὸς πᾶν ἀναιδεύεται κοὐ μεθίστησι τοῦ χρώματος

2 cr

τοῦ παρεστηκότος.

400–1   tro tetram cat II

4 da

ὦ περὶ πάντ' ἐπὶ πᾶσί τε πράγμασι

4 da

δωροδόκοισιν ἐπ' ἄνθεσιν ἵζων,

tro tetram cat

εἴθε φαύλως, ὥσπερ ηὗρες, ἐκβάλοις τὴν ἔνθεσιν.

ia dim

405   ᾄσαιμι γὰρ τότ' ἂν μόνον·

lec = glyc

"πῖνε πῖν' ἐπὶ συμφοραῖς."

407–8   ia tetram cat II

In both strophe and antistrophe the change to dactyls at 328 = 402 is marked by a clear break in sense and a heightening of emotional tone. One might compare the single dactylic (?) verse in a trochaeo-cretic stanza at *Ach.* 285 = 336. The reversal of rhythm from trochaic to iambic at 330–1 = 404–5 must have been striking in performance (Introduction, p. 35).

The correspondence of lecythion to glyconic at 332 = 406 is unique
and designed to admit the quotation from Simonides at 406 (see Page,
PMG 512). No conclusions about the nature of Greek rhythm should be
drawn from it.

At 325, all the MSS have τῶν ῥητόρων. Σ *vet.* (322a), however,
analyses 324–5 as four cretic dimeters, and so is based on a text that

$$551\text{--}64 = 581\text{--}94$$

$$-\cup\cup- \quad \cup-\cup|-$$

ἵππι' ἄναξ Πόσειδον, ᾧ

$$-\cup\cup- \quad \overline{\cup}-|\cup-$$

χαλκοκρότων ἵππων κτύπος

$$-\cup\cup- \quad \cup|-\cup-$$

καὶ χρεμετισμὸς ἀνδάνει

$$-\cup\cup- \quad \cup-\cup-$$

καὶ κυανέμβολοι θοαὶ

$$-\cup\cup- \quad \cup--$$

555   μισθοφόροι τριήρεις,

$$-\cup\cup- \quad \cup-\cup|-$$

μειρακίων θ' ἅμιλλα λαμ-

$$-\cup\cup- \quad \cup-\cup-$$

πρυνομένων ἐν ἅρμασιν

$$-\cup\cup- \quad \cup--$$

καὶ βαρυδαιμονούντων,

$$---\cup\cup--\cup\cup--$$

δεῦρ' ἔλθ' εἰς χορόν, ὦ χρυσοτρίαιν', ὦ

$$---\cup\cup--\cup\cup-\underset{\smile}{}\;||^{\text{H}}$$

560   δελφίνων μεδέων Σουνιάρατε,

$$-\underset{\smile}{}-\cup\cup-\cup-$$

ὦ Γεραίστιε παῖ Κρόνου,

did not have it. τῶν was introduced before the time of Triclinius (322b), who analyses 325 as a 'trochaic hephthemimer' ($- \cup - \times \quad - \cup -$). The interpolation could easily have been made accidentally by someone with a poor ear, perhaps accustomed to mention of οἱ ῥήτορες (e.g. Plato, *Apol.* 32c, Demosthenes 18. 170).

cho ia dim
ὦ πολιοῦχε Παλλάς, ὦ

+ cho ia dim
τῆς ἱερωτάτης ἀπα-

+ cho ia dim
σῶν πολέμῳ τε καὶ ποιη-

+ cho ia dim
ταῖς δυνάμει θ' ὑπερφερού-

+ arist
585 σης μεδέουσα χώρας,

cho ia dim
δεῦρ' ἀφικοῦ λαβοῦσα τὴν

+ cho ia dim
ἐν στρατιαῖς τε καὶ μάχαις

arist
ἡμετέραν ξυνεργὸν

asclepiad cat (ion?)
Νίκην, ἢ χορικῶν ἐστιν ἑταίρα

+ asclepiad cat (ion?)
590 τοῖς τ' ἐχθροῖσι μεθ' ἡμῶν στασιάζει.

glyc
νῦν οὖν δεῦρο φάνηθι· δεῖ

$- \underset{\smile}{\ } - \smile \smile - \smile -$

Φορμίωνί τε φίλτατ᾽ ἐκ

$- - - \smile \smile - \smile -$

τῶν ἄλλων τε θεῶν Ἀθη-

$- - - \smile \smile - \smile \ |||$

ναίοις πρὸς τὸ παρεστός.

The parabasis-song of the Knights, the representatives of true patriotism and civic decency, is a hymn to Poseidon (in the strophe) and Athene (in the antistrophe). The stanza falls into four sections, of which the first two are constructed metrically in the same way: a sequence of choriambo-iambic dimeters, with their own catalectic form, the aristophanean, as clausula. The third section stands out rhythmically, forming a climax: in the strophe there is the invocation, in the antistrophe the reference to victory. Throughout the song the chorus maintain a delicate ambiguity of identification between their dramatic role as knights and their real-life character as chorus-men. It is in the third section, in both strophe and antistrophe, that they clearly step outside their dramatic role (εἰς χορόν 559, χορικῶν 589). The antistrophe brings together city, chorus, and poet. The stanza ends with the same simple structure of repeated acatalectic colon with its own catalectic form as clausula (Introduction, pp. 22–5), but this time the colon is glyconic.

The formal resemblance of this song to the parabasis-song of *Clouds* (563–74 = 595–606), a hymn to four gods, is evident (cf. Fraenkel, *Beobachtungen*, 191 ff.). The hymn to Athene at *Thesm.* 1136 ff., with its rhythmically contrasting climax in the fourth section, also invites comparison. The paean to Dionysus of Philodamus of Scarphaea (J. U. Powell, *Collectanea Alexandrina*, 167), a poem composed around 330, also has a marked resemblance to this song, as its first editor, Weil, observed (*BCH* 19 (1895), 411):

$- \smile \smile - \quad \smile - \smile -$

$- \smile \smile - \quad \smile - \smile -$

$- \smile \smile - \quad \smile - \smile -$

$- \smile \smile - \quad \smile - -$

$- - - \smile \smile - - \smile \smile - -$

+ glyc

γὰρ τοῖς ἀνδράσι τοῖσδε πά-

+ glyc

ση τέχνῃ πορίσαι σε νί-

+ pher

κην εἴπερ ποτὲ καὶ νῦν.

$$-\times-\cup\cup-\cup-$$
$$-\times-\cup\cup\underset{\smile}{\cup}\cup\underset{\smile}{\cup}\cup--$$
$$-\times-\cup\cup-\cup-$$
$$-\times-\cup\cup-\cup-$$
$$-\times-\cup\cup--$$

ephymnium: $\cup\cup--\cup\cup--$

$$---\cup\cup-\cup-$$
$$---\cup\cup--$$

The fifth colon,

εὐοῖ ὦ Ἰόβακχ᾽, ὦ ἰὲ Παιάν

$$---\cup\cup--\cup\cup--,$$

is, like the first colon of the ephymnium,

ἰὲ Παιάν, ἴθι σωτήρ

$$\cup\cup--\cup\cup--,$$

a recurrent invocation. The apparently unambiguous ionic form of the latter led Fraenkel to conclude that $---\cup\cup--\cup\cup--$ both in the paean and in *Knights* 559–60=589–90 must be ionic too. But this is a dangerous conclusion to draw from a single line of a poem composed so long after the golden age of Greek choral lyric. The colon is of a type not uncommonn in Sophocles in contexts which suggest aeolo-choriambic and iambo-choriambic affiliations (Introduction, p. 72). That traditional hymn-forms lie behind the compositions of both Aristophanes and Philodamus is less dubious, although it is still worth reflecting that Philodamus was clearly an educated man, and such literary amateurs usually follow literary models. It is also interesting to compare the constituents of Aristophanes' stanza with Sophocles' song in praise of Colonus at *OC* 668–719, a poem which has something of the character of a hymn to Poseidon and Athene. The first strophe there is a highly sophisticated version of the same type of four-section choriambic stanza as *Knights* 551 ff. = 581 ff., with a passage in other metres (dactylic and iambic) making up the third section (see further, Introduction, p. 25). Sophocles' second strophe combines iambic with the same type of choriambic sequence as *Knights* 559–60 = 589–90:

$$- - - \cup\cup - - \cup\cup - - \cup\cup - -$$
$$- - - \cup\cup - - \cup\cup - - \cup\cup - - \cup\cup - -$$
$$\cup - \cup - \quad - \cup - \quad \cup - \smile \ \|$$
$$- - \cup - \quad \cup - \cup -$$
$$\cup - \cup - \quad - \cup - \quad \cup - -$$
$$- - - \cup\cup - - \cup\cup - -$$
$$\underset{=}{\cup} - \cup - \quad \overset{\frown\frown}{}\cup - \quad \cup - -$$
$$- - - \cup\cup - - \cup\cup - -$$

616–23=683–90

$$- \cup - \cup \quad - \cup| - \cup \quad - \cup \underset{\frown\frown}{}\cup \quad - \smile \ \| \, \text{н}$$

νῦν ἄρ’ ἄξιόν γε πᾶσίν ἐστιν ἐπολολύξαι.

$$- \cup \overset{\frown}{\smile} \quad - \cup \overset{\frown}{\smile} \quad - \cup \overset{\frown}{\smile} \quad - \cup -$$

ὦ καλὰ λέγων, πολὺ δ’ ἀμείνον’ ἔτι τῶν λόγων

$$- \cup \overset{\frown}{\smile} \quad - \cup - \quad - \cup - \cup \quad - \cup -$$

ἐργασάμεν’ εἴθ’ ἐπέλθοις ἅπαντά μοι σαφῶς·

$$- \cup - \quad - \cup -$$

620 ὡς ἐγώ μοι δοκῶ

$$- \cup - \cup \quad - \cup - - \quad - \cup - \overset{\smile}{} \quad - \cup - \overset{\smile}{}$$

κἂν μακρὰν ὁδὸν διελθεῖν ὥστ’ ἀκοῦσαι. πρὸς τάδ’, ὦ βέλ-

$$- \cup - - \quad - | \cup - \underset{=}{\cup} \quad - \cup - \cup \quad - \cup - \ \|$$

τιστε, θαρρήσας λέγ’, ὡς ἅπαντες ἡδόμεσθά σοι.

In the strophe of this song the chorus hail the news that the Sausage-seller has triumphed over the Paphlagonian in Council, while the antistrophe follows the victor's narration of how it was done. The song opens with a trochaic verse of congratulation, separated from what follows by rhetorical pause, verse-end, and double syncopation. One may surmise that the final spondaic metron, especially if delivered in

⏑ – ⏑ ⏑ – ⏑ –

– – – ⏑ ⏑ – ⏑ –

– – – ⏑ ⏑ – –

The use of these rhythms in two songs infused with patriotic cult association, despite the difference of stylistic level, seems more than accidental.

551–4 and 581–3 are preserved in *P. Berol.* 13929 + *P. Berol.* 21105 of the fourth century AD. The fragments are extensive enough to show that the colometry was, not surprisingly, that described in *Σ vet.* (551b) and given above. The song is free of textual problems. At 557, R alone of the pre-Triclinian MSS preserves the metrically necessary ephelcystic *ν* of ἅρμασιν.

       3 tro   sp
   πάντα τοι πέπραγας οἷα χρὴ τὸν εὐτυχοῦντα·

       4 cr
   ηὗρε δ' ὁ πανοῦργος ἕτερον πολὺ πανουργίαις

       2 cr + lec
685–6 μείζοσι κεκασμένον καὶ δόλοισι ποικίλοις

       2 cr
687   ῥήμασίν θ' αἱμύλοις.

       7 tro + cr
   ἀλλ' ὅπως ἀγωνιεῖ φρόντιζε τἀπίλοιπ' ἄριστα·

689–90   συμμάχους δ' ἡμᾶς ἔχων εὔνους ἐπίστασαι πάλαι.

the rhythm ⌣ ⌣ ⌣, will have had a particular appropriateness to ἐπολολύξαι. The rest of the stanza is made up of a cretic section and a trochaic section. However, the lecythion which forms the second limb of the dicolon at 619 = 685 introduces trochaic rhythm just before the close of the cretic section. In the strophe, the chorus pass from congratulation to inviting the Sausage-seller to tell his story. In the antistrophe, their warnings and exhortations serve to introduce the triple contest which takes up most of the rest of the play. In content, the song belongs to a type characteristic of plays which make a major feature of a formal contest (see Dover, *Aristophanic Comedy*, 66–8).

In the MSS these stanzas have suffered from a number of minor omissions and transpositions. In 616, γε is Triclinian (LVp2AldB), ἐπολολύξαι is the reading of the majority of the MSS against RM (ὀλο-) and Vp3 (ἀπολο-). Σ *vet.* (616) describes the verse as an acatalectic

$$756{-}60 = 836{-}40$$

‒ ‒ ∪|‒   ⏕ ‒|∪ ‒| ⏒ ‒ ∪ ‒   ∪ ‒ ⏗ ‖
νῦν δή σε πάντα δεῖ κάλων ἐξιέναι σεαυτοῦ,

‒ ‒ ∪|‒   ⏕ ‒ ∪ ‒| ‒ ∪ ‒   ∪ ‒ ‒
καὶ λῆμα θούριον φορεῖν καὶ λόγους ἀφύκτους,

∪ ‒ ∪ ‒   ⏕ ‒ ∪ ‒| ‒ ∪ ‒   ∪ ‒ ‒
ὅτοισι τόνδ᾽ ὑπερβαλεῖ. ποικίλος γὰρ ἀνὴρ

‒ ‒ ∪ ‒   ⏕ ‒ ∪ ‒| ‒ ‒ ∪ ‒| ∪ ‒ ⏗ ‖
κἀκ τῶν ἀμηχάνων πόρους εὐμήχανος πορίζειν.

‒ ‒ ∪ ‒   ⏒ ‒ ∪ ‒| ‒ ‒ ∪|‒   ∪ ‒ ⏘ ‖‖
760   πρὸς ταῦθ᾽ ὅπως ἕξει πολὺς καὶ λαμπρὸς εἰς τὸν ἄνδρα.

The strophe of this song follows the episode of the introduction of Demus (which is in iambic trimeters) and precedes the first instalment of the contest between the Paphlagonian and the Sausage-seller before the assembly (which is in catalectic anapaestic tetrameters). It is the chorus that introduces anapaests, with a pair of verses (760–1). The scene closes with a sort of shared pnigos of twenty-four metra (824–35), in which the Sausage-seller gets the last word. In the antistrophe, the chorus looks forward with some confidence to his future accession to power. The song is followed, again, by two verses from the chorus in which they introduce the metre of the next instalment of the contest: catalectic iambic tetrameters.

The song itself is very close to recitative: the first, fourth, and fifth verses are catalectic tetrameters, the second and third dicola consisting of iambic dimeter and ithyphallic, a verse called 'euripidean' by

trochaic trimeter, which is neither what we have in the pre-Triclinian MSS, nor what we want. At 617 ἀμείνον᾿ is Bergler's emendation for the MSS᾿ ἄμεινον and, at 618, ἐργασάμεν᾿ Bentley's for εἰργασμέν᾿. At 683, τοι is peculiar to R, and suits the personal style of address (see Denniston, *Particles*, 539–40). The other MSS have δή. At 687, αἱμύλοις is a good Triclinian reading (LVp2AldB) for αἱμυλίοις. At 623 (ἡδόμεσθα for ἡδόμεθα), and 689 (ἡμᾶς ἔχων for ἔχων ἡμᾶς), VE share the metrically necessary readings with the Triclinian MSS.

>ia tetram cat
>ὦ πᾶσιν ἀνθρώποις φανεὶς μέγιστον ὠφέλημα,
>
>euripid
>ζηλῶ σε τῆς εὐγλωττίας. εἰ γὰρ ὧδ᾿ ἐποίσει,
>
>euripid
>μέγιστος Ἑλλήνων ἔσει, καὶ μόνος καθέξεις
>
>ia tetram cat
>τὰν τῇ πόλει τῶν συμμάχων τ᾿ ἄρξεις ἔχων τρίαιναν,
>
>ia tetram cat
>840 ἢ πολλὰ χρήματ᾿ ἐργάσει σείων τε καὶ ταράττων.

Hephaestion (Cons. 53. 6 cf. *Wasps* 248–72, *Lys.* 256 ff. = 271 ff.). All the verses have diaeresis after the opening iambic dimeter. Only in the fourth verse of the antistrophe is there elision at this point.

At 759, εὐμήχανος πορίζειν is Bentley's emendation for the MSS's εὐμηχάνους πορίζων.

The metrician whose work is preserved here in Σ vet. failed to observe correspondence in this song. Indeed, he overlooked the antistrophe completely, describing 836–910 as 75 catalectic trochaic tetrameters. 756–60 is described (Σ vet. 756a) as '5 stichoi', but the dicola at 757–8 are correctly identified. Triclinius' description of 756–60 shows his indebtedness to Hephaestion. He uses the term 'euripidean' for 757–8, and notes in illustration the same verse of Euripides. Like Σ vet., he misses the antistrophe. This gives us a measure of the lack of finesse of ear of the metrician of Σ vet., and of the reliance of Triclinius upon him.

973–84 = 985–96

$$- \smallsmile - \cup \cup - \cup -$$
ἥδιστον φάος ἡμέρας

$$- - - \cup \cup - \cup -$$
ἔσται τοῖσι παροῦσι καὶ

$$- - - \cup \cup - \cup -$$
975 †τοῖσιν ἀφικνουμένοισιν†

$$- \cup - \cup \cup - -$$
ἢν Κλέων ἀπόληται.

$$- - - \cup \cup - \cup -$$
καίτοι πρεσβυτέρων τινῶν

$$- - - \cup \cup - \cup -$$
οἵων ἀργαλεωτάτων

$$- - - \cup \cup - \cup -$$
ἐν τῷ δείγματι τῶν δικῶν

$$- \smallsmile - \cup \cup - -$$
980 ἤκουσ' ἀντιλεγόντων,

$$- - - \cup \cup - \cup -$$
ὡς εἰ μὴ 'γένεθ' οὗτος ἐν

$$- \smallsmile - \cup \cup - \cup -$$
τῇ πόλει μέγας, οὐκ ἂν ἤ-

$$- \smallsmile - \cup \cup - \cup -$$
στην σκεύει δύο χρησίμω,

$$- - - \cup \cup - \frown ||\!|$$
δοῖδυξ οὐδὲ τορύνη.

The contest in catalectic iambic tetrameters (843–910) also ends with a shared pnigos, this time in iambic (911–40), in which, again, the Sausage-seller gets the last word (at considerable length). The chorus do not, however, sing at this point. They merely express their approval very briefly and in prose. In the short scene in iambic trimeters that

glyc
985 ἀλλὰ καὶ τόδ' ἔγωγε θαυ-
+ glyc
μάζω τῆς ὑομουσίας

+ glyc
αὐτοῦ· φασὶ γὰρ αὐτὸν οἱ

+ pher
παῖδες οἳ ξυνεφοίτων,

glyc
τὴν Δωριστὶ μόνην ἂν ἁρ-

+ glyc
990 μόττεσθαι θαμὰ τὴν λύραν,

+ glyc
ἄλλην δ' οὐκ ἐθέλειν μαθεῖν·

+ pher
κᾆτα τὸν κιθαριστὴν

glyc
ὀργισθέντ' ἀπάγειν κελεύ-

+ glyc
ειν, ὡς ἁρμονίαν ὁ παῖς

+ glyc
995 οὗτος οὐ δύναται μαθεῖν

+ pher
ἢν μὴ Δωροδοκιστί.

follows, the contest seems about to come to an end when Demus proposes to dismiss the Paphlagonian from his stewardship and substitute
the Sausage-seller. An excuse is, however, devised to produce one more
instalment. The contestants have gone indoors to fetch their oracles,
when the chorus bursts into song in anticipation of the destruction of—

Cleon. This is the only mention of Cleon by name in the play. The audience can have had no doubt about whom the Paphlagonian was meant to represent, but the explicit identification makes a climax, and also makes the song into a self-contained anti-Cleon ditty suitable for performance at drinking-parties (Introduction, p. 10).

Metrically, the song is aeolo-choriambic at its simplest, which is consistent with the intention that it should catch on. The stanza falls into three sections, each made up of three glyconics and a pherecratean (Introduction, p. 22). The first colon is said by Σ *vet.* (973c) to be a quotation from Euripides. There is no hiatus (or *brevis in fine versus*)

$$1111-1120 = 1121-1130 = 1131-1140 = 1141-1150$$

$- - \cup \cup - \cup -$

X. ὦ Δῆμε, καλήν γ᾽ ἔχεις

$- - \cup \cup - \cup -$

ἀρχήν, ὅτε πάντες ἄν-

$- - \cup \cup - \cup -$

θρωποι δεδίασί σ᾽ ὥσ-

$\underset{\smile}{} - \cup \cup - \underset{\smile}{} \parallel_{\text{H}}$

περ ἄνδρα τύραννον.

$- - \cup \cup - \cup -$

1115   ἀλλ᾽ εὐπαράγωγος εἶ,

$- - \cup \cup - \cup -$

θωπευόμενός τε χαί-

$- - \cup \cup - \cup -$

ρεις κἀξαπατώμενος,

$- - \cup \cup - \cup -$

πρὸς τόν τε λέγοντ᾽ ἀεὶ

$\underset{\smile}{} - \cup \cup - \cup -$

κέχηνας· ὁ νοῦς δέ σου

$\underset{\smile}{} - \cup \cup - -$

1120   παρὼν ἀποδημεῖ.

except at the end of 984 and 996, which tends to confirm that the song is really in two stanzas, not, as *Σ vet.* (973a) thought, in six.

Emendation at 975 is rendered problematic by uncertainty about who is meant by οἱ ἀφικνούμενοι. Cobet's εἰσαφικνουμένοις would mean temporary residents of some kind. Dobree's

$$\text{ἔσται τοῖσι παροῦσι }\langle\text{πᾶ-}$$
$$\text{σιν}\rangle\text{ καὶ τοῖς ἀφικνουμένοις}$$

leaves the matter open. Other, more complicated, solutions have been proposed.

tel
Χ. οὕτω μὲν ἂν εὖ ποιοῖς,

tel
εἴ σοι πυκνότης ἔνεστ᾽

+ tel
ἐν τῷ τρόπῳ, ὡς λέγεις,

+ reiz
τούτῳ πάνυ πολλή,

tel
1135   εἰ τούσδ᾽ ἐπίτηδες ὧσ-

+ tel
περ δημοσίους τρέφεις

+ tel
ἐν τῇ πυκνί, κᾆθ᾽ ὅταν

+ tel
μή σοι τύχῃ ὄψον ὄν,

tel
τούτων ὃς ἂν ᾖ παχύς,

reiz
1140   θύσας ἐπιδειπνεῖς.

‒ ‒ ◡ ◡ ‒ ◡ ‒

Δ. νοῦς οὐκ ἔνι ταῖς κόμαις

‒ ‒ ◡ ◡ ‒ ◡ ‒

ὑμῶν, ὅτε μ' οὐ φρονεῖν

◡̲ ‒ ◡ ◡ ‒ ◡ ‒

νομίζετ'· ἐγὼ δ' ἑκὼν

‒ ‒ ◡ ◡ ‒ ‒ ‖ ᴴ

ταῦτ' ἠλιθιάζω.

‒ ‒ ◡ ◡ ‒ ◡ ‒

1125   αὐτός τε γὰρ ἥδομαι

‒ ‒ ◡ ◡ ‒ ◡ ‒

βρύλλων τὸ καθ' ἡμέραν,

‒ ‒ ◡ ◡ ‒ ◡ ‒

κλέπτοντά τε βούλομαι

◡̲ ‒ ◡ ◡ ‒ ◡ ‒

τρέφειν ἕνα προστάτην·

‒ ‒ ◡ ◡ ‒ ◡ ‒

τοῦτον δ' ὅταν ᾖ πλέως,

‒ ‒ ◡ ◡ ‒ ◡̲ ‖‖‖

1130   ἄρας ἐπάταξα.

This duet fills the time while the Sausage-seller and the Paphlagonian prepare competing treats for Demus. The chorus and Demus are alone together on stage, and Demus reveals that his senility is not as complete as it seems, and is, indeed, part of a strategy for exploiting the politicians who think that *they* are exploiting *him*. The song is highly significant in the play (and unique in Aristophanes) in offering an interpretation of the action which the audience would otherwise have no reason to think of. It can be seen as providing an alternative dénouement, more plausible than the return to old Athens and the rejuvenation of Demus.

The metre is, again, aeolo-choriambic, and almost as simple as in the preceding song. Instead of glyconic and pherecratean, Aristophanes uses the telesilean with its own catalectic form, the reizianum. It can be inter-

        tel
Δ. σκέψασθε δέ μ', εἰ σοφῶς

        tel
   αὐτοὺς περιέρχομαι

        + tel
   τοὺς οἰομένους φρονεῖν

        + reiz
   κἄμ' ἐξαπατύλλειν.

        tel
1145 τηρῶ γὰρ ἑκάστοτ' αὐ-

        + tel
   τοὺς οὐδὲ δοκῶν ὁρᾶν

        + tel
   κλέπτοντας· ἔπειτ' ἀναγ-

        + tel
   κάζω πάλιν ἐξεμεῖν

        tel
   ἅττ' ἂν κεκλόφωσί μου,
        reiz
1150 κἠμὸν καταμηλῶν.

preted as four stanzas, or as two stanzas divided between the singers. There is rather less synartesis between cola in Demus' part. The pattern based on his verses alone would be:

$$-- \cup \cup - \cup -$$
$$-- \cup \cup - \cup -$$
$$\underset{\smile}{} - \cup \cup - \cup -$$
$$-- \cup \cup - -$$
$$-- \cup \cup - \cup -$$
$$\quad -- \cup \cup - \cup -$$
$$-- \cup \cup - \cup -$$
$$\underset{\smile}{} - \cup \cup - \cup -$$
$$-- \cup \cup - \cup -$$
$$-- \cup \cup - -$$

Whether this difference is rhythmically significant or not we do not
know. For a telesillean song, compare *Peace* 1329 ff. and *Ecc.* 289 ff. =
300 ff.

1127–41 is preserved in *P. Mich.* inv. 6035 of the 2nd–3rd
century AD (see A. Henrichs, *ZPE* 4 (1969), 216–18). There, the
chorus's stanza, 1131–40, and the first colon of Demus' stanza, 1141–50,
are both recessed by the space of seven letters in relation to the four

1264–73 = 1290–9

◡̆ – ◡ ◡|– ◡ ◡ –   ◡| – ◡ ◡ – ◡ ◡ –   ◡̆

1264–5 τί κάλλιον ἀρχομένοισιν ἢ καταπαυομένοισιν

– ◡ –   –   – ◡ ◡ – ◡ ◡ –   –

ἢ θοὰν ἵππων ἐλατῆρας ἀείδειν

– ◡ –   ◡̄   – ◡ –

μηδὲν εἰς Λυσίστρατον,

– ◡ –   –   – ◡ ◡ – ◡ ◡ –

μηδὲ Θούμαντιν τὸν ἀνέστιον αὖ

◡̄   – ◡ –   – | – ◡ –

λυπεῖν ἑκούσῃ καρδίᾳ;

– ◡ –   ◡̆   – ◡ ◡ – ◡ ◡ –

1270 καὶ γὰρ οὗτος[ι], ὦ φίλ' Ἄπολλον, ⟨ἀεὶ⟩

–   – ◡ ◡ – ◡ ◡ –̄

πεινῇ θαλεροῖς δακρύοις

◡̄   – ◡ ◡ – ◡ ◡ –

σᾶς ἁπτόμενος φαρέτρας

–   – ◡ |–   –   – ◡ –   ◡ – – |||

Πυθῶνι [ἐν] δίᾳ ⟨μὴ⟩ κακῶς πένεσθαι.

After the final defeat of the Paphlagonian, the chorus, alone on stage, fill
the time taken by the Sausage-seller to rejuvenate Demus indoors with
a second parabasis. The epirrhematic sections are in catalectic trochaic
tetrameters. The chorus maintain their dramatic character throughout,
and devote themselves to attacks on four people: Thumantis (ode),

preserved cola of 1121–30. This, perhaps, suggests an interpretation of the song as one strophic pair, rather than as four stanzas (as in Σ. *vet.*).

At 1118, R and the *Suda* (s. εὐπαράγωγος) have the metrically correct πρὸς τόν τε. The other MSS offer πρός τε τὸν, producing an accidental lecythion. At 1129, however, R alone is wrong with ὅταν δ᾽, where the other MSS and the papyrus offer δ᾽ ὅταν.

⏑D⏑D⏑
1290–1 ἦ πολλάκις ἐννυχίαισι φροντίσι συγγεγένημαι,

e–D–
καὶ διεζήτηχ᾽ ὁπόθεν ποτὲ φαύλως

e⏜e
ἐσθίει Κλεώνυμος.

e–D
φασὶ ⟨μὲν⟩ γὰρ αὐτὸν ἐρεπτόμενον

⏜e–e
1295 τὰ τῶν ἐχόντων ἀνέρων

e⏑D
οὐκ ἂν ἐξελθεῖν ἀπὸ τῆς σιπύης·

–D
τοὺς δ᾽ ἀντιβολεῖν ἂν ὁμῶς·

⏝D
ἴθ᾽, ὦ ἄνα, πρὸς γονάτων,

–e–e + ba (ia trim cat)
ἔξελθε καὶ σύγγνωθι τῇ τραπέζῃ.

Ariphrades (epirrheme), Cleonymus (antode), Hyperbolus (antepirrheme).

The ode and antode are in pure dactylo-epitrite, the only such stanzas in Aristophanes (Introduction, p. 89), and the first verses are, according to Σ *vet.* (1264b), adapted from Pindar (Snell–Maehler, fr. 89a). The song may be compared with *Ach.* 1150ff. = 1163ff. as an elaborate lampoon-song, depending for its effect on literary and musical allusion and parody. The choice of metre and the Pindaric reference suit the Knights' typically aristocratic interest in equitation. Verbal parody is confined to the beginning of the stanza, where the allusion to Pindar at 1264–5 is balanced by a probable allusion to Euripides at 1290–1 (Σ *vet.* 1290b, cf. *Frogs* 932–3). There is an interesting discussion of the song by Fraenkel (*Beobachtungen*, 204–7). Within the stanza there is no indication of verse-end.

The text has suffered some minor mutilations, apparently after the composition of Σ *vet.* (1264a). In 1270, the deletion of ι and the supplement $\dot{\alpha}\epsilon\dot{\iota}$ are Dindorf's and at 1273 $[\dot{\epsilon}\nu]$ $\delta\dot{\iota}\alpha$ $\langle\mu\dot{\eta}\rangle$ is also his. At 1294, $\mu\dot{\epsilon}\nu$ is Bentley's supplement. 1271 = 1297 is described by Σ *vet.* as a 'prosodiac dodecaseme' which confirms $--\cup\cup-\cup\cup-$. Zacher's combination of $\ddot{\alpha}\nu$ from RM ($\ddot{\alpha}\nu$ $\dot{\delta}\mu o\dot{\iota}\omega s$) with $\ddot{o}\mu\omega s$ from AΘ ($\dot{\alpha}\lambda\lambda'$ $\ddot{o}\mu\omega s$) restores correspondence at 1297. Triclinius seems to have noticed the failures of correspondence, but his attempts at emendation are inept. At 1268, LAldB omit $\tau\acute{o}\nu$. At 1270, LAld (at least) omit $\ddot{\omega}$. At 1273, LVp2AldB read $\dot{\epsilon}\nu$ $\delta\iota\dot{\alpha}$ $\tau\dot{o}$ $\kappa\alpha\kappa\hat{\omega}s$ and at 1296 LVp2AldB omit $\tau\hat{\eta}s$. There is no Triclinian metrical scholium. Triclinius, then, registered the failures of correspondence, perhaps by syllable-counting, but either did not have or could not interpret Σ *vet.*

Clouds

SYNOPSIS

275–90=298–313	*Dactyls.*
457–75	*Trochees, dactyls,* modulating through syncopated *iambo-cretic* to *dactylo-epitrite.*
510–17	*Anapaests,* introducing *iambo-choriambic.*
563–74=595–606	*Iambo-choriambic, dactylic,* then again *iambo-choriambic,* modulating into *aeolo-choriambic.*
700–6=804–13, 706–7	*Iambo-choriambic,* with colon $- \cup - \cup \cup - \cup \cup -$. Final section of strophe missing.
949–58=1024–33	*Iambo-choriambic.*
1154–70	Strepsiades: *Iambic* trimeters, with some syncopation, two *hemiepe, dochmiacs, anapaests.*
1206–13	Strepsiades: *Ionic,* introducing syncopated *iambic.*
1303–10=1311–20	*Iambic* (with lecythia) and one *aeolo-choriambic* colon (reizianum). Problems of correspondence.
1345–50=1391–6	*Iambic* trimeters and *aeolo-choriambic* (reiziana). Problems of correspondence.

The chorus of *Clouds* is consistently dignified and detached: it never succumbs to emotional excitement and is never involved in any rough and tumble. It does not use metres associated either with virility and aggression (cretics) or with passion (dochmiacs).

The metrical style and rhythms of the lyric mark out the play very clearly into three sections. In the two songs that precede the parabasis and Strepsiades' full enrolment as Socrates' pupil (275 ff. = 298 ff. and 457 ff.), the chorus uses metres with dignified associations, and, as far as their metrical patterns are concerned, both songs (except, perhaps, for the trochees at 457) would be compatible with contemporary tragedy.

The κομμάτιον (510–17) that introduces the parabasis moves from the anapaests usual in such a context into iambo-choriambic, the rhythm which dominates the chorus's songs until 1033, the mid-point of the contest between the two Λόγοι. In our version of the play, this contest is not rounded off by a lyric stanza. The chorus limits itself to a single, menacing euripidean dicolon:

χωρεῖτε νῦν. οἶμαι δέ σοι ταῦτα μεταμελήσειν.

Σ *vet.* (Vb3Vs1) says, with reference to the first version of *Clouds*, that five lines of lyric are missing here (See further Dover, *Clouds*, pp. lxxxv–lxxxvi, Holwerda, *Mnemosyne*, 11 (1958), 38 ff.). The lyric stanza that would have rounded off this section of the play seems never to have been provided for the revised version.

What special associations, if any, iambo-choriambic may have had to account for its dominance in this part of the play we do not know. The metre is relatively more common in Aristophanes than in tragedy, but it is by no means specifically comic. Particularly striking, by contrast, is the almost complete absence of aeolo-choriambic, which is so often associated with iambo-choriambic (Introduction, pp. 81–2), but here makes only one brief appearance at the end of the parabasis-hymn. As distinct from its accompanying lyric, the parabasis proper is, of course, in a variety of aeolo-choriambic, eupolideans (See Parker, *PCPS* 214 (1988), 115–22). Whatever the significance of the choice of metre, the whole development of the plot from the moment when Strepsiades enters the Reflectory to that when Pheidippides goes the same way is punctuated by songs which make up a set of variations on a single rhythm.

After the brief second parabasis (1115–30), the chorus watches in silence while wrong appears to triumph for the space of over 170 lines. Within this episode, Strepsiades' two short, paratragic songs ingeniously provide musical diversion and variety.

In their last two songs (1303 ff. = 1311 ff. and 1345 ff. = 1391 ff.), the Clouds declare themselves frankly on the side of conventional morality. Again, the two songs are variations on the same rhythmic theme: this time, iambic, with occasional reiziana. Both songs are simple, and keep strictly within the limits of comic metrical style. After 1396 the chorus sing no more, and only intervene through their leader's curt explanation of their behaviour (1454–5, 1458–61) and her bleak, departing anapaestic tetrameter:

ἡγεῖσθ' ἔξω· κεχόρευται γὰρ μετρίως τό γε τήμερον ἡμῖν.

275–90 = 298–313

$- \cup \cup - \cup \cup - \| $ ʜ

275   ἀέναοι Νεφέλαι,

$- - \quad -|\cup\cup \quad -|\cup\cup \quad -\cup\cup| \quad - - \quad - -$

ἀρθῶμεν φανεραὶ δροσερὰν φύσιν εὐάγητον

$- \cup \cup \quad - \cup \cup \quad -|\cup \cup \quad - \cup \cup$

πατ|ρὸς ἀπ' Ὠκεανοῦ βαρυαχέος

$- \overline{\cup\cup} \quad - \underline{\overline{\cup\cup}} \quad -|\cup\cup \quad - \cup\cup \quad - \cup\cup \quad -|\cup\cup$

279–80   ὑψηλῶν ὀρέων κορυφὰς ἔπι δενδροκόμους, ἵνα

$- \cup\cup \quad -|\cup\cup \quad -|\cup\cup \quad - \cup\cup$

τηλεφανεῖς σκοπιὰς ἀφορώμεθα,

$- \overline{\cup\cup} \quad - \cup\cup \quad -|\underline{\overline{\cup\cup}} \quad - \cup\cup$

καρπούς τ' ἀρδομέναν ἱερὰν χθόνα,

$- \underline{\overline{\cup\cup}} \quad - \cup\cup \quad -|\cup\cup \quad - \cup\cup$

καὶ ποταμῶν ζαθέων κελαδήματα,

$- \overline{\cup\cup} \quad -|\cup\cup \quad - \cup\cup \quad - \cup\cup$

καὶ πόντον κελάδοντα βαρύβ|ρομον·

$- \cup\cup \quad - \cup\cup \quad - \cup\cup \quad -|\cup\cup \quad - \smile \|$

285–6   ὄμμα γὰρ αἰθέρος ἀκάματον σελαγεῖται

$- \cup\cup - \cup | - -$

μαρμαρέαισιν αὐγαῖς.

$- \cup\cup \quad - \cup\cup \quad -|\cup\cup \quad - \cup\cup$

ἀλλ' ἀποσεισάμεναι νέφος ὄμβριον

$- \cup\cup \quad - \cup\cup \quad -|\cup\cup \quad - \cup\cup$

ἀθανάτας ἰδέας ἐπιδώμεθα

$- - \cup\cup - \cup\cup| - - \|\|$

290   τηλεσκόπῳ ὄμματι γαῖαν.

Socrates' anapaestic invocation (263–74) is followed by the sound of
the chorus singing off stage. Strophe and antistrophe are separated by
a short burlesque exchange in anapaestic tetrameters between Socrates
and Strepsiades (291–7). The chorus do not actually enter until 327.

hem
παρθένοι ὀμβροφόροι,

da hex
299–300 ἔλθωμεν λιπαρὰν χθόνα Παλλάδος, εὔανδρον γᾶν

da tetram B
Κέκ|ροπος ὀψόμεναι πολυήρατον·

10 da
οὗ σέβας ἀρρήτων ἱερῶν, ἵνα μυστοδόκος δόμος

ἐν τελεταῖς ἁγίαις ἀναδείκνυται·

da tetram B
305 οὐρανίοις τε θεοῖς δωρήματα,

da tetram B
ναοί θ' ὑψερεφεῖς καὶ ἀγάλματα,

da tetram B
καὶ πρόσοδοι μακάρων ἱερώταται

da pent
εὐστέφανοί τε θεῶν θυσίαι θαλίαι τε

arist
310 παντοδαπαῖσιν [ἐν] ὥραις,

da tetram B
ἦρί τ' ἐπερχομένῳ Βρομία χάρις

da tetram B
εὐκελάδων τε χορῶν ἐρεθίσματα

paroem
καὶ μοῦσα βαρύβ|ρομος αὐλῶν.

The song, except for the clausular aristophanean (287=310) and, possibly, the very last colon, is in pure dactylic, and its closest metrical affinities are with Euripidean lyric (Introduction, pp. 51–2). At 315, Strepsiades refers to the song he has just heard as τοῦτο τὸ σεμνόν, and dactylic, the metre of epic, is indeed dignified in its associations. The diction, too, is dignified, featuring, in particular, lavish use of compound epithets. Dover (on 137) points out the tendency to verbal echo between strophe and antistrophe. There is also much correspondence of word-end. The epic metre brings with it, as usual, certain epic prosodic features: there are five examples of epic correption (τηλεσκόπῳ, παρθένοῐ, ἀναδείκνυτᾱι, κᾱι, ἱερώτατᾱι). Lengthening before mute and liquid (πατ|ρός, Κέκ|ροπος, βαρύβ|ρομος) belongs to high poetry rather than to colloquial Attic (Introduction, pp. 91–2).

From a literary point of view, the problem is whether the song is to be taken seriously, and if so, whether it is 'one of the most beautiful lyric passages in Attic literature' (C. Segal, *Arethusa* 2 (1969), 148) or merely inflated and trite, or whether it is parody (perhaps of the products of those κυκλίων χορῶν ἀσματοκάμπται whom the Clouds are said at 333 to nourish). The antistrophe at least, with its early intimations of a religious orthodoxy wholly at variance with Socrates' views, seems serious. The combination of parodic strophe with serious antistrophe is unparalleled in Aristophanes (see further M. Silk, *YCS* 26, (1980), 106–10 and Introduction, pp. 14–15). It is, however, possible that, in this instance, the metrical pattern was adaptable to both bogus and real solemnity.

The final colon of the stanza, $--\cup\cup-\cup\cup--$, is puzzling from the theoretical point of view. It can be called a 'paroemiac', but it is unlikely in this context to be anapaestic. Acephalous dactylic occurs in

457–475

$-\cup-\cup \quad -\cup-\cup \quad -\cup-\cup \quad -\cup-\cup$

X. λῆμα μὲν πάρεστι τῷδέ γ' οὐκ ἄτολμον ἀλλ' ἕτοιμον.

$-\cup-$

ἴσθι δ' ὡς

$-\cup\cup \quad -\cup\cup \quad -\cup\cup \quad -\cup\cup \quad -\cup \,\|$

460–1 ταῦτα μαθὼν παρ' ἐμοῦ κλέος οὐρανόμηκες

$-\cup- \quad \cup--$

ἐν βροτοῖσιν ἕξεις.

$\cup-\cup-$

Στ. τί πείσομαι;

Attic drama (Introduction, p. 54), and the same colon appears in a dactylo-iambic context at *OT* 154 = 162 (whether it is there interpreted as $\times - \cup \cup - \cup \cup - -$ depends on the scansion of ἵηιε). But there is no parallel for acephalous dactylic following on a trisyllabic dactyl ($- \cup \cup | \overline{\cup\cup} - \cup \cup$ . . .). Taking the colon as the dactylo-epitrite $\times - \cup \cup - \cup \cup - \times$ following . . . $- \cup \cup$ would involve *breve iuxta anceps*. That sequence is occasionally found, especially in transitions from dactylic to iambic. The closest parallel to this passage is *OT* 171–2 = 182–3 (Introduction, pp. 53–4). At any rate, this exotic rhythm brings a touch of sophistication to the stanza which, again, suggests tragic style.

At 287, μαρμαρέαισιν αὐγαῖς is the reading of V, whereas R and other pre-Triclinian MSS have μαρμαρέαις ἐν αὐγαῖς (equally an aristophanean, $- \cup \cup - \cup - -$). In the corresponding verse, 310, V shares παντοδαπαῖς ἐν ὥραις with the other pre-Triclinian MSS. The reading of the Triclinian MSS is μαρμαρέαισιν ἐν αὐγαῖς (LVv5Ald), while at 310 LAld (with E corr. and the 14th-c. Np2) have παντο-δαπαῖσιν ἐν ὥραις. These latter versions, which produce corresponding $- \cup \cup - \cup \cup - -$, are typical Triclinian regularizations. Both passages are linguistically better without ἐν, and the aristophanean is a common all-purpose clausula (Introduction, pp. 82–4). The text of 310 as printed follows Blaydes. At 299 too, some MSS interpolate a preposition: χθόνα is the reading of M4 and Triclinius (LAld), while the rest have ἐς χθόνα.

4 tro

cr

+ da pentam

ith

$\cup$ e (ia)

‒ ‒∪∪‒∪∪‒

X. τὸν πάντα χρόνον μετ᾽ ἐμοῦ

‒ ‒∪∪‒∪∪‒ ‒ ‒∪‒ ‒

465   ζηλωτότατον βίον ἀνθρώπων διάξεις.

‒∪∪‒∪∪‒ ∪ ‒∪∪‒∪∪‒

Στ. ἆρά γε τοῦτ᾽ ἄρ᾽ ἐγώ ποτ᾽ ὄψομαι; X. ὥστε γέ σου

‒ ‒∪∪‒∪∪‒ ∪ ‒∪‒ ‒

πολλοὺς ἐπὶ ταῖσι θύραις ἀεὶ καθῆσθαι,

‒∪∪‒∪∪‒ ‒ ‒∪∪‒∪∪‒

470–1 βουλομένους ἀνακοινοῦσθαί τε καὶ εἰς λόγον ἐλθεῖν

‒∪∪‒∪∪‒ ‒ ‒∪‒ ‒

πράγματα κἀντιγραφὰς πολλῶν ταλάντων,

‒∪∪‒∪∪‒ ‒ ‒∪∪‒∪∪‒ ‖‖‖

474–5 ἄξια σῇ φρενὶ συμβουλευσομένους μετὰ σοῦ.

The substantial anapaestic section (tetrameters ending in a long πνῖγος, 439–56) in which Socrates introduces the Clouds to Strepsiades is followed by a short duet between Strepsiades and the Clouds. The song marks his formal acceptance as the Clouds' protégé, and leads, through a pair of anapaestic tetrameters (476–7), into the short, propaedeutic dialogue between Socrates and Strepsiades (478–509).

Metrically, the stanza proceeds from trochaic and dactylic into true dactylo-epitrite, a metre of high lyric. There is no parallel in tragedy for the trochaic opening of the stanza, and that is probably to be seen as reflecting the comic context. For stanzas which move from a mixture of *iambic* and dactylic to datylo-epitrite, compare *Aj.* 172 ff. = 182 ff. and 221 ff. = 245 ff. In the lyric dialogues of tragedy, dactylo-epitrite lengths can lend themselves to situations where one partner in a duet is more emotional than the other (e.g. *Her.* 1184–8). Here, the chorus's tone is of exaltation rather than excitement. Their matter-of-fact opening in trochaic modulates into a dactylic burst, accompanied by epic phraseology. Strepsiades' first utterance is equivalent to an iambic metron, and could have been spoken, which would have made it as bathetic in rhythm as in diction. The Clouds' promise (464–5), however, makes him soar, briefly, into unambiguous song (466).

−D

−D−e−

D⌣D

−D⌣e−

D−D−

D−e−

D−D

At 466, the change of speaker within a dactylo-epitrite phrase
(− ⌣ ⌣|− ⌣ ⌣ −) is, I think, unparalleled (Cf. West, *GM* 135). *Σ vet.*
V51 (457 and 467) provides a full analysis of the stanza with verse-end at
that point:

Στ. ἆρά γε τοῦτ᾽ ἄρ᾽ ἐγώ ποτ᾽   − ⌣ ⌣ − ⌣ ⌣ − ⌣
        ὄψομαι;   − ⌣ − ‖ ʜ
X. ὥστε γέ σοῦ.   − ⌣ ⌣ −

The *Suda*'s ἐπόψομαι is at least worth mentioning: it produces a
straight dactylic sequence, with a change of spaeaker after the fourth
metron:

− ⌣ ⌣   − ⌣ ⌣   − ⌣ ⌣   − ⌣ ⌣| − ⌣ ⌣   −

The future of ἐφοράω is appropriate in prophetic expressions (*Ag.* 1246,
or, of something desirable, *Il.* 14. 145, *Od.* 20. 233). This would, however, disrupt the attractively neat pattern of varied dactylo-epitrite
verses at 462–75 (Introduction, p. 21).

At 471, V has εὐλόγους and the other pre-Triclinian MSS have ἐς
λόγους. ἐ(ἰ)ς λόγον in the Triclinian MSS restores the metre. Triclinius
may have been guided by the analysis of *Σ vet.* or, more probably, by his
own taste for uniform rhythm (− ⌣ − ⌣ . . . or − ⌣ ⌣ − ⌣ ⌣ . . .).

510–17

```
       – ⏑ ⏑ – –
```

510 ἀλλ᾽ ἴθι χαίρων

```
       – – – – |    – ⏑ ⏑ – –
```

τῆς ἀνδρείας οὕνεκα ταύτης.

```
       – ⏑ ⏑ – |    ⏑ – ⏑ –
```

εὐτυχία γένοιτο τἀν-

```
       – ⏑ ⌒·    ⏑ – –
```

θρώπῳ ὅτι προήκων

```
       – ⏑ ⏑ –    – ⏑ ⏑ –
```

εἰς βαθὺ τῆς ἡλικίας

```
       ⏑ – ⏑ – |    – ⏑ ⏑ –
```

515 νεωτέροις τὴν φύσιν αὐ-

```
       – – ⏑ – |    – – ⏑ –
```

τοῦ πράγμασι⟨ν⟩ χρωτίζεται

```
       – ⏑ ⏑ –    ⏑ – – |||
```

καὶ σοφίαν ἐπασκεῖ.

As Strepsiades, accompanied by Socrates, goes into the school, the chorus wish him well with the formula used for the same purpose at *Knights* 498, *Wasps* 1009, and *Peace* 729. In those three plays, the valedictory κομμάτιον is in anapaests throughout, and leads into the parabasis proper in anapaests. The parabasis which follows here is unique in Aristophanes in being in eupolideans:

$$\cdots\ \cdots -\times-\cup\cup-\quad\cdots\ \cdots-\times-\cup-$$

The κομμάτιον prepares the way by changing, after the first three metra, into iambo-choriambic, which shares both choriambic and iambic rhythms with the following verses. The ode and antode too are in iambo-choriambic.

At 512–13, R and some other MSS read γένοιτο τἀνθρώπῳ, while V, the *Suda* and LAld read γένοιτ᾽ ἀνθρώπῳ. Triclinius' colometry is, however, the same as that of R (not the very disturbed V). He either did not have or did not choose to follow the Σ *vet.* of Vs1 (512b), for there the first two cola are correctly described as anapaestic, while he devises a choriambic analysis.

an

an dim

cho ia dim

+ ith

2 cho

ia   cho dim

+ ia dim

arist

The chief problem of the stanza is 513. The scansion offered requires epic correption (-ρῷ ὅτι), which is very rare in iambo-trochaic in Aristophanes' lyric (see *Wasps* 1065, 1338, and Introduction, pp. 91–2). The alternative is to take the colon as $- \cup \cup - \cup - -$ (Triclinius and White). Metrically, this is attractive: the choriambo-iambic dimeter at 512 would then be followed by its own catalectic form. Prosodically, however, it is even more difficult, since it requires the scansion ὅτῑ π|ροήκων. Lengthening by mute and liquid is very rare in Aristophanes' lyric, except in dactylic and dactylo-epitrite (see, however, πέτ|ραν at 597 below, and Introduction p. 93), and can only take place within a word. ὅτι is prepositive, but only weakly so. It is occasionally found at the end of iambic trimeters in Sophocles and Aristophanes, though only once (*Eum.* 98) in Aeschylus (apart from *PV*. See E. C. Yorke, *CQ* 30 (1936), 153–4) and only very rarely in Euripides.

At 516, Hermann's addition of ephelcystic ν restores the metre. οὕνεκα for the MSS's εἵνεκα at 511 is Brunck's correction (see Barrett on *Hipp.* 453–6).

Clouds

563–74 = 595–606

‒ ‿ ‿ ‒   ‿ ‒ ‿ ‒

ὑψιμέδοντα μὲν θεῶν

‒ ‿ ‿ ‒   ‿ ‒ ‿ ‒

Ζῆνα τύραννον εἰς χορὸν

‒ ‿ ‿ ‒   ‿ ‒ ‒

565   πρῶτα μέγαν κικλήσκω·

‒ ‿ ‿ ‒   ‿ ‒ ‿ ‒

τόν τε μεγασθενῆ τριαί-

‒ ‿ ‿ ‒| ‒ ‿|‿ ‒   ‿ ‒ ‿ ‒

νης ταμίαν, γῆς τε καὶ ἁλμυρᾶς θαλάσ-

‒|‿ ‿ ‒   ‿ ‒ ⌣ ‖

σης ἄγριον μοχλευτήν·

‒ ‿ ‿   ‒ ‿ ‿| ‒ ‿ ‿   ‒|‿ ‿

καὶ μεγαλώνυμον ἡμέτερον πατέρ᾽,

‒ ‿ ‿| ‒ ‿ ‿   ‒|‿ ‿   ‒ ‿ ‿   ‒ ‒

570   Αἰθέρα σνμνότατον, βιοθρέμμονα πάντων·

‒ ‒ ‿ ‒   ‒ ‿ ‿ ‒

τόν θ᾽ ἱππονώμαν, ὃς ὑπερ-

⌣ ‒|‒ ‒ ‒|‿ ‿ ‒

λάμπροις ἀκτῖσιν κατέχει

‒ ⌣ ‒ ‿ ‿|‒ ‿ ‒

γῆς πέδον, μέγας ἐν θεοῖς

‒ ‒ ‒ ‿ ‿ ‒ ⌣ ‖‖‖

ἐν θνητοῖσί τε δαίμων.

The religious orthodoxy of the Clouds emerges strikingly in the ode and antode of the parabasis, an invocation to several gods. Metrically, the song has a strong resemblance to the parabasis-song of *Knights* (551 ff. = 581 ff.), another cletic hymn. Both songs begin with two sections in iambo-choriambic, followed by a third section in a distinctive rhythm (asclepiadic in *Knights*, dactylic in *Clouds*) and end in aeolo-

cho ia dim
595 ἀμφί μοι αὖτε, Φοῖβ᾽ ἄναξ

cho ia dim
Δήλιε, Κυνθίαν ἔχων

arist
ὑψικέρατα πέτ|ραν·

cho ia dim
ἤ τ᾽ Ἐφέσου μάκαιρα πάγ-

+ cho ia trim
χρυσον ἔχεις οἶκον ἐν ᾧ κόραι σε Λυ-

+ arist
600 δῶν μεγάλως σέβουσιν·

9 da
ἤ τ᾽ ἐπιχώριος ἡμετέρα θεός

αἰγίδος ἡνίοχος, πολιοῦχος Ἀθάνα,

ia cho dim
Παρνασσίαν θ᾽ ὃς κατέχων

+ pol
πέτραν σὺν πεύκαις σελαγεῖ

glyc
605 Βάκχαις Δελφίσιν ἐμπρέπων,

pher
κωμαστὴς Διόνυσος.

choriambic. The Clouds' song is, however, slightly more sophisticated metrically than the Knights'. The second section just avoids repeating the colon-forms of the first, and the final section makes a subtle transition from iambo-choriambic to glyconic through a polyschematist (see Introduction, p. 24).

Rhetorically, the song is highly formal: each god invoked has a

metrical section to him- or herself, and strophe is balanced against antistrophe with careful parallelism:

Strophe	Antistrophe
I Zeus (elder brother)	Apollo (brother)
II Poseidon (younger brother)	Artemis (sister)
III Aether (father of the chorus)	Athene (guardian of the city)
IV Helios (whose beams shine by day)	Dionysus (whose torches shine by night)

As in the Clouds' first song, there is verbal parallelism between strophe
and antistrophe: 569 ἡμέτερον = 601 ἡμετέρα, 572 ἀκτῖσιν κατέχει =
604 σὺν πεύκαις σελαγεῖ. There is also frequent correspondence of
word-end.

Metrically, the song is a careful composition in comic style, combining two major classes of metre in well-defined sections. The stanza
begins with a verse of three cola: two choriambo-iambic dimeters, with
their own catalectic form as clausula. The second verse repeats this
pattern, varied only by the addition of one choriamb. The preferred
colometry of *Σ vet.* (563a) at 566–8 = 598–600 is preserved in the antistrophe by R and by the 3rd c. AD papyrus, *PSI* 1171:

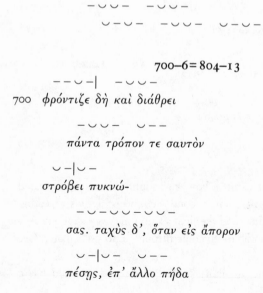

700–6 = 804–13

700   φρόντιζε δὴ καὶ διάθρει

πάντα τρόπον τε σαυτὸν

στρόβει πυκνώ-

σας. ταχὺς δ᾽, ὅταν εἰς ἄπορον

πέσῃς, ἐπ᾽ ἄλλο πήδα

Σ vet. seems, however, to envisage an alternative colometry, which actually appears in the strophe in R:

$$- \cup \cup - \cup - \cup - - \cup \cup -$$
$$- \cup \cup - \cup - \cup - - \cup \cup - \cup - -$$

This latter division, which follows word-end a little more closely, was adopted by Triclinius, and has remained entrenched in printed texts, in spite of the general convention that cola are printed on different lines and of the principle that once an iambo- or aeolo-choriambic colon has moved from double-short rhythm to single short it does not move back again. Greek lyric was, of course, designed to be sung, not to be set out on the page. The lay-out I have adopted seems to me to show best the rhythmic structure of the verse in its relation to the rest of the stanza. It also obviates analyses like $- \cup \cup - \times - + \cdot \cdot \quad \cdot \cdot - \cup \cup -$ (Dale, *LM²*, 139), which wrecks the coherence of the passage. Unfortunately, *PSI* 1171 does not preserve enough of the strophe to cast any light on the question of when alternative colometries came to be adopted for strophe and antistrophe.

The scansion $\pi \epsilon \tau | \rho a \nu$ is necessary at 597; possible, but not necessary, at 604.

At 572, the metrically necessary ephelcystic ν of $\dot{a} \kappa \tau \hat{\iota} \sigma \iota \nu$ was provided by Triclinius.

       ia cho dim
    $\hat{a} \rho'$ $a \dot{\iota} \sigma \theta \acute{a} \nu \epsilon \iota$ $\pi \lambda \epsilon \hat{\iota} \sigma \tau a$ $\delta \iota'$ $\dot{\eta}$-

         + arist
805   $\mu \hat{a} s$ $\dot{a} \gamma \acute{a} \theta'$ $a \dot{v} \tau \acute{\iota} \chi'$ $\check{\epsilon} \xi \omega \nu$

       ia
  $\mu \acute{o} \nu a s$ $\theta \epsilon \hat{\omega} \nu;$

         + aeol da
  $\dot{\omega} s$ $\check{\epsilon} \tau o \iota \mu o s$ $\ddot{o} \delta'$ $\dot{\epsilon} \sigma \tau \dot{\iota} \nu$ $\ddot{a} \pi a \nu$-

         + ia dim cat
  τa $\delta \rho \hat{a} \nu$ $\ddot{o} \sigma'$ $\ddot{a} \nu$ $\kappa \epsilon \lambda \epsilon \acute{v} \eta s.$

$\cup - \cup | \underline{\underline{\cup}} \qquad \cup - \cup -$

705　νόημα φρενός· ὕπνος δ' ἀπέ-

$- \cup \cup - \qquad \cup - \cup -$

στω γλυκύθυμος ὀμμάτων.

$- \cup \cup - \qquad - \cup \cup - \qquad - \cup \cup -$

$\cup \cup - \cup - \qquad - - \cup -$

$- \cup \cup - \qquad \cup - - \; \|\|$

706–7

$- \cup - \qquad - \cup -$

Στ.　ἀτταταῖ ἀτταταῖ

$\cup - - \qquad \cup - -$

Χ.　τί πάσχεις; τί κάμνεις;

The strophe of this song, together with Strepsiades' short anapaestic lament over his sufferings from bed-bugs, make up a brief lyric and recitative interlude separating Socrates' two attempts to educate Strepsiades. After trying to instruct his pupil in metre and grammar, Socrates orders him into bed to think his way out of his difficulties. The chorus offer encouragement. The antistrophe follows Socrates' final loss of patience and the chorus's suggestion that Strepsiades substitute his own son as pupil. Here the Clouds appear at their most manipulative and disingenuous, and their final utterance:

> φιλεῖ γάρ πως τὰ τοι-
> αῦθ' ἑτέρᾳ τρέπεσθαι

is heavily ironical.

　　The metre is still iambo-choriambic, used in a freer structure than in the formal hymn, 563 ff. = 595 ff. Apart from the more varied rhythm, there are striking divergences of rhetorical from metrical divisions, especially in the strophe (strong stops after πύκνωσας 703, φρενός 705, θεῶν 806). The final section is missing in the strophe, which, as it stands,

ia dim
σὺ δ' ἀνδρὸς ἐκπεπληγμένου

+ cho ia dim
καὶ φανερῶς ἐπηρμένου

3 cho
810   γνοὺς ἀπολάψεις ὅτι πλεῖστον δύνασαι

ia dim (ᴧ dodrans A   ia?)
ταχέως· φιλεῖ γάρ πως τὰ τοι-
+ arist
αὖθ' ἑτέρᾳ τρέπεσθαι.

2 cr

2 ba

ends most implausibly with the acatalectic $- \cup \cup - \quad \cup - \cup -$. This is followed, at 707, by Strepsiades' yell, ἀτταταῖ ἀτταταῖ, and it is just possible that we have here a unique metrical joke: the absence of a clausular rhythm and, indeed, of the end of the stanza, marks the brutality of the interruption (see Romano, *Responsioni libere nei canti di Aristofane*, 107). But other explanations are possible. It may be, as Dover suggests (*Clouds* 187) that Aristophanes removed the original end to the stanza when revising the play and failed to produce a substitute (Cf. *Σ vet.* Vb3Vs1 1115a), or the lines may simply have been lost by accident. Accidental losses of stanzas and parts of stanzas in transmission have happened elsewhere in the plays (see, in particular, *Wasps* 1265 ff.). *Σ vet.* (700c) recognizes that the strophe is ἑπτάκωλος ἀντὶ δεκακώλου.

The aeolic colon at 703 = 807 ($\cdot \cdot \quad \cdot \cdot - \cup \cup - \cup \cup -$) is found with the base $- \cup$ at E. *El.* 439 = 449, and with the base $\cup \cup \cup$ at *Thesm.* 1153 (cf. *Ba.* 112 = 127, 115 = 130). The most interesting parallel, however, is *Aj.* 231 = 255, where the colon (in synartesis, as here, with a catalectic iambic dimeter) rounds off a passage in a blend of iambo-choriambic and asclepiad, 229–31 = 251–6:

$$- - \cup - \quad - \cup \cup - \quad - \cup \cup - \quad \cup - -$$
$$\cup - \quad - \cup \cup - \quad - \cup \cup - \quad \cup - -$$
$$\cup - \quad - \cup \cup - \cup \cup -$$
$$\cup - \cup - \quad \cup - -$$

949–58 = 1024–33

$$- - \cup - \quad - \cup \cup -$$
νῦν δείξετον τὼ πισύνω

$$- \cup \cup - \quad \cup - -$$
950 τοῖς περιδεξίοισιν

$$\underset{\smile}{} - \cup - \quad - \cup \cup -$$
λόγοισι καὶ φροντίσι καὶ

$$- \cup \cup - \quad \cup - \frown \|$$
γνωμοτύποις μερίμναις

$$- - \cup - \quad - \cup \cup -$$
†ὁπότερος αὐτοῖν λέγων

$$- - \cup \frown \quad - \cup \cup -$$
ἀμείνων φανήσεται.† νῦν γὰρ ἅπας

$$- \cup \cup - \quad - \cup \cup - \quad - \cup \cup -$$
955 ἐνθάδε κίνδυνος ἀνεῖται σοφίας,

$$- \cup \cup - \quad \cup - \cup -$$
ἧς πέρι τοῖς ἐμοῖς φίλοις.

$$- \cup \cup - \quad \cup - \smile \|$$
ἐστὶν ἀγὼν μέγιστος.

The arrival of Strepsiades and his son at Socrates' school is followed by a slanging match in anapaests between the two Λόγοι (889–932). The chorus-leader then proposes a regular contest, and the chorus sing the strophe as an introductory stanza, without, apparently, committing themselves to support either side. The first instalment of the contest, in which the Κρείττων Λόγος states his case, is in catalectic

For ⌣⌣ for ✕ in iambic at 811, see Introduction, p. 33. The alternative would be synizesis: ταχεως.

At 813, ἑτέρᾳ is Ernesti's emendation of ἑτέρα R+ or ἕτερα V+.

Although Σ *vet.* (700 and 804) shows awareness of correspondence, the Triclinian scholia show none. Triclinius offers an analysis into a jumble of 'feet' derived from Hephaestion.

ia cho dim
ὦ καλλίπυργον σοφίαν

arist
1025   κλεινοτάτην ἐπασκῶν,

ia cho dim
ὡς ἡδύ σου τοῖσι λόγοις

   + arist
σῶφρον ἔπεστιν ἄνθος.

ia cho dim
εὐδαίμονές γ' ἦσαν ἄρ' οἱ

   + ia cho dim
ζῶντες τότ' ἐπὶ τῶν προτέρων.

3 cho
1030–1   πρὸς τάδε σ', ὦ κομψοπρεπῆ μοῦσαν ἔχων,

cho ia dim
δεῖ σε λέγειν τι καινόν, ὡς

   + arist
ηὐδοκίμηκεν ἀνήρ.

anapaestic tetrameters, ending in a long πνῖγος. The chorus then express their warm approval in the antistrophe, and invite the Ἥττων Λόγος to think up something original by way of refutation.

Once again the metre is iambo-choriambic, the stanza opens with the same pair of cola as 700 ff. = 804 ff., and the last three cola are identical with 810–13, except that the second colon of the three is pure iambic in the earlier passage and iambo-choriambic here. But the run of three choriambs at 810 and at 955 = 1030 will have been distinctive enough to draw the audience's attention to the similarity.

Part of the passage (955–9) survives in *P. Berol.* 13219 (5th–6th c. AD, Dover *Π4*), and this is one of the three passages in which a papyrus diverges in colometry from R. The divergence looks, however, like the result of scribal carelessness (Introduction, p. 100).

Σ vet. on the strophe remarks that there is an antistrophe διαφόρως κεκωλισμένην, and adds θήσω δὲ ὡς φέρονται νῦν. Another *Σ* (on Vs1, marked *vet.?* by Holwerda) is a little more explicit: ἰστέον ὅτι ἡ ᾠδὴ τῇ ἀντῳδῇ τῶν ἴσων κώλων ἐστίν, τὰ δὲ κῶλα πῆ μὲν ἔοικεν ἀλλήλοις πῆ δὲ ἐνήλλακται.

There is a genuine textual problem at 953–4 = 1028–9, and it is probably this that accounts for the remarks of *Σ vet.* The antistrophe is open to serious suspicion at only one point: at 1028 the MSS have the inappropriate particle εὐδαίμονες δ'. This, however, is very easily remedied by Blaydes's γ'. For exclamatory γε without irony, compare

1154–70

⏑–⏑– –⏑– ⏑–⏑–

Στ. βοάσομαι τἄρα τὰν ὑπέρτονον

⏑–⏑– –⏑– ⏑–⏑– ‖ ᴴ

1155 βοάν. ἰώ, κλάετ' ὠβολοστάται,

––⏑– ––⏑– ⏑–⏑–

αὐτοί τε καὶ τἀρχαῖα καὶ τόκοι τόκων.

––⏑– ⏑–⏑– ⏑–⏑⌣ ‖ ᴴ

οὐδὲν γὰρ ἄν με φλαῦρον ἐργάσαισθ' ἔτι,

–⏑⏑–⏑⏑–

οἷος ἐμοὶ τρέφεται

–⏑⏑–⏑⏑–

τοῖσδ' ἐνὶ δώμασι παῖς

–––– –––

1160 ἀμφήκει γλώττῃ λάμπων,

Ach. 836, *Peace* 856, *Ecc.* 558. In contrast, the strophe is highly prosaic and metrically shapeless:

$$\cup \,\widehat{\cup\cup}\, \cup - \quad - \cup -$$
$$\cup - - \quad \cup - \cup - \quad - \cup\cup -$$

Any emendator disposed to make major changes to the antistrophe should first ask himself how likely it is that corruption should have produced a pair of iambo-choriambic dimeters which are not only metrically correct in themselves but absolutely right for the context. Bergk's re-writing of the strophe is worth quoting *exempli gratia*:

λέγων ἀμείνων πότερος $\cup - \cup - \quad - \cup\cup -$
   φανήσεται. νῦν γὰρ ἅπας $\cup - \cup - \quad - \cup\cup -$

Cf. Wilamowitz, *GV* 325.

At 1030, the pre-Triclinian MSS offer πρὸς οὖν τάδ᾽, ὦ . . ., an iambic metron corresponding to a choriamb. But here there is good linguistic reason for adopting Hall–Geldart's emendation, as printed (see Dover, ad loc.). Triclinius made a move in the right direction metrically: L+ (but not the Aldine) have πρὸς τάδε δ᾽, ὦ . . .

ia trim sync

ia trim sync

ia trim

ia trim

hem

hem

an dim cat

∪⌣|∪ –| – –|∪ –| – –|∪ –

πρόβολος ἐμός, σωτὴρ δόμοις, ἐχθροῖς βλάβη,

– ∪ ∪ – ∪ –   – ∪ ∪ – ∪ –

λυσανίας πατρῴων μεγάλων κακῶν·

– ∪ ∪ – ∪ –   – ∪ ∪ – ∪ ⌣ ‖ ᴴ

ὃν κάλεσον τρέχων ἔνδοθεν ὡς ἐμέ.

– ∪ ∪ – –   – – – –

1165   ὦ τέκνον, ὦ παῖ, ἔξελθ' οἴκων,

⌣ ∪ ∪ – ∪ ⌣ ‖

ἄϊε σοῦ πατρός.

∪ ∪ – ∪ ∪ –

Σω. ὅδ' ἐκεῖνος ἀνήρ.

– ∪ ∪ – ∪ ⌣ ‖

Στ. ὦ φίλος, ὦ φίλος.

∪ ⌣ ∪ –

Σω. ἄπιθι λαβών.

∪ ∪ ∪ – ∪ ⌣ ‖‖

1170 Στ. ἰὼ ἰώ, τέκνον.

Strepsiades greets the news that his son has mastered the ἥττων λόγος with a jubilant burst of song combining iambs (syncopated and unsyncopated), hemiepe, anapaests, and dochmiacs. Towards the end of the song, Socrates, who is not a singing character, interjects one anapaest (presumably delivered as recitative) and one iambic metron. At 1166 and 1168, the combination of change of speaker and following short or anceps is decisive in favour of the dochmiac scansion, with *brevis in longo* as against – ∪ ∪ – ∪ ∪| ∪ ∪ – ∪ ∪ –   and – ∪ ∪ – ∪ ∪| ∪ ⌣ ∪ –.

The paratragic character of the passage is obvious, and the first words, βοάσομαι . . . βοάν, are variously attributed by Σ *vet*. to Sophocles' *Peleus* (V 1154b, where, however, reference to Sophocles is emended away by Holwerda), to Euripides' *Peleus* (REVs1) and to Phrynichus, σατύροις (EVs1). This is usually taken to mean that Phrynichus, the comedian, quoted the same tragic verse in a play called

ia trim

2 δ

2 δ

an dim

δ

an monom

δ

ia

δ

Satyrs (see Phrynichus, *PCG* 48), but could, as Dover (ad loc.) points out, mean 'in a satyr play'. The verse, whatever its source, still echoes, some thirty years later, in the dochmiac song of joy at *Plutus* 637 ff.

Exactly what is being parodied and with what degree of precision is more controversial. Rau (*Paratragodia*, 149) suggests a comparison with the moments of mistaken joy characteristic of Sophocles, and develops his argument to the point of suggesting that Strepsiades' solo is based on a choral song at such a moment in Sophocles' *Peleus*. This can be ruled out with virtual certainty on metrical grounds. The existing Sophoclean songs of mistaken joy are either predominantly aeolo-choriambic (*Aj.* 693 ff., *Ant.* 1115 ff.), or dactylo-epitrite (*OT* 1086 ff.), or iambic (*Trach.* 205 ff.). None of them includes dochmiacs or anapaests. For a less controversial allusion to Sophocles' *Peleus*, see on *Birds* 851 ff. = 895 ff.

Dochmiac does not become a metre for rejoicing until late in the fifth century. The chorus's use of it at *Cho.* 935 ff. = 946 ff. reflects the distraught and ambiguous character of their song of triumph. Strepsiades' metres are appropriate to the songs of tumultuous joy mingled with recollection of past distress which belong, as far as we know, to late tragedy. Such songs feature dochmiacs in particular, and are, in general, metrically similar to passages of solo lamentation. There is one surviving example in Sophocles, *El.* 1232–87. The rest are Euripidean: *IT* 827–99, *Ion* 1445–1500, and *Hel.* 625–97. *Hypsipyle* fr. 64. 68 ff. resembles the latter part of such passages, when the first explosions of joy are past. The occasion is always a recognition, and the episode a duet between a woman who sings and a man (in *Hypsipyle* two men) who speaks, as does Socrates here. In Euripides, the predominant metres are dochmiac and iambic, with an admixture of anapaests. There are also occasional phrases with dactylo-epitrite affinities, like the hemiepe here at 1158–9 (cf. *IT* 888–9, *Ion* 1441, 1504–5). Since none of the extant examples is certainly earlier than even the second version of *Clouds*, it can be assumed that Aristophenes is parodying something new in tragedy. But problems remain. Did a *male* character (an old man, perhaps) ever take the singing role in such a scene? Or is Strepsiades behaving in a manner that, on the tragic stage, was peculiar to women? And did the character in Aristophanes' model burst, like Strepsiades, into a

1206–13

⏑⏑ – –   ⏑⏑ ⌣ ‖

Στ. "μάκαρ ὦ Στρεψίαδες.

– – ⏑ –   – ⏑ –

αὐτός τ᾽ ἔφυς ὡς σοφός,

– – ⏑ –   – ⏑ –

χοῖον τὸν υἱὸν τρέφεις,"

– – ⏑ –   – ⏑ –| – – ⏑ –

φήσουσι δή μ᾽ οἱ φίλοι χοἰ δημόται

– – ⏑ –   ⏑ – ⏑ –

1210   ζηλοῦντες ἡνίκ᾽ ἂν σὺ νι-

– ⏑ –   – ⏑ –

κᾷς λέγων τὰς δίκας.

song of misguided rejoicing in the presence of a boding and potentially hostile chorus? Such a situation seems suitable to tragedy, but there is no extant parallel.

Finally, it is worth considering the possibility that Aristophanes' model was, in fact, a lament, so that, for example, κλάετ', ὠβολοστάται, would be a perversion of the ordinary call to fellow-sufferers and sympathizers to join in lamentation. The resemblance of 1165–6 to *Hec.* 173–4 has been noted (see, in particular, L. Settler Spatz, *QUCC* 13 (1972), 77).

At 1161, where RV and the *Suda* have βλάβη, the majority of MSS have ἀνιαρός, a notable example of the true reading being driven out by a gloss. At 1163, RV reverse the order of τρέχων ἔνδοθεν. The hiatus after παῖ at 1165 is exclamatory (cf. *Frogs* 37, in dialogue). At 1169, RV have the unmetrical ἄπιθι λαβὼν τὸν υἱόν σου, and the rest the equally unmetrical ἄπιθι σὺ λαβὼν ($\cup \cup \cup \cup \cup -$), except that Ernesti claimed to find ἄπιθι συλλαβών in a 'Paris MS'. This last reading would scan as a dochmiac, producing a wholly inappropriate burst of excitement from Socrates, who, in any case, does not otherwise sing. Dover's ἄπιθι λαβών is convincing. σύ is likely to have slipped in by accident. Sommerstein's ἄπιθί σφε λαβών would produce another anapaestic metron, but that degree of metrical uniformity is unnecessary.

ion dim cat

ia dim sync

ia dim sync

ia trim sync

ia dim

+ 2 cr

‒ ‒ ◡ ‒   ◡ ‒ ◡ ‒

ἀλλ' εἰσάγων σε βούλομαι

‒ ◡ ‒   ◡ ‒ ‒ |||

πρῶτον ἑστιᾶσαι,

After Pheidippides' first demonstration of his newly acquired intellectual agility, Strepsiades sings a short encomium on himself (see C. W. Macleod, *Phoenix*, 35 (1981), 142–4 = *Collected Essays*, 49–51).

There is no surviving parallel for a stanza in pure syncopated iambic opening with an ionic colon, but E. *Supp.* 778 ff. = 786 ff. is in very similar syncopated iambic and opens with an alien colon:

◡ ◡ ‒ ◡ ◡ ‒ ◡ ‒

◡ ‒ ◡ ‒   ‒ ◡ ‒

‒ ◡ ‒   ◡ ‒ ◡ ‒

◡ ‒ ◡ ‒   ‒ ‒ ||

◡ ‒ ◡ ‒   ‒ ◡ ‒   ◡ ‒ ◡ ‒

◡ ‒ ◡ ‒   ◡ ‒ ◡ ‒   ◡ ‒ ◡ ‒

‒ ◡ ‒   ◡ ‒ ◡ ‒

◡ ‒ ◡ ‒   ‒ ◡ ‒   ◡ ‒ ‒ |||

1303–10 = 1311–20

‒ ‒ ◡ ‒   ◡ ‒ ◡ ‒   ‒ ‒ ◡ ‒

οἷον τὸ πραγμάτων ἐρᾶν φλαύρων· ὁ γὰρ

◡ ‒ ◡ ◡ ‒ ‒ ||ₕ

γέρων ὅδ' ἐρασθεὶς

◡ ‒ ◡ ‒   ‒|‒ ◡ ‒

1305 ἀποστερῆσαι βούλεται

◡ ‒ ◡ ‒   ◡ ‒ ◡ ◡ ‒ ||

τὰ χρήμαθ' ἀδανείσατο.

‒ ‒ ◡ ‒   ‒ ‒ ◡ ‒

κοὐκ ἔσθ' ὅπως οὐ τήμερον

‒ ◡ ‒   ◡ ‒ ◡ ‒

λήψεταί τι πρᾶγμ' ὃ τοῦ‑

ia dim

ith

The iambic dimeter ×–ᴗ– –ᴗ– occurs in sequence in the same
play at 73–5 = 81–3 (it is also quite common in Aeschylus). The opening
μακαρισμός, though a standard encomiastic motif (Dover, ad loc.),
may have a Euripidean ring: compare Nauck², fr. 446 (anapaests).
There are other examples in plays later than *Clouds*: *Hel.* 375, *Ba.* 72,
565, 1180, *IA* 543. For the tragedian's recurrent interest in defining
blessedness, see *Ion* 623, Nauck², frs. 256, 793, 1057.

Σ *vet.* V (1209) has ὦ μάκαρ ὦ Στρεψιάδης, but there is no reason
to regard this as anything but a private mistake. At 1208, VE+ and
Triclinius have ἐκτρέφεις, producing an unsyncopated dimeter.
τρέφεις comes from RM+, and was also read by the metrician of Σ *vet.*
(1206a). At 1212, εἰσάγων is shared by RV, while most other MSS have
εἰσαγαγών. Through Triclinius, the latter prevailed in printed texts
until that of Hermann, who adopted εἰσάγων, following Elmsley on
Ach. 1210.

           ia trim
    οἶμαι γὰρ αὐτὸν αὐτίχ᾽ εὑρήσειν ὅπερ

         + reiz
      πάλαι ποτ᾽ ἐπήτει,

         ia dim
    εἶναι τὸν υἱὸν δεινόν οἱ

         ia dim
1315 γνώμας ἐναντίας λέγειν

         ia dim
    τοῖσιν δικαίοις, ὥστε νι-

          + lec
      κἂν ἅπαντας, οἷσπερ ἂν

$$- \cup - \quad - - \cup -$$

τὸν ποιήσει τὸν σοφι-

$$- \cup - \quad \cup - \cup - \quad - - \cup -$$

στὴν ∪ - ✕ ὢν πανουργεῖν ἤρξατ' ἐξ-

$$- - \cup - \quad \cup - - \; \||\|$$

1310   αἴφνης †τι κακὸν λαβεῖν.†

Having driven away the two creditors, Strepsiades has gone into the house, and the chous is left alone on stage. With their last utterance in their dramatic character (1114), they have cryptically suggested that things will not turn out as Strepsiades imagines. They now express open disapproval of Strepsiades' behaviour and predict that he will regret the education he has imposed on his son.

The opening iambic trimeter and reizianum, almost in synartesis (word-end after ὁ γὰρ and ὅπερ is very weak), prefigure the next song (1345 ff. = 1391 ff.). The rest of the song is in very simple iambic of comic type, admitting syncopation only in the form of lecythia. Syncopation of tragic type (as in 1154 ff., for example) would have suggested parody and detracted from the seriousness of tone. The chorus convey their earnestness through simple language and simple metre.

The latter part of the strophe is mutilated beyond hope of plausible emendation. Apart from the failure of correspondence, the awkwardness

1345–50 = 1391–6

$$\underset{\smile}{\cup} - \cup | - \quad \cup - \cup - \quad - - \cup -$$

1345   σὸν ἔργον, ὦ πρεσβῦτα, φροντίζειν ὅπῃ

$$\underset{\smile}{\cup} - \cup \cup - - \; \|_H$$

τὸν ἄνδρα κρατήσεις,

$$- - \cup - \quad \cup - \cup - \quad - - \cup -$$

ὡς οὗτος, εἰ μή τῳ 'πεποίθειν, οὐκ ἂν ἦν

$$\cup - \cup \cup - \underset{\smile}{\smile} \;\|$$

οὕτως ἀκόλαστος.

$$\cup - \cup - \quad \cup - \cup - \quad \cup - \cup \smile \;\|$$

ἀλλ' ἔσθ' ὅτῳ θρασύνεται· δῆλον†∪—

+ lec

ξυγγένηται, κἂν λέγῃ

+ lec ia (ia trim sync)

παμπόνηρ'. ἴσως δ' ἴσως βουλήσεται

+ ia dim cat

1320   κἄφωνον αὐτὸν εἶναι.

of expression at 1307–10 is effectively demonstrated by Dover (ad loc.). At 1312, most MSS have ἐζήτει producing $\smile - \smile - - -$. Apart from the failure of correspondence, this heavily syncopated colon is stylistically inappropriate to the stanza. RV+ have ἐπεζήτει, which very probably preserves the traces of an ancient variant: ἐζήτει. ἐπήτει, proposed by Hermann, restores correspondence. ἐπαιτέω is used of the activity of a mendicant at *OC* 1364 and *Rhes*. 715, but at *OT* 1416 it seems to mean no more than 'request' or 'beg' in the non-technical sense (not, *pace* LSJ, 'ask in addition'). ἐζήτει could well have appeared as a gloss on the relatively rare word. To fill the gap at 1309 Austin suggests ἁπάντων *exempli gratia*.

Σ *vet*. (1319, Vs1 only) notes the failure of correspondence: τὰ β′ κῶλα ταῦτα ἄνισά εἰσι ⟨τοῖς⟩ τῆς ᾠδῆς . . . Σ *vet*. on 1303a, however, describes the song as a single stanza of eighteen cola, an interpretation adopted by Triclinius (1303a and b).

ia trim

1391 οἶμαί γε τῶν νεωτέρων τὰς καρδίας

reiz

πηδᾶν ὅ τι λέξει.

ia trim

εἰ γὰρ τοιαῦτά γ' οὗτος ἐξειργασμένος

reiz

λαλῶν ἀναπείσει,

ia trim

1395 τὸ δέρμα τῶν γεραιτέρων λάβοιμεν ἄν

$$-- \cup \cup -- \;|||$$
1350 τὸ λῆμ' ἐστὶ τἀνθρώπου.†

The strophe introduces and the antistrophe punctuates the contest between Strepsiades and Pheidippides. In contrast with the earlier contest between the two Λόγοι, the episode is asymmetrical. In the first section, between the two lyric stanzas, Strepsiades, instead of making his case, recites his grievances. The inadequacy of Strepsiades as contestant is underlined by the way in which the chorus in both stanzas concentrate on Pheidippides, building up curiosity about how he is going to argue his case.

The pair of cola, iambic trimeter and reizianum, that opened the last strophic pair, are here repeated three times over to produce a very simple and very formal stanza.

The end of the strophe is corrupt and the corruption is ancient. Hence the analysis of the strophe in Σ *vet.* E (1345a) as a miniature triad (strophe, antistrophe, and epode). The last two cola, the 'epode', are described as iambic dimeter, iambic 'basis', and 'trochaic penthemimer':

ἀλλ' ἔσθ' ὅτῳ θρασύνεται·
δῆλον τὸ λῆμ' ἐστὶ τἀνθρώπου.

$$-- \cup - \quad \cup - \cup -$$
$$-- \cup - \quad - \cup ---$$

Σ *vet.* Vs1 (1350) shows some awareness of failure of correspondence at 1349 = 1395. Triclinius also was aware of the need for correspondence, and sought to improve it by re-division and, typically, the addition of γε:

reiz
ἀλλ' οὐδ' ἐρεβίνθου.

> ἀλλ' ἔσθ' ὅτῳ θρασύνεται· δῆλόν ⟨γε⟩ τὸ
> λῆμ' ἐστὶ τἀνθρώπου.

$$-- \cup - \quad \cup - \cup - \quad --⟨\cup⟩\smallsmile$$
$$-- \cup ---$$

Brevis in longo and verse-end within τὸ ‖ λῆμα is impossible, but the Triclinian text led Hermann to propose ⟨γέ τοι⟩ for the end of 1349, which has gained wide acceptance. Combined with Hermann's τὸ λῆμα τὸ τἀνδρός ('One thing at least is clear, the man's λῆμα') it restores the metre plausibly. For the substitution of ἀνθρώπου for ἀνδρός, compare R's substitution of ἄνθρωποι for ἄνδρες (other MSS) at *Lys.* 615. The evidence of verse-end provided by the antistrophe rules out Hermann's alternative suggestion:

> δῆλόν ⟨γε⟩ τἀν-
> θρώπου 'στι τὸ λῆμα.

In view of Prato's attempts to cite parallels for this, it is worth stating emphatically that there is none. Verse-end within an enclosed phrase (λασίων μετὰ ‖ θηρῶν *Phil.* 184), or even after a preposition (see Dale on *Alc.* 232) is irrelevant. Dover is consistent in accepting × – ∪ – – –
= × – ∪ ∪ – – both here and at 1304 = 1312, but emendation in the earlier passage is very easy, and here there are more pointers to corruption than the irregularity of correspondence.

*W*asps

273–80 = 281–9	*Ionic* and *dactylo-epitrite*, with, apparently, correspondence of ⏑⏑– with –⏑–.
291–302 = 303–16	Chorus-leader and Boy: *Ionic*.
317–33	Philocleon: *Aeolo-choriambic* and *anapaestic*.
334–45 = 365–78	Chorus and Philocleon: *trochaic* and *cretic*, the latter corresponding with *dochmiac*.
403–87	*Trochaic* and *cretic*. Song interspersed with recitative tetrameters.
526–45 = 631–47	*Iambo-choriambic*. Correspondence of –⏑⏑– with ×–⏑–.
729–35 = 743–9	*Iambic, dochmiac, cretic*.
868–74 = 885–90	*Iambic* and *aeolo-choriambic*.
1009–14	*Anapaestic* and *trochaic*.
1060–70 = 1091–1101	*Trochaic* and *cretic*. Correspondence of –⏑–⏑ with –⏑⌢.
1226–48	Bdelycleon and Philocleon: *Aeolo-choriambic*.
1265–74	*Trochaic*.
1326–40	Philocleon and the Angry Man: *Trochaic* and *iambic*.
1450–61 = 1462–73	*Iambo-choriambic* and *aeolo-choriambic*.
1518–37	*Archilochean*.

While dramatically *W*asps is rich in comic fantasy and invention, it is not particularly adventurous metrically. However, the idea of opposition in musical taste between the old and the young is fitfully present as a subordinate theme. It is used early in the play to produce an exceptionally varied and elaborate parodos in the form of a sort of paratragic cantata, beginning with the Old Jurymen's 'aubade' in the metrical style, presumably, of Phrynichus. Then follows the duet between the chorus-leader and his son and Philocleon's solo. At this point (334), there is an abrupt change to distinctively comic metres: trochaic and cretic. From here onwards, trochaic, with some aeolo-choriambic and iambo-choriambic, becomes the dominant metre of the play. A short musical diversion from these basic metres of comedy is provided by the scene at 1224–48 in which Philocleon practises symposiastic songs under the tuition of his son. The opposition of old rhythms versus new surfaces once more, in a form incomprehensible to us, with the dancing competition between Philocleon and the sons of Carcinus at the end of the play.

The lyric parts of the play present some major textual and metrical difficulties. In particular, there is an exceptional number of passages with imperfect correspondence: 273 ff. = 281 ff., 339 = 370, 526 ff. = 631 ff., 1060 ff. = 1091 ff. These difficulties may or may not be linked to certain unexplained peculiarities in the transmission of the text. Grenfell and Hunt (*P. Oxy.* xi. 146) note that 'the *Wasps*, like the *Knights*, is one of the plays in which V tends to disagree most with R'. It is also the more reliable of the two (Sommerstein, *Wasps*, p. xx), and agrees much more closely with the 5th-century papyrus, *P. Oxy.* 1374 (Grenfell and Hunt, ad loc.). There are hardly any surviving metrical Σ *vet.* on the play, but an important one that does survive (on 1283 d e) notes a serious mutilation of the text going back to an early period (see on 1265–74). Nor is there anything in Triclinius' metrical scholia to suggest that he had access to earlier scholia. On 365a, 415, 863, 1009a, 1091, 1450a he produces characteristic analyses into a medley of feet. He shows no awareness even of the important Σ *vet.* on 1283 d e. Finally, the colon-division of RV is highly disordered, with an unusual number of failures of correspondence, even where the transmitted text in fact corresponds.

$$275\text{–}90 = 298\text{–}313$$

‿‿− ‿‿−− ‿‿−− ‿‿−− ‿‿−◡

τί ποτ' οὐ πρὸ θυρῶν φαίνετ' ἄρ' ἡμῖν ὁ γέρων οὐδ'

[ὑπακούει;

−‿‿−‿‿−
−‿‿− −‿−

μῶν ἀπολώλεκε τὰς

−‿‿−‿‿−−
−‿‿− −‿−−

ἐμβάδας; ἢ προσέκοψ' ἐν

−‿−| − −‿− −||ᴴ

275   τῷ σκότῳ τὸν δάκτυλόν που,

−‿− −‿− −
‿‿− ‿‿−−

εἶτ' ἐφλέγμηνεν αὐτοῦ

−‿−| ◡ −‿− −

τὸ σφυρὸν γέροντος ὄντος;

−‿−| − −‿− −||ᴴ

καὶ τάχ' ἂν βουβωνιῴη.

− −‿‿−‿‿− − −‿− ◡

ἦ μὴν πολὺ δριμύτατός γ' ἦν τῶν παρ' ἡμῖν,

−‿‿−‿‿− ◡ −‿‿−‿‿− −

καὶ μόνος οὐκ ἀνεπείθετ', ἀλλ' ὁπότ' ἀντιβολοίη

−‿− − −‿− −||

τις, κάτω κύπτων ἂν οὕτω

‿‿−− ‿‿−|||

280   "λίθον ἕψεις" ἔλεγεν.

‿‿−− ‿‿‿|||

The chorus enter, making their way painfully through the darkness, chanting in catalectic iambic tetrameters. With the intervention of the boy at 248, the metre changes to euripideans (ia dim + ith). In this section, even the pre-Triclinian MSS contain small interpolations which

ion sync + 4 ion
τάχα δ' ἄν διὰ τὸν χθιζινὸν ἄνθρωπον, ὃς ἡμᾶς †διεδύετ†

+D = cho cr (d e)
ἐξαπατῶν καὶ λέγων

+D − = cho tro (d e −)
ὡς φιλαθήναιος ἦν καὶ

+ e − e −
τὰν Σάμῳ πρῶτος κατείποι,

e e − = ion dim sync
διὰ τοῦτ' ὀδυνηθεὶς

e ⏑ e −
εἶτ' ἴσως κεῖται πυρέττων.

e − e −
285   ἔστι γὰρ τοιοῦτος ἀνήρ.

− D −e ⏑
ἀλλ' ὦγαθ', ἀνίστασο μηδ' οὕτω σεαυτὸν

D ⏑ D −
ἔσθιε, μηδ' ἀγανάκτει. καὶ γὰρ ἀνὴρ παχὺς ἥκει

+ e − e −
τῶν προδόντων τἀπὶ Θρᾴκης·

ion dim cat
ὃν ὅπως ἐγχυτριεῖς.

ion dim cat
290   ὕπαγ', ὦ παῖ, ὕπαγε.

seem designed to turn the verses into full catalectic tetrameters (248 σὺ
before τουτονὶ codd.; 249 σὺ before τὸν RBVp3+; 254 κονδύλοισι(ν)
for κονδύλοις codd.). It may be recalled that at *Knights* 756 ff. = 836 ff.,
Σ *vet.* fails to distinguish euripideans from catalectic iambic tetrameters.

It is much less surprising that the scholar who has left his mark on the 16th century MS B indulged in a private orgy of interpolation (251 σὺ τὴν B: τὴν rell.: 252 νῦν ὠνόητε B: ὠνόητε rell.: 253 δέῃ τί B: δέῃ rell.: 256 σκότῳ γε B: σκότῳ rell.: etc.) The correction of 248 and 263 by another 16th century scholar, Florent Chrestien, is the more creditable.

The lyric stanzas which follow the euripideans are in an unparalleled combinatinon of ionic and dactylo-epitrite. At 219–20, Bdelycleon has described the habitual arrival of his father's comrades:

> λύχνους ἔχοντες καὶ μινυρίζοντες μέλη
> ἀρχαιομελισιδωνοφρυνιχήρατα

It can safely be assumed that, metrically and musically, this song aims to reproduce the elegant tragic style of Phrynichus, with which the content and diction would contrast to excellent comic effect.

Fragments of Phrynichus' lyric are few (see on 1518–37 below), but *TrGF* 9, from Φοίνισσαι (quoted in part by Σ *vet.* 220c), seems to be in dactylo-epitrite:

> Σιδώνιον ἄστυ λιποῦσα καὶ δροσερὰν Ἄραδον
> − −∪∪−∪∪− ∪ −∪∪−∪∪−

(λιποῦσαι Porson)

TrGF 14, from an unidentified play, is in catalectic ionic tetrameters:

> ∪∪−− ∪∪−− ∪∪−− ∪∪−.

The song contains a number of metrical oddities. Given the strophe only, it would be natural to take the initial ionic pentameter as an independent introductory verse, and, indeed, the short syllable at the end of the verse in the antistrophe (διεδύετ') might seem to confirm that. However, elision at verse-end is not acceptable. On the other hand, a metron of the form ∪ ∪ − ∪ in ionics is not attested unless followed

291–302=303–16

∪∪−−   ∪∪−−   ∪∪−−   ∪∪−−
Π. ἐθελήσεις τί μοι οὖν, ὦ πάτερ, ἤν σού τι δεηθῶ;

∪∪−−   ∪∪−−
Χ. πάνυ γ' ὦ παιδίον. ἀλλ' εἰ-

∪∪−−   ∪∪−−
πέ, τί βούλει με πρίασθαι

by – ∪ – – or – –. Dindorf proposed removing the elision with διέδυ πως (based on Bentley's διέδυ). The active form is less common, but it is used at 212 in this play (cf. Dem. 18. 133 τὸ δίκην δοῦναι διαδύς). As the more familiar form, the middle could have slipped in.

The repeated correspondence between ∪ ∪ – and – ∪ – seems too systematic to have been produced by any ordinary process of corruption. The explicit association of the song with Phrynichus makes it difficult to invoke 'comic' correspondence by syllable-counting as an explanation. In any case, something more than syllable-counting is involved. If the stanzas are as Aristophanes composed them it is best to admit that there is something here that is beyond us.

For the elision of -αι in φαίνεται (273), compare *Peace* 392 (χάρισ') and *Ecc.* 495 (ὄψεθ') and 913 (λείπομ'). See also Platnauer on *Peace* 392 and Dover on *Clouds* 7.

As usual in this play, there are no metrical Σ *vet*. R has, however, preserved a colometry which corresponds throughout, except for 273=281, which is split between two lines in the antistrophe, but not in the strophe. Thus, in spite of the eccentricities of correspondence, the stanzas were recognized as corresponding in later antiquity.

In 281, χθιζινὸν is Hermann's emendation for the unmetrical χθεσινὸν of the MSS (cf. *Frogs* 987, where also the MSS have χθεσινὸν where χθιζινὸν is metrically necessary). The fact that ∪ ∪ – – ∪ ∪ ∪ – –, which is produced here by χθεσινὸν, also scans the MS text at 314 below is of no significance, since emendation is necessary in the latter passage for other reasons. Triclinius perceived the metrical difficulty, and attempted χθεσινόν γ'. In the received text, the strophe ends with one catalectic ionic dimeter, the antistrophe with two. Hermann suggested reading ὕπαγ', ὦ παῖ, ὕπαγε as a refrain after 280.

4 ion
Π. ἄγε νῦν, ὦ πάτερ, ἢν μὴ τὸ δικαστήριον ἄρχων

6 ion
305   καθέσῃ νῦν, πόθεν ὠνη-

σόμεθ' ἄριστον; ἔχεις ἐλ-

‿‿|‐‐　‿‿‐|‐

295　καλόν; οἶμαι δέ σ᾽ ἐρεῖν ἀ-

‿‿‐‐‐‐‿‐‐

στραγάλους δήπουθεν, ὦ παῖ.

‿‿‐‐　‿‿‐‐

Π. μὰ Δί᾽, ἀλλ᾽ ἰσχάδας, ὦ παπ-

‿‿|‐‿‐‿|‐‐

298　ία· ἥδιον γάρ — Χ. οὐκ ἂν

‿‿‐‿‐‿‐‐

μὰ Δί᾽, εἰ κρέμαισθέ γ᾽ ὑμεῖς.

‿‿‐‐　‿‿‐‐　‿|‿‐‿||

Π. μὰ Δί᾽, οὐ τἄρα προπέμψω σε τὸ λοιπόν.

‿‿‐‐　‿‿|‐‐　‿‿‐

300　Χ. ἀπὸ γὰρ τοῦδέ με τοῦ μισθαρίου

‿‿‐　‿‿‐‐　‿‿‐|‐　‿‿‐⌣||ₕ

τρίτον αὐτὸν ἔχειν ἄλφιτα δεῖ καὶ ξύλα κὥψον·

‿‿‐‿‐‐

σὺ δὲ σῦκά μ᾽ αἰτεῖς.

This duet with paratragic overtones between the chorus-leader and his young son is in pure ionic. It is worth recalling here the well-known scholium on *PV* 128 (Introduction, p. 62). Metrically, however, there is nothing closely comparable in surviving tragedy. The anacreontic of the form ‿‿‐‐‐‿‐‐ is occasionally found in tragedy; relatively more frequently in Aristophanes (Introduction, pp. 62–3). ‿‿‐‿‐‐ is found as clausula to ionics at *Ba.* 385 = 401. At 536 = 555 in the same play, there is a version lengthened by initial ‿‿‐‐ (cf. Anacreon, *PMG* 346).

The duet is unusual in that change of speaker fails to correspond, so that the second to fifth and the last two cola are sung by the father in the strophe and by the son in the antistrophe. Particularly striking, however, is the angry irruption of the father in mid-colon at 298—undoubtedly a metrical and musical joke.

RV preserve a corresponding colometry up to 297 = 309, up to the

πίδα χρηστήν τινα νῷν ἢ
+ anac (=ion dim cat?)
†πόρον Ἕλλας ἱερόν;†

2 ion
X. ἀπαπαῖ φεῦ, ⟨ἀπαπαῖ φεῦ,⟩

+ anac
310   μὰ Δί', οὐκ ἔγωγε νῷν οἶδ'

+ anac
ὁπόθεν γε δεῖπνον ἔσται.

3 ion
Π. τί με δῆτ', ὦ μελέα μῆτερ, ἔτικτες;

3 ion cat
X. ἵν' ἐμοὶ πράγματα βόσκειν παρέχῃς.

ion sync + 3 ion
Π. ἀνόνητον ἄρ', ὦ θυλάκιόν, σ' εἶχον ἄγαλμα.
315   ἒ ἔ.

ion colarion
πάρα νῷν στενάζειν.

point, that is, where there is a lacuna in our text in the antistrophe, closely followed by the exceptional change of speaker in mid-colon in the strophe. These two cola may have baffled Alexandrian colometricians.

At 308, a quotation from Pindar has been introduced nonsensically (compare the introduction of δόμους Ἀμφίονος at *Birds* 1247), with, in addition, a play on the figurative and topographical meanings of πόρος. Correspondence is also broken. An acatalectic ionic dimeter in correspondence with an anacreontic would be relatively unsurprising, given the close association of the two cola (Introduction, p. 61, and *Frogs* 327 = 344). The catalectic dimeter (◡ ◡ – – ◡ ◡ –) is much more peculiar. At *Knights* 406, correspondence is violated for the sake of introducing a quotation, but there attention is drawn to the fact that the chorus is quoting: one can imagine a snatch from a different tune being incorporated. The fact that the words of Pinder being quoted here are given in a different order by Σ *vet.* 308b (cf. Snell–Maehler, 189) adds to the uncertainties. Moreover, in Pindar the scansion ἱερόν is a possibility (*Ol.* 3. 30, but not, as Slater claims, *Pyth.* 9. 39). This scansion (or ἱρόν), followed by a lacuna equal to two longs, would produce an anacreontic. Blaydes proposed εὑρεῖν to fill such a lacuna (for πόρον εὑρίσκειν in Euripides, cf. *Med.* 260, *IT* 876, *IA* 356, and, of course, the verses which conclude *Alc.*, *Andr.*, *Med.*, *Hel.*, and *Ba.*). Rather than emending the antistrophe, Hermann proposed re-writing the strophe to produce

317–33

‿ — —   ‿ — —

φίλοι, τήκομαι μὲν

‿ — ‿ ‿ — ‿ —

πάλαι διὰ τῆς ὀπῆς

— — ‿ ‿ — —

ὑμῶν ἐπακούων.

— — ‿ ‿ — —

318   ἀλλ'—οὐ γὰρ οἷός τ' εἴμ'

— — ‿ ‿ — —

ᾄδειν—τί ποιήσω;

— — — ‿ ‿ — ‿ —

τηροῦμαι δ' ὑπὸ τῶνδ' ἐπεὶ

— ‿ — ‿ ‿ — ‿ —

320   βούλομαί γε πάλαι μεθ' ὑ-

— — — ‿ ‿ — ‿ —

μῶν ἐλθὼν ἐπὶ τοὺς καδί-

— ‿ — ‿ ‿ — — ‖ ʜ

σκους κακόν τι ποιῆσαι.

— — — ‿ ‿ — ‿⌣ ‖ ʜ

ἀλλ' ὦ Ζεῦ μεγαβρόντα,

— ‿ ‿ — —   ‿ ‿ — — —

ἤ με ποίησον καπνὸν ἐξαίφνης

$$\cup\cup--\quad\cup\cup--$$
$$\cup\cup--\quad\cup\cup-$$

But it is unlikely that the metrically-acceptable anacreontic of the received text would have been produced by accidental transposition.

At 314, the MSS offer ἀνόνητον ἄρα σ' ὦ θυλάκιόν γ' εἶχον ἄγαλμα ($\cup\cup-\cup\cup\cup--\ldots$). Hermann improved both language and metre by deleting γ' (both unnecessary and misplaced after the vocative) and transferring σ' to its place after θυλάκιον.

    2 ba

    tel

    reiz

    reiz

      + reiz

    glyc

      + glyc

      + glyc

      + pher

    pher

    an dim

‒ ‒ ◡ ◡ ‒　　‒ ‒ ‒ ‒
325　ἢ Προξενίδην ἢ τὸν Σέλλου

‒ ‒ ‒ ‒　　◡ ◡ ‒ ‒
τοῦτον τὸν ψευδαμάμαξυν·

‒ ‒ ◡ ◡ ‒　　◡ ◡ ‒ ‒ ‒
τόλμησον, ἄναξ, χαρίσασθαί μοι

◡ ◡ ‒ ‒ ‒　　‒ ◡ ◡ ‒ ‒
πάθος οἰκτίρας· ἤ με κεραυνῷ

◡ ◡ ‒ ◡ ◡ ‒　　◡ ◡ ‒ ◡ ◡ ‒
διατινθαλέῳ σπόδισον ταχέως,

‒ ‒ ◡ ◡ ‒　　◡ ◡ ‒ ‒ ‒
330　κἄπειτ' ἀνελών μ' ἀποφυσήσας

‒ ‒ ‒ ‒　　‒ ◡ ◡ ‒ ‒
εἰς ὀξάλμην ἔμβαλε θερμήν·

‒ ‒ ◡ ◡ ‒　　◡ ◡ ‒ ◡ ◡ ‒
ἢ δῆτα λίθον με ποίησον, ἐφ' οὗ

‒ ‒ ‒ ‒　　◡ ◡ ‒ ‒ |||
τὰς χοιρίνας ἀριθμοῦσιν.

Philocleon's aria is simple metrically, but interesting. Two bacchiacs serve as introduction to four aeolo-choriambic cola: a telesillean (acatalectic) followed by three reiziana (catalectic). Then follow another four aeolo-choriambic cola: three glyconics (acatalectic) and a pherecratean (catalectic). Thus, the two groups of four have inverse structure: ABBB AAAB. After verse-end (marked by hiatus), another pherecratean (also marked off as a separate verse by hiatus and b.f.v.), introduces a new section, this time in anapaests which are either recitative, or at least approximate very closely to the recitative type. Repeated bacchiac introducing aeolo-choriambic is found at E. *Supp.* 990 = 1012 and *Ion* 190 = 202. For repeated bacchiacs among aeolo-choriambic, see *Thesm.* 1136 ff.

Transitions into anapaests in tragic monody may sometimes, perhaps, signal a more positive and resolute frame of mind, without, however, any diminution of passion. See S. *El.* 236 ff., possibly also *Phil.* 1198–9 (where, if Philoctetes is still using dactyls, the rhythm is at least closely assimilated to anapaests). In these passages, however, it is only a matter

an dim

an dim cat

an dim

an dim

an dim

an dim

an dim

an dim

+ an dim cat

of a few lines. On threnetic anapaests in general, see Introduction, p. 57.

At 318, the pre-Triclinian MSS (except for V: ἀλλ' ἀτὰρ) have ἀλλὰ
γὰρ which breaks the metrical pattern by producing:

$$- \cup \cup - \cup - -$$
$$- - \cup \cup - -$$

'Complex' ἀλλὰ γὰρ, in which γὰρ applies to the subordinate and ἀλλὰ
to the main clause (e.g. S. *Ant.* 148 ἀλλὰ γὰρ ἁ μεγαλώνυμος ἦλθε
Νίκα) is, according to Denniston (*Particles*, 99), 'exceedingly rare'. The
alternative of taking ἀλλὰ γὰρ as 'breaking off' (Denniston, 102) would
require Philocleon actually to break off after ᾄδειν, leaving τί ποιήσω;
isolated, with very harsh asyndeton. Bentley's transposition ἀλλ' οὐ
γὰρ restores both language and metre.

Triclinius (LVp2BAld) converts 317 into unsyncopated iambic
(φίλοι, πάλαι μὲν τήκομαι), and, more perceptively, deletes γὰρ at
318. As so often, he shows himself better at spotting corruption than at
curing it.

The pherecratean introducing anapaests at 323 was regarded with suspicion by nineteenth-century scholars, and Hall–Geldart adopt supplements by Dindorf and Porson so as to turn the verse into a full

$$334–45 = 365–78$$

‒∪‒∪ ‒∪‒◡

X. τίς γάρ ἐσθ' ὁ ταῦτά σ' εἴργων

‒∪‒◡ ‒∪‒◡ ‒∪‒◡ ‒∪‒

335   κἀποκλῄων τῇ θύρᾳ; λέξον· πρὸς εὔνους γὰρ φράσεις.

Φ.   336–7   tro tetram cat II

‒∪‒∪ ‒∪‒∪ ‒∪‒∪ ‒∪‒

X. τοῦ δ' ἔφεξιν, ὦ μάταιε, ταῦτα δρᾶν σε βούλεται;

∪∪∪∪∪∪‒
‒∪∪∪‒∪‒

339   τίνα πρόφασιν ἔχων;

Φ.   340–1   tro tetram cat II

‒∪‒‒ ⌒∪‒∪

342 *X.* τοῦτ' ἐτόλμησ' ὁ μιαρὸς χα-

‒∪‒∪ ⌒∪‒∪

νεῖν, ὁ Δημολογοκλέων ⟨ὅδ'⟩

⌒∪‒∪ ⌒∪‒∪

ὅτι λέγεις ⟨σύ⟩ τι περὶ τῶν νε-

‒∪‒∪ ‒∪‒∪

343–4 ῶν ἀληθές; οὐ γὰρ ἄν ποθ'

‒∪‒◡ ‒∪‒‒

οὗτος ἀνὴρ τοῦτ' ἐτόλμη-

‒∪‒◡

σεν λέγειν, εἰ

‒∪‒∪ ‒∪◠|||

345   μὴ ξυνωμότης τις ἦν.

dimeter. This is, however, unnecessary. The association between anapaest and pherecratean is well authenticated, even if its nature is not fully understood (Introduction, p. 60).

           tro dim
X. ἀλλὰ καὶ νῦν ἐκπόριζε

           tro tetram cat
    μηχανὴν ὅπως τάχισθ'· ἕως γάρ, ὦ μελίττιον.

Φ.   367–8   tro tetram cat II

           tro tetram cat
X. ταῦτα μὲν πρὸς ἀνδρός ἐστ' ἄνοντος ἐς σωτηρίαν.

           δ = 2 cr
370   ἀλλ' ἔπαγε τὴν γνάθον.

Φ.   371–2   tro tetram cat II

           13 tro cat
X. μηδέν, ὦ τᾶν, δέδιθι, μηδέν·

    ὡς ἐγὼ τοῦτόν γ' ἐὰν γρύ-

    ξῃ τι, ποιήσω δακεῖν τὴν

375–6   καρδίαν καὶ τὸν περὶ ψυ-

376–7   χῆς δρόμον δραμεῖν, ἵν' εἰδῇ

    μὴ πατεῖν τὰ

    ταῖν θεαῖν ψηφίσματα.

This pair of stanzas and the passage of anapaestic recitative between them (346–64) serve to carry the plot forward. Philocleon at last explains what is detaining him, and the chorus breaks into fulminations against Bdelycleon (strophe); they urge Philocleon to devise some means of escape, and Philocleon describes the odds against him (recitative); the chorus offers further encouragement and Philocleon decides to gnaw through the net (antistrophe). The metre of the lyric stanzas is very simple: pure, unsyncopated trochaic, except for the one colon, 339 = 370. Philocleon confines himself to catalectic tetrameters, presumably recitative, while the chorus diversifies with the inital dimeter, the lyric colon, 339 = 370, and, finally, a pnigos-like run of thirteen trochees ending in catalexis.

The curious correspondence of dochmiac with two cretics at 339 = 370 is paralleled by *Birds* 333–5 = 349–51, where the same phenomenon is repeated five times. There, while various forms of dochmiac and cretic are used, the number of syllables in each dochmiac matches that in the corresponding pair of cretics. Here, too, the corresponding cola are both of seven syllables. If the MS text at 342 is sound, a cretic of the form $\widehat{\smile\smile}\ \smile\ -$ twice corresponds with a full trochee of the form $-\ \smile\ -\ -$. It is very easy to supplement: ⟨ὅδ'⟩ was supplied by Hermann and Dindorf, ⟨σὺ⟩ by Meineke. See, however, below, 1060 ff. = 1091 ff.

In the anapaestic recitative, τουδὶ for τοῦδε at 347 again bears witness to the metrical skill of Florent Chrestien.

The colometry of the stanza shared by RV completely fails to correspond. Thus, 334–5 are divided:

τίς γὰρ ἐσθ' ὁ ταῦτά σ' εἴργων κἀποκλῄων τῇ θύρᾳ;
λέξον· πρὸς εὔνους γὰρ φράσεις.

$-\smile-\smile\quad -\smile--\quad -\smile--\quad -\smile-$

$--\smile-\quad --\smile-$

403–87

403–4

$-\smile-\smile\quad -\smile-\smile$

405 νῦν ἐκεῖνο νῦν ἐκεῖνο

$-\smile-\smile\quad -\smile-\smile\quad -\smile-\smile\quad \dagger-\smile\smile-\smile\dagger$

τοὐξύθυμον, ᾧ κολαζόμεσθα, κέντρον †ἐντέτατ' ὀξύ.†

The corresponding verses, 365–6, become:

ἀλλὰ καὶ νῦν ἐκπόριζε
μηχανὴν ὅπως τάχισθ᾿· ἕως γάρ, ὦ μελίττιον.

⏤ ⏑ ⏤ ⏤   ⏤ ⏑ ⏤ ⏑

⏤ ⏑ ⏤ ⏑   ⏤ ⏑ ⏤ ⏑   ⏤ ⏑ ⏤ ⏑   ⏤ ⏑ ⏤

Thereafter, the colometry of the strophe, 342–5, seems even more strongly influenced by rhetorical division:

⏤ ⏑ ⏤ ⏤   ⏗ ⏑ ⏤ ⏑   ⏤ ⏑ ⏤ ⏑   ⏗ ⏑ ⏤

⏗ ⏑ ⏤   ⏗ ⏑ ⏤ ⏑   ⏤ ⏑ ⏤ ⏑

⏤ ⏑ ⏤ ⏑   ⏤ ⏑ ⏤ ⏤   ⏤ ⏑ ⏤ ⏤   ⏤ ⏑ ⏤

⏤ ⏤ ⏑ ⏤   ⏑ ⏤ ⏑ ⏤

The corresponding verses, 373–9, are divided into a catalectic trochaic tetrameter, iambic dimeter, iambic monometer, and three further dimeters. These divisions look deliberate. They look, indeed, like the work of someone with some understanding of metre who, working on a text which did not fully correspond, failed to recognize correspondence altogether. The same division is reproduced in the Triclinian L (and Ald). Triclinius did, nevertheless, perceive correspondence: ἡ ἀμοιβαία αὕτη στροφὴ ἔοικεν εἶναι ἀντιστροφὴ τῆς ἄνω ῥηθείσης ὁμοίας στροφῆς (Σ LAld 365a). It could be conjectured that Triclinius had before him Σ *vet.* that are lost to us, but that would do little to clarify the matter. Since Σ *vet.* generally accord with the colon-division preserved more or less imperfectly by RV, we should not expect the Σ to note correspondence where the MS colometry fails so patently to correspond.

tro tetram cat II

tro dim

tro tetram (?)

408–9

‒ ᴗ ‒ ᴗ   ‒ ᴗ ‒ ‒

410 καὶ κελεύετ᾽ αὐτὸν ἥκειν

‒ ᴗ ‒ ᴗ   ‒ ᴗ ⌢

ὡς ἐπ᾽ ἄνδρα μισόπολιν

‒ ᴗ ‒ ᴗ   ‒ ᴗ ⌢ᴗ

ὄντα κἀπολούμενον, ὅτι

‒ ᴗ ⌢   ‒ ᴗ ‒

τόνδε λόγον εἰσφέρει,

‒ ᴗ ‒   ‒ ᴗ ‒

[ὡς χρὴ] μὴ δικάζειν δίκας.

415–17

‒ ᴗ ‒   ‒ ᴗ ‒   ‒ ᴗ ‒   ‒ ᴗ ‒

418 ὦ πόλις καὶ Θεώρου θεοισεχθρία,

‒ ᴗ ‒   ‒ ᴗ ‒   ‒ ᴗ ‒   ‒ ᴗ ‒

κεἴ τις ἄλλος προέστηκεν ἡμῶν κόλαξ.

420–27

‒ ᴗ ‒   ‒ ᴗ ‒   ‒ ᴗ ‒   ‒ ᴗ ‒

428 ἀλλ᾽ ἀφίει τὸν ἄνδρ᾽· εἰ δὲ μή, φήμ᾽ ἐγὼ

‒ ᴗ ‒   ‒ ᴗ ⌢   ‒ ᴗ ‒   ‒ ᴗ ‿ ‖

τὰς χελώνας μακαριεῖν σε τοῦ δέρματος.

430–62

‒ ᴗ ‒ ‒   ‒ ᴗ ‒ ᴗ

463 ἆρα δῆτ᾽ οὐκ αὐτόδηλα

‒ ᴗ ‒ ᴗ   ‒ ᴗ ‒ ᴗ   ‒ ᴗ ‒ ᴗ

465 τοῖς πένησιν, ἡ τυραννὶς ὡς λάθρᾳ γ᾽ ἐ-

‒ ᴗ ⌢   ‒ ᴗ ‿ ‖

λάμβαν᾽ ὑπιοῦσά με

tro tetram cat II

tro dim

tro cr

tro dim

    + 2 cr

2 cr

tro tetram cat III

4 cr

4 cr

tro tetram cat VIII

4 cr

4 cr

tro tetram cat XXXIII

2 tro

3 tro

    + 2 cr

466–7

‒ ⏑ ⏖   ‒ ⏑ ⏖

468   οὔτε τιν' ἔχων πρόφασιν

‒ ⏑ ⏖   ‒ ⏑ ⏖

οὔτε λόγον εὐτράπελον,

‒ ⏑ ‒   ‒ ⏑ ⏑ ‖

470   αὐτὸς ἄρχων μόνος;

471–2

‒ ⏑ ‒ ‒   ‒ ⏑ ‒ ⏑

473   σοὺς λόγους, ὦ μισόδημε

‒ ⏑ ‒ ⏑   ‒ ⏑ ‒ ⏑

καὶ μοναρχίας ἐραστὰ

‒ ⏑ ‒   ‒ ⏑ ‒   ‒ ⏑ ‒   ‒ ⏑ ‒

475   καὶ ξυνὼν Βρασίδᾳ καὶ φορῶν κράσπεδα

‒ ⏑ ‒   ‒ ⏑ ‒   ‒ ⏑ ‒   ‒ ⏑ ‒

στεμμάτων τήν θ' ὑπήνην ἄκουρον τρέφων;

478–85

‒ ⏑ ⏖   ‒ ⏑ ‒   ‒ ⏑ ‒   ‒ ⏑ ‒ ‖ ᴴ

486   οὐδέποτέ γ', οὔχ, ἕως ἄν τί μου λοιπὸν ἦ—

‒ ⏑ ‒   ‒ ⏑ ⏖   ‒ ⏑ ‒   ‒ ⏑ ‒

ὅστις ἡμῶν ἐπὶ τυραννίδ' ⟨ἐξ⟩εστάλης.

Metrically, this knock-about scene has affinities with the scuffle-scene at
Ach. 204 ff. There, except in the intermission where Dicaeopolis performs his phallic ceremony, cretic and trochaic predominate. Here, they
are used exclusively. Here, too, the action is more prolonged and more
characters are involved. There is a degree of symmetry of structure,
but not enough to justify division into strophe and antistrophe. All the
characters, including the chorus, use recitative-type tetrameters, but
only the chorus uses lyric metre: trochaic (in lengths other than tetrameters) and cretic. The structure is as follows:

tro tetram cat II

2 cr

2 cr

2 cr

tro tetram cat II

2 tro

2 tro

4 cr

4 cr

tetram cat VIII

4 cr

4 cr

403–4	2 tetrameters		463–5	7 metra (trochaic and cretic)
405–7	6 metra? (trochaic)			
408–9	2 tetrameters		466–7	2 tetrameters
410–14	10 metra (trochaic and cretic)		468–70	6 metra (cretic)
415–17	3 tetrameters		471–2	2 tetrameters
418–19	8 metra (cretic)		473–4	4 metra (trochaic)
420–7	8 tetrameters		475–7	8 metra (cretic)
428–9	8 metra (cretic)		478–85	8 tetrameters
430–62	33 tetrameters		486–7	8 metra (cretic)

After 487, the chorus falls silent and there is no more lyric. Bdelycleon and Philocleon (with one intervention from Xanthias) carry on an exchange in trochaic tetrameters to 525. These 38 lines roughly balance the 33 lines at 430–62.

Part of the passage (443 onwards) is preserved in fragmentary form in *P. Oxy.* 1374, of the 5th century AD. The lyric portions are very fragmentary, but the text and colon-division, as far as discernible, agree with RV.

At 407, the MSS' ἐντέτατ᾽ ὀξύ is highly dubious for several reasons, which are well expounded by A. H. Sommerstein (*CQ* 27 (1977), 263–4).

Metrically, the text combines three rarities: verse-end without catalexis in trochaic (Introduction, p. 35), double short for single short in lyric (Introduction, p. 39) and elision of -αι (see on 273 above). ὀξύ has most probably slipped in from τοὐξύθυμον, but ἐντέταται alone is a very awkward word to accommodate in trochees. The only alternative for double short in place of short or for elision is epic correption, as in Sommerstein's proposal *exempli gratia*, ἐντέταται εἰς μάχην, making a

$$526\text{–}45=631\text{–}47$$

$$-\,-\,\cup\,-\quad-\,\cup\,\cup\,-$$
νῦν δὴ τὸν ἐκ θἠμετέρου

$$-\,\cup\,\cup\,-\quad\cup\,-\,\cup\,-$$
$$-\,\cup\,\cup\,-$$
527 γυμνασίου λέγειν τι δεῖ

$$-\,\cup\,\cup\,-\quad-\,\smile\,\|\,\mathrm{H}$$
καινόν, ὅπως φανήσει—

$$529\text{–}31\qquad\text{ia tetram cat II}$$

$$-\,\cup\,\cup\,-\quad\cup\,-\,\cup\,-$$
532 μὴ κατὰ τὸν νεανίαν

$$-\,\cup\,\cup\,-\quad\cup\,-\,\cup\,-$$
$$-\,-\,\cup\,-\quad\cup\,-\,\cup\,-$$
533 τόνδε λέγειν. ὁρᾷς γὰρ ὡς

$$-\,\cup\,\cup\,-\quad\cup\,-\,-$$
σοι μέγας ἐστὶν ἀγών

pair of cretics, like 413. But epic correption, although it occurs more than thirty times in Aristophanes' lyric, is never otherwise used to produce a short in resolution, except in dochmiacs (*Clouds* 1170, *Thesm.* 915, 1028; see Introduction, pp. 91-2). D. M. Jones's ἐντατέον, either with his own ὀξέως or with Sommerstein's εἰς μάχην, removes that problem (Sommerstein, op. cit. 264 n. 1).

At 414, ὡς χρὴ, an obvious attempt at linguistic simplification which would produce a dochmiac completely out of context, was excised by Dindorf. θεοισεχθρία at 418 is Bentley's emendation of θεοσεχθρία (θεὸς ἐχθρία RV). At 487, ⟨ἐξ⟩εστάλης is Meineke's supplement (ὧδ' ἐστάλης Hermann). The syllable seems to have been lost early in the process of transmission. In *P. Oxy.* 1374 there is a hole betweeen τυρ- and ἐστάλης, but not, according to Grenfell and Hunt, enough space for ἐξ or ὧδ'.

Emendations without metrical implications are: 463 αὐτόδηλα L. Dindorf, for αὐτὰ δῆλα of the MSS; 473 σοὺς Dindorf, for σοὶ MSS.

There is split resolution at 412.

       ia cho dim
631   οὐπώποθ' οὕτω καθαρῶς

       cho ia dim = cho cho
632   οὐδένος ἠκούσαμεν οὐ-

        + arist
633   δὲ ξυνετῶς λέγοντος.

     634-5   ia tetram cat II
       cho ia dim
636 ὡς δ' ἐπὶ πάντ' ἐλήλυθεν

       cho ia dim = ia dim
       κοὐδεν παρῆλθεν, ὥστ' ἔγωγ'

        + arist
       ηὐξανόμην ἀκούων.

‒∪∪‒ ∪‒‒

καὶ περὶ τῶν ἁπάντων.

‒∪∪‒ ∪‒‒

536 εἰ γάρ, ὁ μὴ †γένοιτο νῦν

‒∪∪‒ ∪‒◡ ‖

οὗτος ἐθέλει κρατῆσαι†

538–9 ia tetram cat II

‒∪∪‒ ‒‒∪‒

οὐκέτι πρεσβυτῶν ὄχλος

‒∪∪‒ ‒∪∪‒

χρήσιμός ἐστ᾽ οὐδ᾽ ἀκαρῆ·

‒∪∪‒ ‒‒∪‒

542 σκωπτόμενοι δ᾽ [ἂν] ἐν ταῖς ὁδοῖς [ἁπάσαις]

‒∪∪‒ ∪‒∪‒

θαλλοφόροι καλούμεθ᾽, ἀντ-

‒∪∪‒ ∪‒◡ ‖‖‖

ωμοσιῶν κελύφη.

The strophe introduces the debate between Philocleon and Bdelycleon, and follows, in content, the familiar pattern in which a chorus encourages a debater with whom they are in sympathy. In the antistrophe, following the first round of the debate, the chorus, still firmly on Philocleon's side, congratulate their champion, and challenge Bdelycleon to extricate himself. The metre is pure iambo-choriambic, with two interventions from the characters in iambic tetrameters. In the strophe, Bdelycleon twice interrupts the chorus in mid-sentence (see Sommerstein, *CQ* 27 (1977), 265–7, whose conjecture εἰ γάρ for εἴπερ at 536 I accept). After the first interruption, he himself invites them to complete what they were going to say; after the second, the invitation to continue comes from Philocleon. It is to be noted, however, that the chorus's utterances, though incomplete syntactically, are rounded off rhythmically by catelexis at 528 and 537. This makes possible the variation in the antistrophe, where the recitative interventions, both by

arist

κἂν μακάρων δικάζειν

arist

640 αὐτὸς ἔδοξα νήσοις,

arist

ἡδόμενος λέγοντι.

642–3   ia tetram cat II

cho ia dim

δεῖ δέ σε παντοίας πλέκειν

cho cho

εἰς ἀπόφευξιν παλάμας·

cho ia dim

τὴν γὰρ ἐμὴν ὀργὴν πεπᾶ-

+ cho ia dim

646 ναι χαλεπὸν ⟨νεανίᾳ⟩

+ arist

μὴ πρὸς ἐμοῦ λέγοντι.

Philocleon, coincide with rhetorical pause, and make up a harmonious duet.

The song as transmitted contains several minor failures of correspondence and other more serious corruptions. Porson (*Notae in Aristophanem*, 131–5) produced a fully corresponding version on which all subsequent editors have drawn to some extent. Wilamowitz made two onslaughts on the passage (*Isyllos von Epidauros*, 137, and *GV* 472–3). In the interests of clarity I have given the MS text where it is tolerable, but the non-metrical evidence of corruption in the passage is enough to suggest that accidental paraphrasing has taken place (Introduction, p. 118) and that quite extensive emendation is justified, if it can be done simply.

At 526, RV and the Triclinian MSS offer νῦν δέ, producing – ‿ ‿ – corresponding with – – ‿ –. Porson restored νῦν δή from 'Brunck's MS' (Ct6; Vp3 also has δή), which is a clear improvement in sense

(Denniston, *Particles*, 206, cf. *Knights* 756), as well as metre. In the other two places in the received text where – ⌣ ⌣ – corresponds with ✕ – ⌣ – (527 and 533) linguistic considerations are not involved, and the freedom of correspondence might be regarded as tolerable (Introduction, p. 78 and *Ach.* 1150 and *Lys.* 326). However, Bentley's transposition δεῖ τι λέγειν at 527 and his τονδί at 533 are simple and plausible. Loss of demonstrative -ι is a common error: compare Bentley's restoration of ταυτηὶ for ταύτῃ at 1330.

At 532 = 636, the MSS offer cho ia dim in the strophe, but a glyconic (ὡς δὲ πάντ᾽ ἐπελήλυθεν) in the antistrophe. Such a correspondence is without reliable parallel. MacDowell notes glyc = ia cho at E. *Supp.* 1000 = 1023, but that is a severely corrupt stanza. Cho ia = glyc appears in the MSS at Pindar, *Pyth.* 8. 97, but is easily removed by Heyne's transposition, φέγγος ἔπεστιν. See further on this and on more or less kindred anomalies, D. L. Page, *Sappho and Alcaeus*, 81, G. W. Bond, *Euripides: Hypsipyle*, 64, D. S. Raven, *AJP* 86 (1965), 228. The solitary glyconic is, in any case, out of place in this stanza. Porson's ὡς δ᾽ ἐπὶ πάντ᾽ ἐλήλυθεν gained the approval of Wilamowitz (Cf. *OT* 265. See W. S. Barrett on *Hipp.* 284). I do not see that ἐπὶ πάντ᾽ ἔρχεσθαι need imply, as MacDowell asserts, that 'most of the attempts fail'. Finally, it is worth emphasizing that examples of glyc = pol are irrelevant.

At 534, the pre-Triclinian MSS have σοι μέγας ἐστ᾽ ἀγών (– ⌣ ⌣ – ⌣ –). Elmsley (on *Hcld.* 722) restored correspondence by accepting the Triclinian ἐστίν, combined with ἀγών. The loss of the article in crasis is ubiquitous in MSS, and scholars of the late 18th and early 19th centuries restored metre in countless passages by its reintroduction. However, while the article makes sense here ('great is the conflict before you'), it is not necessary. Compare *Clouds* 958–9:

> . . . σοφίας,
> ἧς πέρι τοῖς ἐμοῖς φίλοις
> ἐστὶν ἀγὼν μέγιστος.

Bentley's proposal, ἐστ᾽ ἀγὼν νῦν still deserves consideration. νῦν would be more meaningful here than in 536, a line which presents a much more difficult problem. Porson, accepting Bentley's treatment of 534, also followed him in deleting νῦν at 536 (which could, as Dobree suggests, have slipped down a line in the process of copying from an MS with two cola per line), adding σ' (rather than Bentley's γ') before ἐθέλει. This produces a pair of aristophaneans in synartesis:

> εἴπερ, ὃ μὴ γένοιθ', οὗ-
> τος σ' ἐθέλει κρατῆσαι

For aristophaneans in synartesis, see Introduction, p. 83. Wilamowitz's remedy was to delete not νῦν but οὗτος. This entails verse-end after γένοιτο, since -το becomes *brevis in longo*. But with both approaches ἐθέλει κρατῆσαι remains a problem. 'If he wishes to win' is nonsense in the context: Bdelycleon's wishes have never been in doubt, and ὃ μὴ γένοιτο points to something in the future. The only way to save ἐθέλει κρατῆσαι is to take it as a periphrastic future, but that is a usage not attested in Attic. At Plato, *Rep.* 370b and 375a, cited by Sommerstein (*CQ* 27 (1977), 267), ἐθέλει means 'can', rather than 'will' (see W. J. Verdenius, 'Notes on Plato's *Phaedo*', *Mnemosyne*, 11 (1958), 231–2). Blaydes's σε λέγων κρατήσει gives the sense needed.

At 542–5 = 645–7, there is again a serious failure of correspondence. The strophe is too long, and Wilamowitz chose to make it even longer by adding ⟨αὐτίκ'⟩ after ἄν. This, with ταῖσιν from RV and the Triclinian MSS (ταῖς ΓVp3), produces:

$$- \cup \cup - \quad \cup - \cup -$$
$$- \cup \cup - \quad \cup - -$$
$$- \cup \cup - \quad \cup - \cup -$$
$$- \cup \cup - \quad \cup - -$$

where the antistrophe provides only:

$$- \cup \cup - \quad - - \cup -$$
$$- \cup \cup -$$
$$- \cup \cup - \quad \cup - -$$

I print Porson's solution, which is preferable linguistically as well as metrically. The future καλούμεθ' (for the MSS' καλοίμεθ') gives the proper apodosis to the 'menacing' conditional at 536–7, and that entails the deletion of ἄν. ἄν may well have been introduced by near-dittography, leading, in its turn, to the introduction of the optative καλοίμεθ'. ἐν ταῖς ὁδοῖς ('in the open street', 'in public') is something of a set phrase in Aristophanes (Cf. *Knights* 348, *Clouds* 362, 964, *Lys.* 523, *Ecc.* 773), but (ἁ)πάσαις never elsewhere forms part of it. Porson's supplement ⟨νεανίᾳ⟩ at 646 perfects correspondence.

729–35 = 743–9

‿–‿–   ‿–‿|–   ‿–‿–
πιθοῦ πιθοῦ λόγοισι, μηδ᾽ ἄφρων γένῃ

⏟⏜–‿–   ⏝⏜–‿–
730   μηδ᾽ ἀτενὴς ἄγαν ἀτεράμων τ᾽ ἀνήρ.

⏟–‿–   ⏟–‿–   ⏟–‿–
εἴθ᾽ ὤφελέν μοι κηδεμὼν ἢ ξυγγενὴς

⏟–‿–   –‿–   ‿–‿⏝‖
εἶναί τις ὅστις τοιαῦτ᾽ ἐνουθέτει.

–‿–   –‿–| ‿–|–‿–
σοὶ δὲ νῦν τις θεῶν παρὼν ἐμφανὴς

––‿–   ––‿–   ––‿–   ⏝|–‿–
ξυλλαμβάνει τοῦ πράγματος καὶ δῆλός ἐστιν εὖ ποιῶν·

⏝⏜–‿–|‖
735   σὺ δὲ παρὼν δέχου.

At 725–6, the chorus, through the mouth of their leader, declare themselves converted, with the suddenness typical of an Aristophanic chorus, to the views of Bdelycleon. In the last verse of his anapaestic tetrameters, the leader addresses Philocleon: ἀλλ᾽ ὦ τῆς ἡλικίας ἡμῖν τῆς αὐτῆς συνθιασῶτα. Then, with whimsical dramatic effect, the chorus join in the address in lyric. They sing in iambic, diversified by syncopation and given urgency by dochmiacs. In 733 = 747, corresponding word-end accentuates the affinity between cretic and dochmiac. The dramatic ambiance of the song is paratragic (Philocleon, sword in hand, is preserving the ominous silence of the tragic hero), and the dochmiacs signal an appropriate emotional level. Between strophe and antistrophe, Bdelycleon interjects a short anapaestic system promising his father various comforts in his old age. This is roughly balanced, after the antistrophe, by the paratragic anapaests with which Philocleon accompanies his suicide *manqué*.

   P. Oxy. 1374 preserves 746–9 in very fragmentary form with the same colometry as RV, who preserve the vestiges of a corresponding division, except that οἷς is transferred from the end of 743 to the begin-

ia trim
νενουθέτηκεν αὐτὸν εἰς τὰ πράγμαθ' οἷς

+ 2 δ
τότ' ἐπεμαίνετ'· ἔγνωκε γὰρ ἀρτίως

ia trim
745 λογίζεταί τ' ἐκεῖνα πάνθ' ἁμαρτίας

ia trim sync
ἃ σοῦ κελεύοντος οὐκ ἐπείθετο.

2 cr δ
νῦν δ' ἴσως τοῖσι σοῖς λόγοις πείθεται

ia tetram
καὶ σωφρονεῖ μέντοι μεθιστὰς εἰς τὸ λοιπὸν τὸν τρόπον

δ
πειθόμενός τε σοι.

ning of 744. This looks like 'correction' by a metrically ignorant person, rather than a simple scribal error. The trimeters at 731–2 are split between lines in the strophe to produce:

$$- - \cup - -$$
$$- \cup - - - \cup -$$
$$- - \cup - -$$
$$\cup - \cup - \cup -$$

Again this follows word-end, seemingly regardless of metre. The corresponding verses in the antistrophe, where the incidence of word-end is different, are left intact.

No Σ *vet.* have survived, and it seems clear that Triclinius had none either. The Triclinian Σ on 725 takes the chorus-leader's anapaests and the following strophe together as στροφὴ στίχων ια'. His colometry survives in the Budé text, except that his last verse is there divided into two. The antistrophe, however, he seems to have taken, with 748, to be five iambic trimeters and two catalectic trochaic tetrameters. At least, he emends freely in characteristic style so as to make the lines approximate to that pattern. This gives an idea of how far Triclinius could be at sea without the aid of *Σ vet.*

The text is free from problems. At 747, the pre-Triclinian MSS have τοῖς ἴσοις (]ι̣σ̣οις *Π*) and the later, but non-Triclinian MSS (Vp3+) have τοῖς ἴσοι καὶ. Triclinius saw the sense required: his τοῖς σοῖς

868–74=885–90

868–9 trim II

⏓ – ⏑ –   ⏑ – – ||^{H}
τὸ πρᾶγμ', ὃ μηχανᾶται

– – ⏑ | –   ⏒ – ⏑ –
ἔμπροσθεν οὗτος τῶν θυρῶν,

⏑ – ⏑ –   – – ⏑ –
ἅπασιν ἡμῖν ἁρμόσαι

– ⏑ ⏑ – ⏑ –
παυσαμένοις πλάνων.

⏑ – ⏑ ⏑ – – |||
ἰήιε Παιάν.

Nearly 250 lines, from 760 to 1008, are taken up with the episode of the domestic trial. This comparatively long sequence of iambic trimeters is interrupted at 863–90 by a passage in recitative and lyric which divides the preparations from the trial itself. The chorus chants a short prelude in anapaests (863–7). Then follows a pair of iambic trimeters (868–9) in which Bdelycleon calls for εὐφημία and the chorus begin their address to Apollo, running straight on into a short and simple lyric stanza (for the absence of rhetorical pause between recitative and song, compare 728–9 above). Bdelycleon's prayer to Apollo (875–84), in anapaests, forms a centre-piece. The two iambic trimeters (885–6) which balance 868–9 are both delivered by the chorus and are syntactically distinct from the antistrophe (887–90). The whole passage is a piece of dramatic punctuation, providing rhythmic and musical variety.

The stanza begins, a little surprisingly, with a catalectic iambic dimeter followed by verse-end, even though there is close syntactic continuity with what follows. Indeed, in the antistrophe, even word-end

(LVp2AldB) prepared the way for Invernizi to restore τοῖσι σοῖς. At 749, Brunck conjectured πιθόμενος to produce exact correspondence in the dochmiac. This, however, is unnecessary (Introduction, p. 66), and πειθόμενος, 'under the guidance of' (cf. *Birds* 5, 7), makes good sense.

885–6   trim II

ia dim cat
εὖνοι γάρ ἐσμεν ἐξ οὗ

ia dim
τὸν δῆμον ᾐσθόμεσθά σου

ia dim
φιλοῦντος ὡς οὐδεὶς ἀνὴρ

dodrans A
890   τῶν γε νεωτέρων.

reiz

after ἐξ οὗ is weak. This may be seen as a touch of the unexpected which saves the stanza from banality. There is another unusual touch at the end of the strophe, where – ∪ ∪ – ∪ – is not followed by its own catalectic form (– ∪ ∪ – –), but by the catalectic equivalent of the telesillean (✕ – ∪ ∪ – –). Meineke may have been right to believe that ἰήιε Παιάν should be repeated after 891 to round off the song with catalexis. The chorus has, however, turned its attention in the antistrophe from Apollo to Bdelycleon, and, to our taste at least, the ritual cry seems intrusive.

At 889, the Triclinian MSS restore the metre with οὐδείς, where the rest have οὐδὲ εἷς. At 890, the pre-Triclinian MSS have τῶν γενναιοτέρων, but Σ *vet.* preserves a variant: εἰ μὲν "γενναιοτέρων", τῶν σπουδαίων, εἰ δὲ "νεωτέρων", τῶν ὁμηλίκων. Triclinius chose the right meaning, but, characteristically, made the colon up to full iambic (τῶν νῦν γε σοῦ νεωτέρων LVp2AldB) without observing correspondence. He pointed the way, however, to Reisig's solution, which I print.

1009–14

‒ ∪ ∪ ‒ ‒ 　 ∪ ∪ ‒ ‒ ‒
ἀλλ' ἴτε χαίροντες ὅποι βούλεσθ'.

‒ ‒ ∪ ∪ ‒
1010　　ὑμεῖς δὲ τέως,

‒ ‒ ∪ ∪ ∪ ∪ 　 ∪ ∪ ‒ ‒
ὦ μυριάδες ἀναρίθμητοι,

‒ ∪ ‒ ‒ 　 ‒ ∪ ‒ ‒
1011　νῦν [μὲν] τὰ μέλλοντ' εὖ λέγεσθαι

‒ ∪ ‒ ‒ 　 ‒ ∪ ‒
1012　μὴ πέσῃ φαύλως χαμᾶζ'

‒ ∪ ‒ ∪
εὐλαβεῖσθε·

‒ ∪ ‒ ‒ 　 ‒ ∪ ‒ ‒
τοῦτο γὰρ σκαιῶν θεατῶν

‒ ∪ ‒ ‒ 　 ‒ ∪ ‒ ‒ |||
ἐστι πάσχειν, κοὐ πρὸς ὑμῶν.

The song combines a send-off for the characters with an introduction to the parabasis. In *Knights* (498–506), the same purpose is served by a short anapaestic system (compare *Ach.* 1143–9, which is also an anapaestic send-off preceding a song, 1150ff.). Here, as in *Clouds* (510ff.), only the opening is in anapaests, the characteristic metre of welcomes and send-offs. The address to the audience is still in anapaests, but then the metre changes to trochaic, ending without catalexis (Introduction, p. 35). White (*VGC* 118) wished to add 1015 to the song because of the sequence ∪ ∪ ∪ ∪ (προσέχετε), which is characteristic of sung anapaests. Rhetorically, however, there is a clear break after 1014 (πρὸς ὑμῶν), and 1015 points forward. προσέχετε causes metrical oddities elsewhere in Aristophanes: in recitative anapaests at *Knights* 503 and *Birds* 688, and at the end of a catalectic trochaic tetrameter at *Clouds* 575 (⁀∪ ∪ ⁀, cf. 581 Παφλαγόνα). The alternatives are to assume that

an dim

+ an

an dim cat

tro dim

tro cr

+ tro

tro tetram

forms of προσέχειν are 'simply allowed as an exception' (Dover on *Clouds* 575) or to emend to πρόσχετε (like B in this passage, cf. Pherecrates, *PCG* 84). If, however, πρόσχετε is right, the systematic corruption to προσέχετε is hard to explain.

With μέν (deleted by Burges) at 1011, the passage could be scanned as iambic as far as χαμᾶζ', but the change to trochaic without full word-end that would become necessary at that point is highly implausible (Introduction, p. 35). Moreover, μέν is unwanted here, and is the sort of word that copyists easily allow to slip in (or out).

The cretic in mid-verse at 1012 may seem a little obtrusive rhythmically, and it is just worth noting that the transpositon χαμᾶζε φαύλως would produce a simple run of unsyncopated trochees. Compare, however, 1063 below.

1060–70=1091–1101

$$-\cup-\cup \quad -\cup-\breve{} \quad -\cup-\cup \quad -\cup-$$

1060   ὦ πάλαι ποτ᾽ ὄντες ἡμεῖς ἄλκιμοι μὲν ἐν χοροῖς,

$$-\cup- \quad -\cup-$$

ἄλκιμοι δ᾽ ἐν μάχαις,

$$-\cup-\cup \quad -\cup\underset{\cup}{\wideparen{}}$$

1062   καὶ κατ᾽ αὐτὸ τοῦτο μόνον

$$-\cup|-\cup \quad -\cup\frown ||$$

ἄνδρες ἀλκιμώτατοι.

$$-\cup-|- \quad -\cup-$$

1063   πρίν ποτ᾽ ἦν πρὶν ταῦτα, νῦν δ᾽

$$-\cup-|\underset{\smile}{} \quad -\cup\underset{\cup}{\wideparen{}}$$

οἴχεται, κύκνου τε πολι-

$$-\cup-\cup \quad -\cup-- \quad -\cup\smile ||$$

1065   ώτεραι δὴ αἵδ᾽ ἐπανθοῦσιν τρίχες.

$$-\cup-- \quad \wideparen{\infty}\cup-|\breve{} \quad -\cup--$$

1066–7   ἀλλὰ κἀκ τῶν λειψάνων δεῖ τῶνδε ῥώμην

$$-\cup-- \quad -\cup-|- \quad -|\cup-\breve{}$$

νεανικὴν σχεῖν· ὡς ἐγὼ τοὐμὸν νομίζω

$$-\cup-\breve{} \quad -\cup-- \quad -\cup--$$

γῆρας εἶναι κρεῖττον ἢ πολλῶν κικίννους

$$-\cup-- \quad -\cup|-\cup \quad -\cup- |||$$

1070   νεανιῶν καὶ σχῆμα κεὐρυπρωκτίαν.

The ode and antode of the parabasis follow the same sequence of ideas
as the recitative. The chorus begin by recalling the prowess of their
youth and end with opprobrious reflections on the younger generation.
The metre is trochaic, diversified by cretic and divided by verse-end into
sections of ten, seven, and twelve metra. In two places (1062 = 1093 and
1064 = 1095), a resolved cretic ($-\cup\wideparen{\infty}$) in the strophe corresponds to
$-\cup-\cup$ in the antistrophe, and there is no simple solution. At 1062, the
presence of δὴ after αὐτὸ in the printed vulgate gave rise to attempts by

tro tretram cat
ἆρα δεινὸς ἦ τόθ' ὥστε πάντα μὴ δεδοικέναι,

2 cr
καὶ κατεστρεψάμην

tro cr = tro tro
1093 τοὺς ἐναντίους, πλέων ἐ-

+ tro cr
κεῖσε ταῖς τριήρεσιν.

tro cr
οὐ γὰρ ἦν ἡμῖν ὅπως

+ tro cr = tro tro
1095 ῥῆσιν εὖ λέξειν ἐμέλλο-

+ tro trim cat
μεν τότ' οὐδὲ συκοφαντήσειν τινὰ

3 tro
φροντίς, ἀλλ' ὅστις ἐρέτης ἔσοιτ' ἄριστος.

3 tro
τοιγαροῦν πολλὰς πόλεις Μήδων ἑλόντες

3 tro
1100 αἰτιώτατοι φέρεσθαι τὸν φόρον δεῦρ'

+ 2 tro cr
ἐσμέν, ὃν κλέπτουσιν οἱ νεώτεροι.

Bentley and Brunck to restore correspondence by transposition. Now, however, the recognition that δὴ is a Triclinian interpolation (LVp2 AldB) makes that course seem unattractive. This passage (together with *Lys.* 781 ff. = 805 ff.) provides the basis for Dale's theory of correspondence by 'syllable-counting' (LM² 89–90 and Introduction, p. 117).

   The song also includes two oddities of prosody. The correption of δὴ at 1065 is highly unusual in trochaic (Introduction, p. 92) and the failure to lengthen final short vowel before ῥ in τῶνδε ῥώμην (1066–7) is said by White (*VGC* 366) to be unique in Aristophanes. It is, indeed, generally very rare in Attic. The most plausible example elsewhere in Old Comedy seems to be Hermippus, *PCG* 77. 8 (dactylic hexameters; see Meineke, *FCG* ii. 303–4). On tragedy, see M. Griffith, *The Authenticity of 'Prometheus Bound'*, 81–2.

1226–48

‒ ‒ ‒ ∪ ∪ ‒ ∪ ‒ ∪ ‒ ‒

1226   *B.* οὐδεὶς πώποτ' ἀνὴρ ἔγεντ' Ἀθήναις

‒ ‒ ‒ ∪ ∪ ‒ ∪ ‒ ∪ ‒ ‒

1227   *Φ.* οὐχ οὕτω γε πανοῦργος ⟨οὐδὲ⟩ κλέπτης.

‒ ‒ ‒ ∪ ∪ ‒ ∪ ∪ ‒ ∪ ∪ ‒ ∪ ⌣ ‖

1232–3 *Φ.* ὤνθρωφ', οὗτος ὁ μαιόμενος τὸ μέγα κράτος,

‒ ‒ ‒ ∪ ∪ ‒ ∪ ∪ ‒ ∪ ∪ ‒ ∪ ‒

1234–5 ἀντρέψεις ἔτι τὰν πόλιν· ἁ δ' ἔχεται ῥοπᾶς.

‒ ‒ ‒ ∪ ∪ ‒ ‒ ∪ ∪ ‒ ‒ ∪ ∪ ‒ ∪ ‒

1238–9 *B.* Ἀδμήτου λόγον, ὦταῖρε, μαθὼν τοὺς ἀγαθοὺς φίλει.

‒ ‒ ∪ ∪ ‒ ∪ ‒ ‒

1241   *Φ.* οὐκ ἔστιν ἀλωπεκίζειν,

‒ ‒ ∪ ∪ ‒ ∪ ‒ ‒ ‒ ∪ ‒

1242   οὐδ' ἀμφοτέροισι γίγνεσθαι φίλον.

‒ ∪ ∪ ‒ ∪ ‒

1245   *B.* χρήματα καὶ βίον

‒ ∪ ∪ ‒ ∪ ‒   ‒ ∪ ∪ ‒ ∪ ‒

1246–7 Κλειταγόρᾳ τε κἀμοὶ μετὰ Θετταλῶν

‒ ∪ ‒ ∪ ∪ ‒ ∪ ‒ ∪ ‒ ‒

1248   *Φ.* πολλὰ δὴ διεκόμπασας σὺ κἀγώ.

The scene (1208 ff.) in which Bdelycleon instructs Philocleon in how to behave at a gentlemanly drinking-party culminates in an exchange of snatches of song. This represents the final stage of the symposium, when the myrtle-branch was passed round and each guest was expected to

At 1063, ἀλκιμώτατοι, Bentley's emendation, is necessary both to sense and metre. The MSS have μαχιμώτατοι.

Despite the eccentric correspondence, RV preserve a corresponding colon-division. Alexandrian scholars could hardly have failed to observe correspondence between the ode and antode of a parabasis.

phal

phal

aeol da

aeol da

greater asclepiad

hag

hag cr or telesill ia

dodrans A

2 dodrans A

phal

perform according to his abilities (on the proceedings and repertoire at symposia, see R. Reitzenstein, *Epigramm und Skolion*, 3–44). Bdelycleon's taste seems highly conservative, compared with that of the thoroughly modern Pheidippides (*Clouds* 1355 ff.)

The snatches of song here are all in aeolic metres. Although fellow-diners seem to have drawn on a wide range of poetic genres for their performances, the symposium was evidently the ambiance in which earlier Greek monodic lyric lived on at Athens, and metres of aeolic type also appear in native Attic drinking-songs, such as the Harmodius songs (Introduction, p. 72). The aeolic hendecasyllable (phal) figures as the first two lines of the Harmodius stanza. × ×– ◡ ◡ – ◡ ◡ – ◡ ◡ – ◡ – was the metre of Sappho's second book, and is also respresented among the fragments of Alcaeus, from whom 1323–5 are adapted (for the original, see *P. Oxy.* 2295 = *PLF* 141). Apart from the line of Praxilla quoted at 1238–9 (*PMG* 749), greater asclepiads appear in fragments of sympotic poetry (*PMG* 902–5, 908). ×– ◡ ◡ – ◡ –×– ◡ –, which combines – ◡ ◡ – ◡ – with iambo-trochaic rhythm in the manner of the sapphic and alcaic stanzas, may appear in Sappho (*P. Oxy.* 2295, fr. 2 = *PLF* 99), combined with the telesillean (×– ◡ ◡ – ◡ –). The metre of the fragment is discussed by Lobel (*P. Oxy.* xxi. 10–14). The double dodrans at 1246–7 is identical with the last verse of the Harmodius stanza. It has nothing to do with dochmiacs.

1265–74

– ◡ – –   – ◡ – –

1265   πολλάκις δὴ 'δοξ' ἐμαυτῷ

– ◡ – ◡   – ◡ – –   – ◡ – ◡   – ◡ ‿ ‖ ʜ

δεξιὸς πεφυκέναι καὶ σκαιὸς οὐδεπώποτε,

– ◡ – ◡   – ◡ – –   – ◡ – –   – ◡ – ‖ ʜ

ἀλλ' Ἀμυνίας ὁ Σέλλου μᾶλλον, οὐκ τῶν Κρωβύλου,

– ◡ – ◡   – ◡ – ◡

οὗτος ὅν γ' ἐγώ ποτ' εἶδον

– ◡ – –   – ◡ – –

ἀντὶ μήλου καὶ ῥοᾶς δειπ-

– ◡ ⌒◡ ◡   – ◡ – –   – ◡ – ◡   – ◡ –

1270   νοῦντα μετὰ Λεωγόρου· πεινῇ γὰρ ἧπερ Ἀντιφῶν.

– ◡ – –   – ◡ – –   – ◡ – ◡

ἀλλὰ πρεσβεύων γὰρ ἐς Φάρσαλον ᾤχετ'·

Scribes have made a number of mistakes in these lines, but the metres are so well defined as to permit restoration with comparative ease and certainty. At 1226, ἔγεντ᾽ Ἀθήναις is Bentley's emendation for the MSS' ἐγένετ᾽ Ἀθηναῖος. At 1227, several scholars (Bergk, Dindorf, Hirschig, Hermann) have proposed οὐδὲ, and priority is doubtful. At 1234, Bentley proposed ἀντρέψεις for the MSS' ἀνατρέψεις. At 1248, V has διεκόμισα and the rest διεκόμισας. διεκόμπασας was proposed by Tyrwhitt (who also corrected βίαν to βίον in 1245). RV divide 1238–9 into two cola, $---\cup\cup--|$ $\cup\cup--\cup\cup-\cup-$, and at 1245–7 take χρήματα . . . κἀ- together and separate -μοι . . . Θετταλῶν, contrary to word-end. Otherwise, their colometry is as printed. Given that the metricians of Alexandria had Lesbian poetry available to them in quantity, the generally correct division is not surprising. The greater asclepiad may have been divided because of its length, but the point chosen for the division is, none the less, curious, and provokes the suspicion that the verse may have been incorrectly analysed as pher + ?.

2 tro

tro tetram cat

tro tetram cat

2 tro

2 tro

+ tro tretram cat

3 tro

$$- \cup - \cup \quad - \cup -$$

εἶτ' ἐκεῖ μόνος μόνοις

$$- \cup - - \quad - \cup - -$$

τοῖς Πενέσταισι ξυνὴν τοῖς

$$- \cup - - \quad - \cup - - \quad - \cup - - \quad - \cup \smile \, |||$$

Θετταλῶν, αὐτὸς πενέστης ὢν ἐλάττων οὐδενός.

The chorus fill the time taken up by the symposium off stage with a short second parabasis. The passage performs a similar function structurally to *Ach.* 1150 ff. = 1162 ff. and the second parabasis of *Knights* (1264–1315), and the ode and epirrheme are, like the song in *Ach.* and the *Knights* parabasis, devoted to personal attack. The antode is lost, but in the antepirrheme the chorus turns to speaking in the person of the poet.

The ode is in pure trochaic, with occasional catalexis. The epirrhematic sections (accepting Bothe's deletion of 1282) consist of seven cretic tetrameters of the form $- \cup \widetilde{} \quad - \cup \widetilde{} \quad - \cup \widetilde{} \quad - \cup -$ rounded off by a catalectic trochaic tetrameter (Introduction, p. 45, and cf. *Ach.* 971 ff. = 988 ff.).

At 1268, γ' is preserved by R alone. The Triclinian MSS have ὄντιν' for ὄν. It is ironical that Triclinius, who so frequently inserted γε, did not think to do so here. At 1272, the Triclinian MSS make up a full trochaic metron with μόνοισι. I see no compelling argument for avoiding catalexis here. On the contrary, there is some case for ending the stanza with a run of six trochees, as it began.

Hall–Geldart's colometry, adopted with minimal corrections from RV, produces a mixture of trochaic and iambic demarcated by verse-end, or at least word-end, which is not impossible:

$$- \cup - - \quad - \cup - - \quad - \cup - \cup \quad - \cup -$$
$$- - \cup - \quad \cup - \cup \smile \, ||$$

1326–40

$$\widetilde{} \cup \widetilde{} \cup$$

Φ. ἄνεχε, πάρεχε,

$$- \cup - - \quad - \cup - \cup \quad \widetilde{} \cup - - \quad - \cup - \, || \text{ H}$$

κλαύσεταί τις τῶν ὄπισθεν ἐπακολουθούντων ἐμοί.

+ tro dim cat

2 tro

+ tro tetram cat

```
–∪–∪   –∪––   –∪––   –∪–‖ᴴ
–∪–∪   –∪–∪   –∪––   –∪–
––∪⁀⁀   ∪–∪–
––∪–   ∪–∪–
–∪––   –∪––   –∪–∪   –∪–
∪–∪–
–∪––   –∪––
–∪––   –∪––   –∪–∪   –∪⌣‖‖
```

This follows rhetorical division closely, but the iambic sections are much shorter than in the iambo-trochaic combination at 1326–40 below. The single iambic metron at 1272 seems particularly odd rhythmically.

The loss of the antode is noted in two Σ *vet.* on the passage, both mutilated. The shorter note (VG, Σ *vet.* 1283d) runs (in V): μετὰ τοῦτο διάλειμμα στίχων ἀνάστατον εἶναι, τῶν πλείστων δὲ εὗρον ἔνδεκα. The author has, apparently, examined more than one manuscript, and the maximum space he has found is of eleven lines. Eleven lines is actually the length of the ode in the colometry of RV. The second note (Σ *vet.* 1283e), which is preserved by V alone, mentions Heliodorus by name, and quotes him as having found traces of seven missing lines. The most useful discussion of these scholia is by D. Holwerda, *Mnemosyne*, 20 (1967), 261–3. Other passages where Σ *vet.* notes missing lines are *Clouds* 888 and *Birds* 1342.

1 tro

tro tetram cat

$$- \cup - - \,. \; - \cup - -$$

οἷον, εἰ μὴ 'ρρήσεθ', ὑμᾶς,

$$- \cup - - \quad - \cup - - \quad - \cup - - \quad - \cup - \, \| \, \text{н}$$

1230–1   ὦ πόνηροι, ταυτηὶ τῇ δᾳδὶ φρυκτοὺς σκευάσω.

1332–4

$$\cup - \cup - \quad \cup - \cup - \, \| \, \text{н}$$

1335   Φ. ἰὴ ἰεῦ, "καλούμενοι".

$$- - \cup - \quad - - \cup - \quad - - \cup - \quad - | \widehat{\cup\cup} \, \cup -$$

ἀρχαῖά γ' ὑμῶν. ἀρά γ' ἴσθ' ὡς οὐδ' ἀκούων ἀνέχομαι

$$\cup - \cup - \quad \cup - - \|$$

δικῶν; ἰαιβοῖ αἰβοῖ.

$$\widehat{\cup\cup} \, \cup - - \quad - \cup - -$$

τάδε μ' ἀρέσκει· βάλλε κημούς.

$$- \cup - - \quad - \cup - - \quad - \cup - \, \| \|$$

1340   οὐκ ἄπει; ποῦ 'στ' ἡλιαστής; ἐκποδών.

Philocleon's drunken and irrascible song, interrupted by three trimeters
from an aggrieved person, is in clearly demarcated blocks of trochaic
and iambic. There is one metrical oddity: word-end after long anceps
preceding resolution ($- | \widehat{\cup\cup} \, \cup -$) at 1337 (Introduction, p. 34).

1450–61 = 1462–73

$$- - \cup - \quad - \cup - -$$

1450   ζηλῶ γε τῆς εὐτυχίας

$$- - \cup - \quad \cup - -$$

τὸν πρέσβυν, οἷ μετέστη

$$\overline{\cup} - | \cup - \quad - \cup \cup -$$

ξηρῶν τρόπων καὶ βιοτῆς.

$$\cup \widehat{\cup\cup} \, \cup - | \quad - \cup \cup -$$

ἕτερα δὲ νῦν ἀντιμαθὼν

2 tro

tro tetram cat

trim III

ia dim

ia tetram

ia dim cat

2 tro

tro trim cat

At 1330, where the MSS have ταύτῃ, the metre is restored by
Bentley's ταυτῃὶ, and, at 1340, ἄπει is Weise's correction of the MS
ἄπεισι.

      ia cho dim
πολλοῦ δ' ἐπαίνου παρ' ἐμοὶ

      ia ba
καὶ τοῖσιν εὖ φρονοῦσιν

      ia cho dim
τυχὼν ἄπεισιν διὰ τὴν

      + ia cho dim
1465   φιλοπατρίαν καὶ σοφίαν

˘ ⏜ ˘ ⏜   ˘ – ⌣ ‖ ᴴ
ἦ μέγα τι μεταπεσεῖται

⌣ ⏜ ˘ –   – ˘ ˘ –
1455 ἐπὶ τὸ τρυφῶν καὶ μαλακόν.

˘ ⏜ ˘ – | – ˘ ˘ –
τάχα δ᾽ ἂν ἴσως οὐκ ἐθέλοι·

˘ ˘ ˘ – – – ˘ ˘ –
τὸ γὰρ ἀποστῆναι χαλεπὸν

˘ ⏒ – ˘ – ˘ ˘ –
φύσεως, ἣν ἔχοι τις, ἀεί.

– – – – | – ˘ ˘ –
καίτοι πολλοὶ ταῦτ᾽ ἔπαθον·

⌣ – – ˘ – ˘ ˘ –
1460 ξυνόντες γνώμαις ἑτέρων

˘ ˘ ⌣ – ⌣ | – ˘ – |||
μετεβάλοντο τοὺς τρόπους.

The chorus in this song deliver their final (though not deeply perceptive) judgements on Philocleon and Bdelycleon.

The stanza combines iambo-choriambic dimeters and polyschematists, but the two are kept in separate blocks (Introduction, pp 81–2). It ends with a eupolidean dicolon. This verse, which belongs typically to comic recitative, is first found in the fragments of Cratinus (*PCG* 75, 105, 357). There, it consists of pol + lec. It may well have been Eupolis who introduced the licence of treating in this context the first two positions of the lecythion as aeolic base (·· ··) on the analogy of the polyschematist (see further, Parker, *PCPS* 214 (1988), 115–22).

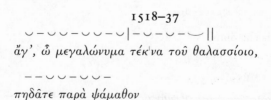

1518–37

˘ – ˘ ˘ – ˘ ˘ – ˘ | – ˘ – ˘ – ⌣ ‖
ἄγ᾽, ὦ μεγαλώνυμα τέκˈνα τοῦ θαλασσίοιο,

– – ˘ ˘ – ˘ ˘ –
1520 πηδᾶτε παρὰ ψάμαθον

ia ba
ὁ παῖς ὁ Φιλοκλέωνος.

ia cho dim
οὐδενὶ γὰρ οὕτως ἀγανῷ

ia cho dim
ξυνεγενόμην, οὐδὲ τρόποις

pol
ἐπεμάνην οὐδ᾽ ἐξεχύθην.

pol
1470 τί γὰρ ἐκεῖνος ἀντιλέγων

pol
οὐ κρείττων ἦν, βουλόμενος

eupol
τὸν φύσαντα σεμνοτέροις

†κατακοσμῆσαι† πράγμασιν;

At 1461, RV have μετεβάλλοντο, which corresponds with κατα-κοσμῆσαι at 1473: ◡◡ – – ◡ – ◡ –. The correspondence might be seen as confirming the soundness of the text, but base in the form ◡◡ – has no reliable parallel (Introduction, p. 71, and *Frogs* 1322). Moreover, at 1461, it is not only easy but linguistically necessary to accept the gnomic aorist, μετεβάλοντο, of the other MSS. At 1473, Meineke proposed κατακομῆσαι, which, however, does not occur in classical Greek. It is, of course, possible that κατακοσμῆσαι is an intrusive gloss which has taken the place of a word which did not resemble it at all palaeographically.

archil

– D

‒ ‒ ◡ ◡ ‒ ◡ ◡ ‒ ◡ | ‒ ◡ ‒ ◡ ‒ ‒
καὶ θῖν᾽ ἁλὸς ἀτρυγέτοιο, καρίδων ἀδελφοί·

◡ ‒ ◡ ◡ ‒ ◡ ◡ ‒ ◡ | ‒ ◡ ‒ ◡ ‒ ◡ ‖
ταχὺν πόδα κυκλοσοβεῖτε, καὶ τὸ Φρυνίχειον

‒ ‒ ◡ ◡ ‒ ◡ ◡ ‒

1525 ἐκλακτισάτω τις, ὅπως

◡ ‒ ◡ ◡ ‒ ◡ ◡ ‒ ‒ ◡ ‒ ◡ ‒ ‒
ἰδόντες ἄνω σκέλος ᾤζωσιν οἱ θεαταί.

◡ ‒ ◡ ◡ ‒ ◡ ◡ ‒ | ‒ ‒ ◡ ‒ ◡ ‒ ‒
στρόβει, παράβαινε κύκλῳ καὶ γάστρισον σεαυτόν·

‒ ‒ ◡ ◡ ‒ ◡ ◡ ‒ | ‒ ‒ ◡ ‒ ◡ ‒ ‒
1530 ῥῖπτε σκέλος οὐράνιον· βέμβικες ἐγγενέσθων.

‒ ‒ ◡ ◡ ‒ ◡ ◡ ‒ | ◡ ‒ ◡ ‒ ◡ ‒ ‒ ‖ н
καὐτὸς γὰρ ὁ ποντομέδων ἄναξ πατὴρ προσέρπει

‒ ‒ ◡ ◡ ‒ ◡ ◡ ‒ ‒ | ‒ ◡ ‒ ◡ ‒ ‒
ἡσθεὶς ἐπὶ τοῖσιν ἑαυτοῦ παισί, τοῖς τριόρχοις.

‒ ‒ ◡ ◡ ‒ ◡ ◡ ‒ | ‒ ‒ ◡ ‒ ◡ ‒ ◡ ‖ н
1535 ἀλλ᾽ ἐξάγετ᾽, εἴ τι φιλεῖτ᾽, ὀρχούμενοι θύραζε

‒ ‒ ◡ ◡ ‒ ◡ ◡ ‒ ‒ ‒ ◡ ‒ ◡ ‒ ◡ ‖
ἡμᾶς ταχύ· τοῦτο γὰρ οὐδείς πω πάρος δέδρακεν,

‒ ‒ ◡ ◡ ‒ ◡ ◡ ‒ ‒ ‒ ◡ ‒ ◡ ‒ ‒ ‖‖
ὀρχούμενος ὅστις ἀπήλλαξεν χορὸν τρυγῳδῶν.

At 1516 the chorus exhort themselves in anapaestic tetrameters to make space for the dancing-contest between Philocleon and the sons of Carcinus, which ends the play. They then accompany the dancing with archilochean dicola and variations on that verse. It is tempting to interpret 1518–27 as a strophe and antistrophe of the form: archil ‒ D archil. One failure of correspondence in the MS text is easily dealt with by Burges's θαλασσίοιο for θαλασ(σ)ίου at 1519. Indeed, considerations of correspondence apart, the hypodochmiac ‒ ◡ ‒ ◡ ‒ produced by θαλασσίου is impossible in this context. The failure of correspondence

archil

archil

– D

⏑ D + ith

archil

archil

archil

archil

archil

archil

archil

between 1521 and 1526 would be removed by Dindorf's ἀτρυγέτου. The epic genitive is, however, much better suited to the epic phraseology. Wilamowitz's suggestion (*GV* 385) that in 1526 the initial ὤ- of ὤζωσιν was extended in delivery to the value of two longs to imitate the expected 'O-oh' of the audience is ingenious and attractive, if unprovable.

What actually happened on stage during these lines has been the subject of much (largely unprofitable) speculation. The choice of the rhythm must have been a matter for collaboration with the dancers.

Our knowledge of the presence of the dicolon in Archilochus is derived from Hephaestion (Cons. 27. 7 ff. and 47. 6 ff.). His account and quotations provide us with the scheme:

$$\text{x} - \underset{\smile\smile}{} - \smile\smile - \text{x} \mid - \smile - \smile - -$$

He also tells us that word-end (τομή) after the internal anceps is universal in Archilochus, but that later poets vary it. In support of this he quotes three verses from Cratinus (*PCG* 360), of which the first two have word-end *before* anceps:

$$\text{x} - \smile\smile - \smile\smile - \mid \text{x} - \smile - \smile - -$$

Most comic dicola are made up of a colon followed by its own catalectic form, with regular word-end between the two (see Parker, *CQ* 26 (1976), 14). This produces a contrasting rhythm between blunt diaeresis and pendent verse-end or the reverse. It is not, therefore, surprising that Attic poets who used the archilochean tended to introduce the familiar contrast. Here, Aristophanes uses pendent and blunt τομή four times each, while the last two verses have no central word-end at all.

The title of the play of Cratinus from which Hephaestion quotes is

unknown, but he also mentions a play by the same author called
Ἀρχίλοχοι, from which he quotes a verse parodied from Archilochus
(*IEG*² 168):

$$\text{Ἐρασμονίδη Βάθιππε τῶν ἀωρολείων}$$
$$\cup - \cup \cup - \cup - \cup \,|\, - \cup - \cup - -$$

The substitution of $- \cup \cup - \cup -$ for $- \cup \cup - \cup \cup -$ is evidently a
unique comic device designed to accommodate the name, and has no
significance beyond that. Other examples of the verse from comedy are
Diphilus, *PCG* 12, Eupolis, *PCG* 148. 1 and 4, 250, 317, Pherecrates,
PCG 77. More surprisingly, there is what appears to be an archilochean
among the fragments of the tragic poet Phrynichus (*TrGF* 13), the
favourite poet of Philocleon's generation (see above on 273 ff. = 281 ff.).
This raises tantalizingly the question of whether the rhythm can have
had any relation to τἀρχαῖ᾽ ἐκεῖν᾽ οἷς Θέσπις ἠγωνίζετο. It is, of
course, possible for an archilochean to appear in a tragic stanza in a
context which robs it of any stylistic association with Archilochus or
comedy (e.g. *IT* 402).

Peace

114–18	Trygaeus' children: *Dactylic*.
346–60 = 385–99 = 582–600	*Cretics, trochaic* tetrameters (possibly, correspondence between cretic and trochaic).
463–72 = 490–9	*Anapaests*, with slight admixture of *iambic* and *cretic*.
512–19	Chorus and Hermes: *Iambic*, with introductory *anapaestic* metron.
775–95 = 796–818	*Dactylo-epitrite, aeolo-choriambic, dactylic*.
856–67 = 909–21	*Aeolo-choriambic* (telesilleans and reiziana), *iambic* tetrameters.
939–55 = 1023–38	*Anapaestic, iambic* and *aeolo-choriambic* (clausular reizianum, and telesilleans corresponding with iambic dimeters).
1127–39 = 1159–71	*Iambo-cretic*, passing through pure *cretic*, to *trochaeo-cretic*.
1329–59	*Aeolo-choriambic* (telesilleans and reiziana).

While not the most comically inventive of Aristophanes' plays, *Peace* exhibits great skill in the use of recurring and contrasting metres to reinforce dramatic structure.

The first song of the play is a brief parody of tragic dactyls sung by

Trygaeus' children (114–18). Dactylic hexameter parody will figure largely later in the play. The main action from the entrance of the chorus to the rescue of Peace is marked off by recurrences of the same stanza-form, at 346ff., 385ff. and 582ff. The stanza combines trochees and cretics, so that these are the rhythms that dominate the first half of the play. Between the first and second antistrophae, the two attempts to rescue Peace are accompanied by songs (463ff.=490ff. and 512ff.) which combine anapaestic, iambic, and (in the first song) cretic in different proportions. The parabasis comes in two parts, 729–818 and 1127–90, and each part has its own parabasis-song which is quite distinct metrically from the songs which belong to the action of the play. The first parabasis-song, 775ff.=796ff., uses metres of tragedy and high lyric for a complex combination of allusion and parody. The recurrent rhythm of the second half of the play is the aeolo-choriambic colon, the telesillean, with its catalectic form the reizianum. It features in 856ff.=909ff., in the antistrophe only of 939ff.=1023ff., and makes up the wedding-song that ends the play.

The second half of *Peace* has a certain resemblance to that of *Ach.*: the comic hypothesis has been established, and we are shown the results. In *Ach.*, however, the continuing controversy between Dicaeopolis and Lamachus produces dramatic contrasts and tension which are lacking in *Peace*. Here, the second part of the parabasis, with its song in syncopated iambic, cretic, and trochaic, separates two episodes of rejoicing: Trygaeus's sacrifice and prayer to Peace, and his wedding with Opora. Each episode includes a burlesque passage in dactylic hexameters: the recurrent metre gives a sense of symmetry.

Unfortunately, the lyric parts of *Peace* contain several very difficult textual and metrical problems which raise tantalizing questions about the processes of corruption.

114–18

— ∪ ∪   — ∪ ∪   — ∪ ∪   — ⌣ ||

ὦ πάτερ, ὦ πάτερ, ἆρ᾽ ἔτυμός γε

— ∪ ∪   — ∪ ∪   —|∪ ∪   — — || ʜ

115   δώμασιν ἡμετέροις φάτις ἥκει,

— ∪ ∪   — —   —|∪ ∪   — ∪ ∪ ʜ

ὡς σὺ μετ᾽ ὀρνίθων προλιπὼν ἐμὲ

— ∪ ∪   — ∪ ∪   —|∪ ∪   — ∪ ∪

ἐς κόρακας βαδιεῖ μεταμώνιος;

— ∪ ∪   — ∪ ∪   —|—   — ∪ ∪| — ∪ ∪   — ⌣ |||

ἔστι τι τῶνδ᾽ ἐτύμως; εἴπ᾽, ὦ πάτερ, εἴ τι φιλεῖς με.

As Trygaeus, mounted on the beetle, rises slowly into the air, his children plead with him in tragic style. Trygaeus answers in five dactylic hexameters, probably recitative. The passage seems to be parodied from an exchange in lyric dactyls in Euripides' *Aeolus*. Σ. *vet.* 114e provides, in addition to some scraps, a whole hexameter: δοξάσαι ἔστι, κόραι· τὸ δ᾽ ἐτήτυμον οὐκ ἔχω εἰπεῖν. This verse provides the first words of Trygaeus' reply (119). For dactyls in passages of lamentation in Sophocles and Euripides, see Introduction, pp 51–2. In a surviving early play of Euripides, Peleus' lament at *Andr.* 1173 ff. = 1186 ff. is made up entirely (except for the sounds of lamentation at 1175 = 1188 and the enigmatic clausula, 1183 = 1196 ∪ ∪ — ∪ ∪ ∪ — —) of dactylic tetrameters, with one hexameter (1177 = 1190). This style of composition in lyric dactyls can be traced back to Alcman, whose *PMG* 56 is, in fact, the closest surviving parallel to this stanza:

— ∪ ∪   — ∪ ∪   —|∪ ∪   — ∪ ∪

— ∪ ∪   — ∪ ∪   — ∪|∪   — —

— ∪ ∪   — ∪ ∪   — ∪|∪   — ∪ ∪

— ∪ ∪   — ∪ ∪   — ∪|∪   — —

— ∪ ∪   — ∪ ∪   — ∪|∪   — ⌣ ||

— ∪ ∪   — —   —|∪ ∪   — ∪ ∪| — ∪ ∪   — —

Like Aristophanes, Alcman uses bucolic diaeresis in the hexameter to harmonize the verse with the preceding tetrameters. Aristophanes, however, also uses repeated penthemimeral caesura (— ∪ ∪ — ∪ ∪ —|) to the

da tetram

da tetram

da tetram

da tetram

da hex

same end. This type of harmonization is common in the lyric dactyls of Attic drama. Compare, for example, *OT* 151 ff. = 159 ff.:

$$- \cup \cup \quad - \cup \cup \quad -| \cup \cup \quad - \cup \cup| \quad - \cup \cup \quad - -$$
$$- - \cup - \quad \cup - \cup -$$
$$- \overline{\cup\cup} \quad - \cup \cup \quad -| \cup \cup \quad - \cup \cup| \quad - \cup \cup \quad - -$$
$$- \quad - \cup \cup - \cup \cup - \quad -$$
$$- \cup \cup \quad - \cup \cup \quad -| \cup \cup \quad - \cup \cup$$
$$- \cup \cup \quad - \cup \cup \quad -|- \quad - \cup \cup \quad - \cup \cup \quad -| \cup \cup$$
$$- \cup \cup \quad - \cup \cup \quad -| \cup \cup| \quad - \cup \cup| \quad - \cup \cup \quad - -$$

The only problem in the stanza is the hiatus after trisyllabic dactyl at 116. Hephaestion's remark that Alcman composed whole stanzas in dactylic tetrameters of the form $- \cup \cup \quad - \cup \cup \quad - \cup \cup \quad - \cup \cup$ (Introduction, p. 48) invites speculation on whether verse-end is possible after trisyllabic dactyls. The first two cola here seem to be metrically independent, while 117 is metrically continuous with the following hexameter. It would be very easy indeed to remove the oddity at 116 by reading με (with *brevis in longo* as well as hiatus, and so unquestionable verse-end). However, there are several examples of hiatus after trisyllabic dactyls in tragedy: *Phil.* 1205 (where there is also change of speaker), E. *Supp.* 277 (twelve dactyls, with hiatus after the sixth), *Ba.* 585, and *Phaethon*, Diggle 111 (both of which are followed by interjections). At *Or.* 1303–4, φάσγανα | ἐκ χερός is dubious for various reasons.

346–60 = 385–99 = 582–600

†εἰ γὰρ ἐκγένοιτ᾽ ἰδεῖν ταύτην με τὴν ἡμέραν ποτέ.†

πολλὰ γὰρ ἀνεσχόμην

πράγματά τε καὶ στιβάδας

ἃς ἔλαχε Φορμίων·

κοὐκέτ᾽ ἄν μ᾽ εὕροις δικαστὴν δριμὺν οὐδὲ δύσκολον

350 οὐδὲ τοὺς τρόπους γε δήπου σκληρὸν ὥσπερ καὶ πρὸ τοῦ,

ἀλλ᾽ ἁπαλὸν ἄν μ᾽ ἴδοις

καὶ πολὺ νεώτερον ἀπ-

αλλαγέντα πραγμάτων.

καὶ γὰρ ἱκανὸν χρόνον ἀπ-

ὀλλύμεθα, καὶ κατατε-

355 τρίμμεθα πλανώμενοι

εἰς Λύκειον κἀκ Λυκείου ξὺν δορὶ ξὺν ἀσπίδι.

ἀλλ᾽ ὅ τι μάλιστα χαρι-

tro tetram cat?

385 X. μηδαμῶς, ὦ δέσποθ' Ἑρμῆ †μὴ μηδαμῶς μηδαμῶς†

2 cr

εἴ τι κεχαρισμένον

2 cr

χοιρίδιον οἶσθα παρ' ἐ-

+ 2 cr

387   μοῦ ⟨γε⟩ κατεδηδοκώς

tro tetram cat

τοῦτο μὴ φαῦλον νόμιζ' ἐν †τῷδε τῷ πράγματι†

tro tetram cat

T. οὐκ ἀκούεις οἷα θωπεύουσί σ', ὦναξ δέσποτα;

2 cr

390a X. †μὴ γένῃ παλίγκοτος

+ 2 cr

390b   ἀντιβολοῦσιν ἡμῖν†

+ lec

ὥστε τήνδε μὴ λαβεῖν·

2 cr

392   ἀλλὰ χάρισ', ὦ φιλαν-

+ 2 cr

θρωπότατε καὶ μεγαλο-

+ 2 cr

δωρότατε δαιμόνων,

tro tetram cat

395 εἴ τι Πεισάνδρου βδελύττει τοὺς λόφους καὶ τὰς ὀφρῦς,

2 cr

καί σε θυσίαισιν ἱε-

$$-\cup\overset{\frown}{\smallsmile}\quad-\cup\overset{\frown}{\smallsmile}$$

οὔμεθα ποιοῦντες, ἄγε,

$$-\cup\overset{\frown}{\smallsmile}\quad-\cup\underset{\smallsmile}{\underset{\frown}{}}$$

φράζε· σὲ γὰρ αὐτοκράτορ᾽

$$-\cup\overset{\frown}{\smallsmile}\quad-\cup-\quad-\cup\equiv\ |||$$

360   εἷλετ᾽ ἀγαθή τις ἡμῖν τύχη.

582   †χαῖρε, χαῖρ᾽, ὦ φίλταθ᾽, ὡς ἀσμένοισιν ἡμῖν ἦλθες.†
        σῷ γὰρ ἐδάμην πόθῳ,
        δαιμόνια βουλόμενος
585   εἰς ἀγρὸν ἀνερπύσαι.
        ⟨ − ∪ − × − ∪ − × − ∪ − × − ∪ − ⟩
        ἦσθα γὰρ μέγιστον ἡμῖν κέρδος, ὦ ποθουμένη,
        πᾶσιν ὁπόσοι γεωργ[ικ]-
            ὸν βίον ἐτρίβομεν·
590   †μόνη γὰρ ἡμᾶς ὠφέλεις.†
        πολλὰ γὰρ ἐπάσχομεν
            πρίν ποτ᾽ ἐπὶ σοῦ γλυκέα
            κἀδάπανα καὶ φίλα.
595   τοῖς ἀγροίκοισιν γὰρ ἦσθα χῖδρα καὶ σωτηρία.
        ὥστε σὲ τά τ᾽ ἀμπέλια
            καὶ τὰ νέα συκίδια
            τἄλλα θ᾽ ὁπόσ᾽ ἐστὶ φυτὰ
            προσγελάσεται λαβόντ᾽ ἄσμενα.

The chorus enter *con brio*, with catalectic trochaic tetrameters, and their
first song mingles trochaic tetrameters with cretics. The combination of
metres is the same as in the parodos of *Ach.*, but there the chorus derived
its animation from anger, instead of joy. The stanza differs from *Ach.*
204ff. = 218ff. in that the trochaic tetrameters are intermingled with the
cretics in a way that tends to blur the transition between recitative and
song. There is a simple numerical structure: 1 tro tetram; 6 cr; 2 tro
tetram; 4 cr + lec, 6 cr (=12 metra); 1 tro tetram; 9 cr. The lecythion in
mid-stanza, at the end of the first of the near-twin sections, produces a
subtle variation that avoids monotony (cf. *Knights* 619=686). Except at
one point of major failure, where corruption is certain (390), correspon-

+ 2 cr

ραῖσι προσόδοις τε μεγά-

+ 2 cr

λαισι διὰ παντός, ὦ

+ 3 cr

δέσποτ᾽, ἀγαλοῦμεν ἡμεῖς ἀεί.

dence between resolved and unresolved longs in the cretics is close. This is the more remarkable in that there are three corresponding stanzas. The first antistrophe differs from the first and last repetitions in that one trochaic tetrameter is delivered by Trygaeus.

Structurally, the song is of crucial importance in the first half of the play, which contains the major development of the plot, the rescue of Peace. The strophe, in which the chorus look forward to the life of peacetime, forms the prelude to the rescue. The first antistrophe (385–99) marks the dangerous moment when Hermes is about to call on Zeus to intervene. The second antistrophe (592–600), the welcome to Peace, rounds off the action.

All three stanzas have suffered serious mutilation by paraphrasing (Introduction, p. 118). They may also exemplify freedoms of responsion, but with so much evidence of corruption, judgement must be reserved.

Firstly, the initial trochaic tetrameter is not attested by the pre-Triclinian MSS in any of the three repetitions, However, Σ. *vet.* V (346. See White, *VGC* 413) describes the first verse as στίχος τροχαικός and a tetrameter seems stylistically right, in view of the preceding tetrameters (553–70) and those interspersed later in the stanza (cf. *Ach.* 204ff.=218ff., 285ff.=335ff.). At 582 all MSS share the text as printed. For the other two corresponding verses I give the text of R. Variants are as follows:

346 ἐκγένοιτ’ : γένοιτο V: γένοιτ’ VP2C. Triclinius proposed μοι γένοιτ’ and excised με (LBAld)

385 μηδαμῶς, ὦ δέσποθ’ Ἑρμῆ is shared by all MSS; then: μηδαμῶς μηδαμῶς V: μὴ μηδαμῶς μὴ μηδαμῶς ΓC: μηδαμῶς μὴ μηδαμῶς Triclinius (LBAld)

385 and 582 present little difficulty. For 385, Triclinius’ emendation will suffice. 582 is easily rearranged, as by Enger:

χαῖρε, χαῖρ’, ὡς ἀσμένοισιν ἦλθες ἡμῖν, φιλτάτη.

(ἡμῖν ἦλθες Bothe),

or Dindorf:

χαῖρε, χαῖρ’, ὡς ἦλθες ἡμῖν ἀσμένοις, ὦ φιλτάτη.

346 poses a less tractable problem. Enger rearranged the words provided by R to produce: εἰ γὰρ ἐκγένοιτ’ ἰδεῖν ταυτήν μέ ποτε τὴν ἡμέραν. But impersonal (ἐκ)γίγνεται with accusative and infinitive and without ὥστε does not seem to be paralleled. Triclinius’ version produces – – – for – ◡ –, but Bentley, using the Triclinian printed vulgate of his day, proposed

. . . εἴθε μοι γένοιτ’ ἰδεῖν τὴν ἡμέραν ταύτην ποτέ.

Porson adopted Bentley’s arrangement of the second half of the line, while suggesting εἰ γὰρ ἐκγένοιτ’ ἰδεῖν for the first half. The omission of the dative pronoun is again hard to parallel. At *Phil.* 324, θυμὸν γένοιτο χειρὶ πληρῶσαί ποτε is a conjecture (Brunck’s). Bentley’s solution still deserves attention. The substitution of εἰ γὰρ for εἴθε and of ἐκγένοιτ’ (R only) for γένοιτ’ would not be beyond the capacity of a careless and metrically ignorant copyist, and such a copyist has undoubtedly operated on this passage.

Another approach, which found favour with Platnauer (on 346–60), is to take V's version of 385 as the model. This scans

$$- \cup - - \quad - \cup - - \quad - \cup - \quad - \cup -$$

which is not impossible in the context, but Platnauer's attempt to transfer the principle of preferring the *lectio difficilior* to metre is misguided (Introduction, p. 119). Moreover, the latter part of 385 is a bad 'anchorpoint' for emendation, being highly at risk of miscopying, as the MS variants show. Further, the necessary reductions in 346 and 582 cannot be made without losing words valuable to the sense. In 346, Platnauer regarded ποτέ as dispensable, but it adds an appropriate plaintiveness to 'may it be granted to me to see . . .' while ἡμῖν in 582 is even less dispensable than μοι in 346.

At 387 ⟨γε⟩ is a Triclinian supplement.

At 388 the MSS offer τοῦτο μὴ φαῦλον νομίζων ἐν τῷδε τῷ πράγματι. The corresponding verse, 349, is a trochaic tetrameter, while at 586–7 there is only one tetrameter where the corresponding stanzas have two. Bentley's νόμιζ᾽ is necessary to the sense. He sought also to perfect correspondence by supplementing the second half of the verse: τῷδε τῷ ⟨νῦν⟩ πράγματι. But Aristophanes never combines ὅδε and ὁ νῦν: the two are alternatives (*Thesm.* 302 ἐκκλησίαν τήνδε καὶ σύνοδον τὴν νῦν). If sound, τῷδε τῷ πράγματι would be an example of $- \cup - - \cup -$ corresponding with $- \cup - \times - \cup -$.

If μὴ γένῃ παλίγκοτος is to stand at 390, that colon would again be a lecythion corresponding with two cretics. But the last syllable of παλίγκοτος would have to be lengthened by a following consonant. *Brevis in longo* is impossible here, when there is no word-end at 588–9. Moreover, the whole pattern of the stanza is against verse-end at this point. Apart from the initial vowel, ἀντιβολοῦσιν ἡμῖν ($- \cup \cup - \cup - -$) is completely out of place in this metrical context. There is no simple and convincing solution. Triclinius seems to have been aware of a problem here, and to have tried, as so often, to solve it by adding monosyllables.

For the elision of -αι in χαρισ᾽ at 392, see on *Wasps* 273.

Σ vet. on 582ff. (VΓ, White, *VGC* 415) does not show any awareness that the stanza he is describing corresponds with any other. The note also mentions as a variant the highly dubious form ἐδάμημεν, which is actually the reading of surviving MSS at 583. ἐδάμην and, in consequence, βουλόμενος for βουλόμενοι (584), were restored by Dindorf, by inference from Σ *vet*. This perfects correspondence between 347–8, 386–7, and 583–4.

At 587–90, taking the first syllable of μόνη (590) as belonging to the penultimate colon produces a scannable text, with repeated correspondence of cretic with trochaic metron:

$$\pi\hat{\alpha}\sigma\iota\nu\ \dot{o}\pi\acuteο\sigma\omicron\iota\ \gamma\epsilon\omega\rho\gamma\iota\text{-} \qquad -\cup\overset{\frown}{}\ \ -\cup-\cup$$

$$\kappa\grave{o}\nu\ \beta\acuteι\omicron\nu\ \dot{\epsilon}\tau\rho\acuteι\beta\omicron\mu\epsilon\nu\cdot\ \mu\acuteο\text{-} \qquad -\cup\overset{\frown}{}\ \ -\cup-\cup$$

463–72=490–99

$$\overline{\cup}-\cup-\ \ -\cup\ \|\ ^{\text{H}}$$

X. ὢ εἶα, ὢ εἶα

$$----\ \ -\cup\cup--$$

T. ἀλλ' οὐχ ἕλκουσ' ἄνδρες ὁμοίως.

$$----\ \ ----$$

465   οὐ ξυλλήψεσθ'; οἷ' ὀγκύλλεσθ'·

$$----\ \ ---\ \|\ ^{\text{H}}$$

οἰμώξεσθ', οἱ Βοιωτοί.

$$-\cup-$$

E. εἶα νῦν.

$$-\cup-\ \|\ ^{\text{H}}$$

X. εἶα ὤ.

$$\cup\cup-\cup\cup-\ \ \cup\cup--\ \|\ ^{\text{H}}$$

ἄγε νῦν, ξυνανέλκετε καὶ σφώ.

$$----|\ \ ----$$

470   T. οὔκουν ἕλκω κἀξαρτῶμαι

$$----|\ \ ----$$

κἀπεμπίπτω καὶ σπουδάζω;

$$----\ \ --\cup\ \||| $$

X. πῶς οὖν οὐ χωρεῖ τοὔργον;

This pair of stanzas accompanies the first (and unsuccessful) attempt to pull Peace out of the cave. Both strophe and antistrophe are preceded by effort-noises, which at 463 continue into the first verse of the song. Effort-noises are resumed briefly in mid-stanza. Pulling is interrupted

νη γὰρ ἡμᾶς ὠφέλεις   − ∪ − −   − ∪ −

The strong stop after ἐτρίβομεν, however, makes a very marked clash
between metrical and rhetorical phrasing. Reading γεωργὸν (Bothe) for
γεωργικὸν (cf. *Ach.* 1036) makes 588 into two cretics. In 590 it is quite
possible that ἡμᾶς is interpolated. On that hypothesis, Platnauer
suggests καὶ γὰρ ὠφέλεις μόνη and Dover καὶ μόνη γὰρ ὠφέλεις
(see Platnauer, ad loc.) Thus correspondence can be restored without
too much difficulty.

              ia sp
490 Χ. μικρόν γε κινοῦμεν.

              an dim
     Τ. οὔκουν δεινὸν ⟨κἄτοπον, ὑμῶν⟩

              an dim
          τοὺς μὲν τείνειν, τοὺς δ᾽ ἀντισπᾶν;

              + an dim cat
          πληγὰς λήψεσθ᾽, Ἀργεῖοι.

              cr
     Ε. εἷα νῦν.

              cr
495 Χ. εἷα ὤ.

              an dim cat
          [ὡς] κακόνοι τινές εἰσιν ἐν ἡμῖν.

              an dim
     Τ. ὑμεῖς μὲν γοῦν οἱ κιττῶντες

              an dim
          τῆς εἰρήνης σπᾶτ᾽ ἀνδρείως.

              an dim cat
     Χ. ἀλλ᾽ εἷσ᾽ οἳ κωλύουσιν.

while Trygaeus and the Chorus comment, in anapaests, on progress or
the lack of it. The distribution of lines between singers is uncertain. Σ
vet. (459d) takes Hermes to be the foreman, and I have followed that
(see, however, Sommerstein, ad loc.). The anapaests are marked as of

lyric type by the predominantly spondaic movement. It would be rash to assume that this song is modelled on the rhythms of genuine work-songs, for here the work is going badly, and the scene is one of considerable disorder. Contrast the rhythm of 512–19 below.

At 469, the MSS have ἄγετον ξυνέλκετον (ξυνᾱ̆λκετον V) καὶ σφώ. The corresponding verse, as it stands in the MSS, is an anapaestic dimeter. Σ *vet*. V (486a) recognizes correspondence, but his description of 469 (469a) is ἀναπαιστικὸν πενθημιμερές. Hense conjectured ἐφθημιμερές, which is, theoretically, a possible way to describe a catalectic anapaestic dimeter. But Σ *vet*.'s normal term is καταληκτικὸν δίμετρον, which, indeed, appears twice in the description of this very stanza, for 466 and 472. No clear guidance, then, is to be had from Σ *vet*. A full dimeter can be produced at 469 by adopting Hermann's supplement ⟨ἀλλ᾿⟩ and Dobree's plurals ἄγετε ξυνανέλκετε (for ἀλλ᾿ ἄγετε

512–19

⏑ ⏑ – ⏑ ⏑ –

X. ἄγε νῦν, ἄγε πᾶς.

– – ⏑ –   ⏑ – –

E. καὶ μὴν ὁμοῦ 'στιν ἤδη.

– – ⏑ –   ⏑ – ⏑ –   – – ⏑ –   ⏑ – ⏑ ‿ ‖

514–5 X. μὴ νῦν ἀνῶμεν, ἀλλ᾿ ἐπεντείνωμεν ἀνδρικώτερον.

– – ⏑ –   ⏑ – ‿ ‖ н

E. ἤδη 'στὶ τοῦτ᾿ ἐκεῖνο.

– – ⏑ –   – – ⏑ –

X. ὢ εἶα νῦν, ὢ εἶα πᾶς.

– – ⏑ –   ⏑ – ⏑ –

ὢ εἶα εἶα εἶα ⟨νῦν⟩

– – ⏑ –   ⏑ – ⏑ – ‖‖

ὢ εἶα εἶα εἶα πᾶς.

Having got rid of the slackers and obstructionists, the chorus return to their task, and, during this song, haul Peace on to the stage. For the use of an isolated anapaestic metron to convey an exhortation, compare *Thesm.* 953 and *Ecc.* 478 (both – – – –). Otherwise, the pure iambic of this stanza contrasts with the anapaests that predominate in 463ff. =

cf. *Lys.* 664). The verse-end with change of speaker and the lack of metron-diaeresis in 469, however, tell in favour of a catalectic dimeter. This can be produced by reading ἄγε νῦν (Austin, cf 512) or ἄγε δή (Zimmermann, *Untersuchungen*, i. 211) and deleting ὡς at 496 (White). The substitution of dual for plural in course of transmission is, of course, much less common than the reverse, and is, perhaps, more likely to have happened through the deliberate intervention of a metrically ignorant pedant than by inadvertence.

491–2 is one anapaestic metron shorter than the corresponding passage in the strophe. ⟨κάτοπον, ὑμῶν⟩ is Merry's supplement. At 497, γοῦν is adapted from Bentley's γ' οὖν. The MSS have οὖν *contra metrum*. At 498, ἀνδρείως is, again, Bentley's correction of the unmetrical ἀνδρικῶς (cf. 515 below).

an monom

ia dim cat

ia tetram

ia dim cat

ia dim

ia dim

ia dim

490ff. The change in rhythm must in some way mark the contrast in action between the successful and unsuccessful attempts.

The effort-noises at 517–19 are variously reproduced by the MSS. The reconstruction printed is that of Richter, guided by Σ *vet.* (512a). The scholiast's note is, however, lacunary.

775–95=796–818

‒ ᴗ ᴗ ‒ ᴗ ᴗ ‒ | ᴗ   ‒ ᴗ ᴗ ‒ ᴗ ᴗ ‒

775   Μοῦσα, σὺ μὲν πολέμους ἀπωσαμένη μετ᾽ ἐμοῦ

‒ ᴗ ‒ | ᴗ ‒ ‒

τοῦ φίλου χόρευσον,

‒   ‒ ᴗ ᴗ ‒ ᴗ ᴗ ‒

κλείουσα θεῶν τε γάμους

‒   ‒ ᴗ ‒   ‒ | ‒ ᴗ ᴗ ‒ | ᴗ ᴗ ‒

ἀνδρῶν τε δαῖτας καὶ θαλίας μακάρων·

ᴗ   ‒ ᴗ ‒ ‒   ‒   ‒ ᴗ ‒ ‖ ᴴ

780   σοὶ γὰρ τάδ᾽ ἐξ ἀρχῆς μέλει.

‒ ᴗ ᴗ ‒ ᴗ ᴗ | ‒   ‒

ἢν δέ σε Καρκίνος ἐλθὼν

‒ ᴗ ᴗ ‒ | ᴗ ᴗ ‒   ‒   ‒ ᴗ ‒   ‒

ἀντιβολῇ μετὰ τῶν παίδων χορεῦσαι,

‒ ᴗ ᴗ ‒ ᴗ ‒ ‒

785   μήθ᾽ ὑπάκουε μήτ᾽ ἔλ-

‒ ᴗ ᴗ ‒ ᴗ | ‒ ‒

θῃς συνέριθος αὐτοῖς,

‒ ᴗ ᴗ ‒ ᴗ ‒ ᴗ ‖

ἀλλὰ νόμιζε πάντας

‒ ᴗ ᴗ | ‒ ᴗ ᴗ   ‒ | ᴗ ᴗ   ‒ ᴗ ᴗ | ‒ ‒   ‒

788–9   ὄρτυγας οἰκογενεῖς, γυλιαύχενας ὀρχηστὰς

‒ ᴗ ᴗ   ‒ | ᴗ ᴗ   ‒ | ᴗ ᴗ   ‒ ᴗ ᴗ | ‒ ᴗ ᴗ   ‒ ‒ ‖ ᴴ

790–1   νανοφυεῖς, σφυράδων ἀποκνίσματα μηχανοδίφας.

‒ ᴗ ᴗ   ‒ ᴗ ᴗ   ‒ | ᴗ ᴗ   ‒ ᴗ ᴗ

καὶ γὰρ ἔφασχ᾽ ὁ πατὴρ ὃ παρ᾽ ἐλπίδας

‒ ᴗ ᴗ ‒ ᴗ ᴗ ‒ | ‒   ‒ ᴗ ‒   ᴗ ‒ ‒ ‖‖

795   εἶχε τὸ δρᾶμα γαλῆν τῆς ἑσπέρας ἀπάγξαι.

D ⌣ D
τοιάδε χρὴ Χαρίτων δαμώματα καλλικόμων

ith
τὸν σοφὸν ποιητὴν

– D
ὑμνεῖν, ὅταν ἠρινὰ μὲν

– e – D
800   φωνῇ χελιδὼν ἡδομένη κελαδῇ,

⌣ e – e
χορὸν δὲ μὴ 'χῃ Μόρσιμος

D –
μηδὲ Μελάνθιος, οὗ δὴ

D – e –
805   πικροτάτην ὄπα γηρύσαντος ἤκουσ',

+ arist
ἡνίκα τῶν τραγῳδῶν

+ arist
τὸν χορὸν εἶχον ἀδελ-

+ arist
φός τε καὶ αὐτός, ἄμφω

da hex cat
810–11 Γοργόνες ὀψοφάγοι, βατιδοσκόποι Ἅρπυιαι,

da hex
γραοσόβαι μιαροί, τραγομάσχαλοι ἰχθυολῦμαι·

da tetram
815   ὧν καταχρεμψαμένη μέγα καὶ πλατὺ

D – ith
Μοῦσα θεὰ μετ' ἐμοῦ ξύμπαιζε τὴν ἑορτήν.

In the parabasis proper the chorus-leader may either speak of the poet (*Knights*) or actually as the poet (*Clouds*), or change from one to the other (*Ach.* and *Peace*). In *Ach.*, the change of person comes with the pnigos at 659; in *Peace* it is much more striking, since it comes before the end of the anapaestic tetrameters, at a point where continuity would be expected. It is important that the audience should note the change if they are to appreciate the song which follows.

The parabasis song here is the poet's own song, and it is highly literary both in form and content. I have discussed it at length in the Introduction (pp. 6–10), and so will only summarize the main points here. The song begins and ends in dactylo-epitrite, and, as in *Knights* 1264ff.=1290ff., the incorporation of quotation shows that the metre is being used allusively. Here, the quotations are from Stesichorus (*PMG* 210, 211, 212), but the passages should not be described as 'parody' of Stesichorus. The quotations have been diluted, and their stylistic level modified by Aristophanic insertions. By a process of semi-identification, Aristophanes is enlisting the grand old poet as an ally against the contemporaries he is about to ridicule. Modification is metrical as well as verbal: in the manner of Attic drama, bacchiacs are admitted into the dactylo-epitrites (Introduction, p. 89).

The first section of the stanza ends with verse-end at 780=801. The second begins in dactylo-epitrite, and passes, without full word-end in the antistrophe, into a run of three aristophaneans in synartesis. Despite its name, the aristophenean is a favourite colon of Aeschylus, who uses it both as a general-purpose clausula and in synartesis. If not decidedly grand, the sequence is at least neutral in style, while the following dactyls certainly suggest high poetry (Introduction, p. 48). For the striking rhythm produced in dactyls by a spondaic metron followed by

$$856\text{–}67=909\text{–}21$$

$$- - \cup \cup - \cup -$$
X. εὐδαιμονικῶς γ' ὁ πρε-

$$- - \cup \cup - \cup -$$
σβύτης, ὅσα γ' ὧδ' ἰδεῖν,

$$\cup - \cup \cup - \smile \parallel$$
τὰ νῦν τάδε πράττει.

catalexis, compare *Eum.* 1035 = 1039, *Andr.* 274 = 284, E. *Supp.* 279, *Rhes.* 26–7 = 44–5. Dale's introduction of a purely hypothetical anceps (−×−) to turn *Peace* 788 = 810 and *Andr.* 274 = 284 into 'prosodiacs' is unjustified (*LM²* 168 and 183).

We know nothing whatever about the lyric of the tragedians under attack in 781 ff. and 801 ff., but both the dactyls and the accumulation of compound epithets and substantives suggest Aeschylus; cf. *Ag.* 154–5:

$$\ldots \; \mu\acute{\iota}\mu\nu\epsilon\iota \; \gamma\grave{\alpha}\rho \; \phi o\beta\epsilon\rho\grave{\alpha} \; \pi\alpha\lambda\acute{\iota}\nu o\rho\tau o\varsigma,$$
$$o\mathring{\iota}\kappa o\nu\acute{o}\mu o\varsigma \; \delta o\lambda\acute{\iota}\alpha, \; \mu\nu\acute{\alpha}\mu\omega\nu \; M\hat{\eta}\nu\iota\varsigma \; \tau\epsilon\kappa\nu\acute{o}\pi o\iota\nu o\varsigma.$$

The passage indicates that Morsimus and Melanthius were brothers. To lambast them in the style of their own great-uncle would have been particularly savorous, and, once again, a great poet of the past would have been enlisted as an ally. The brief return of dactylo-epitrite rhythm at the end of the stanza is combined, in the antistrophe, with the return to the Muse. This skilfully composed song, rich in allusion, with its attacks on inferior tragedians, provides a lyrical development of the anapaests, in which Aristophanes has asserted, in humorous terms, the artistic seriousness of his comedy.

Peace 721–87 is partially preserved in *PSI* vi. 720, of the third century AD, and 781–6 is one of the four passages where a papyrus colometry differs from that of R (Introduction, p. 101). At 785, the papyrus apparently shared the unmetrical ὑπακούσῃς with RV+. ὑπάκουε is Bentley's emendation. Like the duals at 469, ὑπακούσῃς may be a deliberate 'normalization' by a metrically ignorant person. At 801, ἡδομένη, which provides an epithet for φωνῇ, is Bergk's suggestion for the MS ἐζομένη. Metre is not involved.

tel

X. ἦ χρηστὸς ἀνὴρ πολί-

+ tel

910   ταις ἐστὶν ἅπασιν ὅσ-

+ reiz

τις ἐστὶ τοιοῦτος.

$$\cup-\cup- \quad --\cup- \quad \underset{\smile}{-}-\cup|- \quad \cup-\smile\|$$

T. τί δῆτ' ἐπειδὰν νυμφίον μ' ὁρᾶτε λαμπρὸν ὄντα;

$$--\cup\cup-\cup-$$

860 *X.* ζηλωτὸς ἔσει γέρων

$$--\cup\cup-\cup-$$

αὖθις νέος ὢν πάλιν,

$$\cup-\cup\cup-\underset{\smile}{\smile}\|$$

μύρῳ κατάλειπτος.

$$--\cup- \quad \cup-\cup-| \quad --\cup-| \quad \cup--\|^{\text{H}}$$

T. οἶμαι. τί δῆθ', ὅταν ξυνὼν τῶν τιτθίων ἔχωμαι;

$$--\cup- \quad \cup-\cup- \quad --\cup- \quad \cup--$$

X. εὐδαιμονέστερος φανεῖ τῶν Καρκίνου στροβίλων.

$$--\cup- \quad -|-\cup- \quad \cup-\cup|- \quad \cup-\cup-$$

865 *T.* οὔκουν δικαίως; ὅστις εἰς ὄχημα κανθάρου 'πιβὰς

$$\underset{\smile}{-}-\cup- \quad --\cup- \quad --\cup- \quad \cup--$$

ἔσωσα τοὺς Ἕλληνας, ὥστ' ἐν τοῖς ἀγροῖς ⟨∪--⟩

$$\underset{\smile}{-}-\cup- \quad \cup-\cup-| \quad \smile-\cup- \quad \cup--\|\|$$

ἅπαντας ὄντας ἀσφαλῶς κινεῖν τε καὶ καθεύδειν.

This duet of congratulation on the part of the chorus and of self-contratulation on that of Trygaeus has close affinities with *Ach.* 1008 ff. = 1037 ff. Metrically, the catalectic iambic tetrameter features in both songs, but the Acharnians' song is purely iambic, while here the chorus begins, in effect, with a miniature strophe and antistrophe within the stanza, each made up of a pair of telesilleans with reizianum as clausula. The choice of metre is significant: the song looks forward to Trygaeus' marriage to Opora, which will actually be solemnized at the end of the play to the accompaniment of a wedding-hymn in telesilleans. The possible appropriateness of that metre to wedding hymns is discussed below, on 1329 ff. = 1359 ff. The second ('epodic') half of the stanza is in catalectic iambic tetrameters, with variation provided by one acatalectic run of four metra in the middle.

At 860, γέρων (nominative: 'You will be enviable, an old man turned young again') is B's reading, instead of the vocative γέρον of the other

ia tetram cat

T. ὅταν τρυγᾶτ᾽, εἴσεσθε πολλῷ μᾶλλον οἷός εἰμι.

tel

X. καὶ νῦν σύ γε δῆλος εἶ·

tel

σωτὴρ γὰρ ἅπασιν ἀν-

+ reiz

915 θρώποις γεγένησαι.

ia tetram cat

T. φήσεις ⟨γ᾽⟩, ἐπειδὰν ἐκπίῃς οἴνου νέου λεπαστήν.

ia tetram cat

X. καὶ πλήν γε τῶν θεῶν ἀεί σ᾽ ἡγησόμεσθα πρῶτον.

ia tetram

T. πολλῶν γὰρ ὑμῖν ἄξιος Τρυγαῖος Ἀθμονεὺς ἐγώ,

ia tetram cat

920 δεινῶν ἀπαλλάξας πόνων τὸν δημότην ὅμιλον

ia tetram cat

καὶ τὸν γεωργικὸν λεών, Ὑπέρβολόν τε παύσας.

MSS (including the Triclinian L). γέρον, with *brevis in longo*, would produce verse-end after 860=913, whereas sequences of aeolic cola of this
type (two or more telesilleans or glyconics rounded off by reizianum or
pherecratean) are normally metrically continuous. At *Ecc.* 292=303, a
pair of telesilleans ends with strong rhetorical pause and verse-end, but
that is a deliberate (and perfectly comprehensible) surprise effect. At
Birds 1734=1740, the telesillean with verse-end preceding the surprise
clausula (pherecratean instead of reizianum) is, again, strategically
placed. At 1351 and 1354 below, and at *Thesm.* 360, the text is open to
doubt. Here, there is clear rhetorical pause in the antistrophe, but I doubt
whether the pause after a vocative inserted in mid-sentence is strong
enough to justify the break in rhythm.

At 865, εἶς is Nenci's emendation of the MS εἰς.

At 866, Triclinius noticed the failure of correspondence, and sought
to remedy it with ἀγροῖσ⟨ιν αὐτούς⟩. The alternative to assuming a

lacuna at 866 is to excise ὅμιλον in 920 (Dindorf), making δημότην
as well as γεωργικόν adjectival with λεών. The effect of this on the
metrical structure of the passage would be to make Trygaeus deliver an
iambic pnigos of eleven metra, ending in catalexis. This is not in itself
implausible, but there are two serious objections to accepting it. Firstly,
how does one account for the interpolation of ὅμιλον? ὅμιλος is an
uncommon word, but not out of place in Attic comedy (cf. Cratinus,
PCG 360), and ὁ δημότης ὅμιλος is a recherché literary expression
(cf. *Hec.* 921 ναύταν . . . ὅμιλον) which suits the exalted tone in
which Trygaeus describes his own exploit. Moreover, it is acceptable
metrically: absence of rhetorical pause at the end of a catalectic iambic
tetrameter presents no problem (see e.g. *Wasps* 242–5). Secondly, both
correspondence and the presence of tetrameters was recognized in
antiquity. Σ *vet.* 856a has suffered some mutilation, but describes the
stanza as ending with two catalectic iambic tetrameters, which accords
with the shared (and, as far as possible, corresponding) colometry of RV:

$$
\begin{array}{lllll}
      & --\cup- & --\cup- & & \\
      & \cup-\cup- & \cup-\cup- & & \\
866   & \cup-\cup- & --\cup- & --\cup- & \\
920   & --\cup- & --\cup- & --\cup- & \cup-- \\
      & \underline{\cup}-\cup- & \cup-\cup- & \overline{\cup}-\cup- & \cup--
\end{array}
$$

939–55 = 1023–38

$$\overline{\cup}-\cup- \quad \cup-\cup-| \quad -\cup- \quad \cup--$$

X. ὡς πάνθ' ὅσ' ἂν θεὸς θέλῃ χἠ τύχη κατορθοῖ

$$--\underline{\underline{\cup}}-| \quad \cup\cup-\cup\cup-$$

940   χωρεῖ κατὰ νοῦν, ἕτερον δ' ἑτέρῳ

$$\overline{\underline{\cup}}-\cup\cup- \quad \cup\cup--\|^{H}$$

τούτων κατὰ καιρὸν ἀπαντᾷ.

$$--\cup- \quad \underline{\cup}-\cup- \quad \overline{\cup}-\cup- \quad \cup--\|^{H}$$

T. ὡς ταῦτα δῆλά γ' ἔσθ'· ὁ γὰρ βωμὸς θύρασι καὶ δή.

$$\underline{\underline{\cup}}-\cup\cup- \quad \cup\cup-\cup\cup-$$

X. ⟨ἄγ'⟩ ἐπείγετε νῦν ἐν ὅσῳ σοβαρὰ

The acatalectic tetrameter, 865=919, was divided into dimeters, but where catalexis was present the metrician recognized the familiar στίχος and made a single line. Even without the testimony of *Σ vet.*, loss of the end of 866 is an easier hypothesis than the interpolation of ὅμιλον in antiquity by someone of considerable metrical and verbal skill, who none the less failed to alter the strophe to match.

φήσεις ⟨γ'⟩ at 916 is Dindorf's emendation of φήσεις (RVG+, *Suda*). A version beginning with τί δῆτ' instead of φήσεις is quoted in garbled form by Athenaeus (11. 485a). Both versions were known to Triclinius, who tries, quaintly, to accommodate both τί δῆτ' and φήσεις by excising νέου. Biset (and Bentley) preferred τί δῆτ' to φήσεις, but this requires the assumption that the chorus continue their utterance of 913–15, ignoring Trygaeus' intervention at 916.

At 919 the MS reading Ἀθμονεύς would require lengthening before mute and liquid, always unusual in iambic and unparalleled in the earlier plays (Introduction, p. 93). The article in crasis, introduced by Dawes, removes the anomaly. Introducing himself at 190, Trygaeus (like Dicaeopolis at *Ach.* 406) used the ordinary official form, with no article before the deme-name. Its presence here shows that he now feels himself to be a well-known person (Kühner–Gerth, i. 600).

euripid
X. σέ τοι θύρασι †χρὴ μένοντα τοίνον†

an dim
σχίζας δευρὶ τιθέναι ταχέως

an dim cat
1025 τά τε πρόσφορα πάντ' ἐπὶ τούτοις.

ia tetram cat
T. οὔκουν δοκῶ σοι μαντικῶς τὸ φρύγανον τίθεσθαι;

an dim
X. πῶς δ' οὐχί; τί γάρ σε πέφευγ' ὅσα χρὴ

∪∪−∪∪− ∪∪−|∪∪∪∪

θεόθεν κατέχει πολέμου μετάτροπος

−−−− ⌒−∪∪−

945   αὖρα· νῦν γὰρ δαίμων φανερῶς

⊙⌒∪⌣ ∪−−‖н

εἰς ἀγαθὰ μεταβιβάζει.

⌣−∪− ∪−∪−| −−∪− ∪−−

T. τὸ κανοῦν πάρεστ᾽ ὀλὰς ἔχον καὶ στέμμα καὶ μάχαιραν,

−−∪− ⊙−∪− −−∪⌣ ∪−−

καὶ πῦρ γε τουτί, κοὐδὲν ἴσχει πλὴν τὸ πρόβατον ἡμᾶς.

⊙−∪− ⊙−∪−

950   *X.* οὔκουν ἁμιλλήσεσθον; ὡς

−−∪− −∪−
∪−∪∪−∪−

†ἣν Χαῖρις ὑμᾶς ἴδῃ,†

∪−∪− −−∪−
−−∪∪−∪−

πρόσεισιν αὐλήσων ἄκλη-

−−∪− −−∪⌣‖
∪−∪∪−∪⌣⌣

τος, κᾆτα τοῦτ᾽ εὖ οἶδ᾽ ὅτι

−−∪− ⌣−∪−

φυσῶντι καὶ πονουμένῳ

−−∪∪−−‖‖‖

955   προσδώσετε δήπου.

This strophe and antistrophe frame the episode of the near-sacrifice on stage of the sheep and of Trygaeus' prayer to Peace. While not a climax in ordinary dramatic terms, the episode is crucial to the ideas and emotions that underlie the play. The song is articulated by catalectic iambic tetrameters delivered by Trygaeus (substitution of ∪∪ for anceps at 947 suggests recitative. See Introduction p. 33). The first half is in anapaests, framed by iambic with the opening euripidean and the closing catalectic dimeter. The final section includes a notable example

4 an

σοφὸν ἄνδρα; τί δ' οὐ σὺ φρονεῖς ὁπόσα χρε-

1030   ὧν ἐστι⟨ν⟩ τόν γε σοφῇ δόκιμον

ia dim cat

φρενὶ πορίμῳ τε τόλμῃ;

ia tetram cat

ἡ σχίζα γοῦν ἐνημμένη τὸν Στιλβίδην πιέζει.

ia tetram cat

καὶ τὴν τράπεζαν οἴσομαι, καὶ παιδὸς οὐ δεήσει.

ia dim

τίς οὖν ἂν οὐκ ἐπαινέσει-

+ ia dim sync (= tel)

εν ἄνδρα τοιοῦτον, ὅσ-

+ ia dim (= tel)

1035   τις πόλλ' ἀνατλὰς ἔσω-

+ ia dim (= tel)

σε τὴν ἱερὰν πόλιν;

ia dim

ὥστ' οὐχὶ μὴ παύσει ποτ' ὢν

reiz

ζηλωτὸς ἅπασιν.

of 'free' correspondence between iambic dimeters and telesilleans. Syllable-counting is of no use here: strophe and antistrophe do not match even in that respect. Both the telesilleans and the clausular reizianum of both strophe and antistrophe hark back to the previous duet, 856ff. = 909ff., and there are other rhythmic references to that song. Iambic tetrameters are again interspersed with lyric, and again the stanza has a suggestion of triadic structure, although the miniature (anapaestic) strophe and antistrophe no longer match in length.

The diversity of tone and stylistic level in Aristophanic lyric produces a connection between type of utterance and type of rhythm not merely closer but different in kind from any in tragic lyric. As a result, strophe and antistrophe generally correspond in content as well as rhythm (see on *Clouds* 275ff.=298ff., and Introduction, p. 14). Here, at 951ff.=1034ff. the difference in metre is clearly combined with difference in tone: the strophe derides Chaeris, where the antistrophe praises Trygaeus in dignified terms. It may be that the use of telesilleans for the praise of Trygaeus merely refers back to 856–62=909–15 and forward to the wedding-hymn, 1329ff. But it is tempting to suspect that

$$\ldots \; \pi \acute{o} \lambda \lambda' \; \mathring{a} \nu a \tau \lambda \grave{a} \varsigma \; \mathring{\epsilon} \sigma \omega \text{-}$$
$$\sigma \epsilon \; \tau \grave{\eta} \nu \; \mathring{\iota} \epsilon \rho \grave{a} \nu \; \pi \acute{o} \lambda \iota \nu \; \ldots$$

may be a quotation. In that case, the departure from correspondence would be comparable with that at *Knights* 332=406. At any rate, the only suspect point, as Bentley rightly saw, is the syncopated dimeter at 951. The correspondence 3A=3B is comprehensible, if remarkable. 1C+2A=3B seems beyond belief. Also, the solitary cretic is out of place in this regular iambic sequence (contrast 1128ff.=1160ff. below). Platnauer makes 1034 correspond with 951 by scanning τοιοῦτον. The scansion is possible: where the quantity can be determined, Aristophanes has τοιοῦτος etc. 26 times, as against τοιοῦτος 16 times (11 of which are in -αυτ- forms). However, beginning the run of cola in synartesis with a syncopated iambic dimeter destroys the metrical coherence of the passage.

Σ. *vet.* V (939–55, White *VGC* 417–18) expresses the belief that the stanza is in correspondence, but observes that the colometry transmitted does not correspond (Introduction, p. 97). Given the divergence at 951ff.=1034ff. and several textual problems, it is perhaps not surprising that the question of correspondence here was controversial in later antiquity. Indeed, the first verse does not correspond in the MS text. Moreover, the metrician of Σ. *vet.* seems to have had before him a different text from ours for both 939 and 1023. At 1023 his θύρασι, which provides the proper contrast with εἴσω (1020), is clearly preferable to the MS θύραισι. Otherwise, his version of the verse has reached us in hopelessly mutilated form. For 939 he envisages two possibilities:

(*a*) A full catalectic tetrameter:

ὡς πάνθ᾽ ὅσ᾽ ἂν θεὸς θέλῃ τε χἠ τύχη κατορθοῖ

The lemma has θέλοι for θέλῃ, but this may be a copyist's misspelling by sound. Zacher distinguished γε (not τε) erased after θέλῃ in V, and θέλῃ γε was adopted by Triclinius (LBAld).

(*b*) An implausible trimeter:

ὡς πάνθ᾽ ὅσ᾽ ἂν θεὸς θέλῃ χἠ τύχη

‒ ‒ ◡ ‒   ◡ ‒ ◡ ‒   ‒ ◡ ‒

Not surprisingly, *Σ vet.* prefers (*a*), apparently because of its compatibility with the rest of the stanza. He shows no knowledge of the euripidean tetrameter of the medieval MSS. The insertion of τε in (*a*) must be designed to simplify the metre, and it is interesting to find maladroit regularization of a typical Byzantine kind appearing before the end of the classical period. The truncation of the verse in (*b*) is apparently the work of an emendator who was aware of correspondence. Unless he was totally incompetent, his version of 1023 must have differed from ours: it cannot have ended with τοίνυν. Enger produced correspondence by the supplement ἐνθαδὶ after θύρασι⟨ν⟩, but the postponement of τοίνυν is unparalleled (Denniston, *Particles*, 579). The history of this passage, as far as it can be traced, is interesting for the light it casts on ancient metrical scholarship and on the hazards to a passage where correspondence is either absent or unrecognized.

At 943, the first syllable of the colon was already missing in *Σ vet.*, for he describes it as προσοδιακὸν ἑνδεκάσημον, i.e. ◡ ‒ ◡◡ ‒ ◡◡ ‒ ◡◡ ‒. ⟨ἄγ᾽⟩ is Dindorf's supplement. Bothe proposed κατεπείγετε. The corresponding anapaestic dimeters at 1028–30 are unusual in their lack of word-end between metra. Also, the MS ἐστι at 1030 is unmetrical. This is simply remedied by ephelcystic ν (Hermann). Triclinius tried transposing ἐστὶ χρεὼν (LBAld), and also made up the last colon into catalectic anapaests with καὶ πορίμῳ τῇ τόλμῃ. This shows a certain understanding of the metre, but failure (in spite of *Σ vet.*) to observe correspondence. There is split resolution in φρενὶ πορίμῳ (Introduction, pp. 34–5).

1127–39=1159–71

‒ ∪ ‒   ‒ ∪ ‒
ἥδομαί γ' ἥδομαι

⏒ ‒|∪ ‒   ‒ ∪ ‒
κράνους ἀπηλλαγμένος

⏑ ‒ ∪ ‒   ‒ ∪ ‒
τυροῦ τε καὶ κρομμύων.

‒ ‒ ∪ ‒   ‒ ∪ ‒
1130   οὐ γὰρ φιληδῶ μάχαις,

‒ ∪ ‒   ‒ ∪ ‒   ‒|∪ ‒   ‒ ∪ ‒   ‒ ∪ ‒
ἀλλὰ πρὸς πῦρ διέλκων μετ' ἀνδρῶν ἑταίρων φίλων

‒ ∪ ‒   ‒ ∪ ‒| ‒ ∪ ‒   ‒ ∪ ⏖   ‒ ∪ ‒
1133–4 ἐκκέας τῶν ξύλων ἅττ' ἂν ᾖ δανότατα τοῦ θέρους

‒ ∪ ‒   ‒ ∪ ⏒||
1135   ἐκπεπρ⟨εμν⟩ισμένα,

‒ ∪ ‒ ‒   ‒ ∪ ‒ ‒   ‒ ∪ ‒ ∪   ‒ ∪ ‒ ‒
κἀνθρακίζων τοὐρεβίνθου τήν τε φηγὸν ἐμπυρεύων

‒ ∪|‒ ⏑   ‒|∪ ‒
χἅμα τὴν Θρᾷτταν κυνῶν

‒ ∪ ‒ ⏑| ‒ ∪ ‒ |||
τῆς γυναικὸς λουμένης.

The second part of the parabasis (see on 775 ff. = 796 ff. above) divides the sacrifice, with its burlesque epilogue, the Hierocles-scene, from the burlesque prologue to the wedding-feast. Visually, the two episodes, 1046–1126 (a simple interplay between two characters) and 1191–1304 (with its multiplicity of characters and slapstick) are quite unlike each other, but Trygaeus' two exchanges in hexameters, first with Hierocles, then with the son of Lamachus, serve to give a feeling of symmetry.

It has already been observed that the songs following the first part of the parabasis are given a certain compatibility by the recurrence of rhythms: telesillean and unsyncopated iambic, in particular catalectic tetrameters. The ode and antode of this (the chorus's) part of the para-

2 cr
ἡνίκ' ἂν δ' ἀχέτας

ia cr (ia dim sync)
1160 ᾄδῃ τὸν ἡδὺν νόμον,

ia cr
διασκοπῶν ἥδομαι

ia cr
τὰς Λημνίας ἀμπέλους.

5 cr
εἰ πεπαίνουσιν ἤδη—τὸ γὰρ φῖτυ πρῷον φύσει—

5 cr
1165 τόν τε φήληχ' ὁρῶν οἰδάνοντ'· εἶθ' ὁπόταν ᾖ πέπων,

2 cr
ἐσθίω κἀπέχω

tro tetram
χἄμα φήμ'· Ὧραι φίλαι·' καὶ τοῦ θύμου τρίβων κυκῶμαι·

tro cr (lec)
1170 κᾆτα γίγνομαι παχὺς

tro cr (lec)
τηνικαῦτα τοῦ θέρους . . .

basis stand out in sharp contrast. As often in Aristophanes' earlier plays, cretics express animation and energy, which here belong to the farmers' festivities. After the cretic opening , the rhythm moves from syncopated iambic, through pure cretic, to trochaic. The cretic–iambic section consists of eight metra, the pure cretic of twelve, and the final, trochaic, section of eight again. The trochees lead smoothly into the trochaic tetrameters of the epirrhematic sections. Indeed, at the end of the antode, Aristophanes whimsically exploits the uniformity of rhythm for a surprise effect: the last section of the antode seems to be syntactically complete, but then turns out to run on unbroken into the epirrheme.

There is some corruption in the MS text, but satisfactory emendation is possible. At 1133, ἐκκέας was eventually restored to the text from RV. The printed vulgate, derived from the Aldine, had shared οὐκ ἐᾷς with Vp2C and the Triclinian edition. Brunck achieved a near-successful restoration with his conjecture συγκέας. ἐκπεπρ⟨εμν⟩ισμένα (1135) is a brilliant conjecture by Bergk. The word had, not surprisingly, spread havoc among copyists. Bothe's ἐκπεπρεμνισμένων (with τῶν for τοῦ in 1134) is not metrically necessary: *brevis in longo* makes a perfectly

1329–59

– – ◡ ◡ – ◡ –

T. δεῦρ᾽, ὦ γύναι, εἰς ἀγρόν,

◡ – ◡ ◡ – ◡ –

1330   χὤπως μετ᾽ ἐμοῦ καλὴ

◡ – ◡ ◡ – – ||

καλῶς κατακείσει.

◡ – ◡ ◡ – – ||

1332   Ὑμήν, Ὑμέναι᾽ ὤ,

◡ – ◡ ◡ – – ||

1332   Ὑμήν, Ὑμέναι᾽ ὤ.

◡ – ◡ ◡ – –

1337 *X.* τί δράσομεν αὐτήν;

◡ – ◡ ◡ – –

τί δράσομεν αὐτήν;

◡ – ◡ ◡ – –

τρυγήσομεν αὐτήν;

◡ – ◡ ◡ – –

1340   τρυγήσομεν αὐτήν.

1341 *X.* ἀλλ᾽ ἀράμενοι φέρω-
          μεν οἱ προτεταγμένοι
          τὸν νυμφίον, ὦνδρες.
          Ὑμήν, Ὑμέναι᾽ ὤ,
1345   Ὑμήν, Ὑμέναι᾽ ὤ.
1351 *X.* τοῦ μὲν μέγα καὶ παχύ
          ⟨× – ◡ ◡ – ◡ –⟩
1352   τῆς δ᾽ ἡδὺ τὸ σῦκον.

acceptable end to the cretic section. At 1159, the pre-Triclinian MSS
have the unmetrical ἡνίκα δ' ἄν. Triclinius' ἡνίκ' ἄν pointed the way
towards Hermann's ἡνίκ' ἄν δ'. At 1165, Bentley restored οἰδάνοντ'
from οἰδαίνοντ'.

Σ *vet.* V (1127–90, White, *VGC*, 419) seems to mention a divergence
of colometry between strophe and antistrophe in the cretic section of the
stanza, but RV preserve a corresponding division.

           tel
1333 X. ὦ τρίσμακαρ, ὡς δικαί-

           + tel
1334   ως τἀγαθὰ νῦν ἔχεις.

           + reiz
       ⟨× − ◡ ◡ − −⟩

           reiz
1335   Ὑμήν, Ὑμέναι' ὤ,

           reiz
1335   Ὑμήν, Ὑμέναι' ὤ.

           reiz

           reiz

           reiz

1346 X. οἰκήσατε γοῦν καλῶς
        οὐ πράγματ' ἔχοντες ἀλ-
        λὰ συκολογοῦντες.
        Ὑμήν, Ὑμέναι' ὤ,
1350   Ὑμήν, Ὑμέναι' ὤ.
1353 T. φήσεις γ' ὅταν ἐσθίῃς
1354   οἶνόν τε πίῃς πολύν.
       ⟨× − ◡ ◡ − −⟩

⟨Ὑμήν, Ὑμέναι' ὤ,
Ὑμήν, Ὑμέναι' ὤ.⟩

T. ὦ χαίρετε, χαίρετ', ἄνδρες, κἂν ξυνέπησθέ μοι

1359   πλακοῦντας ἔδεσθε.

⟨Ὑμήν, Ὑμέναι' ὤ,
Ὑμήν, Ὑμέναι' ὤ.⟩

This song and *Birds* 1731 ff. = 1737 ff., both featuring telesilleans, are the sole survivers in Greek of a type of processional wedding-song which must have provided the model for Catullus (61) and for his fellow-neoteric, Ticidas (Morel, fr. 1). From their testimony it is reasonable to deduce that short, aeolo-choriambic stanzas of the type we associate with Anacreon (Introduction, p. 22) were commonly used in such songs. Both the Latin poems use glyconic. Of Ticidas' only a line and a half survive, but Catullus' is in stanzas of four glyconics with pherecratean as clausula, frequently, but not universally, in the form of the refrain 'O Hymen Hymenaee'. Corroborative evidence for the use of glyconics in wedding-songs is provided by Cassandra's monody at *Tro.* 308 ff. = 325 ff. In this weird and anguished parody, Euripides exploits the surprise use of metre to powerful effect. The hymeneal refrain at 331 = 314 introduces an isolated glyconic among dochmiac and iambic, and the stanza ends with the familiar sequence of glyconic and pherecratean, followed by a curious appendage: a single, resolved iambic metron:

δίδους' ὦ Ὑμέναιε, σοί,   ∪ − − ∪ ∪ − ∪ −
δίδους', ὦ Ἑκάτα, φάος   ∪ − − ∪ ∪ − ∪ −
παρθένων ἐπὶ λέκτροις   − ∪ − ∪ ∪ − −
ᾇ νόμος ἔχει.   − ⌢ ∪ −

The very inappropriateness of the aeolic cola to the metrical context marks them as allusive.

Sappho is, of course, the best-known composer of wedding-songs of the pre-classical to classical age, but the form cannot be connected with her. Telesilleans appear in one fragment, *PLF* 99, col. i, but that is not a wedding-song, and the stanza-form there is, as far as can be ascertained, of Lesbian type:

× − ∪ ∪ − ∪ −
× − ∪ ∪ − ∪ − × − ∪ −

1355   Ὑμήν, Ὑμέναι' ὤ,
        Ὑμήν, Ὑμέναι' ὤ.

Indeed, the simple sequence of from two to four acatalectic cola rounded off by the appropriate catalectic colon does not seem to have been used by the Lesbian poets. One suspects that it is of popular origin, and was adopted into literary poetry by Anacreon and, possibly, Telesilla (*PMG* 717, quoted by Hephaestion, (Cons. 35. 10–11) is a pair of telesilleans without clausula).

Aristophanes' use of telesilleans rather than glyconics for his wedding-songs remains to be explained. A scholiast's note on the Antinoë papyrus of Theocritus mentions Telesilla in connection with 15. 64: πάντα γυναῖκες ἴσαντι, καὶ ὡς Ζεὺς ἀγάγεθ' Ἥραν. This led the first editors of the papyrus to the plausible conjecture that Telesilla was the author of a poem about the marriage of Zeus and Hera (A. S. Hunt and J. Johnson, *Two Theocritus Papyri* (London, 1930), 46 and 76). If Telesilla used her eponymous metre for the poem and it enjoyed some celebrity (as the quasi-proverbial allusion in Theocritus would indicate), Aristophanes' use of telesilleans here and, even more significantly, at *Birds* 1731 ff. = 1737 ff. would be explained. The song of *Birds*, however, is dignified and consciously literary, while that of *Peace* is earthy and akin to folk-song, as befits the chorus and the bride and bridegroom.

In particular, the sequence of question and answer in four reiziana at 1337–40 is very much in the manner of folk-song, as it still survives in children's games: 'Whom will you have for nuts-in-May? ... We'll have X for nuts-in-May.' Compare Page, *PMG* 852, 876, and, in a hymeneal context in literary poetry, Sappho, *PLF* 115. Suspicion of the sequence has been encouraged by the statement of Σ *vet.* that it is not present in some texts διὰ τὰ μέτρα. Yet, although it interrupts the over-all pattern, it is not metrically incompatible with the rest of the song. Holwerda (*Mnemosyne*, 20 (1967), 271 ff.) argues that the words διὰ τὰ μέτρα in Σ *vet.* are corrupt, and suggests transferring the four cola to follow 1352. The problem is thoroughly explored by Dover (*ICS* 2 (1977), 158ff.= *The Greeks and their Legacy*, ii. 218ff.)

Apart from 1337–40, the song as preserved in the MSS is not in stanzas of equal length, and the refrain does not appear regularly. In the interest of clear presentation of the evidence, I have shown in my text the lacunae and repetitions of the refrain that would have to be assumed to produce regularity. The metrician of Σ *vet.* (1329) apparently thought that the song ought to follow a regular pattern: διπλῆ καί †ἐπιτέλει† (ἑπτάς Holwerda) μονοστροφικὴ περιόδων πεντακώλων ἰωνικῶν διμέτρων, δύο καταληκτικῶν, τριῶν δὲ βραχυκαταλήκτων. There is also some evidence among the mutilated remains of Σ *vet.* that the text before him did not fully conform to the required pattern (1346). Also, Heliodorus is quoted by name as authority for the view that the play should end with the refrain. The fragments are, however, inadequate to show how far the text of Σ *vet.* coincided with ours. All that can be said is that most of the major textual difficulties of Aristophanes' lyric seem to have been already present in the text of Σ *vet.*, and that there is no evidence in the surviving notes of a general propensity to identify correspondence on the basis of inadequate evidence. H. J. Newiger's outright dismissal of the testimony of Σ *vet.* (*Aristophanes und die Alte Komödie*, 225–55=*RhM* 108 (1965), 241–54) is imprudent.

Even if the idea of regular stanzas is abandoned, the MS text at 1351–6 is implausible:

X. τοῦ μὲν μέγα καὶ παχύ,   – – ⏑ ⏑ – ⏑ ⌣ ‖
    τῆς δ᾿ ἡδὺ τὸ σῦκον.   – – ⏑ ⏑ – – –

T. φήσεις γ᾿, ὅταν ἐσθίῃς   – – ⏑ ⏑ – ⏑ –
    οἶνόν τε πίῃς πολύν.   – – ⏑ ⏑ – ⏑ ⌣ ‖

X. Ὑμήν, Ὑμέναι᾿ ὦ,   ⏑ – ⏑ ⏑ – – ‖
    Ὑμήν, Ὑμέναι᾿ ὦ,   ⏑ – ⏑ ⏑ – – ‖

The telesillean with verse-end at 1354 could, perhaps, be justified as preceding a genuine pause, but that at 1351 seems wholly misplaced (see above on 860). Moreover, the sequence of catalectic and acatalectic cola lacks any intelligible pattern. The fragments of ancient Greek folk-poetry are too exiguous to give us any idea of its distinctive rhythmic structures, but the practice of literary poetry at all levels indicates that patterns of contrast between catalexis and acatalexis are natural and fundamental to Greek poetic rhythm. Generally, surprise effects produced by the disruption of common rhythms belong to sophisticated, not to popular poetry. Newiger's suggestion that the irregularity of structure can be explained by the function of the song as an accompaniment to action is not founded on Aristophanes' practice. See, for example, the 'packing' and 'cooking' duets at *Ach.* 929 ff.=940 ff. and 1008 ff.=1037 ff. It should be admitted that we lack both the knowledge and the material to solve the problem of the structure of this song.

At 1342 προτεταγμένοι is Bentley's emendation of the MSS's non-metrical προστεταγμένοι.

Birds

SYNOPSIS

229–259	Hoopoe's solo: *Iambic, dochmiac, dactylo-epitrite, trochaic, ionic, anapaestic, cretic, dactylic.*
327–35=343–51	*Anapaestic,* correspondence of *dochmiac* with *cretic.*
406–34	Hoopoe and chorus: *Iambic, iambo-cretic, dochmiac.*
451–9=539–47	*'Free' dactylo-epitrite.*
629–36	*Iambic,* with resolution and syncopation.
676–84	*Aeolo-choriambic.*
737–52=769–84	*Dactylic, trochaic, iambic* clausula.
851–8=895–902	*Iambic,* with resolution and syncopation.
904–52	The lyric poet: *Aeolo-choriambic,* – ᴗ – ᴗ –, *dactylo-epitrite* (eccentric), *iambic* (a few bacchiacs).
1058–71=1088–1101	*Anapaestic* (of lyric type), *cretic.*
1188–95=1262–6	*Dochmiac.*
1313–22=1325–34	*Dactylic* (acephalous) and *Iambic.*
1337–9	The father-beater: *Dactylo-epitrite* and *iambic.*
1372–1400	Cinesias: *Iambo-choriambic, iambic, aeolo-choriambic, anapaestic.*
1410–15	The sycophant: *Aeolo-choriambic* (greater ascelepiad), *enoplian.*
1470–81=1482–93	*Trochaic.*
1553–64=1694–1705	*Trochaic* (corresponding, or nearly so, with the preceding strophic pair).
1720–5	*Trochaic, molossi, choriambic.*
1731–6=1737–42	*Aeolo-choriambic* (telesilleans, with pherecratean clausula).
1748–54	*Dactylic, aeolo-choriambic* (clausular pherecratean).
1755–65	Chorus and Peisetaerus: *Iambic* (dicola: iambic dimeter + lecythion).

In *Birds* Aristophanes seems to have set out to dazzle his audience with a display of metrical and musical virtuosity. Here, in consequence, we face most painfully our inability to appreciate what he was doing, except theoretically and intellectually. The repeated use of certain rhythms with structural and thematic functions, which is so common a feature of Aristophanes' plays, is absent here. On the contrary, the chief metrical characteristic of the play is diversity: every major type of metre found in Attic drama is represented, with, in addition, some rarities (see, in particular, 451 ff. = 539 ff., 737 ff. = 769 ff., 1313 ff. = 1325 ff.). The first song of the play, the Hoopoe's solo (229 ff.), sets the tone: that song in itself includes every type of metre except choriambic. Two scenes of parody (904 ff. and 1372 ff.) enable Aristophanes to move outside the metrical style of drama, with particularly puzzling results for us. The father-beater (1337 ff.) and the sycophant (1410 ff.) sing snatches of lyric from the archaic age which probably formed part of the symposiastic reper-toire (see Introduction, p. 4). The play includes at one extreme virtuoso compositions which make a feature of imitating bird-song (229 ff., 737 ff. = 769 ff.), and at the other a cycle of lampoon-songs of traditional simplicity (1470 ff. = 1482 ff., 1553 ff. = 1694 ff.).

Dochmiacs are used with their normal emotional connotations at 1188 ff. = 1262 ff. and, perhaps, at 333 ff., but it is a unique feature of *Birds* that dochmiacs are also found interspersed in passages where the singer or singers show no signs of extraordinary excitement (229 ff., 427 ff., and, possibly, 629 ff.).

Twittering, especially at moments of emotion, is mimicked by resolu-tion. There is a highly resolved passage in trochees and anapaests in the Hoopoe's song (240–1). In the chorus's first utterances (310, 315) bird-noises merge into speech in a string of shorts, although the exact number of shorts and the type of metre remain open to dispute. It is, however, worth remarking that the version of 310 as a trochaic tetrameter which has gained wide acceptance (by e.g. Kock, Schroeder, and Coulon) involves a very harsh split resolution (-σε; | τίνα τόπον ἄρ-, ◡◡◡◡◡). Fraenkel (*KB* i. 434) proposes anapaestic trimeters, anti-cipating 327 ff. = 343 ff., where, indeed, the Birds open in highly resolved anapaests, and go on, in the strophe, to highly resolved dochmiacs (333–5). Other concentrations of short syllables are delivered by the chorus at 853–4 = 897–9 (iambic), 1191 = 1265 (dochmiac), 1720–3 (trochaic).

229–59

‿ − ‿ −　　‿ − ‿ −　　‿ − ‿ −

ἴτω τις ὧδε τῶν ἐμῶν ὁμοπτέρων·

‿ − − ‿ −　　‿ − − ‿ −

230　ὅσοι τ᾽ εὐσπόρους ἀγροίκων γύας

‿　− ‿ −　‿　− ‿ ‿ − ‿ ‿ −

νέμεσθε, φῦλα μυρία κριθοτράγων

− ‿ ‿ − ‿ ‿ −

σπερμολόγων τε γένη

⁀ ‿ ⁀ ‿　− ‿ − −　− ‿ − ‿ ‖ a.a.

ταχὺ πετόμενα μαλθακὴν ἱέντα γῆρυν·

‿ ⁀ ⁀ ‿ ⁀

ὅσα τ᾽ ἐν ἄλοκι θαμὰ

− ‿ − ‿　− ‿ − ‿　− ‿ − ‿ ‖ a.a.

235　βῶλον ἀμφιτιττυβίζεθ᾽ ὧδε λεπτὸν

− ‿ ‿ − − −

ἡδομένᾳ φωνᾷ·

τιὸ τιὸ τιὸ τιὸ τιὸ τιὸ τιὸ τιό.

‿ ‿ − −　　‿ ‿ − −　　‿ ‿ − −

ὅσα θ᾽ ὑμῶν κατὰ κήπους ἐπὶ κισσοῦ

‿ ⁀ ⁀ ‿ −

κλάδεσι νομὸν ἔχει,

⁀ ‿ ⁀ ‿　⁀ ‿ ⁀ ‿　⁀ ‿ ⁀ ‿ ‖ н

240　τά τε κατ᾽ ὄρεα τὰ [τε] κοτινοτράγα τὰ [τε] κομαροφάγα,

‿ ‿ ‿ ‿ ‿ ‿　　‿ ‿ − − −

ἀνύσατε πετόμενα πρὸς ἐμὰν αὐδάν·

τριοτὸ τριοτὸ τοτοβρίξ.

− ‿ −　　− ‿ −　　− ‿ −　　　− ‿ −

οἵ θ᾽ ἑλείας παρ᾽ αὐλῶνας ὀξυστόμους

ia trim

2δ

iambel (– e – D)

hem (D)

tro trim

δ

tro trim

δ

ion trim

δ

tro trim

an dim

4 cr

‒◡‒ ‒◡⌒   ‒◡‒   ‒◡‒

245 ἐμπίδας κάπτεθ', ὅσα τ' εὐδρόσους γῆς τόπους

⌒◡‒   ‒◡⌒   ‒◡⌒   ‒◡†‒

ἔχετε λειμῶνά τ' ἐρόεντα Μαραθῶνος †ὄρ-

‒‒◡◡‒◡†‒◡‒   ‒◡‒

νις ⟨τε⟩ πτεροποίκιλος† ἀτταγᾶς ἀτταγᾶς·

‒◡◡   ‒◡◡   ‒◡◡   ‒‒

250 ὧν τ' ἐπὶ πόντιον οἶδμα θαλάσσης

‒◡◡   ‒◡◡   ‒◡◡   ‒‒

φῦλα μετ' ἀλκυόνεσσι ποτῆται,

‒◡◡   ‒◡◡   ‒◡◡   ‒◡◡

δεῦρ' ἴτε πευσόμενοι τὰ νεώτερα·

‒◡◡   ‒◡◡   ‒◡◡   ‒◡◡

πάντα γὰρ ἐνθάδε φῦλ' ἀθροΐζομεν

‒‒‒‒   ◡◡‒‒

οἰωνῶν ταναοδείρων.

‒‒‒‒   ‒‒‒‒

255 ἥκει γάρ τις δριμὺς πρέσβυς

‒‒‒‒

καινὸς γνώμην

‒‒‒‒   ‒‒‒‒

καινῶν ἔργων τ' ἐγχειρητής.

‒◡‒◡   ‒◡‒◡

ἀλλ' ἴτ' εἰς λόγους ἅπαντα,

‒◡‒◡   ‒◡‒◡

δεῦρο δεῦρο δεῦρο δεῦρο.

The Hoopoe has gone back into his 'thicket' at 208 to rouse the
Nightingale. He begins with a prelude in anapaests (209–22), with no
apparent lyric features: metron-diaeresis and synapheia are preserved
throughout (for Ἴτῡν at 212, compare S. *El.* 148), there is no catalexis

4 cr

4 cr

?

da tetram

da tetram

da tetram

da tetram

an dim cat (paroem)

an dim

an

an dim

tro dim

tro dim

until the clausula, and the incidence of double short is as in recitative. The evidence that these anapaests are sung is Peisetaerus' remark at 226: οὔποψ μελῳδεῖν αὖ παρασκευάζεται (which presumably gave rise to the pronouncement of Σ vet. 209: μελικῶς δὲ ἄρχεται). It is tempting to see a connection between the nightingale (the 'mourning bird') and the anapaestic metre. These anapaests are not, however, of the distinctive type used in tragic lamentation (Introduction, p. 57).

The Hoopoe's second song (229ff.) is unambiguous lyric and an extraordinary composition: within its thirty lines every type of metre is represented, except choriambic. The different metres are, however, clearly demarcated, and, except where there is corruption, each individual section is metrically simple and coherent. The fact that the Hoopoe leaves the stage in order to sing has led to the suggestion that the performance called for a virtuoso singer, who happened to be unable to act. It is true that exigencies of this kind have left their mark on masterpieces of music and drama (see e.g. *Twelfth Night* II. iv). But on the Attic stage a high degree of skill as a singer was evidently part of the normal equipment of both the comic and the tragic actor, and this song was probably no more demanding than, say, the monody at *Frogs* 1331 ff. Craik's suggestion (in Craik, '*Owls to Athens*', 83–4) that the Hoopoe made an exit through the skene door, climbed up backstage, and sang from the roof is much more plausible.

The song begins with bird-noises which merge into words (ἰτώ turns to ἴτω. See Sommerstein, ad loc.). The opening iambic trimeter is followed by a pair of dochmiacs, then a short passage in dactylo-epitrite. Then follows a curious alternation between trochaic trimeters and dochmiacs. The sequence trochee–dochmiac places anceps beside anceps, and so requires intervening verse-end: $- \cup -\times \mid\mid \times - -\times -$. Verse-end after acatalectic trochees is rare (Introduction, p. 35). At 238, a single ionic trimeter is again followed by a dochmiac. The sequence of 18 short syllables at 240 makes up another trochaic trimeter, again followed by verse-end, as the hiatus shows. The anapaestic dimeter at 241 is very clearly marked as of lyric type by consecutive double short. 244–7 should, in all probability, be a sequence of four cretic tetrameters, balancing the four dactylic tetrameters that follow, but corruption is evident on linguistic as well as metrical grounds. The text of the pre-Triclinian MSS gives a singular bird in apposition to ὅσα. The Triclinian supplement ⟨τε⟩ (LBVp2) patches up the passage linguistically, but does nothing for the metre. The general metrical clarity of the song demands cretics, but the word πτεροποίκιλος cannot be fitted into cretics, and the cretic of the form $\widehat{\cup\cup} \cup -$ comes as a surprise in such a sequence (see above on *Ach.* 284 ff. = 335 ff.). The extent of rewriting needed to produce cretics must make any proposed solution problematic. With the scansion τᾱναοδείρων, 254 is a catalectic anapaestic dimeter, which serves both as a sort of substitute-clausula to the dactyls (to which it belongs rhetorically) and as an introduction to the following anapaests. For the drift from dactyls into anapaests, compare S. *El.* 236 ff. The occasional lengthening of the first of a sequence of three short syllables in single-long–double-short metres seems to have been a licence on the analogy of epic that Greek poets continued occasionally to allow themselves (cf. Πρῑαμίδαισιν *Ag.* 747, δῡσοδοπαίπαλα *Eum.* 387, ᾱπαράμυθον *PV* 185; see Wilamowitz, *Homerische Untersuchungen*, 325). Scanning τᾰναοδείρων would produce – – – ◡ ◡ ◡ – –, analysable as mol tro, which might seem acceptable in view of the trochees both earlier and later in the passage. But the syncopation is stylistically out of place in this song. Moreover, when the words recur at 1394 there are anapaests in the passage, but no trochees. The purely spondaic rhythm of the anapaests at 255–7 is, again, characteristic of lyric. The song ends with trochees and bird-noises.

Undoubtedly, this metrical and musical *tour de force* is designed to imitate bird-song, but there is also literary allusion: 251 seems to echo Alcman, *PMG* 26. 3. It would be interesting, in this connection, to know more about the poem to which Alcman, *PMG* 39, belonged.

Apart from 244–7, the chief textual problem is presented by 240. The solution I adopt was put forward by A. M. Dale in a short note which cannot be bettered as an appreciation of the metrical character of this song ('The Hoopoe's Song', *CR* 9 (1959), 199–200 = *Collected Papers*, 11). On one technical point, however, Dale is at fault: 240 cannot be iambic, since verse-end cannot follow resolution. × || in trochaic is odd, but ◡ ◡ || in iambic is impossible. Equally, Sommerstein (*CR* 35 (1985), 15) is wrong to object to Dale's solution because of 'hiatus within a metrical period'. Hiatus here indicates verse-end, and the verse-end is neither more nor less strange than that after the other trochaic trimeters at 233 and 235.

At 247 I have included in the text the Triclinian supplement ⟨τε⟩ because it has some linguistic justification and has enjoyed fairly wide acceptance, although I do not believe that it is right. In fact, it is one of a number of minor interpolations shared by LVp2 and, sometimes, B,

e.g.: 244 ⟨τὰς⟩ ὀξυστόμους LVp2B; 245 εὐδρόσους ⟨τε⟩ LVp2; 246–7
ἔχετε ⟨καὶ⟩ λειμῶνα ⟨τὸν⟩ ἐρόεντα LVp2B. These supplements taken
together look like a systematic attempt to turn the cretics into trochees.

$$327–35 = 343–51$$

ἔα ἔα

∪∪∪∪ ∪∪∪∪ ∪∪∪∪

προδεδόμεθ᾽ ἀνόσιά τ᾽ ἐπάθομεν·

– –|∪ ∪ –| ∪ ∪ ∪ ∪ – –

ὃς γὰρ φίλος ἦν ὁμότροφά θ᾽ ἡμῖν

∪∪∪∪| ∪∪∪∪ – –||ₕ

330   ἐνέμετο πεδία παρ᾽ ἡμῖν,

‿ – – –   – – – –

παρέβη μὲν θεσμοὺς ἀρχαίους,

‿ – – –   – – –

παρέβη δ᾽ ὅρκους ὀρνίθων.

– ⌒ ⌒ ∪ ⌒
– ∪ ⌒   – ∪ ⌒

333a   ἐς δὲ δόλον ἐκάλεσε

∪ ⌒ ⌒ ∪ ⌒
– ∪ ⌒   – ∪ ⌒

333b   παρέβαλέ τ᾽ ἐμὲ παρὰ

∪ ⌒ ⌒ ∪ ⌒
– ∪ ⌒   – ∪ ⌒

334a   γένος ἀνόσιον ὅπερ

– ⌒ ⌒ ∪ –
– ∪ ⌒   – ∪ –

334b   ἐξότ᾽ ἐγένετ᾽ [ἐπ᾽] ἐμοὶ

∪ ⌒ ⌒ ∪ –
– ∪ ⌒   – ∪ ‿|||

335   πολέμιον ἐτράφη.

The Birds begin to sing in anapaests, with a furious rush of short
syllables. There is a tendency here to divide by word-end κατὰ πόδα,
which becomes even more marked if word-end with elision is included:

At 254, ⟨τῶν⟩ ταναοδείρων (LVp2) is probably intended to equalize the
colon with 253 and 255.

ἰὼ ἰώ·

　　　an trip
ἔπαγ' ἔπιθ' ἐπίφερε πολέμιον

　　　an dim
345　ὁρμὰν φονίαν, πτέρυγά τε παντᾷ

　　　an trip
περίβαλε περί τε κύκλωσαι·

　　　an dim
ὡς δεῖ τώδ' οἰμώζειν ἄμφω

　　　an dim cat (paroem)
καὶ δοῦναι ῥύγχει φορβάν.

　　　δ = 2 cr

349a　οὔτε γὰρ ὄρος σκιερὸν

　　　　　+δ = 2 cr

349b　οὔτε νέφος αἰθέριον

　　　　　+δ = 2 cr

350a　οὔτε πολιὸν πέλαγος

　　　　　+δ = 2 cr

350b　ἔστιν ὅ τι δέξεται

　　　　　+δ = 2 cr

　　　τώδ' ἀποφυγόντε με.

　　　　∪∪∪∪| ∪∪∪∪| ∪∪∪∪
　　　　－－|∪∪－| ∪∪∪∪|－－
　　　　∪∪∪∪| ∪∪∪∪ －－

Then, at 331–2=347–8, they change to a more resolute spondaic rhythm. This passage has affinities with the anapaests of the angry old men at *Lys.* 479–82=543–6. There, too, there are tripodies and runs of consecutive shorts. The spondaic rhythm, however, is lacking.

The song falls clearly into two halves, and in the second half there is a striking departure from normal correspondence. The antistrophe presents no problem: it is a sequence of ten cretics, with frequent resolution of the second long and a tendency to fall into dimeters. The strophe does not, in itself present any problem either. 333–4 consist of four dochmiacs:

$$- \widehat{\smile\smile} \; \widehat{\smile\smile} \; \smile \; \widehat{\smile\smile}$$
$$\smile \; \widehat{\smile\smile} \; \widehat{\smile\smile} \; \smile \; \widehat{\smile\smile}$$
$$- \widehat{\smile\smile} \; \widehat{\smile\smile} \; \smile \; -$$
$$\smile \; \widehat{\smile\smile} \; \widehat{\smile\smile} \; \smile \; -$$

These are all common (or reasonably common) forms of dochmiac, and were seen to be so by White (*VGC*, 213), and cretics and dochmiacs clearly had rhythmic affinities (Introduction pp.43, 67). Here, as Dale observed, the syllable-count of each dochmiac equals that of its corresponding pair of cretics. This is the same sort of compatibility that is to be observed in correspondence between different forms of

406–34

$$\smile - \smile - \quad \smile - \smile -$$
X. ἰὼ ἔποψ, σέ τοι καλῶ.

$$\smile - \smile - \quad \smile - \smile -$$
E. καλεῖς δὲ τοῦ κλυεῖν θέλων;

$$\smile - \smile - \quad \smile - \smile -$$
X. τίνες ποθ' οἴδε καὶ πόθεν;

$$\smile - \smile - \quad \smile - \smile -$$
E. ξένω σοφῆς ἀφ' Ἑλλάδος.

$$\smile - \smile - \quad - \smile - \quad - \smile -$$
410   X. τύχη δὲ ποία κομίζει ποτ' αὐ-

$$- \smile - \quad - \smile - \quad - \smile -$$
τὼ πρὸς ὄρνιθας ἐλθεῖν; E. ἔρως

dochmiac (Introduction, p. 66). the analysis of 333–5 has been bedevilled by attempts not only to establish syllable-for-syllable correspondence, but also to identify anapaests. Correspondence of dochmiac to cretic is, however, also found at *Wasps* 339 = 370, where there are no anapaests in the context. This passage accords better, perhaps, than any other with White's theory of 'intentional variation of melody' (Introduction, p. 116). One can see that the dochmiacs of the strophe could fitly express the distress and sense of betrayal of the Birds, and the cretics of the antistrophe their aggressive firmness and resolution. This would be entirely consistent with the use of the two metres elsewhere (cf., in particular, *Ach.*). However, as with correspondence by syllable-counting, the problem remains of why, if such a convenient device was open to Aristophanes, he did not use it more often.

At 334, ἐπ' was deleted by Blaydes.

At 346, περίβαλε is Reisig's proposal for the MS ἐπίβαλε, which involves hiatus after παντᾷ at 345, which is exceptional after an acatalectic anapaestic dimeter, and much harsher here than after the tripody at *Lys.* 479. Moreover, περίβαλε has positive advantages from the point of view of meaning. The movement in the first clause is of attack (ἐπί), that in the second of encircling (περί). ἐπίβαλε could easily have been introduced by a scribe with ἐπί on the brain.

ia dim

ia dim

ia dim

ia dim

ia + 5 cr

　　　∪−∪−　　−∪−　　−∪−

　　　βίου διαίτης τέ σου καὶ ξυνοι-

　　　　　　−∪−　　−∪−　　−∪−

415　　　κεῖν τέ σοι καὶ ξυνεῖναι τὸ πᾶν.

　　　∪−†∪−∪∪−†　∪−∪−

Χ. τί φής; †λέγουσι δὲ δὴ† τίνας λόγους;

　　　∪−∪−　　∪−∪−

Ε. ἄπιστα καὶ πέρα κλύειν.

　　　∪−∪−　　∪−∪−　　∪−∪−

Χ. ὁρᾷ τι κέρδος ἐνθάδ᾽ ἄξιον μονῆς

　　　∪−∪−　　∪−∪−

　　　ὅτῳ πέποιθ᾽ ἐμοὶ ξυνὼν

　　　∪−∪−　　∪−∪−

420　　　κρατεῖν ἂν ἢ τὸν ἔχθρον ἢ

　　　　　　∪−∪−　　∪−∪−

　　　φίλοισιν ὠφελεῖν ἔχειν;

　　　∪−∪−　　∪−∪−　　∪−∪−

Ε. λέγει μέγαν τιν᾽ ὄλβον οὔτε λεκτὸν οὔ-

　　　　　　∪−∪−　　∪−∪−　　∪−∪−

　　　τε πιστόν· ὡς σὰ [γὰρ ταῦτα] πάντα καὶ τὸ τῇδε καὶ

　　　　　　∪−∪−　　∪−∪−　　∪−∪−

425–6　　τὸ κεῖσε καὶ τὸ δεῦρο προσβιβᾷ λέγων.

　　　∪⌢−∪⌢

Χ. πότερα μαινόμενος;

　　　∪⌢−∪⌢

Ε. ἄφατον ὡς φρόνιμος.

　　　∪⌢−∪⌢

Χ. ἔνι σοφόν τι φρενί;

　　　∪∪∪−∪∪−̣

430　Ε. πυκνότατον κίναδος,

ia + 5 cr

ia dim?

ia dim

ia trim

ia dim

ia tetram

9 ia

δ

δ

δ

dodrans B? δ?

$$\cup - \cup - \quad \cup - \cup - \quad \cup - \cup -$$
σόφισμα, κύρμα, τρῖμμα, παιπάλημ' ὅλον.

$$\cup - \cup - \quad \cup - \cup -$$
X. λέγειν λέγειν κέλευέ μοι.

$$\cup - \cup - \quad \cup - \cup -$$
κλυὼν γὰρ ὧν σύ μοι λέγεις

$$\cup - \cup - \quad \cup - - |||$$
λόγων ἀνεπτέρωμαι.

The moment of extreme danger for Peisetaerus and Euelpides has passed, and the birds have agreed to parley with the Hoopoe. The ensuing dialogue, though not in full correspondence, is constructed with a high degree of symmetry. After the opening exchange in iambic dimeters, there follows a pair of verses, each made up of an iambic metron and five cretics. Here, however, symmetry is broken by change of singer just before the end of 411. Syntactically, the chorus's utterance is complete; musically, the Hoopoe interrupts. The iambic 'base' for a cretic verse appears here for the first time. It becomes a repeated rhythmic motif in *Lys.* (476 ff. = 541 ff., 614 ff. = 636 ff., 1043 ff. = 1058 ff. = 1189 ff. = 1203 ff.). 416 is corrupt, and would have to be reduced to a dimeter if it were to balance 417 (see below). The chorus's utterance at 418–21 and the Hoopoe's answer at 422–6 are each of nine iambic metra, but the first sequence is divided by coincidence of word-end and metron-end into 3 + 2 + 4, while the second is in synartesis throughout. In the brisk exchange of 427–30, there is, again, a break in symmetry with the last colon. Double short for anceps in dochmiacs is exceedingly rare (Introduction, p. 66), and if 430 is such a dochmiac, it is the only one in Aristophanes (cf. below on *Thesm.* 675). $\cup \cup \cup - \cup \cup -$ is found within a sequence of dochmiacs at A. *Supp.* 350=361 (ἴδε με τὰν (με τὰν Stephanus: μέγαν M) ἱκέτιν = σὺ δὲ παρ' ὀψιγόνου). The duet ends with a third group of nine iambic metra, divided asymmetrically between the Hoopoe (3) and the chorus (6, ending in catalexis).

In the iambic metra, short anceps is universal.

This last fact helps to confirm Dindorf's correction at 409 of the MS ξείνω to ξένω (ξεν- being, in any case, normal in Aristophanes). σου καί at 412 is Reiske's transposition for the MSS' καὶ σοῦ. At 420, τὸν

ia trim

ia dim

ia dim

ia dim cat

ἐχθρὸν is a Triclinian correction (LVp2+) for τῶν ἐχθρῶν. Bergk's excision of γὰρ ταῦτα at 424 is a terse and elegant solution. The elimination of asyndeton by the introduction of γάρ is typical of the paraphraser, deliberate or accidental. Meineke's ὡς σὰ γὰρ τὰ πάντα ταῦτα restores iambic rhythm, but destoys symmetry by producing ten metra, and is no less clumsy and prosaic than the MS text. With ὡς σὰ ταῦτα γὰρ δὴ πάντα (LVp2+), Triclinius tried, characteristically, to emend by addition rather than subtraction.

A harder textual problem is presented by 416. R omits δὴ and U δέ, but these are simple mistakes of haplography. δὲ δὴ in 'surprised, or emphatic and crucial questions' (Denniston, *Particles*, 259, P. T. Stevens, *Colloquial Expressions in Euripides*, (*Hermes* Einzelschrift 38, 1976), 46) and 'always with postponed interrogative' belongs to popular language, and is entirely appropriate here (cf. 67, 112 above). Wilamowitz's λέγουσιν produces ∪ – ∪ –   – ∪ –   ∪ – ∪ –, which seems theoretically possible, but inappropriate in the context: the iambic in this passage is unsyncopated, and the two verses 410–12 and 413–15, where an iambic metron introduces cretics, are quite distinct. Symmetry requires a dimeter here, balancing 417, and this can, in a manner, be produced by reading λέγει (Dindorf) and treating τί φῄς; as extra metrum. At some point between 412 and 418 the dual signifying Peisetaerus and Euelpides is dropped in favour of the singular referring to Peisetaerus alone. It is odd, however, that the change should be initiated by the chorus, who as yet know nothing of the relative importance of the two Athenians. And taking τί φῄς; as extra metrum smacks of subterfuge. This is, however, a plausible remedy.

451–9=539–47

⏑⏑ – ⏑⏑ –|⏑⏑ –   ⏑ –|⏑ –

δολερὸν μὲν ἀεὶ κατὰ πάντα δὴ τρόπον

⏕   – ⏑|–   –   – ⏑⏑ – ⏑⏑ –|⏑⏑ –

πέφυκεν ἄνθρωπος· σὺ δ' ὅμως λέγε μοι. τάχα γὰρ

⏑ –   –   – ⏑|–   –   –|⏑⏑ –|⏑⏑ –

τύχοις ἂν χρηστὸν ἐξειπὼν ὅ τι μοι παρορᾷς

            – ⏑⏑ – ⏑⏑ –   –

455   ἢ δύναμίν τινα μείζω

⏑⏑ – ⏑⏑ – ⏑⏑ – ⏑⏑ – ⏑⏑ –

παραλειπομένην ὑπ' ἐμῆς φρενὸς ἀξυνέτου·

⏑⏑ –   –   – ⏑ –   – ⏖ ||

σὺ δὲ τοῦθ' οὐρᾶς λέγ' εἰς κοινόν.

⏑⏑ – ⏑⏑ –   – ||^H

ὃ γὰρ ἂν σὺ τύχῃς μοι

⏑⏑ – ⏑⏑ –   – ⏑ –   ⏑ – – |||

ἀγαθὸν πορίσας, τοῦτο κοινὸν ἔσται.

This strophe precedes and its antistrophe follows the crucial turning-point in the early part of the play. In the intervening episode, Peisetaerus uses his demagogic talents to convince the chorus of his good faith and to rouse their resentment against their own supposed loss of status. The humour lies in the situation: in the fact that the beings who give vent to these classic human sentiments of injured nationalism are birds. The song is one of Aristophanes' two surviving compositions (cf. *Ran.* 674 ff. = 706 ff.) in a rare type of tragic metre which Dale correctly classified with dactylo-epitrite (*LM*² 191–4; cf. West, *GM* 133). Later in the play, 1313 ff. = 1325 ff. has affinities with the present passage, but the rhythmic phrases are there much simpler and more clearly defined. It is a pity that in discussing these rhythms Dale allowed the term 'iambo-anapaestic' to slip in. Taken up by less skilled metricians, it has led to analyses into formless mixtures of iambs and anapaestic 'feet', much in the manner of Hephaestion. Dale was writing before the discovery of major fragments of Stesichorus, and so had, in particular, no analogy in

$_\wedge$D prol ‿ e (‿ ‿ D ‿ e)
πολὺ δὴ πολὺ δὴ χαλεπωτάτους λόγους

‿ e – D prol
540 ἤνεγκας, ἄνθρωφ', ὡς ἐδάκρυσά γ' ἐμῶν πατέρων

$_\wedge$e – e – D
κάκην, οἳ τάσδε τὰς τιμὰς προγόνων παραδόν-

+ D –
των ἐπ' ἐμοὶ κατέλυσαν.

$_\wedge$D prol (‿ ‿ D prol)
σὺ δέ μοι κατὰ δαίμονα καί ⟨τινα⟩ συντυχίαν

$_\wedge$d – e – –
545 ἀγαθὴν ἥκεις ἐμοὶ σωτήρ.

$_\wedge$D –
ἀναθεὶς γὰρ ἐγώ σοι

$_\wedge$D ith
τὰ νεόττια κἀμαυτὸν †οἰκήσω.†

dactylo-epitrite outside Attic drama for long sequences in single-long–double-short rhythm. It is now possible to recognize the metre as an Attic version of undeveloped dactylo-epitrite (Introduction, p. 88).

Dactylo-epitrite characteristics are most clearly apparent in 452–5 = 540–3. There, the first verse is a prolonged version of the common 'iambelegus' (× – ‿ – × – ‿ ‿ – ‿ ‿ –). The temptation to follow rhetorical division in the strophe by making a separate colon of τάχα γὰρ τύχοις ἄν (‿ ‿ – ‿ – –) should be resisted. It produces a metrical phrase which is at home only in ionic (see *Wasps* 302–16) and a corresponding division in the antistrophe which cuts harshly *against* the sense: πατέρων κάκην, οἳ. It must simply be accepted here that rhetorical divisions in strophe and antistrophe differ strikingly. Compare πέφυκεν ἄνθρωπος· = ἤνεγκας ἄνθρωφ'. ὡς (‿ – ‿ – – –) at the beginning of the verse. The next verse (454–5 = 541–2) comes close to developed dactylo-epitrite: the only un-Pindaric feature is the sequence of two hemiepe with no intervening anceps. 457 = 545, too, resembles the bolder forms of developed dactylo-epitrite found in Pindar (cf. *Ol.* 7. 1. Introduction, p. 87).

The closest metrical parallel in tragedy to this stanza is *PV* 545 ff. = 552 ff. (which follows a strophic pair in standard dactylo-epitrite:

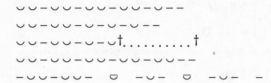

It is interesting, moreover, that the metrical resemblance is probably not fortuitous, for the song from *PV* seems to have been in Aristophanes' mind when he wrote this play: *PV* 547–9 is echoed verbally at *Birds* 686–7 (see Rau, *Paratragodia*, 176–7).

629–36

　　∪ – –　　– ∪ | –　　∪ – ∪ –

　　ἐπαυχήσας δὲ τοῖσι σοῖς λόγοις

　　∪ – –　　– ∪ | –　　∪ – ∪ ‿ || ʜ

630　ἐπηπείλησα καὶ κατώμοσα,

　　　∪ – ∪ | ‿　∪ | ‿ ∪ | ‿　∪ – | ∪ –

　　　ἐὰν σὺ παρ' ἐμὲ θέμενος ὁμόφρονας λόγους

　　　∪ – ∪ | ‿　∪ | ‿ ∪ | ‿　∪ – | ∪ –

　　　δίκαιος, ἄδολος, ὅσιος ἐπὶ θεοὺς ἴῃς,

　　　∪ – | ∪ – |　∪ – ∪ | –　∪ – ∪ –

635　ἐμοὶ φρονῶν ξυνῳδά, μὴ πολὺν χρόνον

　　　∪ – | ∪ – |　– ∪ | –　∪ – – |||

　　　θεοὺς ἔτι σκῆπτρα τἀμὰ τρίψειν.

In the anapaestic scene, 548–626, Peisetaerus has propounded his new order, in which birds are to take the place of gods. In a pair of anapaestic tetrameters (627–8), the Birds ecstatically affirm their devotion to him, then, in a short song, look forward to their victory over the gods—provided that Peisetaerus will keep his faith with them.

The version that I give of 631–4 includes Meineke's emendation of

At 457, οὐρᾷς is Bothe's emendation for the MS ὁρᾷς (or -ας). At 543, ⟨τινα⟩ is Bentley's supplement. The pre-Triclinian MSS have τά τε νεόττια at 547. τε is omitted in LVp2+. οἰκήσω at the end of the antistrophe raises problems both of metre and meaning. Hermann proposed οἰκετεύσω, a word found only at *Alc.* 437 in classical Greek: χαίρουσά μοι . . . τὸν ἀνάλιον οἶκον οἰκετεύοις (cf. the possible allusion to *Alc.* 442 at 539). But can the word be used with no indication of locality? Can 'I will become resident in ⟨your⟩ house' be supplied from the context? And, if it can, does it make sense for the Birds to say it? The Platonic use of οἰκεῖν for 'to manage one's affairs' would make sense, but seems implausible both so early and transferred to οἰκετεύειν. If οἰκετεύσω is accepted, it is better taken as 'I shall be your servant' (οἰκέτης). Ironically, the Birds (like other victims of demagogy) would then be demonstrating their inherent ἀνελευθερία.

ia trim sync

ia trim sync

ia trim

ia trim

ia trim

ia trim sync cat

ἤν to ἐάν and Bergk's of δικαίους, ἀδόλους, ὁσίους to nominative singular, applying to Peisetaerus. The merits of this version are well described by Fraenkel (*Beobachtungen*, 94), and its metrical neatness is striking. The stanza consists of six iambic trimeters, which fall into couplets in which the two verses that make up each couplet are assimilated to each other by matching patterns of syncopation, resolution, and word-end. Only in the last couplet is there divergence, so that the clausular verse contrasts with its predecessor. The use of syncopated trimeters gives a suggestion of solemnity (Introduction, pp. 30–2).

The one possible inducement to hesitation is the curious absence in classical Greek of examples of ἄδολος applied to people, as distinct from words, treaties, and the like. It is also worth noting that the MS version of 631–4, while untidy by comparison with the emended version, is not metrically impossible:

ἦν σὺ παρ' ἐμὲ θέμενος	– ⏜ ⏜ ⏑ ⏜	δ
ὁμόφρονας λόγους δικαίους	⏑ ⏜ – ⏑ – ⏑ – –	δ ba
ἀδόλους ὁσίους	⏑ ⏑ – ⏑ ⏑ –	an
ἐπὶ θεοὺς ἴῃς . . .	⏑ ⏜ – ⏑ –	δ

676–84

– ⏑ ⏑ – – – ‖ ʜ

ὦ φίλη, ὦ ξουθή,

– – ⏑ ⏑ – ⏑ –

ὦ φίλτατον ὀρνέων

– – – ⏑ ⏑ – ⏑ –

πάντων, ξύννομε τῶν ἐμῶν

– – – ⏑ ⏑ – – ‖ ʜ

ὕμνων, ξύντροφ' ἀηδοῖ,

– ⏑ – ⏑ – –

680   ἦλθες, ἦλθες, ὤφθης,

– – – ⏑ ⏑ – ⏑ –

ἡδὺν φθόγγον ἐμοὶ φέρουσ'·

– – – ⏑ ⏑ – ⏑ –

ἀλλ' ὦ καλλιβόαν κρέκουσ'

– – – ⏑ ⏑ – ⏑ –

αὐλὸν φθέγμασιν ἠρινοῖς,

– – – ⏑ ⏑ – – ‖‖‖

ἄρχου τῶν ἀναπαίστων.

For anapaests among dochmiacs, compare *Clouds* 1165 ff. Conservative critics have been known to champion readings more metrically ungainly than this. The passage offers a particularly apt illustration of the difficulties and inadequancies of modern judgement in metrical matters.

In any case, it should be observed that when the chorus comes to touch on the subject of the good faith of their human ally, the rhythm shows signs of heightened emotion: dochmiacs in the MS text, resolution in the emended version.

Minor emendations elsewhere in the text are the Triclinian τοῖσι for τοῖς in 629 (LVp2+) and Brunck's ἴῃς for ἴοις in 634.

dodrans (dragged)

tel

glyc

pher

ith

glyc

   + glyc

   + glyc

pher

In the prelude to the parabasis, the chorus invites a piper, who has entered disguised as Procne, to accompany 'the anapaests'. Although the chorus of *Birds* never abandon their dramatic role in the parabasis, the mention of τῶν ἀναπαίστων makes a fleeting break in dramatic illusion.

The song begins with a single colon followed by hiatus. A possible alternative to the dragged dodrans would be a cretic and molossus, divided from each other by yet another hiatus ($- \cup -$н $- - -$), but there is no reason to avoid the correption (Introduction, p. 91). The address to the Nightingale continues in three further aeolo-choriambic cola, of which the last is a clausular pherecratean. It is interesting to note how in 677–9 the familiar cola, telesillean, glyconic, and pherecratean, overlie a different pattern, which is marked out by rhetorical division, anaphora and rhyme:

$$737–52=769–84$$

$- \cup \cup \quad - -$

Μοῦσα λοχμαία,

    738   *bird-noises*

$- \cup -|\cup \quad - \cup -|\cup$

ποικίλη, μεθ᾽ ἧς ἐγὼ νά-

    $- \cup \cup \quad - \cup \cup \quad - \cup \cup \quad - -$

740   παισί ⟨τε καὶ⟩ κορυφαῖς [τ᾽] ἐν ὀρείαις,

    741   *bird-noises*

    $- \cup \cup \quad - \cup \cup \quad -|\cup \cup \quad - \cup \cup. \quad -$

742   ἱζόμενος μελίας ἔπι φυλλοκόμου,

    743   *bird-noises*

    $\cup \cup \quad - \cup \cup \quad -|\overline{\cup\cup} \quad - \cup \cup \quad -$

744   δι᾽ ἐμῆς γέννος ξουθῆς μελέων

    $- \cup \cup \quad - \cup \cup \quad - \cup \cup \quad - -$

745   Πανὶ νόμους ἱεροὺς ἀναφαίνω

    $- \cup \cup \quad - \cup \cup \quad - \cup \cup \quad - -$

σεμνά τε μητρὶ χορεύματ᾽ ὀρεία,

ὦ φίλτατον ὀρνέ<u>ων</u> πάντ<u>ων</u>,   − − ∪ ∪ − ∪ − − −
ξύννομε τ<u>ῶν</u> ἐμ<u>ῶν</u> ὕμν<u>ων</u>,   − ∪ ∪ − ∪ − − −
ξύντροφ' ἀηδοῖ, . . .   − ∪ ∪ − −

The ithyphallic at 680 marks the climax of the invocation: ἦλθες, ἦλθες, ὤφθης (compare the hymns at *Knights* 551 ff. = 581 ff. and *Thesm.* 1136ff.). There follows a dislocation between metrical and rhetorical division. 681 belongs rhetorically to what precedes, but metrically it is the first colon of a group of three glyconics and a pherecratean (in fact, the basic aeolo-choriambic stanza-form (Introduction, p. 22). The pherecratean with double-long base leads easily into the anapaests of the parabasis. Compare *Wasps* 323, and, on the compatibility of pherecrateans and anapaests, see Introduction, pp. 60–1.

      da dim
τοιάδε κύκ¹νοι,

    770 *bird-noises*

      tro dim
771 συμμιγῆ βοὴν ὁμοῦ πτε-

        + da tetram
ροῖσι κρέκοντες ἴαχον Ἀπόλλω,

    773 *bird-noises*

      da pent cat
ὄχθῳ ἐφεζόμενοι παρ' Ἕβρον ποταμόν,

    775 *bird-noises*

      ∧da pent cat
776 διὰ δ' αἰθέριον νέφος ἦλθε βοά·

      da tetram
πτῆξε δὲ φῦλά τε ποικίλα θηρῶν,

      da tetram
κύματά τ' ἔσβεσε νήνεμος αἴθρη·

747　*bird-noises*

−∪−∪　−∪−∪

ἔνθεν ὡσπερεὶ μέλιττα

−∪∪|　−∪∪　−∪∪　−∪∪　−∪∪　−∪∪　−

Φρύνιχος ἀμβροσίων μελέων ἀπεβόσκετο καρπὸν ἀεὶ

∪−∪−　∪−−

750　φέρων γλυκεῖαν ᾠδάν.

751　*bird-noises*

The parabasis-song seems completely dissociated from the plot of the
play at this point, when the Birds are in fact planning a coup against the
gods in association with a man. Here, instead, men, with the exception
of the poet, Phrynichus, are excluded, and birds and their song are dignified by association with the gods. In the strophe, the Birds, like other
choruses, address their own muse, who inspires them, as, in the parts of
the countryside remote from men, they sing to the gods of wild nature,
Pan and the Great Mother. The mention of Phrynichus tempts one to
wonder whether a metrical or musical debt is being acknowledged.
Complimentary allusion to an earlier poet is not out of place in a
parabasis-song (cf. *Knights* 1264 ff. = 1290 ff., *Peace* 775 ff. = 796 ff.).
There are no dactyls among the (exiguous) fragments of Phrynichus'
lyric. The antistrophe takes up a theme typical of high poetry: the song
of the swan. In particular, there are several references to it in plays of
Euripides which belong (or probably belong) to the same decade as
Birds: *Her.* 692, *Phaethon* 78 (Diggle), *Ion* 161 ff., *El.* 151, *IT* 1104 (these
last two plays being probably a little later than *Birds*).

The song is an elegant composition, serious, but avoiding a level of
elevation discordant with comedy. The key to its distinctive quality and
to the particular kind of enjoyment it will have afforded lies in the bird-
noises, and, no doubt, the piper's accompaniment (see further, Introduction, p. 13).

Dactylic and iambic are regularly blended in Aeschylus and else-

779   *bird-noises*

tro dim
780   πᾶς δ' ἐπεκτύπησ' Ὄλυμπος·

7 da cat
εἷλε δὲ θάμβος ἄνακτας· Ὀλυμπιάδες δὲ μέλος Χάριτες

ia dim cat
Μοῦσαί τ' ἐπωλόλυξαν.

783   *bird-noises*

where in Attic drama (Introduction, pp. 50–2), but there is no parallel
there for the close association of dactylic and trochaic that appears in this
stanza. In Aeschylus, in particular, lecythia are often used as clausulae to
dactyls (see below on *Frogs* 814 ff.), but the lecythion is an ambigous
colon, with as much claim to be classed as iambic as trochaic. To us,
the rarity of the association may seem surprising, as both metres move
from long to short. The first colon here is better described as 'dactylic
dimeter' than as adonean, so as to distinguish it from the aeolo-
choriambic colon, the catalectic version of $- \cup \cup - \cup -$. The sequence
at 742–4 is curious: it is as if the bird-noises were inserted in the middle
of a dactylic metron. The sequence of catalectic colon followed by
acephalous colon in dactyls is, however, guaranteed by *Eum.*
1042–3 = 1046–7, where there is metrical pause between the two cola:

$- \underset{\smile}{\smile} \quad - \cup \cup \quad - \cup \cup \quad \underset{\smile}{\smile} \parallel_H$ da tetr cat
λαμπάδι τερπόμενοι καθ' ὁδόν.   οὕτω Μοῖρά τε συγκατέβα.

$\cup \cup \quad - \cup \cup \quad - \cup \cup \quad - -$ $_\wedge$da tetr
ὀλολύξατε νῦν ἐπὶ μολπαῖς   ὀλολύξατε νῦν ἐπὶ μολπαῖς.

At 740, τε was suggested by Brunck and καὶ by Thiersch. For the
combination of locatival dative and ἐν with dative, compare *Ach.* 533,
Knights 610. At 769, ΓU share τοιάνδε with the Triclinian LVp2 and B.
Here, Triclinius allowed a failure of correspondence to pass. At 777,
φῦλα τε ποικίλα is Hermann's transposition of the MS ποικίλα φῦλα
τε.

851–8=895–902

⏒ – ⏑ –   – ⏑ –

ὁμορροθῶ, συνθέλω,

– ⏑ –   ⏑ – | ⏑ –

συμπαραινέσας ἔχω

⏒ ⏔ ⏑ ⏔   ⏑ | ⏔ ⏑ | ⏔   ⏑ – | ⏑ –

προσόδια μεγάλα σεμνὰ προσιέναι θεοῖ-

⏑ | ⏔ ⏑ | ⏔   ⏑ ⏔ ⏑ ⏒

σιν, ἅμα δὲ προσέτι χάριτος ἔνε-

⏑ ⏔ ⏑ –   ⏑ – –

855–6   κα προβάτιόν τι θύειν.

⏑ – ⏑ –   ⏑ – ⏑ –   ⏑ – ⏑ –

ἴτω ἴτω ἴτω δὲ Πυθιὰς βοὰ [τῷ θεῷ],

⏑ – –   – ⏑ | –   ⏑ – ⌣ |||

συναυλείτω δὲ Χαῖρις ᾠδᾷ.

This mock-solemn strophic pair appropriately frames the burlesque scene of sacrifice to the new bird-gods. Σ *vet*. VEΓ on ὁμορροθῶ (851) identifies a quotation from Sophocles' *Peleus*, although its precise extent is not clear (see Radt, *TrGF*, Sophocles 489). Σ *vet*. VE derives ἴτω δὲ Πυθιὰς βοὰ from the same source. Metrically, the restrained, but strategic, use of syncopation, the passage featuring lavish resolution, and the heavily syncopated clausular trimeter following an unsyncopated sequence can all be paralleled from Sophocles' iambic (compare *Ant*. 586 ff. = 597 ff., 847 ff. = 866 ff., 953 ff. = 964 ff., *El*. 126–7 = 142–4, 1085 ff. = 1093 ff.). In both strophe and antistrophe, dignity is maintained until the second half of the resolved middle section. Then begins the descent into bathos with the prosaic προβάτιόν τι in the strophe and the overtly comic invitation to only *one* god in the antistrophe. The rhythm, however, remains stately, and the distinctively tragic trimeter which ends the song coincides with a climax of absurdity of content, with the naming of Aristophanes' favourite target, Chaeris, in the strophe and the punch-line to the description of the victim in the antistrophe. The corresponding stanzas are very slightly differentiated by the recurrence of the high

ia dim sync
εἶτ᾽ αὖθις αὖ τἄρα σοι

lec
δεῖ με δεύτερον μέλος

6 ia ba
χέρνιβι θεοσεβὲς ὅσιον ἐπιβοᾶν, καλεῖν

δὲ μάκαρας, ἕνα τινὰ μόνον, εἴ-

900   περ ἱκανὸν ἕξετ᾽ ὄψον.

ia trim + ia trim sync
τὰ γὰρ παρόντα θύματ᾽ οὐδὲν ἄλλο πλὴν

γένειόν τ᾽ ἐστὶ καὶ κέρατα.

tone in 857, throwing the final verse into sharper relief. For a similar, but more uproarious, use of tragic iambic rhythm, compare *Ach.* 1150 ff. = 1162 ff.

There is a tendency for word-end to coincide in strophe and antistrophe, especially in the resolved passage. There are two metrical oddities in the antistrophe. At 899, the phrase ἕνα τινὰ μόνον produces split resolution (Introduction, p. 34). It is tempting to suspect that the inelegant rhythm serves to emphasize the prosaicness of the expression. At 901–2, since there can hardly be full word-end after πλὴν, the following bacchiac is neither preceded nor followed by word-end (Introduction, p. 28).

At 856, προβάτιον is Bentley's correction of the MS πρόβατον. At 857, MSS vary, not surprisingly, in the number of repetitions of ἴτω. Bentley's solution was to read ἴτω twice and delete the article with θεῷ. The version I have adopted is Dindorf's. The triple ἴτω gives an appropriate suggestion of bird-song.

At 858, the MSS have συναδέτω δὲ Χαῖρις ᾠδάν (∪–∪–∪–∪––), which is unmetrical. συναυλείτω . . . ᾠδᾷ (Hermann) is surely right.

Chaeris (unless there was more than one musician of the name) seems to have been a versatile performer, since he is mentioned as a singer at *Ach.* 16 and as the world's second worst lyre-player by Pherecrates (*PCG* 6),

904–52

⌒ ‿ –   – ‿ –

904a   Νεφελοκοκκυγίαν

– – – ‿ ‿ – ‿ –

904b   τὰν εὐδαίμονα κλῆσον, ὦ

– ‿ ‿ – ‿ – –

905   Μοῦσα, τεαῖς ἐν ὕμνων

‿ – –

   ἀοιδαῖς.

907   trim I

‿   – ‿ –   –   – ‿ ‿ –   –   – ‿ –   –

908   ἐγὼ μελιγλώσσων ἐπέων ἱεὶς ἀοιδὰν

– – – ‿ ‿ – ‿ –

   Μουσάων θεράπων ὀτρη-

– ‿ ⌒ ‿ – ‿ ||

910   ρὸς κατὰ τὸν Ὅμηρον.

911–12   trim II

– – – ‿ ‿ – ‿ ‿ –

913   Μουσάων θεράποντες ὀτρη-

– ‿ ⌒ ‿ – ‿ ||

   ροὶ κατὰ τὸν Ὅμηρον.

915–23   trim IX

– ‿ ‿ –   – ‿ –   –   – ‿ ‿ ||

924   ἀλλά τις ὠκεῖα Μουσάων φάτις

but he earns his most frequent mentions as a piper: *Ach.* 866, Cratinus, *PCG* 126, and *Peace* 950ff. (where, as here, he threatens to accompany a sacrifice).

e e (cr cr)

glyc +

   arist

ba

trim I

$\smile$ e – d – e –

glyc +

   Ē – (ith)

trim II

– – D

   E – (ith)

trim IX

d e – e

⏑⏑– –⏑⏑– –

925　οἷαπερ ἵππων ἀμαρυγά.

⌢⏑– –⏑– –

σὺ δὲ πάτερ, κτίστορ Αἴτνας,

⏑⏑–⏑⏑– ⏑ –⏑⌣ ‖

ζαθέων ἱερῶν ὁμώνυμε,

⏑⏑–͡⏑⏑– ⏑–⏑⏑–⏑–

928–9　δὸς ἐμὶν ὅ τι περ τεᾷ κεφαλᾷ θέλῃς

– –⏑⏑†.....†

930　πρόφρων δόμεν †ἐμὶν τείν†

931–5　　　　trim V

⏑⏑⏑ –⏑⏑–⏑⏑–

936　τόδε μὲν οὐκ ἀέκουσα φίλα

–⏑– –⏑⏑–

Μοῦσα δῶρον δέχεται·

⌢⏑–⏑⏑⌢ –⏑–⏑⏑⌣ ‖

938–9　τὺ δὲ τεᾷ φρενὶ μάθε Πινδάρειον ἔπος

940　　　　trim I

⏑⏑–⏑⏑– ⏑ –⏑– –⏑–

941　νομάδεσσι γὰρ ἐν Σκύθαις ἀλᾶται Στράτων,

⏑⏑–⏑⏑– ⏑ –⏑– ⏑– –

ὃς ὑφαντοδόνατον ἔσθος οὐ πέπαται.

–⏑–⏑–

ἀκ|λεὴς δ’ ἔβα

⌢⏑–⏑– –

σπολὰς ἄνευ χιτῶνος.

⌢⏑–⏑–

945　ξύνες ὅ τοι λέγω.

d d –

e e –

$\wedge$D $\smile$ e

$\wedge$D tel

?

trim V

$\wedge$e D

e d

2 dodrans B

trim I

$\wedge$D $\smile$ e e

$\wedge$D $\smile$ e ba

E

E – (ith)

E

946–9 　　　trim IV

$$- \cup - \quad - \quad - \cup \cup - \cup \cup - \cup \cup -$$

950　κλῇσον, ὦ χρυσόθρονε, τὰν τρομερὰν κρυεράν.

$$\overset{\frown}{} \cup \overset{\frown}{} \cup \overset{\frown}{} \quad \overset{\frown}{} \cup - \cup \smile \parallel$$

νιφόβολα πεδία πολύπορά τ' ἤλυθον.

ἀλαλαί.

Having got rid of the priest, Peisetaerus is starting to officiate himself, when a poet appears, delivering snatches of song, which are, at least partly, quoted from Pindar. No metrical coherence is discernible, nor is there any reason to expect it. Scansion is, moreover, complicated by alternative possibilities: we do not know how far the victim of Aristophanes' parody will have adopted Pindaric prosody (Attic poets were usually free in their treatment of their models), nor do we know how far quotations have been garbled. If Σ *vet.* on 926 is to be believed, the Pindaric original there was metrically quite different from Aristophanes' version. Most of the rhythmic phrases used by the 'poet' can, however, be paralleled individually from Pindar.

904a: $\overset{\frown}{} \cup - \quad - \cup -$. This is quite a common phrase in Pindar. See especially *Ol.* 2, a predominantly cretic poem, e.g. Χρόνος ὁ πάντων πατήρ.

904b: $- - - \cup \cup - \cup -$. Pindar does not favour aeolic base in the form $- -$, but in *Ol.* 9 the fourth verse of the strophe begins with a glyconic with spondaic base in all repetitions, and the seventh verse, another glyconic, has spondaic base in seven repetitions out of eight.

905: $- \cup \cup - \cup - -$. Compare the end of the final verse of the epode of *Ol.* 1, e.g. ἐξαπατῶντι μῦθοι.

908: $\cup e - d - e -$. There is no exact parallel in Pindar's surviving poems, but there are a number of verses made up of e, d, and anceps, e.g.: $e - e - d$ (*Ol.* 12, str. 4 and ep. 8, *Pyth.* 4, ep. 6, *Isth.* 5, str. 2, etc.), $- e - e - d$ (*Pyth.* 3, str. 5), $d - d - e - e$ (*Ol.* 6, ep. 3).

909–14. The scansion I offer approximates to Attic usage, although not impossible in Pindar. The glyconic at 909 echoes 904, and 913–14 is very similar to *Ol.* 5, str. 2:

$$- \overline{\cup} - \cup \cup - \cup \cup - \cup \cup - - \cup - \cup - -$$

trim IV

e – D prol

E E

An alternative would be to divide following word-end, making κατὰ τὸν Ὅμηρον into a separate colon:

– – – ∪ ∪ – ∪ – –   hipp
∪ ⁀∪ –   ⌣ || ∪ e ⌣ ||

and

– –   – ∪ ∪ – ∪ ∪ –   –   – – D –
∪ ⁀∪ –   ⌣ || ∪ e ⌣ ||

κατὰ τὸν Ὅμηρον is not actually part of the poet's song, but whether the phrase was spoken or sung in performance is a different question. If spoken, it would have to be taken as an iambic trimeter cut short at the caesura. If sung, × e × can be easily paralleled from Pindar, and *Pyth.* 6. 16 has the same resolution: δύο δ᾽ ἀπὸ Κίρρας.

Again, the scansion of ὀτρηρός is open to question. I have adopted Attic scansion, whereas in Homer it is ὀτρηρός. There is no surviving example of the word in Pindar, but he uses parts of ὀτρύνω a number of times, always scanning ὀτ|ρυν-, except once, at *Ol.* 6. 87 (note that Slater's *Lexicon to Pindar* is not to be relied on in this matter). Scanning ὀτ|ρηρ- here would produce less easily classifiable patterns.

924–5. The sequence d e is not uncommon in Pindar. See, for example, *Ol.* 9, str. 10, *Pyth.* 1, str. 2, *Pyth.* 5. 11, *Pyth.* 7, str. 2, *Pyth.* 10, str. 2, etc. The closest approximation to this colon is *Ol.* 13, ep. 6, which differs only in that the opening choriamb is acephalous: ∧ ∪ ∪ –   – ∪ –   –   – ∪ –. ἀμαρυγά is found neither in Pindar nor anywhere in Attic poetry, except for this passage (for ἀμάρυγμα, see Bacchylides 8. 36). The Homeric scansion is ἀμαρῡγή. For d d in Pindar, compare *Ol.* 4, str. 5 (–d d–), and *Pyth.* 8, ep. 4 (–d d ∪e). Without verse-end after 924, 924–5 would run –∪∪– –∪– – –∪∪–∪∪– –∪∪– – (d e–D d –). D d is found at *Isth.* 1, str. 6 (e–D d e–e).

Reading οἷάπερ at 925 produces –   – ◡ –   – ◡ ◡ –   –, which is
extremely hard to parallel in Pindar. There are several examples of
– ◡ –   – ◡ ◡ –, but the only example of the phrase flanked by longs
is *Nem.* 1, ep. 4 (– e d e – e), where there is consistent word-end after d
and the last long of the phrase belongs to a following cretic (–   – ◡ –
– ◡ ◡ –| – ◡ –   –   – ◡ –). Running together 924–5 would
produce an unparalleled sequence, . . . – ◡ ◡ –   – ◡ –   – ◡ ◡ – . . .

926–7. According to Σ *vet.*, the relevant passage, from a hyporcheme
of Pindar, ran:

ξύνες ὅ τοι λέγω, ζαθέων ἱερῶν
ἐπώνυμε πάτερ, κτίστορ Αἴτνας

⌒ ◡ –   ◡   – ◡ ◡ – ◡ ◡ –
◡ –   ⌒ ◡ –   – ◡ –   –

926 is identical metrically with the second Pindaric colon, less the initial
◡ – (ₐe). 927 is a possible segment of a Pindaric verse (e.g. *Nem.* 3. 37,
Τελαμὼν Ἰόλᾳ παραστάτας).

928–30. There are two possibilities for 928–9, depending on whether
the final syllable of ἐμίν is long or short (see Kühner–Blass i. 1. 583 n. 2).
The form is not commonly used by Pindar. His one example, at *Paean*
10. 19, falls before a consonant, so reveals nothing. Scanning ἐμῖν gives
initial ◡ ◡ – ◡ ◡ –, which is found in Pindar both in dactylo-epitrite
(*Pyth.* 3, ep. 9, *Nem.* 8, str. 5) and non-dactylo-epitrite contexts (*Ol.* 5,
str. 3, *Ol.* 13, str. 1, *Pyth.* 10, str. 6, etc.). It is, however, never followed
by ◡ – ◡ ◡ – ◡ –.

Scanning ἐμῐ́ν produces ⌒ ◡ ⌒   – ◡ – ◡ ◡ – ◡ –. Fully resolved
cretics are occasionally found in Pindar's non-dactylo-epitrite poems.
At *Nem.* 7, str. 6, such a cretic follows a telesillean, – – ◡ ◡ – – ◡ –
⌒ ◡ ⌒   ◡   – ◡ –, but, again, there is no exact parallel.

In Pindar, the first syllable of πρόφρων (and related words) is always
long. τείν at the end of 930 is clearly corrupt, while δόμεν ἐμίν seems
clumsy after δὸς ἐμίν in the previous colon, and such obvious clumsi-
ness does not seem to be the sort of fault that Aristophanes is parodying
here. M. L. West's suggestion (*CR* 18 (1968), 8) that ἐμὶν τείν is part
of a gloss on ἐμίν at 928 which has found its way into the text is
plausible. The snatch of song could simply end with πρόφρων δόμεν
(–   – ◡ ⌣ ||), or ἐμὶν τείν could have replaced something else.

936–9. Initial ◡ ◡ ◡ is not uncommon in Pindar, but it is never found preceding – ◡ ◡ – ◡ ◡ – (D). This is not surprising, since D is a characteristically dactylo-epitrite phrase, and resolution is rare in dactylo-epitrite (see, however, *Isth.* 5). For e D, compare *Ol.* 8, ep. 7: ἔνθα Σώτειρα Διὸς ξενίου. At 937, all the MSS except A have τόδε δῶρον. On this basis, Meineke conjectured τὸ δῶρον. Metrically, both δῶρον and τὸ δῶρον are acceptable. For – ◡ –   – ◡ ◡ – (e d), see *Pyth.* 5, str. 5 and 10; for – ◡ ◡ –   – ◡ ◡ – (d d), see above on 925. For the repeated reversed dodrans at 938–9, compare *Ol.* 4, str. 7 (– ◡ – ◡ ◡ –   ⌢ ◡ – ◡ ◡ –). A dodrans with *two* resolved longs is unparalleled in Pindar.

941–5. According to Σ *vet.*, the Pindaric original of 941–2 (Snell–Maehler 105b) was identical in scansion with the Aristophanic parody. While there is no exact parallel for either verse in the complete poems, there are several Pindaric verses which share essential features with one or both. For the sequence e e in a verse beginning ◡ ◡ – ◡ ◡ –, compare:

Ol. 5, str. 3	◡ ◡ – ◡ ◡ – ◡ – – ◡ – – ◡ – ◡ – –
Ol. 10, str. 1	◡ ◡ – ◡ ◡ – – ◡ – – ◡ –

For ◡ ◡ – ◡ ◡ – followed by an uninterrupted sequence in ×–×–... compare:

Pyth. 10, str. 6	◡ ◡ – ◡ ◡ – ◡ –×–×– ◡ –
Nem. 3, str. 8	◡ ◡ – ◡ ◡ – ◡ – ◡ – ◡ – ◡ – –.

An exact parallel for 942 is, however, to be found in tragedy: *PV* 546=554 (see above on 451 ff.=539 ff.). *Alc.* 437=446, 442=452 are similar, but shorter.

The phrase – ◡ – ◡ – (943 and 945), which would in dochmiac contexts be classified as a hypodochmiac, is found in non-dactylo-epitrite contexts in Pindar. For the resolved and unresolved forms together, see *Ol.* 2, ep. 2:

– ◡ – ◡ –   ⌢ ◡ – ◡ –   – ◡ – –

944 is evidently not a quotation from Pindar, and it is natural to take it in Attic poetry as an ithyphallic. It is, however, a perfectly possible segment of Pindaric verse, eg. *Ol.* 1, str. 2: ἐπιφέροισα τιμὰν (καὶ ἄπιστον ἐμήσατο πιστόν) ◡ ◡ ◡ – ◡ – – (◡ ◡ – ◡ ◡ – ◡ ◡ – ⌣ ||).

950–3. For $- \smile - \quad - \quad - \smile \smile - \smile \smile - \smile \smile -$ compare *Pyth.* 4, str. 6, e.g.: 167:

(ὅρκος ἄμμιν) μάρτυς ἔστω Ζεὺς ὁ γενέθλιος ἀμφοτέροις
($- \smile - \quad -$) $- \smile - \quad - \quad - \smile \smile - \smile \smile - \smile \smile -$

or *Nem.* 1, ep. 4, e.g. 17:

λαὸν ἵππαιχμον, θαμὰ δὴ καὶ Ὀλυμπιάδων (φύλλοις ἐλαιᾶν
[χρυσέοις)
$- \smile - \quad - \quad - \smile \smile - \smile \smile - \smile \smile - \quad (- \quad - \smile - \quad - \quad - \smile -)$

1058–71 = 1088–1101

$- - -|- \quad - - -$
ἤδη 'μοὶ τῷ παντόπτᾳ

$- - - - \quad - - - -$
καὶ παντάρχᾳ θνητοὶ πάντες

$- - - - \quad - - -\|_H$
1060   θύσουσ' εὐκταίαις εὐχαῖς.

$- - - -| \quad - - - -$
πᾶσαν μὲν γὰρ γᾶν ὀπτεύω,

$- - - - \quad -|--\|$
σώζω δ' εὐθαλεῖς καρποὺς,

$- - - - \quad - - -$
κτείνων παμφύλων γένναν

$- - - - \quad - - -\|_H$
θηρῶν, ἃ πᾶν τ' ἐν γαίᾳ

$- \smile \widehat{} \quad - \smile \widehat{} \quad - \smile \widehat{}| \quad - \smile -$
1065   ἐκ κάλυκος αὐξανόμενον γένυσι παμφάγοις

$- \smile \widehat{} \quad - \smile -$
δένδρεσί τ' ἐφημένα

$- \smile \widehat{} \quad - \smile -$
καρπὸν ἀποβόσκεται.

$- - - - \quad - - - -$
κτείνω δ' οἳ κήπους εὐώδεις

951 is open to more than one analysis. An alternative to the one offered would be e e ⏑ e. But, in any case, a sequence of eleven short syllables is unparalleled in Pindar. As at 938, one suspects burlesque exaggeration of some kind.

Although there are minor variations between MSS, there is very little that is of metrical significance, and signs of Triclinian activity are scarce.

an dim cat
εὔδαιμον φῦλον πτηνῶν

an dim
οἰωνῶν, οἳ χειμῶνος μὲν

an dim cat

1090

χλαίνας οὐκ ἀμπισχνοῦνται·

an dim
οὐδ᾽ αὖ θερμὴ πνίγους ἡμᾶς

an dim cat
ἀκτὶς τηλαυγὴς θάλπει·

an dim cat
ἀλλ᾽ ἀνθηρῶν λειμώνων

an dim cat
φύλλων ⟨τ᾽⟩ ἐν κόλποις ναίω,

4 cr

1095

ἡνίκ᾽ ἂν ὁ θεσπέσιος ὀξὺ μέλος ἀχέτας

2 cr

1096a

θάλπεσι μεσημβρινοῖς

2 cr

1096b

ἡλιομανὴς βοᾷ.

an dim
χειμάζω δ᾽ ἐν κοίλοις ἄντροις

```
    ‒ ‒ ‒ ‒   ‒|‒ ‒ ‒
```
φθείρουσιν λύμαις ἐχθίσταις·

```
    ‒ ◡ ⌢|   ‒ ◡ ⌢|   ‒ ◡ ⌢|
```
ἑρπετά τε καὶ δάκετα ⟨πάνθ'⟩ ὅσαπερ

```
    ‒ ◡ ⌢   ‒ ◡ ⌢
```
1070　　ἔστιν, ὑπ' ἐμᾶς πτέρυγος

```
    ‒ ◡ ‒   ‒ ◡ ⌣|||
```
ἐν φοναῖς ὄλλυται.

The poet is followed by a procession of professionals (oracle-monger, town-planner, inspector, decree-salesman) all hoping to profit from the foundation of Cloudcuckooborough, until, at 1055–7, Peisetaerus decides to sacrifice off stage. The chorus are left to perform a second parabasis, in which in ode and antode the Birds deliver encomia on themselves.

Metrically, this is a remarkable composition. It combines anapaests of tragic-lyrical type (Introduction, p. 57) with cretics of Aristophanes' characteristic pattern, with frequent resolution of the second long. The two metres are kept apart in well-defined sections, in Aristophanes' manner. The anapaests are wholly spondaic. There is no parallel for the combination of anapaest and cretic either in Aristophanes or elsewhere in Attic drama, except earlier in this play, at 229 ff. and 327–35, and at *Lys.* 476 ff. = 541 ff. (Introduction, p. 46).

The strophe is preserved, in mutilated form, in the 6th-century P. Louvre (ed. Weil, *RPh* 6 (1882), 179). The only improvement in the papyrus on the MS text is τ' in 1066, which is shared only by the Aldine (by conjecture, one supposes) and B¹ erased. The other MSS have δ'. At 1065, παμφάγοις is Dobree's emendation for the MS πολυφάγοις (which produces the unparalleled sequence ‒ ◡ ⌢　⌢ ◡ ‒). ἐφημένα in 1066 is also Dobree's conjecture for ἐφεζόμενα (or -οι) in the MSS. The papyrus has]φιζομεν[. In 1069 ⟨πάνθ'⟩ is Dissen's

1188–95 = 1262–6

```
    ◡ ⌢ ‒ ◡ ‒|   ◡ ⌢ ‒ ◡ ‒
```
πόλεμος αἴρεται, πόλεμος οὐ φατὸς

```
    ⌣ ⌢|‒ ◡ ‒|   ◡ ⌢ ‒ ◡ ‒
```
1190 πρὸς ἐμὲ καὶ θεούς. ἀλλὰ φύλαττε πᾶς

an dim
νύμφαις οὐρείαις ξυμπαίζων·

7 cr
ἠρινά τε βοσκόμεθα παρθένια

1100   λευκότροφα μύρτα Χαρί-

των τε κηπεύματα.

supplement, but Triclinius observed the failure of correspondence in
1068–9, adding the metrically necessary ephelcystic ν to φθείρουσι (L,
but not, if White and Cary are to be trusted, the other Triclinian MSS)
and produced the desired sequence of cretics by small supplements:

ἕρπετά τε καὶ δάκεθ᾿ ⟨ὀπ⟩όσ⟨σ⟩απερ ⟨ἂν⟩ . . .
– ∪ ⌒⌒   – ∪ ⌒⌒   – ∪ ⌒⌒

Musurus adopted this with one change: ὁπόσαπερ, thereby retaining
Triclinius' linguistic oddities, while destroying their metrical justification. At 1071, ἐν φοναῖς ὄλλυται is the reading of the Triclinian MSS
(LVp2+) and Ald., and, again, does credit to Triclinius' ability to use
correspondence. The pre-Triclinian MSS have the unmetrical φοναῖσιν
ἐξόλλυται (-όλυται V). At 1094, I accept the Triclinian ναίω with
Bentley's supplement ⟨τ᾿⟩. An alternative is to retain the pre-Triclinian
ἐνναίω, reading φύλλ᾿ for φύλλων (Desrousseaux). This is attractive,
but ἐνναίω with *acc. loci* does not seem to be attested before the
Alexandrian period.

At 1095, ὀξὺ μέλος is Brunck's emendation of the MSS' unmetrical
ὀξυμελὴς (ὀξυβελὴς R). At 1096b, ἡλιομανὴς is the reading of the
Suda. The MSS have ὑφ᾿ ἡλίῳ μανείς (ὑφηλιομανὴς R), to all appear-
ances an intruding gloss.

2 δ
ἀποκεκλήκαμεν διογενεῖς θεοὺς

2 δ
μηκέτι τὴν ἐμὴν διαπερᾶν πόλιν,

$$- \widehat{\smile\smile} \smile \widehat{\smile\smile} \mid \quad \smile \widehat{\smile\smile} \widehat{\smile\smile} \smile \widehat{\smile\smile}$$

ἀέρα περινέφελον, ὃν Ἔρεβος ἐτέκετο

$$- \widehat{\smile\smile} - \mid \smile - \quad \circ \mid - - \mid \smile - \mid\mid\mid$$

1195 μή σε λάθῃ θεῶν τις ταύτῃ περῶν.

The great comic fantasy of the play, the messenger's description of the building of the walls of Cloudcuckooborough, is immediately followed by the news that a god has penetrated the defences. A strophe, containing the Birds' declaration of war, and an antistrophe proclaiming their triumph frame the episode of the capture and expulsion of Iris.

Birds contains more dochmiacs than any other play of Aristophanes, but this is the only concentrated use of the metre with its ordinary function of expressing violent excitement (Introduction, p. 67). As usual in Aristophanes, there is close correspondence between types of dochmiac. While the stanza is in synapheia throughout, all the dochmiacs, except the last two, are marked off by word-end. There is a certain correspondence of ideas at the close of the stanza (let no god pass = let no smoke pass), and this is reflected in close correspondence of word-end, with θεῶν τις in the strophe and θεοῖσι in the antistrophe occupying the same metrical position. For this sort of reflection of content and verbal parallelism in strophe and antistrophe, compare, for example, A. *Cho.* 345–6=363–4:

εἰ γὰρ ὑπ᾽ Ἰλίῳ   μηδ᾽ ὑπὸ Τροίας
πρός τινος Λυκίων, πάτερ, . . .   τείχεσι φθίμενος, πάτερ . . .

$$- \smile\smile - \smile -$$
$$- \smile - \mid \smile\smile - \mid \smile -$$

1313–22=1325–34

$$\smile\smile \quad - \mid \smile\smile \quad - \smile\smile \quad - \smile\smile \quad -$$

Χ. τάχα δὴ πολυάνορα τάνδε πόλιν

$$\smile - \smile \mid - \quad - -$$

καλεῖ τις ἀνθρώπων·

$$\underline{\smile} - \smile - \quad \smile - -$$

1315 Π. τύχη μόνον προσείη.

2 δ

1265   μηδέ τιν' ἱερόθυτον †ἀνὰ δάπεδον ἔτι

2 δ

τῇδε βροτῶν θεοῖσι πέμπειν καπνόν.

The only significant textual problem is the lack of one short syllable at 1265. Blaydes's μηδέ γέ τιν' ('nor yet . . .' cf. *Wasps* 62) breaks the pattern of word-end and metron-end. Dunbar's ἀνὰ δάπεδον ⟨ἐν⟩ fits, and seems preferable to Coulon's ⟨ἐν'⟩, which is awkwardly placed to go with καπνόν. An unmetrical Triclinian supplement in 1266, ⟨ἂν⟩ after πέμπειν (LVp2+ κἂν B), prompted Meineke's ἀνὰ δάπεδον ⟨ἂν⟩ (Kock: 'unabhängig οὐδεὶς ἂν ἔτι πέμποι').

It is interesting to note that, while ancient metrical writings show very scant evidence of any understanding of dochmiacs, these stanzas are correctly divided into monometers and dimeters in RV, except for the division of 1195:

μή σε λάθῃ
θεῶν τις ταύτῃ περῶν

which splits a dochmiac: $- \cup \cup -|\cup -$.

There is a divergence of lay-out between strophe and antistrophe at the beginning of the stanza, where πόλεμος . . . φατός is set out as a dimeter and ἀποκεκλήκαμεν . . . θεούς as two monometers. Σ vet. observes, with meticulous incomprehension: ἔν τισι δὲ τῶν ἀντιγράφων εἰς δύο κῶλα διῄρηται τὸ ἔν, ἐν δὲ ἄλλοις συνῆπται. We may suspect that RV preserve the confounding of two distinct colometries in late antiquity.

⋀da pent cat

1325   Χ. φερέτω κάλαθον ταχύ τις πτερ⟨ύγ⟩ων.

ia sp

σὺ δ' αὖθις ἐξόρμα—

ia ba

Π. τύπτων γε τοῦτον ὡδί.

∪∪   −∪∪   −∪∪   −∪∪   −

Χ. κατέχουσι δ' ἔρωτες ἐμᾶς πόλεως.

− − ∪ −   ∪ − −

Π. θᾶττον φέρειν κελεύω.

∪ ∪| −∪∪   − −

Χ. τί γὰρ οὐκ ἔνι ταύτῃ

∪∪   −∪∪   − −

καλὸν ἀνδρὶ μετοικεῖν;

∪∪   −∪∪   −∪∪   −∪∪   −∪∪

1320   Σοφία, Πόθος, ἀμβρόσιαι Χάριτες τό τε

−∪∪   −∪∪   −∪∪   −

τῆς ἀγανόφρονος Ἡσυχίας

⌣ − ∪ −| ∪ − − |||

εὐήμερον πρόσωπον.

This song accompanies Peisetaerus' preparations to receive the rush of would-be immigrants whose arrival has been announced by the messenger (1277–1307). A slave is evidently running hither and thither during the song, under constant urging. Between strophe and antistrophe, Peisetaerus interjects an extra address to the slave in a catalectic iambic tetrameter (or dim, dim cat). While the Birds in the first stanza celebrate their future city, Peisetaerus' interventions (even 1315) are strictly practical (and all in iambic, the less lyrical of the two metres used). The markedly more exalted tone of the strophe in comparison with the antistrophe is unusual in Aristophanes (see Introduction, p. 14).

Metrically, the passage looks simple and coherent, yet to us it presents an enigma from the point of view of classification. The sequences in single-long–double-short rhythm are certainly not anapaestic: the regularity of the movement (∪∪ − ∪∪ − . . .) and the absence of diaeresis between metra are both uncharacteristic of that metre. Nor is ∪∪ − ∪∪ − − an anapaestic length. The closest parallel to these sequences is to be found in 'free dactylo-epitrite' contexts (cf. above, on 451ff.=539ff.). They are also compatible with aeolo-choriambic, and ∪∪ − ∪∪ − − could be interpreted as reizianum with ∪∪ for × in the

$_\wedge$da pent cat

X. πάνυ γὰρ βραδύς ἐστί τις ὥσπερ ὄνος.

ia ba

Π. Μανῆς γάρ ἐστι δειλός.

$_\wedge$da trim

1330 *X. σὺ δὲ τὰ πτερὰ πρῶτον*

$_\wedge$da trim

διάθες τάδε κόσμῳ·

$_\wedge$9 da cat

τά τε μουσίχ᾽ ὁμοῦ τά τε μαντικὰ καὶ τὰ θα-

λάττι᾽. ἔπειτα δ᾽ ὅπως φρονίμως

ia ba

πρὸς ἄνδρ᾽ ὁρῶν πτερώσεις.

base (cf. Aristophanes, *PCG* 516, and Introduction, p. 71). The best key we have to the stanza is to be found, however, in the fragments of Cratinus' *Χείρωνες*, a play which ante-dated *Birds* by over fifteen years (see *PCG* iv. 245). *PCG* 256 ends with the dicolon

$$\smile \smile - \smile \smile - \smile \smile - \smile \smile - \times - \smile - \smile - -$$

and, more interestingly, 257 consists of the same verse twice in sequence. This looks like one of the quite numerous dicola used (and sometimes invented) by the poets of old comedy (see Parker, *PCPS* 214 (1988), 115 ff.). The combination of single-long–single-short and single-long–double-short metres suggests Archilochus as the model, and this very dicolon is indeed attributed to him in Marius Victorinus (*Gramm. Lat.* vi. 142, 31 ff. cf. *IEG*² 317), although initial $\smile \smile$ is not found in the actual fragments. Aristophanes' stanza is comprehensible as a set of variations on this dicolon. In 1313–14 = 1325–6, the iambic second colon defeats expectation by ending in $- -$, instead of $\smile - -$. Then follows (1315 = 1327) the second half of the dicolon in its ordinary form, then (1316–17 = 1328–9) the whole dicolon. 1318–19 = 1330–1 are, in effect, a couple of false starts. The rhythmic suspense is maintained by 1320–1 = 1332–3, where the sequence of $\smile \smile - \ldots$ is extended to twice its normal length before resolving itself in the expected clausula. The problem of classifying the non-iambic parts of the song remains, and I have chosen dactylic because of the affinities that I see with Archilochus and with 'free dactylo-epitrite'. Dactylic is the only single-long–double-short metre used by Archilochus.

At 1313, τάχα ('soon') is Blaydes's emendation for the MS ταχύ ('quickly'. See Hipp. 182–3, and Barrett, ad loc.). Porson proposed δή for the MSS' δ' ἄν. The presence of ἄν is presumably the reason for καλοῖ in 1314 in Vp2B and Γ² (but not L). Triclinius added another ἄν (LVp2+B) to the end of 1314, presumably to equalize the number of

$$1337-9$$

‿ – –

γενοίμαν

– ‿ ‿ – ‿ ‿ –

1337 αἰετὸς ὑψιπέτας

– – ‿ –   –   – ‿ ‿ – ‿ ‿ –

ὡς ἀμποταθείην ὑπὲρ ἀτρυγέτου,

– – ‿ –   ‿ – – |||

γλαυκᾶς ἐπ᾽ οἶδμα λίμνας.

The first would-be immigrant, the 'father-beater', enters singing a snatch of lyric which Σ *vet.* attributes to Sophocles' *Oenomaus* (*TrGF* 476). The fragment suggests the theme of escape more familiar from Euripides (e.g. *Hipp.* 732 ff., *Andr.* 862 ff., *Ion* 796 ff., *Hel.* 1479 ff., *Ba.* 403 ff.). There is a Sophoclean example at *Aj.* 1217 ff., where γενοίμαν, an opening bacchiac (as here), leads into glyconic. The motif is, of course, traceable to Alcman (*PMG* 26). A Sophoclean variant is the wish of the chorus at *OC* 1081 ff. to be in a position to obtain a bird's-eye view of interesting events off-stage. The collective singular, common in these

$$1372-1400$$

‿ ‿ ‿ ‿ –   – ‿ ‿ –   – ‿ ‿ –   ‿ – –

K. ἀναπέτομαι δὴ πρὸς Ὄλυμπον πτερύγεσσι κούφαις·

‿ ‿ – ‿ ‿ – ‿ ‿ – – ‿ ‿ – ||

1373–4   πέτομαι δ᾽ ὁδὸν ἄλλοτ᾽ ἐπ᾽ ἄλλαν μελέων.

syllables with 1315. He lengthened the corresponding 1326 by reading αὖτις αὖ γ᾽ for αὖθις (LVp2+B). At 1325, Porson restored the metre with πτερύγων (πτερῶν MSS), and at 1328, ἐστί τις is Bentley's transposition of the MS τις ἐστιν (LVp2+B omit τις). The MSS generally attribute 1315 to Peisetaerus, but only C attributes 1327 to him. Bergk, Meineke, Kock, and Dindorf sought to produce a corresponding distribution by assigning both 1315 and 1327 to the chorus, but C's distribution is clearly better: 1315 looks like an interjection, and ὡδί in 1327 should (as Lenting pointed out) be uttered by the person doing the beating.

ba

hem (D)

iambel ($-$e$-$D)

ia ba

passages, is convenient for the father-beater.

As the text stands, the metre is straightforward dactylo-epitrite, with a typically Attic admixture of iambic. The passage has, however, excited suspicion on linguistic grounds because of the use of ἀτρυγέτου as a substantive (on which see Sommerstein, ad loc.) and the double mention of the sea. It was presumably such considerations that led Triclinius to delete ὑπέρ (LVp2B¹Ald.), so as to make ἀτρυγέτου into another epithet of λίμνας. ἀμποταθείην is Shilleto's emendation of the MS ἀν ποταθείην (-ασθείην Triclinius).

ia cho cho ba

꭯

1375   trim I

ᴗᴗ‒ᴗᴗ‒ᴗᴗ͡ᴗ‒ᴗᴗ‒ ||

1376–7 *K.* ἀφόβῳ φρενὶ σώματί τε νέαν ἐφέπων.

1378–9   trim II

‒‒ᴗ‒   ‒‒ᴗ‒

1380 *K.* ὄρνις γενέσθαι βούλομαι

ᴗ‒‒ᴗᴗ‒‒

λιγύφθογγος ἀηδών.

1381–92   trim XI

‒‒ᴗᴗ‒‒

1393 *K.* εἴδωλα πετηνῶν

‒͡ᴗᴗ‒

αἰθεροδρόμων

‒‒‒‒   ᴗᴗ‒‒ ||

οἰωνῶν ταναοδείρων

1395 *Π.* ὠόπ.

†   †‒͡ᴗᴗ͡ᴗ   ᴗ‒ᴗ‒   ᴗ‒‒

K. †τὸν ἀλάδρομον† ἁλάμενος ἅμ' ἀνέμων πνοαῖσι βαίην.

1397   trim I

ᴗᴗ‒ᴗᴗ‒   ‒‒ᴗᴗ‒

1398 *K.* τοτὲ μὲν νοτίαν στείχων πρὸς ὁδόν,

ᴗᴗ‒ᴗᴗ‒   ‒ᴗᴗ‒‒

τοτὲ δ' αὖ βορέᾳ σῶμα πελάζων

ᴗᴗᴗᴗ‒ᴗᴗ   ‒ᴗᴗ‒‒ ||

ἀλίμενον αἰθέρος αὔλακα τέμνων.

1401–9   trim IX

trim I

?

trim II

ia dim

pher

trim XI

reiz

ia

an dim cat

extra metrum

? 2 ia ba

trim I

an dim

an dim

an dim

trim IX

As we should expect from *Clouds* 333, Cinesias, the dithyrambic poet, claims to derive his art from the clouds, but that is no guide to his metrical practice. It might have been expected that Aristophanes would make him deliver snatches from his own poetry, yet there are no attempts in *Σ vet.* to identify quotations from that source, and there is, indeed, very little evidence that Cinesias' poems were known after his own lifetime (see *PGM* 774–6). The only quotation identified by *Σ vet.* is from Anacreon (*PMG* 378, cf. Hephaestion, Cons. 30. 10).

The first metron of 1372 could in theory, as Hephaestion observed, be a resolved choriamb ($\overset{\frown}{} \cup \cup -$), but resolution in choriambs is extremely rare, and not attested outside Attic poetry. According to Hephaestion, *all* the lines of the poem from which 1372 comes began with $\cup \cup \cup \cup -$. An iambo-choriambic combination would be typical of Anacreon. He also used a verse of the form $- \cup \cup - \quad - \cup \cup - \quad - \cup \cup - \quad \cup - -$ (*PMG* 381(b)), and both that verse and $\cup - \cup - \quad - \cup \cup - \quad - \cup \cup - \quad \cup - -$ occur at *Lys.* 321 ff. = 335 ff. In the same stanza, 328 provides a very close parallel to *Birds* 1372: $\cup \cup \cup \cup - \quad - \cup \cup - \quad - \cup \cup - \quad - \cup \cup - \quad \cup - -$. There, 342 in the antistrophe begins $- \cup \cup \cup -$, securely identifying the first metron as iambic (Introduction, p. 79).

Cinesias' next two verses pose an insoluble problem. The reversal of direction (... $\cup \cup - - \cup \cup$ ...) suggests anapaests, and Cinesias does, apparently, use anapaests in his last snatch of song (1398–1400), but the length of these verses is unparalleled in anapaests. The combination of anapaestic tripody and choriamb is equally unparalleled. C. J. Ruijgh, (*Mnemosyne*, 13 (1960), 318–21) ingeniously suggests that Aristophanes is parodying Cinesias' eccentric use of resolution and contraction in choriambs. Thus, 1373–4 would be three choriambs, of which the first

1410–15

$- - - \cup \cup - - \cup \cup - - \cup \cup - \cup -$

Σ. ὄρνιθες τίνες οἵδ᾽ οὐδὲν ἔχοντες πτεροποίκιλοι,

$\cup \cup - \cup \cup - \cup - \cup - - \parallel$

τανυσίπτερε ποικίλα χελιδοῖ;

1413–14   trim II

has both its longs resolved and its double short contracted. 1376 pushes eccentricity a step further: it begins with the same 'inside-out' choriamb as 1373 and follows it with a choriamb in which the second long is resolved. This explanation would suggest that, whatever Anacreon intended, Aristophanes is to be seen here as choosing to imply that the initial $\cup \cup \cup - $ of 1372 is also a resolved choriamb. One other type of metre which admits the sequence . . . $\cup \cup - - \cup \cup -|$ is ionic, but these cola are at least as recalcitrant to ionic analysis as to anapaestic or choriambic. There is, perhaps, one parallel (*Pers.* 952=965) for a pair of syncopated metra in synartesis both with each other and with what follows ($\cup \cup \frown \cup \cup \frown \cup \cup - -$), and 1376 adds the exceedingly rare resolution, $\cup \cup \cup \cup -$ (Introduction, p. 62).

The scansion of ταναοδείρων has been discussed on 254 above. Scanning τᾰν- would here produce $- - - \cup \cup \cup - -$, which could be interpreted as mol tro (awkward after the iamb at 1394) or sp cr sp.

At 1396, Σ *vet.* seeks to explain τὸν ἀλάδρομον (or ἅλα δρόμον) as 'the path to the sea', adding desperately χλενάζει δὲ τοὺς διθυραμβοποίους. Accepting this meaning, Hermann conjectured τὸν ἅλαδε δρόμον ($\cup \frown \cup \frown$). Sommerstein suggests τὰν ἀναδρομὰν ($- \frown \cup -$), 'my upward way'. Both these conjectures produce a catalectic iambic tetrameter, which may seem rather pedestrian for the context. Blaydes proposed τὸν ἁλίδρομον, which produces three trochees and a spondee, but the word is not attested before Nonnus.

The four consecutive shorts that open 1400 mark the anapaests as of lyric type. Absence of catalexis, of the normal rhythmic rounding-off, at the end of the anapaestic section perhaps marks Cinesias' excitement: he interrupts himself to burst into congratulating Peisetaerus.

greater asclep

enopl?

trim II

ᴗᴗ−ᴗᴗ−ᴗ−ᴗ−⏑ ‖

1415 *Σ. τανυσίπτερε ποικίλα μάλ' αὖθις.*

The sycophant enters singing a greater asclepiad verse (Introduction, p. 76) based, according to *Σ vet.*, on Alcaeus (*PLF* 345, Z 21). His other two verses are identical with *Alc.* 437=446, 442=452, and resemble

1470–81=1482–93

−ᴗ−|−　　−ᴗ−−

1470 *πολλὰ δὴ καὶ καινὰ καὶ θαυ-*

　　−ᴗ−⏕　−ᴗ−

μάστ' ἐπεπτόμεσθα καὶ

　　−ᴗ−ᴗ　−ᴗ⏖‖н

δεινὰ πράγματ' εἴδομεν.

−ᴗ−−　−ᴗ−⏕

ἔστι γὰρ δένδρον πεφυκὸς

　　−ᴗ−⏕　−ᴗ−ᴗ

ἔκτοπόν τι, Καρδίας ἀ-

　　−ᴗ−⏕　−ᴗ−

1475 *πωτέρω, Κλεώνυμος,*

　　−ᴗ−ᴗ　−ᴗ−

χρήσιμον μὲν οὐδέν, ἄλ-

　　−ᴗ−−　−ᴗ⏖‖

λως δὲ δειλὸν καὶ μέγα.

−ᴗ−ᴗ　−ᴗ|−−

τοῦτο ⟨τοῦ⟩ μὲν ἦρος ἀεὶ

−ᴗ−|−　−ᴗ−−

βλαστάνει καὶ συκοφαντεῖ,

−ᴗ−−　−|ᴗ−−

1480 *τοῦ δὲ χειμῶνος πάλιν τὰς*

　　−ᴗ−⏕　−ᴗ⏖‖‖

ἀσπίδας φυλλορροεῖ.

enopl?

451=539 above, both 'free dactylo-epitrite' contexts. The lines could also be interpreted as aeolo-choriambic with initial ◡◡ for × (Introduction, p. 71).

       tro dim
  ἔστι δ' αὖ χώρα πρὸς αὐτῷ

           + tro dim cat (lec)
    τῷ σκότῳ πόρρω τις ἐν

           + tro dim cat (lec)
    τῇ λύχνων ἐρημίᾳ,

       tro dim
1485 ἔνθα τοῖς ἥρωσιν ἄνθρω-

           + tro dim
    ποι ξυναριστῶσι καὶ ξύν-

           + tro dim cat (lec)
    εισι πλὴν τῆς ἑσπέρας.

      tro dim cat (lec)
    τηνικαῦτα δ' οὐκέτ' ἦν

           + tro dim cat (lec)
    ἀσφαλὲς συντυγχάνειν.

       tro dim
1490 εἰ γὰρ ἐντύχοι τις ἥρῳ

       tro dim
    τῶν βροτῶν νύκτωρ Ὀρέστῃ,

       tro dim
    γυμνὸς ἦν πληγεὶς ὑπ' αὐτοῦ

           + tro dim cat (lec)
    πάντα τἀπιδέξια.

$$1553\text{–}64 = 1694\text{–}1705$$

‒ ∪ ‒ ∪   ‒ ∪ ‒ ‒

πρὸς δὲ τοῖς Σκιάποσιν λί-

‒ ∪ ‒ ∪   ‒ ∪ | ‒

μνη τις ἔστ᾿, ἄλουτος οὗ

‒ ∪ ‒ ◡   ‒ ∪ ⌣ ‖

1555   ψυχαγωγεῖ Σωκράτης·

‒ ∪ ‒ ‒   ‒ ∪ | ‒ ⌣

ἔνθα καὶ Πείσανδρος ἦλθε

‿‿ ∪ ‒ ‒   ‒ ∪ ‒ ‒

δεόμενος ψυχὴν ἰδεῖν ἢ

‒ ∪ ‒ ‒   ‒ ∪ ⌣ ‖

ζῶντ᾿ ἐκεῖνον προὔλιπε,

‿‿ ∪ ‒ ⌣   ‒ ∪ ‒

σφάγι᾿ ἔχων κάμηλον ἀ-

‒ ∪ ‒ ◡   ‒ ∪ ‒ ‒

1560   μνόν τιν᾿, ἧς λαιμοὺς τεμὼν ὥσ-

‒ ∪ ‒ ‒   ‒ ∪ ‒ ∪

περ ⟨ποθ᾿⟩ οὑδυσσεύς, ἀπῆλθε,

‒ ∪ ‒ ‒   ‒ ∪ ‒ ‒

κᾆτ᾿ ἀνῆλθ᾿ αὐτῷ κάτωθεν

‒ ∪ ‒ ⌣   ‒ ∪ ‒ ‒

πρὸς τὸ †λαῖμα† τῆς καμήλου

‒ ∪ ‒ ‒   ‒ ∪ ‒ |||

Χαιρεφῶν ἡ νυκτερίς.

These lampoon-songs are very simply constructed metrically, using two cola, the trochaic dimeter and its catalectic form, the lecythion. Both stanzas consist of twelve cola, and the close similarity between them and the pattern of variation can be shown clearly, notating the dimeter by A and the lecythion by B:

tro dim
ἔστι δ' ἐν Φάναισι πρὸς τῇ

+ tro dim cat (lec)
1695   Κλεψύδρᾳ πανοῦργον ἐγ-

+ tro dim cat (lec)
γλωττογαστόρων γένος,

tro dim
οἳ θερίζουσίν τε καὶ σπεί-

+ tro dim
ρουσι καὶ τρυγῶσι ταῖς γλώτ-

+ tro dim cat (lec)
ταισι συκάζουσί τε·

tro dim cat (lec)
1700   βάρβαροι δ' εἰσὶν γένος,

+ tro dim
Γοργίαι τε καὶ Φίλιπποι,

+ tro dim
κἀπὸ τῶν ἐγγλωττογαστό-

+ tro dim
ρων ἐκείνων τῶν Φιλίππων

tro dim
πανταχοῦ τῆς Ἀττικῆς ἡ

+ tro dim cat (lec)
1705   γλῶττα χωρὶς τέμνεται.

1470 ff. = 1482 ff.	ABB	AAB	BB	AAAB
1553 ff. = 1694 ff.	ABB	AAB	BAAA	AB

Exact correspondence of all four stanzas can be achieved by emendation
(see below).

The episodes 1494–1552 and 1565–1693 develop the third 'movement'
of the plot, the resolution of Peisetaerus' contest with the gods in
victory and marriage with Basileia. In content, the stanzas which
punctuate this part of the play have nothing to do with the action, and
in this respect they resemble other lampoon-songs that occur late in
Aristophanes' comedies. Compare the songs of the second parabases at
Knights 1264 ff. = 1290 ff. and *Wasps* 1265 ff. (where, as here, there is a
plurality of victims). However, the lampoon-song formally and stylistically closest to this one is *Ach.* 836 ff. = 842 ff. = 848 ff. = 854 ff.

The function of marking out the dramatic structure is fulfilled by
repeated rhythm and music alone. The consecutive strophe and antistrophe at 1470 ff. introduce a major change of direction in the action, the
strophe at 1553 ff. divides the Prometheus scene (a sort of prelude) from
the scene of negotiation with the divine embassy, and the antistrophe
(1694 ff.) completes the musical 'frame'.

There are a very few minor slips in the text of the pre-Triclinian MSS.
At 1478 ⟨τοῦ⟩ was proposed by Grynaeus. At 1561, the unmetrical
ὥσπερ Ὀδυσσεύς was emended by Bentley (οὐδυσσεύς) and Hermann
(⟨ποθ'⟩). With Bentley's supplement, but without Hermann's, 1560–1
becomes:

-μνόν τιν', ἧς λαιμοὺς τεμών   – ∪ – –   – ∪ –
ὥσπερ οὐδυσσεὺς ἀπῆλθε   – ∪ – –   – ∪ – ∪

The pattern of 1553–64 then becomes identical with that of 1470 ff. =
1482 ff., leaving 1694 ff. as the odd stanza, in which BAAA corresponds

1720–5

⁀∪⁀∪ ⁀∪⁀∪

1720 ἄναγε δίεχε πάραγε πάρεχε,

⁀∪–∪ ⁀∪⁀∪ –∪–||ʜ

περιπέτεσθε [τὸν] μάκαρα μάκαρι σὺν τύχᾳ.

– – –| – – –| – – –

ὦ φεῦ φεῦ τῆς ὥρας, τοῦ κάλλους,

–∪∪– –∪∪– –∪∪– – –|||

1725 ὦ μακαριστὸν σὺ γάμον τῇδε πόλει γήμας.

to BBAA. At *Frogs* 1486 = 1495, the MSS offer tro dim corresponding to lec, but that is easily emended (see below, ad loc.). Robert (*Hermes*, 38 (1903), 156–60) proposed to reduce 1701 to a lecythion by reading καὶ φίλιπποι Γοργίου (φίλιπποι being treated jokingly as an ethnic term, parallel to βάρβαροι). For Philippus as a pupil of Gorgias, see *Wasps* 421. By these means, all four stanzas can be brought into full correspondence.

At 1563, Sommerstein recognizes in λαῖμα an otherwise unknown word 'which may well have been used in sacral language for the act of slaughter'. The (rather shaky) basis for this is provided by Hesychius (Latte, ii. 565, λ 126) λαίεται· καταλεύεται, and Theognostus (Cramer, *Anecdot. Ox.* ii. 9) λαῖγμα τὸ ἱερόν· λαίω τὸ βλέπω, ἢ τὸ φονεύω. At any rate, the word poses no metrical problem.

For 1553–64 the Triclinian MSS have a highly disordered text (with an unusual amount of minor disagreement between themselves). It would seem that the failure of correspondence in his sources at 1561 caused Triclinius completely to lose his bearings in dealing with the stanza. With unaccustomed judiciousness, Musurus refrains from adopting several Triclinian readings. He accepts from Triclinius the notion that the stanza is in itself a strophe and antistrophe of six cola each, and prints τοῖσι for τοῖς (1553) and λιμνητὴς for λίμνη τις, but retains ἄλουτος (ἀλλ᾽ οὗτος Vp2 ἄλλος οὗτος LH) and ἧς λαιμοὺς τεμὼν (ἧς (ἧ Vp2) τεμὼν τοὺς λαιμοὺς LVp2+). He preserves οὗ (1554), which LVp2+ omit, and does not adopt Triclinius᾽ ⟨γὰρ⟩ after Σωκράτης in 1555 (LVp2+).

2 tro

3 tro cat

3 mol

3 cho sp

1731–6=1737–42

‿ − ‿ ‿ − ‿ ‿ −

Ἥρᾳ ποτ' Ὀλυμπίᾳ

⏒ − ‿ ‿ − ‿ ‿ −

τὸν ἠλιβάτων θρόνων

− − ‿ | ‿ − ‿ ‿ −

ἄρχοντα θεοῖς μέγαν

− − | ‿ ‿ − ‿ ⏑̲ ||

Μοῖραι ξυνεκο⟨ί⟩μισαν

− − − ‿ ‿ − − || ᴴ

1735   ἐν τοιῷδ' ὑμεναίῳ.

‿ − − ‿ ‿ − − || ᴴ

1736a   Ὑμὴν ὢ Ὑμέναι' ὤ.

‿ − − ‿ ‿ − − |||

1736b   ⟨Ὑμὴν ὢ Ὑμέναι' ὤ.⟩

1748–54

− ‿ ‿ − ‿ ‿ − ‿ ‿ − ‿ ‿

ὢ μέγα χρύσεον ἀστεροπῆς φάος,

− ‿ ‿ − ‿ ‿ − −

ὢ Διὸς ἄμβροτον ἔγχος

− ‿ ‿ − ‿ ‿ − ‿ ‿ − ‿ ‿

1750   πυρφόρον, ὢ χθόνιαι βαρυαχέες

− ‿ ‿ − ‿ ‿ − − || ᴴ

ὀμβροφόροι θ' ἅμα βρονταί,

− ‿ ‿ − ‿ ‿ − −

αἷς ὅδε νῦν χθόνα σείει,

†‿ ‿ ‿ ‿ − ‿́ ‿ − −

†διὰ σὲ τὰ πάντα κρατήσας

− ‿ ‿ − ‿ ‿ − ‿ ‿ − ‿ ‿

καὶ πάρεδρον Βασίλειαν ἔχει Διός.

tel
ὁ δ' ἀμφιθαλὴς Ἔρως

tel
χρυσόπτερος ἡνίας

tel
ηὔθυνε παλιντόνους,

tel
1740   Ζηνὸς πάροχος γάμων

pher
τῆς τ' εὐδαίμονος Ἥρας.

pher
Ὑμὴν ὢ Ὑμέναι' ὤ.

pher
Ὑμὴν ὢ Ὑμέναι' ὤ.

da tetram

da trim

da tetram

da trim

da trim

da trim

da tetram

$\cup--\cup\cup--\parallel$

Ὑμὴν ὦ Ὑμέναι' ὤ.

1755–65

$\cup-\cup-\quad\cup-\cup-\quad-\cup-\quad\cup-\cup-$

1755–6   Χ. ἔπεσθε νῦν γάμοισιν, ὦ φῦλα πάντα συννόμων

$\cup\overline{\cap}\cup\overline{\cap}\quad\cup-\cup-\quad-\cup-\quad\cup-\cup\smile\parallel$

πτεροφόρ', ἐπὶ ⟨δά⟩πεδον Διὸς καὶ λέχος γαμήλιον.

$\cup-\cup-\quad\cup-\cup-\quad-\cup-\quad\cup-\cup-$

1759–60   Π. ὄρεξον, ὦ μάκαιρα, σὴν χεῖρα καὶ πτερῶν ἐμῶν

$\cup-\cup-\quad\cup-\cup-\quad-\cup-\quad\cup-\cup-\parallel^{\text{H}}$

λαβοῦσα συγχόρευσον· αἴρων δὲ κουφιῶ σ' ἐγώ.

$\overline{\cap}\cup-^{\text{H}}\quad\cup-\cup-$

Χ. ἀλαλαλαὶ ἰὴ παιών,

$--\cup-\quad\cup-\cup-\quad-\cup-\quad\cup-\cup\smile\parallel\parallel$

1764–5   τήνελλα καλλίνικος, ὦ δαιμόνων ὑπέρτατε.

The grand finale combines song with recitative, in which Peisetaerus joins. On the extent of his interventions, see Zimmermann (*Untersuchungen*, i. 192–4), Perusino (Maia, 18 (1966), 60–3) and Sommerstein (ad loc.). The pattern is as follows:

1720–5   Astrophic lyric prelude.

1726–30   Anapaestic system of nine metra ending in catalexis, delivered, presumably, by the chorus-leader.

1731–42   Wedding-hymn in strophe and antistrophe sung by the chorus.

1743–7   Anapaestic system of ten metra ending in catalexis. Exact symmetry with 1726–30 could be produced by deleting ἐχάρην ᾠδαῖς, which could well be a variant absorbed into the text (Helbig). The attribution of ἄγε νῦν . . . κεραυνόν to the chorus-leader depends essentially on αὑτοῦ at 1744, which Peisetaerus cannot use of himself. Willems' αὐτοῦ (third person reflexive for first person) is not comparable with αὐτῶν in 807, where ἠκάσμεσθα in the previous line makes the meaning clear.

pher

ia dim + lec

ia dim + lec

ia dim + lec

ia dim + lec

lec

ia dim + lec

1748–54 Astrophic song by the chorus, celebrating Peisetaerus' possession of Zeus' thunder.

1755–65 Exodus in dicola. 1755–8 could well, as in most modern texts, be delivered by Peisetaerus. The invitation to follow the wedding procession comes appropriately from the bridegroom (cf. *Peace* 1356), and the birds are now Peisetaerus' σύννομοι. The argument that the chorus-leader should give *all* instructions to the chorus is no more than secondary (cf. 1744 above). The asyndeton at 1759, however, with the symmetry of the two summonses, tilts the balance in favour of change of singer at that point. 1759–61 must in any case be uttered by Peisetaerus.

The chorus begin their prelude in trochaic, with much twittering resolution. Compare, however, the highly-resolved opening of *Lys.* 1279, where the singers are human. *Σ vet.* sees parody here of the opening of Cassandra's hymenaeal monody at *Tro.* 308, ἄνεχε πάρεχε· φῶς φέρω· σέβω φλέγω, and Euripides' play was indeed produced a year before *Birds*. However, ἄνεχε πάρεχε seems to have been a formula associated with torchlight processions (see Seaford on *Cyc.* 203). The sequence of molossi at 1724 is unusual (far more unusual than a sequence of bacchiacs). Sequences of long syllables are most commonly found in dochmiacs and anapaests, and analysis is a matter of context and arithmetic. Dionysius of Halicarnassus quotes, as an example of the metre, a sequence of four molossi (without attribution): *PMG* 1027 (c) (see West, *GM* 55). There are six consecutive molossi at *Ion* 125–7, probably four at A. *Supp.* 163–4, three at Phil. 837=853, and, possibly, at *Ant.* 1121=1132 (but here an alternative scansion is plausible). The question of whether − − − here could represent a contracted form of − ∪ ∪ − arises irresistibly, but cannot be answered. A. *Supp.* 163–4 may be followed by choriambs, but text and scansion there are full of uncertainty. Here, the metra are clearly marked out by word-end.

The metrically-redundant τὸν in 1721 was deleted by Dindorf.

For the use of telesilleans in the wedding hymn, see on *Peace* 1329ff. The greater literary sophistication of the Birds' song is matched by a touch of metrical sophistication: the use of pherecratean as clausula instead of reizianum (the exact catalectic counterpart of the telesillean). On verse-end after the acatalectic colon at 1734=1740, see on *Peace* 856ff. In 1734, ξυνεκο⟨ί⟩μισαν is Bentley's emendation for the MSS' ξυνεκόμισαν. Dindorf proposed the repeat of the refrain at 1736b.

For their hymn to Zeus' thunderbolt, the chorus use an appropriately dignified metre: dactylic (Introduction, p. 48). However, as the triteness of diction shows, the dignity is appropriately bogus. Rhythmically, however, the repeated use of an uncommon dactylic length, the trimeter

(Introduction, p. 50), gives the song some distinctiveness, the alternation here has some affinity with that between dactylic tetrameter and ibycean at *Lys.* 1286–90, and at *Thesm.* 1136ff. the dactylic trimeter is again found, this time in a context which seems to exploit ambiguity between the trimeter, catalectic ibycean, and pherecratean. The first half of the stanza, by the alternation of tetrameter and trimeter, sets up the expectation of a repeating pattern, which is teased in the second half. The fully resolved dactyl of the MS text at 1752 is scarcely paralleled. At *Ecc.* 1171, two consecutive metra are resolved, but that is a metrically fantastic passage. The most comprehensive collection of tragic examples is provided by Diggle (*PCPS* 200 (1974), 26). Fraenkel (*KB* i. 182–3, 451) defends διὰ σὲ as a sacral formula. Dale (*LM*²25 n. 2) suggests the possibility that διὰ could sometimes be scanned as a single long (cf. West, *GM* 14, on consonantalization). But the most serious objection to the passage is on grounds of sense. The MS text makes the Birds say that Peisetaerus has won Basileia by means of the thunderbolt, whereas the reverse has actually happened. (cf. Sommerstein, ad loc.).

The exodos, 1755–65, is in dicola, consisting of iambic dimeter + lecythion (cf. *Lys.* 286–7=296–7. Hephaestion calls the verse εὐριπίδειον (Cons. 53.2 ff.), and quotes a specimen from 'Archilochus' Ἰόβακχοι' (*IEG*² 322, under spuria). It seems, at first sight, tempting to posit a lacuna in the penultimate verse (cf. *Ach.* 1232), but ἀλαλαλαὶ ἰὴ παιών seems justifiable on its own as an interjected ritual cry.

In 1757, ⟨δά⟩πεδον is Meineke's supplement.

Lysistrata

256–65 = 271–80	Old Men: *Iambic*.
286–95 = 296–305	Old Men: *Iambic*.
319–20, 321–34 = 335–49	Old Women: *Iambo-choriambic* (correspondence of $- \cup \cup -$ with $\cup - \cup -$ and, perhaps, with $\cup \cup - \cup -$).

In the following four songs, the Old Men sing the strophe and the Old Women the antistrophe:

476–83 = 541–8	*Cretic*, with *iambic* opening, *anapaests*, with $\cup \cup \cup \cup$, and tripodies.
614–25 = 636 –47	*Cretic*, with *iambic* opening, *trochaic*.
658–71 = 682–95	*Cretic*, *trochaic*.
781–96 = 805–20	*Cretic*, *trochaic* (correspondence of $- \cup \overset{\frown}{\cup\cup}$ with $- \cup - \times$).

The two semichoruses join together for the rest of the play:

1043–57 = 1058–71 = 1189–1202 = 1203–15	*Trochaic, cretic, iambic*.
1247–72	The Spartan: *Aeolo-choriambic, cretic, trochaic, iambic, dactylic*.
1279–94	*Trochaic, iambic, dactylic, ibycean*.
1296–1321	The Spartan: *Iambic, aeolo-choriambic, cretic, anapaestic*.

There is little metrical variety in *Lysistrata*, but different types of rhythm are used structurally, as in *Clouds*, to mark off the main divisions of the action. Again as in *Clouds*, the play falls into three sections. A point of difference, however, is that the dominant metres of *Lysistrata*, trochaic and cretic, are characteristically, even boisterously, comic. An exceptional feature of the play is the antagonism of the two semichoruses.

The first section, the parodos, marks the initiation of the women's plot, and the metre is iambic, with an admixture of choriambs in the parts sung by the Old Women. For the central part of the play, from 387 to

979, the action is punctuated by the instalments of a running confrontation between the semichoruses. Here, the recitative is in catalectic trochaic tetrameters, and the songs almost exclusively trochaic and cretic. It is only necessary to look back at some of the lyric of *Acharnians* (the parodos, 284 ff. = 335 ff., 971 ff. = 988 ff.) to appreciate the freedom and sophistication with which Aristophanes handles the two metres in *Lysistrata*. A peculiar feature shared by 614 ff. = 636 ff. and 658 ff. = 682 ff. is a clausular pair of cretics following trochees. 781 ff. = 805 ff. varies the pattern slightly by ending with three cretics. That this clausula has expressive significance of some kind becomes clear at 1014 ff., the recitative dialogue which culminates in the reconciliation of the two semichoruses. Up to 1035, the singers use an unparalleled variation on the trochaic tetrameter in which the second half of the verse is made up of two cretics:

$$- \cup - \times \quad - \cup - \times \quad - \cup \widehat{\cup} \quad - \cup -$$

At the moment when the kiss of peace is imposed on the Old Men (1036) the double cretic gives place to a lecythion, producing ordinary trochaic tetrameters. In the song which follows (1043 ff. = 1058 ff. = 1189 ff. = 1203 ff.), which is performed by the united chorus, the lecythion is a recurrent clausula. This song is still in trochaic and cretic, but is metrically much simpler than the stanzas of confrontation. It frames the peace negotiations, and serves as a kind of interlude, having no explicit connection with the plot. The final section introduces more metrical variety with the two Spartan monodies and the Athenian hymn.

The end of the play is problematic. Various solutions that have been proposed are summarized by Henderson in his note on 1273–1321. The suggestion of Wilamowitz that the hymn to Athene called for in 1320–1 was supplied by a now lost antistrophe to 1279–94 is at least highly plausible. The stanza has the clarity of structure of choral song, and the ritual cries with which it ends would suit an exodos.

The only MS to contain the whole surviving text of *Lysistrata* is R (with its copy, Mu2). In 1871, W. G. Clark (*Journal of Philology*, 3, 153 ff.) and A. von Velsen (*Über den Codex Urbinas der Lysistrata und der Thesmophoriazusen des Aristophanes*) proved independently that the first printed text of *Lysistrata* and *Thesmophoriazusae*, the Juntine edition of 1516, was based on R. The first edition reproduces the colon-division of R, and thence it passed down through successive printed texts.

256–65 = 271–80

⏑ – ⏑ –   ⏑ – ⏑ –   – ⏑ –   ⏑ – – || ᴴ

ἦ πόλλ' ἄελπτ' ἔνεστιν ἐν τῷ μακρῷ βίῳ φεῦ,

⏑ – ⏑ ⏖   ⏑ – ⏑ –   – ⏑ –   ⏑ – ᴗ ||

ἐπεὶ τίς ἄν ποτ' ἤλπισ', ὦ Στρυμόδωρ', ἀκοῦσαι

⏑ – ⏑ | –   ⏑ – ⏑ –   ⏑ – ⏑ –   ⏑ – | ⏑ –

260–1   γυναῖκας, ἃς ἐβόσκομεν κατ' οἶκον ἐμφανὲς κακόν,

⏑ ⏖ ⏑ ⏖   ⏑ – ⏑ –

κατὰ μὲν ἅγιον ἔχειν βρέτας,

⏑ ⏖ ⏑ ⏖   ⏑ – ⏑ –

κατὰ τ' ἀκρόπολιν ἐμὰν λαβεῖν,

– – ⏑ –   ⏖ ⏑ –

κλῇθροισί τ' αὖ καὶ μοχλοῖ-

⏑ ⏖ ⏑ –   ⏑ – ᴗ |||

265   σι τὰ Προπύλαια πακτοῦν;

The separate entrances of the two semichoruses together make up an elaborately constructed parodos:

Old Men:	254–5	Two catalectic iambic tetrameters.
	256–65	Strophe (iambic).
	266–70	Five catalectic iambic tetrameters.
	271–80	Antistrophe.
	281–5	Five catalectic iambic tetrameters.
	286–305	Strophe and antistrophe (iambic).
	306–18	Thirteen catalectic iambic tetrameters.
Old Women:	319–20	Two catalectic iambo-choriambic tetrameters.
	321–49	Strophe and antistrophe (iambo-choriambic).
Dialogue:	350–86	Catalectic iambic tetrameters, ending in a run of twelve metra.

Like other Aristophanic choruses who enter slowly (compare *Wasps* and *Wealth*), the Old Men, weighed down by their faggots, use iambic tetrameters. Their lyric stanzas, too, are purely iambic, and 256 ff. = 271 ff. opens with a dicolon consisting of iambic dimeter + ithyphallic,

euripid

οὐ γάρ, μὰ τὴν Δήμητρ', ἐμοῦ ζῶντος ἐγχανοῦνται·

euripid

ἐπεὶ οὐδὲ Κλεομένης, ὃς αὐτὴν κατέσχε πρῶτος,

ia tetram

275–6　ἀπῆλθεν ἀψάλακτος, ἀλλ' ὅμως Λακωνικὸν πνέων

ia dim

†ᾤχετο θὤπλα παραδοὺς ἐμοί,

ia dim

σμικρὸν ἔχων πάνυ τριβώνιον†,

ia cr

πεινῶν ῥυπῶν ἀπαράτιλ-

+ ia ba

280　τος, ἐξ ἐτῶν ἄλουτος.

which Hephaestion calls εὐριπίδειον τεσσαρεσκαιδεκασύλλαβον (Cons. 53. 6). This is used as a recitative verse at *Wasps* 248–72 and combined with ordinary catalectic tetrameters to make up a lyric stanza at *Knights* 756 ff. = 836 ff. At 256 the Old Men turn from practical exhortation to reflection, and at 271 the statement of determination leads from present back to past. Rhythmically, however, the transition from recitative to song could not be more subtle. While it is convenient to use the terms 'recitative' and 'song' when writing about Aristophanes, it is vital not to import with them the clear distinction between the two types of delivery in modern European opera (cf. on 614 ff. = 636 ff. below). This section of the parodos is in some ways reminiscent of *Ach.* 204 ff. = 219 ff., but the modes of entry of the two parties of old men and the metres they use are completely different.

The altercation in catalectic iambic tetrameters which rounds off the parodos (350–86) reaches a climax when the Old Women douse the Old Men. It closes with a brief, shared pnigos, in which the Women get the last word (a full tetrameter).

262–5 = 277–80 together present one of the most intractable problems in the text of Aristophanes' lyric. The last two cola, 264–5 = 279–80, are the less problematic, and for them the antistrophe offers a metrically acceptable model. πεινῶν is the reading of Γ, where R has πινῶν (on the poor credentials of which see Holzinger on *Plutus* 297, *SAWW* 218.3 (1940), 115). The text of 264–5 survives only in R, which offers μοχλοῖσιν δὲ καὶ κλήθροισιν. The *Suda* (s. πακτοῦν) has μοχλοῖσι τὰ προπύλαια πακτοῦν. This is of no great significance in itself, but transposing κλήθροισι and μοχλοῖσι (Hermann and Reisig) does help towards a possible solution. Wilamowitz proposed:

> κλήθροις δὲ ⟨δὴ⟩ καὶ μοχλοῖ-
> σι τὰ προπύλαια πακτοῦν;

δὲ δὴ is, indeed, used by Aristophanes (and Euripides) in 'surprised or emphatic and crucial questions' (Denniston, *Particles*, 259), but it is found only in *short* questions in dialogue, where it follows the first word. In addition to the examples listed by Denniston, see *Peace* 226–7 (where εἰπέ μοι precedes the question proper), *Lys.* 599, *Thesm.* 608, *Frogs* 158, *Ecc.* 542, *Wealth* 264. *Birds* 1660 is the sole occurrence not definitely in a question. Henderson's and Sommerstein's κλήθροισί τ' αὖ . . ., with μοχλοῖσι rather than μοχλοῖσιν, is a satisfactory solution (see also Parker in Craik, *'Owls to Athens'*, 347–8). There is no need to introduce trochees.

262–3 = 277–8 remain insoluble. The strophe is entirely straight-forward and appropriate to the metrical context. For the antistrophe, Γ provides the linguistically preferable ᾤχετο θὤπλα where R has ᾤχετ' ὅπλα. By adopting the transpositions of Brunck and Meineke, it is possible to produce a pair of iambic dimeters to match 262–3:

> θὤπλ' ᾤχετο παραδοὺς ἐμοὶ
> σμικρὸν πάνυ τριβώνιον ἔχων
>
> – – ᴗ 𝕏   ᴗ – ᴗ –
> – – ᴗ 𝕏   – ⌢ ᴗ –

Both cola, however, have split resolution (the second before long anceps). Denniston ('Lyric Iambics', 129) found this incredible, and it would certainly be imprudent to adopt it (see Parker, *CQ* 18 (1968), 252, 254; and Introduction, p. 34). As it stands, the MS text scans as:

$$- \cup \cup - \cup \cup \cup - \cup -$$
$$- \cup \cup - \cup \cup \cup - \cup -$$

This is analysable as δ cr, but (*a*) $- \cup \cup - \cup \cup \cup$ is a very rare form of δ unparalleled in Aristophanes (see Conomis, *Hermes*, 92 (1964), 23, and Introduction, p. 68) and (*b*) the freedom of responsion between iambic and dochmiac–cretic seems very hard to justify here (contrast *Birds* 333–5 = 349–51 above). The alternative is to take $- \cup \cup - \cup \cup \cup - \cup -$ as cho δ, but this is in itself a strange combination, and even less convincing in correspondence with iambs than δ cr. None the less, the repetition seemed so compelling to Dale (*LM*² 78 n. 1) that she was prepared to explain $- \cup \cup - \cup \cup$ (tentatively, it should be noted) as *iambic*, assuming that an iambic metron with both longs resolved could become $- \cup \cup - \cup \cup$, if it also had long anceps and *long instead of short*. But substitution of long for short in iambic is an extreme rarity confined to dochmiac contexts (see Parker, *CQ* 18 (1968), 246 n. 1), and there is no example of an iambic metron with long for short *and* long anceps. Further, Dale confuses the issue by superimposing the idea of 'inversion' of 'the usual $\cup \cup -$'. This seems to introduce a different and incompatible explanation. We are invited to imagine that an iambic metron of comic *spoken* type, with double short substituted for both anceps and short (Dale cites *Frogs* 937, but there is no parallel in lyric, where substitution is exceedingly rare) has, by some process otherwise unknown to Greek metre, been reversed from $\cup \cup - \cup \cup -$ into $- \cup \cup - \cup \cup$. Dale's authority seems to have secured general acceptance for these *bizzareries*, even by scholars who attempt to conflate them with analyses of $- \cup \cup - \cup \cup$ as two dactyls, which Dale herself explicitly rejected (see Stinton, *CR* 15 (1965), 142 = *Collected Papers* (1990), 11, Zimmermann, *Untersuchungen*, 1. 44–6, Henderson, *CQ* 29 (1979), 53–5, and his commentary, 100). Henderson's attempt to adduce as parallel an ineptly emended version of 338 below can be dismissed. The least incredible explanation of the passage is corruption by paraphrase, which has, by fluke, produced a pair of matching 'cola'.

286–95=296–305

‒ ‒ ∪ ‒   ‒ ‒ ∪ ‒| ‒ ∪ ‒   ⏑ ‒ ∪ ‒

ἀλλ' αὐτὸ γάρ μοι τῆς ὁδοῦ λοιπόν ἐστι χωρίον

⏑ ‒ ∪ ‒| ⏑ ‒ ∪|‒   ‒ ‒|∪ ‒

τὸ πρὸς πόλιν τὸ σιμόν, οἷ σπουδὴν ἔχω.

‒ ‒ ∪ ‒   ⏒ ‒ ∪ ‒| ‒ ∪ ‒   ‒ ‒ ∪ ‒ ||н

289–90 [χὦ]πῶς ⟨δή⟩ ποτ' ἐξαμπρεύσομεν τοῦτ' ἄνευ κανθηλίου;

‒ ∪ ‒   ∪ ‒ ∪ ‒| ∪ ‒ ∪ ‒   ‒ ‒ ∪ ⏗ ||

ὡς ἐμοῦ γε τὼ ξύλω τὸν ὦμον ἐξιπώκατον.

‒ ∪ ‒   ∪ ‒ ∪ ‒

ἀλλ' ὅμως βαδιστέον,

‒ ∪ ‒   ‒ ‒ ∪ ‒ ||н

καὶ τὸ πῦρ φυσητέον,

‒ ∪ ‒   ‒ ‒ ∪ ‒   ‒ ‒ ∪ ‒   ⏒ ‒ ∪ ‒

μή μ' ἀποσβεσθὲν λάθῃ πρὸς τῇ τελευτῇ τῆς ὁδοῦ.

‒ ‒   ⌢∪ ‒   ‒ ∪ ‒ |||

295   φῦ φῦ. ἰοὺ ἰοὺ τοῦ καπνοῦ.

This pair of stanzas sung by the Old Men, which forms the centre-piece of the parodos, is a simple exercise in variation on the iambic dicolon made up of ia dim + lec, one of the related verses called 'euripidean' by Hephaestion (see above on *Birds* 1755 ff.). The most remarkable feature is the ambiguity of 291=301 and 294=304. In any other context one would unhesitatingly classify them as cata-lectic trochaic tetrameters. Here, however, they look more like a reversed version of 286=296 and 289=299, that is lec + ia dim. Aristophanes has, indeed, given a pointer towards that analysis: in three out of the four verses (291, 294, 301), word-end after the

319–20, 321–34=335–49

‒ ‒ ∪ ‒   ‒ ∪ ∪ ‒| ‒ ∪ ∪ ‒   ∪ ‒ ⌣ ||

λιγνὺν δοκῶ μοι καθορᾶν καὶ καπνόν, ὦ γυναῖκες,

ia dim + lec

ὡς δεινόν, ὦναξ Ἡράκλεις, προσπεσόν μ' ἐκ τῆς χύτρας

ia trim

ὥσπερ κύων λυττῶσα τὠφθαλμὼ δάκνει·

ia dim + lec

299–300 κἄστιν γε Λήμνιον τὸ πῦρ τοῦτο πάσῃ μηχανῇ.

lec + ia dim

οὐ γὰρ ⟨ἄν⟩ ποθ' ὧδ' ὀδὰξ ἔβρυκε τὰς λήμας ἐμοῦ.

lec

σπεῦδε πρόσθεν εἰς πόλιν

lec

καὶ βοήθει τῇ θεῷ.

lec + ia dim

ἢ πότ' αὐτῇ μᾶλλον ἢ νῦν, ὦ Λάχης, ἀρήξομεν;

sp cr cr?

305 φῦ φῦ. ἰοὺ ἰοὺ τοῦ καπνοῦ.

opening lecythion replaces the normal diaeresis of the trochaic tetrameter.

At 289, πῶς δή ποτ' is Fraenkel's emendation for the MSS' χὤπως ποτ'. Radt has proposed πῶς πῶς ποτ', but I doubt whether the order is acceptable. Contrast *Knights* 82 πῶς δῆτα πῶς . . ., *OT* 1210 πῶς ποτε πῶς ποθ' . . ., *Phil.* 175 πῶς ποτε πῶς . . ., 686–7 πῶς ποτε πῶς ποτ' . . . At 301, ⟨ἄν⟩ is Brunck's supplement. At 304, ἢ πότ' . . . for the MSS' εἴ ποτ' . . . is a renaissance conjecture, by Ellebodius. Also at 304, ἀρήξομεν is a good reading provided by B (also Zanetti, 1538, ἀρηξόμην R: ἀρήξωμεν Γ).

ia cho tetram cat

‾ ‾ ◡ ‾   ‾ ◡ ◡ ‾| ‾ ◡ ◡ ‾   ◡ ‾ ‾

320   ὥσπερ πυρὸς καομένου· σπευστέον ἐστὶ θᾶττον.

◡͞ ‾ ◡ ‾| ‾ ◡ ◡ ‾

πέτου πέτου, Νικοδίκη,

◡ ‾ ◡ ‾   ‾|◡ ◡ ‾

πρὶν ἐμπεπρῆσθαι Καλύκην

◡ ‾ ◡ ‾   ‾ ◡ ◡ ‾   ‾ ‿||ᴴ

τε καὶ Κρίτυλλαν περιφυσήτω

◡ ⌢ ◡ ‾   ‾ ◡ ◡ ‾

ὑπό τ' ἀνέμων ἀργαλέων

◡͜ ⌢ ◡ ‾   ‾ ◡ ◡ ‾

325   ὑπό τε γερόντων ὀλέθρων.

‾ ◡ ◡ ‾   ‾ ◡ ◡ ‾   ‾ ◡ ◡ ‾   ◡ ‾ ‾
                      ◡ ‾ ◡ ‾

ἀλλὰ φοβοῦμαι τόδε, μῶν ὑστερόπους βοηθῶ.

‾ ‾ ◡ ‾   ‾ ◡ ◡ ‾| ‾ ◡ ◡ ‾   ◡ ‾ ‿||ᴴ

νῦν δὴ γὰρ ἐμπλησαμένη τὴν ὑδρίαν κνεφαία

◡͜ ⌢ ◡ ‾   ‾ ◡ ◡ ‾| ‾ ◡ ◡ ‾| ‾ ◡ ◡ ‾   ◡ ‾ ‾

328-9   μόλις ἀπὸ κρήνης ὑπ' ὄχλου καὶ θορύβου καὶ πατάγου
                                                    [χυτρείου,

◡͞ ‾ ◡|‾   ‾ ◡ ◡ ‾

330   δούλαισιν ὠστιζομένη

‾ ◡ ◡ ‾ ◡ ‾   ‾ ◡ ◡ ‾

στιγματίαις θ', ἁρπαλέως

‾ ◡ ◡ ‾   ‾ ◡ ◡ ‾

. . . .

‾ ◡ ◡ ‾   ‾ ◡ ◡ ‾

ἀραμένη ταῖσιν ἐμαῖς

‾ ◡ ◡ ‾   ‾ ◡ ◡ ‾

δημότισιν καομέναις

◡ ‾ ◡ ‾| ◡ ‾ ‾|||

φέρουσ' ὕδωρ βοηθῶ.

ia cho tetram cat

ia cho dim
335 ἤκουσα γὰρ τυφογέρον-

+ ia cho dim
τας ἄνδρας ἔρρειν, στελέχη

+ ia cho sp
φέροντας ὥσπερ βαλανεύσοντας

ia cho dim
338 †ἐς πόλιν ὡς τριτάλαντον βάρος,†

ia cho dim
δεινότατ' ἀπειλοῦντας ἐπῶν

ia cho tetram cat
340 ὡς πυρὶ χρὴ τὰς μυσαρὰς γυναῖκας ἀνθρακεύειν.

ia cho tetram cat
ἅς, ὦ θεά, μή ποτ' ἐγὼ πιμπραμένας ἴδοιμι,

ia cho pentam cat
342–3 ἀλλὰ πολέμου καὶ μανιῶν ῥυσαμένας Ἑλλάδα καὶ
[πολίτας.

ia cho dim
ἐφ' οἷσπερ, ὦ χρυσολόφα

2 cho = ia cho dim
345 πολιοῦχε, σὰς ἔσχον ἕδρας

6 cho
καί σε καλῶ ξύμμαχον, ὦ

Τριτογένει', ἤν τις ἐκεί-

νας ὑποπιμπρῆσιν ἀνήρ,

ia dim cat
φέρειν ὕδωρ μεθ' ἡμῶν.

The Old Women use iambo-choriambic, a rhythm at once related to and distinct from the pure iambic of the Old Men. It is clear that, within a harmonious whole, there is a deliberate differentiation of movement, tone, and mood between the songs of the two semichoruses. One would guess from the words that the Women's movements are the more sprightly.

For the tetrameters of 319–20, compare Anacreon, *PMG* 378 (see above on *Birds* 1372) and also *Aj.* 227–8=251–2 (see Introduction, p. 79). 326 is paralleled by Anacreon, *PMG* 381(b) (cf. Aristophanes, *PCG* 111), and the pentameter, 329=343, by Cratinus, *PCG* 184. This stanza nicely illustrates the problems inherent in dividing Greek lyric into lines on the page. 326 is genuinely an undivided sequence of four metra, but all the other 'tetrameters' have median diaeresis, and the 'pentameter' at 328–9=342–3 is divided by word-end on both sides of the central choriamb. Thus, one aspect of the poet's phrasing could, perhaps, be better revealed by the lay-out:

$$\times - \cup - \quad - \cup \cup -$$
$$- \cup \cup - \quad \cup - -$$

and
$$\times - \cup - \quad - \cup \cup -$$
$$- \cup \cup -$$
$$- \cup \cup - \quad \cup - -$$

On the other hand, while the passage 321–5=335–9 reveals itself clearly, even without intervening word-end, as a series of dimeters ($\times - \cup - - \cup \cup -$ with clausular $- -$ at 323=337), the tetrameters, with their chiastic structure (ia cho cho ia) and catalectic second member, are rhythmic wholes: dicola.

The phrasing of the song is easy to appreciate. After the prelude of two tetrameters, the colon which forms the first half of the tetrameter recurs five times, the series being articulated into two sections by the spondee, with pause, at the end of 323=337. At the end of 325=339 there is a surprise: instead of reverting to $\times - \cup -$, the choriambs continue, building up a tension which is eventually released by the catalectic iambic close of 326–340. The middle section of the stanza (327–9=341–3) repeats (with one extra choriamb) the prelude. 330 begins as if to repeat 321ff.=335ff., but $\times - \cup - \quad - \cup \cup -$ is not, after all, repeated (except, perhaps, once in the antistrophe). Instead, we move immediately into a long sequence of choriambs, the same device as closed the first part of the stanza. This time, however, the build-up of tension is longer and the resolution into iambic rhythm is more leisurely and decisive.

Apart from the disparity in length between strophe and antistrophe at 332–3 = 346–8, the major problem of the song is 338. As it stands in the MSS, the colon scans – ∪ ∪ – ∪ ∪ –   – ∪ –. Zimmermann (*Untersuchungen* i. 52) seeks to justify this as an example of 2 da = ia, following his interpretation of 262–3 = 277–8 (see above). This involves accepting not only 2 da = ia in the first half of the colon, but ia = cho in the second half. Herkenrath's τριτάλαντα, producing – ∪ ∪ – ∪ ∪ – ∪ ∪ –, adopted by Henderson, is an attempt to remedy this second (and less serious) failure of correspondence. Neither scholar concerns himself with the question of why Aristophanes should suddenly have chosen to disrupt his elegant pattern of rhythmic expectations deluded and fulfilled and to throw to the winds rules of correspondence that he is universally agreed to have observed in at least the vast majority of his compositions. Wilamowitz's ὡς τριτάλαντον εἰς πόλιν (– ∪ ∪ –   ∪ – ∪ –) restores the ordinary constituents of the stanza, choriamb and iamb, but in the wrong order. While there are a few examples of – ∪ ∪ – = × – ∪ – (see Introduction, p. 78, and below on 326 = 340), there is none of × – ∪ –   – ∪ ∪ – = ∪ ∪ –   × – ∪ –. Reisig produced exact correspondence with δεῦρο, τριτάλαντόν τι βάρος (– ⌢ ∪ –   – ∪ ∪ –), assuming ἐς πόλιν to be an intrusive gloss on δεῦρο (as δεῦρο is glossed by ἐπὶ τὴν ἀκρόπολιν at 738 below). The emendation is interesting *exempli gratia*, but produces a split resolution (Introduction, pp. 34–5).

At 324, ὑπό τ' ἀνέμων is Oeri's emendation of the MSS' ὑπό τε νόμων.

At 326 = 340 the MSS offer correspondence between choriamb and iamb, which is rare, but not unparalleled (Introduction, p. 78). Meineke proposed to restore perfect correspondence by substituting τὰς κύνας for γυναῖκας in 340. 331 = 345 seems to be an example of the same freedom of responsion, but the apparent substitution of ∪ ∪ for × in the iambic metron πολιοῦχε, σὰς presents a further problem. There are a few other examples of this licence in Aristophanes' lyric (Introduction, p. 33). There is also the possibility that ι is consonantalized in πολιοῦχε

(see West, *GM* 14, and cf. σιῶν below at 1306). Tiny fragments of line-
ends of 342–6 are preserved in P. Antin. 75 (5th–6th c. AD, Barns and

$$476-83=541-8$$

ō–◡⏝ –◡⏝ –◡– –◡–||ₕ

ὦ Ζεῦ, τί ποτε χρησόμεθα τοῖσδε τοῖς κνωδάλοις;

–◡⏝ –◡⏝ –◡⏝ –◡‿||

478 οὐ γὰρ ἔτ᾽ ἀνεκτὰ τάδε γ᾽, ἀλλὰ βασανιστέον

◡◡– ◡◡–| ◡◡–||ₕ

τόδε σοι τὸ πάθος μετ᾽ ἐμοῦ,

◡◡–◡◡– ◡◡|–◡◡⏝

480 ὅ τι βουλόμεναί ποτε τὴν Κραναὰν

◡◡◡◡|◡◡◡◡| ◡◡◡◡◡◡◡◡

κατέλαβον ἐφ᾽ ὅ τι τε μεγαλόπετρον ἄβατον

◡◡◡◡| ◡◡–| ◡◡‿|||

ἀκρόπολιν ἱερὸν τέμενος.

This strophic pair frames the first instalment of Lysistrata's anapaestic
altercation with the πρόβουλος. The strophe expresses the anger of the
Old Men, the antistrophe the enthusiastic resolution of the Old Women.
The opening cretics are well suited to both (Introduction, pp. 45–6), and
the anapaestic second half of the stanza harmonizes with the anapaests of
the agon. Metrically, the stanza reproduces two motifs which feature in
the agonistic section of *Birds*. The iambic opening to a cretic verse
appears in that play at 406–34 (cf. 614 ff.=636 ff. below, and see Introduction, pp. 42–3), and, in the anapaests, the tripodies and long sequences
of shorts recall *Birds* 327 ff.=343 ff. It is tempting to imagine that, as the
Birds twitter, so the Old Men stammer and splutter with rage. If, however, the rhythm is expressive in that way, it must be acknowledged that
the words of the antistrophe are far less appropriate to it. It is also worth
noting that the spondees which feature in the Birds' song are absent here.

    The colometry of the anapaests that I adopt is based on the division
of 480–3 found in the Bodleian papyrus (*P. Bodl.* Gr. class. e 87, 4th–
5th c.) and in R. It was printed by White, but, unfortunately, ignored
by Dale (*LM*² 56), who, while rightly condemning 'Wilamowitz's

Zilliacus, *Antinoopolis Papyri*, ii. 63–4), which show the same colon-division as R.

ia 3 cr
ἐγώ⟨γε⟩ γὰρ ⟨ἂν⟩ οὔποτε κάμοιμ' ἂν ὀρχουμένη,

4 cr
542 οὐδὲ καματηρὸς ἂν ἕλοι γόνατά μου κόπος.

an trip
ἐθέλω δ' ἐπὶ πᾶν ἰέναι

an dim
μετὰ τῶνδ' ἀρετῆς ἔνεχ', αἷς ἔνι φύσις,

an dim
545 ἔνι χάρις, ἔνι θράσος, ἔνι δὲ ⟨τὸ⟩ σοφόν, ἔνι

an trip
φιλόπολις ἀρετὴ φρόνιμος.

amorphous dimeters', set the seal of her approval on the procrustean tripodies into which R divides 544–6, which require colon-division at τὴν | Κραναὰν and αἷς | ἔνι. The question of colometry here is complicated by textual problems, but it is important to bear in mind the known frequency of diaeresis in anapaests and the tendency for sequences of shorts to be articulated by word-end (cf., again, *Birds* 327 ff. = 343 ff.).

The MS text is corrupt at several points in both strophe and antistrophe, but satisfactory emendation is possible. In 476, τοῖς, conjectured by Bentley and Reisig, is the reading of *P. Bodl.*, against τοῖσι(ν) in RΓ (here the papyrus happens to be right against the MSS, but it is wrong at 470 in having τοῖς where RΓ have τοῖσιν and at 471 in having τοῖσι where they have τοῖς). The supplementation of 541 is by Enger. For the latter verse, B offers ἐγὼ γὰρ οὔποτ' ἂν κάμοιμ' ὀρχουμένη, a simple emendation of the reading of RΓ to produce an iambic trimeter. By a remarkable lapse of judgement, Wilamowitz accepted B's version of 541 and mutilated 476 to fit it. At 478, however, ἔτ' ἀνεκτὰ τάδε γ' is the reading of B. RΓ have οὐ γὰρ ἔτ' (ἔστ' R) ἀνεκτὰ τάδ', and *P. Bodl.* has . . . .]ρ α[ν]εκτα ταδ[ε]τ. Dobree conjectured οὐ γὰρ ἔτ᾽ ἀνεκτέα τάδ᾽. For the corresponding verse, 542, I print the transposition by Jackson (*MS* 46) of the MSS' οὐδὲ (οὔτε Γ) τὰ γόνατα κόπος ἐλεῖ (ἔλοι B) μου καματηρός. At 545, R has ἔνι δὲ θράσος. The supplement ⟨τὸ⟩ is Hermann's. Reisig proposed ἔνι ⟨δὲ⟩ φιλόπολις, and Henderson's text at this point is based on confusion about both the MS reading and Reisig's conjecture. For δὲ within a list

614–25=636–47

614–15   tro tetram cat II

     – – ∪ | –   – ∪ –   – ∪ –

616   ἤδη γὰρ ὄζειν ταδὶ πλειόνων

     ∪ – ∪ – | – ∪ –   – ∪ –

     καὶ μειζόνων πραγμάτων μοι δοκεῖ,

     – ∪ – ∪   – ∪ – ∪   – ∪ – | ∪   – ∪ ⌣ ‖ ₕ

     καὶ μάλιστ᾽ ὀσφραίνομαι τῆς Ἱππίου τυραννίδος·

     – ∪ ⌣͡   – ∪ –   – ∪ –   – ∪ –

620   καὶ πάνυ δέδοικα μὴ τῶν Λακώνων τινὲς

     – ∪ ⌢͡   – ∪ ⌢͡ | – ∪ | –   – ∪ ⌣ ‖

     δεῦρο συνεληλυθότες ἄνδρες εἰς Κλεισθένους

     ⌢͡ ∪ – ∪   – ∪ – ∪ | – ∪ – –   – ∪ ⌣ ‖

623   τὰς θεοῖς ἐχθρὰς γυναῖκας ἐξεπαίρουσιν δόλῳ

     ⌣͡ ∪ – ∪   – ∪ – ∪ | – ∪ – ⌣

     καταλαβεῖν τὰ χρήμαθ᾽ ἡμῶν τόν τε μισθὸν

     – ∪ –   – ∪ ⌣ ‖‖

625   ἔνθεν ἔζων ἐγώ.

From 614 to 705, the two semi-choruses are left alone on stage, but, instead of a normal parabasis, they perform a sort of agonistic duet, in which lyric stanzas alternate with 10-line sequences of catalectic trochaic tetrameters delivered by the leaders. Both lyric stanzas are composed in trochees and cretics, so that they blend easily into their rhythmic setting of trochaic tetrameters. The metrically harmonious combination of song and recitative recalls the parodos (254–349).

otherwise in asyndeton, compare *Birds* 586. The first editors of *P. Bodl.*, Grenfell and Hunt (*Mélanges Nicole*, 217–20), remark that ὅ τι βουλόμεναί ποτε (480) is 'a little long' for the space in the papyrus, which is adequate for 12 or 14 letters. One should, however, set beside this their general conclusion that the quality of the papyrus text is 'not high'.

636–7   tro tetram cat II

       ia 2 cr
638   ἡμεῖς γάρ, ὦ πάντες ἀστοί, λόγων

       ia 2 cr
    κατάρχομεν τῇ πόλει χρησίμων·

       tro tetram cat
640   εἰκότως, ἐπεὶ χλιδῶσαν ἀγλαῶς ἔθρεψέ με·

       4 cr
    ἑπτὰ μὲν ἔτη γεγῶσ᾽ εὐθὺς ἠρρηφόρουν·

       4 cr
    εἶτ᾽ ἀλετρὶς ἦ ᾽δεκέτις οὖσα τἀρχηγέτι

       tro tetram cat
645   †καταχέουσα τὸν κροκωτὸν ἄρκτος ἦ Βραυρωνίοις·

       3 tro
    κἀκανηφόρουν ποτ᾽ οὖσα παῖς καλὴ ᾽χουσ᾽

        +2 cr
    ἰσχάδων ὁρμαθόν.

The first stanza is clearly divided into four sections by verse-end at 515=637, 619=640, and 623=645. The introductory pair of trochaic tetrameters ends with hiatus in both strophe and antistrophe. It is something of a surprise in a trochaic context to find again in the next section the motif of *iambic* metron introducing cretics (see above on 476 ff.= 541 ff.). At the end of the stanza, the double-cretic clausula is introduced by trochees. This same clausula also ends the companion strophic pair,

658 ff. = 682 ff., and the recitative sections at 797–804 = 821–8, and the rhythm foreshadows the sequence of dicola of the form

$$-\cup-\times \quad -\cup-\times \quad -\cup\widetilde{} \quad -\cup-$$

at 1014–35 which leads up to the reconciliation of the two semi-choruses.

At 623, ἐξεπαίρουσιν ('I fear that they are inciting . . .') is Sommerstein's emendation of the MSS' ἐξεπαίρωσιν ('I fear that they

658–71 = 682–95

$$-- \quad -\cup-\underline{\cup} \quad -\cup-\underline{\cup} \quad --$$

ταῦτ' οὖν οὐχ ὕβρις τὰ πράγματ' ἐστὶ πολλή;

$$-\cup-- \quad -\cup-\underline{\cup} \quad -\cup-\underline{\cup}$$

660 κἀπιδώσειν μοι δοκεῖ τὸ χρῆμα μᾶλλον.

661–3   tro tetram cat III

$$-\cup\widetilde{} \quad -\cup\widetilde{} \quad -\cup\widetilde{} \quad -\cup\widetilde{}$$

664–5 ἀλλ' ἄγετε λ⟨ε⟩υκόποδες, οἵπερ ἐπὶ Λειψύδριον

$$-\cup\widetilde{} \quad -\cup\widetilde{}$$

666 ἤλθομεν ὅτ' ἦμεν ἔτι,

$$-- \quad -\cup-\smile \quad -|\cup-|\smile \quad -\cup-\smile$$

667–9 νῦν δεῖ, νῦν ἀνηβῆσαι πάλιν κἀναπτερῶσαι

$$-\cup-\underline{\cup} \quad -\cup-\smile \quad -\cup- \quad -\cup\smile|||^{\text{H}}$$

670–1 πᾶν τὸ σῶμα κἀποσείσασθαι τὸ γῆρας τόδε.

Although there is no apparent metrical pause within the stanza, 658 ff. = 682 ff., like its companion strophic pair, 614 ff. = 636 ff., falls rhythmically into four sections. The third section is, again, purely cretic. The clausula (trochees + double cretic) is similar, except that rhetorical division marks off two trochees preceding the cretics, which prefigures still more closely the dicola of 1014–35. Instead of appearing as a metrically and syntactically distinct prelude, trochaic tetrameters make up the second section, and in the antistrophe they are syntactically continuous with the preceding verse. The motif of iambic metron introducing cretics is not repeated. Instead, in the first and last sections, a spondee introduces trochees (Introduction, p. 35). Both sections also include five full

are going to incite . . .'). The MS text at 644–5 offers two sentences in
intolerably harsh asyndeton. The only variant is that R has καταχέουσα
where the other MSS have κατέχουσα. Emendation is complicated by
the particularities of Attic cult practices. See C. Sourvinou, *CQ* 21
(1971), 339–42, T. C. W. Stinton, *CQ* 26 (1976), 11–13 (= *Collected
Papers* (1990), 186–9), and, again, C. Sourvinou-Inwood, *Studies in
Girls' Transitions* (1988), with further references on p. 68 of that work.

	sp 2 tro sp
	εἰ νὴ τὼ θεώ με ζωπυρήσεις, λύσω

	3 tro
684	τὴν ἐμαυτῆς ὗν ἐγὼ δή, καὶ ποιήσω

685–7	tro tetram cat III

	4 cr
688–9	νῦν πρὸς ἔμ' ἴτω τις, ἵνα μή ποτε φάγῃ σκόροδα,

	2 cr
	μηδὲ κυάμους μέλανας.

	sp 3 tro
692–3	ὡς εἰ καὶ μόνον κακῶς ἐρεῖς, ὑπερχολῶ γάρ,

	2 tro 2 cr
694–5	αἰετὸν τίκτοντα κάνθαρός σε μαιεύσομαι.

trochaic metra. In the first section, however, they are divided into 2 + 3
by a second spondee, while in the final section they run uninterrupted to
the double-cretic clausula. The opening section can equally well be laid
out:

$$-\,-\quad -\cup-\cup\quad -\cup-\cup$$
$$-\,-\quad -\cup-\,-\quad -\cup-\cup\quad -\cup-\cup$$

660=684 then becomes sp 3 tro, like 667=692. The colometry I give is
more sympathetic to rhetorical division in the strophe. But the passage
illustrates how setting out lyric in lines may force us to make choices that
the poet himself may not have seen as such (cf. 321 ff. = 336 ff. above).

At 664, λ⟨ε⟩υκόποδες is Hermann's conjecture. The MSS' λυκόποδες seems, though unmetrical, to be a fairly early corruption, since it is elaborately explained in Σ *vet.*

An odd feature of R's colometry is that both at 660=684 and

781–96=805–20

$$-- | \quad -\cup - |- \quad -\cup -- | \quad -\cup --$$

μῦθον βούλομαι λέξαι τιν' ὑμῖν, ὅν ποτ' ἤκουσ'

$$-\cup \widehat{\cup\cup} \quad -\Longleftarrow ||$$

αὐτὸς ἔτι παῖς ὤν.

$$-- | \quad -\underset{=\cup\widehat{\cup\cup}}{\cup} \quad -\cup \widehat{\cup\cup} \quad -\smile ||$$

785–6   οὕτως ἦν νεανίσκος Μελανίων τις,

$$-- \quad -\cup \widehat{\cup\cup} \quad -\cup \widehat{\cup\cup} \quad -\underset{=\cup\widehat{\cup\cup}}{\cup}$$

ὃς φεύγων γάμον ἀφίκετ' ἐς ἐρημίαν κἀν

$$-\underset{=\cup-\cup}{\cup\widehat{\cup\cup}} \quad --$$

788   τοῖς ὄρεσιν ᾤκει·

$$-\underset{=\cup-\cup}{\cup\widehat{\cup\cup}} \quad --$$

κᾆτ' ἐλαγοθήρει

$$-\cup \widehat{\cup\cup} \quad --$$

790   πλεξάμενος ἄρκυς

$$-\cup \widehat{\cup\cup} \quad --$$

καὶ κύνα τιν' εἶχεν

$$-\cup \widehat{\cup\cup} \quad -\cup \widehat{\cup\cup}| \quad -\cup \widehat{\cup\cup} \quad --$$

κοὐκέτι κατῆλθε πάλιν οἴκαδ' ὑπὸ μίσους.

$$-- | \quad -\cup - \smile | \quad -\cup --$$

οὕτω τὰς γυναῖκας ἐβδελύχθη

$$-\cup -- \quad -\cup --$$

795   'κεῖνος, ἡμεῖς τ' οὐδὲν ἧττον

$$-\cup \widehat{\cup\cup} \quad -\cup |- \quad -\cup - |||$$

τοῦ Μελανίωνος οἱ σώφρονες.

667–9=692–3 three trochees are divided as:

$$- \cup - \times \quad - \cup -$$
$$\times - \cup - \times$$

       sp 3 tro

805   κἀγὼ βούλομαι μῦθόν τιν' ὑμῖν ἀντιλέξαι

        + cr sp
       τῷ Μελανίωνι.

       sp tro cr sp = sp 2 cr sp

808–9   Τίμων ἦν τις ἀίδρυτος ἀβάτοισιν

       sp 2 cr tro = sp 3 cr

810   ἐν σκώλοισι τὰ πρόσωπα περιειργμένος Ἐ-

        + cr sp = tro sp

     ρινύων ἀπορρώξ.

       cr sp = tro sp

     οὗτος οὖν ὁ Τίμων

        cr sp
   ᾤχεθ' ὑπὸ μίσους

       cr sp

.   .   .   .

       3 cr sp

815   πολλὰ καταρασάμενος ἀνδράσι πονηροῖς.

       sp 2 tro
   οὕτω 'κεῖνος †ὑμῶν† ἀντεμίσει

        + 2 tro
    τοὺς πονηροὺς ἄνδρας ἀεί,

       3 cr

820   ταῖσι δὲ γυναιξὶν ἦν φίλτατος.

The contest between the two semi-choruses is interrupted by the entrance of Lysistrata after 705, with the news that the women are deserting. The complementary and contrasting scenes of the attempted desertions and the seduction of Cinesias are divided from each other by a further passage of contest between the semichoruses (781–828) in a combination of lyric with trochaic recitative.

The lyric stanza consists of further, and yet freer, variations on the trochaeo-cretic rhythm. The opening and closing spondee, introduced in 658 ff. = 682 ff., is here a repeated motif, and the signature clausula of this part of the play is extended from two to three cretics. The distinctive feature of the stanza is, however, the free intermixture of trochees and cretics, even in correspondence with each other. This phenomenon is paralleled at *Wasps* 1060 ff. = 1091 ff., where, again, the cretics which correspond with trochees are of the form $- \cup \widehat{\cup\cup}$. Here, it is worth noting, *all* the cretics in the song are of that form, except the two last (on Dale's theory of syllable-counting, see Introduction, p. 117).

At 785–6 = 809–10, I follow Dale (*LM²* 98) in dividing into two verses, taking τις = -σιν as *brevis in longo*. This adds another example of the cadence $- \cup \widehat{\cup\cup} \quad - -$, which features repeatedly in the stanza. The alternative, with τις = -σιν scanned as short, is a long and rather shapeless verse: sp tr (= cr) cr tr cr cr tr (= cr) cr (= tr) sp.

The short cola which at 811–12 correspond to $- \cup \widehat{\cup\cup} \quad - -$ should not here be called ithyphallics, for the ithyphallic is ordinarily understood as a syncopated *iambic* colon $((\times)- \cup - \quad \cup -(\cup)-)$, which would be completely out of place in the context.

Strophe and antistrophe are followed by a quick-fire exchange which is hard to categorize as either song or recitative:

1043–57 = 1058–71 (= 1189–1202 = 1203–15)

$- \cup - \overset{\smile}{} \quad - \cup - \cup \quad - \cup - \overset{\smile}{} \quad - \cup - -$

οὐ παρασκευαζόμεσθα τῶν πολιτῶν οὐδέν᾽, ὦνδρες,

$- \cup - \overset{\smile}{} \quad - \cup \underset{\asymp}{}\|$

1045   φλαῦρον εἰπεῖν οὐδὲ ἕν,

$- \cup \widehat{\cup\cup} \quad - \cup - \quad - \cup \widehat{\cup\cup} \quad - \cup -\|$

ἀλλὰ πολὺ τοὔμπαλιν πάντ᾽ ἀγαθὰ καὶ λέγειν

$$- \cup - \underset{\smile}{} \quad - \cup -$$
$$- \cup - \cup \quad - \cup \smile \frown \|_{\text{H}}$$
$$- \cup - - \quad - \cup -$$
$$- \cup - \overline{\cup} \quad - \cup -$$
$$- \cup - \cup \quad - \cup -$$
$$- \cup - - \quad - \cup - -$$
$$- \cup - - \quad - \cup - \underset{\smile}{}$$
$$- \cup - \quad - \cup -$$

Note, again, the double-cretic clausula.

At 788, *Γ rec.* offer ἐνῴκει for R's ᾤκει. This would produce correspondence of $- \cup \frown \cup$ to $- \cup - \cup$. In this stanza, however, there is no resolution otherwise in the trochaic metra, and ἐνῴκει is most probably the result of dittography of *-ιν*. At 808, Bentley sought to eliminate correspondence of trochee to cretic by the transposition *Τίμων ἦν ἀίδρυτός τις*. This is accepted by Henderson, on the grounds that $- \cup - \cup = - \cup \frown$ is acceptable, but not $- \cup - - = - \cup \frown$ (which, however, he accepts at 1048 = 1062 = 1193 = 1207). There is, however, too much uncertainty about what is and is not acceptable in this type of correspondence to warrant emendation which involves the scansion ἀίδρυτος and removes the symmetry of *Μελανίων τις / Τίμων τις*. At 809–10, the MSS offer: ἀβάτοισιν εὐσκώλοισι τὸ πρόσωπον περιεργμένος. I give the emended version produced by Hermann, using the *Suda*'s paraphrase (s. *Τίμων*): ἀβάτοις ἐνὶ σκώλοισι περιεργμένος. Wilamowitz, in rewriting the passage, introduced two free responsions between $- \cup \frown$ and $- \cup - \cup$ in addition to those already present in the MS text of the stanza. Between 814 and 815 a colon (presumably giving Timon's destination) has been lost. 820 is preserved only by R.

6 tro cat (4 tro + lec)
ἑστιᾶν δὲ μέλλομεν ξένους τινὰς Καρυστίους ἄν-

1060   δρας καλούς τε κἀγαθούς.

4 cr
κἄστιν ⟨ἔτ᾽⟩ ἔτνος τι· καὶ δελφάκιον ἦν τί μοι

$- - \cup \frown \quad - \cup \frown \quad - \cup \frown \quad - \cup \smile \parallel$ H

1048 καὶ δρᾶν· ἱκανὰ γὰρ τὰ κακὰ καὶ τὰ παρακείμενα.

$- \cup - \quad - \cup - | \quad - \cup - \quad - \cup - \parallel$ H

ἀλλ' ἐπαγγελλέτω πᾶς ἀνὴρ καὶ γυνή,

$- \cup - \cup - \cup -$

1050 εἴ τις ἀργυρίδιον

$- - \cup - \quad \ \ \overline{\cup} - \cup -$

δεῖται λαβεῖν, μνᾶς ἢ δύ' ἢ

$- - \cup - \quad \underset{\cdot}{\cup} - \cup - \quad \underset{\cdot}{\cup} - \cup \smile \parallel$ H

τρεῖς, ὡς [πόλλ'] ἔσω 'στὶν κἄχομεν βαλλάντια.

$- \cup - - - \cup \Rightarrow \parallel$ H

κἄν ποτ' εἰρήνη φανῇ,

$- \cup - \overline{\cup} \quad - \cup - - \quad - \cup - -$

1055 ὅστις ἂν νυνὶ δανείσηται παρ' ἡμῶν,

$- \cup - \overline{\cup} \quad \frown \cup - | \parallel$

ἂν λάβῃ, μηκέτ' ἀποδῶ.

1189–1202=1203–15 (=1043–57=1058–71)

$- \cup - \underset{\cdot}{\cup} \quad - \cup - - \quad \frown\!\!\frown \cup - - \quad - \cup - -$

1189–90 στρωμάτων δὲ ποικίλων καὶ χλανιδίων καὶ ξυστίδων καὶ

$- \cup - \cup \quad - \cup \Rightarrow \parallel$ H

χρυσίων ὅσ' ἐστί μοι,

$- \cup \frown \quad - \cup - \quad - \cup \frown \quad - \cup \Rightarrow \parallel$

οὐ φθόνος ἔνεστί μοι πᾶσι παρέχειν φέρειν

$\overline{\cup} - \cup \frown \quad - \cup \frown \quad - \cup \frown \quad - \cup - \parallel$

1193 τοῖς παισίν, ὁπόταν τε θυγάτηρ τινὶ κανηφορῇ.

$- \cup - \quad - \cup - | \quad - \cup - \quad - \cup - \parallel$ H

πᾶσιν ὑμῖν λέγω λαμβάνειν τῶν ἐμῶν

$- \cup - \overline{\cup} - \cup -$

1195 χρημάτων νῦν ἔνδοθεν,

ia 3 cr

1062 καὶ τοῦτο τέθυχ᾽, †ὥστε τὰ κρέα ἔξεσθ᾽ ἁπαλὰ καὶ καλά.

4 cr

ἥκετ᾽ οὖν εἰς ἐμοῦ τήμερον· πρῷ δὲ χρὴ

lec

τοῦτο δρᾶν λελουμένους

5 ia

1065 αὑτούς τε καὶ τὰ παιδί᾽, εἶτ᾽

εἴσω βαδίζειν, μηδ᾽ ἐρέσθαι μηδένα,

lec

ἀλλὰ χωρεῖν ἄντικρυς

5 tro cat (3 tro + lec)

1070 ὥσπερ οἴκαδ᾽ εἰς ἑαυτῶν γεννικῶς, ὡς

ἡ θύρα κεκλήσεται.

6 tro cat (4 tro + lec)

εἰ δέ τῳ μὴ σῖτος ὑμῶν ἐστι, βόσκει δ᾽ οἰκέτας καὶ

1205 σμικρὰ πολλὰ παιδία,

4 cr

ἔστι παρ᾽ ἐμοῦ λαβεῖν πυρίδια λεπτὰ μέν,

ia 3 cr

1207 ὁ δ᾽ ἄρτος ἀπὸ χοίνικος ἰδεῖν μάλα νεανίας.

4 cr

ὅστις οὖν βούλεται τῶν πενήτων ἴτω

lec

εἰς ἐμοῦ σάκους ἔχων

$$- - \cup -\quad - - \cup -$$

καὶ μηδὲν οὕτως εὖ σεση-

$$- - \cup -\quad \underset{\smile}{-} - \cup -\quad \underset{\smile}{-} - \cup - \,||$$

μάνθαι τὸ μὴ οὐχὶ τοὺς ῥύπους ἀνασπάσαι,

$$- \cup - \underset{\smile}{-} - \cup - \,||$$

χἄττ᾽ ⟨ἂν⟩ ἔνδον ᾖ φορεῖν.

$$\overline{\smile\smile} \cup - -\quad - \cup - -\quad - \cup - -$$

1200   ὄψεται δ᾽ οὐδὲν σκοπῶν, εἰ μή τις ὑμῶν

$$- \cup \underset{\smile\smile}{\smile} \cup\quad - \cup \,\frown\!|||$$

ὀξύτερον ἐμοῦ βλέπει.

The arrival of the herald from Sparta (980) begins the dénouement, the
reconciliation of the two semi-choruses follows rapidly (1014–42), and
the united chorus frames the scene of reconciliation between Athens and
Sparta (1076–1188) with matching pairs of stanzas in which they tease
the audience. The song has no explicit connexion with the plot, but one
may perhaps sense beneath the humour a sour hint that the revelry of
comedy is illusory.

The thematic combination of trochaic and cretic continues, but the
iambic element (absent since 614ff. = 636ff.) reappears. In 1048 = 1062 =
1193 = 1207, resolution of the second long is used to harmonize iamb with
cretic ($\times - \cup \widetilde{}\quad - \cup \widetilde{}$ ...) in the same way as in 476 = 541. Failure
to recognize metrical pause at the end of 1046 = 1061 = 1092 =
1206 (revealed by *brevis in longo* in the last repetition) produces the
correspondence $- \cup - - = - \cup \widetilde{}$ (see, most recently, Zimmermann,
Untersuchungen, ii. 187–8, iii. 66, Henderson, 190). On the evidence of
the four repetitions taken together, the stanza divides into at least seven
verses: (1) 6 tr cat (2) 4 cr (3) ia + 3 cr (4) 4 cr (5) lec, 5 ia (6) lec
(7) 5 tro cat (3 tr, lec). Only 5 is at all problematic. It could be taken
as an uninterrupted sequence of seven trochees ending with catalexis,
which might be felt to harmonize with the (only slightly shorter)
trochaic sequences with which the stanza begins and ends. On the other
hand, (6) is certainly an independent lecythion, and the way in which
word-end consistently marks out another lecythion at the beginning of
(5) looks significant. After the reconciliation of the two semichoruses,

5 ia

1210 καὶ κωρύκους· ὡς λήψεται

πυρούς. ὁ Μανῆς δ' οὑμὸς αὐτοῖς ἐμβαλεῖ.

lec
πρὸς γε μέντοι τὴν θύραν

5 tro cat (3 tro + lec)
προαγορεύω μὴ βαδίζειν τὴν ἐμήν, ἀλλ'

1215 εὐλαβεῖσθαι τὴν κύνα.

the double cretic has given way to the lecythion as clausula: rhythmic normality has been restored.

At 1052, Coulon's deletion of πόλλ', understanding instead ἀργυρίδιον from 1051, is simple palaeographically: 'we have (money) at home, and we have wallets'. Burges's ὡς πλέα 'στιν ἄχομεν βαλλάντια makes good sense, but is harder to account for palaeographically. At 1056, ἂν is Sophianus' emendation for the MSS' ἄν. ⟨ἐτ'⟩ at 1061 is Reisig's supplement. The MS text would require the scansion ἔτ'νος which is unparalleled in Aristophanes. The first syllable of the word is definitely short at *Ach.* 246, *Knights* 1171, *Frogs* 62, *Ecc.* 845, *PCG* 419 and 514. It occupies an anceps position at *Ach.* 245 (ἐτνήρυσιν), *Birds* 78, and *Frogs* 63, 65, and 505. 1062 defies easy emendation. Palmer ingeniously conjectures ὥστε γεύσεσθ' ἁπαλὰ ... on the basis of the varient γενέσθ' found in Σ *vet.* R and in the text of C, a 16th-century copy of Vp2. τὰ κρέα can then be ejected as an interpolation or intrusive gloss.

The text of Γ ends at 1034, but 1043 ff. and 1058 ff. survive in BHVp2, as well as in R. 1189 ff. and 1203 ff. are preserved only in R, with a number of minor errors. ἐστί μοι at 1191 is Daubuz's correction of ἔστιν ἐμοί, and παισίν at 1193 Zanetti's for πᾶσιν. Bergler corrected κανηφορεῖ to κανηφορῇ in 1193. In 1199, ⟨ἂν⟩ was supplied by Bothe. In 1211, the metrically necessary transposition of αὐτοῖς οὑμὸς was made by Bentley, and προαγορεύω in 1214 is Biset's correction of προσαγορεύω.

1247–72

‒‒‒‒‒◡◡‒

ὅρμαόν τῷ κυρσανίῳ,

‒◡‒ ‒◡‒

[ὦ] Μναμόνα, τὰν τεὰν

‒◡‒◡ ‒◡‒◡ ‒◡‒‒

1249–50 Μῶάν, ἅτις οἶδεν ἁμὲ τώς τ' Ἀσαναί-

‒◡◡‒◡◡‒ ◡ ‒◡‒

    ως, ὅκα τοὶ μὲν ἐπ' Ἀρταμιτίῳ

‒◡‒◡ ‒◡‒

πρώκροον σιείκελοι

‒◡‒◡

1253a ποττὰ κᾶλα

‒‒ ‒◡‒‒

1253b τὼς Μήδως τ' ἐνίκων·

‒◡‒◡ ‒◡‒

ἁμὲ δ' αὖ Λεωνίδας

‒◡‒‒ ‒◡‒

1255 ἆγεν ᾇπερ τὼς κάπρως

‒ ‒◡◡‒◡◡‒◡◡‒

σάγοντας, οἰῶ, τὸν ὀδόντα· πολὺς δ'

‒◡‒ ⌒◡⌒ ‒◡‒

ἀμφὶ τὰς γένυας ἀφρὸς ἄνσεεν,

◡‒◡‒ ‒‒◡‒ ‒◡‿ ‖ ᴴ

πολὺς δ' ἁμᾶ [καὶ] καττῶν σκελῶν [ἄφρος] ἵετο.

‒‒ ‒◡‒ ◡‒‒

1260 ἦν γὰρ τῶνδρες οὐκ ἐλάσσως

‒‒‒ ‒‒‒ ‖ ᴴ

τὰς ψάμμας τοὶ Πέρσαι.

⌒◡‒‒ ‒◡⌒◡

ἀγροτέρα [Ἄρτεμι] σηροκτόνε, μόλε

pol

2 cr

3 tro

$\quad$ + D $\smile$ c

lec

tro

sp tro?

lec

lec

−D prol

$\quad$ + 3 cr

ia ia cr

sp cr ba?

mol mol

2 tro

‒ ∪ ‒   ⌒ ∪ ‒

δεῦρο, παρσένε σιά,

‒ ‒   ‒ ‒

ποττὰς σπονδάς,

‒ ∪ ∪   ‒ ∪ ∪   ‒ ∪ ∪   ‒ ‒

1265   ὡς συνέχῃς πολὺν ἁμὲ χρόνον. νῦν δ᾽

‒ ∪ ∪   ‒ ∪ ∪   ‒ ∪ ∪   ‒ ‒

αὖ φιλία τ᾽ ἀὲς εὔπορος εἴη

‒ ∪ ‒ ‒   ‒ ∪ ‒ ‒   ‒ ∪ ‒ ∪

ταῖσι συνθήκαισι, καὶ τᾶν αἱμυλᾶν ἀ-

‒ ∪ ‒ ‒   ‒ ∪ ‒ ⌣ ‖ ᴴ

λωπέκων παναίμεθα,

‒ ‒ ∪ ∪ ‒ ⌣ ‖ ᴴ

ὦ, δεῦρ᾽ ἴθι, δεῦρο,

‒ ∪ ‒ ∪   ‒ ∪ ⌣ ‖

1270   ὦ κυναγὲ παρσένε.

For the end of the play, Aristophanes contrives a change in the character of the lyric. In particular, the two 'Spartan' monodic hymns provide an opportunity for virtuosity and exoticism. There is little point in speculating on how far the songs are pastiche or parody, or on how the Athenian audience was intended to react.

The first song seems to be predominantly trochaic, with some iambic and dactylic. The first and penultimate cola are, formally, aeolo-choriambic, but neither features single short or short anceps. The sequences at 1251 and 1256 are most easily described by means of dactylo-epitrite symbols, but they lack typical dactylo-epitrite features: in 1251 the 'link' anceps is short, and in 1256 the prolonged dactylic phrase is followed either by a sequence of cretics with no ancipitia at all (for the fully-resolved cretic, see Introduction, p. 47), or, scanning ἀφρός, by ‒ ∪ ‒   ⌒ ∪ ‒ ∪   ‒ ∪ ‒ (cr tro cr), with resolution and, again, short anceps. 1265–6 could be seen in dactylo-epitrite terms as a pair of prolonged 'D' phrases linked and followed by long anceps. The verse is, however, most obviously analysed as a pair of dactylic tetrameters in synartesis.

2 cr

2 sp

da tetram

+ da tetram

5 tro cat (3 tro + lec)

reiz

lec

Our only surviving Spartan lyric poetry, that of Alcman, is upwards of two centuries earlier than Aristophanes, and these rambling astropha are structurally completely unlike the shapely stanzas of the Louvre partheneion (*GLP* 1). None the less, dactylic, trochaic, aeolo-choriambic, and lecythia feature together there as here. Also among the fragments of Alcman are some curious verses (*GLP* 14 (b), (c)) apparently of the form

$$- - \cup - \cup - \underset{\times}{-} - \cup - -$$

These are quoted by Priscian (*De metr. Terent.*, Keil iii. 428) as having been cited by Heliodorus in support of his theory that Simonides and Alcman admitted iambic metra of the form $\cup - - -$ in mid-verse. The theory itself is implausible, but it is tempting to wonder whether that type of rhythm, whatever it really was, may lie behind 1253b and 1260. In any case, sequences of three or more longs are a feature of this song.

The MSS (RBHVp2) show a persistent tendency to atticize, and I do not list corrections which do not affect metre or sense. τῷ κυρσανίῳ is a correction (variously attributed to Voss and Bergler), based on Σ *vet.* R, of τὼς κυρσανίως. For the scansion of the word, see 983. In 1248, ὦ was deleted by Wilamowitz. The form Μναμόνα is in R (Μναμοσύνα BHVp2), as is also τὰν τεὰν. τὰν τ' ἐμὰν in BHVp2 looks like an emendation designed to make some sort of sense of τὼς κυρσανίως. At 1252, σιείκελοι is Blaydes's emendation of the MSS' θείκελοι (Σ *vet.* R: θεοῖς ὅμοιοι προέκρουον). Wilamowitz's συείκελοι (cf. *Il.* 24. 253) is ingenious, but spoils the effect of the simile at 1255 ff. At 1257, Wilamowitz's ἄνσεεν for ἥνσει (ἥρσει Vp2) makes a sequence of 3 cretics. In

1279–94

⏒⏑⏒⏑ ⏒⟨⏑⟩⏒⏑

πρόσαγε χορόν, ἔπαγε ⟨δὲ⟩ Χάριτας,

⏒⏑⏒⏑ —⏑⏑‿ ||

1280 ἐπὶ δὲ κάλεσον Ἄρτεμιν,

⏒⏑⏒⏑ —⏑⏒⏑ —⏑‿ ||

ἐπὶ δὲ δίδυμον ἀγέχορον Ἰήιον

—⏑⏒⏑ —⏑‿ ||

εὔφρον', ἐπὶ δὲ Νύσιον,

—⏑⏑—⏑⏑—⏑⏑—⏑—

ὃς μετὰ μαινάσιν [βακχειο(ι)ς] ὄμμασι δαίεται,

⏒⏑⏒⏑ ⏒⏑⏒⏑

1285 Δία τε πυρὶ φλεγόμενον, ἐπὶ δὲ

⏒⏑⏒⏑ —⏑—

πότνιαν ἄλοχον ὀλβίαν·

—⏑⏑ —⏑⏑ —⏑⏑ —⏑⏑

εἶτα δὲ δαίμονας, οἷς ἐπιμάρτυσι

—⏑⏑—⏑⏑—⏑‿ ||

χρησόμεθ' οὐκ ἐπιλήσμοσιν

—⏑⏑ —⏑⏑ —⏑⏑ —⏑⏑

ἡσυχίας πέρι τῆς ἀγανόφρονος

—⏑⏑—⏑⏑—⏑‿ ||

1290 ἣν ἐπόησε θεὰ Κύπρις.

⏑⏒⏑— ——

ἀλαλαί, ἰὴ παιών.

1259, Bergk corrected ἅμα to ἁμᾶ, and Reisig καὶ κατὰ τῶν to καττῶν. Brunck deleted ἀφρός. Ἄρτεμι at 1262 was deleted by Dindorf. At 1266, τ᾿ is Schaefer's correction of δ᾿, and ἀὲς Burges's of αἰές. Hermann restored trochees in 1267 with ταῖσι συνθήκαισι for ταῖσιν συνθήκαις. The MSS make 1268–70 continuous by eliding α of παναΐμεθα (1268) and ο of the second δεῦρο (1269). *Scriptio plena*, and with it verse-end, was introduced by Thiersch at 1268 and by Bergk at 1269.

tro dim

lec

tro trim cat

lec

enopl

tro dim

lec

da tetram

ibyc

da tetram

ibyc

ia sp

$- - \smile - \,||\,$ ᴴ

αἴρεσθ’ ἄνω,
ἰαί

$- \smile \smile - - \,||\,$ ᴴ

ὡς ἐπὶ νίκῃ

ἰαί
εὐοῖ εὐοῖ, εὐαῖ εὐαῖ.

The Athenian song contrasts with the Spartan by its much higher proportion of short syllables, suggesting a lighter and faster rhythm. In the
absence of correspondence, there must be a degree of uncertainty about
text and colometry. None the less, it is not particularly difficult to analyse
the stanza into rhythmic phrases well attested in Greek metre. Lecythia
are clearly identifiable, and they are set in a context of highly resolved
trochaic. Enger's ⟨δέ⟩ in 1279 removes a serious metrical difficulty.
Without it, the colon is a fully resolved lecythion ($\overset{\frown}{\smile} \smile \overset{\frown}{\smile} \smile \overset{\frown}{\smile} \smile \overset{\frown}{\smile}$),
an extreme rarity. The only two possible examples elsewhere in drama
(*Cho.* 153 and *Phoen.* 1288 = 1299) are both in iambic contexts. With ⟨δέ⟩,
1279–80 becomes identical with 1285–6, which gives definition to the
first half of the stanza. 1284 is, in effect, a lengthened form of the ibycean
(cf. *PMG* 317(a). 3), foreshadowing the second half. 1287–90 could be
scanned as a single, long, dactylic sequence. However, the strong sense-
pause at the end of 1290 indicates verse-end, with the final syllable of
Κύπρις as *brevis in fine versus*. Both the incidence of word-end and the
symmetry of the pattern then combine to suggest that 1288 and 1290
are ibyceans. The combination of ibyceans with dactylic tetrameters
goes back to Ibycus himself (*PMG* 286, Introduction, p. 77). In
Aristophanes, ibyceans are also found at *Thesm.* 1136ff., where there is
dactylic in the context. This may reflect current metrical fashion (see
further below on *Thesm.* 1136 ff.). The scansion of the ritual cries which
close the stanza is altogether uncertain.

Recent discussions of this song have suffered from the wilful treatment of it by Dale (LM² 89–90), who fancied that she saw in it 'a dance
to a skipping three-time measure in which the first step is given double
the time of the second (as in Sir Roger de Coverley)'. The harm here lies
not so much in the invitation to imagine Aristophanes' chorus bouncing

ia

adon

round like an English school dancing-class as in giving that vision precedence over what observation and logic have taught us about Greek metre. There is indeed, as Dale observed, a tendency to trisyllabic groupings in the passage, not only in the resolved trochees (which is common, see Introduction, p. 38), but also in the dactyls. This is not, however, adequate reason for turning 1281–2 into a single verse of the form: ⌣⌣⌣⌣⌣ −⌣⌣⌣

−⌣⌣−⌣⌣⌣⌣−⌣⌣

Zimmermann (*Untersuchungen* , ii. 45–6, iii. 67) and Henderson, who accept this, analyse the second colon as two trochees, with double short for short in the first and for anceps in the second (− ⌢ − ⌣ ⌢ ⌣ − ⌢), which Dale herself stopped short of. Substitution of ⌣ ⌣ for ⌣ or × is occasionally found in the recitative trochees of comedy, but it is excluded from song (Introduction, p. 39). Of the examples adduced by Henderson (215–16), *Knights* 332 is an exceptional responsion of lecythion to glyconic (see further above, ad loc.), *Wasps* 407, and *Thesm.* 437 are corrupt, *Ecc.* 1177 is not trochaic, *Thesm.* 436 is at least dubious, and *Birds* 396 and the passages he adds from tetrameters are irrelevant, since they are recitative.

1279–94 survive in RBHVp2. At 1281, ἀγέχορον (ἠγέχορον Wilamowitz) was proposed by Hermann and Bergk for R's ἄγε χορὸν (ἄγετε χορὸν *rec.*). The emendation seems easy, but it should not be accepted without reserve. It is not impossible that ἄγε χορόν is derived from πρόσαγε χορόν at 1279. Enger proposed deleting the words and reading Ἤϊον (from epic ἤϊε Φοῖβε) which produces another lecythion ending with *brevis in fine versus*. In 1284, the unmetrical βάκχειος (R) or βακχείοις (BHVp2), which could well have been derived from a gloss, was deleted by Thiersch. Burges's βάκχιος would produce a still more

prolonged version of the ibycean. In 1285, ἐπὶ δέ was derived by
Thiersch from ἔπιδε (HVp2, ἔπιδε twice B). R has ἐπί τε. ἀγανό-

1296–1321

– ⏜ ⌣ –   ⌣ – ⌣ –   ⌣ – ⌣ ‖

Ταΰγετον αὖτ᾽ ἐραννὸν ἐκ λιπῶά

– ⏒ ⌣ ⟨⏜⟩   ⌣ – ⌣ –   ⌣ – –

Μῶά, μόλε, ⟨μόλε,⟩ Λάκαινα, πρεπτὸν ἁμὶν

⌣ – ⌣ ⏜   ⌣ – ⌣ –

κλέωά τὸν Ἀμύκλαις [Ἀπόλλω] σιὸν

– – ⌣ – ⌣ ⌣ –

1300 καὶ Χαλκίοικον Ἀσά-

–   – ⌣ ⌣ – ⌣ ⌣ –

ναν, Τυνδαρίδας τ᾽ ἀγασώς,

– – ⌣ –   – – ⌣ –

τοὶ δὴ παρ᾽ Εὐρώταν ψιάδ-

– – ⌣ ⌣ – – ‖ ᴴ

δοντ᾽. εἶα μάλ᾽ ἔμβη,

– – ⌣ –   ⌣ – ⌣ –

ὢ εἶα κοῦφα πᾶλον, ὡς

– – –   ⌣ – –

1305 Σπάρταν ὑμνίωμες·

– – ⌣ –   ⌣ – ⌣ –   ⌣ – ⌣ ⌣ ‖

τᾷ σιῶν χοροὶ μέλοντι καὶ ποδῶν κτύπος,

⟨⌣⟩ – ⌣ –   – – ⌣ –

1308 ⟨ὄχ᾽⟩ ἇτε πῶλοι ταὶ κόραι

– ⌣ –   – –

πὰρ τὸν Εὐρώταν

– – –   ⌣ ⏜ ⌣ –

1310 ἀμπάλλοντι πυκνὰ ποδοῖν

– ⌣ –   – –

ἀγκονίωαί

φρονος at 1289 was proposed by Reisig for the MSS' inappropriate μεγαλόφρονος.

        ia trim cat

        ia trim cat

        ia dim

        aeol heptasyll

           + – D

        ia dim

           + reiz

        ia dim

           + mol ba

        ia trim

        ia dim

        cr sp

        mol ia

        cr sp

–∪∪–   –––‖ ᴴ

ταὶ δὲ κόμαι σείονται

––––| ––––

1313 ᾇπερ Βακχᾶν θυρσαδδωᾶν

––––

καὶ παιδδωᾶν

––––   –––

ἀγῆται δ' ἁ Λήδας παῖς

––∪–   ∪–∪–

1315 ἀγνὰ χοραγὸς εὐπρεπής.

–⌢∪–   ∪–∪–   ∪⌢∪–   ∪––‖ ᴴ

ἀλλ' ἄγε κόμαν παραμπύκιδδε χερὶ ποδοῖν τε πάδη

–⌢∪–   ∪–∪–   ∪–∪–   ∪––

ᾇ τις ἔλαφος· κρότον δ' ἁμᾷ ποίη χορωφελήταν,

––∪–   ––∪–   ––∪–   ∪––

1320 καὶ τὰν σιὰν δ' αὖ τὰν κρατίσταν Χαλκίοικον ὕμνη,

––∪–

τὰν πάμμαχον . . .

In the second Spartan monody, text and metre are even more uncertain than in the first. It is, however, clear that iambic replaces trochaic as the basic metre. There is some aeolo-choriambic, and a short section (1313–14) in purely spondaic anapaests. The iambs of the song lead into catalectic tetrameters, still delivered by the Spartan, though perhaps in recitative.

In 1297, ⟨μόλε⟩ is Hermann's supplement. Valckenaer deleted Ἀπόλλω at 1299. At 1302–3, an alternative treatment is to read ψιάδδοντι with verse-end, so adding a spondee to the end of 1302. εἶα μάλ' ἔμβη would then be an adonean. At 1304, πᾶλον is Bergk's emendation of the MSS' πάλλων. Wilamowitz proposed to create a reizianum at 1305 by scanning ὑμνίωμες on the authority of Hephaestion (Cons. 6. 2 ff.), who quotes examples of vowels short before μν from Cratinus (*PCG* 162) and Epicharmus (Kaibel 91). At 1308, R offers αἴτε and B *rec.* ἄτε. Wilamowitz's ⟨ὄχ'⟩ with Brunck's ἆτε produces 'there . . . when arist dragged (cho mol)

an dim

an

an dim cat

ia dim

ia tetram cat

ia tetram cat

ia tetram cat

ia

like . . .'. Henderson's χᾷ τε (Enger χᾷτε), requiring ᾷ τε to do double duty as 'where' and 'like' (cf. Denniston, *Particles*, 523) seems very strained linguistically. Metrically, it produces a lecythion. At 1310, ἀμπάλλοντι has to be taken as intransitive (like uncompounded πάλλω). Coulon's ἀμπαδίοντι (Wilamowitz: -δέοντι) produces an iambic dimeter. The MSS make 1312–13 continuous by the dubious elision σείονθ' (-οντ' R). σειόνται, with metrical pause, was proposed by Thiersch. At 1316, the MS reading is παραμπυκίδδετε. Hermann restored the singular. He also provided χορωφελήταν in 1319 for χορωφελέταν (B *rec.*) or χοροφελέταν (R). It is perfectly possible to reduce 1320–1 to a plausible tetrameter (see Henderson, ad loc.), but, given the uncertainty surrounding the end of the play, there is no adequate case for doing so. The MS text as it stands makes sense, and is not unmetrical, but merely truncated.

*Thesmophoria*zusae

SYNOPSIS

101–29	Agathon (and chorus?): *Ionic, choriambic, iambo-choriambic, trochaic, dactylo-epitrite* (one iambelegus), *dactyls*, with *iambic* dimeter in synartesis, *aeolo-choriambic* clausula.
312–30	*Iambic, dactylic* (adonean).
352–71	*Iambic, ionic* (one dimeter), *choriambic, aeolo-choriambic.*
434–42 = 520–30	*Anapaestic* (one colon), *trochaic* (with ‿‿ for ×?).
459–65	*Trochaic* (with ‿‿ for ‿?).
663–6	*Trochaic.*
667–86	*Anapaestic, trochaic, dochmiac, iambic.*
700–1	*Dochmiac.*
707–25	Kinsman and chorus: *Anapaestic, trochaic, dochmiac, iambic.*
914–15	Kinsman: *Dochmiac.*
953–8	*Anapaestic* (one metron), *aeolo-choriambic, iambic.*
959–62 = 963–5	*Trochaeo-cretic.*
966–8	*Trochaeo-cretic.*
969–76 = 977–84	*Iambic, aeolo-choriambic* (two reiziana).
985–9	*Iambic, iambo-choriambic* (one aristophanean).
990–4 = 995–1000	*Aeolo-choriambic, iambic.*
1015–55	Kinsman: *Iambic, aeolo-choriambic, dactylo-epitrite, dochmiac, trochaic, dactylic.*
1136–59	*Enoplian* (ibycean), *aeolo-choriambic, iambic* (bacchiacs).

In its elaborate polymetry, *Thesm.* is more akin to *Birds* than to Aristophanes' other play of 411, *Lys.* Extended parody features prominently and repeatedly (101–29, 707–25, 1015–55), and here again *Thesm.* recalls

Birds and points forward to *Frogs*. Parts of the play are marked by the predominance, or significant presence, of particular metres. Again, however, *Thesm.* differs from *Lys.* in that changes of metre seem to have little structural function. The choice of metre reflects subject-mattter: trochaic for comment, dochmiacs for emotion, etc.

The lyric of *Thesm.* falls into three types. Most specifically comic are the two passages of extended parody, 101–29 and 1015–55, and these are performed by actors. These burlesques of avant-garde lyric are, as we should expect, metrically complex and problematic.

Throughout the central portion of the play, which extends from the opening of the women's assembly at 372 to the formal arrest of the Kinsman at 930–46, the songs spring directly from the action. The earlier, and calmer, songs are trochaic with a few anapaests, but as the excitement mounts after the discovery of the Kinsman (from 667 onwards) the anapaestic element increases, and dochmiacs are, predictably, introduced.

The third type of lyric is liturgical. Indeed, the first lyric of the play, the parody of Agathon, is a cult-song. The chorus, in their character as celebrants of the Thesmophoria, turn repeatedly to prayer and celebration of the gods. It is also symptomatic of their particular character that, like the Clouds, they maintain a certain dignity and decorum and sing no lampoon-song (note 962–4). Their first songs (312 ff. and 352 ff.) are endorsements of the prayers at the opening of the assembly, and here it is noticeable that, while the utterances of the Heraldess (especially 331–51) are burlesque, the songs of the chorus are not manifestly so. After the arrest of the Kinsman, the chorus punctuate the action with an extended sequence of cult-songs and dances (959–1000). Finally, at 1136, they interrupt, with seeming arbitrariness, the process of rescuing the Kinsman with their hymn to Athene and the goddesses of the Thesmophoria. An address to a divine patron (or patrons) of the chorus is common in parabasis-songs, but this play has no parabasis-song. Instead, the hymn which could appropriately have served that purpose has been, as it were, displaced to near the end of the play. In *Lys.*, the final songs are antiphonal Spartan and Athenian hymns, expressing the community of religion between Greeks. Here, the chorus's final act of worship is distinctively Athenian. The liturgical lyric of *Thesm.* tends to be more elaborate metrically than the songs directly related to the central action.

In particular, it includes aeolo-choriambic. The final hymn is highly unusual metrically, synthesizing, as it seems, features of the metrical styles of Anacreon and Ibycus (see below, ad loc.). It would be piquant if, after the parody of Agathon at the beginning of the play, this were Aristophanes' own experiment in the rhythms of 'the famous Ibycus and Anacreon of Teos' (161).

There is much non-corresponding lyric in *Thesm.*, at least as we have it, and this, together with the fact that the play survives only in R and a fifteenth-century copy of R, Mu2 (see above on *Lys.*), makes the text

101–29

⏑⏑‒　⏑⏑‒

ἱερὰν χθονίαις

‒⏑⏑‒　‒⏑⏑‒　‒⏑⏑‒⏑‒

δεξάμεναι λαμπάδα, κοῦραι, ξὺν ἐλευθέρᾳ

⏑⏔⏑‒　‒⏑⏑‒

πραπίδι χορεύσασθε βοάν.

⏑⏑‒⏑‒⏑‒‒

τίνι δαιμόνων ὁ κῶμος;

⏔⏑‒‒　‒⏑‒‒‖a.a.

105 λέγε νιν. εὐπ(ε)ίστως δὲ τοὐμὸν

‒⏔⏑‒⏑⏑‒

δαίμονας ἔχει σεβίσαι.

⏑⏑‒⏑‒⏑‒‒

†ἄγε νῦν ὅπλιζε Μοῦσα†

⏑⏑‒‒　⏑⏑‒‒

χρυσέων ῥύτορα τόξων

‒⏑⏑‒　‒⏑⏑‒‒

Φοῖβον, ὃς ἱδρύσατο χώρας

⏑⏔⏑‒⏑⏑‒

110 γύαλα Σιμουντίδι γᾷ.

‒⏑‒‒　‒⏑‒‒

χαῖρε καλλίσταις ἀοιδαῖς,

highly problematic and difficult. The third printed edition of the play (by B. Zanetti (Venice, 1538)) offers a number of useful corrections. The editions of Fritzsche (Leipzig, 1838) and Enger (Bonn, 1844) first brought modern metrical scholarship to bear on the text. Valuable treatments of a number of problems in the text are to be found in C. Austin, 'Textual Problems in Ar. *Thesm.*' *Dodone*, 16 (1987), 61–92, and 'Observations critiques sur les *Thesmophories* d'Aristophane', *Dodone*, 19 (1990), 9–29. References to these works in the commentary are given in the form 'Austin, *Dodone* 16' or '19', with page number.

ion dim sync

cho trim

ia cho dim

anac

tro dim

aeol heptasyll

anac

ion dim

cho dim cat

aeol heptasyll

tro dim

‒ ◡ ‒ ‒   ‒ ◡ ‒ ‒ || a.a.

Φοῖβ', ἐν εὐμούσοισι τιμαῖς

◡ ⌢ ‒ ◡ ◡ ‒

γέρας ἱερὸν προφέρων.

‒ ◡ ⌢ ◡   ⌢ ◡ ‒ ‿ || a.a.

τὰν τ' ἐν ὄρεσι δρυογόνοισι

◡ ‒ ◡ ‒   ◡ ‒ ◡ ◡ ‒ ◡ ◡ ‒

115–16 κόραν ἀείσατ' Ἄρτεμιν ἀγροτέραν.

◡ ◡ ‒ ‒ ‒ ◡ ‒ ‒

117   ἕπομαι κλῄζουσα σεμνὰν

◡ ◡ ‒ ‒ ‒ ◡ ‒ ‒

γόνον ὀλβίζουσα Λατοῦς,

‒ ⌢ ◡ ‒ ◡ ◡ ‒

Ἄρτεμιν ἀπειρολεχῆ.

‒ ‒ ◡ ‒ ◡ ◡ ⌢ ◡ ‒

120   Λατώ τε κρούματά τ' Ἀσίαδος

◡ ◡ ◡ ◡ ‒ ◡ ◡ ◡ ‒

†ποδὶ παράρυθμ' εὔρυθμα Φρυγίων

◡ ◡ ‒ ◡ ◡   ◡ ◡ ‒

122   διανεύματα Χαρίτων.

◡ ◡ ‒ ‒ ‒ ◡ ‒ ‒

σέβομαι Λατώ τ' ἄνασσαν

◡ ◡ ‒ ◡ ‒ ◡ ‒ ‒

κίθαρίν τε ματέρ' ὕμνων

‒ ⌢ ◡ ‒ ◡ ◡ ‒

125   ἄρσενι βοᾷ δοκίμων·

‒ ◡ ◡   ‒ ◡ ◡   ‒ ◡ ◡   ‒

τᾷ φάος ἔσσυτο δαιμονίοις

‒ ◡ ◡   ‒ ◡ ◡   ‒ ◡ ◡   ‒ ◡ ◡   ‒ ◡ ◡   ‒ ◡ ◡

ὄμμασιν, ὑμετέρας τε δι' αἰφνιδίου ὀπός. †ὧν χάριν

tro dim

aeol heptasyll

tro dim

iambel ($\smile$ e $\smile$ D)

anac

anac

aeol heptasyll

aeol enneasyll.

?

ion dim cat?

anac

anac

aeol heptasyll

da tetram cat (enopl? D prol?)

6 da

$$\cup - \cup - \quad \cup - -$$

ἄνακτ᾽ ἄγαλλε Φοῖβον [τιμᾷ].

$$- - \cup \cup - - - |||$$

χαῖρ᾽, ὄλβιε παῖ Λατοῦς.

The key to interpretation of this parody is lost, since we know nothing about Agathon's lyric. Not even fragments of it survive (if *TrGF* 39 F 31 = *PMG* 773 is lyric and Agathon's, it leaves us none the wiser). Moreover, since the song is astrophic, the received text can neither be relied on nor emended with confidence. Metrical analysis can only be tentative. Some ionic cola are clearly identifiable and a well-established way of dealing with the song (see especially White, *VGC* 189 and Schroeder, *AC* 58–9) is to force it as far as possible into ionic. The most systematic treatment of this kind is White's, which is also expounded with a degree of lucidity that betrays its weakness. In order to accommodate his analysis, White has to invent a special type of 'free ionic' not otherwise found in Aristophanes, or, indeed, anywhere else. The least strange feature of this 'free ionic' is the lavish use of resolution ($\cup \cup - \widehat{\cup\cup}$, $\cup \cup \widehat{\cup\cup} -$), which Euripides used sparingly and Aristophanes, otherwise, never. It *may* by that Agathon admitted frequent resolution in ionic, and it *may* be that in parodying him Aristophanes would have permitted it too, but this is entirely hypothetical. There is not a shred of independent evidence for it. I have tried a different approach. If one adopts minimal emendation and allows the song to divide more or less with the sense, certain recurrent phrases emerge, phrases which are, moreover, quite normal in Attic lyric. The resulting division may not be authentic, but it is relatively harmless in that it does not provide bogus 'parallels' which can be used to devastate the text elsewhere, and it does reveal patterns which are inherent in the words.

There are anacreontics at 104 and 124, and, at 117, 118 and 123, a variation on the anacreontic ($\cup \cup - - - - \cup - -$) which is found in Aeschylus and, just possibly, in Anacreon himself (Introduction, pp. 61–3). 108 is a standard ionic dimeter and 122 a catalectic dimeter with resolution (the only example in Aristophanes (Introduction, p. 62). Compare from late Euripides (later, of course, than *Thesm.*) *Ba.* 151:

ἅμα δ᾽ εὐάσμασι τοιάδ᾽ ἐπιβρέμει

$$\cup \cup - - \quad \cup \cup - \cup \cup \quad \cup \cup -$$

+ ia dim cat

tel dragged

The opening colon, 101, can also be compared wtih *Ba.* 64. There are five occurrences of $\times \overparen{\smile\smile} \smile - \smile \smile -$ (106, 110, 113, 119, 125), an aeolo-choriambic colon which stands in the same relation to the poly-schematist ($\cdots \cdots - \times - \smile \smile -$) as the telesillean ($\times - \smile \smile - \smile -$) to the glyconic ($\cdots \cdots - \smile \smile - \smile -$). Aristophanes uses it elsewhere in the later plays, but without resolution (Introduction, p. 74). 120 resolves the seventh position and adds the coda $\smile -$, so that $\times - \smile - \smile \smile -$ becomes $\times - \smile - \smile \smile \overparen{\smile\smile} \smile -$ (cf., possibly, *Pers.* 549=559). The song, then, is predominantly in the metres of the eastern Aegean, which is consistent with Agathon's association of himself with Ibycus, Anacreon, and Alcaeus at 160 ff. below.

There are also four trochaic dimeters (105, 111, 112, 114), and three of these (105, 112, and 114) must coincide with verse-end, since the following cola begin with anceps. This is a metrical rarity, but it would be rash to assume specific parody of Agathon, since the phenomenon is found elsewhere in Aristophanes as well as in surviving tragedy (Introduction, p. 39 and Parker in Craik, *'Owls to Athens'*, 332–7).

The song takes the form of a cult hymn in dialogue between a celebrant and a chorus of female worshippers. A fragment of such a song, generally attributed to Sappho (*PLF* 140), is in ionics, and belongs to the oriental cult of Adonis.

The problem remains of who the chorus are. Does Agathon himself take the role of chorus as well as celebrant (Σ *vet.* 101; cf. Muecke, *CQ* 32 (1982), 41–55)? Are the κοῦραι addressed human worshippers, or the Muses, as suggested by 41 (Wilamowitz, Austin, *Dodone* 16. 73)? The latter would be a nice literary conceit. For arguments in favour of the view that the imaginary chorus consists of Trojan maidens, see Sommerstein, ad loc.

For the nonsensical MS text of 107, Fritzsche combined Bentley's ὄλβιζε and Bergk's μούσᾳ to produce a fourth example of $\smile \smile - - - \smile - -$. I do not think that the abstract use of μοῦσα (song) in an address to the Muses (if that is what this is) would be intolerable in Aristophanes' pseudo-grand style. A plural imperative, however, seems desirable. Wilamowitz's ἄγετ' ὦ κλῄζετε Μοῦσαι (∪∪ – –   ∪∪ – –) provides one (and makes the addressees definitely the Muses), but at the expense of drastic rewriting. Austin would accept Gannon's ἄγε νῠν ὀλβίζε⟨τε⟩ Μοῦσαι (∪∪∪ – – ∪∪ – –). Metrically, this colon would be a pendent version of 106, 110, etc. (× – ∪ – ∪∪ – –), except that the reversed dodrans would take the form – × – ∪∪ –, as in the polyschematist it not infrequently does (Introduction, p. 71). But a complicating factor, both here and in the MS text of 105 (λέγε νυν) is the scansion of νυν. νῦν is found in tragedy (e.g. *Andr.* 91, *Hipp.* 952, *Ion* 1039, *Ba.* 1279), and this song is paratragic. There is, however, no other place in comedy where νυν is demonstrably short (two passages are cited by LSJ, but on Cratinus, *PCG* 151. 1, see Kassel–Austin, ad loc., and at *Clouds* 141, λέγε νυν ἐμοὶ scans ∪∪ – ∪ –; cf. *Knights* 1028 and many similar verses with other disyllabic imperatives). At 105, νιν was proposed by Meineke (it appears earlier as a misprint in Dindorf's edition). For MS confusion between νυν and νιν, compare *Med.* 1365. Apart from metre, 'Name him' (cf. *OC* 128 ἃς τρέμομεν λέγειν) seems more pointed here than 'Speak, then'.

The obelus at 121 indicates uncertainty, rather than conviction that the verse is extensively corrupt. Bothe's Ἀσίδος would remove the rare resolution from 120, but that is not necessary (Introduction, p. 72). Austin (*Dodone* 19. 16) accepts Fritzsche's διὰ νεύματα with White's ionic interpretation of 120–2:

$$\Lambda ατώ \ τε \ κρούματά \ τ' \ \mbox{Ἀσίαδος} \ ποδὶ$$
$$παράρυθμ' \ εὔρυθμα \ Φρυγίων$$
$$διὰ \ νεύματα \ Χαρίτων$$

– – ∪ –   ∪∪ –   ∪∪ – ∪∪

∪∪ – –   ∪∪ ⏜ –

∪∪ – ⏜   ∪∪ –

The syncopated metron (∪∪ –) neither preceded nor followed by word-end is highly unusual (Parker, *CQ* 26 (1976), 21) and the concentration of resolved ionic metra would be unique in Aristophanes (see above). There are also prosodic oddities. Ἀσίαδος is unparalleled in drama, and in Aristophanes the syllable -ρυθμ- in ῥυθμός and related words always falls, where scansion is certain, on short or anceps. The problem here, as elsewhere in the elaborate paradies of later Aristophanes, is that we do not know how outrageous the poet was prepared to be.

At 128, R again offers a singular imperative. Austin (cf. 107 above) suggests ἀγάλλε⟨τε⟩. Assuming that the colon begins with ἄνακτ᾽, this would again produce ⤬ – ◡ – ◡ ◡ – –, like Gannon's version of 107 (above). There are, however, other problems here. Both the MS text and Austin's version offer a run of dactyls ending in ◡ ◡ followed immediately by anceps. This is possible, but highly unusual (Introduction pp. 53–4). An alternative would be verse-end, with *brevis in longo* and the ibycean coda . . . – ◡ ◡ – ◡ – (see below on 1135ff.), followed by ὧν . . . Φοῖβον as a separate verse. Perhaps:

> ὄμμασιν, ὑμετέρας τε δι᾽ αἰφνιδίου ὀπός.
> ὧν χάριν ἄνακτ᾽
> ἄγαλλε⟨τε⟩ Φοῖβον

> – ◡ ◡ – ◡ ◡ – ◡ ◡ – ◡ ◡ – ◡ ◡ ‖
> – ◠ ◡ –
> ◡ – ◡ ◡ – –

It cannot be said that the iambic metron fits particularly well into the context. Note here the epic hiatus (digamma) at αἰφνιδίου ὀπός.

There are several less difficult textual points. In 103, πραπίδι is Wecklein's emendation of R's πατρίδι (which could, however, be retained if the 'chorus' are Trojan), and χορεύσασθε is an anonymous sixteenth-century correction of χορεύσασθαι. At 105, εὐπ⟨ε⟩ίστως was proposed by Reiske. At 115, Zanetti offers ἀείσατ᾽ for R's ἀείσαντ᾽. At 116, Fraenkel (*Beobachtungen*, 114) suggests that Aristophanes may have written ἕπομαι· κλῄζω δὲ σεμνὰν . . ., κλῄζουσα having come from ὀλβίζουσα below. At 125, δοκίμων is Schöne's emendation of δοκίμῳ, and at 126, φάος Burges's for φῶς. On Nietzsche's ὑμετέρας for ἡμετέρας (R) at 127, see Austin, *Dodone* 16. 74. τιμᾷ at 128 was excised, as a gloss, by Dindorf. Dindorf also corrected R's σεμνὸν to σεμνὰν at 117.

‿⏜‿‒ ‿‒‿‒
δεχόμεθα καὶ θεῶν γένος

‿⏜‿‒ ‿‒‒
λιτόμεθα ταῖσδ᾽ ἐπ᾽ εὐχαῖς

‿‒‿⏜ ‿‒‒
φανέντας ἐπιχαρῆναι.

‒‿‿‒‿‿‒‿‿‒
315 Ζεῦ μεγαλώνυμε χρυσολύρα

‿‒‿⏜ ‒‿‿‒
τε Δῆλον ὃς ἔχεις ἱεράν,

‒‿‒ ‿‒‿‒
καὶ σύ, παγκρατὲς κόρα

‒‒‿‒ ‿‒‿⏜
γλαυκῶπι χρυσόλογχε πόλιν

‒‒‿⏜ ‿‒‿‒ ‿‒⏝ ‖
οἰκοῦσα περιμάχητον, ἐλθὲ δεῦρο·

‒‿‿‒‿‿‒‿‿‒
320 καὶ πολυώνυμε θηροφόνη [παῖ],

‒‒‒‒‿‿‒‒
Λατοῦς χρυσώπιδος ἔρνος,

‿‿‒‿‿‒‿‿‒⏝ ‖
σύ τε, πόντιε σεμνὲ Πόσειδον

⏜‿‒
ἁλιμέδον,

‿‿‒‿‿‒‿‿‒⏝ ‖ ᴴ
προλιπὼν μυχὸν ἰχθυόεντα

‒‿‿‒‒
οἰστροδόνητον,)

‒‿‿‒‿‿‒‿‿‒
325 Νηρέος εἰναλίου τε κόραι

ia dim

ia dim cat

ia dim cat

enopl (D prol)

   + ia cho dim

lec

ia dim

ia trim cat

enopl (D prol)

an dim cat ($_\wedge$ da tetram or mol da dim?)

an dim cat ($_\wedge$ da tetr?)

cr

an dim cat ($_\wedge$ da tetr?)

an (da dim?)

enopl (D prol)

‒ ‒ ∪ ‒   ‒ ‒
Νύμφαι τ' ὀρείπλαγκτοι.

‒ ∪ ‒   ∪ ‒ ∪
χρυσέα δὲ φόρμιγξ

∪ ‒ ‒
ἰαχή-

‒ ∪ ∪ ‒ ‒
σειεν ἐπ' εὐχαῖς

‒ ∪ ∪ ‒ ∪ ∪ ‒   ‒   ‒ ∪ ∪ ‒ ∪ ∪ ‒   ‒
330 ἡμετέραις· τελέως δ' ἐκκλησιάσαιμεν Ἀθηνῶν

‒ ∪ ‒   ∪ ‒ ⌣ |||
εὐγενεῖς γυναῖκες.

The opening of the female assembly forms the (highly unorthodox) parodos. The cletic hymn with which the chorus follows the announcement of the Heraldess is of some metrical sophistication, although it is easier to see the pattern than to name the constituents. Iambic is diversified by single-long–double-short cola which do not quite fit into any standard classification. ‒ ∪ ∪ ‒ ∪ ∪ ‒ ∪ ∪ ‒ seems to occur at 315, 320, and 325. At 315, it is in synartesis with the following colon, which precludes the idea of a catalectic dactylic tetrameter. 320–1 could be run together as seven dactyls, while reading ὀρῐπλαγκτοι at 326 (Austin, *Dodone* 19. 21) makes 325–6 into a dactylic hexameter. But the spondaic fourth metron in both sequences seems odd and disruptive. ‒ ∪ ∪ ‒ ∪ ∪ ‒ ∪ ∪ ‒ is, perhaps, best seen as a prolongation of the dactylo-epitrite hemiepes (‒ ∪ ∪ ‒ ∪ ∪ ‒). This would be compatible with 330, a simple dactylo-epitrite verse (which could also be taken as a dactylic hexameter, but, again, with a disruptively placed spondee). 321–4 are puzzling. One obvious analysis would be anapaestic: three

352–71

∪ ‒ ∪ ‒   ∪ ⌢ ∪ ‒
ξυνευχόμεσθα τέλεα μὲν

∪ ‒ ∪ ⌢   ∪ ‒ ‒
πόλει, τέλεά τε δήμῳ

ia sp

ith

ba

+ adon

D–D–

ith

catalectic dimeters, with an intercalated cretic and a monometer at 324. But, given the presence of dactylo-epitrite in the context and the absence of the reversals of rhythm that characterize anapaests (Introduction, p. 55), it is tempting to take 320–1, 323 as acephalous dactylic tetrameters and 324 as a dimeter. Alternatively, the three longs that open 321 could be interpreted as a molossus, producing a pattern of imperfect alternation. Instead of mol da dim, ∧ da tetr‖ cr da dim, ∧ da tetr ‖, we have mol da dim, ∧ da tetr cr ∧ da tetr ‖ da dim. On the scansion of ἰαχήσειεν in 328, see on *Frogs* 216b, below.

At 312–14, Dindorf corrected δεχόμεσθα and λιτόμεσθα to δεχόμεθα, λιτόμεθα. At 320, R has θηροφόνε παῖ. θηροφόνη, with παῖ deleted, is Hermann's emendation. At 324, Wilamowitz introduced verse-end where R has ἰχθυόεντ᾽ οἰστροδόνητον. εἰναλίου at 325 is Bentley's correction of R's ἐναλίου, δὲ at 327 Blaydes's of τε, and Ἀθηνῶν at 330 Reisig's of Ἀθηναίων.

ia dim

ia dim cat

⏑ – ⏑ ⏔   ⏑ – –
τάδ' εὔγματ' ἀποτελεῖσθαι,

⏑ ⏑ – ⏑ – ⏑ – –
355 τὰ δ' ἄρισθ' ὅσαις προσήκει

– – ⏑ –
νικᾶν λεγού-

– ⏑ ⏑ –   – ⏑ ⏑ –   – ⏑ ⏑ –   – ⏑ ⏑ –
σαις· ὁπόσαι δ' ἐξαπατῶσιν παραβαίνουσί τε τοὺς

– – – ⏑ ⏑ – ⏑ –
ὅρκους τοὺς νενομισμένους

– – – ⏑ ⏑ – ⏑ – || ɥ
360 κερδῶν οὕνεκ' ἐπὶ βλάβῃ,

– – – ⏑ ⏑ – ⏑ –
ἢ ψηφίσματα καὶ νόμον

– – – ⏑ ⏑ – ⏑ –
ζητοῦσ' ἀντιμεθιστάναι,

– – – ⏑ ⏑ – ⏑ –
τἀπόρρητά τε τοῖσιν ἐ-

– – – ⏑ ⏑ – ⏑ –
χθροῖς τοῖς ἡμετέροις λέγουσ',

– – – ⏑ ⏑ – ⏑ –
365   ἢ Μήδους ἐπάγουσι †τῆς

– – – ⏑ ⏑ – ⏑ – || ɥ
χώρας οὕνεκ' ἐπὶ βλάβῃ,

ἀσεβοῦσιν ἀδικοῦσίν τε τὴν πόλιν.†

– –   – ⏑ –
ἀλλ', ὦ παγκρατὲς

– – ⏑ –   – – ⏑ –   – – ⏑ –   ⏑ – ⏑ –
370 Ζεῦ, ταῦτα κυρώσειας, ὥσθ' ἡμῖν θεοὺς παραστατεῖν,

– – ⏑ –   ⏑ – – |||
καίπερ γυναιξὶν οὔσαις.

ia dim cat

anac

ia

   + 4 cho

   + glyc

glyc

glyc

glyc

glyc

   + glyc

   + glyc

   + glyc

sp cr

ia tetram

ia dim cat

In a song which roughly balances 312–30 in length, without (for the most part) corresponding metrically, the chorus endorses the prayers of the Heraldess at 330–51. The metres are predominantly iambic and aeolo-choriambic. It is simpler to take 355 as an anacreontic than as an iambic dimeter with ‿ ‿ for × (Introduction, p. 33). The song opens and closes with iambic, but the two sequences are quite different in effect. The first reproduces the opening of the companion-song, 312 ff.: a full dimeter followed by a double clausular rhythm (see below on the text). The closing address to Zeus has an arresting introduction: a very heavily syncopated dimeter. Then follow four full metra followed by a single catalectic dimeter, producing a long build-up to the clausula. Long anceps predominates.

At 352, R has ξυνευχόμεθα and at 354 τάδ᾽ εὔγματα γενέσθαι. ξυνευχόμεσθα (Daubuz) is an easy correction (cf., in reverse, 312–13). At 353, τε is the reading of R (δὲ Mu2). For γενέσθαι at 354, Willems proposed ἀποτελεῖσθαι (cf. Plato, *Rep.* 4. 443b: τέλεον ἄρα ἡμῖν τὸ ἐνύπνιον ἀποτετέλεσται). R's reading is defended by Dale, who analyses:

$$\text{‿}-\widehat{=}\qquad\text{‿}\widehat{=}\,\text{‿}-$$
$$\text{‿}-\text{‿}\,\widehat{=}\qquad\text{‿}--$$
$$\text{‿}-\widehat{=}\qquad\text{‿}--$$

For resolution in bacchiacs she offers as parallel *Ach.* 1196, which is, however, clearly identified as ia cr ia by the context. Bacchiac with resolution is a rarity even in tragedy, and some examples are produced

434–42=520–30

$$------\,\text{‿}\,\|$$
οὔπω [τε] ταύτης ἤκουσα

$$\widehat{=}\,\text{‿}-\text{‿}\quad-\text{‿}-\text{‿}$$
435   πολυπλοκωτέρας γυναικὸς

$$-\text{‿}-\widehat{=}\quad-\text{‿}--$$
οὐδὲ δεινότερον λεγούσης.

$$-\text{‿}-\text{‿}\quad-\text{‿}-\text{‿}$$
437a   πάντα γὰρ λέγει δίκαια·

(like *Ach.* 1196) by rigid application of the dubious principle that resolution cannot precede a position suppressed by syncopation (e.g. *Trach.* 218, *Tro.* 319=335, *Hel.* 335). The best attested example is *Tro.* 564, which is preceded by a sequence of four ◡ – –   ◡ – ◡ –. Apart from the problem of resolved bacchiacs, there is a positive aesthetic case for correspondence between 312–14 and 352–5, the cola in which, in both songs, the chorus endorses the prayers of the Heraldess.

In 357, Hermann perfected the sequence of choriambs by adding ephelcystic ν to ἐξαπατῶσι. The hiatus at the end of 360, within a sequence of glyconics, is suspect (see above on *Peace* 860), nor is the repetition of . . . οὔνεκ᾽ ἐπὶ βλάβῃ at 366 at all plausible. An added problem in that colon is the meaning of τῆς χώρας οὔνεκ᾽. Austin's solution (*Dodone* 16. 77–8), deleting 360 and τῆς χώρας in 365–6, and reading there:

$$\text{ἢ Μήδους ἐπάγουσι τῶν}$$
$$\text{κερδῶν οὔνεκ᾽ ἐπὶ βλάβῃ}$$

$$– – – ◡ ◡ – ◡ –$$
$$– – – ◡ ◡ – ◡ –$$

is elegant and persuasive. He offers an alternative in *Dodone* 19. 21–2. 367 is difficult to emend with any confidence because it is not obvious what the metre ought to be. The hiatus after 366 indicates discontinuity. Bothe's ἀσεβοῦσ᾽ ἀδικοῦσί τε τὴν πόλιν (◡ ◡ – ◡ ◡ – ◡ ◡ – ◡ –) looks metrically like a shortened version of *Frogs* 1352.

       paroem
520 τουτὶ μέντοι θαυμαστόν,

          tro dim
    ὁπόθεν ηὑρέθη τὸ χρῆμα,

          tro dim
    χἤτις ἐξέθρεψε χώρα

          tro dim
    τήνδε τὴν θρασεῖαν οὕτω.

⏕ ⏑ – –   – ⏑ – –

437b †πάσας δ' εἰδέας ἐξήτασεν

⏕ ⏑ ⏕ ⏑   – ⏑ – –

πάντα δ' ἐβάστασεν φρενὶ πυκνῶς τε†

– ⏑ – ⏑   – ⏑ – ⏒

ποικίλους λόγους ἀνηῦρεν

– ⏑ – –   – ⏑ ⏖ ‖

εὖ διεζητημένους.

– ⏑ – ⏑   – ⏑ – –

440 ὥστ' ἄν εἰ λέγοι παρ' αὐτὴν

⏖ ⏑ – ⏑   – ⏑ – ⏒   – ⏑ – ⏒

Ξενοκλέης ὁ Καρκίνου, δοκεῖν ἄν αὐτόν,

⏕ ⏑ – – | – ⏑ – –

ὡς ἐγᾦμαι, πᾶσιν ὑμῖν

– ⏑ – –   – ⏑ – ‖‖‖

ἄντικρυς μηδὲν λέγειν.

The scene in the women's assembly is formally balanced, but without perfect symmetry. The strophe of this song follows the fifty-line speech of the First Woman. The antistrophe follows the fifty-four-line speech of the disguised Kinsman, and rounds off the scene. Between the two long speeches with their following choral songs, comes the short speech (sixteen lines) of the Second Woman and the short (non-corresponding) stanza (459ff.) in which the chorus registers its reaction. The songs are trochaic throughout, except for the anapaestic opening colon, 434=520. The recurrence of that striking opening rhythm at 520 will have alerted the audience to the arrival of the antistrophe of 434ff., and so to an important piece of dramatic punctuation. After the anapaestic opening, the song is simply constructed in two periods, each ending in catalexis. The first is of fourteen metra, and falls into dimeters. The second is of nine metra, and, except after 440=527, colon-division is much less clear. In spite of some coincidence of word-end and metron-end, 441–2=528–30 is probably best seen as an uninterrupted build-up to the clausula.

tro dim
τάδε γὰρ εἰπεῖν τὴν πανοῦργον

tro dim
525 κατὰ τὸ φανερὸν ὧδ᾽ ἀναιδῶς

tro dim
οὐκ ἂν ᾠόμην ἐν ἡμῖν

lec
οὐδὲ τολμῆσαί ποτ᾽ ἄν.

tro dim
527 ἀλλὰ πᾶν γένοιτ᾽ ἂν ἤδη.

tro trim
τὴν παροιμίαν δ᾽ ἐπαινῶ τὴν παλαιάν·

tro dim
ὑπὸ λίθῳ γὰρ παντί που χρὴ

lec
530 μὴ δάκῃ ῥήτωρ ἀθρεῖν.

At 434, τε (R, οὐπώποτε R²Mu2) was deleted by Dindorf. At 436, R's text offers a metrical rarity: ∪ ∪ for × (Introduction, p. 39). This could be removed by Hermann's δεινότερα, but the licence is, perhaps, tolerable in trochaic which approximates in its simplicity to recitative.

At 437–8, R's text is thoroughly garbled. The *Suda*'s (s. ἐβάστασεν) is equally unmetrical: πάσας δ᾽ ἰδέας ἐξήτασε πάντα δ᾽ ἐβάστασε φρενί, πυκνῶς τε ποικίλως λόγους ἀνεῦρεν. It is worth observing here that while the antistrophe, 520ff., is set out correctly as trochaic in R, the colometry of the strophe is wildly disordered:

```
− −(∪)∪ − −
− − ∪ ∪ ∪ ∪ − ∪ −
∪ − ∪ − ∪ − ∪ ∪ − ∪ − −
− ∪ − ∪ − ∪ − ∪ − − − ∪ −
− − ∪ − − ∪ ∪ − ∪ − ∪ ∪
∪ − ∪ − ∪ − ∪ −
∪ − ∪ − ∪ − − − ∪ −
− ∪ − ∪ − ∪ − − ∪ ∪ − ∪ − ∪ −
∪ − ∪ − ∪
− ∪ − − − ∪ − − − ∪ − − − ∪ −
```

It seems unlikely that a mere copyist could have turned a correctly divided text corresponding to 520ff. into that. An easier hypothesis is that the text received by the Alexandrian editor was already garbled, that he did not recognize correspondence with 520ff., but did the best he could on the assumption that the stanza was more or less iambic (Introduction, p. 104). R's colometry survived the editions of Brunck and Bekker. Correspondence was perceived by Hermann and Dindorf, but White

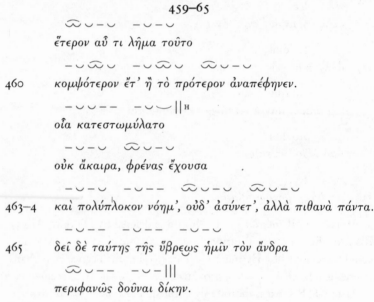

459–65

ἕτερον αὖ τι λῆμα τοῦτο

460   κομψότερον ἔτ᾽ ἢ τὸ πρότερον ἀναπέφηνεν.

οἷα κατεστωμύλατο

οὐκ ἄκαιρα, φρένας ἔχουσα

463–4   καὶ πολύπλοκον νόημ᾽, οὐδ᾽ ἀσύνετ᾽, ἀλλὰ πιθανὰ πάντα.

465   δεῖ δὲ ταύτης τῆς ὕβρεως ἡμῖν τὸν ἄνδρα

περιφανῶς δοῦναι δίκην.

The chorus expresses its appreciation of the Second Woman's speech in a simple trochaic stanza. The one metrical oddity is ◡◡ for ◡ in 461, the most convincing specimen in Aristophanes' lyric trochees, for at *Wasps* 406 there are strong non-metrical reasons for doubting the received text. Here, 461 could theoretically be taken as a choriambo-iambic dimeter, but such a colon would be alien to the trochaic context (Introduction, p. 39). Dobree proposed κἀστωμύλατο, but the καὶ seems to lack justification. Attempts to remove the lengthening by mute and liquid in πολύπλοκον (463) were made by Dobree (καί ⟨τι⟩) and Hermann (πολύστροφον). A cretic (καὶ πολύπλο-, ‒◡⌒) would seem out of place in this stanza, in which there is otherwise no syncopation, except at the catalectic clausula.

still refused to recognize it, and produced an extraordinary combination of iambic and trochaic, with repeated substitution of ◡ ◡ for × and ◡.

In the latter part of the strophe corruption is minor. At 440, παρ᾽ αὐτὴν is Zanetti's correction of R's παραυτῆς. At 441, Ξενοκλέης is Bentley's of ξενοκλῆς.

The antistrophe is free of serious corruption. Cobet corrected R's ἀλλ᾽ ἅπαν at 527 to ἀλλὰ πᾶν.

      tro dim

      tro trim

      lec?

      tro dim

      tro tetram

      tro trim

      lec

At 462, ἄκαιρα is Zanetti's correction of the MS ἄκερα.

Hermann propounded the idea that 459 ff. ought to correspond with 663 ff., suggesting that there must either be a lacuna between 664 and 665, or that 465 (δεῖ δὲ . . .) must be a mesode. Enger sought to establish correspondence by reading νόημα followed by verse-end at 463, emending 464 to οὐδ᾽ ἀσύνετα, πιθανὰ πάντα, and following Hermann in taking 465 (δεῖ . . . δίκην) as a mesode. This treatment was adopted by Schroeder. Enger also noted that, with the same modifications, the stanza itself could be seen as constructed to an A B A pattern: A tro dim, tro trim, lec; B tro dim, tro dim; A tro dim, tro trim, lec. This treatment is by no means compelling, but it stimulates reflection.

663–6

$$-\cup-\cup\quad-\cup-\cup$$

εἷα νῦν ἴχνευε καὶ μά-

$$-\cup\overparen{-\cup}-\quad-\cup-\cup\quad-\cup-\cup$$

663–4a   τευε ταχὺ πάντ᾿, εἰ τις ἐν τόποις ἑδραῖος

$$-\cup-\cup\quad-\cup-$$

664b   ἄλλος αὖ λέληθεν ὤν.

$$-\cup--\quad-\cup-\cup$$

665   πανταχῆ δὲ ῥῖψον ὄμμα,

$$-\cup-\cup\quad-\cup-\cup$$

καὶ τὰ τῆδε καὶ τὰ δεῦρο

$$-\cup-\cup\quad-\cup-\;|||$$

πάντ᾿ ἀνασκόπει καλῶς.

This simple trochaic stanza, marked off into two periods by catalexis in 664, follows the definitive unmasking of the Kinsman, and leads on to the next stage of the action, the search for other men and the parodic baby-snatching.

In the received text the first period (663–4) is one metron longer than the second. It is tempting (if not strictly necessary) to try to equalize the periods, to produce, in fact, a pair of short corresponding stanzas. Enger proposed to reduce the first period to match the second by deleting καὶ μάτευε, but the single imperative seems unrealistically concise for this kind of excited self-exhortation (cf. *Ach.* 203–4, *Knights* 251–2, *Birds*

667–86

$$----\quad-\cup\cup\cup\cup$$

ἢν γὰρ ληφθῆ δράσας ἀνόσια,

$$--\cup\cup-\quad----$$

δώσει τε δίκην καὶ πρὸς τούτῳ

$$----\quad\cup\cup--$$

τοῖς ἄλλοις ἀνδράσιν ἔσται

5 tro

lec

tro dim

tro dim

lec

344–6). The alternative of expanding the second period is achieved by Kaibel's supplement in 666: καὶ τὰ τῆδε ⟨καὶ τὰ κεῖσε⟩ (cf. *Birds* 425), which may also be desirable on grounds of sense.

On attempts to make 663 ff. and 459 ff. correspond, see above on 459 ff.

At 664a, τόποις comes from R² (also Mu2). R has τούτοις. Blaydes's cumbersome attempt to accommodate both readings by ἐν ⟨τούτοισι τοῖς⟩ τόποις adds a metron and increases the disparity between the first and second parts of the stanza. At 665, δὲ ῥῖψον is Hermann's correction of R's διάρριψον.

an dim

an dim

an dim cat

670   παράδειγμ' ὕβρεως

ἀδίκων τ' ἔργων ἀθέων τε τρόπων·

φήσει δ' εἶναί τε θεοὺς φανερῶς,

δείξει τ' ἤδη

πᾶσιν ἀνθρώποις σεβίζειν δαίμονας

675   δικαίως τ' †ἐφέποντας† ὅσια καὶ νόμιμα

μηδομένους ποιεῖν ὅ τι καλῶς ἔχει.

κἄν μὴ ποιῶσι ταῦτα τοιάδ' ἔσται·

αὐτῶν ὅταν ληφθῇ τις †ὅσια δρῶν†

680–2   μανίαις φλέγων λύσσῃ παράκοπος εἴ τι δρῴη πᾶσιν

                                 [ἐμφανὴς ὁρᾶν

ἔσται γυναιξὶ καὶ βροτοῖς

ὅτι τὰ παράνομα τὰ τ' ἀνόσια

685–6   θεὸς †ἀποτίνεται· παραχρῆμά τε τίνεται† |||

The short and simple trochaic song, 663–6, is followed immediately by this much more complicated stanza, which combines anapaestic, trochaic, dochmiac, and iambic. The two facts of general importance

an

an dim

an dim

an

tro trim cat

2 δ (?)

2 δ

ia trim cat

2 ia . . .

5 ia

2 ia

2 ia

δ . . .

about the stanza are that it is quite heavily corrupt and that it has a strong resemblance to 707–25. This later song marks the climax of action and emotion in the baby-snatching scene. The seven opening cola (667–73 and 707–13) are in pure anapaests and can be made to correspond fully (on the text, see below on 707 ff.). Thereafter, the songs run metrically as follows:

	674–86		714–25
	tro trim cat		tro tetram cat
675	2 δ	715	2 δ
	2 δ		2 δ
	ia trim cat		ia trim cat
	2 ia + ?		ia tetram
680	5 ia	720	ia dim
	ia dim		δ
	ia dim		tro tetram
	δ + ?	725	3 δ

Substantial re-writings of 667 ff. by Reisig, Fritzsche, and Hermann are clearly laid out in Enger's commentary. The case for battering the two stanzas into perfect correspondence is not, however, compelling. While 667 ff. is sung by the chorus alone, 707 ff. is a dialogue between the Kinsman and the chorus, and there, it will be seen, the changes of metre between trochaic, iambic, and dochmiac look significant. The opening anapaests, which, except for the consecutive double shorts in the first colon, are of recitative rather than lyric type (Introduction, p. 57), seem to suit the resolute tone of 667–73 better than the excited exchange of 707–13. It may be that while, for structural reasons, Aristophanes made the second stanza reminiscent of the first, he also chose, in the interests of dramatic expressiveness, to allow himself a degree of freedom from

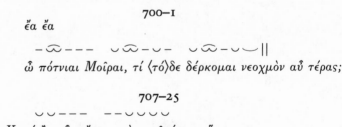

700–1

ἔα ἔα

‒ ⌒ ‒ ‒ ‒   ∪ ⌒ ‒ ∪ ‒   ∪ ⌒ ‒ ∪ ‿ ||

ὦ πότνιαι Μοῖραι, τί ⟨τό⟩δε δέρκομαι νεοχμὸν αὖ τέρας;

707–25

∪ ∪ ‒ ‒ ‒   ‒ ‒ ∪ ∪ ∪

Χ. τί ἂν οὖν εἴποι πρὸς ταῦτά τις, ὅτε

‒ ‒ ∪ ∪ ‒   ∪ ∪ ‒ ‒ ‒

τοιαῦτα ποιῶν ὅδ' ἀναισχυντεῖ;

strict responsion. Such a technical experiment would not be out of place in this play.

In 667, ἦν γὰρ ληφθῇ is Reisig's emendation of R's ἦν γὰρ μὴ λάθῃ, which is silly as well as unmetrical. Bergk's ἦν γὰρ με λάθῃ, corrects the metre, but does little for the sense ('For if he commits impious deeds unobserved by me, he shall be punished . . .'). At 669, ἀνδράσιν is Beer's correction. R has ἅπασιν ἅπασιν ἔσται, with the second ἅπασιν crossed out. At 675, Hermann's ἐφέπειν is simple and attractive, except that it produces a dochmiac with ‿ ‿ for the second ×. The only parallel for this in Aristophanes is *Birds* 430 (Introduction, p. 69). At 679, Hermann's ἀνόσιόν τι δρῶν for the corrupt ὅσια δρῶν would complete a full iambic, and Burges's ὅσια ⟨μὴ⟩ δρῶν a catalectic trimeter, but there can be no certainty here. The passage as it stands seems rambling and prolix, and δρῶν in 679 followed by εἴ τι δρώῃ in 681 is infelicitous. For the rare substitution of ‿ ‿ for × in lyric iambic in 680, see Introduction, p. 33. Von Velsen reads ἢ μανίαις making, with φλέγων, a dochmiac. In 681, ἔσται is Bothe's correction of ἐστὶν, and γυναιξὶ Brunck's of γυναιξὶν.

At 685, R has ἀποτίνεται on a line by itself, above παραχρῆμά τε τίνεται, suggesting a mistake in copying what was in its source a correction above the line (see Rogers, Appendix 209, and Wilamowitz, *GV* 591). Hermann's θεὸς παραχρῆμ' ἀποτίνεται (‿ – ‿ ‿ – ‿ ⌢ ‿ –) seems simple and attractive, but involves creating by emendation an example of ‿ ‿ for ‿, for which there is no secure parallel in Aristophanes' lyric iambic (Introduction, p. 33). We do not know how much is missing from the text here.

3 δ

an dim

an dim

–––– ‿‿––‖ʜ

Κ. κοὖπω μέντοι γε πέπαυμαι.

–––– ‿‿–‿

710   Χ. ἀλλ᾽ οὖν ἥκεις γ᾽ ὅθεν ἥκεις.

––‿‿– –––

φαύλως δ᾽ ἀποδρὰς οὐ λέξεις

–––– ‿‿–––

οἷον δράσας διέδυς ἔργον,

––‿‿–

λήψει δὲ κακόν.

–‿–– –‿–‿ –‿–‿ –‿–

Κ. τοῦτο μέντοι μὴ γένοιτο μηδαμῶς, ἀπεύχομαι.

‿––‿– –⁓–‿–

715   Χ. τίς ἄν σοι, τίς ἂν σύμμαχος ἐκ θεῶν

–⁓––– ‿⁓–––

ἀθανάτων ἔλθοι ξὺν ἀδίκοις ἔργοις;

‿–‿– ‿–‿– ‿––‖ʜ

Κ. μάτην λαλεῖτε· τήνδ᾽ ἐγὼ‿οὐκ ἀφήσω.

––‿– ‿–‿– ––‿– ‿–‿–

Χ. ἀλλ᾽ οὐ μὰ τὼ θεὼ τάχ᾽ οὐ χαίρων ἴσως ἐνυβριεῖς

‿–‿– –|⁓‿–

720   λόγους τε λέξεις ἀνοσίους

‿⁓–––

⟨ἐπ᾽⟩ ἀθέοις ἔργοις.

–‿–‿ –‿–‿ –‿–‿ –‿–‿‿‖

⟨καὶ⟩ γὰρ ἀνταμειψόμεσθά σ᾽ ὥσπερ εἰκὸς ἀντὶ τῶνδε.

‿⁓⁓‿– ‿⁓⁓‿⁓ ‿⁓–‿–‖‖

724–5   τάχα δὲ [σε] μεταβαλοῦσ᾽ ἐπὶ κακὸν ἑτερότροπος ἐπέχει
         [τις] τύχη.

At 700–1, the chorus respond to the baby-snatching with a horrified cry in dochmiacs. Then follows a short dialogue between chorus and

an dim cat

an dim cat

an dim cat

an dim

an

tro tetram cat

2 δ

2 δ

ia trim cat

ia tetram

ia dim

δ

tro tetram

3 δ

Kinsman in catalectic trochaic tetrameters, leading up to the lyric stanza which resembles, if it does not actually correspond with, 667 ff. (see below on the text). It has already been remarked that the anapaestic opening seems rhythmically better suited to 668–73 than to 707–13. In the paratragic action that accompanies this song, the dochmiacs come into their own, and it is significant that they are used only by the chorus. The Kinsman utters a catalectic trochaic tetrameter and a catalectic iambic trimeter, rhythms much more akin to recitative or speech. This is a variation on the type of dialogue found in tragedy where a relatively calm character responds to a highly agitated character who uses the typical metre of agitation, dochmiacs. See, for example, *Sept.* 686–711, *OT* 1328–68. As the preceding examples show, either party to the exchange may be the chorus. In addition to parody in action, there may also be parody here in words and metre of Euripides' *Telephus* (see Rau, *Paratragodia*, 48, Austin, *Dodone* 19. 23). Certainly, the highly resolved dochmiacs (indicative, one supposes, of a climax of rage) in 725 are forms particularly favoured by Euripides (Introduction, p. 65).

In 700, ⟨τό⟩δε is Dobree's correction.

At 710–11, I print the nearest passable approximation to the MS text, but without conviction. ἥκεις γ' in 710 is the *Suda*'s reading (ἥκεις τ' R). The passage has been explained by Bentley and others (see Austin *Dodone* 19. 25) as meaning 'I neither know nor care where you have come from, but you will not easily escape and say . . .'. This requires an adversative in the second clause, hence Boissonade's φαύλως δ' for the MS φαύλως τ'. The meaning posited for ἥκεις γ' ὅθεν ἥκεις is not really paralleled by such euphemistic expressions as ἱκόμην ἵν' ἱκόμην (*OC* 273), but Willems's ἥκων γ' ὅθεν ἥκεις is no improvement, although it has enjoyed some success with editors (Coulon, Gannon). 'Having returned to the place you came from' requires the chorus to assume that the Kinsman will get away, whereas the threat 'You will not easily escape' means 'You will not escape'. It is worth noting that the author of the *Suda* (s. ἥκεις) interpreted the text before him quite dif-

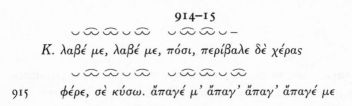

914–15

∪ ⌢ ⌢ ∪ ⌢   ∪ ⌢ ⌢ ∪ –

Κ. λαβέ με, λαβέ με, πόσι, περίβαλε δὲ χέρας

∪ ⌢ ⌢ ∪ ⌢   ∪ ⌢ ⌢ ∪ ⌢

915   φέρε, σὲ κύσω. ἄπαγέ μ' ἄπαγ' ἄπαγ' ἄπαγέ με

ferently: ἥκεις, φησίν, εἰς τὰς χεῖρας ἡμῶν, ὅθεν οὐ φεύξῃ. Reisig proposed:

> ἀλλ' οὖν ἥκεις
> ὅθεν οὐ φαύλως γ' ἀποδρὰς λέξεις ...

With γ' following ἥκεις, this was accepted by Meineke and Hall–Geldart. The proposal has significant merits. It makes the chorus say what, even without the *Suda*, we should expect them to say. It places οὐ more naturally (cf. *Ach.* 214–15 οὐκ ἂν ... ὧδε φαύλως ... ἐξέφυγεν). Finally, and interestingly, it makes 707–13 correspond metrically with 667–73.

720–2 present another problem. In the text I have adopted, ⟨ἐπ'⟩ is Enger's supplement, and ⟨καὶ⟩ Hermann's. Austin (*Dodone* 19. 25–6) places a stop after ἀνοσίους and accepts Burges's transposition γὰρ ἔργοις to give the following:

> ἀθέοις γὰρ ἔργοις ἀνταμει-
> ψόμεσθά σ', ὥσπερ εἰκός, ἀντὶ τῶνδε

⌒ – ∪ –   – – ∪ –
∪ – ∪ –   ∪ – ∪ –   ∪ – ∪ ||

But the substitution of double short for anceps in iambic is so rare that one should hesitate to introduce it by emendation (Introduction, p. 33). More subjectively, an announcement by the chorus of intent to commit 'godless deeds' strikes me as implausible, rather than comic. Under the *lex talionis* the gods are deemed to be on the side of the avenger: *you* perpetrate godless deeds, *I* exact just vengeance.

Other emendations are minor. At 715, τίς ἄν σοι is (according to Meineke) Brunck's correction of τίς οὖν σοι, and ἐνυβρίεις at 719 is Reisig's of ἐνυβρίσεις. Fritzsche deleted σε in 724, and ἑτερότροπος is Blaydes's emendation of ἑτερότροπον. At the end of the same line, τύχη is Bergk's emendation. R has the unmetrical τις τύχη.

2 δ

2 δ

In *Hel.* 625 ff., the Euripidean original that Aristophanes parodies at 869–919, Helen expresses her ecstatic joy in dochmiacs, while Menelaus, as becomes a man, keeps to spoken trimeters (See on 707 ff. above, and on *Clouds* 1154 ff.). Aristophanes' 'Helen' is allowed just this one burst of dochmiacs, in which the characteristic Euripidean repetitions (*Hel.* 640, 650–1, 664, 670, 684) and runs of short syllables are grossly parodied,

953–8

‒ ‒ ‒ ‒

ὅρμα, χώρει,

‒ ᴗ ⌢　ᴗ‒ᴗ‒

κοῦφα ποσὶν ἄγ᾽ ἐς κύκλον,

‒ᴗᴗ‒ᴗ‒‒

955　χειρὶ σύναπτε χεῖρα,

†ῥυθμὸν χορείας ὕπαγε πᾶσα†

‒ᴗ‒ᴗᴗ‒ᴗ‒

βαῖνε καρπαλίμοιν ποδοῖν·

ᴗ‒ᴗ‒　ᴗ‒ᴗ‒

ἐπισκοπεῖν δὲ πανταχῇ

ᴗ‒ᴗ‒　ᴗ‒ᴗ‒　ᴗ‒ᴗ⌣ |||

κυκλοῦσαν ὄμμα χρὴ χοροῦ κατάστασιν

Between the Kinsman's departure with the Magistrate at 946 and his return, with the Archer, to the pillory, at 1000, the chorus performs an elaborate cult-song and dance. The best treatment of the structure is that of Enger:

947–52	anapaests
953–8	proode
959–62 = 963–5	strophic pair
966–8	mesode
969–76 = 977–84	strophic pair
985–9	mesode
990–4 = 995–1000	strophic pair

even when in the original passage one might suspect Euripides of parodying himself. 915 leads, without metrical pause, into iambic trimeters.

At 914, περίβαλε is Biset's correction of R's περίβαλλε. At 915, the correption κύσω. ἄπαγε is harsh, and unusual in dochmiacs, but, unlike 1028 below, it is not easily removed (Introduction, p. 92).

an

lec

arist

glyc

ia dim

ia trim

Enger points out the programmatic function of the mesodes: the chorus precedes each strophic pair with an exhortation to itself to change the dance-movement. Fritzsche noted the similarities of sound between the end of the proode and that of the first mesode:

958: κυκλοῦσαν ὄμμα χρὴ χοροῦ κατάστασιν
968: πρῶτον εὐκύκλου χορείας εὐφυᾶ στῆσαι βάσιν

953 opens impressively with a sequence of four longs. For an anapaestic opening (even more emphatically spondaic) to a stanza which contains no other anapaests, compare 434 ff. = 520 ff. The rest of the stanza seems to fall naturally into iambic and choriambic cola, leaving only an intractable residue at 956, which as it stands, scans ⏑–⏑––⏑⏑⏑–⏑. R sets out 955–6 as

χειρὶ σύναπτε χεῖρα, ῥυθμὸν χορείας
ὕπαγε πᾶσα· βαῖνε καρπαλίμοιν ποδοῖν

‒ ◡ ◡ ‒ ◡ ‒ ‒ ◡ ‒ ◡ ‒ ‒

◡ ◡ ◡ ‒ ◡ ‒ ◡ ‒ ◡ ◡ ‒ ◡ ‒

and this division is confirmed by *P. Oxy.* 3839 of the 2nd–3rd century.
The division that I offer, without strong conviction, is based on this. At
least it avoids the concatenation of solecisms produced by the 'trochaic'
colometry found in Rogers's edition, and, apparently, accepted by Dale
(LM² 91):

χειρὶ σύναπτε χεῖρα, ῥυθ-
μὸν χορείας ὕπαγε πᾶσα

‒ ◡ ◡ ‒ ◡   ‒ ◡ ‒

‒ ◡ ‒ ‒   ⌒ ◡ ‒ ◡

χεῖρᾰ ῥῡθμ- is dubious prosody (see on 121 above, and on *Wasps*
1066). In addition, we have to accept ◡ ◡ substituted for ◡ *and* split by
word-end (χειρὶ | σύναπτε), as well as a catalectic colon in synartesis
with the following colon.

Schroeder sought to avoid the split substitution by reading χερὶ

959–62=963–5

⌣ ◡ ‒

ἅμα δὲ καὶ

⌣ ◡ ‒ ◡   ‒ ◡ ‒

960   γένος Ὀλυμπίων θεῶν

⌣ ◡ ‒ ◡   ‒ ◡ ‒ ◡| ‒ ◡ ⌣ ◡   ‒ ◡ ‒|||

μέλπε καὶ γέραιρε φωνῇ πᾶσα χορομανεῖ τρόπῳ.

966–8

‒ ◡ ‒ ||ʜ

ἀλλὰ χρή

‒ ◡ ‒ ◡   ‒ ◡ ‒ ‒

967   ὡς πρὸς ἔργον αὖ τι καινὸν

‒ ◡ ‒ ◡   ‒ ◡ ‒ ‒| ‒ ◡ ‒ ‒   ‒ ◡ ‒|||

πρῶτον εὐκύκλου χορείας εὐφυᾶ στῆσαι βάσιν.

σύναπτε (࿇ | ◡ – ◡), but the other oddities remain. The analysis cho ia dim + tro dim produces reversal of rhythm from iambic to trochaic without intervening word-end (Introduction, p. 35). The prize for ineptitude in dealing with this stanza, must, however, go to Wilamowitz (*GV* 475 n. 2). His 'schöne Trochäen, die sich sogar in Tetrameter abteilen lassen' produce a 'trochee' of the form – – – – (ὅρμα, χώρει), a split resolution (χέρ᾽ ⟨ἱερᾶς⟩ ῥυ- ࿇◡ – ◡) and ◡ ◡ for × (βαῖνε καρπαλί- – ◡ – ◡ ◡). They are also both metrically and rhetorically shapeless. The prudent course is to allow the song to fall into what seems to be its natural division. We do not have the information to decide whether that division is actually correct, nor, if it is, what has happened to 956. It can be said that there is no reason to eliminate aeolochoriambic here (it reappears later at 985–9 and 990–1000), nor to introduce trochees. Further, χειρ- forms in Aristophanes are far more common than χερ-forms (52 to 7); initial ῥ tends to 'make position', and υ in ῥυθμός and its cognates is not demonstrably long elsewhere in Aristophanes (see above on 101–29). Dr Austin has suggested to me the transposition ῥυθμὸν χορείας πᾶσ᾽ ὕπαγε (◡ – ◡ – – – ◡ ࿇ ia dim; cf. 970), which is both simple and possible.

cr
εἰ δέ τις

+ lec
προσδοκᾷ κακῶς ἐρεῖν

tro tetram cat

965   ἐν ἱερῷ γυναῖκά μ᾽ οὖσαν ἄνδρας, οὐκ ὀρθῶς φρονεῖ.

cr

tro dim

tro tetram cat

The evident similarity of these three trochaic stanzas constitutes a temptation to see them all as corresponding. However, the initial cretic is in synartesis with the following lecythion at 959–60, whereas in 966 hiatus after χρή indicates verse-end. The second colon of the stanza

$$969\text{–}76=977\text{–}84$$

∪ – ∪ ⌢   ∪ – ∪ –
πρόβαινε ποσὶ τὸν Εὐλύραν

– – ∪ –   – – ∪ ⌣
970   μέλπουσα καὶ τὴν τοξοφόρον

⌣ ⌢ ∪ –   ∪ – –
Ἄρτεμιν, ἄνασσαν ἁγνήν.

– – ∪ ∪ – ⌣ ||ᴴ
χαῖρ᾽, ὦ Ἑκάεργε,

∪ – ∪ ∪ – –
ὄπαζε δὲ νίκην.

– – ∪ –   ∪ – –
Ἥραν τε τὴν τελείαν

⌣ – ∪ –   ∪ – ⌣ ||
μέλψωμεν ὥσπερ εἰκός,

– – ∪ –   ∪ – ∪ –   ⌣ – ∪ –   – – ∪ –   ∪ – – |||
975–6   ἢ πᾶσι τοῖς χοροῖσιν ἐμπαίζει τε καὶ κλῇδας γάμου
[φυλάττει.

This simple stanza falls into four sections: six iambs with catalexis, two reiziana, two catalectic iambic dimeters, five iambs with catalexis. In the strophe, the two aeolo-choriambic cola, the one departure from iambic, embody the prayer to Apollo for victory. For the inset prayer in contrasting rhythm, compare 1144 below, and see on *Knights* 551 ff. = 581 ff. It is striking that the greeting to the god is marked off from the prayer by verse-end. When the pair of reiziana recur in the antistrophe, how-

at 967 also diverges from 960=964 (full trochaic dimeter instead of lecythion). Both facts lend support to Enger's identification of 966–8 as a mesode (see above on 953–68).

In 967, ὡς πρὸς is Austin's correction of R's ὥσπερ (*Dodone* 16. 84).

ia dim
Ἑρμῆν τε νόμιον ἄντομαι

ia dim
καὶ Πᾶνα καὶ Νύμφας φίλας

ia dim cat
ἐπιγελάσαι προθύμως

reiz
980   ταῖς ἡμετέραισ⟨ι⟩

reiz
χαρέντα χορείαις.

ia dim cat
ἔξαιρε δὴ προθύμως

ia dim cat
982   διπλῆν χάριν χορείας.

4 ia ba
983–4   παίσωμεν, ὦ γυναῖκες, οἷάπερ νόμος· νηστεύομεν δὲ
                                                   [πάντως.

ever, they carry no such significance. The hiatus (digamma) in ὦ Ἑκάεργε follows Homeric practice (e.g. *Il.* 1. 479, 7. 34, etc.).

For 969 R has πρόβαινε ποσὶν τὸν ἐλύραν. ποσὶ is Bothe's emendation, Εὐλύραν Zanetti's. At 980, ἡμετέραισι is Hermann's correction of R's ἡμετέραις. In 982, the change of χαίρειν (R) to χάριν is Ellebodius'. In 984, Bentley corrected R's νηστεύωμεν to νηστεύομεν.

985–9

‒‒◡‒   ◡‒◡‒   ◡‒◡◡‒ ‖

985 ἀλλ' εἶα, πάλλ', ἀνάστρεφ' εὐρύθμῳ ποδί·

◡‒◡‒   ◡‒‒

τόρευε πᾶσαν ᾠδήν.

‒‒◡‒   ‒‒◡‒ ‖

ἡγοῦ δέ γ' ὧδ' αὐτὸς σύ,

‒◠◡‒   ‒◡‒ ‖

κισσοφόρε Βακχεῖε

‒◡◡‒   ◡‒‒

δέσποτ'· ἐγὼ δὲ κώμοις

◡◠◡‒   ◡‒‒ ‖‖‖

σὲ φιλοχόροισι[ν] μέλψω.

The second mesode (see above on 953 ff.) is iambic, except for the penultimate colon, an aristophanean, which is interpretable as a catalectic
choriambo-iambic dimeter (Introduction, p. 82). Its presence here points
forward to the stronger choriambic element in 990 ff. = 995 ff. After the
opening trimeter and catalectic dimeter, the two cola addressed to the
god stand out by their heavy accumulation of longs. Both are metrically
isolated by verse-end (*brevis in longo*). For the metrically distinctive
invocation in a hymn, compare 1143–4 below.

990–4=995–1000

‒◡◡‒◡‒‒

990 †εὔιον ὦ Διόνυσε†

◡◠‒◡◡‒‒

Βρόμιε, καὶ Σεμέλας παῖ,

◡‒‒◡◡‒

χοροῖς τερπόμενος

◡◠◡‒

993 κατ' ὄρεα Νυμ-

‒◡◡‒◡‒‒

φᾶν ἐρατοῖς ἐν ὕμνοις

ia trim

ia dim cat

ia mol

ia sp (cr mol?)

arist

ia dim cat

At 985, ἀλλ' εἶα, πάλλ' (cf. *Frogs* 345, *Tro.* 325) is Blaydes's emendation of R's ἀλλ' ειαπάλλ', which became in the first printed edition ἀλλ' εἶ' ἐπ' ἀλλ'. τόρευε at 986 is defended by R. E. Wycherley (*CR* 9 (1959), 205–6. See also Thomsen, *C&M* Diss. 9 (1973), 35–6). Scaliger deleted the ephelcystic ν in 989. Retaining it would produce another heavy verse-end in − − −, like 987–8. Whether this is felt to detract from the distinctive effect of the invocation or to reinforce it is a matter of taste.

      arist
995 ἀμφὶ δὲ σοὶ κτυπεῖται

      pher
Κιθαιρώνιος ἠχώ,

    aeol hexasyll
μελάμφυλλά τ' ὄρη

      ia
998 δάσκια πετρώ-

      + arist
δεις τε νάπαι βρέμονται·

∪−∪⏜ ∪−‿‖

†εὔιον εὔιον εὐοῖ

−⏜∪⏜ ∪−−⫴

. . . . . . †ἀναχορεύων.

953 ff., 969 ff. = 977 ff. and 985 ff. are all predominantly iambic stanzas with some choriambic admixture. In this stanza, choriambic predominates over iambic. In the pherecratean at 991 = 996, the correspondence of ∪∪∪ to ∪ − in aeolic base is an extreme rarity (see Itsumi, *CQ* 34 (1984), 67–9, and Introduction, p. 71). The colon ∪ − − ∪ ∪ − (992 = 997) is most easily interpreted in this context as a sort of truncated version of the preceding pherecratean:

.. .. − ∪ ∪ − −

.. .. − ∪ ∪ −

Compare *Ba.* 865 = 885, 873 = 893. On the unusual 'trimeter', 993 = 998, see Introduction, pp. 79–80.

     The received text of the strophe is badly mutilated. Apart from major failures of correspondence at the beginning and end, there is no main

1015–55

∪ − −   ∪ − ∪ −

1015   φίλαι παρθένοι, φίλαι,

− ∪ ∪ −   − ∪ −

πῶς ἂν ἀπέλθοιμι καὶ

− ∪ −   ∪ − ‿ ‖

τὸν Σκύθην λάθοιμι;

∪ − −   ∪ − −   ∪ − −   ∪ − −

1018–19 κλυεῖς, ὦ προσᾴδουσ᾽ ἀϋτὰς ἐν ἄντροις;

∪ ∪ − ∪ ∪ − ∪ −

1020   κατάνευσον, ἔασον ὡς

− ∪ −   ∪ − −

τὴν γυναῖκά μ᾽ ἐλθεῖν.

∪ − ∪ −   ∪ − ∪ −

ἄνοικτος ὅς μ᾽ ἔδησε, τὸν

ia dim cat

κύκλῳ δὲ περί σε κισσὸς

ia dim cat

1000 εὐπέταλος ἕλικι θάλλει.

verb. At 990, it is likely, as Hermann, Fritzsche, and Enger supposed, that Διόνυσε is corrupt, and conceals Διὸς (to be combined with καὶ Σεμέλας παῖ). Correspondence and sense can be patched up by accepting Enger's Εὔιε, ὦ Διὸς σύ at 990, Hermann's ὦ Εὔι' Εὔι', εὐοῖ at 994, and von Velsen's ⟨ἥκεις γὰρ⟩ ἀναχορεύων to end the stanza. Wilamowitz's rewriting, which is accepted by Coulon, does much greater violence to the MS text, without even restoring correspondence.

The text of the antistrophe is comparatively unproblematic. σοὶ in 995 and Κιθαιρώνιος in 996 are Zanetti's corrections of R's συὶ and κιθαρώνιος. At 998, πετρώδεις τε νάπαι is Enger's emendation of R's καὶ νάπαι· πετρώδεις. At this point it is the strophe that provides an acceptable model, while the MS version of the antistrophe, – ∪ ∪ – ∪ – ∪ – – ∪ – –, defies metrical analysis.

ba ia

cho cr

+ ith

4 ba

tel?

+ ith

ia dim

⌢‿– ‿–‿–
πολυπονώτατον βροτῶν,

‿–‿– ‿⌢‿–
μόλις δὲ γραῖαν ἀποφυγὼν

‿–‿– ‿–‿–
1025 σαπρὰν ἀπωλόμην ὅμως.

‿⌢–‿– ‿–⌢‿– –⌢⌢‿⌢
ὅδε γὰρ ὁ Σκύθης φύλαξ πάλαι ἐφεστὼς ὀλοὸν ἄφιλον ἑ-

‿⌢‿– ‿–‿ ‖
κρέμασε κόραξι δεῖπνον.

‿–– ‿–‿– ‿–‿– ‿–‿–
1030 ὁρᾷς; οὐ χοροῖσιν οὐδ' ὑφ' ἡλίκων νεανίδων

–‿– –‿–
†[ψῆφον] κημὸν ἕστηκ' ἔχουσ',

––‿– ––‿– ‿–‿–
ἀλλ' ἐν πυκνοῖς δεσμοῖσιν ἐμπεπλεγμένη

––‿– –‿– ‿––
κήτει βορὰ Γλαυκέτῃ πρόκειμαι.

‿–‿– ‿––
γαμηλίῳ μὲν οὐ ξὺν

––‿– ‿–‿ ‖
1035 παιῶνι δεσμίῳ δὲ

‿–‿– ‿–‿–
γοᾶσθέ μ', ὦ γυναῖκες, ὡς

⌢‿– ‿–‿⌢
μέλεα μὲν πέπονθα μέλε-

‿–‿– ‿–‿–
ος, ὦ τάλας ἐγώ, τάλας,

‿⌢–‿– ‿⌢⌢‿⌢
1039a ἀπὸ δὲ συγγόνων ἄνομ' ἄνομα πάθεα,

+ lec

ia dim

ia dim

3 δ

+ ia dim cat

ba 3 ia

2 cr

+ ia trim

ia trim sync cat

ia dim cat

+ ia dim cat

ia dim

+ lec

+ ia dim

2 δ

‒ ◡ ⌢ ◡ ‒

1039b   φῶτα λιτομένα,

◡ ⌢ ‒ ◡ ⌢   ‒ ◡ ‒   ◡ ‒ ◡ ‖ ᴴ

1040   πολυδάκρυτον Ἄϊδα γόον φλέγουσα

αἰαῖ αἰαῖ ἒ ἔ,

⌢ ◡ ‒ ◡   ‒ ◡ ‒ ◡

ὃς ἔμ' ἀπεξύρησε πρῶτον,

1044   †ὃς ἐμὲ κροκόεντ' ἐνέδυσεν†

⌢ ◡ ‒ ◡   ⌢ ◡ ‒ ◡

1045   ἐπὶ δὲ τοῖσδε τόδ' ἀνέπεμψεν

◡ ◡ ◡ ‒ ◡ ◡ ‒ ◡ ‖

ἱερόν, ἔνθα γυναῖκες.

◡ ‒ ‒ ‒ ‒

ἰώ μοι μοίρας

‒ ◡ ‒   ◡ ‒ ‒

1047   ἃν ἔτικτε δαίμων.

‒ ◡ ◡ ‒ ◡ ◡ ‒

ὦ κατάρατος ἐγώ·

⌢ ◡ ‒   ◡ ‒ ◡ ‒

τίς ἐμὸν οὐκ ἐπόψεται

◡ ⌢ ◡ ‒   ◡ ⌢ ◡ ‒   ◡ ‒ ◡ ‒ ‖ ᴴ

πάθος ἀμέγαρτον ἐπὶ κακῶν παρουσίᾳ;

‒ ◡ ◡   ‒ ◡ ◡   ‒ ◡ ◡   ‒ ‒

1050   εἴθε με πυρφόρος αἰθέρος ἀστὴρ

‒   ‒ ◡ ◡ ‒ ◡ ◡ ‒   ◡ ‖

τὸν δύσμορον ἐξολέσειεν.

‒ ◡ ◡   ‒ ◡ ◡   ‒ ◡ ◡   ‒ ‒

οὐ γὰρ ἔτ' ἀθανάταν φλόγα λεύσσειν

‒ ◡ ◡   ‒ ◡ ◡   ‒ ◡ ◡   ‒ ‒

ἐστὶν ἐμοὶ φίλον, ὡς ἐκρεμάσθην,

hypod

δ cr ba

extra metrum
tro dim

tro dim

pher

δ

ith

hem (D)

lec

ia trim

da tetram

enopl (– D –)

da tetram

   + da tetram

$$ \_ \cup \_ \cup \_ \quad \_ \cup \cup \_ \cup $$

λαιμότμητ' ἄχη δαιμόνι', αἰόλαν

$$ \widetilde{\smile} \cup \widetilde{\smile} \quad \cup \_ \_ ||| $$

1055   νέκυσιν ἔπι πορείαν.

This song, like *Frogs* 1331–64, parodies on a grand scale a Euripidean monody. It is important here to note that surviving Euripidean monodies are very diverse. It is wrong to suppose that there is a single type of aria, even in the later plays of Euripides, which can easily be identified as Aristophanes' target. The Phrygian's monody at *Or.* 1369 ff., called by Rau (*Paratragodia*, 131) 'das Paradestück dieser Art', is exceptional not only in its length and metrical elaboration, but in that the singer is not a major character and that the song takes the place of a messenger's speech. In any case, *Or.* was not staged until three years after *Thesm.* For a fuller discussion of Euripidean monody, see on *Frogs* 1331ff. Unlike the *Frogs* parody, this song does not indulge in an un-Euripidean excess of metrical diversity and it does have some resemblance to a single, surviving Euripidean monody, Jocasta's solo at *Phoen.* 301ff., which combines iambic and dochmiac with occasional cretic sequences, and has a dactylic passage at the end, just before the dochmiac clausula. However, *Phoen.* (like *Or.*) was staged later than *Thesm.* Aristophanes' model here would seem to have been a lost composition of similar type.

The song is full of uncertainties of text and, in consequence, of metre. At a number of points, quite small (and plausible) alterations to the text would produce major changes to the metrical pattern. The very beginning of the song provides an example. By a monosyllabic supplement, Hermann was able to produce a neat sequence of three dochmiacs and ithyphallic:

> φίλαι παρθένοι,
> φίλαι, πῶς ἂν ⟨οὖν⟩ ἀπέλθοιμι καὶ
> τὸν Σκύθην λάθοιμι;

$$ \cup \_ \_ \cup \_ $$
$$ \cup \_ \_ \cup \_ \quad \cup \_ \_ \cup \_ $$
$$ \_ \cup \_ \quad \cup \_ \smile || $$

However, the dimeter ⌣ – – ⌣ – ⌣ – (1015) is found in later Euripides, and almost nowhere else (Stinton, *BICS* 22 (1975), 93–4 = *Collected Papers* (1990), 126 f., and see below, on *Ecc.* 913a), and Aristo-

hypod δ

ith

phanes may have chosen the rhythm deliberately for that reason (Σ *vet.* here identifies a quotation from *Andromeda* (Nauck², Eur. 117)).

λάθοιμι (1017) is Ellebodius' emendation of R's λάβοιμι.

1018–19 present an interesting problem. R offers προσαιδουσσαι τὰς both in the text and in Σ *vet.*'s version of the Euripidean original. The text I print combines Elmsley's προσᾴδουσα with Burges's αὖτάς. The resulting run of four bacchiacs, which makes the invocation stand out rhythmically (see below on 1144), is elegant and attractive (see Mitsdörffer, *Philologus*, 98 (1954), 70). Sommerstein's αὖταῖς ('Thou that singest in response to my cries') gives a similar result. Runs of bacchiacs feature in later Euripidean monody (*Ion* 1446, *Hel.* 642–3, *Phoen.* 1536, *Or.* 1437–40 (cf. below on 1136). Nauck observed that, with Bothe's προσαυδῶ σε τὰν, 1019–21 seems to correspond with a quotation from *Andromeda* in Stobaeus (Nauck², Eur. 118, 119). If this is more than a coincidence, it would suggest that the Euripidean original was in strophic correspondence, like *Tro.* 308ff. However, the single dochmiac between bacchiacs required by Bothe (as also by Seidler–von Velsen) is metrically rather odd.

The colon ∪∪–∪∪–∪– (1020) is found in aeolo-choriambic contexts in Euripides (*Hec.* 905ff.=914ff., *Hel.* 1114=1128; Introduction, p. 73).

The text and metre of 1026–8 are highly problematic. I print the nearest (possible) approximation to R. The correption παλαῐ may, however, be regarded as suspect (Introduction, p. 92). Dindorf's πάλιν is plausible. Meineke proposed ἐφεστὼς for ἐφέστηκ', removing a rather harsh asyndeton. 1026–7 has commonly been taken as a lecythion followed by a pair of trochaic dimeters, either reading ἐκρέμασεν (Bothe) or adding ⟨με⟩ (Mehler) after ἐκρέμασε ('hung me up as a meal', instead of 'hung up a meal'):

ὅδε γὰρ ὁ Σκύθης φύλαξ
πάλιν ἐφεστὼς ὀλοὸν ἄφιλον
ἐκρέμασέ ⟨με⟩ κόραξι δεῖπνον.

Sommerstein's ἄφιλόν ⟨μ᾽⟩, with ἐκρέμασεν, produces the rare trochaic metron, ⌒ ∪ ⌒ – twice over (Introduction, p. 39). Trochees would not be out of place in a Euripidean lament (see 1042–5 below, and *Hel.* 330 ff.). This analysis involves a transition from acatalectic trochee to iamb at δεῖπνον. | ὁρᾷς . . ., which is very rare, though not absolutely unparalleled, especially with strong sense pause. But the only possible parallel for trochee followed by bacchiac (as here) is *PV* 694–5, which is easily emended (see further Parker, in Craik, *'Owls to Athens'* 332–5, 339). The same metrical rarity is produced by Zimmermann's solution (*Untersuchungen*, iii. 78). He follows Jackson (*MS* 94) in substituting ὅς for ὁ Σκύθης (ejected as a gloss), and accepts Hermann's ⟨ἐμοὶ⟩ after φύλαξ. Jackson's own version requires an unwanted definite article with κόραξι (contrast *Ant.* 29–30 οἰωνοῖς . . . θησαυρὸν) and produces a rare form of dochmiac (∪ – – ∪ ⌒) unparalleled in Aristophanes (Introduction, p. 68).

Meaning and metre are in doubt in 1030–1. The unusual rhythm ∪ – –   ∪ – ∪ – (see on 1015) opens 1030. By transposing ἡλίκων and ὑπὸ, Hermann again managed to produce a series of dochmiacs:

ὁρᾷς; οὐ χοροῖσιν οὐδ᾽ ἡλίκων ὑπὸ νεανίδων
∪ – – ∪ –   ∪ – – ∪ –   ∪ ∪ ∪ – ∪ –

Mitsdörffer would delete ὑφ᾽ in 1030 on the grounds that ὑπὸ with the genitive means 'accompanied by' only in the musical sense. The musical sense cannot, however, be excluded here, given the state of the text. The deletion of ψῆφον (as an intrusive gloss) is Hermann's. It may well be that ψῆφον has displaced some word or words which would have made better connected sense.

The pair of catalectic cola in synartesis at 1034–5 is unusual, but acceptable (see Parker, *CQ* 26 (1976), 20).

1036–8 is usually divided into ia dim (ending with ὡς), tro dim (μέλεα . . . μέλεος), lec (ὦ . . . τάλας), but an acatalectic iambic dimeter ending with a subordinating conjunction followed immediately by trochees is highly dubious (see Parker, in Craik, *'Owls to Athens'*, 348).

At 1039a, ἄνομ᾽ ἄνομα is Blaydes's suggestion for ἀλλὰν ἄνομα R. Scaliger's ἀλλ᾽ ἄνομα, which has enjoyed some popularity recently (Coulon, *RhM* 100 (1957), 189, Rau, *Paratragodia*, 75 n. 140, Zimmermann, *Untersuchungen*, ii. 8, Sommerstein), produces a hypodochmiac of unparalleled form (at *Tro.* 309 = 326, there is verse-end in the strophe, giving – ⌒ ⌒ ◡ ⌣ || rather than – ◡ ⌒ ◡ ⌒ = – ⌒ ⌒ ◡ –). In fact, the only hypodochmiacs in Aristophanes are in this song (1039b and 1054).

In the following colon (1039b), *Σ. vet.* offers the variant φῶτ᾽ ἀντομένα (– – ◡ ◡ –). λίτομαι also occurs at 313 of this play, but never in tragedy. Mitsdörffer, (*Philologus*, 98 (1954), 83 n. 2) traces the word to liturgical language. The main problem here, already recognized by *Σ vet.*, is whether the participles should be accusative (following γοᾶσθε μ᾽ at 1036) or nominative (agreeing with the subject of πέπονθα). I offer the nearest scannable alternative to the MS text, but the whole passage is in doubt. At 1040, R reads φεύγουσαν. Enger's linguistically bold φλέγουσα (following Musgrave, φλέγουσαν) is attractive (cf. Bacchylides, fr. 4. 80 Snell). χέουσα (following Casaubon, χέουσαν) is suggested by Rau (*Paratragodia*, 75 n. 139).

At 1044, Hermann produced a trochaic dimeter by adopting ἀμφέδυσεν from *Σ vet.* in place of ἐνέδυσεν, taking κροκόεντ᾽ as neuter plural, 'these saffron things'. The alternative of assuming that κροκόεις can stand on its own for κροκόεις πέπλος or χιτών is hard to support. Sappho, *PLF* 92. 8 is too fragmentary to make clear how the word is being used. Bergk proposed κροκόεν τόδ᾽, retaining ἐνέδυσεν (⌒ ◡ ⌒ – ⌒ ◡ – ◡). Again, the rare ⌒ ◡ ⌒ – is involved.

At 1047, ἂν ἔτικτε is Casaubon's conjecture for R's ἀνέτικτε. The ingenious ἄτεγτε δαῖμον of Biset and Ellebodius may well have been inspired by Zanetti's ἀνάτεγτε. Taken with 1046, this makes ba ia ba.

δύσμορον at 1051 is Brunck's conjecture for R's βάρβαρον. The MS text has been retained by some editors on the supposition that the Kinsman launches into a typical tragic prayer that he may be struck by lightning, only to reflect midway that he would much rather that the Scythian were struck instead. But ancient writers are aware of the imperatives of inflected languages and say what they mean (compare Catullus 44. 20, 'non mihi sed ipsi Sestio', in a joke of this kind). For a different view, however, see Austin, *Dodone* 19. 28–9.

1136–59

−∪∪−∪∪⌢∪−

Παλλάδα τὴν φιλόχορον ἐμοὶ

−∪∪−∪∪−∪−

1137–8   δεῦρο καλεῖν νόμος εἰς χορόν,

−∪∪−∪∪−−

παρθένον ἄζυγα κούρην,

−∪∪−∪∪−∪−

1140   ἢ πόλιν ἡμετέραν ἔχει

−∪−∪∪−∪−

καὶ κράτος φανερὸν μόνη

−−−∪∪−−

κληδοῦχός τε καλεῖται.

     ∪−−   ∪−−   ∪−−   ∪−−

1143–4   φάνηθ', ὦ τυράννους στυγοῦσ', ὥσπερ εἰκός·

−−−∪∪−∪−

1145   δῆμός τοί σε καλεῖ γυναι-

−∪−∪∪−∪−

κῶν· ἔχουσα δέ μοι μόλοις

−−−∪∪−‿ ‖

εἰρήνην φιλέορτον.

−∪∪−∪∪−∪−

ἥκετ⟨έ τ'⟩ εὔφρονες, ἵλαοι,

−∪∪−∪∪−∪⌢

πότνιαι, ἄλσος ἐς ὑμέτερον,

−∪∪−∪∪−∪−

1150   [οὗ δὴ] ἀνδράσιν οὐ θεμίτ'[ον] εἰσορᾶν

−∪∪ −∪∪ −∪∪ −∪∪

ὄργια σεμνὰ θεαῖν ἵνα λαμπάσι

−∪∪−∪∪−−

φαίνετον ἄμβροτον ὄψιν.

ibyc

ibyc

ibyc cat (da trim)

ibyc

glyc

pher

4 ba

glyc

   + glyc

pher

ibyc

ibyc

ibyc

da tetram

ibyc cat (da trim)

1155   ⏑⏑⏑ − ⏑⏑ − ⏑⏑ −
        μόλετον, ἔλθετον, ἀντόμεθ᾽, ὦ

        − ⏑⏑ − − ⏑⏑ − ⏑ − ‖ ᴴ
        Θεσμοφόρω πολυποτ᾽νία.

        − − ⏑⏑ − ⏑⏑ − ⏑⏑ − ⏑ −
        εἰ καὶ πρότερόν ποτ᾽ ἐπηκόω ἤλθετον

        †νῦν ἀφίκεσθον, ἱκετεύομεν, ἐνθάδ᾽ ἡμῖν.†

Between the extended parody of *Andromeda* and the rapidly concluded agreement between Euripides and the women which opens the way to the rescue of the Kinsman, the chorus sing a hymn to Athene and to the goddesses of the Thesmophoria, Demeter and Persephone. The diction is simple (contrast *Clouds* 299 ff.), the metre sophisticated. In fact, there is nothing else quite like it in surviving drama. The thematic colon of the stanza, − ⏑⏑ − ⏑⏑ − ⏑ −, has acquired the name 'ibycean' from Ibycus, *PMG* 286, and the combination of that colon with dactylic in the latter half of the stanza is definitely suggestive of Ibyus (cf. *Lys.* 1279 ff., above). Dale (*LM*² 166) was justified in seeing 'the dominant movement' here as 'ibycean-dactylic'.

Ibycus' metres share with aeolo-choriambic the cadence . . . − ⏑⏑ − ⏑ −. He seems to use initial biceps (*PMG* 282, the fourth colon of the strophe, perhaps 287. 1, 3, and 5), and there is one example among his fragments of a single-short prefix (287. 4 ⏑ − ⏑⏑ − ⏑⏑ − − −). But it is not clear that he admitted disyllabic aeolic base. The initial − ⏑ at 298 (*P. Oxy.* 2260) and 282. 8, 21, 34, 47 could be so interpreted, but the absence of any form other than − ⏑ suggests, rather, a reversed form of the ibycean cadence (− ⏑ − ⏑⏑ − . . . instead of − ⏑⏑ − ⏑ −). Compare ⏑⏑⏑ − ⏑⏑ − ⏑⏑ − at 1155 in this song. The common aeolic cola, glyconic and pherecratean, which figure largely among the fragments of his colleague in Samos, Anacreon, are not found among Ibycus' fragments.

It is worth noting the fact that in origin the ibycean and glyconic are quite distinct, because, following Wilamowitz (*GV* 592), the ibyceans in this song are sometimes treated as glyconics with base of the form − ⏑ ⏑. Twice in a single song (*IT* 1092 = 1109, 1129 = 1144), Euripides seems to introduce such a base, making − ⏑⏑ − ⏑⏑ − ⏑ − correspond

aeol da

+ ibyc

aeol da

once with polyschematist and once with glyconic (both with triple-short base). Also, at *El.* 150–6, ibyceans alternate with glyconics (again with triple-short base). Itsumi (*CQ* 34 (1984), 72 n. 17) lists five passages in late Euripides where – ‿ ‿ seems to correspond with ‿ ‿ ‿ in the base of polyschematists (*Hel.* 1347=1363, *Ba.* 410=425, *IA* 553=568, 753=764, 754=765). Of these, the *Hel.* example is easily eliminated by reading τύπανα at 1347. *IA* is notable for the eccentricity of its aeolo-choriambic. But to treat ibycean and glyconic here as identical is to conceal the subtlety of variation in the song. The exploitation of ambiguity is a different matter.

The first half (1136–47), addressed to Athene, is relatively simple. There are three periods, each of three cola, following Anacreon's familiar pattern of two acatalectic cola rounded off by one with catalexis. The first period is purely ibycean; the second begins with an ibycean, but turns to glyconic and pherecratean; the third is pure glyconic-pherecratean. The introduction of resolution (1136, 1149) is a distinctively Attic touch (Introduction, p. 72), one might even say late-Euripidean.

Between the second and third periods, the bacchiac invocation to Athene intervenes with startling effect. This is the only bacchiac sequence in surviving Aristophanes, except for the pair at *Wasps* 317 and (not certainly) the four in this play at 1019. For both of these the context is paratragic monody (see above, on 1019). In tragedy, except for the sequence of four among dochmiacs at *Phil.* 396=511, repeated bacchiacs are found only in Aeschylus and Euripides and in two plays of uncertain authorship, *PV* and *Rhes.* Bacchiacs sharply divided from each other by rhetorical pause or change of speaker are found at *Sept.* 105, *Eum.* 788–9, *Tro.* 587–8=591–2, and, almost to the point of parody, at *Rhes.* 706–9=724–6. Otherwise, there are sequences of more than two bacchiacs at

Ag. 1104–5=1111–2, *Cho.* 350=368, 390=415, 607=618, *PV* 579=597, *Ion* 1446, *Hel.* 642–3, *Or.* 1437–40, and *Ba.* 993, 1014. Almost all the tragic examples occur in iambic, dochmiac, or iambo-dochmiac contexts. Only in *Cho.* 390=415 and 607=618 is there a choriambic element in the passage. Only in *Wasps* 317 (where the two bacchiacs open the stanza, so do not interrupt an established rhythm) and *Thesm.* 1143 is there no iambic or dochmiac in the passage whatever. Only the most dedicated exponent of the view that Aristophanes' plays are wholly devoid of serious content could avoid the conclusion that the audience of *Thesm.* were meant to leave the theatre with this invocation resounding in their minds.

　　At 1139, κούρην is Hermann's correction of κόρην R. After 1143, R has the words στυγνὰς ὤσσε, which are crossed out by R² (Mu2 has στυγνὰς ὡς ἐ). The supplementation of 1148 to make an ibycean is Enger's. The loss of -ε τ’ is easily explained by haplography. For the connective τε in a hymn addressed to several gods, compare 322, 325, 326 above. On the other hand, the glyconic of the MS text is not impossible in the context, and the asyndeton could perhaps be defended as marking a major change of addressee (cf. *Knights* 581, at the beginning of a stanza). In 1150, Hermann deleted οὗ δὴ and Bothe proposed θεμίτ’. οὗ δὴ looks like an attempt at emendation by someone baffled by the postponement of ἵνα. θεμιτὸν presumably came by attraction from ἄλσος. 1151–4 could, of course, be taken as an unbroken sequence of seven dactyls (cf. Ibycus, *PMG* 288, 3–4). The colon ⏑⏑⏑–⏑⏑–⏑⏑– is found (later than this play) at *Ba.* 112=127 and 115=130 among a variety of choriambic cola. –⏑–⏑⏑–⏑⏑– occurs at *Clouds* 703= 807 in an iambo-choriambic context. The metrical context of *Birds* 936 is indeterminate. At 1150–1, Hermann's ἄνδρας ἵν’ οὐ θέμις εἰσορᾶν | ὄργια σεμν’ [θεαῖν] ἵνα λαμπάσι⟨ν⟩ . . . deserves very serious consideration. Dr Austin points out to me in a private communication that, apart from the dubious postponement of ἵνα, ‘θεαῖν needs to be deleted (as a gloss from 948), as it sounds odd in a call to the two goddesses, and ὄψιν is best taken as referring to the goddesses themselves in the divine epiphany’. Metrically, this produces a sequence of four ibyceans (1148–51) rounded off by the catalectic form (in fact, an extended repetition of the opening section, 1136–9).

　　The text and metre of 1157–9 cannot be decided with any degree of certainty. Double καί is characteristic of this type of prayer (e.g. *OT* 165–6 εἴ ποτε καὶ προτέρας ἄτας ὕπερ . . . ἔλθετε καὶ νῦν, *Clouds* 356–7 καὶ νῦν, εἴπερ τινὶ κἄλλῳ . . . ῥήξατε κἀμοὶ φωνήν). The first καί may be omitted (Demosthenes 32. 3: εἴπερ ἄλλῳ τινὶ πώποτε . . . καὶ τούτῳ προσέχειν), and Van Leeuwen's proposal to delete it here, combined with Hermann's ἤλθετε, could turn 1157 into a dactylic tetrameter. This, however, brings little benefit if the following colon begins with anceps or biceps, which it must do to accommodate the second καί. This καί is indispensable, and must go where Blaydes put it, before νῦν, for the second καί is always placed immediately before the word which makes precise the circumstances of the help now required, as distinct from the help given on another occasion (καὶ νῦν contrasted with 'previously', κἀμοί contrasted with 'to someone else'). So, with πρότερον in the first clause, Hermann's ἐνθάδε χἠμῖν, which, with his own ἤλθετε and Reisig's ἀφίκεσθ', would produce a pure dactylic sequence, will not do. Wilamowitz (*GV* 592) sought to preserve the MS text, adding only καί:

> εἰ πρότερόν ποτ' ἐπηκόω
> ἤλθετον, ⟨καὶ⟩ νῦν ἀφίκεσ-
> θον, ἱκετεύομεν, ἐνθάδ' ἡμῖν.
>
> – ⏑ ⏑ – ⏑ ⏑ – ⏑ –
> – ⏑ – – – ⏑ ⏑ –
> ⏑ ⏑ ⏑ – ⏑ ⏑ – ⏑ – –

This is unacceptable for two reasons. Firstly, the polyschematist (– ⏑ – – – ⏑ ⏑ –) is out of place in this context. Ibycus does not seem to have used the colon, and Aristophanes uses it only sparingly and in particular contexts (Introduction, p. 74). Secondly, Itsumi (*CQ* 34 (1984), 70) has made the important observation that triple-short base in glyconics is hardly ever found in synartesis with the preceding colon. He finds only *IA* 186 in tragedy, and there all three shorts belong to the same word. I can find no example in hipponacteans anywhere. Turning ἤλθετον and ἀφίκεσθον into second person plurals with verse-end after ἤλθετε produces a tolerable solution. οὖ δή at 1150 may be evidence of interventionist and metrically ill-informed editing in later antiquity. Duals are unlikely to be introduced casually, but they could have been introduced here deliberately for the sake of consistency. 1158–9 then becomes a pendent version of 1157 (the so-called 'archeboulean'):

⟨καὶ⟩ νῦν ἀφίκεσθ᾽ , ἱκετεύομεν, ἐνθάδ᾽ ἡμῖν.

－－◡◡－◡◡－◡◡－◡－－

Ibycus *PMG* 298. 3 is ◡◡－◡◡－◡◡－◡◡－◡－－, and the poet's

practice elsewhere (*PMG* 282, perhaps 287. 1, 3, 5) suggests that the initial ‿ ‿ might be contracted to −. To our eyes, the aeolic dactyls of *Wasps* 1232–5 are distinguished from these verses only by the disyllabic aeolic base.

Frogs

SYNOPSIS

209–67	Frogs and Dionysus: *Iambic, trochaic,* isolated *choriambic* cola, *dactylo-epitrite.*
323–36=340–53	*Ionic*, with *bacchiacs* and one *cretic.*
372–6=377–82	*Anapaestic.*
384–8=389–93	*Iambic.*
398–403=404–8=409–13	*Iambic.*
416–39	Chorus and Dionysus: *Iambic* (8 corresponding 3-verse stanzas).
448–53=454–9	*Iambic, aeolo-choriambic.*
534–48=590–604	Chorus, Dionysus, Xanthias: *Trochaic.*
674–85=706–16	*Dactylo-epitrite.*
814–17=818–21=822–5=826–9	*Dactylic*, with *lecythion* as clausula.
875–84	*Dactylic*, with *ithyphallic* as clausula.
895–904=992–1003	*Anapaestic*, introducing *trochaic.*
1099–1108=1109–18	*Trochaic.*
1251–60	*Aeolo-choriambic.*
1264–77, 1284–95	Euripides: *Dactylic*, sometimes preceded by an *iambic* metron.
1309–28	Aeschylus: *Iambic, aeolo-choriambic, iambo-choriambic.*
1331–63	Aeschylus: *Aeolo-choriambic, anapaestic, dactylic, trochaic, cretic, iambic, dactylo-epitrite, enoplian.*
1370–7, 1482–90=1491–9	*Trochaic.*

The dramatic action of *Frogs* is articulated with exceptional clarity, and metrical patterning plays only a subsidiary structural role. The introductory sub-plot of Dionysus' descent into Hades contains two major musical set-pieces: the Frogs' boating song (209–67) and the miniature religious festival (316–459). The stylized, symmetrical comedy of the clothes-changing episode (460–604) is given extra definition by the trochaic comment-song, which the chorus shares in the strophe (534–48) with Dionysus and in the antistrophe (590–604) with Xanthias.

With the exit of Dionysus, Xanthias, and Aeacus at 673, the sub-plot reaches its dénouement, and the parabasis marks a sharp break in the action. The solemn-seeming invocation to the Muse (674 ff.) leads into a stylistically ornate lampoon-song, perhaps reminiscent metrically of Euripides (see below, ad loc.) and a pair of sombre epirrhemes.

The contest between Aeschylus and Euripides, which occupies the second half of the play, is preceded by three preliminary scenes: first a 'prologue' between Xanthias and Aeacus, then a short initial exchange between Aeschylus and Euripides with Dionysus as mediator, and, finally, the prayers of the two contestants to their patron-divinities. Each of the three scenes is rounded off by a short song, in which the chorus looks forward to the ensuing competition. The first two songs (814–29 and 875–84) are high-flown in diction and dignified in metre. Both are dactylic, and there is a stong probability that echoes of Aeschylus' metrical style are to be detected at least in the first. The third scene is followed by a trochaic strophe (895 ff.) opening with a single anapaestic dimeter. The antistrophe (992 ff.) marks the middle of the recitative agon between the two poets, and a longer trochaic strophic pair (1099 ff. = 1109 ff.) its close. In fact, from 895 onwards, the chorus are confined to quite simple songs of comment on the action, and, but for the single anapaestic colon, 895 = 992, and the short aeolo-choriambic stanza, 1251 ff., they use only trochees. The major metrical set-pieces of the second half of the play are, of course, Aeschylus' and Euripides' parodies of each other's lyric.

209–67

     ⌒ ∪ – ∪ – ∪ –

B. βρεκεκεκὲξ κοὰξ κοάξ,

     ⌒ ∪ – ∪ – ∪ –

210   βρεκεκεκὲξ κοὰξ κοάξ,

     – – ∪ –   – ∪ –

     λιμναῖα κρηνῶν τέκνα,

     ∪ – ∪ –   – ∪ –

     ξύναυλον ὕμνων βοὰν

     – – ∪ –   – ∪ ∪ –

     φθεγξώμεθ᾽, εὔγηρυν ἐμὰν

     ∪ – –

     ἀοιδάν,

     ∪ – ∪ –

     κοὰξ κοάξ,

     – – ∪ –   – ∪ –

215   ἣν ἀμφὶ Νυσήϊον

     ∪ – ∪ ∪ – ∪ –

     Διὸς Διόνυσον ἐν

        – – ∪ –   – ∪ ⌣ ‖

        Λίμναις[ιν] ἰαχήσαμεν,

     – ∪ ∪ – ∪ ∪ – –

     ἡνίχ᾽ ὁ κραιπαλόκωμος

     – ∪ ∪ – ∪ ∪ – –

219   τοῖς ἱεροῖσι Χύτροις[ι] χω-

     – ∪ ∪ – ∪ ∪ –

     ρεῖ κατ᾽ ἐμὸν τέμενος

     – – ∪ –

     λαῶν ὄχλος.

     ⌒ ∪ – ∪ – ∪ –

220   βρεκεκεκὲξ κοὰξ κοάξ,

lec

lec

ia cr

ia cr

ia cho dim

ba

ia

ia cr

tel

+ ia cr

D –

D – D

– e (ia)

lec

ᴗ－ᴗ－　－－ᴗ－

Δ. ἐγὼ δέ γ᾽ ἀλγεῖν ἄρχομαι

ᴗ－ᴗ－　ᴗ－ᴗ－

222　τὸν ὄρρον, ὦ κοὰξ κοάξ·

－－ᴗ－　－－ᴗ－

224　ὑμῖν δ᾽ ἴσως οὐδὲν μέλει.

⌢ᴗ－ᴗ－ᴗ－

225　Β. βρεκεκεκὲξ κοὰξ κοάξ.

－－ᴗ－　－－ᴗ－

Δ. ἀλλ᾽ ἐξόλοισθ᾽ αὐτῷ κοάξ.

－－ᴗ－　－－ᴗ－

οὐδὲν γάρ ἐστ᾽ ἀλλ᾽ ἢ κοάξ.

－ᴗ－－　－ᴗ－－

Β. εἰκότως γ᾽, ὦ πολλὰ πράττων.

⌢ᴗ－－　－ᴗ－ᴗ　－ᴗ－－

ἐμὲ γὰρ ἔστερξαν ⟨μὲν⟩ εὔλυροί τε Μοῦσαι

－ᴗ⌢－　－ᴗ⌢－　－ᴗ－－

230　καὶ κεροβάτας Πάν, ὁ καλαμόφθογγα παίζων·

⌢ᴗ－ᴗ　－ᴗ－－　－ᴗ－－

231–2　προσεπιτέρπεται δ᾽ ὁ φορμικτὰς Ἀπόλλων,

⌢ᴗ⌢ᴗ　⌢ᴗ⌢ᴗ

ἕνεκα δόνακος ὃν ὑπολύριον

⌢ᴗ－－－ᴗ

ἔνυδρον ἐν λίμναις τρέφω.

⌢ᴗ－ᴗ－ᴗ－

235　βρεκεκεκὲξ κοὰξ κοάξ.

ᴗ－ᴗ－　－－ᴗ－

Δ. ἐγὼ δὲ φλυκταίνας γ᾽ ἔχω,

－－ᴗ－　ᴗ－ᴗ－

χὠ πρωκτὸς ἰδίει πάλαι,

ia dim

ia dim

ia dim

lec

ia dim

ia dim

tro dim

tro trim

tro trim

tro trim

tro dim

lec

lec

ia dim

ia dim

‒ ‒ ◡ ‒   ‒ ‒ ◡ ‒
κᾆτ' αὐτίκ' ἐκκύψας ἐρεῖ—

⌢ ◡ ‒ ◡ ‒ ◡ ‒
Β. βρεκεκεκὲξ κοὰξ κοάξ.

‒ ‒ ◡ ‒   ‒ ◡ ‒
240   Δ. ἀλλ', ὦ φιλῳδὸν γένος,

‒ ‒ ◡ ‒   ‒ ◡ ‒
παύσασθε. Β. μᾶλλον μὲν οὖν

‒ ◡ ‒ ‒ ‒ ◡ ‒
242a   φθεγξόμεσθ', εἰ δὴ ποτ' εὐ-

‒ ◡ ‒ ◡   ‒ ◡ ‒ ◡
242b   ηλίοις ἐν ἁμέραισιν

‒ ◡ ‒ ◡   ⌢ ◡ ‒ ‒
ἡλάμεσθα διὰ κυπείρου

‒ ◡ ‒ ‒   ‒ ◡ ‒ ‒
καὶ φλέω, χαίροντες ᾠδῆς

⌢ ◡ ‒   ‒ ◡ ⌢ ◡
245   πολυκολύμβοισι μέλεσιν,

‒ ◡ ‒ ‒   ‒ ◡ ‒ ◡
ἢ Διὸς φεύγοντες ὄμβρον

⌢ ◡ ‒ ◡   ‒ ◡ ‒ ‒
ἔνυδρον ἐν βυθῷ χορείαν

‒ ◡ ‒ ‒   ‒ ◡ ‒ ◡
αἰόλαν ἐφθεγξάμεσθα

‒ ◡ ⌢ ◡ ‒ ◡ ‒
πομφολυγοπαφλάσμασιν.

⌢ ◡ ‒ ◡ ‒ ◡ ‒
250   Δ. βρεκεκεκὲξ κοὰξ κοάξ.

‒ ‒ ◡ ‒   ‒ ‒ ◡ ‒
τουτὶ παρ' ὑμῶν λαμβάνω.

ia dim

lec

ia cr

ia cr

lec

  + tro dim

tro dim

tro dim

cr tro

tro dim

tro dim

tro dim

lec

lec

ia dim

‒ ⏑ ‒ ⏑   ‒ ⏑ ‒ ⏑

B. δεινά τἄρα πεισόμεσθα.

‒ ⏑ ⌢ ⏑   ‒ ⏑ ‒ ‒

253–4   Δ. δεινότερα δ' ἔγωγ', ἐλαύνων

‒ ⏑ ‒ ⏑ ‒ ⏑ ‒

255   εἰ διαρραγήσομαι.

⌢ ⏑ ‒ ⏑ ‒ ⏑ ‒

B. βρεκεκεκὲξ κοὰξ κοάξ.

‒ ‒ ⏑ ‒   ‒ ‒ ⏑ ‒

Δ. οἰμώζετ'· οὐ γάρ μοι μέλει.

‒ ⏑ ‒ ⏑   ‒ ⏑ ‒ ⏑

258a   B. ἀλλὰ μὴν κεκραξόμεσθά γ'

⌢ ⏑ ‒ ⏑   ‒ ⏑ ‒ ‒

258b   ὁπόσον ἡ φάρυξ ἂν ἡμῶν

‒ ⏑ ‒ ⏑ ‒ ⏑ ‒

χανδάνῃ δι' ἡμέρας—

⌢ ⏑ ‒ ⏑ ‒ ⏑ ‒

260   Δ. βρεκεκεκὲξ κοὰξ κοάξ.

‒ ‒ ⏑ ‒   ‒ ‒ ⏑ ‿ ‖ ᴴ

τούτῳ γὰρ οὐ νικήσετε.

‒ ⏑ ‒ ‒   ‒ ⏑ ‒ ‒

B. οὐδὲ μὴν ὑμᾶς σὺ πάντως.

‒ ⏑ ‒ ‒ ‒ ⏑ ‿ ‖ ᴴ

Δ. οὐδὲ μὴν ὑμεῖς γ' ἐμὲ

‒ ⏑ ⌢ ⏑   ‒ ⏑ ‒ ‒

οὐδέποτε· κεκράξομαι γάρ,

‒ ⏑ ‒ ⏑   ‒ ⏑ ‒ ⏑

265   κἄν με δῇ, δι' ἡμέρας, ἕ-

‒ ⏑ ‒ ‒   ⌢ ⏑ ‒ ‒

ως ἂν ὑμῶν ἐπικρατήσω

tro dim

tro dim

lec

lec

ia dim

4 tro

lec

lec

ia dim

tro dim

lec

tro dim

4 tro

$- \smile -$

τῷ κοάξ.

$\widehat{} \smile - \smile - \smile - |||$

βρεκεκεκὲξ κοὰξ κοάξ.

The lyric of *Frogs*, like that of *Thesm*., begins with a major comic set-piece. Here, however, the metre is relatively simple, in the comic style, but very far from artless. Play is made, in particular, with transition between iambic and trochaic and with the ambiguous colon, the lecythion.

From 209 to 220, the Frogs perform a prelude, which is much the most rhythmically sophisticated part of the duet. The first section (marked off by κοὰξ κοάξ at 214), features the syncopated iambic dimeter, $\times - \smile - \quad - \smile -$, varied, immediately before the clausular bacchiac, by $\times - \smile - \quad - \smile \smile -$. The syncopated dimeter appears again opening the short middle section (215–17). The next two cola are problematic. Hermann's Διώνυσον in 216 would produce a repetition of ia cr, but the form is unparalleled in Attic poetry. Kock's Λίμναισ[ιν] ἰαχήσαμεν could, on the other hand, be made to produce another telesillean, by scanning ἰαχήσαμεν. But where the scansion of ἰαχέω and ἰάχω can be ascertained in Attic drama, the ι is almost invariably short, even in past tenses, and the α long. ἰαχεῖν occurs in anapaests at *Sept.* 868 (Lachmann: ἀχεῖν, accepted by Page), and ἰάχεῖ is confirmed by correspondence at E.*El.*707 (which Denniston takes as unaugmented imperfect of ἰαχέω). Diggle introduces ἰαχοῦσιν by emendation at *Phaethon* 82. In Aristophanes, ἴαχεν starts a hexameter at *Knights* 1016 (cf. *Od.* 9. 395: ... περὶ δ' ἴαχε πέτρη), but at *Birds* 772, there is an unaugmented imperfect ἴαχον. At *Thesm.* 327, ἰαχήσειεν, the quantity of α is uncertain, but it is probably long (ἰαχήσειεν would turn 329 into a solitary ionic dimeter).

The final section (218–19) is made up of dactylo-epitrite phrases (mostly dactylo-). Radermacher's deletion of ι from the MSS' Χύτροισι is a considerable simplification metrically. The received text produces anceps next to anceps, and so, presumably, verse-end in an inappropriate position.

Dionysus answers with ten iambic metra (221–27, interrupted by the Frogs' call at 225), of which the last six have long anceps. One may con-

cr (tro cat)

lec

jecture that this is not a good rowing rhythm. Since Dionysus ends with a full metron, not with catalexis, the Frogs' outraged trochees seem to break in before he has properly finished. Without Hermann's ⟨μὲν⟩ in 229, the run of trochees would begin with a syncopated metron (ἐμὲ γὰρ ἔστ-). A smooth, rapid run of full metra seems more suitable to the style of the song and the mood of the Frogs. Moreover, $\overline{\smile\smile}\ \smile -$ is rare everywhere in Aristophanes (Introduction, p. 47), and there is no parallel for it in immediate proximity to trochees ($\overline{\smile\smile}\ \smile -\quad -\smile-\times$) except in, at most, three passages in this play (here, 245, and 896b= 993b). Here emendation is easy and 896b=993b presents a serious problem of correspondence.

Dionysus (236–41) perseveres in iambic, picking up, after the Frogs' interruption at 239, the syncopated dimeter of their prelude (211–12, 215, 217). In the middle of 241 there is a remarkable change of singer (see further Parker , in Craik, *'Owls to Athens'*, 343–4). The Frogs continue in full trochees until 248, except, in the received text, for a single syncopated metron at the beginning of 245, which is harder to remove than $\overline{\smile\smile}\ \smile -$ in 229 (see above). Reisig proposed πολυκολύμβοισιν μέλεσσιν ($\overline{\smile\smile}\ \smile --\quad -\smile-\smile$), but dative plurals in -εσσι seem to be confined to quotation and parody in Aristophanes (*Peace* 1075, 1093, 1106, *Birds* 251, 941, 1372, *Lys.* 520, 774).

While taking over the Frogs' lecythion refrain at 250, Dionysus still follows it with an iambic dimeter. At 253 he slips into trochees, but returns to iambic at 257 and 261. In the received text, the last utterance of the Frogs, 262, is acatalectic, and Dionysus steals, as it were, the clausula lecythion that should have been theirs. He has now firmly grasped trochaic rhythm, and finishes the song in it. Wilamowitz was the first to perceive the 'war of metres' in the song (*GV* 593). Without attempting to be precise, one can reasonably guess that the reversals of rhythm are comically reflected in some way in Dionysus' rowing movements. It is also just possible that there is an element of parody of Euripidean iambo-trochaic. For a notable example in late Euripides of movement to and fro by way of the ambiguous lecythion, see *Hel.* 229–51 (and see further Parker, in Craik, '*Owls to Athens*', 331–48).

Part of the song (234–45 and 249–62) is preserved in fragmentary form in *P. Berol.* 13231 (5th c. AD). This provides one good reading not found in the MSS: ἐκκ[ύψας] for ἐγκύψας at 238.

The following are minor, but metrically significant, textual points. At 242, the metrically necessary φθεγξόμεσθ' comes from R. The Aldine shares φθεγξόμεθ' with VAU, while ML have φθεγξώμεθ' (which may have appealed to Triclinius because it would make 242a scan

$$323–36=340–53$$

$$\cup - - \quad \cup \cup - - - \cup - \quad \cup \cup - -$$

323–4 Ἴακχ', ὦ πολυτιμήτοις [ἐν] ἕδραις ἐνθάδε ναίων,

$$\cup - - \quad \cup - \smile \, ||^{\text{H}}$$

325 Ἴακχ', ὦ Ἴακχε,

$$- \cup - - \quad \cup \cup - -$$

ἐλθὲ τόνδ' ἀνὰ λειμῶνα χορεύσων

$$\cup \cup - \overline{\cup} \, \underline{\cup} \, \cup - -$$

ὁσίους εἰς θιασώτας,

$$\cup \cup - \overline{\cup} - | \cup - -$$

πολύκαρπον μὲν τινάσσων

$$\cup \cup - \underline{\cup} - \cup - -$$

περὶ κρατὶ σῷ βρύοντα

$$\cup \cup - \overline{\cup} - | \cup - - \quad \cup \cup - -$$

330–1 στέφανον μύρτων, θρασεῖ δ' ἐγκατακρούων

$$\cup \cup - \quad \cup \cup - -$$

ποδὶ τὰν ἀκόλαστον

$$\cup \cup - \quad \cup \cup - -$$

φιλοπαίγμονα τιμάν,

$$\cup \cup - | - \quad \cup \cup - - \quad \cup \cup - -$$

334–5 χαρίτων πλεῖστον ἔχουσαν μέρος, ἁγνάν,

$$\cup \cup - | \quad \cup \cup - - \overline{\cup} \cup - - |||$$

ἱερὰν ὁσίοις μύσταις χορείαν.

‒ ‒ ◡ ‒   ‒ ◡ ‒, like the preceding cola). At 243, ἠλάμεσθα comes from the Aldine (the pre-Triclinian MSS have -μεθα), but the metrical expertise behind the reading is that of Triclinius: L has ἠλλάμεσθα. At 248 and 252, the MSS are divided between -μεσθα and -μεθα with LAld choosing the metrically correct -μεσθα.

There is some MS variation in the incidence of the βρεκεκεκέξ-refrain. RUAM have it between 222 and 224. Fritzsche's belief that the Frogs ought to deliver it after 249 and 259, before it is taken up by Dionysus, is worth bearing in mind.

	ba anac ion
340-1	†ἔγειρε φλογέας λαμπάδας ἐν χερσὶ γὰρ ἥκει τινάσσων†
	2 ba
	Ἴακχ᾽, ὦ Ἴακχε,
	cr 2 ion
	νυκτέρου τελετῆς φωσφόρος ἀστήρ.
	ion dim = anac
	φλογὶ φέγγεται δὲ λειμών·
	anac
345	γόνυ πάλλεται γερόντων
	anac
	ἀποσείονται δὲ λύπας
	anac
347-8	χρονίους τ᾽ ἐτῶν παλαιῶν ἐνιαυτοὺς
	ion dim sync
	ἱερᾶς ὑπὸ τιμᾶς.
	ion dim sync
350	σὺ δὲ λαμπάδι φέγγων
	ion trim
351-2	προβάδην ἔξαγ᾽ ἐπ᾽ ἀνθηρὸν ἕλειον
	ion sync anac= ion trim sync
	δάπεδον χοροποιόν, μάκαρ, ἥβαν.

The parodos of *Frogs* takes the form of a miniature cult-performance, a sequence of songs and dances, like *Thesm.* 947–1000. The opening ionic hymn to Iacchus is the most metrically sophisticated part of the performance. The stanza is discussed briefly by Wilamowitz in *Isyllos von Epidauros* (37–8). On the possible connection of ionics with the cult of Dionysus, see Dodds on *Ba.* 64–169 and Introduction, p. 63). The rare version of the anaclomenon with long fourth position ($\cup\cup---\cup--$, 323, 328–30) is found in Aeschylus (*Pers.* 951=965, *Supp.* 1021=1029), in *PV* (399?, 405=414), and elsewhere in Aristophanes at *Thesm.* 116–17, 123 (the parody of Agathon). For a bacchiac introducing ionic (323), compare *Phoen.* 1539, 1541.

The stanza offers, in the received text, some exceptional freedoms of responsion. Ionic dimeter corresponding with anaclomenon (327=344) is found at *Ba.* 530=549 (where Bothe proposed σκοτίαισι κρυπτὸν εἰρκταῖς for the latter line.). There may be correspondence between anaclomenon with long fourth position and normal anaclomenon (328=345, 329=346) at *Sept.* 723=730 (unless one is prepared to scan εὐκταΐαν in 723 or ὠμόφρων in 730). The only possible example outside this passage of anaclomenon with long fourth position corresponding with ionic dimeter (336=353) is the MS reading at *PV* 399=408 (δακρυσίστακτον δ' ἀπ' ὄσσων = μεγαλοσχήμονά τ' ἀρχαι-). On these responsions, see further below, in the discussion of the text.

In 323, ἐν is omitted by the Triclinian MSS and the Aldine. For ναίων with *dat. loci*, compare *OT* 1451. Reisig chose to retain ἐν and read ὦ πολυτίμητ' (cf. 398 below), but this leaves ἐν ἕδραις ἐνθάδε to be interpreted as ἐν ταύταις ταῖς ἕδραις, unless we assume (with Dover) the loss of an epithet for ἕδραις. It seems credible, however, that πολυτίμητος (= 'worthy of high honour'), although normally an epithet of

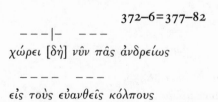

372–6=377–82

$---|-$ $---$

χώρει [δὴ] νῦν πᾶς ἀνδρείως

$----$ $---$

εἰς τοὺς εὐανθεῖς κόλπους

gods, could be transferred to the god's dwelling. The corresponding verse, 340, poses major problems, both of metre and meaning. Triclinius seems to have made an inept attempt at emendation by deleting τινάσσων (omitted by LVv5. The Aldine retains the word, but Σ Ald notes ἐν δέ τισιν ἐκλέλοιπε τὸ τινάσσων). Hermann (who prints a full text of the passage at *EDM* 501–2) more promisingly deletes γὰρ ἥκει (ἥκεις AMU Triclinius), which produces exact correspondence with Reisig's version of 323, or correspondence of ionic dimeter with anaclomenon with long fourth position (as in 336=353): ἔγειρε φλογέας λαμπάδας ἐν χερσὶ τινάσσων. But the lengthening -ρε̄ φλογέας would be unparalleled, even within the same word (Introduction, pp. 92–3), and the nominative ἀστήρ etc. in 342 then has to be accounted for. Zimmermann (*Untersuchungen*, i. 127) adduces *Clouds* 264 ff. There, however, a vocative precedes the verb, and λαμπρός τ᾽ Αἰθήρ is added like an afterthought. An exclamatory nominative (Kühner–Gerth, i. 46. 3) is, perhaps, more promising. γὰρ ἥκει could have been introduced in a maladroit attempt to simplify the syntax. Radermacher's solution (also adopted by Coulon) has nothing to recommend it. He takes from Fritzsche the idea of treating ἔγειρε as intransitive (citing *IA* 624; see Kühner-Gerth, i. 95). He then deletes λαμπάδας and derives φλογέας from a hypothetical form φλογεύς. The result does not correspond with 324 and is itself unmetrical.

At 344, the MSS show evidence of early variants: R has φέγγεται (corrected from φθέγγεται), VAU have φλέγεται, and M φλέγγεται (with λ erased). Hermann proposed φλέγεται δὴ φλογὶ λειμών, and δή (rather than δέ) has much to commend it here: 'There, the meadow is really ablaze' (Denniston, *Particles* 204; cf. Tucker, ad loc.). At 350, φέγγων was proposed by Bothe (and, later, by Hermann and Voss). The MSS have φλέγων *contra metrum*.

> an dim cat
> ἀλλ᾽ ἔμβα χὤπως ἀρεῖς
>
> an dim cat
> τὴν Σώτειραν γενναίως

$- - - \mid - - -$

374a λειμώνων ἐγκρούων

$- - - -$

374b κἀπισκώπτων

$- - - - \quad - - -$

375 καὶ παίζων καὶ χλευάζων·

$- - \overline{\smile\smile} - \quad - - - - \parallel\parallel\parallel$

ἠρίστηται δ' ἐξαρκούντως.

The chorus-leader formally opens the rites in a recitative passage of eighteen catalectic anapaestic tetrameters, in which he warns off a list of 'sinners'. The processional song which follows is also in anapaests, but of an emphatically lyric type (Introduction, p. 57). The reference to Thorycion, mentioned as a sinner at 363, comes as a comic surprise at the end of an apparently 'straight' passage.

The use of catalectic dimeters in sequence and without clausular function is characteristic of lyric anapaests. Here, an unsyncopated dimeter is actually used as a contrasting clausular. Odd as this is, there is no reason to suspect it. 374a=379 is problematic. It could be seen, following word-end, as 2 mol, implying iambic or trochaic in an otherwise purely anapaestic stanza. An anapaestic tripody suits the context better,

384–8=389–93

$- - \smile - \quad \overline{\smile} - \smile -$

Δήμητερ, ἁγνῶν ὀργίων

$\smile - \smile - \quad \smile - \smile -$

385 ἄνασσα, συμπαραστάτει,

$- - \smile - \quad - - \smile -$

καὶ σῷζε τὸν σαυτῆς χορόν·

$- - \smile - \quad \smile - \smile -$

καί μ' ἀσφαλῶς πανήμερον

$- - \smile \mid - \quad \smile - - \parallel\parallel\parallel$

παῖσαί τε καὶ χορεῦσαι.

an trip?

τῇ φωνῇ μολπάζων

an

380 ἢ τὴν χώραν

an dim cat

σώσειν φήσ' εἰς τὰς ὥρας,

an dim

κἂν Θωρυκίων μὴ βούληται.

although no other anapaestic tripody in Aristophanes is made up exclusively of longs (Introduction, p. 60). The MS text of Euripides offers examples of − − − − − − among anapaests: *Tro.* 144 (with Musurus' κοῦραι) and 148, *Ion* 904. The ritual-cry which serves as ephymnium at *Ion* 125 ff. and 141 ff. is not metrically classifiable (see further Introduction, p. 58).

At 372, δὴ is deleted by the corrector of E. Deletion was conjectured by Bentley.

At 377, ἀρεῖς was proposed by Scaliger (ὑψώσεις *Σ vet.* V *Σ* Ald). The MSS are much divided: αἴρεις RU (αἰρεῖς Ald), αἰρήσεις V, αἴροις A, αἴρῃς M (αἴρῃς L).

At 381, σώσειν is Cobet's emendation of the MSS' σῴζειν (σώσει V).

6 ia

καὶ πολλὰ μὲν γέλοιά μ' εἰ-

390 πεῖν, πολλὰ δὲ σπουδαῖα, καὶ

τῆς σῆς ἑορτῆς ἀξίως

3 ia ba (ia tetram cat)

παίσαντα καὶ σκώψαντα νι-

κήσαντα ταινιοῦσθαι.

Two catalectic anapaestic dimeters divide the anapaestic processional song from the iambic hymn to Demeter. There is no syncopation in the song except for the clausular bacchiac (compare Dicaeopolis' processional hymn to Phales at *Ach.* 263 ff.). The stanza is articulated into 6 metra and 4 metra by rhetorical pause in the strophe and word-end in the antistrophe. Fraenkel (*Beobachtungen*, 201–2) points to the formal resemblance between this song and Eupolis, *PCG* 99. 1–22. In metrical style, Eupolis' song is indeed very similar: it is made up of sequences of iambic metra, articulated by bacchiacs into 8 + 6 + 6. It is, however, a lampoon-song on a variety of individuals, and, as such, its real affinities

398–403=404–8=409–13

⏑‒⏑ 〰 ⏑‒⏑|〰 ⏑‒≝ ||

Ἴακχε πολυτίμητε, μέλος ἑορτῆς

‒‒⏑‒ ‒|〰 ⏑ 〰 ⏑‒‒

ἥδιστον εὑρών, δεῦρο συνακολούθει

‒‒⏑‒

400 πρὸς τὴν θεὸν

≝‒⏑‒ ⏑‒⏑‒ ‒‒⏑‒ ⏑‒≝ ||

401–2 καὶ δεῖξον ὡς ἄνευ πόνου πολλὴν ὁδὸν περαίνεις.

⏑‒⏑〰 ⏑‒⏑|‒ ⏑‒⏑⏑ |||

Ἴακχε φιλοχορευτά, συμπρόπεμπέ με.

καὶ γὰρ παραβλέψας τι μειρακίσκης
410 νῦν δὴ κατεῖδον καὶ μάλ' εὐπροσώπου,
συμπαιστρίας,
χιτωνίου παραρραγέντος τιτθίον προκύψαν.
Ἴακχε φιλοχορευτά, συμπρόπεμπέ με.

Again, a pair of recitative verses, this time 'euripideans' (ia dim + ith) (see on *Lys.* 256 ff.=271 ff.), introduces the next song. 395 begins with temporal νῦν, marking the next stage in the proceedings.

This jocular processional hymn to Iacchus is, again, in pure iambic, although the pattern of catalexis suggests slightly more sophistication

are with 416 ff. The prayers of Aristophanes' chorus are in some degree ambiguous: they are in part adaptable to their real persons as comic chorusmen.

In the antistrophe, V is more reliable both in text and colometry than R. At 390, R (with A) adds an extra καὶ after πολλὰ δὲ, and slips into changing line prematurely at word-end after σπουδαῖα and again after σκώψαντα. Stopping short is a less easy mistake to make than running on, but here R, or an ancestor of R, has demonstrably made it (Introduction, p. 101). LAld share the correct text and colon division with V.

> ia trim cat
>
> σὺ γὰρ κατεσχίσω μὲν ἐπὶ γέλωτι
>
> ia trim cat
>
> 405 κἀπ' εὐτελείᾳ τόδε τὸ σανδαλίσκον
>
> ia
>
> καὶ τὸ ῥάκος.
>
> ia tetram cat
>
> κἀξηῦρες ὥστ' ἀζημίους παίζειν τε καὶ χορεύειν.
>
> ia trim
>
> Ἴακχε φιλοχορευτά, συμπρόπεμπέ με.

here than in the previous song. The acatalectic refrain contrasts with the catalectic close of the stanza proper (cf. 372 ff. = 377 ff. above).

The text of 404–8 survives in very fragmentary form in *P. Berol.* 13231, but the only variant offered there, μοι for με at the end of 408, is wrong.

At 405, τόδε τὸ is Bergk's correction of τόνδε τὸν.

At 407, κἀξηῦρες is Meineke's emendation for κἀξεῦρες (VAMUL Ald). R has ἔξευρες, which Kock accepted, proposing κατασχισάμενος

416–18=419–21=422–4=425–7=428–30=431–3=434–6=437–9

×–◡– ◡–◡ || н

Χ. βούλεσθε δῆτα κοινῇ

––◡ ◠◠ ◡–◡ || н

σκώψωμεν Ἀρχέδημον

×–◡– ×–◡– ×–◡◡ |||

ὃς ἑπτέτης ὢν οὐκ ἔφυσε φράτερας;

νυνὶ δὲ δημαγωγεῖ
420　ἐν τοῖς ἄνω νεκροῖσι,
κἀστὶν τὰ πρῶτα τῆς ἐκεῖ μοχθηρίας.

τὸν Κλεισθένους δ' ἀκούω
ἐν ταῖς ταφαῖσι πρωκτὸν
τίλλειν ἑαυτοῦ καὶ σπαράττειν τὰς γνάθους.

425　κἀκόπτετ' ἐγκεκυφώς,
κἄκλαε κἀκεκράγει
Σεβῖνον ὅστις ἐστὶν Ἀναφλύστιος.

καὶ Καλλίαν γέ φασι
τοῦτον τὸν Ἱπποβίνου
430　κύσθῳ λεοντῆν ναυμαχεῖν ἐνημμένον.

Δ. ἔχοιτ' ἂν οὖν φράσαι νῷν
Πλούτων' ὅπου 'νθάδ' οἰκεῖ;
ξένω γάρ ἐσμεν ἀρτίως ἀφιγμένω.

Χ. μηδὲν μακρὰν ἀπέλθῃς,
435　μηδ' αὖθις ἐπανέρῃ με,
ἀλλ' ἴσθ' ἐπ' αὐτὴν τὴν θύραν ἀφιγμένος.

Δ. αἴροι' ἂν αὖθις, ὦ παῖ.
Χ. τουτὶ τί ἦν τὸ πρᾶγμα
ἀλλ' ἢ Διὸς Κόρινθος ἐν τοῖς στρώμασιν;

for κατασχίσω μὲν at 404. This, however, turns the iambic metron at
400=406=411 into an independent verse by requiring *brevis in longo* at
406: ῥάκο̆ς.

ia dim cat

ia dim cat

ia trim

The interlude (414–15) following the second hymn to Iacchus (398 ff. = 404 ff. = 409 ff.) is not delivered by the chorus-leader, but by Dionysus and Xanthias. Since the other sections of the song are divided from each other by recitative couplets, it is virtually certain here that ⏑ – – (to make a second iambic tetrameter) is needed at the end of Xanthias' intervention. Beck's excision of *μετ᾽ αὐτῆς*, turning 414b into an iambic trimeter ending with *καὶ* is injudicious (see further, Fraenkel, *Beobachtungen*, 26 n. 1).

The lampoon-song at 416 ff. is in extremely simple, three-verse stanzas. In the course of repetition, the verses are all marked off from each other by *brevis in longo*, or hiatus, or both, as well as (in the first two verses) by catalexis. Once again, acatalexis, contrasting with catalexis, provides the clausular rhythm. In literary poetry, the three-line stanza takes us back to Archilochus. So does the relative lack of resolution. Precisely this stanza-form is not found among Archilochus' fragments, but, allowing for differences of time and region, we may see here a pastiche of the kind of folk-poetry from which the early lampoon-song developed. For the association of iambic *αἰσχρολογία* with the cult of

448–53 = 454–9

⏓ – ⏑ –   ⏒ – ⏑ – | – – ⏑ ⏕   ⏑ – ⏓ ||

448–9 χωρῶμεν εἰς πολυρρόδους λειμῶνας ἀνθεμώδεις,

⏑ – ⏑ ⏑ – ⏑ –

450 τὸν ἡμέτερον τρόπον,

⏓ – ⏑ ⏑ – ⏑ –

τὸν καλλιχορώτατον,

⏓ – ⏑ ⏑ – ⏑ –

παίζοντες, ὃν ὄλβιαι

– – ⏑ ⏑ – – |||

Μοῖραι ξυνάγουσιν.

The final processional song of the Initiates is introduced by a recitative interlude in 'euripideans' (like 398–413 above). The song itself begins with a full catalectic tetrameter, before changing from iambic to aeolo-choriambic. The colon-division I give is that of V (and, in intention, of

Demeter, see N.J. Richardson, *The Homeric Hymn to Demeter* (Oxford, 1974), 213–17.

The intervention of Dionysus at 431 with his request for directions in the same metre as the song cuts across the ordinary ritual lampoon with another kind of joke (*Peace* 1063 ff.).

Textual corruption in this song is minor. At 418, φράτερας is Dindorf's correction of the MSS' φράτορας (cf. Meisterhans, *GAI*³ 131). At 421, RAV and L have κἀστὶν, while the Aldine, characteristically, follows MU with κἄστι *contra metrum*. At 422, Κλεισθένους is the reading of RVAM. U has Κλεισθένην, and LAld Κλεισθένη. At 426, κἀκεκράγει comes from A (also LAld; καὶ κεκράγει RVM¹U: κἀγκεκράγει M²). At 427 Porson corrected the metre by adding the article in crasis to the MSS' Ἀναφλύστιος. κύσθῳ ('to do battle with a κύσθος') at 434 is Bothe's emendation of κύσθου ('a lion-skin made of a κύσθος'). At 437, RAMU incorporate a gloss, τὰ στρώματα, into the text, after ὦ παῖ. This caused Triclinius (LAld) to emend to αὖ γε παῖ, so as to make a complete iambic trimeter, like the preceding verse.

        ia tetram cat
454–5 μόνοις γὰρ ἡμῖν ἥλιος καὶ φέγγος ἱερόν ἐστιν,

        tel
    ὅσοι μεμνήμεθ' εὐ-

          + tel
      σεβῆ τε διήγομεν

        tel
    τρόπον περὶ τοὺς ξένους

        reiz
    καὶ τοὺς ἰδιώτας.

R, who, however, makes a couple of slips to word-end in the antistrophe). It would be perfectly justifiable to write out the stanza as three dicola, of which the second would then be acatalectic, the first and third catalectic. The usual modern division into dimeters throughout is less satisfactory in that it conceals the affinity between the first verse of the song and the preceding recitative.

At 455, ἱλαρόν is the reading of AMULAld, while RV have ἱερόν. At

$$534\text{--}48 = 590\text{--}604$$

‒ ◡ ‒ ◡　　‒ ◡ ‒ ◡

534a　X. ταῦτα μὲν πρὸς ἀνδρός ἐστι

‒ ◡ ‒ ‒　　‒ ◡ ‒ ◡

534b　　　νοῦν ἔχοντος καὶ φρένας καὶ

‒ ◡ ◡◡ ◡　‒ ◡ ◡ ‖

535　　　πολλὰ περιπεπλευκότος,

◠ ◡ ‒ ‒　‒ ◡ ‒ ‒

μετακυλίνδειν αὐτὸν ἀεὶ

‒ ◡ ‒ ‒　‒ ◡ ‒ ‒

537a　　πρὸς τὸν εὖ πράττοντα τοῖχον

‒ ◡ ‒ ◡　‒ ◡ ◡ ‖

537b　　μᾶλλον ἢ γεγραμμένην

‒ ◡ ‒ ◡　‒ ◡ ‒ ◡

εἰκόν' ἑστάναι, λαβόνθ' ἐν

‒ ◡ ◠◡ ◡　‒ ◡ ‒ ‒

539a　　σχῆμα· τὸ δὲ μεταστρέφεσθαι

‒ ◡ ‒ ◡　‒ ◡ ◡ ‖

539b　　πρὸς τὸ μαλθακώτερον

‒ ◡ ‒ ◡　‒ ◡ ‒ ◡　‒ ◡ ‒ ‒　‒ ◡ ◡ ‖ₕ

540‒1　δεξιοῦ πρὸς ἀνδρός ἐστι καὶ φύσει Θηραμένους.

‒ ◡ ‒ ◡　‒ ◡ ‒ ‒

542a　Δ. οὐ γὰρ ἂν γέλοιον ἦν, εἰ

‒ ◡ ‒ ‒　‒ ◡ ‒ ‒

542b　　　Ξανθίας μὲν δοῦλος ὢν ἐν

‒ ◡ ‒ ◡　‒ ◡ ◡ ‖

543a　　στρώμασιν Μιλησίοις

458, περὶ τοὺς ξένους is the reading of R and the *Suda* (s. ἰδιῶται). VAMU have περὶ τε τοὺς ... *contra metrum*. Triclinius chose the wrong way to mend the metre: he expelled τοὺς (LAld).

tro hex cat

590   Χ. νῦν σὸν ἔργον ἔστ', ἐπειδὴ

591a   τὴν στολὴν εἴληφας ἥνπερ

591b   εἶχες, ἐξ ἀρχῆς πάλιν

tro hex cat

592a   ἀνανεάζειν ⟨– ◡ – ×⟩

592b   καὶ βλέπειν αὖθις τὸ δεινόν,

593a   τοῦ θεοῦ μεμνημένον

tro hex cat

593b   ᾧπερ εἰκάζεις σεαυτόν.

        εἰ δὲ παραληρῶν ἁλώσει

595   κἀκβαλεῖς τι μαλθακόν,

tro tetram cat

596–7   αὖθις αἴρεσθαί σ' ἀνάγκη 'σται πάλιν τὰ στρώματα.

tro hex cat

598a   Ξ. οὐ κακῶς, ὦνδρες, παραινεῖτ',

598b   ἀλλὰ καὐτὸς τυγχάνω ταῦτ'

599a   ἄρτι συννοούμενος.

$\widetilde{} \cup - \underset{\smile}{} \quad - \cup - \overline{}$

543b ἀνατετραμμένος κυνῶν ὀρ-

$- \cup - - \quad - \cup \underset{\smile\smile}{}$

544a χρηστρίδ᾽ εἶτ᾽ ᾔτησεν ἀμίδ᾽, ἐ-

$- \cup - - \quad - \cup \smile \|_{\text{H}}$

544b γὼ δὲ πρὸς τοῦτον βλέπων

$- \cup - \overline{} \quad - \cup - -$

545 τοὐρεβίνθου ᾿δραττόμην, οὗ-

$- \cup - - \quad - \cup - \cup$

546a τος δ᾽ ἅτ᾽ ὢν αὐτὸς πανοῦργος

$- \cup - \overline{} \quad - \cup -$

546b εἶδε, κᾆτ᾽ ἐκ τῆς γνάθου

$- \cup - \overline{} \quad - \cup - \underset{\smile}{} | \quad - \cup - - \quad - \cup - \|\|$

547-8 πὺξ πατάξας μοὐξέκοψε τοῦ χοροῦ τοὺς προσθίους;

This song of comment on the action serves to punctuate the sequence of encounters with alternately hostile and welcoming residents of the Underworld. Typically, it is metrically simple. Three verses, each of six trochees rounded off by catalexis, are followed by a trochaic tetrameter. The whole pattern is repeated four times. It is typographically convenient to set out the trochaic 'hexameters' as dimeters, but in most instances word-end between the dimeters is either very weak or absent altogether in strophe or antistrophe or both. Full word-end after acatalectic metra coincides in strophe and antistrophe at 537a=592b, 539a= 594, and 546a=602b. It is tempting to compare this song with *Birds* 1470ff.=1482ff. and 1553ff.=1694ff. There, however, the four stanzas (or half-stanzas) are not identical, and dimeter-division is indicated by the frequent lecythia, some of which are in sequence. So the effect of the two songs in performance may have been markedly different.

At 539a, μεταστρέφεσθαι is the reading of V (and LAld). A has -στρέφειν, RMU -στρέφεσθ᾽ ἀεὶ. At 543a, the pre-Triclinian MSS have

tro hex cat
599b   ὅδε μὲν οὖν, ἢν χρηστὸν ᾖ τι,

600   ταῦτ' ἀφαιρεῖσθαι πάλιν πει-

         ράσεταί μ' εὖ οἶδ' ὅτι.

tro hex cat
602a   ἀλλ' ὅμως ἐγὼ παρέξω

602b   'μαυτὸν ἀνδρεῖον τὸ λῆμα

603a   καὶ βλέποντ' ὀρίγανον.

tro tetram cat
603b–4   δεῖν δ' ἔοικεν, ὡς ἀκούω τῆς θύρας καὶ δὴ ψόφον.

στρώμασι *contra metrum*. Triclinius (L) added the necessary ephelcystic
ν, but the Aldine did not follow him, and ν disappeared from the printed
vulgate until restored by Brunck (Introduction, pp. 110–11). At 545–46a,
οὗτος δ' . . . αὐτός are preserved correctly by V (and LAld). RU have
αὐτὸς δ' at 545 and omit αὐτός at 546a. At 548, τοῦ χοροῦ is Kock's
emendation of τοὺς χορούς.

At 592a, Triclinius noted the lacuna, and proposed σαυτὸν αἰεί
(LAld), attempting to take ἀνανεάζω as transitive. At 594, there are
signs of variation early in the tradition between different types of conditional. A, with Σ *vet.* V, has ἢν and ἁλῷς, on which Radermacher
based ἢν . . . ἁλῷς ἢ κἀκβάλῃς . . . . RVM have εἰ with ἁλώσει (RM¹)
or ἁλώσῃ (VM²). At 595, V has κἀκβάλῃς, RA have καὶ βάλῃς, and M
καὶ βάλλεις. κἀκβαλεῖς is Hermann's emendation. At 596, 'σται was
supplied by Dawes. The pre-Triclinian MSS have 'στι (V) or nothing
(RAMU). Triclinius supplied τις (LAld). At 599b, ὅδε is Blaydes's
conjecture for the MS ὅτι (redundant, in view of εὖ οἶδ' ὅτι at 600b).

674–85=706–16

‒ ᴗ ᴗ   ‒ ᴗ ᴗ   ‒|ᴗ ᴗ   ‒ ᴗ ᴗ   ‒ ᴗ ᴗ   ‒ ᴗ|ᴗ

Μοῦσα, χορῶν ἱερῶν ἐπίβηθι καὶ ἔλθ' ἐπὶ τέρψιν ἀ-

‒ ‒ ᴗ ‒ ||ₕ

675 οιδᾶς ἐμᾶς,

‒ ᴗ ᴗ ‒ ᴗ ᴗ ‒   ᴗ   ‒ ᴗ ᴗ ‒ ᴗ ᴗ ‒

τὸν πολὺν ὀψομένη λαῶν ὄχλον οὗ σοφίαι

‒ ᴗ ‒   ᴗ ‒ ᴗ ||

μυρίαι κάθηνται

ᴗ ᴗ ‒ ᴗ ᴗ ‒|ᴗ ᴗ ‒ ᴗ ᴗ ‒   ᴗ   ‒ ᴗ ᴗ ‒ ᴗ ᴗ ‒

678–9 φιλοτιμότεραι Κλεοφῶντος, ἐφ' οὗ δὴ χείλεσιν ἀμφιλάλοις

‒ ᴗ ᴗ ‒ ᴗ ᴗ ‒

680 δεινὸν ἐριβ|ρέμεται

‒ ᴗ ‒   ᴗ ‒ ‒

Θρηκία χελιδών

ᴗ ᴗ ‒ ᴗ ᴗ ‒ ᴗ ᴗ ‒ ᴗ ᴗ ‒   ‒

ἐπὶ βάρβαρον ἑζομένη πέταλον· τρύ-

‒ ᴗ ᴗ ‒ ᴗ ᴗ ‒ ᴗ ᴗ ‒ ᴗ ᴗ ‒ ᴗ ᴗ ‒   ᴗ

ζει δ' ἐπίκλαυτον ἀηδόνιον νόμον ὡς ἀπολεῖται

‒ ᴗ ‒   ᴗ ‒ ‒ |||

685 κἂν ἴσαι γένωνται.

The parabasis of *Frogs* consists only of an ode and antode and pair of epirrhemes, and both fantasy and scurrility are strikingly absent from the latter. By contrast, the ode and antode belong to the genre of the sophisticated lampoon-song.

Metrically, the song is quite recherché. The nearest thing to it elsewhere in Aristophanes is *Birds* 451 ff. = 539 ff. 676 = 708 is clearly dactylo-epitrite, and the link-anceps between dactylic phrases at 679 = 710 points in the same direction. However, the long dactylic runs, some opening with double short, suggest the early dactylo-epitrite of Stesichorus, in particular the *Geryoneis* (Introduction, p. 85), rather than Pindar and Bacchylides or Attic lyric, in their metrical manner. But the ithyphallics at 677 = 709, 681 = 713, and 685 = 716 introduce an Attic element alien to

6 da

εἰ δ' ἐγὼ ὀρθὸς ἰδεῖν βίον ἀνέρος ἢ τρόπον ὅστις ἔτ'

+ ia

οἰμώξεται,

D – D

οὐ πολὺν οὐδ' ὁ πίθηκος οὗτος ὁ νῦν ἐνοχλῶν,

ith

Κλειγένης ὁ μικρός,

⏑ ⏑ D prol � D

710–11   ὁ πονηρότατος βαλανεὺς ὁπόσοι κρατοῦσι κυκησίτεφροι

D

ψευδολίτρου κονίας

ith

καὶ Κιμωλίας γῆς,

⏑ ⏑ D prol –

χρόνον ἐνδιατρίψει· ἰδὼν δὲ τάδ' οὐκ εἰ-

D prol �

715   ρηνικός ἐσθ', ἵνα μή ποτε κἀποδυθῇ μεθύων ἄ-

+ ith

νευ ξύλου βαδίζων.

dactylo-epitrite (Introduction, p. 89). While *Birds* 451 ff. = 539 ff. has an affinity with *PV* 545 ff. = 552 ff., the only more or less comparable stanzas to this song elsewhere in Attic poetry are in two early plays of Euripides. *Hipp.* 1102 ff. = 1111 ff. runs thus:

```
 – ⏑ ⏑    – ⏑ ⏑    – ⏑ ⏑       – ⏑ ⏑    – ⏑ ⏑    – –
 ⏑ – ⏑ –
            – ⏑ ⏑    – ⏑ ⏑    – ⏑ ⏑      – –
 – ⏑ ⏑ – ⏑ ⏑ –    –    – ⏑ ⏑ – ⏑ ⏑ –    –
 – ⏑ ⏑    – ⏑ ⏑
              ⏑ – ⏑ –
 ⏑ ⏑    – ⏑ ⏑    – ⏑ ⏑    – –
 ⏑ – ⏑ –    ⏑ – –
```

Here, there are dactylic runs (including one beginning with ⏑ ⏑), an unmistakable dactylo-epitrite compound (verse 3) and the unusual conjunction of short next to anceps produced by dactyl followed by iamb (compare verse 4 with *Frogs* 674–5 = 706–7, and see Introduction, pp. 53–4). On the other hand, the *Hipp.* stanza has features which are absent from the *Frogs* stanza and which tend to assimilate it to Aeschylean dactylo-iambic: the use of normal dactylic lengths (hexameter, tetrameter), the compound of iambic metron + dactylic tetrameter (see below on 1264 ff.). Even the acephalous colon, ∪∪ –∪∪ –∪∪ – – (cf. *Hipp.* 1123 = 1134), can be paralleled in Aeschylus at *Eum.* 1043 = 1047. For these Aeschylean features, compare *Andr.* 117 ff. = 126 ff. A slightly closer parallel in some respects to the *Frogs* song is *Med.* 991 ff. = 996 ff.:

$$∪ \quad –∪∪–∪∪– \quad ∪ \quad –∪– \quad ∪– –$$
$$–∪– \quad ∪– –$$
$$∪∪–∪∪–∪∪–∪∪– \quad ∪ \quad –∪∪–∪∪–$$
$$– –∪– \quad –∪– \quad ∪– –$$

Note, in particular, the ithyphallic at verse 2 followed by a verse of the same form as *Frogs* 678–9 = 710 (a form for which I have found no other parallel). A distinctive feature of *Med.* is the extensive use of dactylo-epitrite. Given the theme of *Frogs*, Euripidean reference here would not be surprising, but the comparative material available is not adequate to prove it. Still less do we know whether even the most musically expert members of the audience would have perceived anything of the kind. Moreover, Σ *vet.* claims that 706 is quoted from Ion of Chios (*TrGF* i, Ion 41), and any metrical reference might be to him.

The first verse forms a prelude (particularly clearly in the strophe, where it embodies the invocation to the Muse). Thereafter, the stanza

$$814–17 = 818–21 = 822–25 = 826–29$$
$$– – \quad –∪∪ \quad –∪∪ \quad –|∪∪ \quad –∪∪ \quad – –||^H$$

ἦ που δεινὸν ἐριβ|ρεμέτας χόλον ἔνδοθεν ἕξει,

$$–∪∪ \quad –∪∪ \quad –∪∪ \quad –|– \quad –∪∪ \quad –⌣||^H$$

815 ἡνίκ᾽ ἂν ὀξύλαλόν περ ἴδῃ θήγοντος ὀδόντα

$$–∪∪ \quad –∪∪ \quad –|∪∪ \quad –∪∪ \quad – –$$

ἀντιτέχνου· τότε δὴ μανίας ὑπὸ δεινῆς

$$–∪– \quad ∪–∪⌣|||^H$$

ὄμματα στροβήσεται.

falls into three sections of increasing length, each rounded off by an ithy-phallic. It is tempting to see the stanza as opening with a dactylic hexameter, ending (with *brevis in longo*) at τέρψιν = ὅστις. This, however, leaves a very awkward metrical residue: ἀοιδᾶς ἐμᾶς = ἐτ᾽ οἰμώξεται (◡ – – ◡ –). *Phil.* 1092=1113 might be cited as a parallel, but there a solitary dochmiac is not grossly inappropriate to the context and type of song.

At 680, ἐπιβρέμεται is the MS reading. The *Suda* (s. χελιδόνων μουσεῖα) and Σ *vet.* RV on 93 offer περιβρέμεται (metrically possible with δεινά, as Radermacher notes). At 683, τρύζει is Fritzsche's emendation. VUAM (with LAld) have κελαδεῖ, which looks as if it originated as a gloss, and R *Suda* κελαρύζει, which could, if τρύζει is right, have resulted from a conflation of gloss and original word. At 711, κυκησίτεφροι is Radermacher's correction of κυκησιτέφρου (MSS and *Suda*), and, at 714, ἰδών Bentley's for the MSS᾽ εἰδώς.

At 712, MSS other than V offer τε before κονίας. Where κονίας occurs elsewhere in Aristophanes (*Ach.* 18 in an iambic trimeter and *Lys.* 470 in a catalectic iambic tetrameter) the ι is long. On that analogy, ψευδολίτρου τε κονίας would scan – ◡ ◡ – ◡ ◡ – –, and 680 would need to be supplemented by one long. Blass proposed τις after ἐριβρέμεται (see Dover, ad loc.). In epic, however, the dative plural κονίῃσι scans ◡ ◡ – ◡, and in tragedy κονίαισι, scanned in the same way, occurs in dactylic and anapaestic contexts reminiscent of epic (*Ag.* 64, *Andr.* 112, E. *Supp.* 821). Here, in pseudo-grandiose dactylo-epitrite, the epic/tragic scansion might seem appropriate. Compare, in the corresponding verse, ἐριβρέμεται.

      da hex

      da hex

      da pent

      lec

ἔσται δ᾽ ἱππολόφων τε λόγων κορυθαίολα νείκη,
σκινδαλάμων τε παραξόνια σμιλεύματά τ᾽ ἔργων
820 φωτὸς ἀμυνομένου φρενοτέκτονος ἀνδρὸς
ῥήμαθ᾽ ἱπποβάμονα.

φρίξας δ᾽ αὐτοκόμου λοφιᾶς λασιαύχενα χαίταν,
δεινὸν ἐπισκύνιον ξυνάγων βρυχώμενος ἤσει
ῥήματα γομφοπαγῆ, πινακηδὸν ἀποσπῶν
825 γηγενεῖ φυσήματι·

ἔνθεν δὴ στοματουργὸς ἐπῶν βασανίστρια λίσπη
γλῶσσ᾽ ἀνελισσομένη, φθονεροὺς κινοῦσα χαλινούς,
ῥήματα δαιομένη καταλεπτολογήσει
πλευμόνων πολὺν πόνον.

After the parabasis, the dialogue of the two slaves constitutes, in effect, a prologue to the second half of the play. The chorus then look forward to the ensuing contest in a song in four identical short stanzas. The closeness of correspondence in these strophae is remarkable. Dactyl corresponds to dactyl and spondee to spondee throughout, and the caesurae marked in the scansion recur in every repetition. While the metrical antecedents of the parabasis-song are in doubt, here several features point to Aeschylean pastiche. For short dactylic stanzas with lecythion as clausula, compare *Eum.* 347 ff. = 360 ff. and 368 ff. = 377 ff. For other examples of lecythion as clausula to dactyls, compare *Ag.* 165–6 = 174–5 and *Pers.* 865–6 = 874–5, 880–1 = 889–90. The dactylic pentameter (816 = 820 = 824 = 828) is a favourite Aeschylean verse. On both this and the spondaic opening to dactylic verses, see below on 1264 ff. and 1284 ff.

The evolution of colometry and text in these strophae casts an interesting light on the vicissitudes of metrical scholarship. In RV the stanza is divided into seven cola (Introduction, pp. 102–3). Brunck established the correct division, following the lead of an Aldine scholium (which, incidentally, shows a higher degree of metrical understanding than one would expect from Musurus).

875–84

‒ ∪ ∪   ‒ ∪ ∪   ‒ ∪ ∪   ‒ ‒
875 ὦ Διὸς ἐννέα παρθένοι ἁγναὶ

At 815, περ ἴδη is the reading of UMAld (περ' ἴδη L: περίδη R: παρίδη V). At 819, σκινδαλάμων is the reading of V and the Triclinian L. The pre-Triclinian MSS other than V have σκινδάλμων, which was injudiciously adopted by Musurus, and passed into the printed vulgate. Until the discovery of V, choice of reading here is something of a test of metrical expertise and powers of observation. Bentley wanted σκινδαλάμων. Brunck reported (without adopting) it from his own MS (Ct 6) which later came under the eyes of Porson (see Th. Gelzer, 'Einer Aristophaneshandschrift und ihre Besitzer', in Koster, *ΚΩΜΩΙΔΟ-ΤΡΑΓΗΜΑΤΑ*, 45). Porson was the first scholar in modern times to point out the strictly-corresponding metrical pattern of these stanzas (*Notae in Aristophanem*, 69), which confirms, as he saw, σκινδαλάμων. The word is also found at *Clouds* 130, where the -αλα- form is guaranteed by metre. Otherwise, MS variation in the stanzas is trivial. The obscure metaphorical expressions tempt emendation, but the consistent metrical pattern preserved by the MSS is evidently sound, and must not be tampered with. From that point of view, Dover's σκινδάλαμοί τε παραξονίων and Stanford's σκινδαλάμων τε παραξονίων (παραξονίων being taken as adjectival) are both acceptable at 819.

da tetram

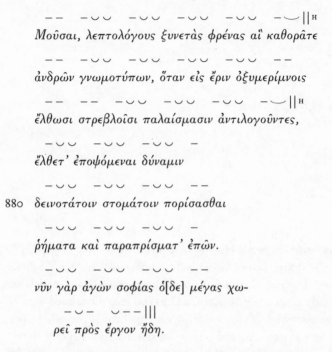

‒ ‒   ‒ ∪ ∪   ‒ ∪ ∪   ‒ ∪ ∪   ‒ ∪ ∪   ‒ ⌣ ‖ ʜ
Μοῦσαι, λεπτολόγους ξυνετὰς φρένας αἳ καθορᾶτε

‒ ‒   ‒ ∪ ∪   ‒ ∪ ∪   ‒ ∪ ∪   ‒ ∪ ∪   ‒ ‒
ἀνδρῶν γνωμοτύπων, ὅταν εἰς ἔριν ὀξυμερίμνοις

‒ ‒   ‒ ‒   ‒ ∪ ∪   ‒ ∪ ∪   ‒ ∪ ∪   ‒ ⌣ ‖ ʜ
ἔλθωσι στρεβλοῖσι παλαίσμασιν ἀντιλογοῦντες,

‒ ∪ ∪   ‒ ∪ ∪   ‒ ∪ ∪   ‒
ἔλθετ' ἐποψόμεναι δύναμιν

‒ ∪ ∪   ‒ ∪ ∪   ‒ ∪ ∪   ‒ ‒
880 δεινοτάτοιν στομάτοιν πορίσασθαι

‒ ∪ ∪   ‒ ∪ ∪   ‒ ∪ ∪   ‒
ῥήματα καὶ παραπρίσματ' ἐπῶν.

‒ ∪ ∪   ‒ ∪ ∪   ‒ ∪ ∪   ‒ ‒
νῦν γὰρ ἀγὼν σοφίας ὁ[δε] μέγας χω-

‒ ∪ ‒   ∪ ‒ ‒ ‖‖
ρεῖ πρὸς ἔργον ἤδη.

This song, which concludes the second introductory scene to the contest of Aeschylus and Euripides, is clearly, both in diction and metre, a companion-piece to 814 ff. Note, in particular, the spondees which open the hexameters at 876–8 (cf. 814 = 818 = 822 = 826). It is, however, less easy to find a close Aeschylean parallel for this song than for 814 ff. *Pers.* 896–907 has, perhaps, some affinity. But almost pure dactylic stanzas are also found in Euripides (see above on *Clouds* 275 ff. = 298 ff., and Introduction, pp. 51–2).

The colometry of RV shows that in the Alexandrian lay-out the hexameters were divided (as in 814 ff.) into two cola at the penthemimeral caesura, so as to turn 875–8 into:

‒ ∪ ∪ ‒ ∪ ∪ ‒ ∪ ∪ ‒ ‒
‒ ‒ ‒ ∪ ∪ ‒
∪ ∪ ‒ ∪ ∪ ‒ ∪ ∪ ‒ ⌣ ‖ ʜ
‒ ‒ ‒ ∪ ∪ ‒
∪ ∪ ‒ ∪ ∪ ‒ ∪ ∪ ‒ ‒
‒ ‒ ‒ ‒ ‒ ∪
∪ ‒ ∪ ∪ ‒ ∪ ∪ ‒ ‒

da hex

da hex

da hex

da tetram cat

da tetram

da tetram cat

da tetram

+ ith

With this colometry before him, Triclinius took the metre to be anapaestic, (*Σ*LAld), and proceeded to inflict minor but systematic mutilation on the text. He deleted the initial ὦ, so as to turn 875 into ᴗ ᴗ – ᴗ ᴗ – ᴗ ᴗ – – (like the third and fifth cola). By adding τε before παλαίσμασιν (878) he again produced ᴗ ᴗ – ᴗ ᴗ – ᴗ ᴗ – – (transferring ι from the end of στρεβλοῖσι to the beginning of the following colon would have produced the same result). At 880, he read πορίσασθε (for πορίσασθαι), like AUM, and deleted καὶ after ῥήματα. All these corruptions passed through the Aldine into the printed vulgate. Brunck restored the initial ὦ and the hexameters. In 882, δε was deleted by Hermann (Introduction, pp. 109–10).

The first ten or so letters of 879–82 are preserved in a papyrus of the 5th century AD, *P. Oxy.* 1372. This, however, contributes nothing to our knowledge of the text.

895–904=992–1003

⏑ – – – | ⏑ ⏑ – –

895 καὶ μὴν ἡμεῖς ἐπιθυμοῦμεν

⏑ ⏑ ⏑ | –   – ⏑ – –

896a παρὰ σοφοῖν ἀνδροῖν ἀκοῦσαι

⏑ ⏑ – ⟨⏑⟩   – ⏑ – –

896b τίνα λόγων, ⟨τίν᾽⟩ ἐμμελείας

⏑ ⏑ – ⏑   – ⏑ –

ἔπιτε δαΐαν ὁδόν.

– ⏑ – ⏝ | – ⏑ – –

γλῶσσα μὲν γὰρ ἠγρίωται,

– ⏑ – ⏑   – ⏑ – ⏝

899a λῆμα δ᾽ οὐκ ἄτολμον ἀμφοῖν

– ⏑ – –   – ⏑ –

899b οὐδ᾽ ἀκίνητοι φρένες.

– ⏑ – – | – ⏑ – ⏝

900 προσδοκᾶν οὖν εἰκός ἐστι

– ⏑ – ⏑   – ⏑ – ⏝

901a τὸν μὲν ἀστεῖόν τι λέξαι

– ⏑ – –   – ⏑ –

901b καὶ κατερρινημένον,

– ⏑ – –   – ⏑ – –

τὸν δ᾽ ἀνασπῶντ᾽ αὐτοπρέμνοις

– ⏑ – ⏝

τοῖς λόγοισιν

– ⏑ – ⏑   – ⏑ – –   – ⏑ – –   – | ⏑ – |||

ἐμπεσόντα συσκεδᾶν πολλὰς ἀλινδήθρας ἐπῶν.

This strophe and antistrophe serve to punctuate the recitative agon between Aeschylus and Euripides (with interventions by Dionysus). The whole episode is constructed as follows:

895–904 Strophe
905–70 Catalectic iambic tetrameters (66 lines)

an dim
τάδε μὲν λεύσσεις, φαίδιμ' Ἀχιλλεῦ·

tro dim
993a σὺ δὲ τί, φέρε, πρὸς ταῦτα λέξεις;

tro dim
993b μόνον ὅπως ⟨× – ◡ – ×⟩

tro dim cat (lec)
μή σ' ὁ θυμὸς ἁρπάσας

tro dim
995 ἐκτὸς οἴσει τῶν ἐλαῶν·

tro dim
δεινὰ γὰρ κατηγόρηκεν.

tro dim cat (lec)
ἀλλ' ὅπως, ὦ γεννάδα,

tro dim
μὴ πρὸς ὀργὴν ἀντιλέξεις,

tro dim
ἀλλὰ συστείλας ἄκροισι

tro dim cat (lec)
1000 χρώμενος τοῖς ἱστίοις

tro dim
εἶτα μᾶλλον μᾶλλον ἄξεις

tro mon
καὶ φυλάξεις,

tro tetram cat
ἡνίκ' ἂν τὸ πνεῦμα λεῖον καὶ καθεστηκὸς λάβῃς.

971–91 Iambic dimeters: Euripides and Dionysus (21 lines)
992–1003 Antistrophe
1004–77 Catalectic anapaestic tetrameters (73 lines)
1078–98 Anapaestic dimeters: Aeschylus and Dionysus (21 lines)
1099–1118 Strophe and antistrophe

It is noteworthy that both these stanzas and the song which marks the transition to the next stage of the contest are in pure, or almost pure, trochaic, a metre excluded from the recitative, so that there is no tendency for song and recitative to merge (contrast *Lys*. 614–705, where the chorus themselves are the contestants).

After the introductory anapaestic dimeter, the song continues in simple sequences of 6, 6, 6, and 7 trochees punctuated by catalexis, in the style typical of songs of comment (compare 534 ff. = 590 ff. above).

In view of the failure of correspondence at 896b=993b, it should be noted that in RV the colometry of strophe and antistrophe are markedly different. In the antistrophe, 993a–b (σὺ δὲ . . . ὅπως) is laid out as a catalectic trimeter, with the rest of the stanza in dimeters until πνεῦμα . . . λάβῃς (1003), which makes a catalectic trimeter. The strophe has two catalectic trochaic trimeters at 896a–b (παρὰ . . . λόγων) and 896b–7 (ἐμμελείας . . . ὁδόν). The rest of the stanza is divided into dimeters and acatalectic tetrameters, except for the last verse, συσκεδᾶν . . . ἐπῶν, which is, again, a trimeter. RV's division of most of the strophe (895–903) is confirmed by a papyrus of the 5th century AD, *P. Oxy*. 1372. Both divisions look deliberate, and this points to the conclusion that the failure of correspondence was in the text early and that correspondence was not recognized in antiquity (Introduction, p. 104).

There is little MS variation at 896a–7. The MSS offer τινα or τινὰ. Π has ϵπιϵ for ἔπιτε. M has ἐπί τε. In the corresponding verse, 993b, V omits μόνον, and R has μόνος. The (partial) solution I adopt is that of Kock: 'Der Streit der beiden Tragiker wird sich erstrecken auf die Angemessenheit des Dialogs (λόγων) und die Eurythmie der Chöre (ἐμμέλειαν)'. The metrical simplicity is in keeping with the rest of the stanza. A different possiblity is offered by RLAld, which have a stop after ἐμμέλειαν:

$$1099–1108=1109–18$$

‿‿ ∪ – ∪| ⁀ ∪ – ∪| ‿‿ ∪ ⁀ ∪ – ∪ –
μέγα τὸ πρᾶγμα, πολὺ τὸ νεῖκος, ἁδρὸς ὁ πόλεμος
                                        [ἔρχεται.

‿‿ ∪ – ⁐ – ∪ – ⁐ ‿‿ ∪ – – –|∪ – –
1100–01 χαλεπὸν οὖν ἔργον διαιρεῖν, ὅταν ὁ μὲν τείνῃ βιαίως,

. . . ἀκοῦσαί
τίνα λόγων ἐμμέλειαν·
ἔπιτε δαΐαν ὅδον.

‿‿ ∪ – – ∪ – ∪

‿‿ ∪ – ∪ – ∪ –

'We wish to hear some harmony of words'. This is accepted by von
Velsen, who assumes a lacuna corresponding to ἐμμέλειαν in the antistrophe, and by Perusino (in F. M. Pontani, *Lirica greca da Archiloco ad
Elitis* (Padua, 1984), 191–5), Dover, and Zimmermann (*Untersuchungen*,
ii. 137), who, in the modern manner, are prepared to accept an antistrophe one metron shorter than the strophe. This, however, produces at
896b the sequence ‿‿ ∪ – – ∪ – ∪ which is never found in Aristophanes,
except in three more or less dubious passages in this play (see above
on 209 ff.). Dindorf's deletion of ἐμμέλειαν is hardly an acceptable
solution (even though it found favour with Radermacher, Coulon, and
Stanford). The introduction of ἐμμέλειαν into the text is inexplicable.
It is an uncommon word, and there is nothing that it could possibly
gloss.

Other textual problems are minor. At 901a, the MSS are divided
between λέξαι (RA) and λέξειν (the rest). It is more likely that λέξαι
should have been changed to the future to match συσκεδᾶν (904), than
that an original λέξειν should have been changed to λέξαι (see, however, Dover, ad loc.). At 993a, Bentley restored the metre with σὺ δέ
where RUMLAld have σὺ δή and V (unknown, of course, to Bentley)
has δὲ δή. At 1000, the metrically necessary τοῖς ἱστίοις is derived
from the *Suda* (s. ἱστίοις) and Σ Ald. RULAld have τοῖς ἱστίοισιν,
making a full trochaic metron, while VMA have completely unmetrical
variations.

4 tro cat
εἰ δὲ τοῦτο καταφοβεῖσθον, μή τις ἀμαθία προσῇ

4 tro
1110–11 τοῖς θεωμένοισιν, ὡς τὰ λεπτὰ μὴ γνῶναι λεγόντοιν,

$$\smile\smile-\smile \quad -\smile-- \quad -\smile-- \quad -\smile-$$

ὁ δ' ἐπαναστρέφειν δύνηται κἀπερείδεσθαι τορῶς.

$$-\smile-\smile \quad -\smile-\smile$$

ἀλλὰ μὴ 'ν ταὐτῷ κάθησθον·

$$-\smile-\smile \quad -\smile--| \quad -\smile-|\smile \quad -\smile\hookleftarrow||_{H}$$

εἰσβολαὶ γάρ εἰσι πολλαὶ χἄτεραι σοφισμάτων.

$$\smile\smile-\smile \quad \smile\smile--$$

1105   ὅ τι περ οὖν ἔχετον ἐρίζειν,

$$\smile\smile\smile\smile\smile\smile \quad \smile\smile\smile\smile\smile$$

λέγετον, ἔπιτον, ἀνὰ ⟨δὲ⟩ δέρετον

$$\smile\smile-\smile \quad -\smile-\smile$$

τά τε παλαιὰ καὶ τὰ καινά,

$$-\smile-\smile \quad -\smile-- \quad -\smile-\smile \quad -\smile-|||$$

κἀποκινδυνεύετον λεπτόν τι καὶ σοφὸν λέγειν.

This strophic pair divides the recitative agon from the long scene in iambic trimeters in which the two poets criticize in detail each other's diction. The stanza is made up of trochaic sequences, marked off by catalexis into lengths of 4, 8, 6, and 10 metra. There is, in addition, a tendency for the long units to subdivide internally by word-end into dimeters and tetrameters, but this is no reason to force a dimeter division throughout, regardless of word-end or lack of it. The lay-out I adopt is that of V, except that the MS divides 1100–1 = 1110–11 into two 'dimeters', which are, however, in synartesis in the strophe. R shares this division with V for the strophe, but divides the antistrophe into 'tetrameters' throughout, producing hiatus (after δεξιά, 1114) in the middle of a verse.

1251–60

$$\smile\smile\smile-\smile\smile-\smile-$$

τί ποτε πρᾶγμα γενήσεται;

$$---\smile\smile-\smile-$$

1252   φροντίζειν γὰρ ἐγὼ οὐκ ἔχω

$$\smile\smile\smile-\smile\smile--||_{H}$$

τίν' ἄρα μέμψιν ἐποίσει

4 tro cat
μηδὲν ὀρρωδεῖτε τοῦθ', ὡς οὐκέθ' οὕτω ταῦτ' ἔχει.

2 tro
ἐστρατευμένοι γάρ εἰσι,

4 tro cat
βιβλίον τ' ἔχων ἕκαστος μανθάνει τὰ δεξία·

2 tro
1115 αἱ φύσεις τ' ἄλλως κράτισται,

2 tro
νῦν δὲ καὶ παρηκόνηνται.

2 tro
μηδὲν οὖν δείσητον, ἀλλὰ

+ 4 tro cat
πάντ' ἐπέξιτον, θεατῶν γ' οὕνεχ', ὡς ὄντων σοφῶν.

This division is evidently a matter of mere scribal error in an ancestor of R. It is worth noting the high incidence of resolution in the strophe: fourteen longs are resolved, as against only two in the antistrophe. At 1105–7 at least, it seems clear that the resolutions in the strophe reflect the much more emotional content. Here, there are seven resolutions, compared with none at all in the corresponding cola (1115–17).

At 1106, ἀνὰ ⟨δὲ⟩ δέρετον is Thiersch's proposal. The MSS, both pre-Triclinian and Triclinian, have ἀναδέρετον, while the Aldine has ἀναδαίρετον. Dobree proposed ἀνά ⟨τε⟩ δέρετον. τε may be more common in a sequence of this kind, but it is harder to account for palaeographically here. For δὲ, compare *OT* 1304–5. 1117 is missing in A.

glyc

glyc

pher

$- \cup - \cup \cup - \cup -$

ἀνδρὶ τῷ πολὺ πλεῖστα δὴ

$- - - \cup \cup - \cup -$

1255 καὶ κάλλιστα μέλη ποιή-

$- \cup - \cup \cup - -$

σαντι τῶν μέχρι νυνί.

$- - - \cup \cup - \cup -$

1257 θαυμάζω γὰρ ἔγωγ' ὅπῃ

$- \cup - \cup \cup - -$

μέμψεταί ποτε τοῦτον

$- - - \cup \cup - \smile \parallel$

τὸν Βακχεῖον ἄνακτα,

$- \cup - \cup \cup - - \parallel\!\parallel$

1260 καὶ δέδοιχ' ὑπὲρ αὐτοῦ.

At 1249–50, Euripides announces that he is going to prove Aeschylus a bad lyric composer, and the chorus mark the moment of transition in the contest with a little song in simple aeolo-choriambic. As we have it, the song consists of two short sections, each made up of two glyconics and a pherecratean, followed by a glyconic and two pherecrateans with verse-end, then one more pherecratean. However, 1252–6 and 1257–9 look like alternative versions. The suitability of 1261 as a following line to 1256 has inclined editors (following Meineke) to condemn 1257–60, although it is hard to see who, other than Aristophanes, could have composed the lines, or why. It is, at least, intriguing that the highly exceptional sequence of three pherecrateans (1258–60) also ends a stanza in Aeschylus' *Dictyulci* (*TrGF* iii. 47a, 802–20). The Aeschylean song is also of simple comic type, composed entirely in glyconics and phere-

glyc

glyc

+ pher

glyc

+ pher

pher

pher

crateans. The sequence of three pherecrateans at Eupolis, *PCG* 175, is attributed by M. Whittaker (*CQ* 29 (1935), 189) to the κομμάτιον of a parabasis. The problem of this stanza is discussed by Dover (*ICS* 2 (1977), 151 and 156 = *The Greeks and their Legacy*, ii. 211–12 and 216), who settles, tentatively, for author's variants.

At 1256, τῶν μέχρι νυνί is the suggestion of Meineke, based on ΣR: τῶν μεχρὶ νῦν ὄντων ποιητῶν. The MS reading is τῶν ἔτι νῦν ὄντων (τῶν νῦν ἔτ᾽ ὄντων U). Bentley proposed τῶν ἔτι νυνί (for the superlative in comparative sense with genitive plural of a class to which the subject does *not* belong, compare *Ant.* 100 κάλλιστον τῶν προτέρων φάος, and see Kuhner–Gerth i. 23). See also Dover, ad loc.

At 1252, ἐγὼ οὐκ (with synecphonesis) is Bentley's emendation of the MSS' ἔγωγ᾽.

1264–77

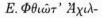

Ε. Φθιῶτ᾽ Ἀχιλ-

$-|\cup\cup\ \ -\cup\cup\ \ -\cup\cup\ \ --$

    λεῦ, τί ποτ᾽ ἀνδροδάϊκτον ἀκούων

$(\cup-)|\cup\cup\ \ -\cup\cup\ \ -\cup\cup\ \ --$

1265   ἰὴ κόπον οὐ πελάθεις ἐπ᾽ ἀρωγάν;

$--\ \ -\cup\cup\ \ -|\cup\cup\ \ -\cup\cup\ \ -\cup\cup\ \ --$

    Ἑρμᾶν μὲν πρόγονον τίομεν γένος οἱ περὶ λίμναν.

$(\cup-)|\cup\cup\ \ -\cup\cup\ \ -\cup\cup\ \ --$

    ἰὴ κόπον οὐ πελάθεις ἐπ᾽ ἀρωγάν;

$\cup\cup\ \ \ -\cup\cup\ \ -\cup\cup\ \ --$

Δ. δύο σοι κόπω, Αἰσχύλε, τούτω.

Ε. κύδιστ᾽ Ἀχαι-

$-\cup\cup\ \ -|\cup\cup\ \ -\cup\cup\ \ -\cup\cup\ \ --\|$ Η

1270   ῶν, Ἀτρέως πολυκοίρανε μάνθανέ μου παῖ.

$(\cup-)|\cup\cup\ \ -\cup\cup\ \ -\cup\cup\ \ --$

    ἰὴ κόπον οὐ πελάθεις ἐπ᾽ ἀρωγάν;

$\cup\cup\ \ -\cup\cup\ \ -\cup\cup\ \ -\cup\|$

Δ. τρίτος, Αἰσχύλε, σοι κόπος οὗτος.

$--\ \ -\cup\cup\ \ -\cup\cup\ \ -|\cup\cup\ \ -\cup\cup\ \ -\cup\cup\ \ --$

1273–4 Ε. εὐφαμεῖτε. μελισσονόμοι δόμον Ἀρτέμιδος πέλας οἴγειν.

$(\cup-)|\cup\cup\ \ -\cup\cup\ \ -\cup\cup\ \ --$

1275   ἰὴ κόπον οὐ πελάθεις ἐπ᾽ ἀρωγάν;

$-\cup\cup\ \ -\cup\cup\ \ -|\cup\cup\ \ -\cup\cup\ \ -\cup\cup\ \ --$

    κύριός εἰμι θροεῖν ὅδιον κράτος αἴσιον ἀνδρῶν.

$(\cup-)|\cup\cup\ \ -\cup\cup\ \ -\cup\cup\ \ --\||$

    ἰὴ κόπον οὐ πελάθεις ἐπ᾽ ἀρωγάν;

ia

   + da tetram

$(\smile -)_\wedge$da tetram

da hex

$(\smile -)_\wedge$da tetram

$_\wedge$da tetram

ia

   + da pent

$(\smile -)_\wedge$da tetram

$_\wedge$da tetram

da hept

$(\smile -)_\wedge$da tetram

da hex

$(\smile -)_\wedge$da tetram

1284–95

∪ – ∪ –

ὅπως Ἀχαι-

– ∪ ∪   – ∪ ∪   – ∪ ∪   – –

1285   ὦν δίθρονον κράτος, Ἑλλάδος ἥβας,

∪ – ∪ –   ∪ – ∪ –

τοφλαττοθρατ τοφλαττοθρατ

– ∪ ∪   – ∪ ∪   – ∪ ∪   – –

Σφίγγα δυσαμεριᾶν πρύτανιν κύνα πέμπει,

∪ – ∪ –   ∪ – ∪ –

τοφλαττοθρατ τοφλαττοθρατ

– ∪ ∪   – ∪ ∪   – ∪ ∪   – –

ξὺν δορὶ καὶ χερὶ πράκτορι θούριος ὄρνις,

∪ – ∪ –   ∪ – ∪ –

1290   τοφλαττοθρατ τοφλαττοθρατ

∪ – ∪ –

κυρεῖν παρα-

– ∪ ∪   – ∪ ∪   – ∪ ∪   – –

σχὼν ἰταμαῖς κυσὶν ἀεροφοίτοις,

∪ – ∪ –   ∪ – ∪ –

τοφλαττοθρατ τοφλαττοθρατ

∪ – ∪ – ∪ – – ∪

†τὸ συγκλινές τ' ἐπ' Αἴαντι,†

∪ – ∪ –   ∪ – ∪ – |||

1295   τοφλαττοθρατ τοφλαττοθρατ

For his specimen of Aeschylean lyric, 'Euripides' chooses a type of dactylo-iambic known to us from *Ag.* 104 ff. = 122 ff. (a type of metre, incidentally, that the real Euripides used occasionally in his earlier plays; see above, on 674 ff. = 706 ff.). Since these stanzas are not so much parodies as centos of genuine Aeschylean lines, it is not surprising that parallels can be found (with one exception) in the surviving plays for the more distinctive metrical features. But the repetition of the refrain after

ia

+ da tetram

ia dim

da pent

ia dim

da pent

ia dim

ia

+ da tetram

ia dim

ia dim

every verse must have made the over-all effect rather different from a real Aeschylean stanza.

The opening iambic metron in synartesis with a dactylic colon (1264, 1269–70, 1284–5, 1291–2) is found twice in *Ag.* 104 ff. = 122 ff. Here, only 1284–5 is actually quoted from that passage. The opening spondee (1266, 1273) is quite common in Aeschylean dactyls (*Pers.* 855 = 861, 864 = 871, 867 = 876, 879 = 886, 896, 904, *Ag.* 111 = 129, 114 = 131, 150,

153, *Eum.* 351=362, 353=364, 1033=1037). The pentameter-length is a favourite with Aeschylus: there are some fourteen corresponding pairs in the complete plays. For the run of seven dactyls at 1274, compare *Pers.* 864=871, 867=876, 896, 904, *Supp.* 45=55, *Eum.* 529=540.

The colon which recurs as a sort of refrain at 1265, 1267, 1271, 1275, and 1277 remains, however, mysterious. Neither ∪–∪∪–∪∪–∪∪––, nor anything like it is found in the surviving plays or fragments. Cola beginning ∪ – ∪ ∪ – ... are very rare in Aeschylus, and are confined to a single, well-defined type of metrical context:

1. *Sept.* 324–5=336–7   ᴗ – ∪ ∪ – – ∪ ∪ – – ∪ ∪ – ∪ – –
2. *Sept.* 751–3=759–61   ∪ – ∪ ∪ – ∪ ∪ – –
                             ∪ – ∪ ∪ – ∪ ∪ –
                             – ∪ –   ∪ – –
3. *Sept.* 756–7=764–5   ∪ – ∪ ∪ – ∪ ∪ – ᴑ
                             – ∪ –   ∪ – –
4. *Supp.* 71–81   ∪ – ∪ ∪ – ∪ – –
(Problematic. I follow Wilamowitz)
5. *Supp.* 525–6=532–3   ∪ – ∪ ∪ – ∪ ∪ –
                             ∪ – ∪ ∪ – ∪ ∪ – ∪ – –
6. *Cho.* 319=336   ∪ – ∪ ∪ – ∪ –
                           – ∪ ∪ – ∪ – –
7. *Cho.* 351–2=368–70   ∪ – ∪ ∪ – ∪ ∪ – –
                             ∪ – ∪ ∪ – ∪ – –
8. *PV* 135=152   ∪ – ∪ ∪ – ∪ ∪ – ∪ – –

Except for *PV* 135=152 (ambiguous ionic/choriambic), all these cola are found in stanzas that combine iambic, iambo-choriambic and aeolo-choriambic. 1 (an asclepiad variation), 4, 6, and the second colon of 7 are all aeolo-choriambic. The remaining cola combine the hemiepes with iambic rhythm in a manner reminiscent of Archilochus (3 is, indeed, an archilochean dicolon). Except that the problematic *Supp.* 69 ff.=77 ff. opens with a dactylic hexameter, there is no ordinary dactylic in any of the stanzas in which these cola occur. All this tends to show that Heath was right to divide the MSS' ἰήκοπον, and, further, that ἰή should be treated as *extra metrum*. Dionysus' use of the colon ∪∪–∪∪–∪∪–– at 1268 and 1272 points the same way. But the problem of identifying

the colon remains. It is conceivable that Dionysus might interject a catalectic anapaestic dimeter, but anapaests would be completely out of place
within the song. There is just one example of what appears to be an
acephalous dactylic tetrameter in Aeschylus: *Eum.* 1043 (1047), which is
preceded by a catalectic colon. It is perhaps worth noting that that is a
refrain. The strange disruptiveness of ἰή inserted *extra metrum* between
verb and object may explain the use Aristophanes makes of the line.
White (*VGC* 145–6) shrewdly observes that every verse of 1264 ff.,
however it begins, ends with ∪ ∪ – ∪ ∪ – ∪ ∪ – –, marked off by word-
end: 'The greater the variety of form of the first part of the period, the
greater would be the monotony of the recurring cadence.' The fact that
Dionysus picks up the phrase would help to bring the point home to the
audience.

By contrast, the problem of τοφλαττοθρατ τοφλαττοθρατ in 1284ff.
has no metrical aspect. The syllables make up an iambic dimeter, which
is perfectly appropriate to Aeschylean dactylo-iambic. Compare *Ag.*
120=138. Deleting initial το (Fritzsche, Kock) produces lec (see Dover
ad loc. and Kassel-Austin on *PCG*, Aristophanes 914).

For neither stanza is there much significant varation in the text of the
pre-Triclinian MSS. 1266–7 are missing in M.

At 1264, Ἀχιλεῦ, the reading of M, was adopted by Triclinius and
passed, through the Aldine, into the printed vulgate. Ἀχιλλεῦ returned
from RV. At 1270, the text of the Aldine is, exceptionally, metrically
better than that of the Triclinian LVv5, who add τε after Ἀτρέως.

In addition to his rather fallible metrical scholarship, Triclinius
brought to bear on the passage his knowledge of the text of Aeschylus,
with varying success. At 1276 he restored ὅδιον, where R preserves
the memory of variants with ὃς δῖον, and VUAM have ὅσιον. Musurus
unwisely adhered to ὅσιον. At 1285, however, it is the MSS of Aristophanes that preserve the right reading, ἥβας, but Triclinius took ἥβαν
from the MSS of Aeschylus, and this time Musurus followed him. At
1289, ξὺν is Triclinian; RVUAM have σὺν. On the unmetrical 1294,
Σ *vet.* V notes Τιμαρχίδας φησὶ τοῦτο ἐν ἐνίοις μὴ γράφεσθαι.
Triclinius (LVv5Ald) deleted τ', giving the construction a sort of logic
('allowing τὸ συγκλινὲς ἐπ' Αἴαντι to encounter . . .'), but this does
little for the metre. In any case, emending deliberate nonsense is an
unrewarding pursuit.

1309–28

$- \cup \, \widehat{\cup \cup} \quad - \cup - \cup \cup - \cup - -$

A. ἀλκυόνες, αἳ παρ' ἀενάοις θαλάσσης

$- \cup - - - \cup \, \smile \, \|$

1310   κύμασι στωμύλλετε

$- - - \cup \cup - \cup -$

τέγγουσαι νοτίοις πτερῶν

$\cup \cup \cup \cup \cup \, | \, \cup \quad - \cup \cup - \, \| \, \text{н}$

ῥανίσι χρόα δροσιζόμεναι·

$- \cup - \cup \cup - \cup \cup - \cup -$

αἵ θ' ὑπωρόφιοι κατὰ γωνίας

$- - \cup \cup - \cup - \cup - \, \smile \, \|$

εἰ(ειειειει)λίσσετε δακτύλοις φάλαγγες

$- \cup \, \widehat{\cup \cup} - - \cup \, \smile \, \|$

1315   ἱστότονα πηνίσματα,

$- \cup \cup \cup - \quad - \cup \cup -$

κερκίδος ἀοιδοῦ μελέτας,

$\cup \cup \cup - \cup \cup - \cup -$

ἵν' ὁ φίλαυλος ἔπαλλε δελ-

$- - - \cup \cup - \cup -$

φὶς πρῴραις κυανεμβόλοις

$- - \cup - \cup \cup \, \_$

μαντεῖα καὶ σταδίους.

$- - - \cup \cup - \cup -$

1320   οἰνάνθας γάνος ἀμπέλου,

$\cup \cup \cup \cup \cup \cup \quad - \cup \cup -$

βότρυος ἕλικα παυσίπονον

$\cup \cup - - \cup \cup - \cup -$

περίβαλλ', ὦ τέκνον ὠλένας.

$\cup - - \cup \cup - \cup \cup -$

ὁρᾷς τὸν πόδα τοῦτον; Ε. ὁρῶ.

cr hipp

lec

glyc

ia cho dim (pol?)

aeol da

aeol decasyll

lec

ia cho dim

glyc

   + glyc

aeol heptasyll

glyc

ia cho dim (pol?)

glyc

aeol da

$$\cup - - \cup \cup - \cup -$$
A. τί δαί; τοῦτον ὁρᾶς; *E.* ὁρῶ.

$$- - - - - \cup \cup -$$
1325 *A.* τοιαυτὶ μέντοι σὺ ποιῶν

$$- - - \cup \cup - \cup -$$
τολμᾷς τἀμὰ μέλη ψέγειν,

$$\cup \cup \cup - \cup \cup - \cup -$$
ἀνὰ τὸ δωδεδαμήχανον

$$- - - \cup \cup - - |||$$
Κυρήνης μελοποιῶν;

If 'Euripides'' Aeschylean stanzas are structurally unlike real Aeschylus, 'Aeschylus'' first Euripidean song is even less like Euripides in that respect. Many of Euripides' aeolo-choriambic stanzas, even in the late plays (see e.g. *Phoen.* 202 ff. = 214 ff., *Ba.* 402 ff. = 416 ff., *IA* 543 ff. = 558 ff.), are made up almost entirely of the most ordinary cola (glyconic, polyschematist, pherecratean) grouped in sequences of acatalectic cola rounded off by a catalectic colon, in the Anacreontic style (Introduction, p. 72). It is the use of resolution that gives these stanzas their modernity and sophistication. That type of structure was, of course, common to all the Attic dramatists, and Aristophanes makes Aeschylus use it at 1325–8, where he is speaking in his own person. But there is nothing of the kind in the parodic part of the song. Again, there is no sign of the sort of rhythmical logic in the juxtaposition of cola (especially the less common ones) that we should expect from Euripides (as from the other tragedians). The first four cola of *Hipp.* 545 ff. = 555 ff. provide an economical illustration of this:

$$- \underset{.}{\cup} - \cup \cup -$$
$$- \cup - \cup \cup - -$$
$$\cup - - \cup - \cup \cup - \cup - -$$
$$- - \cup - \cup \cup -$$

Euripides announces his theme, as it were, with the opening reversed dodrans, then varies it by additions at beginning and end. These devices, together with successive repetitions of the same colon, serve to articulate even so elaborate a stanza as *IA* 164 ff. and its epode, 206 ff. By com-

glyc

pol

glyc

glyc

+ pher

parison, *Frogs* 1309 ff. is a jumble of cola. Aristophanes is clearly not interested in imitating the architectonics of Euripidean lyric: he may even be insinuating that they do not exist.

For the most part, Aristophanes uses cola (and forms of those cola) that are common in Euripides. 1313 and 1314 are, however, unusual. The decasyllable $\times - \cup \cup - \cup - \cup - -$ may occur at *Alc.* 462 = 472 (see Dale, *MATC* i. 43). The closest parallel to 1313 is, again, in *Alc.*, at 570–1 = 580–1: $\cup - \cup \cup - \cup \cup - \cup - | \cup - -$. Allowance must, however, be made for distortion of the metre by the introduction of words which do not belong to the Euripidean originals. Thus, στωμύλλετε (1310) cannot be genuine and the spinners of 1313 ff. will not in Euripides have been spiders, nor will they have operated κατὰ γωνίας. Here, Fritzsche's attempt to reconstruct the Euripidean original usefully illustrates how Aristophanes could have turned common metre into uncommon metre:

αἵ θ' ὑπωρόφιοι κατ' οἴ-
κους εἰλίσσετε δακτύλοις . . .

$$- \cup - \cup \cup - \cup -$$
$$- - - \cup \cup - \cup -$$

Compare Cratinus' well-known substitution, for the sake of a joke, of $\cup - \cup \cup - \cup -$ for $\cup - \cup \cup - \cup \cup -$ in the first half of the archilochean (*PCG* vi. 11). On 1312 and 1321, see Introduction, p. 74.

The major difficulty of the song is 1322. The problem could easily be removed by adopting περίβαλ' from M (compare Biset on *Thesm.* 914), and most editors would doubtless have concurred with Triclinius in choosing that course, but for ὁρᾷς τὸν πόδα τοῦτον (1324), which seems to indicate a metrical anomaly. Dain (*Traité de métrique grecque*, (Paris 1965), § 11) proposes (not entirely convincingly) a non-metrical explanation for 1322–4. It has also been suggested that 1322 is a quotation from Euripides, *Telephus* (Dobree) or *Philoctetes* (Ruijgh, *Mnemosyne*, 13 (1960), 320 n. 1). In any case, there is no sure parallel for a glyconic of the form ∪ ∪ – – ∪ ∪ – ∪ – in surviving Euripides (see Itsumi, *CQ* 84 (1984), 74–5). The nearest (possible) parallel is Bacchylides 18. 1: ∪ ∪ – – ∪ ∪ – ∪ – in all repetitions. So if the metrical explanation of the passage is right, Aristophanes will have picked out a colon which was genuinely altogether exceptional. The possibility remains, however, that we may be cherishing a simple scribal error in an attempt to explain a now incomprehensible joke.

Metrically, 1323 is a possible Euripidean colon in view of *El.* 439=449 and *Ba.* 112=127 and 115=130 (·· ·· – ∪ ∪ – ∪ ∪ –), but the line is still likely to be Aristophanes' own. The triple-short base of 1327 is, of

1331–63

– – – ∪ – ∪ ∪ –　– –

1335a　Α. ὦ Νυκτὸς κελαινοφαὴς ὄρφνα,

∪ ∪ – – –　∪ ∪ – –

τίνα μοι δύστανον ὄνειρον

– – ∪ ∪ –　∪ ∪ – ∪ ∪ –

πέμπεις [ἐξ] ἀφανοῦς Ἀίδα πρόπολον

– – – –　∪ ∪ – ⌣ ‖

ψυχὰν ἄψυχον ἔχοντα

– – – ∪ ∪ – –

1335a　Νυκτὸς παῖδα μελαίνας

– – – –　　– – –

1325b　φρικώδη δεινὰν ὄψιν

⌢ ∪ ⌢　– ∪ ⌣ ‖

1336a　μελανονεκυείμονα

∪ ∪ ∪ ∪　∪ ∪ –　∪ ∪ –

1336b　φόνια φόνια δερκόμενον

course, a form used in later tragedy, hardly by the real Aeschylus (Introduction, p. 71), but this is still quotation from Euripides (Nauck², 755).

ὁρῶ in 1323 and 1324 is generally attributed to Dionysus by the MSS (U has failed to write the name in 1323 and V omits 1324 altogether). The attribution to Euripides is Enger's (see Coulon, *RhM* 105 (1962), 29–30). Dover would attribute the first ὁρῶ to Euripides and the second to Dionysus. In 1324, R has τί δέ (without following punctuation) for τί δαί; The latter is preferable on grounds of metre as well as sense: ◡◡−◡◡−◡− is not in itself an uncommon colon (e.g. E. *El.* 733 = 743, *Her.* 1055, *Ion* 468–9 = 488–9), but all the other aeolic cola in this song have full base. This is the only occurrence of base in the form ◡− in Aristophanes' glyconics (Introduction, p. 73), but in this parody he also admits ◡◡◡ which otherwise occurs only at 1251 in this play.

Not surprisingly, the number of repetitions of ει at 1314 differs between MSS (as it does at 1349 below). The significant point is that repetition is not metrically necessary in either place.

pol + − −

an dim cat

an dim

an dim cat

an trip? pher?

an dim cat

2 cr

an trip

⏑⏑‒   ⏑⏑⏑⏑   ‒⏑‿ ‖ ʜ

μεγάλους ὄνυχας ἔχοντα;

‒⏑⏑   ‒⏑⏑   ‒⏑⏑   ‒⏑⏑

ἀλλά μοι, ἀμφίπολοι, λύχνον ἅψατε

‒⏑⏑   ‒⏑⏑   ‒⏑⏑   ‒⏑⏑   ‒⏑⏑   ‒‒

κάλπισί τ' ἐκ ποταμῶν δρόσον ἄρατε θέρμετέ θ' ὕδωρ,

‒‒   ‒⏑⏑   ‒⏑⏑   ‒⏑⏑

1340   ὡς ἂν θεῖον ὄνειρον ἀποκλύσω·

‒‒‒⏑⏑‒‒

ἰὼ πόντιε δαῖμον.

‒⏑‒‒

τοῦτ' ἐκεῖν'· ἰ-

‒⏑‒   ‒⏑⏡   ‒⏑‒   ‒⏑⏡   ‒⏑⏡

1343a   ὦ ξύνοικοι, τάδε τέρα θεάσασθε· τὸν ἀλεκτρυόνα

‒⏑‒⏑

1343b   μου ξυναρπά-

‒⏑‒   ‒⏑‒

1343c   σασα φρούδη Γλύκη·

‒⏑⏑‒⏑⏑‒ ‖ ʜ

Νύμφαι ὀρεσσίγονοι—

‒‒⏑‒   ‒⏑‿ ‖ ʜ

1345   ὦ Μανία, ξύλλαβε—

⏑‒‒   ⏑‒‿ ‖

1346   ἐγὼ δ' ἁ τάλαινα

⏑⏑‒   ⏑⏑⏑⏑   ‒‒

προσέχουσ' ἔτυχον ἐμαυτῆς

‒‒⏑⏑‒‒⏑⏑‒‿ ‖

ἔργοισι λίνου μεστὸν ἄτρακτον

‒‒‒⏑⏑‒

εἱ(ειει)λίσσουσα χεροῖν,

an trip

da tetram

da hex

da tetram

pher? da trim?

tro

   + 5 cr

   + tro

   + 2 cr

hem (D)

ia cr

2 ba

an trip

asclepiadic decasyll

dodrans B

‒ ‒ ∪ ∪ ‒ ∪ ‒

1350a   κλωστῆρα ποιοῦσ', ὅπως

∪ ‒ ∪ ‒ ∪ ∪ ‒

1350b   κνεφαῖος εἰς ἀγορὰν

∪ ‒ ∪ ∪ ‒ ‒

φέρουσ' ἀποδοίμαν.

∪ ∪ ‒ ∪ ∪ ‒ ∪ ∪ ‒ ∪ ∪ ‒ ∪ ∪ ‒ ∪ ∪ ‒ ∪ ‒

ὁ δ' ἀνέπτατ' ἀνέπτατ' ἐς αἰθέρα κουφοτάταις

∪ ‒ ∪ ⏢   ∪ ⏢ ∪ ⏗   [πτερύγων ἀκμαῖς,

ἐμοὶ δ' ἄχε' ἄχεα κατέλιπε,

∪ ⏗ ∪ ⏗   ∪ ‒ ∪ ‒

δάκρυα δάκρυά τ' ἀπ' ὀμμάτων

∪ ⏗ ∪ ⏗   ‒ ‒ ‒

1355   ἔβαλον ἔβαλον ἁ τλάμων.

‒ ‒   ‒ ∪ ‒   ‒ ∪ ⏗   ‒ ∪ ⏗

ἀλλ', ὦ Κρῆτες, Ἴδας τέκνα, τὰ τόξα ⟨τε⟩ λα-

‒ ∪ ⏗   ‒ ∪ ⏗   ‒ ∪ ‒   ‒ ∪ ⏗

βόντες ἐπαμύνατε τὰ κῶλά τ' ἀμπάλλετε κυ-

‒ ∪ ‒ ‒ ‒ ∪ ‒

κλούμενοι τὴν οἰκίαν.

⏗ ∪ ‒   ‒ ∪ ‒   ‒ ∪ ‒

ἅμα δὲ Δίκτυννα παῖς ⟨ἁ⟩ [Ἄρτεμις] καλὰ

‒ ∪ ‒   ‒ ∪ ‒   ‒ ∪ ‒   .⏗ ∪ ‒   ‒ ∪ ‒

1360   τὰς κυνίσκας ἔχουσ' ἐλθέτω διὰ δόμων πανταχῇ.

∪ ‒ ∪ ‒ ∪ ‒ ∪ ∪ ‒ ∪

1361a   σὺ δ', ὦ Διὸς διπύρους ἀνέχουσα

‒ ∪ ∪ ‒ ∪ ∪ ‒   ∪   ‒ ∪ ∪ ‒ ∪ ∪ ‒   ∪

1361b   λαμπάδας ὀξυτάτας χεροῖν, Ἑκάτα, παράφηνον

‒ ∪ ‒ ͺ∪   ‒ ∪ ‒ ‒

εἰς Γλύκης, ὅπως ἂν εἰσελ-

‒ ∪ ‒   ‒ ‒ |||

θοῦσα φωράσω.

tel

   + aeol heptasyll

reiz

enopl

ia dim

ia dim

ia mol

sp + 7 cr

   + lec

3 cr

5 cr

?

D ⌣ D ⌣

tro dim

   + cr sp

'Aeschylus'' version of Euripidean monody is an interesting specimen of metrical invention in its own right. As often with astropha, there are considerable textual uncertainties. None the less, sections in different rhythms can be identified.

In considering this song, it is natural to turn to *Or.* 1369 ff., not least because of the narrative element. The *Or.* monody features recurrent anapaestic passages (1395, 1398, 1403–6, 1426–9, 1434–5, 1485–8) and also two runs of cretics (1376–8, which ends with a lecythion, and 1419–24). On the other hand, there is a good sprinkling of dochmiacs in *Or.*, but none in *Frogs* 1331 ff. Dactylic is present in *Frogs*, absent in *Or.* There is highly-resolved iambic at *Frogs* 1353–5, as at *Or.* 1414, but otherwise there is very little iambic or trochaic in the *Frogs* song, while iambo-trochaic could fairly be seen as the basic rhythm of the *Or.* monody. To turn from the particular to the general, eight different metres can be identified in the thirty-two lines of *Frogs* 1331 ff., while in more than a hundred and thirty lines in *Or.* 1369 ff. there are no more than six.

As has already been pointed out à propos of *Thesm.* 1015 ff., it is wrong to generalize about Euripidean monody. White's summary description at *VGC* 277 is thoroughly misleading. Euripides' monodies fall, roughly, into three groups. Firstly, there are the strophic songs of the early to middle plays: *Alc.* 244–72, 393–415, *Andr.* 1173–96, *El.* 112–66, *Tro.* 308–41, *Ion* 112–40. In most of these, aeolo-choriambic is the predominant rhythm, although dactylic and iambic are also present. Indeed, *Andr.* 1173 ff. is almost purely dactylic. There are two exceptions: Eumelus' lament at *Alc.* 393 ff. (dochmiac, iambic and, possibly, ionic) and Cassandra's song at *Tro.* 308 ff. (a significantly bizarre combination of dochmiac and aeolo-choriambic, with some iambic; see above on *Peace* 1329 ff.). Only these last two songs feature as many as three types of metre. The rest confine themselves to two.

The songs of the second group, which belong to the same period of Euripides' career, are astrophic, and their characteristic rhythms are anapaestic and dochmiac. Aeolo-choriambic is almost totally absent. *Hipp.* 1370–88 combines anapaests with some dochmiac and iambic and, if the text is sound, one choriambo-iambic dimeter. *Hec.* 1056–1106 is the most polymetric monody of this period: it features six metres (dochmiac, anapaestic, iambic, trochaic, cretic, and, more unexpectedly, aeolo-choriambic, in the shape of a single glyconic at 1097). A distinctive subgroup, belonging to the middle plays, is almost purely anapaestic (*Tro.* 122–52, *IT* 143–77, 203–35, *Ion* 144–83, 859–922), and can be seen as a simple development from recitative anapaestic laments like *Med.* 96 ff. and *Hec.* 59 ff. Between the middle and late plays chronologically, the monodies of *Hel.* are *sui generis*. At 167–252, Helen sings the strophae and the (very long) epode, but the chorus the antistrophae. Both these stanzas and Helen's substantial solo passages at 330–74 are in pure iambo-trochaic, with much resolution. 375–85 is purely dactylic (except for the last colon), like the much earlier song at *Andr.* 1173 ff.

The astrophic monodies of the later plays (*Phoen.* 301–53, 1485–1538, *Or.* 960–1021, 1369–1502, *IA* 1279–1335, 1475–99) seem more metrically various at first sight. The shortest and simplest, *IA* 1475 ff., uses three metres; the most ornate, *Phoen.* 1485 ff., *Or.* 1369 ff., and *IA* 1279 ff., use as many as six. Yet detailed analysis shows that even in these songs the major part or at least long sections are in a single metre or a blend of mutually compatible metres, with just a few alien cola. Thus *Or.* 960 ff. is iambo-trochaic (somewhat in the manner of the *Hel.* monodies), with a run of three hypodochmiacs (992–3) and a dactylic coda. *IA* 1475 ff. is a blend of iambic, trochaic, and dochmiac, metres with well-established affinities. To this same blend, *Phoen.* 301 ff. adds one apparently ana-paestic colon (330) and a short closing section in dactyls. *IA* 1279 ff. adds cretics to the blend, with a short anapaestic section at 1294–7, a longer one at 1321–9, and two dactylic cola (1330–2) before the iambic close. *Phoen.* 1485 ff. begins in dactylic (with two isolated trochaic metra at 1498 and, possibly, 1501). Then, at 1508, follows a metrically enigmatic passage in which the dominant rhythm may be choriambic. The song closes with a mixture of iambic and dochmiac. *Or.* 1369 has been treated above.

This conspectus points to the conclusion that *Frogs* 1331 ff. is not a consistent parody of any one type of Euripidean monody, but rather a medley of specimens of almost every type—with, one suspects, the inherently comic quality of a medley.

The anapaests which follow the opening address recall the anapaestic monodies of the middle plays. I discussed these lines in detail in *CQ* 8 (1958), 87–8, proposing the deletion of ἐξ and the adoption of πρόπολον from A (πρόσπολον Triclinius). The other MSS offer πρόμολον ('comer forth'), which is not found elsewhere. Its credentials are discussed by Dover, ad loc. The MS text at 1335, μελαίνας Νυκτὸς παῖδα ($\cup------\cup$) is unmetrical. The transposition I print (which was proposed by Dindorf) suits the context well, as will be seen. The colon $---\cup\cup--$ would, of course, normally be taken as a pherecratean, but Pherecrates himself (*PCG* vii. 84) claimed to have invented the use of cola of this form in sequence, which he called σύμπτυκτοι ἀνάπαιστοι (cf. Hephaestion, Cons. 32. 9, 55. 7). It seems clear that there *was* an anapaestic colon of this form (whether or not it is right to conceive of it as a tripody), and that the catalectic form of the glyconic ($\cdot\cdot\ \cdot\cdot-\cup\cup--$) is distinct, and should never have been called 'pherecratean'. But the usage goes back to late antiquity (see e.g. Hephaestion, Cons. 32. 9, and *Σ vet. Clouds* 563a). Aristophanes' use of the tripody may be genuinely late-Euripidean. At *IA* 1296, just such a colon occurs in a context which is probably anapaestic, although dactyls cannot be ruled out:

ἀμφὶ τὸ λευκὸν ὕδωρ, ὅθι κρῆναι
νυμφᾶν κεῖνται
λειμών τ᾽ ἔρνεσι θάλλων

$-\cup\cup-\cup\cup-\cup\cup--$

$----$

$---\cup\cup--$

The tripody appears twice more (1337, 1347) in the form $\cup\cup-\cup\cup\cup\cup--$. To interpret this as aeolic pherecratean would require us to accept not only resolved long (not impossible in pastiche of very late Euripides: see Introduction, p. 72), but also the highly problematic base $\cup\cup-$ (see above on 1324). 1336b is theoretically analysable in more than one way: pol or ia cho dim, as well as an trip. But there is a well-authenticated anapaestic tripody of this form at *Lys.* 482=547 (see further, Introduction, p. 60). Finally, $---\cup\cup--$ returns at 1341 at the end of a dactylic sequence, where it could be taken as a dactylic tripody or an aeolic pherecratean ($\cup--\cup\cup--$, clearly aeolic, follows a dactylic tetrameter at *Birds* 1753–4).

Although cretics occur in Euripidean monodies, the overall proportion of cretic here is much higher than anywhere in surviving Euripides. Fully resolved cretics, as at 1336a, are found in middle to late Euripides, although mostly in dochmiac contexts (Introduction, p. 45). It is worth noting that while Aristophanes here resolves both the first and the second long, he never admits both ⌢ ⌣ – and – ⌣ ⌢ in the same sequence. ⌢ ⌣ – is confined to 1359–60. The long verse at 1342 ff. could also be scanned as iambo-cretic:

– ⌣ –

– – ⌣ –   – ⌣ ⌢   – ⌣ –   – ⌣ ⌢   – ⌣ ⌢   – ⌣ –

⌣ – ⌣ –   – ⌣ –

For the colon ⌣ – ⌣ –   – ⌣ –, compare 1345.

For 1346–7, Stinton (*BICS* 22 (1975), 106 n. 23 = *Collected Papers*, 127 n. 23) suggested analysis into two dochmiacs and a bacchiac: ⌣ – – ⌣ –   ⌣ ⌢ – ⌣ ⌢   ⌣ – –. However, the colometry and analysis I offer are more compatible with the rest of the song. 1348 is a curious colon suggestive of the type of rhythm which predominates in *Phoen.* 1508 ff. But there is no exact parallel for it there.

The sequence beginning from double short, with single-short coda at 1352 is of a type that can be recognized in Euripides. It may be suspected that the absurdity lies in the length of the verse. There is a short version at *Hel.* 640: ⌣ ⌣ – ⌣ ⌣ – ⌣ ⌣ – ⌣ –. The 'archebulean' at *Hcld.* 356=365 is a longer and pendent version: ⌣ ⌣ – ⌣ ⌣ – ⌣ ⌣ – ⌣ ⌣ – ⌣ – –. What appears to be an acatalectic version of the same verse is found at *Ion* 1466 and *Her.* 1017: ⌣ ⌣ – ⌣ ⌣ – ⌣ ⌣ – ⌣ ⌣ – ⌣ – ⌣ –. *Ion* 1507–9 runs to six double shorts (like *Frogs* 1352), and has a longer coda: ⌣ ⌣ – ⌣ ⌣ – ⌣ ⌣ – ⌣ ⌣ – ⌣ ⌣ – ⌣ – ⌣ – – –. There are textual uncertainties at *Her.* 1205–11, but the double-short sequence there may be longer still.

1353–5 continue the burlesque of Euripides' use of emotional repetition, which began with ἀνέπτατ᾽ ἀνέπτατ᾽ in 1352. 1353 is remarkable for its double split resolution (the only case in Aristophanes' lyric). If this is deliberately and perceptibly bad metre, the implication that Euripides was prone to such rhythmic infelicities is unjust (see *CQ* 18 (1968), 251, and Introduction, p. 30).

1361a is reminiscent metrically of *Alc.* 252–3 = 259–60:

ὁρῶ δίκωπον ὁρῶ σκάφος ἐν λίμ-
νᾳ νεκύων δὲ πορθμεὺς

⌣ – ⌣ – ⌣ ⌣ – ⌣ ⌣ – ⌣

– ⌣ ⌣ – ⌣ – –

In neither *Alc.* nor *Frogs* is there any way of determining whether the anceps between the two cola belongs with what follows or with what precedes. The context in Alcestis' monologue (in spite of Dale's lavish use of the term 'enoplian' in her analysis, *MATC* 2. 72–3) is aeolochoriambic. 1361a has provoked some suspicion. Radermacher replaces ἀνέχουσα by κρατοῦσα from M, to produce ⏑ – ⏑ – ⏑ ⏑ – ⏑ – ⏑, and Wilamowitz proposed, in Triclinian style, the insertion of παῖ after Διός, making

$$\cup - \cup -$$

$$- \cup \cup - \cup \cup - \cup$$

Neither is an improvement on the MS text.

At the end of the stanza, Aristophanes moves into what seems to be a sort of dactylo-epitrite, lightened by short anceps. A possible alternative analysis of the final cola would be:

1370–7

$$\widehat{\cup\cup} \cup - - \quad - \cup -$$

1370 ἐπίπονοί γ᾽ οἱ δεξιοί.

$$\widehat{\cup\cup} \cup \widehat{\cup\cup} \cup \quad - \cup -$$

τόδε γὰρ ἕτερον αὖ τέρας

$$\widehat{\cup\cup} \cup \widehat{\cup\cup} \cup \quad - \cup -$$

νεοχμόν, ἀτοπίας πλέων,

$$\widehat{\cup\cup} \cup \widehat{\cup\cup} \cup \quad - \cup - -$$

ὃ τίς ἂν ἐπενόησεν ἄλλος;

$$\widehat{\cup\cup} \cup - \cup \quad - \cup - \cup$$

μὰ τόν, ἐγὼ μὲν οὐκ ἂν εἴ τις

$$\widehat{\cup\cup} \cup - - \quad \widehat{\cup\cup} \cup - -$$

1375 ἔλεγέ μοι τῶν ἐπιτυχόντων,

$$\widehat{\cup\cup} \cup - - \quad - \cup - \cup$$

ἐπιθόμην, ἀλλ᾽ ᾠόμην ἂν

$$- \cup - \cup \quad - - |||$$

αὐτὸν αὐτὰ ληρεῖν.

$$- \cup \cup - \cup \cup -$$
$$\cup - \cup \cup - \cup \cup - \cup - \cup -$$
$$\cup - \cup - \quad - - \cup - \quad - -$$

This would give a heavy, iambic finale.

There are a few minor textual points and metrically significant variants. At 1343a, τάδε τέρα is the emendation of L. Dindorf for the MSS' τάδε (or τὰ δὲ) τέρατα (R has the misdivision, τὰ δ' ἔτερα). In 1344, ὀρεσσίγονοι is the reading of RV²U. V¹AM Triclinius have ὀρεσίγονοι. At 1345, M adds μοι after ξύλλαβε. At 1350b, Triclinius inserted τὴν before ἀγορὰν. At 1352, however, he restored the ∪ ∪ – sequence by reading ἐς for εἰς. At 1353, κατέλιπε is the reading of M. RAU Triclinius have κατέλιπεν *contra metrum* (V has κατέλειπεν). At 1356, ⟨τε⟩ is Bergk's supplement. The deletion of Ἄρτεμις and the addition of ⟨ἁ⟩ in 1359 are Kock's.

tro dim cat (lec)

tro dim cat (lec)

tro dim cat (lec)

tro dim

tro dim

tro dim

tro dim

tro sp

1482–90=1491–9

⏑ – ◡   – ⏑ –

μακάριός γ' ἀνὴρ ἔχων

⏑ – ◡   – ⏑ –

ξύνεσιν ἠκριβωμένην.

⏑ – ◡   – ⏑ –

πάρα δὲ πολλοῖσιν μαθεῖν,

⏑ – ⏑   ⏖ ⏑ – ◡

1485   ὅδε γὰρ εὖ φρονεῖν δοκήσας

⏓ ⏑ – ⏑   – ⏑ – ‖ᴴ

πάλιν ἄπεισιν οἴκαδ' αὖ[θις],

⏑ – –   – ⏑ – ◡

ἐπ' ἀγαθῷ μὲν τοῖς πολίταις,

⏓ ⏑ – ◡   – ⏑ – –

ἐπ' ἀγαθῷ δὲ τοῖς ἑαυτοῦ

⏖ ⏑ ⏖ ◡   – ⏑ – ◡

ξυγγενέσι τε καὶ φίλοισ⟨ι⟩,

⏑ ⏑ ⏖ ⏑   – ⏖ ‖‖‖

1490   διὰ τὸ συνετὸς εἶναι.

1370–77 forms the prelude to the last phase of the competition between the poets and, but for the lack of a lecythion between the fourth and fifth cola, it corresponds with 1482 ff. = 1491 ff., the strophic pair which marks the end of the contest and the definitive victory of Aeschylus. The similarity between the single stanza and the later strophic pair is made particularly striking by the highly unusual use of resolution to create a pattern. It is these simple but satisfying rhythmic variations that raise these stanzas metrically above the level of the ordinary comment-song. The device has, perhaps, more in common with the patterning use of resolution in some of Aristophanes' early cretic songs (*Ach.* 204 ff. = 218 ff., 665 ff. = 692 ff., 971 ff. = 988 ff., *Knights* 303 ff. = 382 ff.) than with anything found elsewhere in his iambic or trochaic. The pattern in the short Sophoclean iambic stanza, *Trach.* 847 ff. = 950 ff., is some-

tro dim cat (lec)
χαρίεν οὖν μὴ Σωκράτει

tro dim cat (lec)
παρακαθήμενον λαλεῖν,

tro dim cat (lec)
ἀποβαλόντα μουσικὴν

tro dim
τά τε μέγιστα παραλιπόντα

tro dim cat (lec)
1495   τῆς τραγῳδικῆς τέχνης.

tro dim
τὸ δ' ἐπὶ σεμνοῖσιν λόγοισι

tro dim
καὶ σκαριφησμοῖσι λήρων

tro dim
διατριβὴν ἀργὸν ποιεῖσθαι,

tro sp
παραφρονοῦντος ἀνδρός.

what similar, but comparatively rudimentary (Introduction, p. 30). The clausula $-\cup-\cup$ $--$ is unusual in trochaic, but, phrased as ithyphallic ($-\cup-$ $\cup--$), exceedingly common in iambic.

At 1372, πλέων is the reading of AUM and Triclinius. RV have πλέον. At 1373, UM have ὅστις, the rest ὃ τίς, with some variation in accentuation. At 1374, A adds δί' after μὰ τόν. οὐκ is Blaydes's emendation of the MSS' οὐδ' ('If just anyone were to tell me . . .', not 'Even if . . .'). At 1376, Triclinius anticipated Bentley in proposing ἐπιθόμην, but the Aldine adhered to the unmetrical ἐπειθόμην of the pre-Triclinian MSS. At 1377, V has ἑαυτὸν, and M αὑτὸν for the other MSS' αὐτὸν.

At 1482, μακάριός γ' is the reading of RVU. AML omit γ' *contra metrum*; the Aldine has μακάριόν γ'. At 1484, R and L have the metrically necessary πολλοῖσιν, while the Aldine follows VUAM in omitting ephelcystic *ν*. At 1486, ἄπεισιν is the reading of VAU and Triclinius; RM have ἄπεισ᾿. At 1486 and 1489, Dindorf restored correspondence with αὖ and Bentley with φίλοισι for the MSS' αὖθις and φίλοις. These trivial corrections should be accepted. At 1493, V has ἀπόβαλλοντα *contra metrum.* At 1494, R has καὶ τὰ for the other MSS' τά τε. At 1496, Triclinius anticipated Brunck's σεμνοῖσιν. The Aldine has the unmetrical σεμνοῖσι of the pre-Triclinian MSS, while accepting λόγοις, wrongly, from Triclinius, for the MSS' λόγοισι.

Ecclesiazusae

SYNOPSIS

289–99 = 300–10	*Iambic, aeolo-choriambic (telesilleans,* with *reizianum* as clausula).
478–82, 483–92 = 493–503	*Anapaestic, iambic.*
571–80	*Aeolic dactyls,* free *dactylo-epitrite.*
893–9	Older Woman: *Trochaic,* with one *choriamb.*
900–5 = 906–10	Girl and Older Woman: *Trochaic,* with *aristophanean* as clausula.
911–23	Girl and Older Woman: *Iambic, aeolo-choriambic.*
938–41 = 942–5	Young Man and Older Woman: *Aeolo-choriambic.*
952–9 = 960–8	Girl and Young Man: *Cretic, iambic, anapaestic* (?), *trochaic.*
969–72 = 973–5	Young Man (?): *Iambo-choriambic, iambic, aeolo-choriambic.*
1168–83	*Iambic, dactylic.*

In *Wealth*, the change in the dramatic role of the chorus is clear and complete, but *Ecclesiazusae* presents a puzzle. Up to 580, the chorus behave in the normal way, and in their song at 571–80 they seem set to play the same sort of role as the chorus of *Knights*: encouraging their champion and offering regular comment on the action. But in fact, after 580, nothing is heard from them in the play as we have it until 1127 ff. R has χοροῦ between 729 (where Chremes goes into his house) and 730 (where he emerges) and between 876 (where the Selfish Man goes off to dinner) and 877 (where the Older Woman enters wondering why the men have not returned from dinner). This, however, casts no light on the problem. Anyone familiar with Aristophanes' plays would recognize these points as suitable for choral intervention, so that the note could have been added conjecturally at any time in later antiquity. Whether Aristophanes for some reason wrote no choral lyric for the part of the play between 581 and 1168, but relied instead on music and dancing to provide the required interludes, or whether his lyrics are lost, we have no means of knowing. Between 877 and 1111, the lack of choral lyric is explicable, for the lyric element is provided by soloists. The effects of Praxagora's reforms on sexual *mores* are demonstrated in a symposiastic and comastic context and the songs sung by the Older Woman, the Girl, and the Young Man are based on popular forms that belong to such occasions. Some of the metres are easily identifiable, and the allusive points being made are clear even to us (see especially 938 ff. = 942 ff.). Elsewhere, we are doubly hampered by textual corruption and inadequate knowledge of popular song. The song which accompanies the exodos (1168–83) features a monstrous, unbroken run of dactyls which may be parodic.

289–99=300–10

⏒ – ⏑ – – – ⏑ – | – ⏑ – – – ⏑ – ||

289–90 χωρῶμεν εἰς ἐκκλησίαν, ὦνδρες· ἠπείλησε γὰρ

⏓ – ⏑ ⏑ – | ⏑ –

291a ὁ θεσμοθέτης ὃς ἂν

⏒ – ⏑ ⏑ – ⏑ –

291b μὴ πρῴ πάνυ τοῦ κνέφους

– – ⏑ ⏑ – ⏑ –

291c ἥκῃ κεκονιμένος,

⏒ – ⏑ ⏑ – ⏖ ||

292a στέργων σκοροδάλμῃ

⏓ – ⏑ ⏑ – ⏑ –

292b βλέπων ὑπότριμμα, μὴ

– – ⏑ ⏑ – ⏑ ⏓ ||

292c δώσειν τὸ τριώβολον.

– – ⏑ ⏑ – ⏑ –

293a ἀλλ', ὦ Χαριτιμίδη

⏒ – ⏑ ⏑ – ⏑ –

293b καὶ Σμίκυθε καὶ Δράκης,

⏓ – ⏑ ⏑ – –

294 ἕπου κατεπείγων,

⏒ – ⏑ ⏑ – ⏑ –

295a σαυτῷ προσέχων ὅπως

– – ⏑ ⏑ – ⏑ –

295b μηδὲν παραχορδιεῖς

– – ⏑ ⏑ – ⏖ ||[H]

295c ὧν δεῖ σ' ἀποδεῖξαι·

⏑ – ⏑ ⏑ – ⏑ –

296 ὅπως δὲ τὸ σύμβολον

⏑ – ⏑ ⏑ – ⏑ –

297a λαβόντες ἔπειτα πλη-

ia tetram sync

300–1 ὅρα δ' ὅπως ὠθήσομεν τούσδε τοὺς ἐξ ἄστεως

tel

302a ἥκοντας, ὅσοι πρὸ τοῦ

+ tel

302b μέν, ἡνίκ' ἔδει λαβεῖν

tel

302c ἐλθόντ' ὀβολὸν μόνον,

reiz

303a καθῆντο λαλοῦντες

tel

303b ἐν τοῖς στεφανώμασιν,

+ tel

303c νυνὶ δ' ἐνοχλοῦσ' ἄγαν.

tel

304a ἀλλ' οὐχί, Μυρωνίδης

tel

304b ὅτ' ἦρχεν ὁ γεννάδας,

reiz

305a οὐδεὶς ἂν ἐτόλμα

tel

305b τὰ τῆς πόλεως διοι-

+ tel

305c κεῖν ἀργύριον φέρων·

reiz

306 ἀλλ' ἦκεν ἕκαστος

tel

307 ἐν ἀσκιδίῳ φέρων

tel

308a πιεῖν ἅμα τ' ἄρτον αὐ-

$$\smile - \cup \cup - \cup -$$

297b   σίοι καθεδούμεθ' ὡς

$$- - \cup \cup - \smile \,||$$

297c   ἂν χειροτονῶμεν

$$\smile - \cup \cup - \cup -$$

298   ἅπανθ' ὁπόσ' ἂν δέῃ

$$- - \cup \cup - \cup -$$

299a   τὰς ἡμετέρας φίλας—

$$- - \cup \cup - \cup -$$

299b   καίτοι τί λέγω; φίλους

$$- - \cup \cup - - \,|||$$

299c   γὰρ χρῆν μ' ὀνομάζειν.

The chorus of women, disguised as men, sing a processional song as they set off for the Assembly. There is a recitative introduction of four catalectic iambic tetrameters (285–8), and the first verse of the song is also an iambic tetrameter, although of a slightly different type: the second colon of the verse is a lecythion, not a catalectic dimeter. A sequence of such verses forms the exodos of *Birds* (1755–65; see further ad loc.).

The rest of the song is in telesilleans, marked off into groups of three or four cola by catalexis (on this simple type of aeolo-choriambic song, see Introduction, p. 22). One pair of cola, 292b–c, is exceptional in that there is no catalectic clausula: verse-end, reinforced by strong rhetorical pause, follows an acatalectic colon. This must be a deliberate surprise-effect. On verse-end after acatalectic cola in aeolo-choriambic, see on *Peace* 856 ff. = 909 ff. The association between telesilleans and iambic is found elsewhere in Aristophanes. The short telesillean processional song at *Frogs* 448 ff. = 454 ff. also opens with an iambic tetrameter. The telesilleans of *Peace* 856 ff. = 909 ff. are set in a context of iambic tetrameters, and at *Peace* 951–3 = 1034–6 telesilleans appear, in a predominantly iambic stanza, actually in correspondence with iambic dimeters.

It is naturally tempting to wonder whether the chosen metre has any special significance in the context. The evidence connecting telesilleans with wedding-songs (see on *Peace* 1239 ff.) can hardly be relevant here. The two specimen cola quoted by Hephaestion from Telesilla herself

+ tel
308b τῷ καὶ δύο κρομμύω

+ reiz
308c καὶ τρεῖς ἂν ἐλάας.

tel
309 νυνὶ δὲ τριώβολον

tel
310a ζητοῦσι λαβεῖν, ὅταν

+ tel
310b πράττωσί τι κοινὸν ὥσ-

+ reiz
310c περ πηλοφοροῦντες.

(*PMG* 717), with the address, ὦ κόραι, seem to come from some sort of girls' cult-song (compare Sappho, *PLF* 140, and *Thesm.* 101 ff., and see C. Calame, *Les Chœurs de jeunes filles en Grèce archaique*, i. 372). Among the fragments of Hermippus' Στρατιῶται (or Στρατιώτιδες) there is a sequence of telesilleans which may come from the parodos (*PCG* 57; see M. Whittaker, *CQ* 29 (1935), 184), and the chorus of that play may have consisted of effeminate young men (see Kassel–Austin's note on the play, *PCG* v. 585). However, the idea that telesilleans have specifically feminine connotations is hardly tenable in view of *Knights* 1111 ff. = 1131 ff.

R divides the song (with occasional slips of a syllable in one direction or the other) into single cola. The source of the Aldine, however, apparently wrote two cola to a line, and the Aldine prints these dicola continuously. Hence the problems of line-numeration in modern texts. The text of R is generally more accurate here than that of ΓB, and the Aldine, fortunately, tends to agree with R. In 290, RAld have ὦνδρες (ὦδρες Γ: ὡδὶ γὰρ B). In 291c, exceptionally, ΓB are right with κεκονιμένος (κεκονισμένος R: -μένοις Ald). At 292a–b the word-order is Porson's. The MSS and Ald have βλέπων ὑπότριμμα· στέργων σκοροδάλμῃ. In 293a, Χαριτιμίδη was reconstituted by Bentley from χάριτι μια ἤ in the MSS and Ald. At 295a, Ald departs from the MSS, with σαυτὸν for σαυτῷ. At 297a–b, RAld have πλησίοι and

καθεδούμεθ' (πλησία Γ: πλησίον Β, καθεδοῦμεν ΓΒ). At 298, RAld
have ὁπόσ', ΓΒ ὅπως. At 301, RAld have ἐξ ἀστειως, where ΓΒ have,
eccentrically, ξένους. At 302b–c ἔδει λαβεῖν ἐλθόντ' is Dawes's emendation. RAld have ἐλθόντ' ἔδει λαβεῖν (corrected in R from ἐλθόντα
δεῖ); Γ has ἐλθόντες ἔδει· λαβεῖν and B a 'corrected' version: ἐλθόντας

478–82, 483–92=493–503

– – – – ||

ἔμβα, χώρει

479

∪ – ∪ –

480   στρέφου, σκόπει,

481–2

– – ∪ –   ∪ – ∪ –   ∪ – ∪ ◠   ∪ – ∪ || ᴴ

483   ἀλλ' ὡς μάλιστα τοῖν ποδοῖν ἐπικτυπῶν βάδιζε.

– – ∪ | –   – – ∪ –

ἡμῖν δ' ἂν αἰσχύνην φέροι

– – ∪ | ∪   ∪ – ∪ – | ∪ – ∪ –   ∪ – – || ᴴ

485   πάσαισι παρὰ τοῖς ἀνδράσι⟨ν⟩ τὸ πρᾶγμα τοῦτ' ἐλεγχθέν.

– – ∪ | –   ∪ – ∪ –   – – ∪ –   ∪ – ∪ –

πρὸς ταῦτα συστέλλου σεαυτὴν καὶ περισκοπουμένη

∪ – ∪ –   ∪ – ∪ –

⟨×– ∪ –⟩ κἀκεῖσε καὶ

∪ – ∪ –   – – ∪ –

488a   τἀκ δεξιᾶς, μὴ ξυμφορὰ

∪ – ∪ –   ∪ – ∪ || ᴴ

488b   γενήσεται τὸ πρᾶγμα.

489–92

The chorus of disguised Women returning from the Assembly deliver
first a short prelude, then a pair of corresponding stanzas each followed
by a four-line epirrheme. Except for the initial command in military

ἔδει λαβεῖν. At 303a, however, the correct καθῆντο is shared by
ΓBAld, while R has a private slip, κάθητο. But RAld have λαλοῦντες,
ΓB λαλοῦσαι. The colon ἐν τοῖς στεφανώμασιν (303b) present in R, is
missing in ΓB and Ald. At 308a–b αὐτῷ is von Velsen's emendation:
RAld have αὖ (αὗ R), ΓB nothing.

        an

           ia tetram cat I

           ia

           ia tetram cat II

           ia tetram cat

493   ὥστ' εἰκὸς ἡμᾶς μὴ βραδύνειν ἔστ' ἐπαναμενούσας

           ia dim
       πώγωνας ἐξηρτημένας,

           ia tetram cat

495   μὴ καί τις †ὄψεθ' ἡμᾶς† χἠμῶν ἴσως κατείπῃ.

           ia tetram

496–7 ἀλλ' εἷα δεῦρ' ἐπὶ σκιᾶς ἐλθοῦσα πρὸς τὸ τειχίον,

           6 ia cat
       παραβλέπουσα θἀτέρῳ,

499a   πάλιν μετασκεύαζε σαυ-

499b   τὴν αὖθις ἥπερ ἦσθα.

           ia tetram cat IV

style(a single anapaestic metron), the whole composition is in simple
iambic. Both the absence of syncopation and the presence of catalectic
tetrameters assimilate the strophae to recitative. Indeed, the song is even

less lyrical in metrical style than the iambic parodos of the Old Men at
Lys. 256 ff. = 271 ff., and we may conjecture that the Women are moving
slowly and awkwardly in their big, heavy boots (Introduction, p. 36).
While telesilleans have been seen to blend readily with iambic (see on
289 ff. = 300 ff. above), the Women's re-entry is clearly differentiated
rhythmically from their exit-song. The analogy of *Frogs* 448 ff. = 454 ff.
suggests that their progress to telesilleans will have been comparatively
jaunty. This may be illogical, as the chorus were already booted at 289,
but a degree of contrast between the two songs would be enjoyable
dramatically. Again, the parodos of *Lys.* offers an informative parallel:
while the Old Men use pure iambic, the Old Women (319 ff.) use
iambo-choriambic, a rhythm which is compatible but probably more
sprightly.

While ΓΒ still tend in this song to diverge from RAld, the disagree-
ments are far fewer. At 484, however, ἄν is preserved by R alone. The
other MSS, except for B, have δ᾽ αἰσχύνην *contra metrum*, which passed
through the Aldine into the printed vulgate. B emends the metre with
δέ γ᾽ αἰσχύνην (which was also proposed by Bentley). Brunck restored
ἄν by conjecture, before the discovery of R. In the following verse,
Brunck again restored the metre by supplying ephelcystic ν to the
MSS' ἀνδράσι. At 487, the MS text is shorter than the antistrophe by one
metron. Dale (*LM*² 207 n. 1) lists this as an example of approximate
responsion, but the καί before περισκοπουμένη indicates the need for
another main verb to balance συστέλλου. Coulon's suggestion τὰ πάντ᾽
ἄθρει mends the metre. Ussher's ἄθρει κύκλῳ introduces hiatus, and so
verse-end, inappropriately after περισκοπουμένη. Blaydes's suggestion, φύλαθ᾽ ὅπως, is designed to normalize μὴ . . . γενήσεται in 488b,
which has worried circumspect editors at least since the scribe of B, who

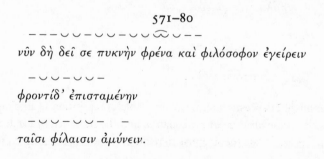

571–80

νῦν δὴ δεῖ σε πυκνὴν φρένα καὶ φιλόσοφον ἐγείρειν

φροντίδ᾽ ἐπισταμένην

ταῖσι φίλαισιν ἀμύνειν.

wrote γένηται *contra metrum*. While ὅπως or ὅπως μή with the future indicative expressing purpose is not uncommon in Aristophanes (see e.g. in this play, 783 and 997), the same usage with μή alone is very rare everywhere, and no parallel is quoted from Aristophanes or anywhere else in Attic poetry, although Goodwin (*SGMT* 115–16 n. 1) mentions 'four undoubted examples' in prose. B's γένηται is accepted by von Velsen, at the cost of further changes.

In 488a, τὰκ δεξιᾶς is the reading of R, while ΓAld have τά τ' ἐκ δεξιᾶς, and B τά τ' ἐκ δεξιῶν. For the asymmetrical κἀκεῖσε καὶ τὰκ δεξιᾶς compare *Trach.* 929 τὸ κεῖσε δεῦρο τ' and *Phoen.* 266 κἀκεῖσε καὶ τὸ δεῦρο.

At 493, ἡμᾶς is preserved in RAld and omitted by ΓB. B also omitted ἔστ', but the scribe apparently noticed that something was amiss, for ἐστι is added above the line in the first hand between εἰκὸς and μή. 495 is problematic: ὄψεθ' ἡμᾶς is the reading of RAld; ΓB have ὄψαιτο ἡμᾶς. A. von Blumenthal's suggestion (*Hermes*, 71 (1936), 455–6), ὄψεθ' ἡμέρας, 'lest someone see us by daylight', is attractive. Elision of -αι in verb-endings is rare, but not unparalleled, in Aristophanes' lyric (see on *Wasps* 273). It must, however, be said, firstly, that the future indicative after μή expressing fear or caution is generally rare (see Goodwin, *SGMT* 132) and suspect in contexts where there is 'real anxiety' (see Jebb, on *Trach.* 550). Secondly, the combination of future and subjunctive (κατείπῃ) is altogether exceptional. The only other example quoted from Attic drama is *Pers.* 115–21, where the two verbs are much farther apart, and where there is corruption in any case (see Broadhead, ad loc. and Appendix I, 258). It is at least curious that the received text of this song offers two syntactical oddities involving μή with the future indicative.

aeol da

D

D –

$$- \quad -\cup\cup-\cup\cup- \quad \cup$$

κοινῇ γὰρ ἐπ' εὐτυχίαισιν

$$-\cup- \quad - \quad -\cup\cup-\cup\cup- \quad - \quad -\cup\cup-\cup\cup- \quad \cup$$

575　ἔρχεται γλώττης ἐπίνοια πολίτην δῆμον ἐπαγλαϊοῦσα

$$-\cup- \quad \cup \quad -\cup\cup-\cup\cup-$$

576a μυρίαισιν ὠφελίαισι βίου·

$$- \quad -\cup\cup-\cup\cup- \quad --$$

576b δηλοῦν ⟨δ'⟩ ὅ τι περ δύναται καιρός.

†δεῖται γάρ τοι (γε R) σοφοῦ τινος ἐξευρήματος ἡ πόλις

[ἡμῶν.

$$-\cup\cup-\cup\cup-$$

ἀλλὰ πέραινε μόνον

$$-\cup\cup-\cup\cup- \quad - \quad -\cup\cup-\cup\cup-$$

μήτε δεδραμένα μήτ' εἰρημένα πω πρότερον.

$$- \quad -\cup\cup-\cup\cup- \quad \cup \quad -\cup- \quad \cup--|||$$

580　μισοῦσι γὰρ ἣν τὰ παλαιὰ πολλάκις θεῶνται.

After Praxagora's return and meeting with her husband and Chremes, the chorus exhort her in song to produce her social and political programme. In the play as we have it nothing more is heard from them until the exodos.

Most of the stanza is in rather free dactylo-epitrite. The first verse, however, looks like a pendent version of Sappho's

$$\times\times-\cup\cup-\cup\cup-\cup\cup-\cup-$$

(see PLF 44). Calling it 'spondee + praxillean' does not cast much light. As far as we know, the cadence . . . $-\cup\cup-\cup-(-)$ belongs to aeolic. Whether Stesichorus admitted it is highly questionable (Introduction, p. 86).

Neither φιλόσοφος nor any of its cognates is found elsewhere in Aristophanes (on the absence of the word from *Clouds*, see J. S. Morrison, *CQ* 8 (1958), 209), but that is not sufficient reason to emend it away here and the resolution is not self-evidently unacceptable. At 574, Meineke's εὐτυχίᾳ for εὐτυχίαισιν would produce hiatus, and so verse-end. 577 is enigmatic. R's version would scan:

– D ⌣

e – D – D ⌣

e ⌣ D

– D – –

D

D – D

– D ⌣ e ba (= archil)

‒ ‒ ‒ ‒ ⌣ ⌣ ‒ ⌣ ⌣ ‒ ‒ ⌣ ⌣ ‒ ⌣ ⌣ ‒ ‒

The initial sequence of three longs is hard to explain in dactylo-epitrite, and the juxtaposition of γάρ τοί γε peculiar (see Denniston, *Particles*², 152). The solution favoured by editors this century (Hall–Geldart, Coulon, Ussher) has been to accept the version of the other MSS, which scans:

‒ ‒ ‒ ‒ ⌣ ‒ ⌣ ⌣ ‒ ‒ ‒ ⌣ ⌣ ‒ ⌣ ⌣ ‒ ‒

Metrically, this is even odder. In addition to the opening triple long, it introduces – ⌣ – ⌣ ⌣ –, instead of the – ⌣ ⌣ – ⌣ ⌣ – appropriate in dactylo-epitrite. In *Ol.* 13, Pindar makes an exceptionally bold transition from aeolo-choriambic to dactylo-epitrite, and there (at str. 6) he seemingly substitutes – ⌣ – ⌣ ⌣ – for – ⌣ ⌣ – ⌣ ⌣ –:

‒ ‒ ⌣ ‒ ⌣ ⌣ ‒ ‒ ‒ ⌣ ‒ ‒ ‒ ⌣ ⌣ ‒ ⌣ ⌣ ‒ ‒ ⌣ ‒

In *Ecc.*, however, the apparent aeolo-choriambic coda to 571 seems too distant to explain the casual introduction of an aeolo-choriambic phrase in 577. The Aldine's δεῖται γάρ τι produces the metrically simple

‒ ‒ ‒ ⌣ ⌣ ‒ ⌣ ⌣ ‒ ‒ ‒ ⌣ ⌣ ‒ ⌣ ⌣ ‒ ‒

which Musurus may well have seen as straight dactyls (if the scholium on *Frogs* 814 is really his, he had some understanding of dactyls; see above, ad loc.). But τι seems redundant. As we have it, the song is marked by both metrical and linguistic oddities, but it would be

893–9

$$- \cup \overgroup{\cup\cup} - \quad - \cup - \cup \quad - \cup \overgroup{\cup\cup} - \quad - \cup - -$$

893–4 Γ. εἴ τις ἀγαθὸν βούλεται παθεῖν τι, παρ' ἐμοὶ χρὴ

[καθεύδειν.

$$- \cup - \cup \quad - \cup \overgroup{\cup\cup} \cup \quad - \cup - - \quad - \cup - -$$

895–6 οὐ γὰρ ἐν νέαις τὸ σοφὸν ἔνεστιν, ἀλλ' ἐν ταῖς

[πεπείροις.

$$- \cup - - \quad - \cup \overgroup{\cup\cup} - \quad - \cup - -$$

οὐδέ τοι στέργειν ἂν ἐθέλοι μᾶλλον ἢ 'γὼ

$$- \cup \cup - \quad - \cup - \cup$$

τὸν φίλον ᾧπερ ξυνείην,

$$- \cup \overgroup{\cup\cup} \cup \quad - \cup - \cup \;|||$$

ἀλλ' ἐφ' ἕτερον ἂν πέτοιτο.

After 876, Chremes sets off for the common dinner, closely followed by the Selfish Man, and R writes χοροῦ. A lapse of time must, indeed, be imagined between 876 and 877, for when the Older Woman speaks at 877 the men are due (indeed overdue) back after the meal. The Older Woman plans to sing an alluring song: μελύδριον . . . τι τῶν Ἰωνικῶν. But, rhythmically at least, there is nothing perceptibly 'Ionian' about the song when it comes. The metre is pure trochaic, except for a single choriamb at 898. Like *Wasps* 1009, the stanza ends with a full trochaic metron (see further, Parker, in Craik, *'Owls to Athens'*, 336).

897–8 are curious both metrically and linguistically. Metrically, the dimeter $- \cup \cup - \quad - \cup - -$ at 898 is exceptional. While choriambs keep regular company with iambs (Introduction, pp. 78–84), they are, for some reason, hardly ever found with trochees. The apparent trochee which opens polyschematists of the form $- \cup - \cup - \cup \cup -$ is, of course, not $- \cup - \times$, but $\cdots \cdots - \times$. The only other example I have found in Attic drama of the colon $- \cup \cup - \; . - \cup - \times$ (or, indeed, of cho tro undivided by word-end) is *Phil.* 1180, ναὸς ἵν' ἡμῖν τέτακται, which is in astropha. R has a dash after τὸν φίλον, raising the possibility that the

irresponsible to resort to extensive emendation in the manner of White and von Velsen. Equally, it will not do to pretend that we know what Aristophanes wrote.

⟨δ᾽⟩ at 576b was proposed by Voss.

4 tro

4 tro

3 tro

cho tro

2 tro

scribe of R or a predecessor found something illegible at that point. Peı and Muı insert ἡ νέα after τὸν φίλον, which suggests that their source interpreted a dash as marking change of speaker. A linguistic oddity in the context is the absence of τις as subject of ἐθέλοι (for which Ussher cites *OC* 1225 ἔπει φάνῃ as parallel). The scribe of B sought to remedy this by οὐδέ τις for οὐδέ τοι in 897. Von Velsen, seeking both to introduce τις and to regularize the metre, takes R's dash as evidence of a lacuna and offers:

> οὐδέ τοι στέργειν τις ἐθέλοι μᾶλλον ἢ 'γὼ
> τὸν φίλον ⟨ἂν⟩ ᾧπερ ξυνείην
>
> $-\cup--\quad-\cup\widetilde{}-\quad-\cup--$
> $-\cup\widetilde{}-\quad-\cup--$

The oddities of the passage are not such as to prove corruption, but the possibility cannot be ruled out.

At 894, χρὴ καθεύδειν is omitted by ΓΒ. πεπείροις at 896 is found in the *Suda* and the Aldine. R has πεπείραις (presumably by assimilation to ταῖς), ΓΒ ἐμπείροις.

900–5＝906–10

－∪－(－)   －∪－∪

900 N^{ιs}. μὴ φθόνει ταῖσιν νέαισι·

⌒∪－∪   ⌒∪－(∪)
τὸ τρυφερὸν γὰρ ἐμπέφυκε

－∪∪－∪－－
τοῖς ἁπαλοῖσι μηροῖς,

－∪－－   －∪－
κἀπὶ τοῖς μήλοις ἐπαν-

－∪－－   ⌒∪－－   －∪－－
θεῖ· σὺ δ᾽, ὦ γραῦ, παραλέλεξαι κἀντέτριψαι

－∪∪－∪－⌣|||
905   τῷ θανάτῳ μέλημα.

The Girl and the Older Woman sing a pair of stanzas which have, at least, close metrical affinities and should probably correspond. 900 ff., where the text is more secure, divides into two sections, both trochaic with aristophanean clausula, the second longer by one metron than the first.

In the first three cola correspondence can be produced quite easily by adopting Hermann's ταῖς for ταισὶν in 900 and Bothe's ἀποβάλοιο ('reject deliberately') at 907. But 907 is problematic in meaning as well as metre. At first sight, 'may you cast away your headrest' seems feeble, and one is tempted to suspect (with Ussher) some further gynecological misadventure. It may, however, be well to notice the pattern of another cumulative Aristophanic curse, that of the chorus upon Antimachus at *Ach.* 1165 ff. There the sequence is: (1) may he be assaulted (2) and in trying to pick up a stone to throw at his assailant, (3) may he, instead, pick up a fresh turd. Here, τό τ᾽ ἐπίκλιντρον ἀποβάλοις may correspond to the second stage in the action, the attempt of the victim to secure a satis-

tro tro = cr tro

Γ. ἐκπέσοι σου τὸ τρῆμα

tro tro = tro cr

τό τ᾽ ἐπίκλιντρον ἀποβάλοις

arist

βουλομένη σποδεῖσθαι,

tro cr

909a κἀπὶ τῆς κλίνης ὄφιν

+ 3 tro

909b †εὔροις καὶ προσελκύσαιο

arist

910 βουλομένη φιλῆσαι.

factory outcome. That interpretation would tend to support the middle, ἀποβάλοιο.

903–4 = 909 pose a much less tractable problem. At 903–4, the absence of word-end after the lecythion (see Parker, *CQ* 26 (1976), 21–2) and the strong pause within the metron after ἐπανθεῖ are striking, but there is nothing to warrant attempts at emendation. At 909, however, the MS text is definitely unmetrical:

$$- \cup - - - \cup -$$
$$- - - \cup - \cup - \cup$$

MS variants are minor and unhelpful (καὶ is reported missing from Pe1 by Ussher. Γ has προσελκύσαι, Β προσελκύσαις). Wilamowitz produced a sequence of three trochees by deleting εὔροις καὶ, but, in view of the evidence for correspondence here it is irresponsible to introduce emendations which tend in the opposite direction.

Other variants are insignificant. At 902, ἀπαλοῖσι comes from R (ἀπαλοῖς ΓΒΑld). μηροῖς comes from Γ (μηρίοις RAld).

911–23

⏑‒ ‒ ⏑ ⌢⏑⏑   ‒ ⏑ ‒ ‖ ʜ

911   αἰαῖ, τί ποτε πείσομαι;

‒ ‒ ‒   ‒ ‒ ‒

 οὐχ ἥκει μοὐταῖρος·

⏑ ‒ ‒   ‒ ‒ ⏑ ‒

913a   μόνη δ' αὐτοῦ λείπομ'· ἡ

‒ ‒ ‒   ‒ ‒ ‒   ⏑ ‒ ⏑⌣ ‖

913b   γάρ μοι μήτηρ ἄλλῃ βέβηκεν.

      914

‒ ‒ ‒ ⏑ ⏑ ‒ ⏑ ‒

915   ἀλλ', ὦ μαῖ', ἱκετεύομαι,

⏑ ‒ ⏑ ‒ ⏑ ⏑ ‒

κάλει τὸν Ὀρθαγόραν,

⏑ ‒ ‒ ‒ ‒ ⏑ ⏑ ‒

917a   ὅπως ⟨ἂν⟩ σαυτῆς κατόναι',

‒ ⏑ ⏑ ‒ ⏑⌣ ‖ ʜ

917b   ἀντιβολῶ σε.

‒ ‒ ⏑ ⌢⏑⏑   ‒ ⏑ ‒

918   ἤδη τὸν ἀπ' Ἰωνίας

⏑ ‒ ⏑ ‒   ⏑ ‒ ⏑ ‒

τρόπον, τάλαινα, κνησιᾷς.

      920

‒ ‒ ‒ ⏑ ⏑ ‒ ⏑ ‒

ἀλλ' οὐκ ἄν ποθ' ὑφαρπάσαι-

⏑ ‒ ⏑ ‒ ⏑ ⏑ ‒

ο τἀμὰ παίγνια· τὴν δ'

⏑ ‒ ‒ ‒ ‒ ⏑ ⏑ ‒

923a   ἐμὴν ὥραν οὐκ ἀπολεῖς

‒ ⏑ ⏑ ‒ ‒ ⦀

923b   οὐδ' ἀπολήψει.

ia cr

2 mol

ba ia

   + 2 mol ba

trim I
glyc

   + aeol heptasyll

   + pol

   + adon

ia cr

ia dim

trim I
glyc

   + aeol heptasyll

   + pol

   + adon

This passage bristles with problems.

Twice, an iambic trimeter (914 and 920) which looks prosaic enough to be spoken, divides an iambic section from an aeolo-choriambic sequence (915–17 and 921–3) which, while preserving the common pattern of three acatalectic cola with catalectic clausula (Introduction, p. 22), is curiously heterogeneous in its components (cf. *Clouds* 571–4= 603–6). This is the colon-division of Wilamowitz (*GV* 478). Most editors (Hall–Geldart, Schroeder, Ussher) print a version, corrected to correspond, of the traditional colometry common to R and the Aldine:

This is an even more unusual combination of cola than Wilamowitz's. Hipponactean in synartesis with the following colon is certainly rare, and may be unparalleled (see Parker, *CQ* 26 (1976), 22–5). The last colon would be a sort of catalectic asclepiad. Asclepiad rhythms are found in convivial songs (see *PMG* 902–5), but in Aristophanes cola of this type are extremely rare and confined to quotation (*Birds* 1238–9) or specific parody (*Birds* 1410). There is one exception, the pair of cola of exactly this form which mark the climax of the hymn at *Knights* 551 ff.= 581 ff. There, however, there is reason to suspect cult associations (see above, ad loc.), which would be thoroughly out of place here.

Willems, followed by Coulon, attributed the whole of 911–23 to the Girl (balancing, in a manner, the Older Woman's song at 893–9), but the strong rhetorical and metrical break after 917, as well as the sequence of ideas, suggests change of singer. Bergk propose an asymmetrical division, giving 911–17 to the Girl, 918–20 to the Older Woman, and 921–3 to the Girl again. This has certain attractions on grounds of sense, but formally the natural pattern would be for the Girl to sing 911–17 and the Older Woman 918–23. Moreover, one would not expect to find a distinctive sequence like 915–17 and 921–3 exactly repeated in Attic lyric except in corresponding strophae. 911 and 918 also correspond, but in answer to the seven metra of 912–13, 919 offers only a dimeter. The case for assuming the loss of cola after 918 and 919 was powerfully put by John Jackson (*MS* 110): 'to question the double lacuna or dream that age failed to answer youth line for line, syllable for syllable, note for note, obscenity for obscenity, is to defy every convention of the stage, ancient or modern or betwixt and between, merely to screen the defects of a written tradition seldom more contemptible than in this play.' For the loss of alternate lines, Jackson compares the loss by A, earlier in this same play, of the even-numbered verses at 158–68 and the odd-numbered verses at 235–9. In lyric the loss would be easier to explain. In an exemplar with two cola to the line, damage to the outer side of the page would result in the loss of the even-numbered cola. Yet sense and syntax at 918–19 discourage the assumption of lacunae. The Girl's double molossi at 912 and 913 are metrically remarkable (see above, on *Birds* 1720–65): can Aristophanes have had some reason for breaking correspondence by not repeating them in the antistrophe? There is no parallel for such semi-correspondence. Apart from the two double molossi at 911–13, 913a (ba ia) does not correspond with 919 (2 ia), and is in itself peculiar in more than one respect. Firstly, the colon ∪ – – × – ∪ – is comparatively rare, as demonstrated by Stinton (*BICS* 22 (1975), 88 ff. = *Collected Papers*, 127). He does not cite this example, but describes the sequence mol ba ia at *IT* 1255 as 'unique in iambics'. Here, there may well be verse-end between mol and ba, in view of the strong rhetorical pause after μοῦταῖρος. Then there is the relatively rare elision λείπομ' (see on 495 above, and on *Wasps* 273). Jackson suggests:

> αὐτοῦ δὲ λείπομαι μόνη,
> ἡ γὰρ [μοι] μήτηρ ἄλλη [βέβηκεν]
>
> – – ∪ –   ∪ – ∪ – ‖ ʜ
> – – –   – – –

Indeed, μοι could well be an accidental insertion and βέβηκεν an incorporated gloss. To introduce emendation on this scale into the text would pass the bounds of prudent editing. None the less, Jackson's treatment usefully highlights the oddities of the received text and demonstrates the likelihood of corruption.

In 911, ΓΒ have πειράσομαι for πείσομαι. In 912, μοῦταῖρος was deduced by Reiske from R's μ' ουτ' αἶρος. The other MSS and the Aldine have μου τοῦρος (one word in B). For the crasis, compare μοῦγκώμιον at *Clouds* 1205. Hermann introduced ἄν in 917, after σαυτῆς. Wilamowitz placed it after ὅπως.

938–41=942–5

$$- - - \cup \cup - \cup - \cup - -$$

N^{as}. εἴθ᾽ ἐξῆν παρὰ τῇ νέᾳ καθεύδειν,

$$- - - \cup \cup - \cup - \cup - - \parallel \text{н}$$

καὶ μὴ 'δει πρότερον διασποδῆσαι

$$\cup \cup - \cup - \quad - \cup \cup -$$

940   ἀνάσιμον ἢ πρεσβυτέραν·

$$- \cup \cup - \cup - \quad - \cup \cup - \cup = \parallel\parallel$$

οὐ γὰρ ἀνασχετὸν τοῦτό γ᾽ ἐλευθέρῳ.

A young man at last arrives from the communal dinner, singing, as might be expected of a reveller, in the rhythm common to a number of popular symposium pieces including, in particular, the Harmodius songs (*PMG* 893–6). The Older Woman answers in the same rhythm, and the choice of metre proves to be not merely appropriate but pointedly allusive: the two singers trumpet out their conflicting assertions of civil

952–9=960–8

$$- \cup - \quad - \cup -$$

952a $N^{\iota s}$. δεῦρο δὴ δεῦρο δή,

$$\underset{\smile}{} \cup - \quad \overline{} \cup -$$

952b   φίλον ἐμόν, δεῦρό μοι

$$\cup - \cup - \quad \cup - -$$

πρόσελθε καὶ ξύνευνος [μοι]

$$- - \cup - \quad \cup - \cup -$$

954a   τὴν εὐφρόνην ὅπως ἔσει.

$$\cup \cup - \cup \cup - \cup \cup -$$

954b   πάνυ γάρ τις ἔρως με δονεῖ

$$- \cup - - - \cup -$$

955   τῶνδε τῶν σῶν βοστρύχων.

$$\cup \cup - - - - - - \cup \cup$$

ἄτοπος δ᾽ ἔγκειταί μοί τις πόθος,

phal
Γ. οἰμώζων ἄρα, νὴ Δία, σποδήσεις.

phal
οὐ γὰρ τἀπὶ Χαριξένης τάδ' ἐστίν.

∧dodrans A cho
κατὰ τὸν νόμον ταῦτα ποιεῖν

2 dodrans A
945   ἔστι δίκαιον, εἰ δημοκρατούμεθα.

rights to the tune of the anthem of Athenian democracy, each conclud-
ing with a key word: ἐλευθέρῳ . . . δημοκρατούμεθα. On the metre of
the Harmodius songs, see on *Wasps* 1226ff., where it serves a similarly
allusive purpose.

At 939, μὴ 'δει is Elmsley's emendation of the MSS' μηδέν.
πρεσβυτέραν at 940 is Bothe's for πρεσβύτερον.

2 cr
960   N^{as}. δεῦρο δὴ δεῦρο δή,

2 cr
961a   καὶ σύ μοι καταδραμοῦ-

+ ia dim cat
961b   σα τὴν θύραν ἄνοιξον

ia dim (– – ᴗ –   ⏓ ᴗ –   – ᴗ –)
τήνδ'· εἰ δὲ μή, †καταπεσὼν κείσομαι.

? (ᴗ ᴗ – – – –)
φίλον, ἀλλ' ἐν τῷ σῷ

lec (– ᴗ – – –)
βούλομαι κόλπῳ

? (– – – – ᴗ ᴗ – – – –)
965   πληκτίζεσθαι μετὰ τῆς σῆς πυγῆς.

$$- \cup \widetilde{\cup} - - \cup -$$

ὅς με διακναίσας ἔχει.

$$\widetilde{\cup} \cup - \quad - \cup -$$

μέθες, ἱκνοῦμαί σ᾽, Ἔρως,

$$- \cup - - \quad - \cup - -$$

959a καὶ ποίησον τόνδ᾽ ἐς εὐνὴν

$$- \cup - \cup \quad - - |||$$

959b τὴν ἐμὴν ἱκέσθαι.

The Girl and the Young Man sing a duet in which amatory common-places familiar from literary poetry are combined with crude explicitness. Comparable literary material is collected by C. M. Bowra (*AJP* 79 (1958), 376–91 = *On Greek Margins*, 149–65), who, however, fails to distinguish between song as dramatic performance on the one hand and on the other as instrument in a real situation. The male serenade is, in origin at least, what it purports to be: a means of attracting a woman's attention and making advances to her. Women's love-songs and male–female duets, whether literary or traditional, are forms of musical drama. It is this confusion that leads Bowra into identifying this duet as pastiche of an otherwise unknown type of popular ditty actually performed in the 'looser quarter' of Athens by young men and the local *filles de joie*. S. Douglas Olson (*CQ* 38 (1988), 328–30) more convincingly identifies the song as literary fantastication of the *paraclausithyron*, designed to express the confusion of sexual roles in Praxagora's new world. In any case, it would be naïve to assume that a highly literary poet, like Aristophanes, would reproduce popular song with formal accuracy. We should expect him both to burlesque and, technically, to improve on his model. To attribute the serious failures of strophic correspondence in the received text to the popular origins of a hypothetical parent form is an intellectually cheap solution.

  The metrical shape of the song can be more or less adduced from the strophe. The stanza opens with cretic and iambic (952–4). There are two lecythia (955 and 957), and the coda is in cretics, which lead, this time, into trochees. The final 'ithyphallic' can be interpreted trochaically as full metron and doubly syncopated metron ($-(\cup)-(\times)$); see above, on *Frogs* 1370 ff.).

lec (∪ ∪ ∪ − − − ∪ ∪ − −)

Κύπρι τί μ' ἐκ|μαίνεις ἐπὶ ταύτῃ;†

2 cr

μέθες, ἱκνοῦμαί σ', Ἔρως,

tro dim

968a   καὶ ποίησον τήνδ' ἐς εὐνὴν

tro sp

968b   τὴν ἐμὴν ἱκέσθαι.

954b is rhythmically perfectly plausible, but the context offers no help in putting a name to it. It is worth remarking that the addition of a spondaic adjective, like δεινός after γὰρ (Dindorf), or after ἔρως (Coulon) would produce an anapaestic dimeter. 956 is theoretically scannable as an anapaestic dimeter but it takes a form without parallel in lyric and exceedingly rare anywhere. The closest approximation I have found in Euripides' recitative is *El.* 1353 (− − − − | − − − ∪ ∪).

Divergences between the MSS are trivial. It is conjectures that swell the apparatuses. Major assaults on the text have been made by Reisig (*Conjecturae*, 322–3) and by Wilamowitz (*GV* 477–8), and the latter's version is adopted by Coulon and, in part, by Ussher. The text I print is that of R. So is the colon-division, except that at 960–1b that MS turns δεῦρο δὴ . . . ἄνοιξον into two trimeters:

When faced with this passage, it is well to bear the following points in mind. Whereas 952–9 is probably more or less sound, a large part of 960–8 has been garbled into prose. Further, there is a strong case for believing that 952–9 originally corresponded with 960–9. However, the rewriting needed to restore correspondence would be more than the most reckless emender would undertake. If 960–8 did not correspond with 952–9, we have absolutely no idea how the passage ought to scan. That being so, it will not do for editors to tinker with the received text in the attempt to produce something which looks metrically acceptable in the light of their own more or less dim perceptions of what constitutes metrical acceptability. The text makes readable sense, and if one does not known what to aim at in metrical emendation, it is best to leave ill alone.

One place at which there is a very strong case for emendation is 953, where deletion of μοι, proposed by Bothe, restores correspondence easily. Bergk's ξύνευνέ μοι which found favour with Wilamowitz and has passed from him to Coulon, Ussher and Zimmermann, requires further emendation in 961 to achieve correspondence, and is in itself implausible syntactically. Examples quoted from Attic of attraction of nominative to vocative are far less harsh than this and seem to be confined to participial phrases. Thus, Ussher cites *Phil.* 759–60:

969–72=973–5

$$- - \cup - \quad - \cup \cup - | \quad \bar{\cup} - \cup \,\overline{\overline{\cup\cup}} \quad \cup - -$$

καὶ ταῦτα μέντοι μετρίως πρὸς τὴν ἐμὴν ἀνάγκην

$$\bar{\cup} - \cup - \quad - \cup \cup - | \quad - \cup \cup \,\underline{\underline{\cup}}? \quad \cup - \bigcirc \,||^{\mathrm{H}}$$

970　εἰρημέν' ἐστίν. σὺ δέ μοι, φίλτατον, ὦ ἱκετεύω,

$$\cup - \cup - \quad - - \smile ||$$

ἄνοιξον, ἀσπάζου με·

$$\cup \cup - \cup \cup - \cup - |||$$

διά τοι σὲ πόνους ἔχω.

Metrically, these stanzas are agreeably free of problems: the problem of who sings them has no metrical aspect. The opening iambo-choriambic dicola are very much in the anacreontic style. Note, in particular, the apparent interchangeability of iamb and choriamb in the second colon (Introduction, p. 79). The last colon appears as the opening of a convivial song in *PMG* 892. The whole of that stanza scans:

The context there suggests that the colon is to be taken as a telesillean with the half-base resolved (cf. *Thesm.* 1020, and see Introduction,

ἰὼ δύστηνε σύ,
δύστηνε δῆτα διὰ πόνων πάντων φανείς

But here the true vocative in 759 smoothes the way for the attracted repetition. Other examples of the attraction, again in participial phrases, are *Pers.* 674 and *Tro.* 1221. *Aj.* 695, adduced by Coulon, is not an example at all (see Lobeck, ad loc., and the punctuation of Lloyd-Jones–Wilson). For anything genuinely comparable with ξύνευνέ μοι . . . ὅπως ἔσει we have to wait for the metrically-convenient conceits of Hellenistic poetry (Theocritus 17. 66 ὄλβιε κοῦρε γένοιο; cf. Callimachus, Pfeiffer, fr. 599). The case for deleting τήνδ᾽ at 962 (Blaydes) is strong, but, amid the general uncertainty, not conclusive.

ia cho dim + ia dim cat
ὦ χρυσοδαίδαλτον ἐμὸν μέλημα, Κύπριδος ἔρνος,

ia cho dim + cho ia dim cat
μέλιττα Μούσης, Χαρίτων θρέμμα, Τρυφῆς πρόσωπον.

ia mol
975a ἄνοιξον, ἀσπάζου με·

tel?
975b διά τοι σὲ πόνους ἔχω.

p. 73). Over all, Aristophanes' stanza is rhythmically suited to a comastic context.

At 970, ὦ ἱκετεύω is much more likely to be an example of crasis than of epic correption. Correption is found characteristically in dignified metres (Introduction, pp. 91–2), and here would require resolution in a choriamb. Crasis of ω (or vocative ὦ, at least) is found in convivial songs (ὦ ἑταῖρε *PMG* 897=*Wasps* 1238).

At 969, μέντοι is the reading of R; the other MSS and the Aldine have μέν μοι. In 971, με comes from B (first hand erased); the other MSS and the Aldine have τε. The scribe of B presumably derived με from 975a. At 973, B alone has χρυσοδαίδαλον, *contra metrum*. At 974, R and the *Suda* (under θρύψις and Χαρίτων θρύμμα) have θρύμμα for θρέμμα.

1168–83

∪ ∪ ∪ ∪ – ⌣ ?

τάχα γὰρ ἔπεισι

∪ ⌢ ∪ ⌢   ∪ ⌢ ∪ ⌢

λοπαδοτεμαχοσελαχογαλεο-

– ∪ ∪   – ∪ ∪   – ∪ ∪   – ∪ ∪

1170   κρανιολειψανοδριμυποτριμματο-

– ∪ ∪   – ∪ ∪   ⌢ ∪ ∪   ⌢ ∪ ∪

σιλφιοτυρομελιτοκατακεχυμενο-

– ∪ ∪   – ∪ ∪   – ∪ ∪   – ∪ ∪

κιχλεπικοσσυφοφαττοπεριστερα-

– ∪ ∪   – ∪ ∪   – ∪ ∪   – ∪ ∪

λεκτρυονοπτοπιφαλλιδοκιγκλοπε-

– ∪ ∪   – ∪ ∪   – ∪ ∪   – ∪ ∪

λειολαγῳοσιραιοβαφητραγα-

– ∪ ∪   – ∪ ∪   – ∪ ∪   – ∪ ∪

1175   νοπτερυγών. σὺ δὲ ταῦτ' ἀκροασάμε-

– ∪ ∪   – ∪ ∪   – ∪ ∪   – ∪ ∪

νος ταχὺ καὶ ταχέως λαβὲ τρύβλιον.

– ∪ ∪ –   – ∪ –

εἶτα κόνισαι λαβὼν

⌢ ∪ ⌢   ∪ – –

λέκιθον, ἵν' ἐπιδειπνῇς.

– ∪ – – – ∪ – || н

ἀλλὰ λαιμάττουσί που.

?

ia dim

+ 28 da

cho cr

ith

lec

$$- - \cup - \quad \text{inter}$$

1180   αἴρεσθ᾽ ἄνω, ἰαί, εὐαί,

$$- - \cup - \quad \text{inter}$$

δειπνήσομεν, εὐοῖ, εὐαί,

$$\underset{\smile}{} - - \cup \cup - -$$

εὐαί, ὡς ἐπὶ νίκῃ.

inter

εὐαί, εὐαί, εὐαί, εὐαί.

The final song of the play features a compound word of at least 98 syllables and a sequence of 28 dactyls unbroken by coincidence of word-end with a spondaic metron. It is the longest such sequence in surviving Attic drama. The second longest, of 26 dactyls, is in *OC* (229–35), a play produced some seven or eight years earlier. Moreover, there as here, after an expository section, the chorus addresses a character on stage with urgent exhortation:

> . . . σὺ δὲ τῶνδ᾽ ἑδράνων πάλιν ἔκτοπος
> αὖθις ἄφορμος ἐμᾶς χθονὸς ἔκθορε . . .

Specific parody of *OC* is not impossible. The case for it is, at least, good enough to be taken into account at 1177, where R offers εἶτα κόνισαι λαβὼν $- \cup \cup - \quad - \cup -$, and PeiMuiAld εἶτα λαβὼν κόνισαι ($- \cup \cup - \quad \cup - -$). The aristophanean seems in itself much simpler and more obvious, but in the same passage of *OC* Antigone both begins and ends another long dactylic sequence (this time of 24 metra) with the colon $- \cup \cup - \quad - \cup -$ (242 ὦ ξένοι, οἰκτίραθ᾽, ἅ . . ., 249 τὰν ἀδόκητον χάριν), and adds a resolved version ($- \cup \cup - \quad \widearc{\cup\cup} \cup -$) at 252. While cho cr seems at first sight the obvious analysis of this colon, da ia cannot be ruled out. The sequence $- \cup \cup \times - \cup -$ seems to occur as a metrical conceit in later tragedy (see D. S. Raven, *AJP* 86 (1965), 229–30, and T. C. W. Stinton, *CR* 15 (1965), 142–5 = *Collected Papers*, 11–15 and Introduction, pp. 53–4). It may, as Stinton suggests, explain the curious cola of the form $- \cup \cup - \cup \cup - \cup \cup \cup -$, which recur earlier in the same *OC* passage at 216, 218, 220, and 222.

ia inter

ia inter

pher

inter

The dactyls with resolved long at 1171 are an extreme rarity (in tragedy, confined, apparently, to Euripides; see above on *Birds* 1720–65 and Introduction pp. 54–5). Dale (*LM*² 25 n. 2) apparently wished to take 1169 as a sequence of three such dactyls. Going yet further in the pursuit of exoticism, Ussher proposes to take 1169 as a tetrameter in which tribrachs represent dactyls. It should not, however, be overlooked that the colon falls quite naturally into a pair of fully resolved iambic metra. Iambic and dactylic make a well-authenticated combination in dramatic lyric (Introduction, pp. 51–2), and iambic reappears at the end of this song.

The monstrous dactylic word has, understandably, suffered some corruption in transmission. At 1171, -τυρο- is Blaydes's suggestion. The MSS have -παραο-, Ussher suggests -λιπαρο-, Sommerstein (*CQ* 34 (1984), 322 n. 54) -παραλο-, to be interpreted as 'slightly salted', on the basis of *Ach.* 1158. The two latter conjectures both produce another metron of the form ∪ ∪ ∪ ∪. At 1172, -κιχλ- is Faber's correction of the MSS' -κινκλ-. -κοσσυφοφαττο- is Dindorf's. R has -κοσσυφατο, MuiPει -κοσσυφαο-, and the Aldine -κοσσυφο-. At 1173, -οπτο- is Meineke's emendation. R has -οπτεγ-, the Aldine -οπτε-. -πιφαλλιδο- is Ussher's suggestion. The MSS have -κεφαλλιο-. At 1176, ταχὺ καὶ ταχέως looks very much like a copying mistake by attraction. Ussher offers the suggestion that it may be a 'stock colloquial expression'. Blaydes suggested τρέχε καὶ ταχέως.

Wealth

SYNOPSIS

290–5 = 296–301	*Iambic.* Carion and chorus.
302–8 = 309–15	*Iambic.* Carion and chorus.
316–21	*Iambic.* Carion.
637–40	*Dochmiac.*

290–5 = 296–301

$$- - \cup - \mid \ \ - - \cup - \mid \ \ - \widetilde{\cup\cup} \mid - \ \ \cup - \smile \parallel$$

290 Κ. καὶ μὴν ἐγὼ βουλήσομαι—θρεττανελὸ—τὸν Κύκλωπα

$$- - \cup - \mid \ \ \sigma - \cup - \mid \ \ - - \cup \widetilde{\cup\cup} \ \ \cup - -$$

μιμούμενος καὶ τοῖν ποδοῖν ὡδὶ παρενσαλεύων

$$- - \cup - \ \ \sigma \widetilde{\cup\cup} \cup \widetilde{\cup\cup} \ \ \cup \mid \widetilde{\cup\cup} \cup \underset{\cup}{\cup} \ \ \cup - \smile \parallel_{\text{H}}$$

ὑμᾶς ἄγειν. ἀλλ᾿ εἶα, τέκεα, θαμίν᾿ ἐπαναβοῶντες

$$- - \cup - \ \ \underset{\cup}{\cup} \widetilde{\cup\cup} \cup -$$

βληχώμενοί τε προβατίων

$$- - \cup \mid \widetilde{\cup\cup} \ \ - - \cup - \parallel^{\text{H}}$$

αἰγῶν τε κιναβρώντων μέλη

$$\cup - \cup - \ \ \sigma - \cup - \mid \ \ \underset{\cup}{\cup} - \cup - \ \ \cup - \smile \parallel\parallel$$

295 ἕπεσθ᾿ ἀπεψωλημένοι· τράγοι δ᾿ ἀκρατιεῖσθε.

The delight of the chorus at Carion's announcement that they are all to become rich provides the slender excuse for a piece of musical and terpsichorean buffoonery. The passage is introduced by recitative in catalectic iambic tetrameters (253–89), and recitative and song make a rhythmically integrated whole, as at *Knights* 478ff. According to Σ *vet.* on 290 and 296 and to the *Suda* (s. θρεττανελώ), Aristophanes is ridiculing in this song a poem by the dithyrambist, Philoxenus of Cythera (whose date is given by the Parian Marble as 436/5 to 380/79). It may be observed that Philoxenus' most notable contribution to the Cyclops' story, his love for Galatea, is ignored by Aristophanes.

In *Wealth*, the use of lyric to provide a running commentary on the action has been altogether abandoned. The role of the chorus in reacting to events with the emotional heightening of lyric is reduced to a single short burst of joy in dochmiacs (637–40). Otherwise, the lyric element has dwindled to a single, self-contained comic set-piece (290–321), only tenuously connected with the plot. Both here and in the dochmiacs, however, lyric continues to allude to and to burlesque poetic forms outside comedy.

ia tetram cat

X. ἡμεῖς δέ γ᾽ αὖ ζητήσομεν—θρεττανελὸ—τὸν Κύκλωπα

ia tetram cat

βληχώμενοι σὲ τουτονὶ πεινῶντα καταλαβόντες,

ia tetram cat

πήραν ἔχοντα λάχανά τ᾽ ἄγρια δροσερά, κραιπαλῶντα

ia dim

ἡγούμενον τοῖς προβατίοις,

ia dim

300   εἰκῇ δὲ καταδαρθόντα που

ia tetram cat

μέγαν λαβόντες ἡμμένον σφηκίσκον ἐκτυφλῶσαι.

The testimony on the poem is to be found in *PMG* 815–21. However, 292 ἀλλ᾽ εἶα . . . ἐπαναβοῶντες is said to be quoted from Philoxenus, and he is said also to be the source of πήραν and λάχανα in 298. Otherwise, the only surviving fragment, *PMG* 821, is of uncertain metre, but contains a high proportion of short syllables. It will be noticed that in Aristophanes' song there is a concentration of resolution at 292=298, precisely the point where there is supposed to be verbal allusion to Philoxenus. There is no other evidence of metrical parody. Indeed, these Aristophanic stanzas are typically comic: all three together make up a simple but artful set of variations on the catalectic iambic tetrameter. Throughout, there is correspondence of word-end between strophe and antistrophe at significant points. Thus, 290 ff.=296 ff. begins with a pair of tetrameters in which the iambic rhythm is strongly marked by coincident word-end. The third tetrameter (293=298) diverges from characteristic recitative rhythm not only by the amount of resolution, but by overlap of one short between the first and second cola of the verse. The following four metra surprise the ear, now accustomed to the pattern of full dimeter + catalectic dimeter. 295 begins with yet another full dimeter, marked off by diaeresis, then, at last, the catalectic dimeter follows.

$$302–8=309–15$$

⏑ – ⏑ –   – – ⏑ | –   ⏑ – ⏑ ⏕   ⏑ – ⏒ ‖

Κ. ἐγὼ δὲ τὴν Κίρκην γε, τὴν τὰ φάρμακ᾽ ἀνακυκῶσαν,

– – ⏑ –   – – ⏑ –   ⏒ – ⏑ –   ⏑ – – ‖

ἢ τοὺς ἑταίρους τοῦ Φιλωνίδου ποτ᾽ ἐν Κορίνθῳ

⏑ – ⏑ | ⏕   ⏒ – ⏑ –

ἔπεισεν ὡς ὄντας κάπρους

⏑ – ⏑ – | – – ⏑ – | – – ⏑ –   ⏑ – –

305   μεμαγμένον σκῶρ ἐσθίειν, —αὐτὴ δ᾽ ἔματτεν αὐτοῖς, —

– – ⏑ –   – – ⏑ –

μιμήσομαι πάντας τρόπους·

– – ⏑ ⏕   – – ⏑ ⏕   ⏒ – ⏑ –

ὑμεῖς δὲ γρυλίζοντες ὑπὸ φιληδίας

⏑ – ⏑ | –   ⏑ | – – ‖‖

ἔπεσθε μητρί, χοῖροι.

Variations on the catalectic iambic tetrameter continue. The distinctive touch here is the uneven number of metra at 306–8=313–15. The expectation of a repetition of 304–5=311–12 (two dimeters + catalectic dimeter) is built up and then frustrated by failure of bacchiac to appear at the end of 307=314.

In 302, γε is omitted by RM. At 306, V adds τοὺς before τρόπους

At 290, V has ἔγωγε *contra metrum* for ἐγώ. At 291, AU have
παρασαλεύων for παρενσαλεύων. At 294, the Aldine has κιναβρῶντα
μέληων, pointing to a predecessor with -ων written above the line. L
does, indeed, write the abbreviation for -ων above the line, but it would
be difficult for a copyist of that MS to misplace the syllable, since it is
very clearly written above -ντ-. At 297, V has βληχώμενόν τε for
βληχώμενοι σέ. At 298, VAMU add καὶ before κραιπαλῶντα.
Holzinger (*SAWW* 218.3 (1940), 114–17) defends the MS readings
πεινῶντα (297) and, less convincingly, καταδαρθέντα (300) from
emendation by Bentley (πίνοντα) or Brunck (πινῶντα) and Porson
(καταδαρθόντα).

ia tetram cat
Χ. οὐκοῦν σέ, τὴν Κίρκην γε, τὴν τὰ φάρμακ’ ἀνακυκῶσαν

ia tetram cat
310   καὶ μαγγανεύουσαν μολύνουσάν τε τοὺς ἑταίρους

ia dim
λαβόντες ὑπὸ φιληδίας

ia tetram cat
τὸν Λαρτίου μιμούμενοι τῶν ὄρχεων κρεμῶμεν

ia dim
μινθώσομέν θ’ ὥσπερ τράγου

ia trim
τὴν ῥῖνα· σὺ δ’ Ἀρίστυλλος ὑποχάσκων ἐρεῖς·

ia dim cat
315   ἕπεσθε μητρί, χοῖροι.

(misread by Coulon as σοὺς). At 307, γρυλίζοντες is preserved by V;
RAMU have γρυλλίζοντες. σέ (instead of σε) at 309 was restored conjecturally by Hemsterhuis, but is present in L (and other Triclinian MSS;
see Koster, *Autour d'un manuscrit . . .*, 146). The Aldine, however, transmitted σε. From 311 to 313 the text of V is markedly inaccurate. At 311,
V (with AM²U) has ἢν λάβωμεν for λαβόντες. At 312, it has Λαερτίου

(with R), instead of Λαρτίου, and is alone in transposing τὸν Λαερτίου μιμουμένοι to follow τῶν ὄρχεων κρεμῶμεν. At 313, V has δ᾽ for θ᾽. In 314, τὴν is omitted by R.

For the purpose of tracing the progress of Triclinius' metrical competence, considerable attention has been focused on *Wealth* 309–15, as it appears in the early Triclinian recension represented by P20. Koster (*Autour d'un manuscrit . . .*, 82–5, with Plate IV) has studied it, and, more recently, O. L. Smith (*C&M* 33 (1981–2), 240–3) has made a meticulous palaeographical analysis, identifying three stages in Triclinius' revisions. Triclinius started at something of a disadvantage with 312–15, in that his exemplar offered the following text and colometry:

τὸν λαερτίου (or possibly λαέρτου) μιμούμενοι τῶν ὄρχεων κρεμῶμεν μινθώσομέν θ᾽ ὥσπερ τράγου
τὴν ῥῖνα σὺ δ᾽ ἀρίστυλλος ὑποχάσκων
ἐρεῖς ἕπεσθε μητρὶ χοῖροι

Triclinius made some progress by moving -μῶμεν, τὴν ῥῖνα and ἐρεῖς

316–21

$$- - \cup - \mid \quad - - \cup - \mid \quad \cup - \cup - \quad \cup - - \mid \mid н$$

Κ. ἀλλ᾽ εἶα νῦν τῶν σκωμμάτων ἀπαλλαγέντες ἤδη

$$- - \cup - \quad - - \cup -$$

ὑμεῖς ἐπ᾽ ἄλλ᾽ εἶδος τρέπεσθ᾽,

$$\cup - \cup - \mid \quad - - \cup - \mid$$

ἐγὼ δ᾽ ἰὼν ἤδη λάθρᾳ

$$- - \cup - \mid \quad - - \cup - \mid$$

βουλήσομαι τοῦ δεσπότου

$$\cup - \cup - \quad - - \cup - \mid$$

320   λαβών τιν᾽ ἄρτον καὶ κρέας

$$\cup - \cup - \mid \quad \cup - \cup - \quad - - \cup - \mid \quad \cup - - \mid \mid \mid$$

μασώμενος τὸ λοιπὸν οὕτω τῷ κόπῳ ξυνεῖναι.

Carion sings a coda, beginning with a catalectic tetrameter. 317–21 is perhaps best thought of as a single *pnigos* of 12 metra. The device of keeping the listeners in suspense while they wait for catalexis has been used before in this song. Here the suspense is maintained for far longer

to the ends of the preceding cola, and, in the case of τὴν ῥῖνα, back again, but he seems to have been baffled by the passage to the point of attempting (on the evidence of his metrical scholium) a trochaic analysis. In contrast, the representative of the final Triclinian recension, Vv5 (with L) has, as Koster triumphantly observes, 'exactement la même colométrie que présente l'édition de Coulon'. But the colometry of Coulon is also the colometry of R. Moreover, at 311, P20 has ἐὰν λαβῶμεν in the text, and ἢν λαβῶμεν, like VAM²U, in the scholia, whereas Vv5L have λαβόντες, like R. It seems more probable that between the earlier and later recensions Triclinius gained access to an exemplar which, like R, preserved both a sounder text and the Alexandrian colometry than that he achieved the leap from bafflement to comprehension purely by increased metrical expertise. This suggests a line of enquiry which may be worth following by anyone who wishes to examine further the evolution of Triclinius' metrical competence between P20 and his final recension.

ia tetram cat

2 ia

+ 2 ia

2 ia

2 ia

ia tetram cat

than in the earlier stanzas.

At 316, ἀλλ' is omitted by RM, while VU have ἄγ'. At 318, ἤδη is defended by Holzinger (*SAWW* 218. 3 (1940), 125). Bamberg proposed εἴσω.

637–40

⏑ – – ⏑ –
λέγεις μοι χαράν,

⏑ – – ⏑ –
λέγεις μοι βοάν.

638

⏑ ⌢ – ⏑ –
ἀναβοάσομαι

⏑ – – ⏑ –   ⏑ ⌢ – ⏑ –   ⏑ – – ⏑ – |||
640 τὸν εὔπαιδα καὶ μέγα βροτοῖσι φέγγος Ἀσκληπιόν.

The trimeters in which the healing of Wealth is announced (627ff.) are tragic in rhythm and stylistic colour, marking an emotional high point in the play. The chorus greet the news with a burst of dochmiacs. For the use of dochmiacs to express tumultuous joy, see above on *Clouds* 1154ff. For a tragic example later than *Clouds*, but earlier than *Wealth*, compare *Ba.* 1153ff.:

δ

δ

trim I

δ

3 δ

> ἀναχορεύσωμεν Βάκχιον,
> ἀναβοάσωμεν ξυμφόραν . . .
> ◡ ◡ ◡ – – –   – ◡ –
> ◡ ◡ ◡ – – –   – ◡ –

Aristophanes here confines himself to the two most common types of dochmiac (Introduction, p. 65).

Select Bibliography

GENERAL

ALEXIOU, M., *The Ritual Lament in Greek Tradition* (Cambridge, 1974).

ALLEN, T. W., 'Miscellanea III', *CQ* 22 (1929), 28–30.

AUBRETON, R., *Démétrius Triclinius et les recensions médiévales de Sophocle* (Paris, 1949).

AUSTIN, C., *Comicorum Graecorum Fragmenta in Papyris Reperta* (Berlin and New York, 1973).

—— review of D. M. MacDowell, *Wasps*, *CR* 23 (1973), 133–5.

—— 'Adnotatiunculae in "Thesmophoriazusas"', *PCPS* 200 (1974), 1–2.

—— 'Textual problems in Ar. *Thesm.*', *Dodone*, 16 (1987), 61–92.

—— Observations critiques sur les *Thesmophories* d'Aristophane', *Dodone*, 19 (1990). 9–29.

BLUMENTHAL, A. VON, 'Beobachtungen zu griechischen Texten', *Hermes*, 71 (1936), 452–8.

BOUDREAUX, P., *Le Texte d'Aristophane et ses commentateurs* (Paris, 1919).

BOWRA, C. M., 'A Love-duet', *AJP* 79 (1958), 376–91 = *On Greek Margins* (Oxford, 1970), 149–63.

BUIJS, J. A. J. M., 'Studies in the Lyric Metres of Greek Tragedy', *Mnemosyne*, 39 (1986), 58–73.

BURGES, G., 'De Carminibus Aristophanis Commentarius', *Classical Journal* 25 (1816), 33–47, 369–81; 28 (1816), 225–40; 39 (1817), 286–92; 31 (1817), 33–43; 36 (1818), 366–70.

CALAME, C., *Les Chœurs de jeunes filles en Grèce archaïque* (Rome, 1977).

CARY, E., 'The Manuscript Tradition of the *Acharnenses*', *HSCP* 18 (1907), 157–211.

CASSIO, A. C., Δαιταλῆς: I frammenti (Pisa, 1977).

—— *Commedia e partecipazione: la Pace di Aristofane* (Naples, 1985).

CLARK, W. G., 'On the History of the Ravenna Manuscript of Aristophanes', *Journal of Philology*, 3 (1871), 153–60.

—— 'Notes on Aristophanes; *Acharnians* 1–578', *Journal of Philology*, 8 (1879), 177–200; 9 (1880), 1–23, 165–85.

COBET, C. G., Novae Lectiones quibus continentur Observationes Criticae in Scriptores Graecos (Leiden, 1858).

COCKLE, W., 'An Unpublished Papyrus of Aristophanes from Oxyrhynchus: *Thesmophoriazusae* 25(?), 742–766, 941–956', in E. M. Craik (ed.), *'Owls to Athens'* (Oxford, 1990).

CONOMIS, N. C., 'The Dochmiacs of Greek Drama', *Hermes*, 92 (1964), 23–50.

COULON, V., *Essai sur la méthode de la critique conjecturale appliquée au texte d'Aristophane* (Paris, 1933).

—— 'Notes critiques et exégétiques sur divers passages controversés d'Aristophane', *REG* 66 (1953), 34–55.

—— 'Beiträge zur Interpretation des Aristophanes', *RhM* 105 (1962), 10–35.

CRAIK, E. M., 'The Staging of Sophocles' *Philoctetes* and Aristophanes' *Birds*', in E. M. Craik (ed.), *'Owls to Athens'* (Oxford, 1990).

DALE, A. M., *The Lyric Metres of Greek Drama* (Cambridge, ²1968). [*LM²*]

—— *Collected Papers* (Cambridge, 1969).

—— *Metrical Analyses of Tragic Choruses*, *BICS* Suppl. 21. 1, 2, 3 1971–83. [*MATC*]

DAWE, R. D., *Studies in the Text of Sophocles* (Leiden 1973–8).

DENNISTON J. D., 'Lyric Iambics in Greek Drama', in *Greek Poetry and Life: Essays presented to Gilbert Murray* (Oxford, 1936), 121–44.

DIGGLE, J., 'On the "Heracles" and "Ion" of Euripides', *PCPS* 200 (1974), 3–36 = *Euripidea: Collected Essays* (Oxford, 1994), 90–136.

—— *Studies on the Text of Euripides* (Oxford, 1981)

DINDORF, W., *Metra Aeschyli, Sophoclis, Euripidis et Aristophanis* (Oxford, 1842).

DOMINGO, E., *La Responsión estrófica en Aristófanes* (Salamanca, 1975).

DOVER, K. J., 'The Poetry of Archilochus', in *Entretiens Hardt*, 10 (Geneva, 1963), 183–212 = *Greek and the Greeks* (Oxford, 1987), 97–121.

—— *Aristophanic Comedy* (London, 1972).

—— 'Ancient Interpolation in Aristophanes', *ICS* 3 (1977), 136–62 = *The Greeks and their Legacy* (Oxford, 1988), 198–222.

—— 'Explorations in the History of the Text of Aristophanes', in *The Greeks and their Legacy* (Oxford, 1988), 223–65.

DUNBAR, N. V., review of Ἀριστοφάνους Ὄρνιθες, ed. Ph. Kakridis, *Gnomon*, 49 (1977), 331–6.

EBERLINE, C. N., *Studies in the Manuscript Tradition of the Ranae of Aristophanes* (Meisenheim am Glan, 1980).

FRAENKEL, E., 'Lyrische Daktylen', *RhM* 72 (1918), 161–97, 321–52 = *Kleine Beiträge zur klassischen Philologie*, i. (Rome, 1964), 165–233. [*KB*]

—— 'Some Notes on the Hoopoe's Song', *Eranos*, 48 (1950), 75–84 = *KB* 453–61.

—— 'Zum Text der *Vögel* des Aristophanes', in *Studien zur Textgeschichte und*

Textkritik (Festschrift G. Jachmann) (Köln–Opladen, 1959), 9–33 = *KB* 427–51.

FRAENKEL, E., *Beobachtungen zu Aristophanes* (Rome, 1962).

FÜHRER, R., 'Muta cum Liquida bei Stesichorus', *ZPE* 28 (1978), 180–6.

GANNON, J. F., 'Thesmophoriazusae Restitutae' (diss. Yale, 1982).

GEISSLER, P., *Chronologie der altattischen Komödie* (Zurich, ³1979).

GELZER, T., 'Eine Aristophaneshandschrift und ihre Besitzer'. in *KΩMΩIΔO-TPAΓHMATA: Studia . . . W. J. W. Koster in honorem* (Amsterdam, 1967), 29–46.

—— 'Aristophanes', in G. A. Seeck (ed.), *Das griechische Drama* (Darmstadt, 1979).

GRENFELL, B.-P., and HUNT, A. S., 'Some Classical Fragments from Hermopolis', in *Mélanges Nicole* (Geneva, 1905), 211–23.

GRIFFITH, M., *The Authenticity of 'Prometheus Bound'* (Cambridge, 1977).

HALDANE, J. A., 'A Scene in *Thesmophoriazusae* (295–371)', *Philologus* 109 (1965), 39–46.

HASLAM, M. W., 'Stesichorean Metre', *QUCC* 17 (1974), 7–57.

—— 'The Versification of the New Stesichorus (P. Lille 75 a b c)', *GRBS* 19 (1978), 29–57.

Henderson, J., 'Conjecturarum in Aristophanis Lysistratam Repertorium', *HSCP* 82 (1978), 87–119.

—— *The Maculate Muse* (New York and Oxford, ²1991).

HENSE, O., *Heliodoreische Untersuchungen* (Leipzig, 1870).

HERINGTON, J., *Poetry into Drama* (Berkeley, 1985).

HERMANN, G., *De Metris Poetarum Graecorum et Romanorum Libri III* (Leipzig, 1796).

—— *Elementa Doctrinae Metricae* (Leipzig, 1816). [*EDM*]

HOLWERDA, D., 'De novo priorum Aristophanis Nubium indicio', *Mnemosyne*, II (1958), 32–41.

—— 'De Heliodori Commentario metrico in Aristophanem', I, *Mnemosyne*, 17 (1964), 113–39; II, *Mnemosyne*, 20 (1967), 247–72.

HOLZINGER, K. VON, *Erklärungen umstrittener Stellen des Aristophanes*, *SAWW* 208. 5 (1928) and 215. 1 (1933).

—— *Vorstudien zur Beurteilung und Erklärertätigkeit des Demetrios Triklinios zu den Komödien des Aristophanes*, *SB Wien* 217. 4 (Vienna and Leipzig, 1939).

—— *Kritisch-exegetischer Kommentar zu Aristophanes' Plutus*, *SAWW* 218. 3 (1940).

HORN, W., *Gebet und Gebetsparodie in den Komödien des Aristophanes* (Nuremberg, 1971).

HOUSMAN, A. E., 'Prosody and Method', *CQ* (1927), 1–12 = *The Classical*

Papers of A. E. Housman, iii, ed. J. Diggle and F. R. D. Goodyear (Cambridge, 1972), 1114–26.

IRIGOIN, J., *Les Scholies métriques de Pindare* (Paris, 1958).

——'Colon, Vers et Période', in *ΚΩΜΩΙΔΟΤΡΑΓΗΜΑΤΑ: Studia . . . W. J. W. Koster in honorem* (Amsterdam, 1967), 65–73.

——'Remarques sur la composition formelle des *Oiseaux* d'Aristophane (vers 1–433)', in W. J. Aerts *et al.*, (eds.), *Σχόλια: Studia . . . D. Holwerda oblata* (Groningen, 1985), 37–52.

ITSUMI, K. 'The "Choriambic Dimeter" of Euripides', *CQ* 32 (1982), 59–74.

——'The Glyconic in Tragedy', *CQ* 34 (1984), 66–82.

——'Enoplian in Tragedy', *BICS* 38 (1991–3), 243–61.

JACKSON, J., *Marginalia Scaenica* (Oxford, 1955). [*MS*]

JONES, D. MERVYN, 'The Manuscripts of Aristophanes, *Knights*'—(I), *CQ* 2 (1952), 168–85; (II), 5 (1955), 39–48.

JORSAL, F., JØRGENSEN, M. K., and SMITH, O. L., 'A Byzantine Metrical Commentary on Aristophanes' *Frogs*', *C&M* 31 (1975), 324–88.

KAPSOMENOS, A., 'Synecphonesis and Consonantalization of Iota in Greek Tragedy', in E. M. Craik (ed.), *'Owls to Athens'*, 321–30.

KÖHNKEN, A., 'Pindar as Innovator: Poseidon Hippios and the Relevance of the Pelops Story in *Olympian I*', *CQ* 24 (1974), 199–206.

KOMORNICKA, A., 'Quelques remarques sur la parodie dans les comédies d'Aristophane', *QUCC* 3 (1967), 51–74.

KOSTER, W. J. W., 'De Codice autographo Triclinii', *Mnemosyne*, 4 (1955), 24.

——*Autour d'un manuscrit d'Aristophane écrit par Démétrius Triclinius* (Groningen, 1957).

KRANZ, W., *Stasimon* (Berlin, 1933).

LANGE, O., 'Variae Lectiones in Scholiis Aristophaneis latentes' (diss. Greifswald, 1872).

LÉVÊQUE, P., *Agathon* (Paris, 1955).

LUPPE, W., 'Literarische Texte unter Ausschluß der Christlichen', *APF* 27 (1980), 232–50.

——'Atlas-Zitate im 1. Buch von Philodems "De Pietate"', *CronErc* 13 (1983), 45–52.

——'Literarische Texte: Drama', *APF* 38 (1992), 75–86.

MAAS, P., 'Die neuen Responsionsfreiheiten bei Bakchylides und Pindar', *Jahresbericht des Philol. Vereins zu Berlin*, 39 (1913), 289–320.

——*Griechische Metrik* (Leipzig and Berlin, ²1929).

——tr. H. Lloyd-Jones, *Greek Metre* (Oxford, 1962).

McEVILLEY, T., 'Development in the Lyrics of Aristophanes', AJP 91 (1970), 257–76.

MAEHLER, H., 'Bruchstücke spätantiker Dramenhandschriften aus Hermu-
polis', *APF* 30 (1984), 5–29.

MITSDÖRFFER, W., 'Das Mnesilochoslied in Aristophanes' Thesmophoriazusen',
Philologus, 98 (1954), 59–93.

MOULTON, C., *Aristophanic Poetry* (Göttingen, 1981).

MUECKE, F., 'A Portrait of the Artist as a Young Woman', *CQ* 32 (1982), 41–55.

NEWIGER, H.-J., 'Retraktationen zu Aristophanes' "Frieden"', *RhM* 108
(1965), 241–54 = H.-J. Newiger (ed.), *Aristophanes und die Alte Komödie*
(Darmstadt, 1975), 225–55.

OLSON, S. D., 'The "Love Duet" in Aristophanes' *Ecclesiazusae*', *CQ* 38 (1988),
328–30.

OPHUIJSEN, J. M. VAN, *Hephaestion on Metre: A Translation and Commentary*
(Leiden, 1987).

PAGE, D. L., 'Ibycus; Stesichorus; Alcman (*P. Oxy.* 2735, 2618, 2737)', *PCPS*
197 (1971), 89–98.

PARKER, L. P. E., 'Some Observations on the Incidence of Word-end in
Anapaestic Paroemiacs and its Application to Textual Questions', *CQ* 8
(1958), 82–9.

——'Some Recent Researches on the Versification of Pindar and Bacchylides',
BICS 5 (1958), 13–24.

——'Split Resolution in Greek Dramatic Lyric', *CQ* 18 (1968), 241–69.

——'Catalexis', *CQ* 26 (1976), 14–28.

——'Eupolis the Unruly', *PCPS* 214 (1988), 115–22.

——'Trochee to Iamb, Iamb to Trochee', in E. M. Craik (ed.), *'Owls to Athens'*
(Oxford, 1990), 331–48.

PARSONS, P. J., 'The Lille Stesichorus', *ZPE* 26 (1977), 7–36.

PERUSINO, F., 'Il finale degli Uccelli di Aristofane', *Maia*, 18 (1966), 66.

——*Il tetrametro giambico nella commedia greca* (Rome, 1968).

——'L' Agone tra Eschilo ed Euripide come "Danza di Parole": Nota ad
Aristofane, *Ran.* 897', in *Lirica greca da Archiloco ad Elitis: Studi in honore di
F. M. Pontani* (Padua, 1984), 191–5.

PLATNAUER, M., 'Antistrophic Variation in Aristophanes', in *Greek Poetry and
Life: Essays presented to Gilbert Murray* (Oxford, 1936), 241–56.

——'Aristophanea', *AJP* 67 (1946), 262–5.

PÖHLMANN, E., '*ΠΑΡΩΙΔΙΑ*', *Glotta*, 50 (1972), 144–56.

PORSON, R., *Ricardi Porsoni Notae in Aristophanem, quibus Plutum Comœdiam
praemisit, et Collationem Appendicem adiecit P. P. Dobree* (Cambridge, 1820).

PRATO, C., *I Canti di Aristofane* (Rome, 1962).

PRETAGOSTINI, R., 'Lecizio e sequenze giambiche o trochaiche', *RFIC* 100
(1972), 257–73.

PRETAGOSTINI, R., 'Sticometria del Pap. Lille 76 a b c (il nuovo Stesicoro)', *QUCC* 26 (1977), 53–8.

PUCCI, P., 'Scoli metrici inediti delle *Nuvole*', *PP* 14 (1959), 56–9.

——'Osservazioni testuali sulle *Nuvole* di Aristofane', *BPEC* 7 (1959), 88–91.

——'Aristofane ed Euripide: ricerche metriche e stilistiche', *MAL* Sci. mor. 10.5 (1961), 227–421.

RAU, P., *Paratragodia* (Munich, 1967).

RAVEN, D. S., 'Metrical Development in Sophocles' Lyrics', *AJP* 86 (1965), 225–39.

REISIG, C., *Coniectaneorum in Aristophanem Libri duo* (Leipzig, 1816).

REITZENSTEIN, R., *Epigramm und Skolion* (Giessen, 1893).

REYNOLDS, L. D., and WILSON, N. G., *Scribes and Scholars* (Oxford, ³1991).

RITCHIE, W., *The Authenticity of the Rhesus of Euripides* (Cambridge, 1964).

ROBERT, C., 'Zu Aristophanes', *Hermes*, 38 (1903), 156–60.

ROMANO, C., *Responsioni libere nei canti di Aristofane* (Rome, 1992).

ROSSI, L.-E., *Metrica e critica stilistica: il termine 'ciclico' e l'ἀγωγή ritmica* (Rome, 1963).

——'Qui te primus "deuro de" fecit (Petron. 58. 7)', *SIFC* 45 (1973), 28–45.

——'Mimica e danza sulla scena comica greca (a proposito del finale delle *Vespe* e di altri passi aristofanei', *RCCM* 20 (1978), 1149–70.

——'P Oxy 9 + P Oxy 2687: Trattato ritmico-metrico', in A. Brancacci and D. Caizzi (eds.), *Aristoxenica, Menandrea, Fragmenta Philosophica* (Florence, 1988), 11–30.

RUIJGH, C. J., 'Aristophane, "Oiseaux" 1372 sqq., "Grenouilles" 1316 sqq., et le sens de πόδα κυλλόν', *Mnemosyne*, 13 (1960), 318–22.

RUSSO, C. F., *Aristofane Autore de Teatro* (Florence, ²1984)=*Aristophanes: An Author for the Stage*, tr. K. Wren (London and New York, 1994).

SCHREIBER, F., 'Unpublished Renaissance Emendations of Aristophanes', *TAPhA* 105 (1975), 313–32.

SCHROEDER, O., *Aristophanis Cantica* (Leipzig, ²1930). [*AC*]

SEIDLER, J. F. A., *De Versibus dochmiacis Tragicorum graecorum* (Leipzig, 1811–12).

SETTLER-SPATZ, L., 'Metrical Motifs in Aristophanes' *Clouds*', *QUCC* 13 (1972), 62–82.

SILK, M., 'Aristophanes as a Lyric Poet', *YCS* 26 (1980), 99–151.

SJÖLUND, R., *Metrische Kürzung im Griechischen* (Uppsala, 1938).

SMITH, O. L., *Studies in the Scholia on Aeschylus* I, *Mnemosyne* Suppl. 27 (1975).

——'Tricliniana', *C&M* 33 (1981–2), 239–62.

SOMMERSTEIN, A. H., 'Notes on Aristophanes' *Wasps*', *CQ* 27 (1977), 261–77.

SOURVINOU-INWOOD, C., 'Aristophanes, *Lysistrata*, 641–647', *CQ* 21 (1971), 339–42.

——*Studies in Girls' Transitions* (Athens, 1988).

STINTON, T. C. W., 'Two Rare Verse-Forms', *CR* 15 (1965), 142–6 = *Collected Papers on Greek Tragedy* (Oxford, 1990), 3–16.

——'More Rare Verse-Forms', *BICS* 22 (1975), 84–108 = *Collected Papers*, 113–42.

——'Iphigeneia and the Bears of Brauron', *CQ* 26 (1976), 11–13 = *Collected Papers*, 186–9.

STOREY, I. C., 'Eupolis 352K', *Phoenix*, 39 (1985), 154–7.

TAILLARDAT, J., *Les Images d'Aristophane: Études de langue et de style* (Paris, 1962).

TESSIER, A., *Scholia metrica vetera in Pindari Carmina* (Leipzig, 1989).

THEIMANN, D., *Heliodori Colometriae aristophaneae quantum superest* (Halle, 1869).

THOMSEN, O., 'Some Notes on the *Thesmophoriazusae* 947–1000', *C&M* Diss. 9 (1973), 27–46.

TURYN, M. A., *The Byzantine Manuscript Tradition of the Tragedies of Euripides* (Urbana, Ill., 1957).

WEST, M. L., 'Two Passages of Aristophanes', *CR* 18 (1968), 5–8.

——'Stesichorus Redivivus', *ZPE* 4 (1969), 135–49.

——*Studies in Greek Elegy and Iambus* (Berlin, 1974).

——'Tragica I', *BICS* 24 (1977), 89–103.

——'Stesichorus at Lille', *ZPE* 29 (1978), 1–4.

——*Greek Metre* (Oxford, 1982).

——*Introduction to Greek Metre* (Oxford, 1987).

WESTPHAL, R., *Metrik der Griechen*, i (Leipzig, ²1867).

WHITE, J. W. 'The Manuscripts of Aristophanes', *CPh* 1 (1906), 1–20, 255–78.

——*The Verse of Greek Comedy* (London, 1912; repr. Hildesheim, 1969). [*VGC*]

——and CARY, E., 'Collations of the Manuscripts of Aristophanes' *Aves*', *HSCP* 29 (1918), 77–131.

—— ——'Collations of the Manuscripts of Aristophanes' *Vespae*', *HSCP* 30 (1919), 1–35.

WHITTAKER, M., 'The Comic Fragments in their Relation to the Structure of Old Attic Comedy', *CQ* 29 (1935), 181–91.

WILAMOWITZ-MOELLENDORFF, U. VON, *Griechische Verskunst* (Berlin, 1921; repr. Bad Homburg vor der Höhe, 1962). [*GV*]

——*Isyllos von Epidauros* (Berlin, 1886).

WILSON A. M., 'A Eupolidean Precedent for the Rowing-Scene in Aristophanes' "Frogs"', *CQ* 24 (1974), 250–2.

—— 'Addendum to a Eupolidean Precedent for the Rowing-Scene in Aristophanes' "Frogs"', *CQ* 26 (1976), 318.

WILSON, N. G., 'The Triclinian Edition of Aristophanes', *CQ* 12 (1962), 32–47.

—— *Scholars of Byzantium* (London, 1983).

ZACHER, K., *Die Handschriften und Classen den Aristophanesscholien*, Bursian Suppl. 16 (Leipzig, 1888).

ZIELIŃSKI, T., *Die Gliederung der altattischen Komoedie* (Leipsig, 1885).

ZIMMERMANN, B., 'The Parodoi of the Aristophanic Comedies', *SIFC* 2 (1984), 13–24.

—— *Untersuchungen zur Form und dramatischen Technik der aristophanischen Komödien*, i and ii (Königstein im Taurus, 1984–5); iii (Frankfurt am Main, 1987). [*Untersuchungen*]

—— 'Parodia metrica nelle *Rane* di Aristofane', *SIFC* 6 (1988), 35–47.

WORKS ON LANGUAGE

DENNISTON, J. D., *The Greek Particles* (Oxford, ²1954). [*Particles*]

GOODWIN, W. W., *Syntax of the Moods and Tenses of the Greek Verb* (London, 1889). [*SGMT*]

KÜHNER, R., *Ausführliche Grammatik der griechischen Sprache*, Part II, rev. B. Gerth (Hanover, 1898–1904, repr. 1966). [Kühner–Gerth]

MEISTERHANS, K., *Ausführliche Grammatik der Attischen Inschriften* (Berlin, ³1900). [*GAI³*]

COLLECTIONS OF FRAGMENTS

DAVIES, M., *Poetarum Melicorum Graecorum Fragmenta*, i (Oxford, 1991).

JACOBY, F., *Die Fragmente der griechischen Historiker* (Berlin, 1926–30; Leiden, 1940–58). [*FGrHist*]

KAIBEL, G., *Comicorum Graecorum Fragmenta*, i (Berlin, 1899–). [*Kaibel*]

KASSEL, R., and AUSTIN, C., *Poetae Comici Graeci* (Berlin and New York, 1983–). [*PCG*]

LOBEL, E., and PAGE, D. L., *Poetarum Lesbiorum Fragmenta* (Oxford, 1955). [*PLF*]

NAUCK, A., *Tragicorum Graecorum Fragmenta: Supplementum adiecit B. Snell* (Hildesheim, 1964). [*Nauck²*]

PAGE, D. L., *Poetae Melici Graeci* (Oxford, 1962). [*PMG*]

PAGE, D. L., *Supplementum Lyricis Graecis* (Oxford, 1974). [*SLG*]

POWELL, J. U., *Collectanea Alexandrina* (Oxford, 1925).

SNELL, B., KANNICHT, R., and RADT, S. L., *Tragicorum Graecorum Fragmenta* (Göttingen, 1971–). [*TrGF*]

VOIGT, E.-M., *Sappho et Alcaeus* (Amsterdam, 1971). [*Voigt*]

WEST, M. L., *Iambi et Elegi Graeci* (Oxford, i, ²1989; ii, ²1992). [*IEG²*]

EDITIONS

Complete Works

Musurus, M. (Venice (Aldus), 1498). [First printed edition of all the plays except *Thesm.* and *Lys.*]

Bonini, E. (Florence (Junta), 1515, new style 1516). [First printed edition of *Thesm.* and *Lys.*]

Zanetti, B. (Venice, 1538).

Küster, L. (Amsterdam, 1710).

Brunck, R. P. F. (Strasbourg, 1783).

Invernizi, P. (Leipzig, 1794–1826).

Bothe, F. H. (Leipzig, 1828–30).

Bekker, I. (London, 1829).

Dindorf, G. [W.] (London, 1830).

Meineke, A. (Leipzig, 1860).

Blaydes, F. H. M. (Halle, 1880–93).

Rogers, B. B. (London, 1902–16).

Hall, F. W., and Geldart, W. M. (Oxford, i, ²1906; ii, ²1907).

Coulon, V. (with Fr. tr. by H. van Daele) (Paris, ²1946–54).

Sommerstein, A. H. (Warminster, 1980–).

Mastromarco, G. (Turin, 1983–).

Selection

Kock, T., *Ausgewählte Komödien des Aristophanes* (Berlin, 1856). [*Clouds, Knights, Frogs, Birds*]

Translation

Willems, A., *Aristophane* (Fr. tr. with critical commentary) (Paris and Brussels, 1919).

Individual Plays

Archarnians

Elmsley, P. (Oxford, 1809).
Mueller, A. (Hanover, 1863).
Leeuwen, J. van (Leiden, ²1901).
Rennie, W. (London, 1909).
Starkie, W. J. M. (London, 1909).
Elliott, R. T. (Oxford, 1914).

Knights

Velsen, A. von, rev. K. Zacher (Leipzig, 1900).
Neil, R. A. (Cambridge, 1901).

Clouds

Hermann, G. (Leipzig, 1830).
Leeuwen, J. van (Leiden, 1898).
Dover, K. J. (Oxford, 1968).

Wasps

Hirschig, R. B. (Leiden, 1847).
Starkie, W. J. M. (London, 1897).
MacDowell, D. M. (Oxford, 1971).

Peace

Herwerden, H. van (Leiden, 1897).
Mazon, P. (Paris, 1904).
Leeuwen, J. van (Leiden, 1906).
Zacher, K. (Leipzig, 1909).
Platnauer, M. (Oxford, 1964).

Birds

Leeuwen, J. van (Leiden, 1902).
Kakridis, Ph. (Athens, 1974).
Dunbar, N. V. (Oxford, 1995)

Lysistrata

Enger, R. (Bonn 1844).
Leeuwen, J. van (Leiden, 1903).
Wilamowitz-Moellendorff, U. von (Berlin, 1927; repr. Zürich/Berlin, 1964).
Henderson, J. (Oxford, 1987).

Thesmophoria{usae
Thiersch, B. (Halberstadt, 1832).
Fritzsche, F. V. (Leipzig, 1838).
Enger, R. (Bonn, 1844).
Velsen, A. von (Leipzig, 1883).
Leeuwen, J. van (Leiden, 1904)
Gannon, J. F. (Bryn Mawr, Pa., 1987–8).

Frogs
Fritzsche, F. V. (Zürich, 1845).
Velsen, A. von (Leipzig, 1881).
Leeuwen, J. van (Leiden, 1896).
Radermacher, L. (Vienna, ²1954).
Stanford, W. B. (London, ²1963).
Dover, K. J. (Oxford, 1993).

Ecclesia{usae
Velsen, A. von (Leipzig, 1883).
Leeuwen, J. van (Leiden, 1905).
Ussher, R. G. (Oxford, 1973).

Wealth
Velsen, A. von (Leipzig, 1881).
Leeuwen, J. van (Leiden, 1904).

Scholia
STEIN, G., *Scholia in Aristophanis Lysistratam* (diss. Göttingen, 1891).
WHITE, J. W., *The Scholia on the Aves of Aristophanes* (Boston and London, 1914).
KOSTER, W. J. W., *et al.*, *Scholia in Aristophanem* (Groningen, 1960–).

See also J. W. White, *The Verse of Greek Comedy* (above), 396–421.

Index of Poets and Passages Cited

For Aristophanes, only references to fragments are indexed.

Adespota:
  PMG:
    856 55
    857 55
    967 40
    1027(c) 356
    1033 60
Aeschylus 32, 36, 43, 52, 56, 63, 66, 151,
      209, 278, 321, 455, 506
  Ag.:
    64 485
    104ff. = 122ff. 500–1
    104–5 = 122–4 9
    107–8 = 126–7 50
    111 = 129 501
    114 = 131 501
    115–16 = 133–4 51
    117 = 135 50
    120 = 138 503
    141 79
    150 501
    153 502
    154–5 9, 279
    165–6 = 174–5 486
    192–7 30
    192 = 205 42
    199–200 = 212–13 83
    201ff. = 214ff. 150
    201–4 = 214–17 80
    225–7 = 235–7 79
    226–7 = 236–7 83
    366ff. 26
    378–9 = 396–7 42
    385–6 31
    407–8 = 424–5 44
    698 = 716 71
    747 303
    750–6 31
    783–809 56
    1104–5 = 1111–12 450

    1142 = 1153 45
    1143 = 1154 67
    1246 191
    1448–1576 57
    1553 55
  Cho.:
    22ff. 30
    152–3 45
    153 390
    319 = 336 502
    325–30 = 357–61 62
    350 = 368 450
    351–2 = 368–70 502
    387–91 = 411–14 83
    390 = 415 450
    467–8 = 472–3 83
    585–6 = 594–5 42
    607 = 618 450
    783 = 794 42
    800ff. = 812ff. 37
    935ff. = 946ff. 206
  Dictyulci, TrGF 47a, 802–20 496
  Eum.:
    98 193
    270–1 67
    323–4 = 336–7 43
    328ff. 44
    347ff. = 360ff. 51, 486
    351 = 362 50, 502
    353 = 364 502
    354ff. 44
    368ff. = 377ff. 51, 486
    372ff. 44
    490ff. = 499ff. 37
    508ff. = 517ff. 37
    529 = 540 502
    556–7 = 564–5 79
    788–9 449
    916ff. = 938ff. 37
    956–7 = 976–7 42

Aeschylus, *Eum. (cont.)*:
996ff. = 1002ff.   37
1033 = 1037   502
1035 = 1039   54, 279
1040ff. = 1044ff.   51
1042 = 1046   54
1042–3 = 1046–7   321
1043   54, 503
1043 = 1047   484
Pers.   63
102–7 = 108–13   62
115–21   533
126–9 = 133–4   42
549 = 559   403
588–9 = 595–6   50
638 = 645   37
647ff. = 652ff.   64
674   549
852ff. = 857ff.   51
855 = 861   501
864 = 871   501–2
864ff. = 871ff.   51
865–6 = 874–5   486
867 = 876   501–2
879 = 886   501
880ff. = 889ff.   51
896   501–2
896–907   51, 488
904   501–2
906   50
932ff. = 940ff.   57
951 = 965   468
952 = 965   62, 345
982–3 = 995–6   42
1007 = 1013   80
1014 = 1026   42
1016 = 1027   79
1017–20 = 1030–2   79
1045 = 1053   82
PV   193, 449
135 = 152   502
185   303
399 = 408   468
405 = 414   468
535 = 544   89
545ff. = 552ff.   314, 483
546 = 554   331
547–9   314

577 = 595   66
579 = 597   450
694   37
694–5   444
Sept.   67
105   449
115 = 132   66
170–1 = 178–9   67
303 = 320   82
324–5 = 336–7   502
326 = 338   80
567 = 630   82
686–711   426
688 = 694   82
701 = 708   82
720ff. = 727ff.   64
723 = 730   468
751–3 = 759–61   502
756–7 = 764–5   502
771 = 777   82
848ff.   30
868   464
918ff. = 929ff.   150
918–21 = 928–30   80
Supp.   67
45 = 55   502
71–81   502
101–3 = 108–11   80
163–4   356
350 = 361   310
352–3 = 363–4   79
375 = 386   80
396 = 406   82
418ff. = 423ff.   42, 44
524 = 531   81
525–6 = 532–3   502
544ff. = 553ff.   150
544–6 = 553–5   80
562–4 = 571–3   80
656ff. = 667ff.   65
659–60 = 670–1   83
1021 = 1029   468
Agathon   49, 75–6, 397–8, 468
Agathon?:
  TrGF 39F31 = *PMG* 773   402
Alcaeus   76, 403
  PLF:
    10   61

141   250
345   346
374   28
Alcman   50, 52–3, 387
PMG:
    1   24, 35, 48, 70
    14   28
    15   28
    16   28
    17   48
    19   28
    20   28
    26   340
    26. 3   303
    27   48
    30   28
    39   303
    46   61
    56   48, 264
    58   40
    59(a)   28
Anacreon   293, 398, 403, 448, 449
PMG:
    346   63, 220
    346, fr. 4. 3   62
    347   36
    349. 1   70
    352   61
    357–61   22
    375   70
    375–77   78
    376   70
    378   70, 368
    378. 1   78
    380   79
    381(b)   71, 77–8, 150, 368
    382   150
    384   79
    385   79, 150
    386   79, 150
    388   79
    395   61
    409   61
    411(b)   61–2
    417   17, 36
    419   36
    427–8   28
    429   28

Archilochus   36, 90, 260, 339–40, 476,
        502
*IEG*²:
    88–167   35
    168   261
    188   48
    190   48
    195   48
    197   35
    215   28
    317   339
    322   357
Aristophanes:
PCG:
    9   83
    29   53
    30   79
    31   79
    36   125
    111   84, 150, 368
    112   45
    113   46, 131
    235   3
    267   53
    284   53
    347   45
    348   163
    419   383
    514   383
    516   339
    520   46
    717   69
    718   59, 69
    719   45, 163
Aristoxenus of Selinus   58

Bacchylides   86, 88, 102 n. 22, 482
    carm.:
    8. 36   329
    18. 1   508
    fr. 4. 80   445
    fr. 15   41, 44
    fr. 16   41

Callimachus:
    fr. 599   549
Carcinus   7, 9, 215, 258

Carmina convivialia:
  PMG:
    884–90   72
    884–917   3
    891   72
    892   71–2, 548
    893–6   72, 250, 544
    897   72, 549
    902–5   72, 250, 542
    903. 1   71
    908   250
Carmina popularia:
  PMG:
    852   293
    876   293
Cinesias   344–5
Cratinus:
  Ἀρχίλοχοι   28
  PCG:
    11   507
    75   256
    94   53
    105   256
    126   325
    149   53
    150   53
    151   404
    183   53
    184   79, 368
    222–4   53
    237   137
    253   53
    255   53
    256   339
    257   339
    258   31
    349   53
    357   256
    360   260, 282

Diphilus:
  PCG 12   261

Epicharmus   36
  Kaibel fr. 114   58
Eupolis   256
  PCG:
    99   29, 140
    148. 1–2   3

148. 1, 4   261
172   79
173   45
175   497
207   63
249   53
250   261
315   53
317   261
386   29, 140
Euripides   9, 32, 43, 51, 56, 65, 66, 71,
    73, 74, 76–8, 173, 176, 182, 187,
    193, 402, 455, 506–9, 514–18
  Alc.:
    120–1 = 130–1   54
    244–72   514
    252–3 = 259–60   517
    266   45
    393–415   514
    402–3 = 414–15   83
    435 ff. = 445 ff.   88
    437 = 446   75, 315, 331, 346
    442 = 452   75, 331, 346
    462 = 472   75, 507
    464–5 = 474–5   54
    465 = 475   42
    570–1 = 580–1   507
  Andr.:
    91   404
    112   485
    117 ff. = 126 ff.   484
    124 = 133   54
    274 = 284   54, 279
    278 = 288   54
    278–9 = 288–9   54
    296 = 303   54
    298 = 306   54
    300 = 308   80
    482 = 490   55
    492–3   30
    766 ff. = 776 ff.   88
    776 = 787   89
    789 ff.   88
    862 ff.   340
    1173 ff. = 1186 ff.   264
    1173–96   52, 514–15
    1204   45
  Ba.   37, 63

64 62
64–169 468
72 209
79–95 62
81 62
105 ff. = 120 ff. 83
112 = 127 199, 450, 508
115 = 130 199, 450, 508
151 402
169 50
344 141
372 62
402 ff. = 416 ff. 506
403 ff. 340
410 = 425 449
414–15 = 431–2 79
530 = 549 468
536 = 555 220
565 209
585 265
589–90 44
600 30
600–3 38
993 450
1014 450
1180 209
1279 404
Cyc.:
73–4 57
79–81 57–8
203 356
360 54
495 ff. 62
El.:
112–66 514
141 = 157 54
150–6 449
151 320
181–2 = 204–5 79
439 = 449 199, 508
452 = 464 54
456–7 = 468–9 54
459–60 = 471–2 54
707 464
710 = 724 83
733 = 743 509
859 ff. = 873 ff. 88
Hec. 83

59–196 57
157 = 200 58
158 = 201 57
167–8 = 209–10 54
173–4 207
185 57
190 57
905 ff. = 914 ff. 443
921 282
1056 = 1106 514
1070–3 58
1076–7 58
Hel. 37–8
59 ff. 515
164–6 52
167–252 515
174–8 37
195 = 214 30
229–51 465–6
232 44
243–4 44
244–51 38
330 ff. 444
330–74 515
335 413
348–52 38
363–6 38
372–4 38
375 209
375–85 52, 515
384–5 54
625 ff. 428
625–97 206
640 517
642–3 443, 450
1114 = 1128 443
1117–18 = 1133–4 30
1137 ff. = 1157 ff. 88
1338–9 = 1353–4 81
1347 = 1363 449
1451 ff. = 1465 ff. 81
1452 = 1466 79
1479 ff. 340
Her.:
113 ff. = 125 ff. 30
131 45
352 = 368 79
637–8 = 655–6 80

Euripides, *Her. (cont.)*
  673 = 687 81
  692 320
  763 ff. = 772 ff. 81
  763–4 = 772–3 79
  763–6 = 772–6 19
  882–3 58
  1017 517
  1055 509
  1184 = 1190 11
  1184–8 190
  1205–11 517
  1399 141
  Hcld. 83
  356 = 365 517
  608 ff. = 618 ff 15, 52
  608–10 = 619–21 50
  Hipp.:
  182–3 340
  545 ff. = 555 ff. 506
  782 ff. 340
  821 = 840 66
  832 = 850 66
  877 79
  952 404
  1102 ff. = 1111 ff. 52, 483
  1108 = 1116 54
  1109 = 1107 54
  1122 = 1133 54
  1123 = 1134 484
  1142 81
  1347 ff. 156
  1347–69 59, 156
  1370–88 514
  1371 57
  Ion:
  1 118
  82–183 57
  112–40 514
  125 ff. 471
  125–7 356
  141 ff. 471
  144–83 515
  147–8 57
  149–50 58
  161 ff. 320
  178 57
  190 = 202 224

  468–9 = 488–9 509
  505–8 58
  623 209
  796 ff. 340
  859–922 57, 515
  894–6 57–8
  904 58, 471
  905 58
  907–9 57
  1039 404
  1095 45
  1370–8 57
  1441 206
  1445–1500 206
  1446 443, 450
  1449 45
  1466 517
  1504–5 206
  1507–9 517
  IA 37
  1–48 57
  115–63 57
  164 ff. = 185 ff. 72, 506
  186 451
  206 ff. 506
  229–30 54
  356 222
  543 209
  543 ff. = 558 ff. 506
  553 = 568 449
  624 469
  753 = 764 449
  754 = 765 449
  1279–1335 57, 515
  1296 516
  1306–9 38
  1319–32 57
  1332 54
  1334 30
  1475–99 515
  1495 38
  IT:
  123–235 57
  126–7 57
  143–77 515
  146 58
  203–35 515
  213 58

220　58
232　58
279–80　133
402　261
827–99　206
863　30
876　222
881　45
1092=1109　448
1104　320
1129=1144　448
1134–5=1149–50　54
1255　543
Med.　83
　96ff.　57, 515
　155=180　66
　206　30
　224ff.=233ff.　88
　260　222
　410ff.=421ff.　88
　420=430　89
　431=439　79
　627ff.=635ff.　88
　634=642　89
　643ff.=652ff.　88
　645–6=654–5　80
　824ff.=835ff.　88
　976ff.=982ff.　88
　981=988　89
　991ff.=996ff.　484
　1252=1262　66
　1365　404
Or.　37
　186　45
　317–18=333–4　43
　330=346　66
　810–11=822–3　81
　811=823　79
　814–15=826–7　81
　960–1021　515
　967=978　37
　992–3　66
　1011–12　54
　1303–4　265
　1369–1502　442, 514–15
　1395ff.　57
　1414–16　30
　1419–24　42

1423　45
1437–40　443, 450
1468–70　38
Phoen.　37
　110　58
　202ff.=214ff.　72, 506
　247–9=258–60　38
　301ff.　442, 515
　638–47=657–66　38
　784ff.=801ff.　52
　794–5=811–12　50
　796=813　55
　825–7　57
　826–31　57
　1023–5=1047–8　66
　1030–1=1054–5　30
　1288=1299　390
　1288–9=1299–300　45
　1295=1307　66
　1485–1538　515
　1489–91　54
　1495–1580　52
　1536　443
　1539　468
　1541　468
　1547–8　54
　1567–9　38
　1580–1　54
　1756–7　38
Rhes.:
　26–7=44–5　54, 279
　242=254　79
　347=356　79
　350=359　83
　369=378　80
　675　129
　706–9=724–6　449
　715　211
Supp.:
　51　62
　179　54
　271ff.　15, 52
　277　265
　279　279
　368=372　37
　374=378　37
　376=380　37
　619=627　80

Euripides, *Supp. (cont.)*
  778 ff. = 786 ff. 208
  798 ff. = 811 ff. 32
  821 485
  918 ff. 32
  990 = 1012 224
  1000 = 1023 238
  1123 ff. = 1132 ff. 32
  1130 = 1137 80
  1139 ff. = 1146 ff. 32
  1153 ff. = 1159 ff. 32
Tro.:
  98–229 57
  122–52 515
  144 58, 471
  148 58, 471
  308 ff. = 325 ff. 292, 443, 514
  308 355
  309 = 326 445
  311 = 328 66
  319 = 335 413
  325 435
  564 413
  587–8 = 591–2 449
  595 ff. = 601 ff. 52
  799 ff. = 808 ff. 88
  1221 549
  1288 30
  1302 ff. = 1317 ff. 32
  1313 = 1329 30
Fragments:
Aeolus N² 18 264
Andromeda:
  N²:
    114 56
    117 443
    118 443
    119 443
Archelaus N² 256 209
Hippolytus I N² 446 209
Hypsipyle:
  Bond 64. 68 ff. 206
  N² 755 509
Peleus 204
Phaethon:
  Diggle:
    78 320
    82 464

    84 = 92 58
    111 265
Philoctetes 508
Telephus 426, 508
Incert. N² 1057 209

Hermippus:
  *IEG*² 267–8 36
  PCG:
    23 53
    57 529
    77 53
Hipponax 36
  *IEG*² 119 28
Homer:
  Il.:
    1. 479 433
    7. 34 433
    14. 145 191
  Od.:
    9. 395 464
    20. 233 191
Homeric Hymn to Demeter 202 ff. 28

Ibycus 390, 398, 403, 451
  PMG:
    282 77, 448, 453
    287 49, 448, 453
    288. 3–4 450
    298 448, 452
Ion of Chios 484

Melanthius 7–9, 279
Morsimus 7–9, 279

Pherecrates:
  PCG:
    6 324
    77 261
    84 60, 245, 516
    162 53
Philodamus of Scarphaea:
  Paean to Dionysus 63, 168–9
Philoxenus of Cythera 554–5
  PMG 821 555
Phrynichus comicus:
  PCG:
    48 204–5
    76 63

Phrynichus tragicus   62, 89, 215, 218–19,
        320
   TrGF:
        3 F 6   72
        9   218
        13   261
        14   218
Pindar   7–8, 18, 65, 89, 94–5, 314,
        328–33, 482
   Ol.:
        1. str. 2   331
        1. ep. 8   328
        1. 101–2   161
        2   41, 44, 328
        2. ep. 2   331
        3. 1–2   85
        3. 30   222
        3. 35   88
        4. str. 5   329
        4. str. 7   331
        5. str. 2   328
        5. str. 3   330–1
        6. ep. 3   328
        6. 6   87
        6. 87   329
        7   87
        8. ep. 7   331
        9. str. 4   328
        9. str. 7   328
        9. str. 10   329
        10. str. 1   331
        12 str. 4   328
        12. ep. 8   328
        13. str. 1   330
        13. str. 6   535
        13. ep. 6   329
   Pyth.:
        1   87
        1. str. 2   329
        1. 2   86
        1. 1–20   13
        1. 40   133
        2. 69   161
        3. str. 5   328
        3. ep. 9   330
        3. 4   87
        3. 23   87
        4   87

        4. str. 6   332
        4. ep. 6   328
        4. 4   87
        4. 184   88
        4. 253   88
        5. str. 5   331
        5. str. 10   331
        5. 11   329
        6. 16   329
        7. str. 2   329
        8. ep. 4   329
        8. 97   238
        9. 39   222
        10. str. 2   329
        10. str. 6   330
   Nem.:
        1   87
        1. ep. 4   330, 332
        2. 16   16
        3   161
        3. str. 8   331
        3. 37   330
        5. 6   88
        5. 10   88
        5. 12   88
        7. str. 6   330
        8. str. 5   330
        10   87
   Isth.:
        1. str. 6   329
        2   88
        3+4. 72b   88
        5   87, 331
        5. str. 2   328
        6   87
   Paean:
        10. 19   330
   fr. 89a   181–2
   fr. 189   221–2
Plato comicus:
   PCG:
        3   53
        173   53
Praxilla:
   PMG 749   250

Sappho:
   PLF:
        44   70, 534

Sappho, *PLF (cont.)*
    47. 2 70
    92. 8 445
    94. 22 70
    95 70, 82
    96. 7 70
    98. 8 70
    99 250, 292
    115 293
    128 78
    140 403, 529
Simonides:
  PMG 512 166
Sophocles 32, 43, 56, 65, 66, 71, 193,
      264
  Aj.:
    172 ff. = 182 ff. 88, 190
    221 ff. = 245 ff. 190
    227–8 = 251–2 79, 368
    228 = 252 71
    228–30 = 252–4 80
    231 = 255 199
    353 = 361 82
    402 = 420 66
    693 ff. 205
    695 549
    705 = 718 79
    1185 = 1192 71
    1185–6 = 1192–3 79
    1199 = 1211 81
    1217 ff. 340
  Ant. 67
    108 = 126 30
    148 225
    155 ff. 56
    364 = 375 37
    376 ff. 56
    526 ff. 56
    582 ff. = 593 ff. 88
    586 ff. = 597 ff. 322
    626 ff. 56
    781 = 791 81
    785 = 795 71
    801 ff. 56
    806 = 823 79
    847 ff. = 866 ff. 322
    856 = 875 32
    953 ff. = 964 ff. 322

    954 = 965 32
    974–6 = 985–7 151
    976 = 987 32
    1115 ff. 205
    1121 = 1132 356
    1257 ff. 56
    1264 = 1286 67
    1320 = 1344
  El.:
    86–250 57
    121–250 51
    126–7 = 142–4 322
    127 = 144 32
    129 = 145 58
    148 300
    172 = 192 32
    205 = 225 58
    209–10 = 229–30 30
    233–42 51–2, 57
    236 ff. 224, 303
    243–5 57
    244–6 66
    823–4 = 862 57
    1066 = 1078 64
    1067–8 = 1077–80 62
    1085 ff. = 1093 ff. 322
    1085–6 = 1093–4 42
    1089 = 1096 32
    1232–87 206
    1281–7 37
    1384–5 = 1391–2 43, 67
    1407 = 1428 42
  OC 37–8
    128 404
    186 30
    207–53 51
    216–22 552
    229–35 51, 552
    538 = 545 30
    668 ff. = 681 ff. 25, 27
    668–719 161, 169–70
    1050 = 1065 79
    1074 ff. = 1085 ff. 88
    1081 ff. 340
    1083 = 1094 89
    1084 = 1095 32
    1225 537
    1251 80

1364 211
1557 = 1569 82
1561 = 1573 66
1567 = 1578 32
1681–3 = 1708–10 43–4
OT 67
  151 ff. = 159 ff. 51, 265
  151–8 = 159–66 50
  154 = 162 189
  165–6 451
  170 = 181 54
  171–2 = 182–3 189
  176–7 = 188–9 53
  190 ff. = 203 ff. 32
  463 = 473 81
  463–6 = 473–6 81
  483 ff. = 498 ff. 64
  649–53 = 678–82 43
  652–3 = 681–2 42
  668 = 696 32
  894–5 = 908–9 37
  1086 ff. = 1098 ff. 88, 205
  1095 = 1107 89
  1208–9 = 1217–19 66
  1210 365
  1212 = 1222 80
  1304–5 495
  1328–68 426
  1337–8 = 1357–8 42
  1416 211
  1451 468
Phil.:
  175 365
  184 213
  324 270
  396 = 511 449
  686–7 365
  687 ff. = 703 ff. 64
  687–90 = 703–6 80
  759–60 548
  828 = 844 58
  837 = 853 356
  839 ff. 52
  1092 = 1113 485
  1099 = 1121 78
  1099–1100 = 1121–3 80
  1138 = 1161 78
  1138–9 = 1161–2 80

1170–1217 51
1178 62
1180 536
1198–9 224
1205 265
1210 30
Trach.:
  94 ff. = 103 ff. 88
  119–21 = 129–31 80
  132–40 32
  133 37
  205–24 32, 205
  218 413
  497 ff. = 507 ff. 88
  499–509 37
  550 533
  821 ff. = 831 ff. 88
  847 ff. = 950 ff. 520
  947–8 30
  1010 ff. 52
Fragments:
Ichneutae:
  235 ff. = 281 ff. 43
  329 ff. = 371 ff. 42, 46
Oenomaus TrGF 476 340
Peleus 204–5
  TrGF 489 322
Sotades comicus:
  PCG I. 32 132
Stesichorus 88–9, 312, 482
  Eriphyle, P. Oxy. 2618 86–7
  Geryoneis, P. Oxy. 2617 85, 90
  Iliou Persis, P. Oxy. 2619 and 2803
    85–6
  Nostoi, P. Oxy. 2360 86
  Syotherae, P. Oxy. 2359 90
  Thebaid, P. Lille 76a b c 86–7
  PMG:
    210–12 278
    211 86
    244 86

Telesilla:
  PMG 717 70, 293, 529
Thaletas of Gortyn 40
Theocritus:
  15. 64 293
  17. 66 549

Theopompus:
   PCG 39   45

Timocreon of Rhodes:
   PMG 731   36